4/14/83

The Origin
of I Corinthians

The Origin
of I Corinthians

BY

JOHN COOLIDGE HURD, JR.

MACON, GEORGIA

Mercer University Press
1983

ISBN 0-86554-046-2

THE ORIGIN OF I CORINTHIANS
first published by S. P. C. K. (London) in 1965
(copyright © 1965 by John Coolidge Hurd, Jr.),
is reprinted—with corrections and a new preface—
by arrangement with S. P. C. K. and with the author.

New edition copyright © 1983
by Mercer University Press, Macon GA.

Printed in the United States of America

All books published by Mercer University Press
are produced on acid-free paper
that exceeds the minimum standards set by the
National Historical Publications and Records Commission.

LIBRARY OF CONGRESS CATALOGING IN PUBLICATION DATA

Hurd, John Coolidge, Jr.
  The origin of I Corinthians.

  Reprint. Originally published: New York: Seabury
Press, 1965.
  Bibliography: p. 306.
  Includes index.
  1. Bible. N.T. Corinthians, 1st—Criticism;
interpretation, etc.   I. Title.
BS2675.2.H8   1982   227'.206   82-20371
ISBN 0-86554-046-2

Table of Contents

PART I
PRELIMINARY HISTORICAL PROBLEMS

PART 2
PAUL'S INFORMATION FROM CORINTH

PART 3
PAUL'S PREVIOUS LETTER TO CORINTH

PART 4
CONCLUSIONS

List of Tables

Abbreviations

Arndt/Gingrich
: William F. Arndt and F. Wilbur Gingrich, *A Greek-English Lexicon of the New Testament* (Cambridge, 1957).

ASV
: American Standard Version of the Holy Bible (1901).

ATR
: *Anglican Theological Review*, Evanston, Ill.

AV
: Authorized Version of the Holy Bible (1611).

BC
: *The Beginnings of Christianity*, ed. F. J. Foakes-Jackson and K. Lake (5 vols.; London, 1920–1933).

Black
: Black's New Testament Commentaries (=Harper's New Testament Commentaries), ed. Henry Chadwick.

Blass/Debrunner
: Friedrich Blass and Albert Debrunner, *A Greek Grammar of the New Testament*, trans. R. W. Funk (Cambridge, 1961).

Camb.
: Cambridge Bible for Schools (and Colleges).

CambGk.
: Cambridge Greek Testament for Schools and Colleges.

Cent.
: The New-Century Bible, ed. Walter F. Adeney.

Clar.
: The Clarendon Bible, ed. T. Strong, H. Wild, and G. H. Box.

CNT
: Commentaire du Nouveau Testament, ed. P. Bonnard *et al.*

DB
: *A Dictionary of the Bible*, ed. James Hastings (5 vols.; Edinburgh, 1899–1904).

*DB*²
: *Dictionary of the Bible*, ed. James Hastings; rev. ed. by F. C. Grant and H. H. Rowley (New York, 1963).

EB
: Études Bibliques.

EnBib
: *Encyclopaedia Biblica*, ed. T. K. Cheyne and J. S. Black (4 vols.; New York, 1899–1903).

ET
: *The Expository Times*, Edinburgh.

ExposGk
: *The Expositor's Greek Testament*, ed. W. Robertson Nicoll (5 vols.; London, 1897–1910).

HCNT
: *Hand-Commentar zum Neuen Testament*, bearb. H. J. Holtzmann *et al.* (4 Bde.; Freiburg I. B., 1891–1892).

HNT
: Handbuch zum Neuen Testament, begründet von Hans Lietzmann, hrsg. Günther Bornkamm.

HSNT
: Die Heilige Schrift des Neuen Testaments, hrsg. Fritz Tillmann.

HTR
: *The Harvard Theological Review*, Cambridge, Mass.

ICC   The International Critical Commentary, ed. S. R. Driver, A. Plummer, and C. A. Briggs.

Internat.   The New International Commentary on the New Testament (=The New London Commentary), ed. Ned B. Stonehouse.

Interp.   *The Interpreter's Bible*, ed. George A. Buttrick *et al.* (12 vols.; New York, 1951–1957).

JBL   *Journal of Biblical Literature and Exegesis*, Philadelphia.

JR   *The Journal of Religion*, Chicago.

JTS   *The Journal of Theological Studies*, London.

Meyer   Kritisch-exegetischer Kommentar über das Neue Testament, begründet von H. A. W. Meyer.

Moffatt   The Moffatt New Testament Commentary, ed. James Moffatt.

Moulton/Milligan
               J. H. Moulton and G. Milligan, *The Vocabulary of the Greek Testament* (London, 1930).

NTD   Das Neue Testament Deutsch, hrsg. Paul Althaus (und Gerhard Friedrich).

NTS   *New Testament Studies*, Cambridge.

RGG³   *Die Religion in Geschichte und Gegenwart: Handwörterbuch für Theologie und Religionswissenschaft*, 3. Aufl. hrsg. H. v. Campenhausen *et al.* (6 Bde.; Tübingen: J. C. B. Mohr [Paul Siebeck], 1957–1962).

RSV   Revised Standard Version of the Holy Bible (1946–1957).

RV   Revised Version of the Holy Bible (1881–1885).

Schrift.   *Die Schriften des Neuen Testaments neu übersetzt und für die Gegenwart erklärt*, begründet von Johannes Weiss, hrsg. Wilhelm Bousset und Wilhelm Heitmüller (4 Bde.; 3. Aufl.; Göttingen, 1917–1918).

SJT   *Scottish Journal of Theology*, Edinburgh.

ThRund   *Theologische Rundschau*, Tübingen.

Torch   Torch Bible Commentaries, ed. J. Marsh, D. L. Edwards, and A. Richardson.

TWNT   *Theologisches Wörterbuch zum Neuen Testament*, hrsg. Gerhard Kittel und Gerhard Friedrich (Stuttgart, 1931——).

Tynd.   The Tyndale New Testament Commentaries, ed. R. V. G. Tasker.

West.   Westminster Commentaries, ed. Walter Lock and D. C. Simpson.

Zahn   Kommentar zum Neuen Testament, hrsg. Theodor Zahn.

ZNW   *Zeitschrift für die Neutestamentliche Wissenschaft und die Kunde der älteren Kirche*, Berlin.

ZThK   *Zeitschrift für Theologie und Kirche*, Tübingen.

Preface to the First Edition

The study which follows is an attempt in one small area to revive a now much neglected concern of Pauline scholarship—the change and development of Paul's thought under the impact of, and in reaction to, the events of his most eventful life. Since the present work is intended as an entering wedge it is by consequence somewhat wedge-shaped. Chapter 1, which deals with the general state of scholarly opinion concerning Pauline chronology, is heavily weighted with citations of the works of scholars past and present. In order that these references might not overburden the reader two conventions have been used for greater brevity. Firstly, in that part of Chapter 1, designated as "The Usual Chronology of Paul's Letters", works cited are referred to in the appended notes (pp. 299–305) by short title, and their authors by surname and initials only. (Since the purpose of this section is to show how many and how important are the scholars listed, their names are capitalized.) Full bibliographical references are given later at the appropriate points for those works used in the remainder of the present study. Those works which are not cited elsewhere are listed in full in the final section of the Bibliography. Secondly, in short titles throughout this study the abbreviation of a New Testament book regularly stands for a given author's commentary on that book, whatever the original title or language of the commentary. Thus, for example, "Lietzmann, *Corr.*" will be understood to mean, "Hans Lietzmann, *An die Korinther I/II* ('HNT,' 9. Bd.; 4. Aufl.; Tübingen: J. C. B. Mohr Verlag [Paul Siebeck], 1949)." In the same manner "*Intro. N. T.*" represents an author's introduction to the New Testament regardless of exact title or original language.

Manuscript authorities for the New Testament text are cited as in Nestle's edition. The Revised Standard Version is used for quotations of English text except where there are particular reasons for modifying this translation.

Gratefully I acknowledge here two special debts. Firstly, it was my privilege to be introduced to the study of Paul by the Very Reverend

Charles H. Buck, Jr, formerly of the Episcopal Theological School, Cambridge, Mass. It is to him that I owe the kind of question which is asked of 1 Corinthians in the following study. His published articles (see the Bibliography) do not do justice to the comprehensiveness of his approach to Paul. His former students, however, will recognize the terms "Corinthian Reply" and "Previous Letter", and will find themselves in a territory with familiar landmarks as they follow the debate between Paul and the Corinthians. To a certain extent these landmarks result from the influence of Dean Buck's conclusions about Paul; however, to a greater extent, I hope, they are the result of asking the same questions of the same material. Conclusions come and go; it is the method which is important. The points where I am conscious of special dependence on Dean Buck are indicated in the footnotes. Here I record my special gratitude to him for showing me the methods, the questions —indeed, the style—of scholarship which were in no small measure responsible both for the present study and for my present vocation.

Secondly, in its original form this study was a dissertation presented for the degree of Doctor of Philosophy in Yale University. That dissertation would not have been possible except for funds graciously made available in memory of Frank Chamberlin Porter, formerly Winkley Professor of Biblical Theology at the Yale Divinity School.

In addition, I wish to thank my colleague, Professor R. Francis Johnson, who kindly read the manuscript and offered numerous suggestions in the interests of greater clarity.

Finally, I mention my wife to whom in another sense this book is due and is here gratefully dedicated.

6 December 1963   JOHN COOLIDGE HURD, JR.

Preface to the New Edition

SUBSEQUENT DEVELOPMENTS

It is now more than twenty years since the original Yale dissertation was completed and seventeen since S.P.C.K. published the revised manuscript. The size of the original printing run was generous for a work of this complexity, but it has been out of print since 1976. That the book has appeared so rarely on the secondhand book market is perhaps the nicest compliment it has received. Now Mercer University Press has made it once more available, and they kindly offered me the opportunity of adding a few words on the situation today. As most reviewers said, the original production was notable for the fullness of its bibliographical citations. (Here lies, I suspect, the real reason why the work has been so hard to obtain.) This feature is explained by the book's history: it was a dissertation and S.P.C.K. generously did not request that I prune the manuscript. In fact no young author could have had a more tolerant and helpful publisher, and their work was a model of accuracy.

Clearly space does not allow a treatment in the same detail of the numerous publications on 1 Corinthians which have appeared in the years since then. However, many of these works seem to me to be further examples of lines of thought already commented upon and set aside, as I shall complain below. In general I am unrepentant of the conclusions I reached then, and thus it did not seem to me necessary to add to the already lengthy lists of the original edition. There are, however, some matters about which I welcome the chance to speak.

The background

In the original preface I gave very inadequate thanks to my first teacher in New Testament, Charles H. Buck, Jr. My difficulty then was that his published articles represented only part of my indebtedness to him. The rest consisted of recollections of his lectures some ten years earlier. Now it is a pleasure to be able to point to his long anticipated book, *Saint Paul: A Study of Development of His Thought.*[1] His collaborator, Greer Taylor, was my classmate at the Episcopal Theological School, and we were introduced to the study of

[1] New York: Charles Scribner's Sons, 1969.

Paul together in Charles Buck's classes. (Greer Taylor had already received his law degree and later went on to teach Christian ethics.) We both were considerably influenced by our teacher, whose approach to Paul, as I later came to realize, was both independent and perceptive.

Buck is not the product of any school of Pauline study. He began his academic carrer in classics and his Ph.D. dissertation was titled A Chronology of the Plays of Plautus.[2] He then took a theology degree and, after a tour as a naval chaplain, studied independently with Henry J. Cadbury and W. H. P. Hatch. (Both these men were exceedingly wise and knew far more than they ever had time to write.) This unorthodox but highly effective introduction to New Testament studies helps to explain the relative lack of interaction between Buck's book and the detailed literature of Pauline research. What is important about the book, however, is not so much whether it takes account of alternative positions nor the particular set of conclusions that are found there (a number of which go beyond positions which I would care to accept), but the method of approach. The present book can be understood as the working out with full scholarly apparatus of some of Buck's suggestions concerning the Previous Letter and the Corinthian Reply. I hasten to add, however, that he is not to be held responsible for the more fanciful aspects of this study, in particular my theory concerning the Apostolic Decree discussed again below.

Pauline chronology

As the reader can see, the first chapter intends to identify and set aside the usual assumptions about the use of Acts for the study of Paul and the resultant dating of the letters. The chapter has, therefore, much wider application than the book's conclusions about 1 Corinthians. Quite naturally I anticipated considerable negative reaction on these points. After all, I had cited as examples of defective method more than a hundred works of Pauline scholars and relegated them to a special section of the bibliography reserved for works mentioned only in chapter 1. My anxiety increased as the original publication date approached. It was with considerable relief, therefore, that I read the kind reviews which began to appear. Naturally and as I expected, many reviewers dissented from many or even most of my conclusions concerning 1 Corinthians.[3] The reaction to chapter 1, however, was to me

[2] Baltimore: Johns Hopkins University Press, 1940.

[3] E.g., Werner Georg Kümmel, in his review of the book (*Theologische Literaturzeitung* 91 [1966]: 505-508), while giving a full summary of its contents and praising its bibliographic completeness, uses terms such as "reine Phantasie" and "völlig unglaubwürdig." Perhaps in consequence Hans Conzelmann takes virtually no notice of the book in his Meyer series commentary on 1 Corinthians published in 1969 and unrevised in its English translation as *1 Corinthians: A Commentary on the First Epistle to the Corinthians*, Hermeneia series (Philadelphia: Fortress Press, 1975).

unexpected. Reviewer after reviewer either passed over the chapter in silence or else took it as the sort of obvious, factual material with which most doctoral dissertations begin. Innocently I entertained the hope that I had helped to move some Pauline scholars toward the position advocated by John Knox, Charles Buck, and others that initially the letters alone are to be used in seeking to discover the course of Paul's career.

In my enthusiasm I enlarged on this theme in my contribution to the John Knox festschrift.[4] It seemed to me that some scholars thought that Knox's position consisted simply of the call for more reliance on the letters and less on Acts. I therefore attempted to argue in a more formal way that primary source material (the letters) and secondary source material (Acts) cannot be laid on the same table at the same time. The difference between these two types of material is qualitative not quantitative. The critical techniques which are used to read the one class of material are rather different from those needed for the other. The primary material is to be squeezed dry of the information it can give before one turns to the secondary material. Again, no counterattack materialized, and I allowed myself to believe that this position was gaining ground.

Moreover, in this period I discovered that there is a considerable consensus among those Pauline scholars who give their opinion concerning the relative order of some or all of the letters without the guidance of Acts.[5] This order is different at a number of points from the usual Acts sequence. That such a consensus exists I took as a good omen.

As the years passed, however, and books and articles on Paul continued to appear which ignored this basic point of method, it became clear that the lack of scholarly objection was not due to agreement but was because few were interested. It appears, therefore, that while scholars have not been inclined to contest this basic issue of method, neither has there been any inclination to abandon the traditional way by which Paul's life is understood on the basis of Acts.[6] Books are still written on the chronology of Paul's life which base

---

[4] "Pauline Chronology and Pauline Theology," in *Christian History and Interpretation: Studies Presented to John Knox*, ed. W. R. Farmer, C. F. D. Moule, and R. R. Niebuhr (Cambridge: The University Press, 1967), pp. 225-48.

[5] See my article, "The Sequence of Paul's Letters," *Canadian Journal of Theology* 14 (1968): 189-200. My purpose there was to identify consensus, not to argue for or against its correctness. In fact I specifically indicated that my position with regard to the apostolic council of Acts 15 (*Origin*, pp. 240-70) ran counter to this opinion. I mention this point because some scholars have assumed that the article presented my own conclusions. Robert Jewett in his recent book, *A Chronology of Paul's Life* (Philadelphia: Fortress Press, 1979), has further confused the issue by describing the article as seeking truth by "using the majority-as-correct principle." As evidence of my inconsistency he then cites the present book's position on the council as though I had made no mention of the point in the article! He dismisses further examination of the main issue which is crucial to his program with the verdict that "the precariousness of deciding historical questions by majority rule is perfectly illustrated."

[6] E.g., C. K. Barrett, in his *A Commentary on the First Epistle to the Corinthians*, Black series

themselves almost entirely on Acts.[7] It seems as if the study of Acts by
Pauline scholars has gotten out of touch with the study of Acts by Acts
scholars. The insights of redaction criticism as applied to Acts seem sometimes forgotten by those whose primary interest is Paul.

For me events took a new turn one day in 1977. A young German scholar,
Gerd Lüdemann, came to see me. He had just taken up the position of
research associate at McMaster University as part of their project to examine
the self-definition of Judaism and early Christianity. As we talked I was
amazed at the extent to which he had mastered the American discussion of
Pauline chronology stemming from the work of John Knox. As he himself
said, this discussion has received very little attention in Germany. I was
delighted to learn that he had written his *Habilitationsschrift* on these issues.
He kindly shared with me a carbon copy of his manuscript. There was very
little except oral tradition that I could add to his exceedingly thorough
research. Since then this work has become available to all in its published
version, *Paulus, der Heidenapostel: I, Studien zur Chronologie*.[8] In it he takes
German scholarship to task for not considering seriously the basic point of

(London: Adam & Charles Black, 1968), begins by describing Paul's dealings with the
Corinthian church "as is right, on the basis of Paul's own certainly genuine writings alone" (p.
4) with a reference to this book. He then settles chronology by using Acts because, like many,
he considers it "consistent" with the letters (pp. 4-5). Thereupon he discusses the present book
appreciatively (pp. 6-7), and sets its major conclusions aside because he considers the time
interval suggested by Acts too short for the developments implied, in my opinion, by 1
Corinthians (p. 8).

To take another example, it is ironic that John A. T. Robinson in his book, *Redating the New
Testament* (London: SCM Press, 1976), somewhat sarcastically rejects Knox et al. (pp. 31, 38),
although his best hope for the early datings he seeks lies with the earlier letters of the Pauline
corpus.

[7] Two particularly pure examples are George Ogg, *The Chronology of the Life of Paul*
(London: Epworth Press, 1968), and John J. Gunther, *Paul: Messenger and Exile: A Study in the
Chronology of His Life and Letters* (Valley Forge PA: Judson Press, 1972). More difficult to assess
is Robert Jewett's *Chronology*. Concerning Knox's hypothesis the reader receives conflicting
signals. Jewett speaks of the "glaring mistakes" which "set most critics against Knox's scheme"
(pp. 79-80; it should be noted that his verdict is the result of his own misunderstanding of
Knox's work, as he admits in a paper soon to be published in the proceedings of the Fort Worth
colloquy mentioned below). But he presents himself as providing a refinement of the "Knox
hypothesis" (pp. 95-96, 100, and 103), which he pronounces "methodologically preferable" to "compromise chronologies" (p. 86). He speaks about method, even about the need for
a "deductive-experimental method" (p. 2), and the reader is lulled into the feeling that here is a
serious attempt to put the best historical method into practice. However, it is emphatically
clear that he has not followed Knox's method at all. He has merely incorporated some of
Knox's conclusions (notably the three-Jerusalem-visit pattern) into his own system. There is
no attempt to present the evidence of the letters independently of Acts and to see how far one
can go solely on the basis of this information towards an account of Paul's life. Instead, Acts gets
into the picture from the beginning, and Jewett ends by accepting from Acts whatever fits his
hypothesis and is not directly contradicted by the letters (as he himself says, p. 24).

[8] Forschungen zur Religion und Literatur des Alten und Neuen Testaments (Göttingen:
Vandenhoeck und Ruprecht, 1980). An English translation is in preparation.

method urged by John Knox. In one leap he has become the leading authority on and most learned exponent of Knox's program.

The work of John Knox and of others who associate themselves with him continues to be discussed. In November 1980, a colloquy was held in Fort Worth immediately preceding the annual meeting of the Society of Biblical Literature in Dallas. Included was a seminar on Pauline chronology titled, "Chapters in a Life of Paul After Thirty Years." Lüdemann was one of the invited speakers, and John Knox contributed an essay, although he was not himself able to attend.[9] The full proceedings of the colloquy will shortly be published by Mercer University Press.

It is my impression that Pauline scholars are increasingly cautious about using Acts to provide the chronological basis for the interpretation of Paul's writings and are increasingly open to the possibility that his thought did change at least in some respects during the period of the letters.[10]

Paul and sexual issues

One issue that has vastly increased in importance since 1965 is the role of women in Christian thought. There is now a growing body of literature on the attitude toward women in the New Testament and in Paul's writings in particular. One strand among the other arguments in the present book is a continued discussion of 1 Corinthians 7. The analysis finally reaches its culmination in a suggested reconstruction of Paul's first preaching in Corinth (chapter 8). There I suggest that Paul originally accepted the apocalyptic view that in the Kingdom sexual differences are eliminated. Since he then believed that the time remaining in the present age was short, he applied to his earliest Christian communities *mutatis mutandis* the attitudes and practices which were to characterize the age to come. I should not care to assess in psychological terms what the unmarried Paul's attitude towards women was, but it seems to me probable that on theological grounds he made no distinction in function between men and women in the life of his churches. Clearly women shared in the ministry of the early Pauline churches, whatever precisely ministry involved at that time. Paul in commenting on the preaching of women was not concerned with their role, but rather with the

---

[9] I have been using Knox's name as a brief designation for a movement. He was, of course, not without antecedents in some respects; there are others whose work was to some extent parallel to his, and there are many who build gratefully on his insights. However, he has focused the issues in a unique way (more than half the battle!) and set the stage for the continued discussion of these matters. Thus it is appropriate to use his name to represent the whole program. In his essay Knox carefully indicates the extent to which he considers his work in this area original.

[10] E.g., Ed Sanders in his recent study, *Paul and Palestinian Judaism: A Comparison of Patterns of Religion* (Philadelphia: Fortress Press, 1977), says simply, "My own position on the use of Acts for the general study of the career of Paul is that of John Knox" (p. 432).

question whether they were modestly veiled. It was Paul's conviction that the church should be as far as possible an anticipation of the coming Kingdom, a view which put him far ahead of his time and led him to a view of the equality of the sexes with which the modern church is only beginning to come to terms.

The relative value of celibacy and marriage is also an issue of current concern, especially within the Roman Catholic communion. Here both parties to the argument can find supporting texts in 1 Corinthians. The problem is more complex than the preceding, for Paul seems to have favored both views. In his earliest preaching he apparently recommended asceticism both for single persons and for married couples. I argued that there is evidence that he even counseled "spiritual marriage," that is, ascetic union, for those who marry as Christians. However, in this period he believed that the nearness of the Kingdom called for unusual measures. He reasoned that there was no purpose in bringing children into a world that was passing away. On the contrary, Christians should devote their energies to preparing for the Parousia. By the time 1 Corinthians was written, however, his attitude had changed. While not abandoning those who had taken his earlier advice, he now recommended normal marriage relationships. In general, time has been on the side of Paul's later attitude.

Speaking in tongues

Charismatic speech is periodically a phenomenon within the Christian church. Invariably its appearance provokes controversy. Here again both sides can point to material in 1 Corinthians to support their case. Again the situation is, it seems to me, that Paul advocated both views, although at different times. Originally he himself spoke in tongues and thus communicated the practice within the churches he founded. Later, however, he came to believe that at least the Corinthians had gone too far in their exaltation of this gift. To moderate their enthusiasm Paul in 1 Corinthians called their attention to the many other (and in his view better) gifts communicated by the Spirit. More profoundly, he held up before them the ideal of Christian love as the standard by which they could value their behavior. By this canon Paul judged their speaking in tongues to be of secondary worth. Once again the modern Christian must decide which of Paul's positions to choose.

Paul's writings as letters

In 1971 the Society of Biblical Literature established a five-year seminar to study the letter structure of Paul's writings. Under the chairmanship of Nils A. Dahl the group addressed itself to the question, what does it mean to our understanding of Paul that Paul wrote letters? The seminar created a subgroup which concentrated on ancient epistolography in general. This group has, for example, collected all examples of Greek common letters, continuing the work done by John L. White in his published dissertation on the structure of the Greek letter.[11] The main seminar devoted its sessions to the analyzing of five of Paul's letters: Philemon, 1 Thessalonians, 1 Corinthians, Galatians, and Romans. The seminar came to agree on several points which relate to the interests of the present book: (1) a number of the epistolary formulae which served as conventional signals within the Greek common-letter tradition do indeed reappear in Paul's letters. There are formulae of introduction, thanksgiving, reproof, disclosure, request, transition, greeting, and farewell—among others. Thus a knowledge of the letter conventions of Paul's day is important to an understanding of the letters which he wrote. Further, (2) although Paul's letters are longer and more elaborate than most Greek common letters, they nevertheless show many of the same structural features. The opening and closing sections relate to past and future personal relationships respectively. The central section concerns the business at hand. Moreover, similarities in the finer structure of these main units can be observed. Thus literary structure is also of importance in understanding Paul.

When the present book first appeared, there was little published material on the structure and conventions of the Greek common letter and still less on the subject as it applied to Paul. In an untutored and preliminary way, however, the book does contribute to this study. It treats a number of the Pauline formulae in 1 Corinthians. Further there is considerable attention to the structure of the letter. I hit upon the expedient of noting for each section of the letter whether the information on which it had been based was in the form of written communication from Corinth or of oral conversation with travelers from Corinth. The result was a nice delineation of what I term Paul's "Reply Letter" form. This analysis is still, I believe, important, although it could be considerably amplified in light of work done subsequently by members of the S.B.L. seminar and others.

Further, an important assumption upon which the seminar based its work was the conviction that Paul's letters should be treated individually. Thus Paul's letters were approached in the way in which one approaches any of the Greek common letters from antiquity. Each letter was considered to have a unique occasion. Each letter was taken to represent a particular stage in the conversation between the writer and the recipient. This emphasis in recent Pauline studies serves to reinforce and amplify the plea of the present book that the letters not be harmonized with each other, but that each be allowed to speak for itself.

[11] *The Form and Function of the Body of the Greek Letter: A Study of the Letter-Body in the Non-literary Papyri and in Paul the Apostle*, SBL Dissertation Series, 2 (Missoula MT: Scholars Press, 1972).

1 Corinthians 1-4

In his contribution to the Knox festschrift Nils A. Dahl quite correctly observed that the present book has little to say about 1 Corinthians 1-4.[12] In a most perceptive article he proceeds to remedy this defect. His work therefore constitutes an important supplement to the present book. I chose to concentrate my attention on 1 Corinthians 7-16, because we know that for the most part these chapters are based on a single text physically in Paul's hands, to which he could refer if necessary. When he quotes the Corinthians' letter, his words are their words, whatever precisely they may have meant. This is what I meant by saying that this material was more objectively known to Paul.[13] By contrast, Paul's oral information may have come from any of several sources and may have reached him in a variety of transformations. I thus proceeded to work my way stage by stage backward in time, attempting to trace the written conversation between Paul and the Corinthians. Having reached the goal of Paul's earliest preaching in Corinth, I closed the book with a summary of the argument. The result is that 1 Corinthians 1-4 received scant attention and chapters 5-6 hardly more. Clearly there was room for much additional work to be done. It is thus with great pleasure that I recommend Dahl's suggestion that these opening chapters constitute Paul's defense of his own mission and status among the Corinthians. These chapters have an important function within the letter, for they provide the basis for his hope that they would recognize his authority and accept the advice he had to give them.

Dahl believes that because the question of Paul's authority is logically prior to the specific advice that he gives, the defense of his authority should stand chronologically before the text that embodies his advice. This may well be so, but since completing the present book I have been examining the Thessalonian letters. It seems to me that 1 Thessalonians has a structure that is strikingly similar to that of 1 Corinthians. Certainly Paul's response to information which he received in oral form appears in the initial chapters of each letter. Further, there is enough similarity between 1 Thessalonians 4-5 and 1 Corinthians 7-16 to suggest (as a number of scholars have argued) that 1 Thessalonians was written in response to a letter Paul had received.[14] If this is in fact the case, then the order of the two main sections in these two letters may well have been due to Paul's sense of form rather than to the logic of his argument.

The apostolic decree

Without doubt the most distinctive conclusion reached in the present book is

---

[12] "Paul and the Church at Corinth According to 1 Corinthians 1:10-4:21," in *Christian History and Interpretation: Studies Presented to John Knox*, pp. 313-35.

[13] See below, p. 62.

[14] See below, p. 64.

the suggestion that the previous letter sent by Paul to the Corinthians contained the substance of the apostolic decree (Acts 15) with little or no explanation as to its origin or suggestions as to its application. There has been a general lack of enthusiasm among scholars over this proposal. Dahl, for example, calls it a "much less attractive hypothesis" than his own suggestion that one should follow up the parallels between 1 Thessalonians 4-5 and the topics upon which Paul elaborated in 1 Corinthians 7-16.[15] I mention these Thessalonian parallels in the present book, as Dahl says, and have examined them still further in the years following its publication. It is certainly true that, taking 1 Thessalonians as evidence, a number of the topics in 1 Corinthians 7-16 could be explained as matters likely to be included in any Pauline discussion of church discipline. Further, I readily grant that the ice has become very thin by the point at which my hypothesis concerning the apostolic decree is reached. I do, however, believe that the parallel nature of the arguments up to that point does increase the probability of the analysis. What I have not heard, however, in the subsequent debate on these issues is an explanation for the inclusion in 1 Corinthians of discussions on idol meat and on the "collection for the poor among the saints at Jerusalem." Pre-Lukan tradition connects the decree with Paul and the Jerusalem church. Reference to the eating of idol meat appears only in Acts and in 1 Corinthians in the literature related to Paul. The collection is clearly for the benefit of the Jerusalem church. Galatians 2 describes a conference between the Jerusalem church leaders and Paul. Further, in the opinion of many scholars, Gal. 2:10 refers to the inception of the collection. I remain convinced that it is worth entertaining the possibility that all these matters are connected. At least, I have yet to hear of a better explanation.[16] On the other hand, I have no quarrel with any who conclude that no explanation has sufficient probability to be seriously considered and that a healthy skepticism is the more reasonable position.

In closing may I say how grateful I am to all those who have entered into conversation with me in person or in print concerning the fascinating matters connected with Paul's early ministry. May I also express the hope for all who study Paul's letters that as we learn of him we may also learn from him.

4 *July* 1982 JOHN COOLIDGE HURD, JR.

---

[15] "Paul and the Church at Corinth," p. 330.

[16] In the present work I discuss at some length (see especially pp. 262-67) the problem that Paul never mentions the decree himself. Some critics, e.g., Barrett, *First Corinthians*, p. 8; and John W. Drane, *Paul: Libertine or Legalist? A Study in the Theology of the Major Pauline Epistles* (London: S.P.C.K., 1975), p. 98, raise the difficulty but do not refer to the above discussion.

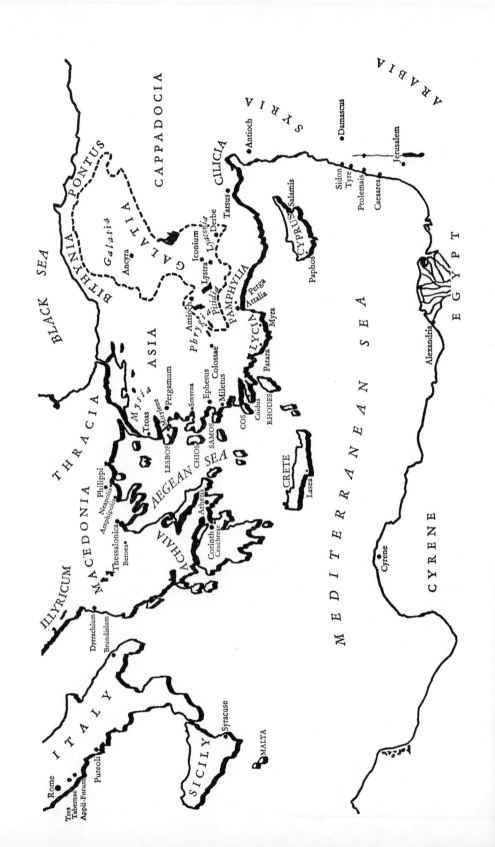

Introduction

The fullest possible understanding of Paul's letters must rest on the fullest possible understanding of the factors which caused Paul to write. For each of Paul's letters we desire to know not simply the meaning of the words Paul used, but the situation which evoked them and the effect Paul intended them to have in the minds of those to whom they were addressed. This perspective is particularly necessary in the case of 1 Corinthians, since, as this study intends to argue, 1 Corinthians is to be understood as but one part of a conversation which took place between Paul and the Church in Corinth. As George G. Findlay put it, "The more closely the Epistle is read in the light of this suggestion, the more evident it becomes that it is, in its construction and main tenor, a *rejoinder*. We are listening, as we read it, to one party of two engaged in a continued dialogue."[1] Or as Kirsopp Lake somewhat more sombrely expressed it, "The [Corinthian] Epistles were not written by St. Paul to illustrate general principles, or to give an *exposé* of Christian practice, but as definite attempts to deal with extremely concrete questions, which gave rise to a violent quarrel between St. Paul and the Corinthians."[2] Thus to read 1 Corinthians in isolation or simply in the context of Paul's other letters inevitably limits or even distorts our understanding of the letter.[3]

---

[1] George G. Findlay, "The Letter of the Corinthian Church to St. Paul," *The Expositor*, Ser. 6; Vol. I (1900), 401.

[2] Kirsopp Lake, *The Earlier Epistles of St. Paul: Their Motive and Origin* (2d ed.; London: Rivingtons, 1914), p. 117.

[3] It is interesting that Robert M. Grant in his recent book, *A Historical Introduction to the New Testament* (New York: Harper & Row, 1963), mentions the metaphor of conversation but appears to reach a conclusion opposed to the one advocated in the present study: "We can describe what Paul said with some measure of confidence. The same confidence must be lacking when we try to state why he said it. . . . When we try to fill in the other side of the conversation, we have the testimony only of Paul himself, and he is hardly an unprejudiced witness. . . . He refers to the opinions of his opponents only in order to refute them. . . . In view of our limited understanding of his environment and his opponents it is difficult to apply this principle [that the background of his letters conditioned his response]; furthermore, he did write what he wrote, not something else. . . . The most important question remains . . . what his gospel was and what he believed it meant for his hearers" (p. 174). In reply three comments need to be made: (*a*) It is of course agreed that Paul's letters themselves are the primary historical evidence and that this evidence cannot be

It is the thesis of this book that the exchanges which lie behind
1 Corinthians may be reconstructed with considerably more clarity
and completeness than has generally been supposed. The mention in
1 Corinthians of a letter from the Corinthians to Paul (1 Cor. 7.1) and
of one from Paul to the Corinthians (1 Cor. 5.9) provide objective
points of departure. Furthermore, a number of passages in 1 Corinthians appear to be direct answers to specific questions put to Paul by the
Corinthian Church. From Paul's answers we shall endeavour to reconstruct the Corinthians' questions. And these questions in turn will lead
us to seek the problems which lie behind them. Thus the background
of 1 Corinthians will resolve into a succession of stages in a somewhat
lengthy exchange between Paul and the Corinthians leading back to
the founding of that Church.

Exchange, however, often involves change. The idea that Paul's
thought developed during the period of his letters was once popular.[1]
To-day, however, for a number of reasons it is out of favour among
scholars. Before beginning to reconstruct Paul's conversation with the
Corinthians, therefore, we must examine these reasons to see how far
they limit or allow the possibility of change in Paul's thought. Specifically we need to know whether we should begin by assuming that Paul
in 1 Corinthians simply restated views which he had held for some
time and which the Corinthians had perhaps misunderstood, or
whether we should leave open the possibility that Paul changed his
ground in the face of Corinthian opposition, in the light of further
experience, or for other reasons. And, more generally, we need to
know the extent to which what can be known about Paul's biography
as a whole contributes to our knowledge of the period which preceded
the writing of 1 Corinthians.

---

subordinated to any theory about their origin. (b) It is necessary, however, in interpreting
any historical text to form some conscious and explicit hypothesis about the background
of the text and the motives of its author. That this task is sometimes difficult affects the
adequacy of our interpretation but not the need for the attempt. (c) Grant himself clearly
goes beyond what Paul wrote to consider why he wrote as he did. To refer to Paul as
"hardly an unprejudiced witness" involves a judgement both about Paul's motives and
about the nature of the controversy in which he was involved. And to suggest that we
seek to understand concerning Paul's gospel "what he *believed* it meant for his hearers"
involves the same kind of judgement. Lastly, Grant's own studies of the background of
Paul's letters are reflected constantly throughout this book (e.g., the section titled " 'Gnostics' at Corinth," pp. 204–6).

[1] For bibliography see p. 8, n. 2.

PART 1

Preliminary Historical Problems

CHAPTER 1

Pauline Biography and Pauline Theology

THE RELATION OF THE OCCASIONS OF PAUL'S LETTERS TO THEIR THEOLOGY

The non-literary aspect of Paul's letters

"Epistles" and "letters." Just before the turn of the century the great papyrus finds of Egypt began to be published.[1] It was not long before scholars led by Adolf Deissmann, George Milligan, James H. Moulton, and Edgar J. Goodspeed awakened all New Testament students to the immense value of these discoveries. To-day these studies are taken for granted. So well did these pioneers work that their books have become the authorities, often replacing the papyri, which were, for them, the real authorities. But whereas these scholars are much honoured in the areas of grammar and lexicography, in another area the implications of their work for New Testament study have received less attention. In 1901 Deissmann wrote, "The author is forced to confess that, previous to his acquaintance with ancient papyrus letters (such as it was—only in facsimiles), he had never rightly known, or, at least, never rightly realized within his own mind, what a letter was."[2] By the word "letter" he was making a sharp distinction between the non-literary letters so abundant in the papyri ("true letters" he called them), and literary letters, that is, "epistles".[3] Turning to Christian writings, he

---

[1] The famous German series, *Ägyptische Urkunden aus den Königlichen Museen zu Berlin: Griechische Urkunden* (Berlin: Weidmann), commenced in 1895. Bernard P. Grenfell and Arthur S. Hunt edited the first volume of *The Oxyrhynchus Papyri* (London: Egypt Exploration Fund) in 1898.

[2] G. Adolf Deissmann, *Bible Studies*, trans. Alexander Grieve (Edinburgh: T. & T. Clark, 1901), p. 21.

[3] Ibid., pp. 3–34. See further Deissmann's *Light from the Ancient East*, trans. Lionel R. M. Strachan (2d ed. rev.; New York: George H. Doran Company, 1927), pp. 148–241; and *Paul: A Study in Social and Religious History*, trans. William E. Wilson (2d ed. rev.; London: Hodder and Stoughton, 1926), pp. 8–11. This distinction was not new with Deissmann, however. He refers to Eduard Reuss and Ulrich von Wilamowitz-Moellendorff on this point (*Bible Studies*, p. 20, n. 1).

then posed the question, "Are the 'Letters' of the New Testament (and further, of early Christianity in general) non-literary letters or literary epistles?" [1] In Paul's case Deissmann answered his own question categorically: "The letters of Paul are not literary; they are real letters, not epistles; they were written by Paul not for the public and posterity, but for the persons to whom they are addressed."[2] Deissmann's answer was generally accepted.[3] Since that time certain studies in the literary form and style of the Pauline Corpus have carried the problem beyond Deissmann's enthusiastic thesis.[4] But in general scholars have adopted Deissmann's emphasis rather than its opposite, either assuming it in their approach to Paul, or explicitly defending it.[5]

The theological importance of the occasions of Paul's letters. The implications of the non-literary character of Paul's letters are far-reaching and

[1] *Light from the Ancient East*, p. 233. See also *Bible Studies*, p. 42; and *Paul*, p. 11.

[2] *Light from the Ancient East*, p. 234. In greater detail see *Bible Studies*, pp. 43–59 and *Paul*, pp. 11–26.

[3] Benjamin W. Bacon was one of the few scholars who expressed reservations: "It is a question of more or less" (*The Story of St. Paul* [Boston: Houghton, Mifflin and Company, 1904], p. 233). William Mitchell Ramsay welcomed Deissmann's work but declared it impossible "to reduce all the letters of the New Testament to one or other of those categories" (*The Letters to the Seven Churches of Asia and Their Place in the Plan of the Apocalypse* [New York: A. C. Armstrong & Son, 1905], p. 24).

It is interesting to notice that the so-called "Dutch radical school" welcomed Deissmann's distinction but applied it in reverse. Already believing that the entire Pauline Corpus was written in the second century, they were quick to give the name "epistles" to "the supposed letters of Paul." See, e.g., W. C. van Manen, "Paul: Later Criticism," *EnBib*, III, 3626.

[4] For example, Rudolf Bultmann, *Der Stil der Paulinischen Predigt und die Kynischstoische Diatribe* (Göttingen: Vandenhoeck und Ruprecht, 1910); Eduard Norden, *Agnostos Theos: Untersuchungen zur Formengeschichte religiöser Rede* (Stuttgart: B. G. Teubner, 1912); Otto Roller, *Das Formular der paulinischen Briefe: Ein Beitrag zur Lehre vom antiken Briefe* ("Beiträge zur Wissenschaft vom Alten und Neuen Testament," Bd. LVIII; Stuttgart: W. Kohlhammer Verlag, 1933); Ernst von Dobschütz, "Zum Wortschatz und Stil des Römerbriefes," *ZNW*, XXXIII (1934), 51–66; Martin Dibelius, *A Fresh Approach to the New Testament and Early Christian Literature* (London: I. Nicholson and Watson, 1936), pp. 142–50; Paul Schubert, *The Form and Function of the Pauline Thanksgivings* ("Beihefte zur ZNW," Beiheft XX; Berlin: Alfred Töpelmann, 1939); Nils W. Lund, *Chiasmus in the New Testament* (Chapel Hill: The University of North Carolina Press, 1942); Rafael Gyllenberg, "Die einleitenden Grussformeln in den paulinischen Briefen," *Svensk Exegetisk Arsbok*, XVI = 1951 (1952), 21–31; and Béda Rigaux, "Les Lettres devant la Formgeschichte," chap. vi of *Saint Paul et ses Lettres: État de la Question* ("Studia Neotestamentica," Subsidia II; Paris: Desclée de Brouwer, 1962), pp. 163–99, a useful survey with a generous bibliography.

[5] For defence of Deissmann's position see, e.g., R. D. Shaw, *The Pauline Epistles* (4th ed.; Edinburgh: T. & T. Clark, 1914), p. 3, n. 1, and pp. 7–10; Ernest Findlay Scott, *The Literature of the New Testament* (New York: Columbia University Press, 1932), pp. 108–11; Frederick C. Grant, *The New Testament: The Letters and the Revelation to John* ("Nelson's Bible Commentary," ed. F. C. Grant, Vol. VII; New York: Thomas Nelson & Sons, 1962), p. 64; and, with special emphasis, Morton Scott Enslin, *Christian Beginnings* (New York: Harper & Brothers, 1938), pp. 213–14; Joseph Klausner, *From Jesus to Paul*, trans. William F. Stinespring (London: George Allen & Unwin, Ltd., 1944), p. 234; and Wilhelm Michaelis, *Einleitung in das Neue Testament* (2. Aufl.; Bern: Berchthold Haller Verlag, 1954), pp. 144–9.

of great importance. Kirsopp Lake summarized the problem in the Preface to *The Earlier Epistles of St. Paul: Their Motive and Origin* (again using "letters" in its technical sense):

> The difficulty which undoubtedly attends any attempt to understand the Epistles of St. Paul is largely due to the fact that they are letters; for the writer of a letter assumes the knowledge of a whole series of facts, which are, as he is quite aware, equally familiar to his correspondent and to himself. But as time goes on this knowledge is gradually forgotten and what was originally quite plain becomes difficult and obscure; it has to be rediscovered from stray hints and from other documents by a process of laborious research, before it is possible for the letters to be read with anything approaching to the ease and intelligence possessed by those to whom they were originally sent. It is necessary to reconstruct the story of the motive and origin of the letters, and create a picture of the background of thought and practice against which they were set in the beginning.[1]

This reconstruction of the "motive and origin" of Paul's letters both precedes and is involved with an understanding of Paul's meaning, and thus of his theology. The importance of the historical setting of a text is a basic principle of modern study of, for example, the Synoptic Gospels. Since the rise of Form Criticism after the First World War no scholar considers it sufficient to ask the meaning of a pericope as it stands. The exegete must seek in so far as possible the *Sitz im Leben* of each saying. Similarly for Paul a *Sitz im Leben* must be sought for each of his letters. And just as it is unsound when interpreting Synoptic sayings to ignore the complex history of the Synoptic tradition and the theologies of the Gospel writers, so it is also unsound to quote Paul to explain Paul from one letter to another with regard neither for the occasions of the letters nor for the original purposes of the passages in question.

The dual occasions of Paul's letters. Strictly speaking, there were two factors involved in the *Sitz im Leben* of each of Paul's letters. On the one hand there was the special situation of each Church to which Paul wrote: its interests, needs, questions, misunderstandings, failures, and triumphs. On the other hand there was Paul's own situation at the

---

[1] P. vii. On this matter John Locke's comments in his "Essay for the Understanding of St. Paul's Epistles" are prophetic: "The nature of epistolary writings in general disposes the writer to pass by the mentioning of many things, as well known to him to whom his letter is addressed, which are necessary to be laid open to a stranger, to make him comprehend what is said. . . . Add to this, that in many places it is manifest he answers letters sent, and questions proposed to him, which, if we had, would much better clear those passages that relate to them than all the learned notes of critics and commentators, who in after-times fill us with their conjectures. . . ." (Quoted by George Milligan, *St. Paul's Epistles to the Thessalonians* [London: Macmillan and Co., 1908], p. xlii, n. 1.) The essay was prefixed to Locke's *A Paraphrase and Notes on the Epistles of Paul*, published 1705–7.

time he wrote: his interests, insights, needs, hopes, fears, and his maturing experience as an ambassador for Christ. These two factors can never be fully separated, for Paul's experience was formed in part by the needs of his Churches, and their needs and questions were in part the result of his preaching. But to the extent to which these factors are distinct we can say that in seeking to understand the occasion of a given letter both the situation of those addressed and of Paul himself must be sought.

Modern Pauline biography and Pauline theology

Recent Pauline scholarship. The desire to recreate the life and times of the Apostle in order to understand him was fundamental to the work of Deissmann and scholars of his period. This approach has never lacked some adherents, especially in England and America.[1]

As Amos N. Wilder put it: "This attitude is not to be construed as a mere survival in America of an exploded historicism. It represents rather a conviction that all aspects of primitive Christianity, not only its external phenomena but the kerygmatic faith itself, are relative to social-cultural factors, and no dichotomy can be made between faith and history."[2] But as Wilder's statement implies, Pauline scholarship whether by reaction or evolution has not followed Deissmann's brand

[1] E.g., George S. Duncan, *St. Paul's Ephesian Ministry* (London: Hodder & Stoughton, 1929), which was written at Deissmann's express suggestion; Wilfred L. Knox, *St. Paul and the Church of Jerusalem* (Cambridge: The University Press, 1925), and *St. Paul and the Church of the Gentiles* (Cambridge: The University Press, 1939); F. J. Foakes-Jackson and K. Lake (eds.), *The Beginnings of Christianity* (5 vols.; London: Macmillan and Co., 1920–33); C. H. Dodd, "The Mind of Paul: II," chap. v of his *New Testament Studies* (Manchester: Manchester University Press, 1953), pp. 83–128; T. W. Manson, *Studies in the Gospels and Epistles*, ed. M. Black (Manchester: Manchester University Press, 1962); John Knox, *Philemon among the Letters of Paul: A New View of its Place and Importance* (New York: Abingdon Press, 1936; rev. ed., 1959); " 'Fourteen Years Later': A Note on the Pauline Chronology," *JR*, XVI (1936), 341–9; "The Pauline Chronology," *JBL*, LVIII (1939), 15–29; *Chapters in a Life of Paul* (New York: Abingdon-Cokesbury Press, 1950); Wilbur Mitchell Franklin, *Die Kollekte des Paulus* (Scottdale, Pa.: Mennonite Publishing House, 1938); Donald W. Riddle, *Paul: Man of Conflict: A Modern Biographical Sketch* (Nashville: Cokesbury Press, 1940); Paul S. Minear, "The Jerusalem Fund and Pauline Chronology," *ATR*, XXV (1943), 389–96; J. R. Porter, "The 'Apostolic Decree' and Paul's Second Visit to Jerusalem," *JTS*, XLVII (1946), 169–74; Charles H. Buck, Jr, "The Collection for the Saints," *HTR*, XLIII (1950), 1–29; "The Date of Galatians," *JBL*, LXX (1951), 113–22; D. T. Rowlingson, "The Jerusalem Conference and Jesus' Nazareth Visit," *JBL*, LXXI (1952), 69–74; R. W. Funk, "The Enigma of the Famine Visit," *JBL*, LXXV (1956), 130–6; M. J. Suggs, "Concerning the Date of Paul's Macedonian Ministry," *Novum Testamentum*, IV (1960), 60–8; R. G. Hoerber, "Galatians 2:1–10 and the Acts of the Apostles," *Concordia Theological Monthly*, XXXI (1960), 482–91; C. E. Faw, "The Anomaly of Galatians," *Biblical Research*, IV (1960), 25–38; H. L. Ramsey, *The Place of Galatians in the Career of Paul* (Ph.D. Thesis, Columbia University, 1960; Ann Arbor, Mich: University Microfilms, Inc., 1961).

[2] "Biblical Hermeneutic and American Scholarship," *Neutestamentliche Studien für Rudolf Bultmann* ("Beihefte zur ZNW," Beiheft XXI; Berlin: Alfred Töpelmann, 1954), p. 25.

of "historicism". Such detailed study of historical origins, it came to be believed, tended to fragment the New Testament analytically, and to particularize its message in a world far different from the modern age. In reaction to this "historical" approach scholars began to re-emphasize the universal, timeless, "theological" elements in the New Testament in order to increase its relevancy for present-day problems. Three notable examples of this more recent emphasis are:

(a) Rudolf Bultmann's programme of "demythologizing" the faith of the early Church, that is, of freeing the gospel from the ancient world view through which it was expressed.[1]

(b) Gerhard Kittel's *Theologisches Wörterbuch zum Neuen Testament*[2] which, by focusing attention on the New Testament usage of individual words, minimizes the element of particularity and individuality in the thought of the various New Testament writers.

(c) C. H. Dodd's attempt to recover a single, general pattern of Apostolic preaching—"the Kerygma"—behind the multiplicity of New Testament documents.[3]

Currently, however, we seem to be entering a period in which more attention is being given in hermeneutical discussions to the relationship and interdependence of faith and history.[4] And the historical problems connected with Paul's letters are receiving renewed attention among both American and European scholars.[5]

Modern assumptions about Pauline theology based on biographical

---

[1] Bultmann's essay, *Offenbarung und Heilsgeschehen: Die Frage der natürlichen Offenbarung. Neues Testament und Mythologie* ("Beiträge zur Evangelische Theologie," Bd. 7; München: A. Lempp) appeared in 1941.

[2] (Stuttgart: W. Kohlhammer Verlag, 1933——). Recently the rationale of the *TWNT* has been questioned by James Barr, *The Semantics of Biblical Language* (London: Oxford University Press, 1961), especially pp. 206–62. His stimulating use of insights from the field of linguistics may be viewed as analogous to Deissmann's cross-fertilization of Biblical studies from the area of papyrology.

[3] See *The Apostolic Preaching and Its Developments* (London: Hodder & Stoughton, 1936). For a criticism of Dodd's work as an attempt to find an "ecumenical" New Testament theology see Henry J. Cadbury, "Acts and Eschatology," *The Background of the New Testament and Its Eschatology*, ed. W. D. Davies and David Daube (Cambridge: The University Press, 1956), pp. 300–21. A rebuttal of this and other criticisms of Dodd's hypothesis is found in W. D. Davies, "A Quest to be Resumed in New Testament Studies," republished as chap. i of his *Christian Origins and Judaism* (London: Darton, Longman & Todd, 1962), pp. 3–7.

[4] See, e.g., Wilder, "Biblical Hermeneutic," pp. 24–32; C. C. McCown, "The Current Plight of Biblical Scholarship," *JBL*, LXXV (1956), 12–18; J. Coert Rylaarsdam, "The Problem of Faith and History in Biblical Interpretation," *JBL*, LXXVII (1958), 26–32; Krister Stendahl, "Implications of Form-Criticism and Tradition-Criticism for Biblical Interpretation," *JBL*, LXXVII (1958), 33–8.

[5] On the Continent, e.g., the following articles appeared in the single collection *Studia Paulina in Honorem Johannis de Zwaan Septuagenarii*, ed. J. N. Sevenster and W. C. van Unnik (Haarlem: De Erven F. Bohn N. V., 1953): A. S. Geyser, "Paul, the Apostolic

conclusions. It is noticeable that recent Pauline study, where it has been concerned with the occasion and motivation of Paul's letters, has concentrated on the first of the two factors distinguished above: the situations within the Pauline Churches. Very little attention has been given to the second factor: the particular state of Paul's mind reflected in each letter.[1] In other words, the study of development in Paul's theology, once a favourite topic,[2] is now largely abandoned.[3] John Lowe

Decree and the Liberals in Corinth," pp. 124–38; Joachim Jeremias, "Zur Gedankenführung in den paulinischen Briefen: (3) Die Briefzitate in 1. Kor 8, 1–13," pp. 151–2; and Bo Reicke, "Der geschichtliche Hintergrund des Apostelkonzils und der Antiochia-Episode, Gal. 2, 1–14," pp. 172–87.

[1] E.g., E. F. Scott writes, "We have to put ourselves into the position of those definite communities to which Paul wrote" (*Intro. N. T.*, p. 110). An extreme example of this tendency to concentrate more on the historical background than on Paul's thought is Walter Schmithals, *Die Gnosis in Korinth: Eine Untersuchung zu den Korintherbriefen* (Göttingen: Vandenhoeck & Ruprecht, 1956).

[2] Albert Schweitzer in assessing Pauline scholarship "From Baur to Holtzmann" says, "There is in works of this period much assertion and little proof regarding the development within Paulinism. One almost gets the impression that the assumption of different stages of thought was chiefly useful as a way of escaping the difficulty about the inner unity of the system" (*Paul and his Interpreters: A Critical History*, trans. W. Montgomery [London: Adam and Charles Black, 1912], p. 32). He lists the following works which deal with theological development in Paul's thought: Auguste Sabatier, *The Apostle Paul: A Sketch of the Development of his Doctrine*, trans. A. M. Hellier (3d ed., London: Hodder and Stoughton, 1896); Hermann Karl Lüdemann, *Die Anthropologie des Apostels Paulus und ihre Stellung innerhalb seiner Heilslehre nach den vier Hauptbriefen* (Kiel, 1872); Eduard Reuss, *History of the Sacred Scriptures of the New Testament*, trans. E. L. Houghton (2 vols.; Boston: Houghton, Mifflin and Company, 1884); Otto Pfleiderer, *Paulinism: A Contribution to the History of Primitive Christian Theology*, trans. E. Peters (2 vols.; London: Williams and Norgate, 1877); Bernhard Weiss, *Biblical Theology of the New Testament*, trans. D. Eaton (2 vols.; Edinburgh: T. & T. Clark, 1885–1893); and, with special emphasis on the development of Paul's eschatological thought, Ernst G. G. Teichmann, *Die paulinischen Vorstellung von Auferstehung und Gericht* (1896); and Heinrich Julius Holtzmann, *Lehrbuch der neutestamentlichen Theologie* (2 vols.; Freiburg i. B.: Mohr, 1897). Schweitzer might well have included the work of four English scholars: Joseph Barber Lightfoot, "The Chronology of Paul's Life and Epistles," *Biblical Essays*, ed. posthum. J. Rendel Harris (London: Macmillan and Co., 1893), pp. 213–33; George Matheson, *The Spiritual Development of St. Paul* (Edinburgh: W. Blackwood and Sons, 1897); and, on Paul's eschatological development: Henry St. John Thackeray, *The Relation of St. Paul to Contemporary Jewish Thought* (London: Macmillan and Co., 1900), pp. 98–135; and R. H. Charles, *A Critical History of the Doctrine of a Future Life in Israel, in Judaism, and in Christianity* (2d ed. rev.; London: Adam and Charles Black, 1913).

[3] Modern scholars who affirm the existence of theological development in Paul's letters may be classified in three groups:

(*a*) There are a number of scholars who believe that the differences between 1 Cor. 15 and 2 Cor. 5 result from a change in Paul's eschatological hopes: Hans Ludwig Windisch, *Der zweite Korintherbrief* ("Meyer," 6. Abt., 9. Aufl.; Göttingen: Vandenhoeck & Ruprecht, 1924), p. 157; W. L. Knox, *Gentiles*, pp. 125–45; W. D. Davies, *Paul and Rabbinic Judaism: Some Rabbinic Elements in Pauline Theology* (2d ed.; London: S.P.C.K., 1955), pp. 317–19, 367; R. F. Hettlinger, "2 Corinthians 5.1–10," *SJT*, X (1957), 184–94; Hans-Joachim Schoeps, *Paul: The Theology of the Apostle in the Light of Jewish Religious History*, trans. H. Knight (London: Lutterworth Press, 1961), p. 103; and F. W. Beare, *St Paul and his Letters* (London: Adam & Charles Black, 1962), pp. 88–90.

(*b*) A second group of scholars attributes a broader eschatological development to Paul. They mention the Thessalonian letter(s) as representing an earlier stage than 1 Cor., and/or

in his article, "An Examination of Attempts to Detect Development in St. Paul's Theology,"[1] begins with an apology for seemingly "flogging a dead horse", but justifies his discussion by saying that with reference to development in Paul's theology, "one still sees suggestions of the kind even in scholarly works". (The scholars to whom he refers are W. L. Knox and C. H. Dodd.) This negative attitude toward the idea of theological development in Paul's letters is not due to any denial by scholars that Paul made an intellectual pilgrimage, or that his thought enlarged and developed during his life. Neither is this lack of interest due to any scarcity of material from which to reconstruct this development. Certainly students of the history of the Synoptic tradition have far less evidence for their reconstructions. Rather it is due to a combination of several items of evidence which makes it appear that Paul wrote all the letters which survive during a relatively brief period after half his Christian ministry was past. Thus it is argued that, however much Paul may have developed since the day of his conversion, little or no development is to be expected in his extant letters. As Lowe put it, "The real question is whether we can observe progress of thought within the period covered by the letters. . . . Every one of the letters

some of the letters after 2 Cor. as representing a later stage or stages: H. Wheeler Robinson, *The Christian Doctrine of Man* (3d ed., Edinburgh: T. & T. Clark, 1926), pp. 129–31, with a reference to R. H. Charles' work listed in the previous footnote; T. W. Manson, *Studies*, pp. 163–5, who accepts what he calls Dodd's theory of "St. Paul's second conversion"; Richard Heard, *An Introduction to the New Testament* (New York: Harper & Brothers, 1950), pp. 182, 193, who advises that the reader "should study the epistles of Paul, in their chronological order to understand . . . how his thought developed as he grew older" (p. 162); John A. T. Robinson, *Jesus and His Coming: The Emergence of a Doctrine* (London: SCM Press Ltd, 1957), pp. 160–1, who believes the development to be real but less radical than C. H. Dodd and W. L. Knox maintain; A. M. Hunter, *Paul and his Predecessors* (rev. ed.; London: SCM Press Ltd, 1961), pp. 98–102, 148, who explicitly reproduces the four stages formulated by R. H. Charles; and Thorleif Boman, "Hebraic and Greek Thought-Forms in the New Testament," in *Current Issues in New Testament Interpretation: Essays in Honor of Otto A. Piper*, ed. W. Klassen and G. F. Snyder (New York: Harper & Brothers, 1962), pp. 5–12.

(c) A third group finds evidence of development in areas other than, or in addition to, the eschatological: William E. Wilson, "The Development of Paul's Doctrine of Dying and Rising again with Christ," *ET*, XLII (1930/31), 562–5; Arthur Darby Nock, *St. Paul* ("The Home University Library"; London: Oxford University Press, 1946), pp. 202–6, who notes development in Paul's eschatology and ethics but warns that Paul's major developments predate his letters (pp. 14–15); Buck, "Date of Galatians," pp. 113–22, who builds on Lightfoot by postulating development of the faith–works antithesis from 2 Cor. 1–9 through Gal. to Rom.; Dodd, "Mind of Paul," pp. 108–28, who describes development in eschatology and in universalism; Faw, "Anomaly of Galatians," pp. 28–32, who summarizes the work of Lightfoot and Buck with approval and sees additional evidence of development in Paul's use of the term "Spirit" and in his death-and-resurrection symbolism; and F. F. Bruce, "The Epistles of Paul," in *Peake's Commentary on the Bible*, ed. M. Black and H. H. Rowley (London: Thomas Nelson and Sons Ltd, 1962), §§805e–807c, who outlines a pattern of development both in Paul's eschatology and in his view of the church as the body of Christ.

[1] *JTS*, XLII (1941), 129–42.

lies within a period of a dozen years, viz. A.D. 50–62. We have none at all from what would presumably be the formative stages in Paul's career as a Christian, the years following his conversion."[1] In saying this Lowe echoes the opinion of the overwhelming majority of modern scholars, an opinion buttressed by the authority of such a great interpreter of Paul as Johannes Weiss: "It cannot be too much insisted upon that the real development of Paul both as a Christian and as a theologian was completed in this [early] period which is so obscure to us, and that in the letters we have to do with the fully matured man. . . . We cannot watch Paul's growth during these [early] years. By contrast, the 'development' which some think they can discern in the period of the letters—ten years, at the most—is not worth considering at all."[2]

This argument is as reasonable as it is widespread. Indeed, as the notes to the next section of this chapter will show, it is difficult to find any writers on Paul who do not agree on these two points:

[1] Ibid., pp. 130, 131.

[2] *The History of Primitive Christianity*, trans. and ed. Frederick C. Grant *et al.* (2 vols.; New York: Wilson-Erickson, 1936), I, 206. His verdict was echoed by James Moffatt: "The extant letters of the apostle fall . . . in the late afternoon of his career" (*An Introduction to the Literature of the New Testament* [3d ed. rev.; "International Theological Library"; Edinburgh: T. & T. Clark, 1918], p. 62); "To arrange the epistles in the order and for the reasons suggested, *e.g.*, by Lightfoot, is to confuse the parade-ground with the battle-field" (ibid., p. 170). So also E. F. Scott, "Attempts . . . to trace out a development of Paul's thought . . . [form] a somewhat futile task" (*Intro. N. T.*, p. 112); George S. Duncan, "Even if we accept Galatians as the earliest of all his letters, we must not forget that at this date Paul had already been a Christian for perhaps seventeen years, and in its essential features his gospel was already formed" (*The Epistle of Paul to the Galatians* ["Moffatt"; London: Hodder and Stoughton, 1934], p. xxi); William Neil, "As is always [to be] pointed out in reply to suggestions of this kind, affecting . . . alleged developments in the apostle's thought, Paul had been a missionary for approximately fifteen years before he wrote anything at all. It is odd, therefore, that [one should believe that] . . . fundamental changes of outlook should have taken all these years to materialize and, when they did, that they should then have taken place within a period of approximately ten years and sometimes within a period of months" (*The Epistle of Paul to the Thessalonians* ["Moffatt"; London: Hodder and Stoughton, 1950], pp. 25–6); and Neill Q. Hamilton, "At the time of the authorship of the first epistle (I Thessalonians) which gives us evidence of Paul's theology, the Apostle, according to Professor Dodd's . . . chronology 'was at least forty years old, probably older. He had been a Christian for fifteen years or more, a trained theologian before that, and an active Christian teacher for at least twelve years, probably longer.' At such an age and with such a background it is highly improbable that Paul's thought would change considerably" (*The Holy Spirit and Eschatology in Paul* ["Scottish Journal of Theology Occasional Papers," No. 6; Edinburgh: Oliver and Boyd Ltd., 1957], p. 61).

R. M. Grant does note differences in the way in which Paul dealt with various topics in his letters, but is agnostic about the possibility of identifying a pattern of theological development. He concludes: "Probably . . . in view of our ignorance about Paul's early life and the occasional nature of his letters we cannot say much about such a development. . . . If we confine our speculations to what can be said *with certainty*, we know only that Paul wrote to the Thessalonians from Corinth about 50, to the Corinthians from Ephesus about 52, and to the Romans, probably from Corinth, about 55" (*Historical Introduction*, p. 173, emphasis added).

(a) The relative lateness of Paul's letters, and therefore,

(b) the unlikelihood of real theological development in the period of the letters.[1]

Scholars are almost unanimous in believing that Paul's significant development took place in the early part of his ministry and that the letters are from the later part of his career. This agreement empties the study of Pauline chronology of theological significance. Scholars of the past have produced innumerable chronologies of Paul's life, but as Massey H. Shepherd, Jr, says of the sister endeavour, the source

---

[1] Those scholars who allow development in Paul's letters can in theory be classified in two groups: (a) those who challenge the usual chronological assumptions which are the premise of this argument, and (b) those who accept the premise but challenge the conclusion drawn from it.

(a) A small group of scholars does not accept the chronological evidence derived mainly from Acts which places Paul's letters in the second half of his career. The work of Riddle, J. Knox, and Buck has been noted above, p. 6, n. 1. H. L. Ramsey, a pupil of Knox's, accepts his main chronological conclusions (Place of Galatians, p. 351). Knox's chronology is also accepted by R. P. C. Hanson, II Corinthians ("Torch Bible Commentaries"; London: SCM Press Ltd, 1954), p. 11; and by Frederic R. Crownfield, A Historical Approach to the New Testament (New York: Harper & Brothers, 1960), p. 259, n. 3. M. J. Suggs ("Paul's Macedonian Ministry") accepts and supplies additional evidence for Knox's proposal of an earlier date for Paul's western mission. Of these scholars, however, only Buck and Suggs, to the present writer's knowledge, have used their chronological conclusions to support a developmental presentation of Paul's theology, but neither of these scholars has published such a reconstruction. Buck's former students at the Episcopal Theological School, Cambridge, Mass. (1945–53), will remember that his courses on Pauline thought were organized around his chronology, the centre section of which he published much compressed in "Collection for the Saints." His other article, "Date of Galatians," is a sample of his close literary reasoning which, in this instance, does not arise from, but leads to, chronological considerations. And Suggs in a personal communication to the writer (dated 15 Jan. 1962) in reference to his article mentioned above indicated that he had been "struck by the possibilities which a revised chronology presents for Pauline theology".

(b) Dodd ("The Mind of Paul"), W. L. Knox (Gentiles), and, except for Buck, all the other scholars listed above, p. 15, n. 1, find room for development in Paul's theology in the period of his mature Christian ministry. (Dodd's chronological conclusions are conveniently found in his article "Chronology of the Acts and Pauline Epistles," Helps to the Study of the Bible, by A. W. F. Blunt et al. [2d ed. rev.; London: Oxford University Press, 1931], pp. 195–7.) Dodd shows (p. 84) that he is well aware of the chronological objection to the development he finds in Paul's letters (written, he believes, A.D. 50–64) by saying, "I should only depreciate any presumption at the onset that the mind of Paul is not likely to have developed in middle age. . . . About A.D. 50 Paul entered upon a new phase of his missionary work. . . .Would it be surprising if his thought took fresh turns?" Although Dodd does not attempt to increase the period of the letters by lowering the date of the earliest, he is zealous in keeping the date of the last as high as possible. Thus he devotes pp. 85–108 of the above essay to a detailed criticism of Duncan's book, St. Paul's Ephesian Ministry. Duncan represents a series of scholars who would place some or all of the captivity letters during an imprisonment at Ephesus (see pp. 14–15, and p. 303, n. 6 below). Such an hypothesis if adopted for all the imprisonment epistles would reduce the span of Paul's letter writing activity to three or four years, making any theory of development impossible. It is noticeable that the list given above of scholars favouring development and the list below of scholars accepting the Ephesian imprisonment hypothesis do not overlap except in one instance. Bruce dates Philippians (only) from such an imprisonment, placing it between 1 and 2 Corinthians ("Epistles of Paul," §809).

analysis of Acts, "The general verdict, accepted by many who had indulged most strenuously in the game, was that nobody could win".[1] The result is that Pauline chronology receives little attention today from scholars. Donald Riddle puts it down to academic laziness:

> It is highly regrettable that at this point the conventionality in the extant "lives" of Paul occurs. This is not merely because of the difficulty of determining the dates and sequence of the letters, or of fixing the letters in their relation to observable statistical facts. It is due to the readiness to determine dates and adjust letters to the simple schematic outline of the secondary traditions [i.e., Acts]. For most scholars the temptation to avail oneself of this too easy system is inescapable.[2]

But it seems more just to say that the principal cause of this neglect is the conviction that these details simply do not matter theologically. It is thus of particular importance to note that the scholars who have worked on the chronological problem recently—Riddle, J. Knox, and Buck—agree in suggesting earlier dates for Paul's first letters. Since it is the period of Paul's early ministry in which it is generally expected that a development in Paul's theological thought took place, their suggestion, although merely chronological, is thus highly significant theologically. Let us examine, therefore, the points of evidence on which the usual late dating of Paul's letters rests.

THE EVIDENCE FOR THE USUAL CHRONOLOGY OF PAUL'S LETTERS

The evidence of Acts

The method. In reconstructing the events of Paul's life the accepted starting point is the book of Acts. Two reasons explain this uniformity in procedure:

(*a*) Acts is the only (relatively) connected account extant of Paul's labours. It has, moreover, the external authority of tradition, and the internal witness of, for example, the "we" sections.

(*b*) Paul's own letters provide such fragmentary biographical data.[3]

---

[1] "A Venture in the Source Analysis of Acts," *Munera Studiosa*, ed. M. H. Shepherd, Jr, and S. E. Johnson (Cambridge, Mass.: Published by the Episcopal Theological School, 1946), p. 91.

[2] *Paul: Man of Conflict*, p. 77.

[3] J. Knox and Johannes Munck both witness to the universality of this method of using Acts by the sweeping nature of their objections to this procedure. Knox says, e.g., "While we tend to harmonize Acts with the letters as regards the inner facts of Paul's life, we tend to harmonize the letters with Acts as regards the outer. Neither instance of harmonization, of course, can be justified" (*Chapters*, p. 32). Munck accepts Knox's evaluation of the

As Edgar J. Goodspeed poetically put it, "The biographer of Paul thus sets himself to weave the letters into the narrative of The Acts as the weaver weaves his threads into the warp on his loom."[1] Although expressed in this way the method appears suspiciously simple, it is the approach adopted by practically every writer on Paul from the Church Fathers to the present day.[2] The footnotes appended to this chapter are by no means complete, but they are intended to give an impression of this uniformity of procedure.

In Acts Paul (Saul) first appears at the martyrdom of Stephen (Acts 7.58; 8.1, 3) as an arch-enemy of the Church. Converted in Acts 9, Paul does not take the centre of the stage again until his first missionary journey, so-called, in Acts 13—14. Not until his second journey (Acts 15.40—18.22) does he establish the first of the Churches to which his letters are addressed.[3] All the letters, however, except Romans and Colossians (and Ephesians), were written to Churches Paul had visited previously.[4] But when Paul wrote Romans he had already penetrated to the west as far as Illyricum (Rom. 15.19). Further, no scholar who accepts Colossians and Ephesians as genuine considers them Paul's earliest letters. Thus none of Paul's letters can be inserted into the Acts narrative before the beginning of the second missionary journey (Acts 15.40) with the possible exception of Galatians for special reasons to be discussed below.

The Thessalonian letters. The Thessalonian correspondence is considered by many scholars to be Paul's earliest. Acts tells of Paul's evangelization of Thessalonica in 17.1–9. Paul is next described as escaping to Athens (Acts 17.15–34). Most scholars take 1 Thess. 3.1 ("Therefore . . . we were willing to be left behind at Athens alone") to refer to this visit to Athens. Thus they place the writing of this letter during the visit to Corinth described in Acts 18.1–18 just after Timothy's return to Paul, which is mentioned both in Acts 18.5 ("When Silas and Timothy arrived from Macedonia . . .")

current situation, and he attributes the general over-reliance on Acts to the persistent influence of the supposedly dead Tübingen school (*Paul and the Salvation of Mankind* [London: SCM Press Ltd, 1959], pp. 77–85).

[1] *Paul* (Philadelphia: John C. Winston Company, 1947), p. vii.

[2] E.g., R. M. Grant says bluntly, "The only way to give a chronological arrangement to the letters is to correlate them with the events described in Acts" (*Historical Introduction*, p. 172).

[3] The theory held by many scholars that Iconium, Lystra, and Derbe (reached by Paul in Acts 14.1–7) are the Galatian Churches to which Paul wrote resulted from the attempt to harmonize Galatians and Acts. This theory, the so-called "South Galatian" hypothesis, affects only Galatians, allowing some scholars to date the letter as early as Acts 14. See the discussion below on the interrelation of Acts and Galatians, pp. 16–19.

[4] Rom. 1.8–15; 15.22–4; Col. 2.1; Eph. 1.5; 3.2, 3; 4.21.

and in 1 Thess. 3.6 ("But now that Timothy has come to us from you . . .").[1]

2 Thessalonians does not connect as neatly with Acts as does 1 Thessalonians, and some scholars reject it as deutero-Pauline. Those who accept it date the letter either immediately before, or more often, just after 1 Thessalonians.

The Corinthian letters. 1 Cor. 16.8 ("I will stay in Ephesus until Pentecost . . .") seems to indicate that the letter was composed while Paul was in Ephesus. 1 Cor. 1.12; 3.4–6; and 16.12 show that Apollos had already worked in Corinth. Therefore scholars date the letter during Paul's stay in Ephesus described in Acts 19 (usually at 19.22) after Apollos had reached Achaia (Acts 18.27, 28).[2]

2 Corinthians has evoked a variety of critical theories concerning its unity or lack of unity. Those scholars, however, who date 1 Corinthians by means of Acts 19 date the subsequent letter(s) during the period from Acts 19 (Ephesus) to Acts 20.2a (Macedonia).

The letter to the Romans. Romans, too, is often regarded as composite. For the most part, however, Rom. 15 is accepted as part of the main letter,[3] so that Rom. 15.14–29 is used to date the letter from Paul's stay in "Greece" (usually assumed to mean Corinth), Acts 20.2b–3a.[4]

The "imprisonment" letters. The "imprisonment" epistles—Philippians, Colossians, Philemon, and Ephesians—are usually grouped (Philippians is sometimes excepted) and referred to a single confinement, which consequently is assumed to be of some seriousness and length.[5] On the basis of Acts, therefore, these letters are dated either from Paul's two-year imprisonment at Caesarea (Acts 24.27),[6] or more usually in Rome (Acts 28.16–31).[7] A group of scholars, however, has followed Deissmann's suggestion that the letters originate from an

---

[1] See appended note 1, pp. 299–300.   [2] See appended note 2, pp. 300–1.

[3] The complicated problem of the long and short recensions is discussed in detail by Lake, *Earlier Epistles*, pp. 324–70. The position of the doxology after 15.33 in P[46] strengthens his argument that Romans 1—15 is the letter Paul sent to Rome. Cf. G. Zuntz, *The Text of the Epistles: A Disquisition upon the Corpus Paulinum* ("The Schweich Lectures of the British Academy," 1946; London: The British Academy, 1953), p. 227; Manson, *Studies*, pp. 225–41; and C. K. Barrett, *A Commentary on the Epistle to the Romans* ("Black"; London: Adam & Charles Black, 1957), pp. 9–13.

On Rom. 16 C. H. Dodd's argument that Paul sent greetings to individuals only in churches he had *not* visited (cf. Col. 4.7–18) is very strong but is not needed to support the present inquiry. See his *The Epistle of Paul to the Romans* ("Moffatt"; New York: Harper and Brothers, 1932), p. xix.

[4] See appended note 3, pp. 302–3.

[5] Manson seems to be alone in arguing that Philippians was not written from prison (*Studies*, pp. 149–67).

[6] See appended note 4, p. 303.   [7] See appended note 5, p. 303.

imprisonment in Ephesus not mentioned by Acts.[1] The theory is important as the only real attempt which has attracted any following to relate Paul's letters by internal evidence rather than by a simple reliance on Acts. However, with Ephesus chosen on the basis of such references as 1 Cor. 15.32 ("I fought with beasts at Ephesus"), these scholars then date the letter(s) in the period of Acts 19.

Over the date of Galatians critical opinion is divided. The major theories by which Galatians and Acts are harmonized remain to be considered next. But all the other Pauline epistles, when they are correlated with Acts in the above manner, definitely appear to be products of the closing years of Paul's active ministry. The Thessalonian letter(s) occur at Acts 18.1 or 5; by Acts 20.4 Paul has embarked on his final and fatal[2] voyage to Jerusalem.

The letter to the Galatians

The chronology of Galatians. Galatians by contrast with Paul's other letters is difficult to date by means of Acts for the very reason that the letter contains so much biographical information. In order to specify the nature of his relationship to the Jerusalem Church Paul summarized his early career at the opening of this letter. His movements may be outlined as follows:

1.13–14	Persecuted the Church.
1.15–16	Converted by God's grace.
1.17*a*	Went to Arabia.
1.17*b*	Returned to Damascus.
1.18–20	"Then after three years" visited Jerusalem for the first time. Remained fifteen days.
1.21	"Then" went to the "regions of Syria and Cilicia".
2.1	"Then after fourteen years" visited Jerusalem again.[3]

[1] See appended note 6, p. 303.

[2] As J. C. O'Neill notes, the theory that Paul was released at Rome, journeyed to Spain, was reimprisoned in Rome and was executed there results from the attempt to find room in the life of Paul for the personal notes found in the Pastoral epistles. This theory he rejects (with most scholars) and points instead to the forebodings of Paul's death which appear in the last chapters of Acts (*The Theology of Acts in its Historical Setting* [London: S.P.C.K., 1961], pp. 55–6). So also Martin Dibelius, *Studies in the Acts of the Apostles*, ed. Heinrich Greeven, trans. Mary Ling (London: SCM Press Ltd, 1956), pp. 157–8.

[3] With reference to the time intervals in Gal. 1.18 and 2.1 it should be noted that each of these periods may be reduced by a year or more if the ancient system of numbering years rather than subtracting dates was used. Thus διὰ δεκατεσσάρων ἐτῶν which literally means "after fourteen years" may also mean "in the fourteenth year", i.e. "after thirteen years". Cf. the equivalence of the two expressions dating the Resurrection: μετὰ τρεῖς ἡμέρας (Mark 8.31; 9.31; 10.34) and τῇ τρίτῃ ἡμέρᾳ (in the parallels in Matt. and Luke). More-

Considered in isolation, Galatians confirms the impression made by Acts that Paul's letters came late in his career. Apparently Paul remained in the east for a considerable length of time (fourteen years if these intervals were intended to refer back to his conversion; more than seventeen years if the periods are consecutive). Of his mission to the west to found the Churches to which he would later write he made no mention in Galatians.

When Galatians and Acts are considered together, however, they strengthen one another's evidence immeasurably, for Galatians supplies definite figures to the time intervals about which Acts is somewhat vague. Paul's conversion is the point of departure for the attempt to transfer the chronological information of Galatians into Acts. Clearly Gal. 1.15, 16 in the above outline corresponds with the account of Paul's conversion in Acts 9.1–19. Further, it seems apparent to most scholars that Paul's visit to Jerusalem "after three years" (Gal. 1.18–20) is to be identified with his first visit in Acts, Acts 9.26–9. But here critical opinion divides in the face of a double obstacle. If the second visits in Galatians and Acts are identified (Gal. 2.1 = Acts 11.27–30) and Galatians is therefore dated before the third visit of Acts 15, then Paul is found writing to Churches which according to Acts he could not yet have established. On the other hand, if Gal. 2.1 is taken to refer to Acts 15, the visit to which it has apparently the most similarity, and Galatians is therefore dated after Acts 15, then the commentator must explain why Paul failed to mention two points vital to his relationship with the Jerusalem Church: the visit of Acts 11.27–30, and the Apostolic Decree of Acts 15.20.

The traditional position on this dilemma (the "North Galatian" hypothesis) is to identify the Γαλατία of Gal. 1.2 with ἡ Γαλατικὴ χώρα of Acts 16.6 and 18.23.[1] And Paul's reference to his "former" visit to Galatia (Gal. 4.13, εὐηγγελισάμην ὑμῖν τὸ πρότερον) is taken to mean the "former" of *two* visits,[2] so that Galatians is dated after Acts 18.23.

Probably the more popular theory at present, however, is the so-called "South Galatian" hypothesis, suggested in 1748 by John Joachim Schmidt, a German grammar school teacher.[3] This theory holds that the "Galatian" Churches to whom Paul wrote were those in Pisidian

over, years were often reckoned from New Year's day and the first fractional year numbered as a whole year. See the detailed discussion by C. W. Emmet, "The Case for the Tradition," *BC*, II, 280–1. Cf. also C. J. Cadoux, "A Tentative Synthetic Chronology of the Apostolic Age," *JBL*, LVI (1937), 184–5, who refers to J. Jeremias, "Sabbatjahr und nt. Chronologie," *ZNW*, XXIX (1928), 101, n. 3.

[1] See appended note 7, pp. 303–4.   [2] See appended note 8, p. 304.
[3] See appended note 9, pp. 304–5.

Antioch, Iconium, Lystra, and Derbe which Paul founded on his first missionary Journey, Acts 13.14—14.23. These cities were not ethnically Gallic, but were included by the Roman Imperial administration within the province of Galatia. Thus it becomes possible to date Galatians before Acts 15, the "Apostolic Council", and thus to identify the two visits to Jerusalem in Gal. 1—2 with the first two visits recorded in Acts (9.26 and 11.27-30).

There are, therefore, actually three decisions to be made in placing Galatians into the narrative of Acts: (a) the destination of the letter, (b) the implication of πρότερον in Gal. 4.13 concerning the number of Paul's visits to Galatia, and (c) the identification of the visit to Jerusalem of Gal. 2.1 with either the second or third visit in Acts.[1] Table 1 shows the possible combinations of these decisions, and the *terminus a quo* for the writing of Galatians resulting from each combination.[2]

Galatians when dated traditionally falls late in Paul's ministry among the other letters. Galatians, therefore, does not increase the span of Paul's letter writing activity, and thus provides no chronological evidence for a theory of theological development in Paul's thought. But if there is any trend to be discerned in the recent study of the introductory problems of Galatians, it is a trend toward the South Galatian hypothesis accompanied, in general, by the identification of Gal. 2.1 and Acts 11.27-30. This theory has two implications for Pauline theology:

[1] G. B. Caird has worked out a neat set of abbreviations to survey and classify the various scholarly identifications of Jerusalem visits. See his *Apostolic Age*, pp. 201-9. A recent and full bibliographical survey of the problem is provided by Rigaux, *Saint Paul et ses Lettres*, pp. 103-23. That he also has his own opinions appears from his comment on Buck, "Collection": "Entre Buck et Luc, on ne peut hésiter" (p. 115).

[2] Note that the first and third decisions above are not equivalent. It is true that if Paul is thought to have been writing to North Galatia he must have done so after the Council of Acts 15 and, conversely, if it is decided that he wrote before the Council he must have addressed churches in South Galatia. However, there are a number of scholars who choose South Galatia, who also equate Gal. 2.1 and Acts 15.4. For them Acts 16.1-5 becomes the *terminus a quo* for the composition of Galatians. So principally J. Weiss, *Primitive Christianity*, pp. 296-9; B. W. Bacon, *Intro. N. T.*, p. 58; and E. de W. Burton, *Gal.* ("ICC"), pp. xliv-xlv.

Note further that, although Table 1 indicates only the earliest point in Acts at which a given combination of assumptions would allow Galatians to stand, in general most scholars place the letter in the interval before the next point in Acts listed at the bottom of the Table. (But notice that there is no interval between Acts 16.1-5 and 16.6.) Thus, for example, one of the reasons which leads scholars to identify the visit of Gal. 2.1 with that of Acts 11.27-30 is the desire to avoid attributing to Paul any incompleteness in his list of visits to Jerusalem. They equate the first two visits in Acts with the two mentioned in Galatians and date the letter *before* the Council visit of Acts 15. To this rule, however, W. M. Ramsay constitutes a notable exception. Although making the above identification of visits, he dated Galatians in a more traditional way; he supposed it to be written during the stay in Antioch mentioned in Acts 18.22. Thus for him Acts 16.1-5 was the second visit to South Galatia implied by Gal. 4.13 (*St. Paul the Traveller*, pp. 184-92).

TABLE 1

The Position of the Epistle to the Galatians in the Narrative of Acts

CRITICAL ASSUMPTIONS

	South Galatia			North Galatia	
Destination	South Galatia			North Galatia	
πρότερον (Gal. 4.13)	"formerly"	"former" (of two visits)		"formerly"	"former"
Jerusalem visits	Gal. 2.1 = Acts 11.27–30			Gal. 2.1 = Acts 15.4	

POSITION OF GALATIANS

Galatians written after:	Acts 14.1–7 Paul's first visit to South Galatia	Acts 14.21 Paul's return trip through South Galatia	Acts 16.1–5 Paul's second tour of South Galatia	Acts 16.6 Paul's first visit to North Galatia	Acts 18.23 Paul's second visit to North Galatia

(*a*) Although in appearance Galatians is placed earlier in Paul's life, actually the result of this identification of visits is that Galatians holds its absolute date (since the chronological information is contained in Galatians), and all the other letters move to later dates. The fourteen (or more than seventeen) years now precede Paul's second rather than his third visit to Jerusalem.

(*b*) Galatians becomes the earliest of Paul's letters. Yet in many ways Galatians is most similar to Romans,[1] which contains Paul's fullest statement of his faith. If, therefore, the earliest letter is so mature, no real development of thought can be expected or allowed in Paul's other letters.

Thus Acts and Galatians separately afford evidence that Paul's letters were written toward the end of his ministry. Taken together, however, with the dates from Galatians inserted in the narrative of Acts the case seems settled beyond reasonable doubt. This is the position of all but a handful of modern New Testament scholars.

THE WEAKNESS OF THE EVIDENCE FOR THE USUAL CHRONOLOGY OF PAUL'S LETTERS

The letter to the Galatians

If Acts had not survived, or had never been written, the evidence that Paul wrote all his letters when a veteran missionary would be confined to Galatians. Only there does Paul describe his early years as a Christian. Yet Paul's description of the interval of fourteen (or more than seventeen) years from his conversion to his return visit to Jerusalem contains only eastern place names. Cilicia is the farthest point to the west mentioned. Is it probable, therefore, that the western mission was not begun until after this long interval? Most scholars answer this question on the basis of their critical decisions concerning the position of Galatians within Acts (see Table 1 above). Those who identify the visits of Gal. 2.1 and Acts 15.4 place the first missionary journey in this period. On the other hand, those who date the letter before Acts 15 refer to this interval as Paul's "silent years". But, Acts to one side, does Galatians imply that the western mission did not precede Paul's visit to Jerusalem "after fourteen years"?

---

[1] See J. B. Lightfoot's classic discussion in *Gal.*, pp. 42–50. His opinion was seconded by Lake, *Earlier Epistles*, p. 299: "The relationship of Galatians to Romans is extraordinarily close. It is similar to, though possibly slightly less marked, than that of Colossians to Ephesians." Additional evidence in support of Lightfoot's thesis is provided by Wilson, "Dying and Rising," p. 565; Buck, "Date of Galatians," pp. 114–16; and Faw, "Anomaly of Galatians," pp. 26–32.

To make such an inference is, admittedly, to argue from silence. Paul said that he "went into the regions of Syria and Cilicia" (Gal. 1.21). Further, his report of the rumour that had reached the Judeans, "He who once persecuted us is now preaching the faith he once tried to destroy" (Gal. 1.23), indicates that Paul spent at least some of the time in missionary work. But he does not define the bounds of his work; he does not say that he did not go beyond Syria and Cilicia. A conclusion based on an "argument from silence" can have considerable probability, of course, but its probability depends on some assumption of completeness in the passage in question. Here we must assume that Paul intended to list at least the main areas in which he worked during this period. What was Paul's purpose in writing this account?

It seems clear, as G. S. Duncan says, that Paul wrote this passage to affirm that "in no sense was he ever in subjection to Jerusalem".[1] Or, as Johannes Weiss put it, "Paul wishes to exclude any idea that he had felt bound to report himself to the original Apostles, or to get himself recognized in some way as though he held his Apostleship by commission from them."[2] The Galatians knew (or would have been expected to know) that he had been in contact with Jerusalem Christianity. Paul's argument, therefore, ran thus (to paraphrase the outline of Gal. 1.13—2.1 given above):

(a) Before my conversion, far from being a catechumen of the Jerusalem Church, or of any other Church, I persecuted Christianity violently.

(b) When I was converted (by God, not by any who were Christians before me) immediately ($\epsilon \mathring{v} \theta \acute{\epsilon} \omega s$):

    (i) I did *not* confer with flesh and blood.

    (ii) I did *not* go up to Jerusalem.

    (iii) I went to Arabia.

(c) When after three years I at last went to Jerusalem I only went to interview ($\mathring{\iota} \sigma \tau o \rho \mathring{\eta} \sigma a \iota$)[3] Cephas.

---

[1] *Gal.*, p. 22.

[2] *Primitive Christianity*, p. 201. So too, e.g., Ernest de Witt Burton, *A Critical and Exegetical Commentary on the Epistle to the Galatians* ("ICC"; Edinburgh: T. & T. Clark, 1921), p. 22, "He affirms his entire independence of all human authority"; and Pierre Bonnard, *L'Épître de Saint Paul aux Galates* ("CNT," Vol. IX; Neuchâtel: Delachaux & Niestlé, 1953), pp. 26–35.

[3] G. D. Kilpatrick maintains that this verb should not be taken as meaning "to pay a social call or a tourist's visit" but in the more serious sense, "to get information from" (within the limits imposed by Gal. 1.12). See his careful article, "Galatians 1.18 *IΣTOPHΣAI KHΦAN*," *New Testament Essays: Studies in Memory of Thomas Walter Manson*, ed. A. J. B. Higgins (Manchester: Manchester University Press, 1959), pp. 144–9.

(i) I did *not* see anyone but Cephas (and James).

(ii) I stayed only fifteen days.

(iii) (Before God I do *not* lie!)

(iv) I did not linger in Judea but immediately went north to Syria and Cilicia.

(v) I remained unknown by sight to Christians in Judea.

(vi) In Judea I was known only by reputation as a converted persecutor of the Church.

(*d*) It was not until fourteen years later that I returned to Jerusalem.

In the above outline "Syria and Cilicia" do not function as a list of Paul's missionary fields during the period between the two visits to Jerusalem. In fact, to have given such a list would have interrupted the flow of his argument with less relevant material. As Johannes Weiss said,

> Gal. 1 and 2 . . . aims at anything but the setting forth of an uninterrupted biographical narrative.[1]
>
> The statement of the Apostle that after his first visit to Jerusalem he went "into the regions of Syria and Cilicia" (Gal. 1.21) is, in its context, just an aside between 1.18ff and 1.22 and has there merely the negative purpose of showing that he had removed himself far from the "sphere of influence" of the original Apostles.[2]

And John Knox is of the same opinion: "What was important in the argument was that he left Judea after his two-weeks' visit; there was no occasion whatever for a description of all his subsequent activities."[3] If Paul had worked in Galatia and to the west during this period, such work would hardly have been interpreted by the Galatians as evidence of a further connection between Paul and the Jerusalem Church. Paul in his letter, therefore, accounted to the Galatians for his activity in the missionary areas on the Jerusalem side of Galatia.[4]

---

[1] *Primitive Christianity*, p. 200, n. 17.   [2] Ibid., p. 203.

[3] *Chapters*, pp. 58–9; and in more detail, " 'Fourteen Years Later,' " pp. 342–5. So, too, Arthur Cushman McGiffert, *A History of Christianity in the Apostolic Age* ("International Theological Library"; Edinburgh: T. & T. Clark, 1897), p. 181: "His argument did not require that he should give an account of himself during all that time, but only that he should omit no occasion on which he came into contact with the Mother Church, or with the older apostles, and on which, therefore, he might be supposed to have received his Gospel." And, more recently, Suggs, "Paul's Macedonian Ministry," pp. 66–7: "It is . . . *a chronology of his relations with Jerusalem and the Jerusalem apostles.* . . . For Paul to say in such a passage, 'Then I went into the regions of Syria and Cilicia,' is not for him to inject a comment about his missionary activity." Notice further that all scholars who equate the visits of Gal. 2.1 and Acts 15.4, and count the latter as Paul's third visit, must assume that Paul was not even complete about his relationship with the Jerusalem Church: he failed to mention in Galatians the visit of Acts 11.27–30.

[4] See map above, p. xiv.

More completeness can not be expected of him. Thus the argument from silence is exceedingly feeble with respect to the western mission.

Clearly the whole argument for the lateness of Paul's letters depends on Acts. The chronological information from Galatians creates the impression of lateness only when placed into the Acts narrative. The crucial question, therefore, is: how much reliance can reasonably be placed in the order of events in Acts? To answer this question there are five points to be considered which concern Acts and three which concern the relationship of Galatians to Acts.

The evidence of Acts

The chronological vagueness of Acts. The narrative of Acts is punctuated by vague references to the passage of time. Such phrases as "about that time" (12.1; 19.23), or "in these days" (6.1; 11.27) are not likely to arouse confidence in the author's chronological information.[1] Kirsopp Lake concludes his essay, "The Chronology of Acts," by saying,

> It cannot escape the attention of any who study the chronology of Acts, how vividly it illustrates the "patchy" nature of the book. Chapters i.–ix. cover not more than three years, but chapters x.–xi. 25 cover fourteen, and the rest of the book (fourteen chapters) covers only nine. . . . For the historian the importance of this observation is clear: we are dealing with selected episodes, not with a continuous history.[2]

Some scholars, however, maintain that the author of Acts had more chronological knowledge than he actually indicated in his narrative. C. J. Cadoux, for example, proposed the theory that the six "panels" into which Acts was divided by C. H. Turner[3] represent in fact consecutive five-year intervals, although the time references are not given in the text.[4] Philip Carrington's hypothesis that Paul's visits to Jerusalem in Acts occurred triennially[5] is a proposal of precisely the same order. But such theories beg the question we are considering, for they depend on the assumption that the order of events in Acts is historically accurate. No attempt is made to consider the tendencies of the author of Acts. Henry J. Cadbury who has made such a study of "Luke-Acts" says of Cadoux's suggestion, "Efforts to detect a subtle plan in

---

[1] Cf. also, e.g., Acts 9.19 ("some days"); 9.23 ("after many days"); 14.28 ("They remained no little time."); 15.36 ("after some days"); and 18.18 ("Paul stayed many days longer.").

[2] *BC*, V, 474.   [3] "Chronology," *DB*, I, 415-25.

[4] "The Chronological Divisions of Acts," *JTS*, XIX (1918), 333-41.

[5] *The Early Christian Church* (2 vols.; Cambridge: The University Press, 1957), pp. 127-8.

the author's arrangement are doubtless misplaced. . . . [Such] a discovery . . . would surprise no one more than the author."[1] No scholar seems to have taken Cadoux's theory seriously but B. W. Bacon,[2] as Cadoux himself complained in a later reaffirmation of his idea.[3] And even Cadoux can say, "The loose articulation of the story in Acts surely allows us to imagine the lapse of two or three years between Acts 12.19a and 20."[4] The verses in question are as follows:

v. 19a And when Herod sought for him [Peter] and could not find him, he examined the sentries and ordered that they should be put to death.

v. 19b And having gone down from Judea to Caesarea he remained there.

v. 20 And he was angry with the people of Tyre and Sidon; . . .

If the author of Acts can ignore a gap of several years here he may have done so at numerous other points in his narrative. In Acts 9.19–26, for example, the "three-year" interval between Paul's conversion (Gal. 1.16), or his return to Damascus (Gal. 1.17), and his first visit to Jerusalem (Gal. 1.18) is represented only by the ἡμέραι ἱκαναί of Acts 9.23 together with the ἡμέρας τινάς of Acts 9.19. Furthermore, the "fourteen-year" interval of Gal. 2.1 is by no means accounted for by Acts whichever way these years are counted. The intervals of time specified in Acts do not add up to fourteen years throughout the entire book! Yet the author of Acts seems by no means unconcerned about the dating of the events he describes. Both his frequent temporal references (indefinite though they are) and his allusions to events in secular history[5] indicate that he intended to give his narrative the form of a history whatever else may have been his motive in writing.

Thus the events in Acts are separated by intervals concerning many of which the author seems uncertain. It is, of course, possible that the process of transmission of the traditions incorporated in Acts preserved the relative order of events without their temporal connection,[6] but the possibility of confusion is high.

Information omitted by Acts. Paul's letters contain relatively little biographical information, yet of the material which they do contain only a small proportion reappears in Acts. The following items are absent from Acts:

---

[1] *The Making of Luke-Acts* (London: Macmillan and Co., 1927, S.P.C.K., 1958), p. 325.
[2] "The Chronological Scheme of Acts," *HTR*, XIV (1921), 137–66.
[3] "Tentative Synthetic Chronology," p. 183, n. 13.   [4] Ibid., p. 185, n. 20.
[5] Discussed by Lake, "Chronology of Acts," *BC*, V, 445–74. Cadbury with Lake and Foakes-Jackson discusses the inaccuracies of some of Acts' references to secular history in *BC*, II, 356–7.
[6] On Dibelius' theory of the "itinerary source" see below, pp. 28, 30.

(i) Five whippings by Jews (2 Cor. 11.24).

(ii) Two beatings by Gentiles (2 Cor. 11.25).[1]

(iii) Three shipwrecks, including one in which Paul did not immediately reach shore but spent a whole day adrift (2 Cor. 11.25).[2]

(iv) An unspecified but sizable number of imprisonments (2 Cor. 11.23 ἐν φυλακαῖς περισσοτέρως).[3]

(v) A contest with wild beasts at Ephesus (1 Cor. 15.32).

(vi) Paul's "affliction in Asia" when he despaired of his life (2 Cor. 1.8).[4]

(vii) The "painful" visit to Corinth before his trip to Macedonia (2 Cor. 2.1; cf. 2 Cor. 12.14; 13.1).

(viii) The sojourn in Arabia (Gal. 1.17).

(ix) All of the events of the fourteen-year interval of Gal. 2.1 except the year in Antioch with Barnabas (Acts 11.26), if the visit of Acts 11.27–30 is to be identified with that of Gal. 2.1.[5]

(x) Paul's collision with Peter in Antioch over table fellowship between Jew and Gentile (Gal. 2.11ff).

(xi) Paul's evangelization of Illyricum (Rom. 15.19).

(xii) The internal discord and divisions in the Corinthian Church (1 Cor. 1.12; 3.4, 22).

(xiii) The Galatian defection caused by opponent(s) of Paul (Gal. 1.6, 7; 5.12).

(xiv) The "collection for the saints" (1 Cor. 16.1; 2 Cor. 9.1, 2; and Rom. 15.25–7), which receives scant notice in Acts. Acts 11.27–30 is a spontaneous burst of generosity, not an organized campaign through the western mission field. Only in Paul's defence before Felix (Acts 24.17, "Now after some years I came

---

[1] 2 Cor. 11.25 has "three"; Acts 16.22–3 at Philippi is the story of one such beating. The author of Acts, it could be argued, was writing an apology to the Gentile world in which miscarriages of Roman justice would not look well and thus he glossed over Paul's other beatings. This line of argument, however, makes the total absence of the Jewish scourgings mentioned above still more difficult to explain except as a result of ignorance.

[2] The shipwreck of Acts 27 occurred after the writing of 2 Cor. 11.25 according to the usual chronology.

[3] Acts has Paul in prison only once (Acts 16.23–39) before his arrest in Jerusalem.

[4] Note that these last two items cannot be equated, for when Paul wrote 2 Cor. his "affliction" apparently lay in the immediate past; 2 Cor. 1.7–10 was his first report to the Corinthians. These items may, of course, correspond with some of the imprisonments and beatings above.

[5] If the visit of Acts 15.4 is chosen, then the rapid narrative of Acts 13 and 14, belongs in this interval together with the χρόνον οὐκ ὀλίγον spent in Antioch in 14.28.

to bring to my nation alms and offerings") is this major project hinted at in retrospect.[1]

Furthermore, at the points where Acts and the letters overlap the disagreements and difficulties are more notable than the agreements:[2]

(i) The problems raised for Acts even by the somewhat sparse outline of events given by Paul in Gal. 1 and 2 have been discussed above.

(ii) The movements of Timothy to and from Thessalonica have occasioned much scholarly ingenuity. According to 1 Thessalonians Paul sent Timothy (presumably alone) from Athens to Thessalonica (3.1, 2), whence he returned to Paul (3.6) with good news. Acts, on the other hand, makes a point of saying that Silas and Timothy did *not* accompany Paul to Athens but remained in Beroea (17.14). Together they rejoined Paul in Corinth (18.5). The customary procedure by which these accounts are "reconciled" is simple conflation. The two stories are dovetailed, neither giving way to the other. They are both referred to one event concerning which it is assumed that what Acts reports Paul omits and vice versa.[3] Since these two accounts have only

[1] Cf. the three backward references in Paul's farewell to the Ephesian elders: that "in every city" the Holy Spirit had repeatedly warned him of what lay ahead in Jerusalem (Acts 20. 23); that he had stayed three years in Ephesus (20.31); and that he had earned his own living there (20.33, 34). So noted by Dibelius, *Studies in Acts*, p. 176. On the importance of the collection trip for Paul see Minear, "Jerusalem Fund," *ATR*, XXV (1943), 389–96.

[2] Rowlingson says flatly, "There is no way of checking many events in Acts, but it is significant that at points at which it can be checked with obviously reliable material in the Letters, it usually proves to be inaccurate, and gives the impression of being a very free and tendentious rendering of events" ("Jerusalem Conference," p. 72).

[3] E.g., Neil, "There is no real contradiction if we explain the situation thus: Paul arrived in Athens alone [Acts, but contrary to the simplest explanation of 1 Thess. 3.1]; Timothy joined him there [omitted by Paul and Acts] and was sent back to Thessalonica when Paul found it impossible to go himself [omitted by Acts]. Paul then went on alone to Corinth [omitted by Paul], and was joined there by Silvanus and Timothy [Acts]" (*Thess.*, p. 62). So also George G. Findlay, *The Epistles to the Thessalonians* ("Camb."; Cambridge: The University Press, 1898), p. 81; E. J. Bicknell, *The First and Second Epistles to the Thessalonians*("West."; London: Methuen & Co. Ltd., 1932), pp. xv–xvi; Charles Masson, *Les Deux Épîtres de Saint Paul aux Thessaloniciens* ("CNT," XIa; Neuchâtel: Delachaux & Niestlé, 1957), p. 39; and Ernst Haenchen, *Die Apostelgeschichte* ("Meyer," 3. Abt., 13. Aufl.; Göttingen: Vandenhoeck & Ruprecht, 1961), p. 471, n. 1.

This theory is but a variant of the one proposed by William Paley (*Horae Paulinae: or the Truth of the Scripture History of St. Paul, Evinced by a Comparison of the Epistles Which Bear His Name with The Acts of the Apostles, and with one Another* [8th ed., London: J. Faulder *et al.*, 1812], chap. IX, sec. 4) by which Timothy and Silas rejoin Paul in Athens. Silvanus (Silas) can then be read into the plural μόνοι of 1 Thess. 3.2. Scholars adopting the theory in this version are G. Wohlenberg, *Der erste und zweite Thessalonicherbrief*("Zahn"; 2. Aufl.; Leipzig: A. Deichert'sche Verlagsbuchhandlung Nachf. [Georg Böhme], 1909), pp. 73–4; Paul W. Schmiedel, "Die Briefe an die Thessalonicher und an die Korinther" ("HCNT"; Freiburg i. B.: J. C. B. Mohr [Paul Siebeck], 1891), II.1, p. 2; James E. Frame, *A Critical and Exegetical Commentary on the Epistles to the Thessalonians* ("ICC"; Edinburgh: T. & T. Clark, 1912), p. 126; Manson, *Studies*, pp. 266–7; F. F. Bruce, *Commentary on the Book of Acts* ("Internat."; Grand Rapids, Mich.: Wm. B. Eerdmans Publishing Company, 1955), p. 347, n. 18; and C. S. C. Williams, *A Commentary on the Acts of the Apostles* ("Black"; London: Adam & Charles Black, 1957), p. 199.

the proper names "Paul", "Timothy", and "Athens" in common, and at every other point either differ or contradict one another more or less directly, there would seem to be more reason for separating these reports than for assuming that they concern a single series of events.[1] And yet this last assumption is the sole basis for the commonly accepted dating of 1 Thessalonians in Corinth during Acts 18.1–18.

On the contrary, 1 Thessalonians considered alone does not sound as though it were composed shortly after Paul's founding visit to the Church addressed. Evidence for the traditional date, however, is usually found in 1 Thess. 2.17, 18 (RSV):

> But since we were bereft of you, brethren, *for a short time*, in person not in heart, we endeavored the more eagerly and with great desire to see you face to face; because we wanted to come to you—I, Paul, again and again—but Satan hindered us.

However, the phrase "for a short time" stands for $\pi\rho\grave{o}s$ $\kappa\alpha\iota\rho\grave{o}\nu$ $\H{\omega}\rho\alpha s$, which may equally well be translated "for the present" or "at the present moment".[2] Indeed, if Paul had left the Thessalonians only shortly before, it is hard to understand how he could have attempted *repeatedly* to revisit them. Furthermore, enough time must be allowed for news of the conversion of the Thessalonians to have preceded Paul beyond Macedonia and Achaia:

> For not only has the word of the Lord sounded forth from you in Macedonia and Achaia, but your faith in God has gone forth everywhere, so that we need not say anything. For they themselves report concerning us what a welcome we had among you, and how you turned from idols, to serve a living and true God.[3]

In addition, the very authenticity of 2 Thessalonians for many scholars depends on the dating of 1 Thessalonians. On the evidence of

---

[1] C. H. Buck even suggests that the author of Acts had access to Paul's letters and added Timothy's name to the source he was following here because he noticed the association of Timothy with Paul in Athens mentioned in 1 Thess. 3.1, 2, 6 ("Collection," pp. 24-5).

[2] See Arndt/Gingrich, p. 395b on $\pi\rho\grave{o}s$ $\kappa\alpha\iota\rho\acute{o}\nu$.

[3] 1 Thess. 1.8–10. It is most natural to take these verses to mean (i) that the Thessalonians have had time to become missionaries themselves and have helped to spread the gospel in Greece, and (ii) that Paul had left Macedonia and Achaia when he met those who already knew of the faith of the Thessalonians. As an alternative to this last it could be supposed that Christians from beyond Greece coming to Paul in Greece brought the information that other Churches knew of the success of the Thessalonian mission (a supposition suggesting still more time). H. L. Ramsey guesses the interval to be two or three years and cites three additional points of evidence: serious afflictions suffered by both Paul and the Thessalonians (3.3–5), the unexpected death of some Christians before the Parousia (4.13–18), and the appearance of opposition to Paul against which 1 Thess. 2.1–12 was a defence (*Place of Galatians*, pp. 187-8).

Acts they believe 1 Thessalonians to be Paul's first letter to Thessalonica written the moment he had news of their situation (Acts 18.5 = 1 Thess. 3.6). And, as Johannes Weiss put it, "The result is that the majority of critical scholars are uncertain as regards the genuineness of 2 Thess. . . . Since they only read it in the shadow, as it were, of the first letter, it seems to them an unimportant and unmeaning copy of 1 Thess."[1] Since Weiss wrote this statement, the majority opinion has probably shifted in favour of the authenticity of 2 Thessalonians, although many modern scholars consider the letter deutero-Pauline.[2] But it is true to say that the exegesis of both the Thessalonian letters has been, and is, almost universally controlled by the chronological information derived from Acts. It is important to notice how really superficial the evidence is by which these letters are customarily dated.

The source analysis of Acts. The usual late dating of Paul's letters rests on the assumption that the narrative of Acts is a single chronological thread. An event which is described after another in Acts is understood to have occurred later in time, and vice versa. Yet as Kirsopp Lake said, "The source criticism of Acts introduces complications which cannot be ignored, even though it be impossible to simplify them.

[1] Primitive Christianity, p. 289, n. 16. Weiss's own solution was to reverse the canonical order of the two epistles and to consider 2 Thessalonians as a letter taken by Timothy from Athens to Thessalonica (ibid.). This suggestion was originally made by Hugo Grotius in 1641 in vol. I of his Annotationes in Novum Testamentum (Amsterdam, 1641), pp. 1032–42 (cited by Manson, Studies, p. 267, n. 2). It is defended by Heinrich Ewald, Die Sendschreiben des Apostels Paulus übersetzt und erklärt (Göttingen: Verlag der Dieterichschen Buchhandlung, 1857), pp. 17, 33; J. C. West, "The Order of 1 and 2 Thessalonians," JTS, XV (1914), 66–74; Hadorn, Abfassung der Thessalonicherbriefe, pp. 116–26; F. J. Badcock, The Pauline Epistles and the Epistle to the Hebrews in Their Historical Setting (London: S.P.C.K., 1937), pp. 43–52; L. O. Bristol, "Paul's Thessalonian Correspondence," ET, LV (1944), 223; Manson, Studies, pp. 267–77; and W. Michaelis, Intro. N. T., pp. 228–30.

[2] Scholars who reject the Pauline authorship of 2 Thess. include Schmiedel, "Thess.," pp. 9–11; H. J. Holtzmann, "Zum zweiten Thessalonicherbrief," ZNW, II (1901), 97–108; William Wrede, Die Echtheit des zweiten Thessalonicherbriefs untersucht ("Texte und Untersuchung zur Geschichte der altchristlichen Literatur," N.S. 9. Bd., 2. Hft.; Leipzig: J. C. Hinrichs, 1903); Georg Hollmann, "Die Unechtheit des zweiten Thessalonicherbriefs," ZNW, V (1904), 28–38; Albert Schweitzer, The Mysticism of Paul the Apostle, trans. William Montgomery (New York: Henry Holt and Company, 1931), p. 42; M. S. Enslin, Beginnings, pp. 239–44; Alfred Loisy, The Origins of the New Testament, trans. L. P. Jacks (London: George Allen and Unwin Ltd, 1950), p. 270; Rudolf Knopf, Hans Lietzmann, and Heinrich Weinel, Einführung in das Neue Testament ("Sammlung Töpelmann," Bd. 2; 5. Aufl.; Berlin: Alfred Töpelmann Verlag, 1949), pp. 81–2; Herbert Braun, "Zur nachpaulinischen Herkunft des zweiten Thessalonicherbriefs," ZNW, XLIV (1952/53), 152–6; Rudolf Bultmann, Theology of the New Testament, trans. Kendrick Grobel (2 vols.; New York: Charles Scribner's Sons, 1951–5), I, 76, 88; Masson, Thess. ("CNT"), pp. 9–13; G. Bornkamm, "Paulus," in RGG³, V, 167; and Karl-Gottfried Echkart, "Der zweite echte Brief des Apostels Paulus an die Thessalonicher," ZThK, LVIII (1961), 30–44, who clearly exaggerates, however, in saying, "Es sollte nicht mehr bezweifelt werden, dass das im Neuen Testament als 2. Thessalonicher-Brief geführte Schreiben nicht von Paulus, sondern so, wie es steht, aus sehr viel späterer Zeit stammt" (p. 30).

Especially is this true of Paul's first and second journeys, and the relation of the 'famine-relief visit' to the Apostolic council."[1]

The fact that the problem is complex and that no scholarly agreement has been, or probably ever will be, reached does not mean that it can be set aside, as does Archibald M. Hunter, for example: "It has been said that in the early decades of the present century splitting the Acts into sources was almost as popular a pastime with the critics, as splitting the atom is nowadays with the scientists. And to tell the plain truth, the scientists have been much more successful than the critics. . . . We have no reason to distrust Luke as an historian."[2] The New Testament does not present merely those problems which may be solved. The problem is there, and it injects a generous measure of uncertainty into the usual dating of the Pauline letters.

Uncertainty concerning the occasion of events in Paul's travels. It may be argued with considerable force that the author of Acts had at his disposal an itinerary of Paul's travels which listed, although it did not

---

[1] "Chronology of Acts," *BC*, V, 473. The literature of the source analysis of Acts is vast and varied. The history of the attempt down to 1916, as well as a full survey of the problem with a suggested solution is presented by Foakes-Jackson and Lake, *BC*, II, 121–175. The following scholars also provide bibliographical surveys: W. Heitmüller, "Die Quellenfrage in der Apostelgeschichte (1886–1898)," *ThRund*, II (1899), 47–59, 83–95, 127–140.; A. Bludau, "Die Quellenscheidungen in der Apostelgeschichte," *Biblische Zeitschrift*, V (1907), 166–89, 258–81; Arthur C. Headlam, "Acts," *DB*, I, 34; Paul W. Schmiedel, "Acts of the Apostles," *EnBib*, I, 37–57; Moffatt, *Intro. N.T.*, pp. 284–96; Werner Georg Kümmel, "Urchristentum," *ThRund*, XIV (1942), 167–73; Jacques Dupont, *The Sources of Acts: The Present Position*, trans. K. Pond (London: Darton, Longman & Todd, 1964); Erich Grässer, "Die Apostelgeschichte in der Forschung der Gegenwart," *ThRund*, XXVI (1960), 94, 123–30; and Haenchen, *Acts* ("Meyer," 13. Aufl.), pp. 13–47, 72–80, 658, and 671–5.

Scholars who have made significant contributions recently include: Martin Dibelius, "Style Criticism of the Book of Acts," *Studies in Acts*, pp. 1–25; Joachim Jeremias, "Untersuchungen zum Quellenproblem der Apostelgeschichte," *ZNW*, XXXVI (1937), 205–21; Harald Sahlin, *Der Messias und das Gottesvolk: Studien zur protolukanischen Theologie* ("Acta Seminarii Neotestamentici Upsaliensis," XII; Uppsala: Almquist & Wiksells, 1945), pp. 347–70; Shepherd, "Source Analysis of Acts"; Wilfred L. Knox, *The Acts of the Apostles* (Cambridge: The University Press, 1948), pp. 16–39; Buck, "Collection," pp. 14–29; Lucien Cerfaux, "Le Chapitre XVᵉ du Livre des Actes à la Lumière de la Littérature Ancienne," *Recueil Lucien Cerfaux* (2 vols.; "Bibliotheca Ephemeridum Theologicarum Lovaniensum," Vols. VI–VII; Gembloux: Éditions J. Duculot, S. A., 1954), II, 105–24; Étienne Trocmé, *Le "Livre des Actes" et l'Histoire* ("Études d'Histoire et de Philosophie Religieuses publiées sous les auspices de la Faculté de Theologie Protestante de l'Université de Strasbourg," No. 45; Paris: Presses Universitaires de France, 1957); Rudolf Bultmann, "Zur Frage nach den Quellen der Apostelgeschichte," in *New Testament Essays: Studies in Memory of Thomas Walter Manson*, ed. A. J. B. Higgins (Manchester: Manchester University Press, 1959), pp. 68–80; and Ernst Haenchen, "Quellenanalyse und Kompositionsanalyse in Act 15," in *Judentum–Urchristentum–Kirche: Festschrift für Joachim Jeremias*, ed. W. Eltester ("Beihefte zur ZNW," Beiheft XXVI; Berlin: Verlag Alfred Töpelmann, 1960), pp. 153–64; and "Das 'Wir' in der Apostelgeschichte und das Itinerar," *ZThK*, LVIII (1961), 329–66.

[2] *Interpreting the New Testament, 1900–1950* (Philadelphia: The Westminster Press, 1951), pp. 110–12.

TABLE 2

Cities in Acts Visited by Paul upon More than One Occasion

	First Visit	Second Visit	Further Visits
Jerusalem	9.26–30 Church afraid Saul preaches	(11.30)	12.25 15.4–30 Council (18.22)
Caesarea	9.30	18.22	21.8–15 Philip's home Agabus
Tarsus	9.30/11.25, 26 Barnabas	(15.41)	
Antioch (Syria)	11.26	13.1 Prophets, etc. Saul chosen	14.26—15.3 Judaizers
Antioch (Pisidia)	13.14–51 Sermon	14.21	(16.4?)
Iconium	13.51—14.6 Almost stoned	14.21	(16.4?)
Lystra (& Derbe)	14.6–21 Cripple healed Hermes & Zeus Paul stoned	16.1–6 Timothy	
Troas	16.8–11 Vision	20.6–13 Delegates Eutychus falls	
Philippi	16.12–40 Lydia Exorcism Jailed Earthquake	(20.1)	20.6
Thessalonica	17.1–10 Synagogue 3 wk. Jason mobbed	(20.1)	(20.3)
Beroea	17.10–14 Noble Jews Jews pursue	(20.1)	(20.3)
Corinth	18.1–18 Aquila, Prisca Titius Justus Crispus won Vision Teaching 18 mo. Gallio	(20.2)	
Ephesus	18.19–21 (Synagogue)	19.1—20.1 John's baptism Argued 2 yr. Sons of Sceva Books burned Timothy sent Riot	

date, the places visited by Paul.[1] Thus it could be concluded that the order of events concerning Paul's travels has a higher historical value than the chronological information of Acts, because this order was not due to the author of Acts but to his source. There is considerable probability in this suggestion, but two limitations should be noted:

(i) The itinerary of Paul's travels, if it is independent of its context in Acts, must be allowed to find its natural place in the reconstruction of Paul's life. The greatest chronological uncertainties occur before Acts 13.1 and after Acts 21.16. How many visits to Jerusalem had Paul made before the itinerary begins? Is Acts 21.16 Paul's final visit to Jerusalem? These are the questions which date Paul's letters, and questions which the itinerary taken by itself cannot answer.

(ii) The itinerary had almost certainly been expanded by the author of Acts by the addition at the proper points of traditions concerning Paul's adventures. The technique is particularly obvious in the case of Acts 14.6–20, Paul's stay at Lystra. In 14.6, 7 Paul and Barnabas flee to "Lystra and Derbe, cities of Lycaonia, and to the surrounding country; and there they preached the gospel". But v. 8 finds them in Lystra: "Now at Lystra there was a man sitting, who could not use his feet." And not until after Paul's stoning do they (again?) reach Derbe (14.20). Clearly the events of the stay at Lystra have been added to the itinerary.[2]

If, however, the account in Acts of Paul's missionary journeys (see Table 2) is examined, a striking fact appears: although Paul may visit a city several times, his adventures occur only on one of his visits, usually his first. There are some minor exceptions to this rule, but in general it holds true.[3] Thus it appears that the author of Acts tended to concentrate all of his additions in one visit.[4] It is possible that all these events

---

[1] So Dibelius, "Style Criticism," *Studies in Acts*, pp. 5–25, for Acts 13.1—14.28; 15.35—21.16.

[2] So Dibelius, *Studies in Acts*, pp. 6, 86, 105.

[3] (i) Events after Acts 21.16 fall outside the itinerary as reconstructed by Dibelius (*Studies in Acts*, p. 5); (ii) it will be suggested in the next section that Acts 15 is a literary creation by the author of Acts; (iii) Paul's vision in Troas may well result from the author's theory that the spread of Christianity was controlled by revelation.

[4] Buck comments, "Luke generally tells all incidents connected with a given town as though they occurred on Paul's first visit there" ("Collection," p. 27, n. 35); and Funk in discussing the geographical plan of the author observes, "It is a curious fact that he seldom mixes the accounts of work in a given locale, preferring on the whole to complete a panel once he has begun" ("Enigma," p. 134).

Furthermore, it appears that the author of Acts tends to gloss over return visits to cities already fully treated. This seems more probable than to suppose that the itinerary omitted the names of cities already evangelized by Paul in, e.g., Acts 20.1–3, a journey from Ephesus through Macedonia to Greece (Corinth presumably), or in Acts 16.4, a tour through South Galatia. Cf. "Syria and Cilicia" (15.41) for Antioch and Tarsus.

occurred during the visits where they now stand in Acts, but it is unlikely that traditions about only one of Paul's visits to each city would
have been preserved. Whatever may be the historical value of these
episodes in Paul's travels,[1] their connection with a particular city will
be of a somewhat lower value. But the connection of an episode with
a particular visit to a particular city has the lowest historical value of all.

This observation indicates still another weakness in the evidence for
the usual dating of the Thessalonian letters. The description of Paul's
stay in Corinth is by no means continuous. In Acts 18.1–4 Paul is the
guest of Aquila and Priscilla, but in vv. 5–11 ("When Silas and Timothy arrived . . .") Paul is staying with Titius Justus. And in v. 18 Paul
sails for Syria with Priscilla and Aquila. In v. 8 Crispus is named as the
ruler of the synagogue, but in v. 17 Sosthenes carries the title. Do all
these items belong to the same visit? And what of the story in vv.
12–17: "But when Gallio was proconsul of Achaia the Jews made a
united attack on Paul . . ." (v. 12)? The proconsulship of Gallio is dated
by the well-known inscription from Delphi,[2] and forms the corner-
stone of almost every Pauline chronology. Thus, for example, such a
careful scholar as Morton S. Enslin says, "This reference to Gallio is
highly important as giving one reasonably sure fixed point for the
Pauline chronology".[3] But on which of Paul's visits to Corinth was he
brought before Gallio's tribunal ($\beta\hat{\eta}\mu\alpha$)? It appears likely that the author
of Acts has composed Acts 18.1–21 from several originally separate
traditions.[4] Therefore, the link between the Gallio inscription and the
date of Paul's first visit to Corinth, and the link between this visit and
the writing of the Thessalonian letters are both extremely tenuous.
One would expect either reverent agnosticism or widespread disagreement over the dating of these letters instead of the general uniformity
of opinion which now obtains.

[1] Dibelius is inclined to be cautious: "While the statements about the actual travelling
[i.e., the itinerary] can be taken as quite reliable, it is only to a limited extent that we can
accept the stories as being of real historical value" (*Paul*, ed. and completed by Werner
Georg Kümmel, trans. Frank Clarke [London: Longmans, Green and Co., 1953], pp. 10–
11).

[2] This inscription has been often published and discussed. Deissmann gives a full biblio-
graphy through 1925 in his *Paul*, p. 270, n. 1. See also Maurice Goguel, *Introduction au
Nouveau Testament* (4 Pts. in 5 vols.; Paris: Ernest Leroux, 1922–6), pp. 101–5; W. L.
Knox, *Jerusalem*, p. 278, n. 36; K. Lake, "Chronology of Acts," *BC*, pp. 460–4; and, most
recently, C. K. Barrett, *The New Testament Background: Selected Documents* (London:
S.P.C.K., 1957), pp. 48–9.

[3] *Beginnings*, p. 246.

[4] As B. Rigaux observes, "Nous ajouterons que le texte de Luc sur le séjour à Corinthe
nous semble une combinaison de deux traditions et que ce travail de rédaction a pu
obscurcir les événements" (*Saint Paul: Les Épîtres aux Thessaloniciens* ["EB"; Paris: J.
Gabalda et Cie, 1956], p. 32).

The purpose of Acts. The discussion of the preceding four points has assumed that the author of Acts intended to deal with his material in as chronological a way as possible, but that his knowledge of the events was limited. There is, however, a growing conviction among scholars that the author had very definite aims in writing Acts and that chronological accuracy was not his primary concern. Burton Scott Easton conveniently summarized some of the points at which the author's interest affected his material:

> In the first place, he simplifies it [i.e., his story] by beginning with a city (Jerusalem) and ending with a city (Rome). . . . From Jerusalem the narrative widens out to Samaria and Judea, moves from there to Cyprus and Asia Minor, from there to eastern Europe, and from there finally to Rome itself. Along with this geographical simplification goes a biographical. The first part is dominated by the figure of Peter, the latter by that of Paul. . . . A third simplification is chronological. Luke does not burden his readers with time sequences.[1]

Easton notes the pattern formed by speeches in Acts: three long, five short (addressed to a carefully chosen variety of audiences), and three long speeches.[2] He further points out what appears to be a conscious parallelism between the series of miracles (eight) performed by Peter and those (eight) performed by Paul.[3] But for Easton the major interest behind the composition of Acts was the author's desire to present Christianity to Roman officials as a *religio licita*, as a party within Judaism.[4]

Martin Dibelius, going further, added a theological interest to Easton's practical analysis of the purpose of Acts:

> In Acts, as in the Gospel, Luke wishes to be an evangelist; he wishes to portray God's leadership of the Christian community within the framework of its history. He certainly had only Paul's itinerary at his disposal as a unified, written source; for the rest, he had to use current stories and accounts which he had discovered. His own special contribution lay in arranging them, linking them together and illuminating them, particularly by means of speeches; it includes also the theological point of the book, which is the acknowledgement that the way the gospel progressed was the way God desired.[5]

And Ernst Haenchen after surveying the history of the criticism of Acts to 1956 concluded by saying,

[1] *Early Christianity: The Purpose of Acts and Other Papers*, ed. Frederick C. Grant (London: S.P.C.K., 1955), pp. 34–5.
[2] Ibid., pp. 36–7.   [3] Ibid., p. 38.   [4] Ibid., pp. 41–67.
[5] "The Acts of the Apostles as an Historical Source," *Studies in Acts*, p. 107.

Damit wandelt sich das Bild der Apg für uns. Bisher las und studierte man sie vor allem, um von ihr etwas über die Apostelzeit zu erfahren, und es fragte sich nur, wie weit ihre historische Zuverlässigkeit reichte. Heute beginnen wir zu sehen, dass sie eine kunstvolle Komposition ist, nicht eine schlichte Erzählung, und dass wir die Gesetze dieser Komposition erfassen müssen, um ihr gerecht zu werden. Zugleich aber wird deutlich, dass uns in ihr eine selbständige Theologie entgegentritt, die—mag sie uns lieb oder leid sein—ernst genommen werden muss. Das wird die Arbeit an diesem neutestamentlichen Buch für die nächsten Jahre bestimmen.[1]

Thus although recent scholars disagree somewhat in their understanding of the motivation of Acts they agree that there was such motivation over and above a simple desire to record "facts" for posterity. But the more of purpose, creativity, and theology that is attributed to the writer of Acts, the less he remains a simple chronicler of events in early Christian history. That is, taken as a whole, recent scholarly work on Acts tends to undercut the confidence in the order of events in Acts which is the basis of the commonly accepted dating of Paul's letters.

The relationship of Galatians to Acts

Paul's visits to Jerusalem. Paul's visits to Jerusalem are the reference points by which Galatians is related to Acts. These visits occur in Acts as follows:

Acts 9.26 Conversion visit
Acts 11.30 Famine visit
Acts 15.4   Council visit
Acts 21.17 Final visit

To this list it seems probable that Acts 18.22 should be added although the name "Jerusalem" does not appear: "When he had landed at Caesarea, he went up and greeted the church, and then went down to Antioch."[2] But there is still another candidate for inclusion in this list.

[1] *Acts* ("Meyer," 10. Aufl.), p. 41.
[2] Scholars fall into three groups on this point:
(*a*) Those who identify Acts 18.22 definitely as a visit to Jerusalem. So Richard Belward Rackham, *The Acts of the Apostles* (3d ed.; "West."; London: Methuen & Co., 1906), p. 334, n. 1; Erwin Preuschen, *Die Apostelgeschichte* ("HNT," Bd. IV. 1.; Tübingen: J. C. B. Mohr [Paul Siebeck], 1912), p. 114; W. L. Knox, *Jerusalem*, p. 289, n. 1; J. Knox, *Chapters*, p. 68; Rowlingson, "Jerusalem Conference," p. 73; Menoud, "Plan des Actes," p. 48, n. 2; G. B. Caird, *The Apostolic Age* ("Studies in Theology"; London: Gerald Duckworth & Co. Ltd., 1955), p. 202; Bruce, *Book of Acts*, p. 379; Hermann Wolfgang Beyer, *Die Apostelgeschichte* ("NTD," 5. Abt., 8. Aufl.; Göttingen: Vandenhoeck & Ruprecht, 1958), p. 113; H. L. Ramsey, *Place of Galatians*, pp. 255–6; and Gustav Stählin, *Die Apostelgeschichte* ("NTD," 5. Abt., 10. Aufl.; Göttingen: Vandenhoeck & Ruprecht, 1962), p. 248.
(*b*) Those who consider the identification probable: Hans Hinrich Wendt, *Die Apostel-*

The text of Acts 12.25. Barnabas and Saul, having gone to Jerusalem in Acts 11.30, next appear in Acts 12.25: "And Barnabas and Saul returned from Jerusalem when they had fulfilled their mission." There are, however, four other readings beside the text translated "from Jerusalem". The principal evidence is as follows:

1(a) $\epsilon\xi$ $I\epsilon\rho o v\sigma a\lambda\eta\mu$: P[74]; A; 33, 330, 547, 1319; bo; Tisch., Souter, von Soden.

(b) $\epsilon\xi$ $I\epsilon\rho o v\sigma a\lambda\eta\mu$ $\epsilon\iota\sigma$ $A v\tau\iota o\chi\epsilon\iota a v$: 35[**], 42, 51, 104, 234, 322, 323, 429, 536, 605, 913, 1522, 1831, 1838, 2298; p; (sy[p]), sa.

2(a) $a\pi o$ $I\epsilon\rho o v\sigma a\lambda\eta\mu$: (B[*]), D; 18, 36[a], 94, 101, 181, 205, 209, 226, 307, 431, 436, 441, 453, 614, 1175, 1827, 1873; gig, vg; Chr[pt].

(b) $a\pi o$ $I\epsilon\rho o v\sigma a\lambda\eta\mu$ $\epsilon\iota\sigma$ $A v\tau\iota o\chi\epsilon\iota a v$: E; 103, 242, 464, 1898; e; (sy[p]).

3. $\epsilon\iota\sigma$ $A v\tau\iota o\chi\epsilon\iota a v$: 97[mg], 110, 328, 424[mg], 425[**].

4. $\epsilon\iota\sigma$ $I\epsilon\rho o v\sigma a\lambda\eta\mu$: ℵ, B, H, L, P, 81; sy[h], aeth; Chr[pt]; Hort[db].

Tischendorf reports that the scribe of B started to write $a\pi o$ but changed it to $\epsilon\iota\sigma$.[1] Readings 1b and 2b clearly result from the conflation of 1 with 3, and 2 with 3 respectively. There are then basically four readings: 1a, 2a, 3, and 4. But 3 cannot be original, since it could not have produced the other readings. Further, as Westcott and Hort said,[2] 1a and 2a are smooth readings which could have given rise neither to 4 nor to each other. They, therefore, reluctantly printed 4, marked it as a doubtful reading, and resorted to conjectural emendation. Their reason is significant: "$\epsilon\iota s$ $\textquoteright I\epsilon\rho o v\sigma a\lambda\acute\eta\mu$ which is best attested, and was not likely to be introduced, cannot possibly be right if it is taken with $\upsilon\pi\acute\epsilon\sigma\tau\rho\epsilon\psi a v$ (see 11.27ff)."[3] In other words, 4 is a reading which has the best attestation, and which by its very difficulty perfectly explains all the other variants. One could hardly ask for better evidence. Yet

geschichte ("Meyer," 3. Abt., 9. Aufl.; Göttingen: Vandenhoeck & Ruprecht, 1913), p. 269; A. W. F. Blunt, *The Acts of the Apostles in the Revised Version* ("Clar."; Oxford: The Clarendon Press, 1923), p. 221; F. J. Foakes-Jackson, *The Acts of the Apostles* ("Moffatt"; London: Hodder and Stoughton, 1931), p. 172; G. H. C. MacGregor, "The Acts of the Apostles," *Interp.* (New York: Abingdon Press, 1954), IX, 247; Dibelius, *Studies in Acts*, p. 197; C. S. C. Williams, *Acts*, p. 214.

(c) Those against the suggestion: B. H. Streeter, "The Primitive Text of Acts," *JTS*, XXXIV (1933), 237; and Kirsopp Lake and Henry J. Cadbury, *The Acts of the Apostles: English Translation and Commentary*, Vol. IV of *BC*, p. 230.

[1] So B. F. Westcott and F. J. A. Hort, *The New Testament in the Original Greek:* Vol. II, *Introduction and Appendix* (New York: Harper & Bros., 1882), p. 94.

[2] Ibid.

[3] Ibid. Other scholars who recognize the textual superiority of reading 4 but who construe or emend the text to harmonize it with 11.27–30 include K. Lake, *Earlier Epistles*, pp. 317–19; J. H. Ropes, *The Text of Acts*, Vol. III of *BC*, p. 114; Lake and Cadbury, *BC*, IV, 141; MacGregor, "Acts," p. 163; and C. S. C. Williams, *Acts*, p. 25.

the reading is rejected, not really because it conflicts with its context,[1] but because it conflicts with Acts 11.27–30 a chapter before. However, the text of Acts is exceedingly problematical.[2] Further, the author's use of sources discussed above adds an element of uncertainty, lessening the level of consistency which can be expected. The textual evidence is that reading 4, $\epsilon\iota\sigma\ I\epsilon\rho o\upsilon\sigma\alpha\lambda\eta\mu$, is the earliest reading which survives. Because of Acts 11.27–30 the preposition was changed to $\epsilon\xi$ in some texts, to $\alpha\pi o$ in others. In still others $A\nu\tau\iota o\chi\epsilon\iota\alpha\nu$ was substituted for $I\epsilon\rho o\upsilon\sigma\alpha\lambda\eta\mu$ to ease the difficulty. Reading 4 may well be the original text. The alternative is conjectural emendation.

The task of reconciling Acts and Galatians is thus complicated by an extra visit before the Council or by the necessity of producing a convincing emendation to eliminate it. Counting visits in Acts becomes a precarious pastime. Those who identify Gal. 2.1 as the Council visit will probably have to assume that Paul neglected to mention *two* visits to Jerusalem, if they are to remain faithful to Acts. On the other hand, those who equate Gal. 2.1 and Acts 11.30 must picture Paul first as largely independent of Jerusalem for some fourteen (or more than seventeen) years. Then with his increasing anger and bitterness over the problem of circumcision he becomes a relatively frequent visitor at Jerusalem (three or four visits). Either of these positions is possible, but it may well be that the author of Acts has failed to consolidate his sources, and thus left his narrative with too many Jerusalem visits. It would seem more reasonable to hold Acts accountable to Paul's letters rather than the reverse.

The historicity of Acts 15. There are four considerations each of which suggests that Acts 15 is largely the literary creation of the author of Acts. None of these arguments is or, by the nature of the case, can be conclusive, but taken together they are further evidence that the order of the events in Acts is not a rock upon which the reconstruction of the dates or sequence of Paul's letters can be built.

(i) More than fifty years ago a number of scholars had already suggested that Acts 11.27–30 and Acts 15.1–33 were originally separate accounts of the same visit.[3] Eduard Schwartz elaborated this theory by

---

[1] The "mission" ($\tau\dot{\eta}\nu\ \delta\iota\alpha\kappa o\nu\acute{\iota}\alpha\nu$) fulfilled by Barnabas and Saul may just as well mean a mission outside Jerusalem as one in Jerusalem. So Buck, "Collection," p. 15; and Funk, "Enigma," p. 133, n. 14. These scholars accept the natural meaning of the text that 12.25 represents a visit to Jerusalem.

[2] See Dibelius, "The Text of Acts: An Urgent Critical Task," *Studies in Acts*, pp. 84–92.

[3] E.g., McGiffert, *Apostolic Age*, pp. 170–2; and Julius Wellhausen, "Noten zur Apostelgeschichte," *Nachrichten von der Königlichen Gesellschaft der Wissenschaften zu Göttingen: Philologisch-historische Klasse* (Berlin: Weidmannsche Buchhandlung, 1907), pp. 19–21.

pointing out the parallels between Acts 11.19–30 and Acts 15.1—16.5, and by suggesting that the journeys which follow each visit are, in fact, the same journey.[1] Foakes-Jackson and Lake in adopting this theory made a special point of the brevity of the narrative in Acts 14.21–8 and 15.35—16.1:

> The story of the first journey stops, so far as any detailed account is concerned, in Lystra and Derbe, and is suddenly wound up by a few sentences which are surely redactorial. The story of the so-called second journey begins with a passage which summarizes the first part, but in Lystra begins again with a detailed narrative. Leave out the summary descriptions at the end of the first journey and the beginning of the second and there is a tolerably full and connected narrative.[2]

Clearly this hypothesis arose from a desire to reduce in Acts the number of Paul's visits to Jerusalem. But the evidence on which it is based cannot be easily dismissed. In Acts 14.20 Paul arrives in Derbe. At this point his missionary progress is interrupted with no reason given, and he returns to Syrian Antioch over the route by which he came (except that he by-passes Cyprus). But the return journey is without a single real event.[3] The account is hardly more than a list of towns. After the council an even briefer summary returns Paul to Derbe, where events begin to happen again. Acts 15, therefore, is not anchored to its context. There are what appear to be editorial seams on either side. What of Acts 15 itself? Does it give evidence of being a composition of the author of Acts?

(ii) The structure of Acts provides a clue. Easton's comment mentioned above that the speeches in Acts are addressed to a varied selection of audiences opens an interesting line of investigation. Acts progresses from Jerusalem to Rome but also from Jew to Gentile. Peter's sermon at Pentecost (2.14–36) is directed to all Judaism as it is represented at Jerusalem ("men of Judea", 2.14; "men of Israel", 2.22).

---

[1] "Zur Chronologie des Paulus," *Nachrichten von der Königlichen Gesellschaft der Wissenschaften zu Göttingen: Philologisch-historische Klasse* (Berlin: Weidmannsche Buchhandlung, 1907), pp. 269–74.

[2] "The Composition and Purpose of Acts," *BC*, II, 154–5. The same point is echoed by Buck, "Collection," pp. 18–19; and by Funk, "Enigma," p. 134. This identification of visits was adopted by Hans Ludwig Windisch, "The Case against the Tradition," in Vol. II of *BC*, p. 322; and by C. H. Dodd, "Chronology," pp. 196–7. In 1937 Joachim Jeremias could say, "Es ist heute fast allgemein anerkannt, dass Act 11,30/12,25 einerseits, Act 15, 1–33 anderseits, ein und dieselbe Jerusalemreise des Paulus beschrieben wird" ("Untersuchungen zum Quellenproblem," p. 217). So also, more recently, Nock, *St. Paul*, pp. 111–17; Porter, "Apostolic Decree," pp. 169–74; and Beyer, *Acts*, pp. 74, 92.

[3] The nearest thing to an event is the appointment of elders at Pisidian Antioch (14.23). However, according to Easton (*Early Christianity*, pp. 67–80) the author of Acts had a special interest in church government and, in particular, the authority of the elders.

Next he speaks to the "rulers of the people and elders" (4.8). Stephen's speech, Acts 7.1–53, represents the final break between Judaism and Christianity resulting, according to the author of Acts, in the rejection of Judaism by God and the persecution of the Church by Judaism. The scattering of the Church, however, furthers God's purposes, for it begins the Gentile mission. In 8.4–13 Philip takes the gospel to Samaria, where Peter and John follow, bringing the gift of the Holy Spirit (8.14–25). The Ethiopian Eunuch is the next Gentile God calls (8.26–40). Then follows the conversion of Saul, the Apostle to the Gentiles (9.1–31). At this point there begins in Acts a double account of God's special choice of the Gentiles, first through Peter (Acts 9.32—11.18) and then through Paul (Acts 13.1ff). Both Peter and Paul perform miracles which reveal that the Holy Spirit works through them.[1] Both convert prominent Roman officials.[2]

In Acts 11 and 15 the parallelism (as Table 3 shows) becomes remarkably close.[3] Each account is preceded by a summary statement to the effect that God had chosen the Gentiles. Peter and Paul each travel to Jerusalem, where they are each challenged by the circumcision party. In each case this challenge is answered with a speech recounting the signs of God's favour toward the Gentiles, his gift of the Holy Spirit to Gentiles, and prophecies concerning Gentiles. (The two speeches in chapter 15 function as two halves of a single speech with a rhetorical pause in the middle.) In each case the Church concludes that if God is for them, who can be against them. Then the Gentile mission spreads. Barnabas and Paul twice evangelize Antioch. Finally, the two missions close with the word of God spoken through prophets from Jerusalem, and Barnabas and Paul move on. And as the final triumph, each account tells of the miraculous freeing of the apostle (Peter, 12.1–17, and Paul, 16.16–40) from prison.

The pattern which underlies these twin accounts, however, occurs once again. These two cycles are the whole book of Acts in microcosm. At the beginning God acts with his gift of the Holy Spirit to "about three thousand souls" (2.41) out of the crowd gathered "from every nation under heaven" (2.5). Those of the circumcision challenge this

---

[1] Peter heals Aeneas, the paralytic, Acts 9.32–5; and resurrects Tabitha, 9.36–43. Paul blinds Elymas, the magician, 13.8–12.

[2] Peter converts Cornelius, the centurion, Acts 10.1–48; Paul converts Sergius Paulus, the proconsul, 13.6–12.

[3] Porter in arguing for the identification of the Jerusalem visit of Acts 15.4 with that of Acts 11.27–30 notes two verbal links which lead him to conclude that "Peter's speech in Acts xv. 7–11 shows a literary dependence on the latter half of his speech in xi. 4–17" ("Apostolic Decree," p. 171).

TABLE 3

A Comparison of the Order of Events in Acts 11 and Acts 15

	Acts 10.44—11.30	Acts 14.27—15.33
God chooses the Gentiles	10.44–7: The Holy Spirit fell on all who heard the word. And the believers . . . were amazed, because the gift of the Holy Spirit had been poured out even on the Gentiles. . . . Then Peter declared, "Can any one forbid water . . . ?"	14.27: They . . . declared all that God had done with them, and how he had opened a door of faith to the Gentiles.
Mission prospers	10.48: Then they asked him to remain for some days.	14.28: And they remained no little time with the disciples.
Judea hears of mission	11.1: Now the apostles and the brethren who were in Judea heard that the Gentiles also had received the word of God.	15.1: But some men came down from Judea.
Delegates to Jerusalem	11.2, 3: So when Peter went up to Jerusalem,	15.2: Paul and Barnabas . . . were appointed to go up to Jerusalem to the apostles and elders about this question.
Circumcision party objects	the circumcision party criticized him, saying, "Why did you go to uncircumcised men and eat with them?"	15.5: But some believers who belonged to the party of the Pharisees rose up, and said, "It is necessary to circumcise them."

Case for the Gentiles:	11.4: But Peter began and explained to them in order:	15.7: After . . . much debate, Peter rose and said to them,
(a) God's choice	11.5–12: "In a trance I saw a vision, . . . a great sheet, let down from heaven. . . . And the Spirit told me to go with them. . . ."	"Brethren, you know that in the early days God made a choice . . . that by my mouth the Gentiles should hear the word of the gospel and believe."
(b) Holy Spirit given	11.15: "The Holy Spirit fell on them just as on us at the beginning."	15.8: "God . . . bore witness to them, giving them the Holy Spirit just as he did us. . . ."
(c) Prophecy fulfilled	11.16: "And I remembered the word of the Lord, . . . 'John baptized with water, but you shall be baptized with the Holy Spirit.'"	15.15: "With this the words of the prophets agree, '. . . that the rest of men may seek the Lord, . . . all the Gentiles who are called by my name. . . .'"
Church accepts Gentiles	11.18: They glorified God, saying, "Then to the Gentiles also God has granted repentance unto life."	15.19: "Therefore . . . we should not trouble those of the Gentiles who turn to God."
Gentile mission spreads	11.20: Some . . . on coming to Antioch spoke to the Greeks also, preaching the Lord Jesus.	15.22: It seemed good . . . to the whole church to choose men . . . and send them to Antioch
Barnabas & Paul to Antioch	11.22, 25f: The church . . . sent Barnabas to Antioch. . . . Barnabas went to Tarsus to look for Saul; and . . . brought him to Antioch.	15.22, 30: with Paul and Barnabas. . . . So . . . they went down to Antioch.
Antioch mission prospers	For a whole year they met with the church and taught a large company of people.	15.35: Paul and Barnabas remained in Antioch teaching and preaching the word of the Lord, with many others also.

act (4.1–7), but God answers with miracles and the gift of the Holy Spirit, thus fulfilling his prophecies concerning the rejection of the old Israel in favour of the new Israel. The Gentile mission spreads in widening circles. And the book closes paradoxically with God's spokesman freely preaching the gospel while in prison where the envy of Judaism has placed him.[1]

The plan of the whole book of Acts is almost certainly the design of its author. The reappearance of the plan in Acts 11 and 15 indicates the importance the author attached to this scheme. And the fact that Acts 15 presents no new material (except the Apostolic Decree, which is also to be found in Acts 21.25) creates the probability that Acts 15 is the literary creation of the author. By this chapter he intended to confirm through Paul the mission to the Gentiles as he had through Peter.

(iii) In 1947 Martin Dibelius published his paper "Das Apostelkonzil."[2] His conclusion about the historicity of Acts 15 is unambiguous: "We . . . have only one account of the meeting between Paul and those in authority in Jerusalem, that of Paul in Gal. 2. We are not justified in correcting it according to the account in Acts. . . . Luke's treatment of the event is only literary-theological and can make no claim to historical worth."[3] He based his argument upon the purely literary relationship of the speeches of Peter and James to the event emphasized by the author earlier in Acts, the conversion of Cornelius. Both Peter and James ignore the immediate historical situation and the presence of Barnabas and Paul. Both refer to Peter's vision and they do so in such an oblique manner that only the *reader* of Acts sees the connection:

Peter: Brethren, you know that in the early days God made choice among you that by my mouth the Gentiles should hear the word of the gospel and believe (15.7).

James: Symeon has related how God first visited the Gentiles (15.14).

On the other hand, the testimony of Barnabas and Paul about the Gentile mission, which would have been of crucial significance if the incident were an historical account, is of no importance in Acts 15. But again the reader can supply what Acts omits, for the two preceding

[1] Note, of course, the parallelism with the Third Gospel: Jesus begotten by the Holy Spirit, his baptism with the Spirit, his rejection by his people, his signs and wonders, the spreading mission of the seventy, and his final victory through apparent defeat at the hands of the Jews.

[2] *Theologische Literaturzeitung*, LXXII (1947), 193–8. It was translated and republished in *Studies in Acts*, pp. 93–101.

[3] *Studies in Acts*, p. 100.

chapters are exactly what Acts 15.12 describes—"signs and wonders God had done through them [Paul and Barnabas] among the Gent-tiles".[1] Acts 15, Dibelius concludes, is merely a re-emphasizing of the Cornelius story with the Decree, which he considers a piece of floating tradition, added at the end. Thus by a somewhat different path Dibelius reaches the conclusion suggested in the preceding section.

(iv) One final point remains to be discussed. We have seen that Acts 15 is free of its context, that it expresses the theological pattern of the author of Acts, and that it can only be understood in a literary, not an historical, connection with preceding events. But why, if this story is indeed the composition of the author of Acts, does it stand in its present position? Why should the author break into a unified travel account at this point? Certainty is, of course, not possible, but unless a plausible answer to this question can be given there will remain the probability that the occasion for this account was the mention of a visit to Jerusalem in the itinerary source used by the author of Acts.

In answer the following points can be suggested: (*a*) Acts 15 is vitally necessary to the purpose of Acts, since official approval of the western mission is not provided by the Cornelius episode. But (*b*) this approval cannot be given until the western mission had grown large enough to be significant. It must in a real sense represent the Gentile world at large to which the book of Acts is addressed. On the other hand, (*c*) this approval if delayed until Paul had reached Corinth and returned would have been both anticlimactic and after the fact. And finally, (*d*) the farther Paul journeyed from Syria, the more difficult it would have been to bring him back to Jerusalem and return him to the mission field. Thus the author, it appears, waited until Paul's second miracle (Acts 14.8–18), and then inserted his own account of the meet-ing which united the original Jewish-Christian Church and the newer Gentile Church.

If what has been said above concerning Acts 15 carries any weight of probability, then here is another rotten plank in the much travelled bridge between Paul's letters and the book of Acts.

CONCLUSION

The purpose of this chapter is threefold:
   (i) To show how much the understanding of Paul's letters must rest

---

[1] Ibid., p. 98.

on an understanding of the circumstances under which they were written.

(ii) To show how widespread among scholars to-day is a conventional reconstruction of these circumstances based on an uncritical use of the narrative of Acts.

(iii) To show how really unsound are the assumptions which underlie the usual dating and suggested sequence of Paul's letters. There is solid evidence that Acts is vague about chronological matters, incomplete in coverage, and built up of sources now probably beyond recovery. It appears probable that its author had an incomplete knowledge of the events he recounted, and, on the other hand, that he had a number of literary and theological motivations which controlled the presentation of his materials.

This chapter has not intended to solve the many problems it has raised. They may never be solved. But they certainly will never be solved if the accepted results of past generations are perpetuated.

The following chapters deal with only a small segment of this larger set of problems. But it is hoped that the way is now clear to examine 1 Corinthians without preconceptions as to its chronological relationship with others of Paul's letters, the possibility or impossibility of change in Paul's thought, and the maturity or immaturity to be expected of Paul's theology.[1] It may be that in reconstructing the exchanges between Paul and the Corinthian Church we shall find ourselves in what appears to be an earlier stage of Paul's thought than the usual dating of the letters allows.

---

[1] Without necessarily agreeing with Johannes Munck's theory of the ubiquitous influence of the Tübingen School we find ourselves in strong support of his conclusions: "1. Paul's letters are to be interpreted as such. Statements from other sources, especially Acts and the post-Pauline letters, . . . must not determine the exposition of the letters. 2. Paul's individual letters, and the situation that forms the background of each individual letter, must be viewed on their own merits in each case . . . (*Paul and the Salvation of Mankind*, p. 85).

CHAPTER 2

The Events which preceded the Writing of 1 Corinthians

THE PROBLEM OF THE INTEGRITY OF I CORINTHIANS

Before beginning to search out the chain of events which lies behind 1 Corinthians it is necessary to discuss the problem of the integrity of 1 Corinthians. Was the canonical 1 Corinthians written at a single time or is it a compilation of two or more letters written at various times? Until 1876 the unity of 1 Corinthians was generally assumed, since there is no manuscript or patristic evidence to the contrary.[1] In that year, however, Hagge suggested that chapters 1—6, 9 (vv. 1–18) and 15 should be taken with 2 Corinthians 10—13 as a vigorous letter written by Paul in defence of his apostleship which he had heard (1 Cor. 1.11; 5.1) had been questioned by the Corinthians.[2] The remainder of 1 Corinthians he considered to be a reply to the letter from Corinth mentioned in 1 Corinthians 7.1. Because of the calm tone of this reply he dated the letter before the vigorous letter first mentioned. Although his particular division of 1 Corinthians did not find acceptance, his attempt was significant in that it recognized the basic difference between Paul's treatment of the oral information unfavourable to Corinth in 1 Cor. 1.11ff, and Paul's reply to the Corinthians' letter beginning at 1 Cor. 7.1ff. On this difference almost all the later theories of the partition of 1 Corinthians are based.

In 1894 Carl Clemen published an elaborate hypothesis which

[1] For an amazingly thorough survey of the first suspicions about the unity of 1 Corinthians see Carl Clemen, *Die Einheitlichkeit der paulinischen Briefe* (Göttingen: Vandenhoeck und Ruprecht, 1894), pp. 19–57.

[2] Hagge, "Die beiden überlieferten Sendschreiben des Apostels Paulus an die Gemeinde zu Korinth," *Jahrbücher für protestantische Theologie*, II (1876), 481–531. From the above sections he excepted 4.16–20, which he put with the rest of Paul's travel plans in chap. 16, and 2 Corinthians 13.11–13, which he used to close 2 Corinthians 1—9.

divided the two canonical epistles into five letters.[1] This theory also proved unacceptable; Clemen himself abandoned it within ten years.[2] But his method of using 2 Cor. 6.14—7.1 as the nucleus of the earliest letter and adding to it similar material from 1 Corinthians has generally been followed by those who divide 1 Corinthians.

The first theory to win approval from other scholars was that of Johannes Weiss in 1910.[3] When his analysis and those of his successors —Alfred Loisy,[4] Paul-Louis Couchoud,[5] Maurice Goguel,[6] Johannes de Zwaan,[7] Walter Schmithals,[8] and Erich Dinkler[9]—are written out by chapter and verse the total effect is complicated and confusing.[10] Table 4, however, shows the relative uniformity of the general approach of these six scholars. All but one of these scholars believed 2 Cor. 6.14—7.1 to be a fragment of Paul's earlier letter ("Letter A") to Corinth referred to in 1 Cor. 5.9 ("I wrote you in my letter ...").[11] To this fragment with its strict exclusiveness ("Do not be mismated with unbelievers ...", 2 Cor. 6.14) they all added 1 Cor. 10.1–22(23), the stricter of Paul's two discussions about the advisability of Christians avoiding meat offered to idols. The more lenient passages (1 Cor. 8; 10.[23]24—11.1) they considered to be his second and later treatment of the problem. 1 Cor. 6.12–20 also concerns the avoidance of immorality. (In fact, 6.12 is a doublet of 10.23.) Thus this passage is added to the early letter also. Finally, 1 Cor. 11.2–34, Paul's strict instructions

---

[1] Clemen, *Einheitlichkeit*, pp. 66–7. Goguel, *Intro. N. T.*, IV.2, p. 87, listed Clemen's divisions incorrectly, an error repeated by E.-B. Allo, *Saint Paul: Seconde Épître aux Corinthiens* ("EB"; Paris: J. Gabalda et Cⁱᵉ, Éditeurs, 1937), p. lv.

[2] In *Paulus: sein Leben und Wirken* (2 Bde.; Giessen: J. Ricker'sche, 1904), I, 85, he maintained the unity of 1 Corinthians, and considered 2 Cor. 6.14—7.1 the only surviving fragment of the earlier letter mentioned in 1 Cor. 5.9.

[3] J. Weiss, *Der erste Korintherbrief* ("Meyer," 5. Abt., 10. Aufl.; Göttingen: Vandenhoeck und Ruprecht, 1925), pp. xl–xliii.

[4] A. Loisy, *Les Livres du Nouveau Testament* (Paris: Émile Nourry, 1922), pp. 39–47. In later works Loisy abandoned this analysis in favour of a theory of extensive pre-Marcionite interpolations.

[5] P.-L. Couchoud, "Reconstitution et Classement des Lettres de Saint Paul," *Revue de l'Histoire des Religions*, LXXXVII (1923), 17–31, who mentions his indebtedness to Loisy.

[6] Goguel, *Intro. N. T.*, IV.2, p. 86.

[7] De Zwaan, *Inleiding tot het Nieuwe Testament* (3 vols.; 2d ed.; "Volksuniversiteits Bibliotheek"; Haarlem: Erven Bohn, 1948), II, 47, 57.

[8] Schmithals, *Gnosis*, pp. 12–18, 22, n. 2. See also his recent article, "Abfassung," p. 230.

[9] Dinkler, "Korintherbriefe," in *RGG*³, IV, 18. (Or his article, "I Cor." in *DB*², 177a.)

[10] Patrick Cleary in his article, "The Epistles to the Corinthians," *The Catholic Biblical Quarterly*, XII (1950), 10–33, offered a source analysis which he declared was completely uninfluenced "by the theorizing of rationalistic critics". His "Letter A" comprises more than twenty-one fragments! In its main outline, however, his hypothesis is similar to that of Schmithals.

[11] Dinkler believes 2 Cor. 6.14—7.1 to be non-Pauline, perhaps under the influence of J. A. Fitzmyer's recent article, "Qumrân and the Interpolated Paragraph in 2 Cor. 6,14—7,1," *The Catholic Biblical Quarterly*, XXIII (1961), 271–80.

TABLE 4

Principal Source Analyses of 1 Corinthians[a]

	Weiss	Loisy	Couc.	Gog'l	Zwaan	Schm.	Dinkler
2 Cor. 6.14—7.1	A	A	A	A	A	A	—[b]
I Cor. 10.1–22(23)	A	A	A	A	A[c]	A	A
6.12–20	A	A	A	A	A	A	A
11.2–34	A	A	A	B	A	A	A
9.24–7	B	A	A	C	A	A	A
I Cor. 5.1—6.11	C[d]	B	B	B	B	B	B
7 & 8	B	B	B	B	B	B	B
9.1–23	B	A	A	C	B	B	B
10.(23)24—11.1	B	B	B	B	B	B	B
12, 13, & 14	B	B[e]	B	B	B	B	A
15	B	C	F[f]	B	B	A	B
I Cor. 1—4	C[d]	C	C	C[g]	B	B	B

a. "A" stands for Paul's first letter to Corinth; "B", his second; and "C", his third.
b. Dinkler considered 2 Cor. 6.14—7.1 an interpolation.
c. De Zwaan placed 10.1–13 in B, however.
d. For uniformity Weiss's letter "B2" is here labelled C.
e. Loisy considered chap. 13 an interpolation.
f. Couchoud placed chap. 15 in a fifth and final letter to Corinth.
g. Goguel was undecided about 1.1–9.

about the veiling of women and the conduct of the Lord's Supper, is assigned to the same letter, both because of its tone and because there is no hint that Paul knew of the spiritualistic excesses of the Corinthians' worship which he later dealt with in 1 Cor. 12, 13, and 14.

Having thus identified the components of "Letter A", these scholars considered the remainder of 1 Corinthians, except for 1 Cor. 1—4, to be a letter ("Letter B") written as Paul's response to the inquiring letter from Corinth mentioned in 1 Cor. 7.1 ("Now concerning the matters about which you wrote . . ."). 1 Cor. 1—4, however, ("Letter C") does not concern the Corinthians' letter, but is solely concerned with the party divisions at Corinth of which Paul had learned from "Chloe's people" (1.11). Paul's indignation over these dissensions appears absent from the rest of 1 Corinthians. 1 Cor. 11.18, for example, contains the calm remark, "I hear that there are divisions among you and I *partly*

($\mu\epsilon\rho$os $\tau\iota$) believe it". Therefore, most of these scholars concluded that "Chloe's people" arrived after the letter from Corinth. To the latter Paul had replied serenely with "Letter B". Upon hearing the news brought by "Chloe's people" he then sent the angry and sarcastic "Letter C" ("We are fools for Christ's sake, but you are wise in Christ," 4.10).[1]

Even when simplified these theories appear radical and somewhat arbitrary. Actually, however, these critics share a large measure of agreement with the usual scholarly assumptions about 1 Corinthians which will be discussed below. That is, almost all scholars understand 1 Cor. 5.9 to mean that Paul wrote a letter which corresponds to "Letter A". Many scholars also believe 2 Cor. 6.14—7.1 to be a fragment of this letter.[2] Even as conservative a scholar as David Smith takes 1 Cor. 6.12–20 in addition to be a part of the letter of 1 Cor. 5.9.[3] And of the same passage James Moffatt said, "Logically it might be taken with 2 Cor. vi. 14–vii. 1 as part of the original first letter".[4] Further, there is widespread agreement that 1 Cor. 7ff was written in answer to a letter from Corinth, and that 1 Cor. 1ff dealt with information brought by "Chloe's people".

On the other hand, the six critics mentioned above who divide 1 Corinthians do not separate "Letter B" from "Letter C" by any great interval. They do not suppose, for example, that Paul had received a reply to "Letter B" before writing "Letter C".[5] In effect then, these two parts may be considered one letter since they represent a single stage in the exchange between Paul and the Church in Corinth. Reduced to essentials what Weiss and his adherents emphasize is:

(i) That letters "B" and "C" had separate occasions although close in time.

---

[1] The major deviations from this scheme are as follows: (a) de Zwaan and Schmithals believe 1 Corinthians to be a unity except for the sections belonging to "Letter A"; (b) chaps. 9 and 15, which are relatively free of their contexts, are variously placed. Concerning chap. 16, where the characteristics used to date the rest of the letter are lacking, there is wide disagreement and uncertainty among these scholars.

[2] See below, pp. 235–7.

[3] The Life and Letters of St. Paul (New York: George H. Doran Company, [1919]), pp. 236, 654.

[4] The First Epistle of Paul to the Corinthians ("Moffatt"; London: Hodder and Stoughton, 1938), p. 67. So also Clarence T. Craig, "The First Epistle to the Corinthians," Interp. (New York: Abingdon Press, 1953), X, 73.

[5] J. Weiss labelled these letters "B 1" and "B 2" to indicate their close relationship. He suggested that Paul had just composed "B 1" when Chloe's people arrived; thereupon he wrote "B 2". Weiss referred to these two parts collectively as "the second letter (B 1–2)" (Primitive Christianity, p. 341).

(ii) That Paul dealt with the problem of idol-meat twice in rather different ways.

Seen in this way the problem of the integrity of I Corinthians is not a matter for proof or disproof, nor of radical against conservative; it is a matter of more or less.[1] Most scholars and the present writer, while recognizing the above points, do not believe that this evidence is strong enough to support the burden of proof which this kind of theory must always bear. Since, however, these hypotheses do not involve essentially new or different interpretations of I Corinthians and its occasion, the problem of integrity may be resolved into the two points given above, which can then be dealt with as they occur naturally in the discussions below.[2]

THE OCCASION OF I CORINTHIANS: INFORMATION FROM CORINTH

The reasons which led Paul to write I Corinthians are clearly visible in the letter. Paul wrote because while absent from Corinth he received news about the situation there to which he desired to speak before he

[1] J. Weiss, for his part, considered his theory only a working hypothesis. As he put it, "Whoever does not find this division of the material into two or three letters convincing must at any rate admit that different points of view or attitudes are apparent in the discussion in these three groups; and this is the important point" (*Primitive Christianity*, p. 341).

Both Smith, *St. Paul*, p. 259, and Ernest Evans, *The Epistles of Paul the Apostle to the Corinthians* ("Clar."; Oxford: The Clarendon Press, 1930), p. 21, represent a *via media*. They suggest that when Paul met "Chloe's people" he began to write, that he was still writing when a letter came from Corinth, and that he completed I Cor. as an answer to this letter.

Moffatt, who decided in favour of the unity of I Corinthians, said mildly, "One may conclude not unfairly, that the present order of First Corinthians at any rate is on the whole as likely to be Paul's as editorial" (*1 Cor.*, p. xxvi). And Craig, also on the side of unity, warned, "Such partition theories are not to be dismissed as ridiculous" ("1 Cor.," p. 6).

[2] An analysis which is partly independent of those in Table 4 is offered by Jean Héring, *The First Epistle of Saint Paul to the Corinthians*, trans. A. W. Heathcote and P. J. Allcock (London: Epworth Press, 1962), pp. xii–xiv. He believes "Letter A" to be entirely lost. For him I Cor. 1—8; 10.23—11.1 is both Paul's answer to the letter from Corinth and his treatment of the news from Chloe's people. I Cor. 9; 10.1–22; 11—15, he suggests, was a letter written shortly later in response to Stephanas' still more unfavourable news about Corinth. Thus Héring adopts the second principle above, while changing the terms of the first.

Further discussion of the problem of integrity will be found below as follows: concerning I Cor. 6.12–20, see pp. 86–9; on I Cor. 9.1–23, see pp. 70–1 and pp. 126–31; and on I Cor. 8.1—11.1, see pp. 131–42.

could visit the Church again.[1] Paul mentioned three sources of information:

1. *"Chloe's people."* In 1 Cor. 1.11 Paul wrote, "For it has been reported to me by Chloe's people that there is quarrelling among you, my brethren". The expression οἱ Χλόης may be translated "the family of Chloe" and understood to mean the children or relatives of this Greek lady otherwise unknown to us. Thus understood there is some probability that she herself was a Christian.[2] Or the phrase may be translated "the household (or people) of Chloe" and interpreted to mean the slaves or freedmen of her establishment.[3] In this case there is no particular reason to suppose that she was a Christian.[4] However the expression is translated, it is clear that Paul had received from this group information about the internal discords of the Church in Corinth. Both because the information is said to come from these persons rather than from the Corinthian Church (contrast 7.1), and because of the unfavourable nature of this news, it is safe to assume that these persons were not sent by the Corinthians to bring this news, and that their report, therefore, was quite unofficial.[5] To the conditions about which they brought news, Paul addressed the first part of 1 Corinthians (at least 1 Cor. 1—3).

2. *The letter from Corinth.* In 1 Cor. 7.1 Paul made a new beginning: "Now concerning the matters about which you wrote . . .". At this point begins a series of what appear to be answers to questions which had come to Paul by letter from the Corinthians. Very probably such a letter formed the occasion for this part of 1 Corinthians. As Kirsopp Lake says, "It seems as though the greater part of 1 Cor. vii–xvi. is directly based on the letter [mentioned in 7.1]."[6]

[1] His intended visit he mentions in 4.19, 21; 11.34; and 16.5–7. Héring, *1 Cor.*, p. xiii, makes much of the difference between "I will come to you soon" in 4.19 and "I will stay in Ephesus until Pentecost" in 16.8, and assigns these sections to different sources. However, in 4.19 Paul was using his intended visit as a threat ("Shall I come to you with a rod . . . ?" 4.21), and he naturally emphasized its imminence. Of the scholars mentioned above who also divide 1 Cor., Loisy, Couchoud, de Zwaan, Schmithals, and Dinkler see no difficulty here, and put these passages in the same letter.

[2] So, e.g., Joseph Barber Lightfoot, *Notes on the Epistles of St. Paul*, ed. posthum. J. Rendel Harris (London: Macmillan and Co., 1895), p. 152.

[3] So, e.g., Lake, *Earlier Epistles*, p. 125; and Arndt/Gingrich, p. 890.

[4] So, e.g., Archibald Robertson and Alfred Plummer, *A Critical and Exegetical Commentary on the First Epistle of St. Paul to the Corinthians* (2d ed.; "ICC"; Edinburgh: T. & T. Clark, 1914), pp. 10–11.

[5] Philipp Bachmann, e.g., wrote, "Diese Quelle war aber nicht offizieller, sondern privater Natur" (*Der erste Brief des Paulus an die Korinther* ["Zahn"; 3. Aufl.; Leipzig: A. Deichertsche Verlagsbuchhandlung (Dr. Werner Scholl), 1921], p. 54).

[6] *Earlier Epistles*, p. 136. So also, e.g., Wilhelm Bousset, "Der erste Brief an die Korinther," *Schrift.* (4 Bde; 3. Aufl.; Göttingen: Vandenhoeck & Ruprecht, 1917–1918), II, 76, "Im ganzen scheint also fast der ganze zweite Teil unseres Briefes von Kap. 7 an eine Beantwortung des Gemeindeschreibens zu sein."

3. *Stephanas, Fortunatus, and Achaicus.* At the close of 1 Corinthians Paul expressed his joy at the arrival of Stephanas, Fortunatus, and Achaicus: "I rejoice at the coming of Stephanas and Fortunatus and Achaicus . . ." (16.17). Since Paul speaks of Stephanas and his household (= Fortunatus and Achaicus?)[1] as the "first fruits of Achaia" (16.15),[2] mentions their ministry to the saints (16.15), and says of them, "They have made up for your absence, for they refreshed my spirit as well as yours" (16.17, 18), it seems clear that these men are members or even leaders[3] of the Corinthian Church who have recently come to Paul. And since Paul urged the Corinthians to subordinate themselves on their part to these men[4] and to all who work and labour with them (16.16), and to give these men recognition (16.18), it is also clear that these men expect to return to Corinth. Because these men appear to be of more importance in the Corinthian Church than Paul's unofficial informants, "Chloe's people", they are usually credited with having brought the letter of the Church from Corinth to Paul.[5] And since

---

[1] Bousset suggested that Fortunatus and Achaicus were the slaves of Stephanas (ibid., p. 76). So also Ernst von Dobschütz, *Christian Life in the Primitive Church*, trans. G. Bremner; ed. W. D. Morrison (London: Williams and Norgate, 1904), p. 57.

[2] P46 reads Aσιασ, which is either an anticipation of 16.19, or a reminiscence of Rom. 16.5, where Epaenetus is called ἀπαρχὴ τῆς 'Ασίας. The opposite confusion is found in Rom. 16.5, where the Koine reads Aχαιασ for Aσιασ.

[3] Their importance is attested to not only by Paul's reference to their "ministry" (16.15) and the recommendation he gives them (16.18), but also by the official ring to the word παρουσία, "arrival". See Moulton/Milligan, pp. xix, 497; and Deissmann, *Light from the Ancient East*, pp. 368–73.

[4] τοιούτοις here in 16.16 can not mean "to (any) men like these", but rather must mean "to *these* men who are like this", because Paul, having referred only to these men, then generalized his admonition by adding, "and every fellow worker and labourer". So also τοιούτους in 16.18. Cf. 1 Thess. 5.12.

[5] So, e.g., Lightfoot, *Notes*, p. 219; F. W. Farrar, *The Life and Work of St. Paul* (New York: E. P. Dutton and Company, 1902), p. 379; George G. Findlay, "St. Paul's First Epistle to the Corinthians," *ExposGk* (5 vols.; London: Hodder and Stoughton, 1897–1910), II, 736; Smith, *St. Paul*, pp. 259, 325; Lake, *Earlier Epistles*, p. 136 ("not unlikely"); Bachmann, *1 Cor.*, p. 476; Evans, *Corr.*, p. 21; Enslin, *Beginnings*, p. 248; Moffatt, *1 Cor.*, p. xv; E.-B. Allo, *Saint Paul: Première Épître aux Corinthiens* ("EB"; Paris: J. Gabalda et Cᵢᵉ, Éditeurs, 1935), p. 464; Goodspeed, *Paul*, p. 119; Hans Lietzmann, *An die Korinther I/II*, rev. Werner Georg Kümmel ("HNT," 9. Bd.; 4. Aufl.; Tübingen: Verlag von J. C. B. Mohr [Paul Siebeck], 1949), p. 90 ("vermutlich"); A. H. McNeile, *An Introduction to the New Testament* (2d ed rev. C. S. C. Williams; Oxford: The Clarendon Press, 1953), p. 137; F. W. Grosheide, *Commentary on the First Epistle to the Corinthians* ("Internat."; Grand Rapids, Mich.: Wm. B. Eerdmans Publishing Company, 1953), p. 154; and Heinz-Dietrich Wendland, *Die Briefe an die Korinther* ("NTD," hrsg. P. Althaus und G. Friedrich, 7. Abt., 8. Aufl.; Göttingen: Vandenhoeck & Ruprecht, 1962), p. 142 ("offenbar"). Schmiedel, "Corr.," pp. xii-xiii, concurs and cites in addition Heinrici, B. Weiss, Klöpper, Hilgenfeld, and Hausrath.

Hausrath's suggestion (ref. by Schmiedel, ibid.) that Stephanas, Fortunatus, and Achaicus *are* Chloe's people has found no support. As Lightfoot said (*Notes*, p. 152), "All such identifications are hazardous." Further, it is improbable that Paul would have rejoiced (16.17) to meet those who told him of the shocking conditions in Corinth (1.11), and that he would have expected the Corinthians to receive these men again with honour

they are returning to Corinth with Paul's high recommendation, it is more than likely that they are the bearers of 1 Corinthians.[1]

Thus there are three sources of information which occasioned 1 Corinthians, an embarrassment of riches for scholars who regard the letter as a unity. Either the arrival of the letter from Corinth (probably with Stephanas, Fortunatus, and Achaicus) or the disturbing news from Chloe's people would have been sufficient reason for Paul to have written a letter. Here scholars must balance two improbabilities: (i) the inherent improbability of the partition theories (which, however, solve the problem of multiple occasions for 1 Corinthians by assigning a separate letter to each occasion) against (ii) the improbability that the households of Chloe and of Stephanas happened to meet Paul within a period brief enough that one letter (1 Corinthians) could deal with both sets of problems. The dilemma is a real one, but most scholars to-day think it more probable that both sets of information arrived within a brief period than that the present text of 1 Corinthians was assembled by a later editor. But in either case it is improbable to suppose that Paul had any further sources of information. The information implied, for example, by 11.18 ("I hear that there are divisions among you and I partly believe it.") and by 5.1 ("it is actually reported that there is immorality among you!") should be identified as coming either from Chloe's people or from Stephanas and his companions.

PAUL'S PREVIOUS LETTER

In 1 Cor. 5.9 Paul wrote, ἔγραψα ὑμῖν ἐν τῇ ἐπιστολῇ μὴ συναναμίγνυσθαι πόρνοις. Taken by itself the phrase ἔγραψα ὑμῖν is ambiguous. It could equally well be translated "I wrote you" (i.e., a completed action), or "I write you" (i.e., an epistolary aorist, action com-

(16.18). And, finally, as Lietzmann points out (Corr., p. 90), the juxtaposition of "those of Chloe" (1.11) and "the household of Stephanas" (1.16) indicates that they are not the same group.

[1] So Robertson and Plummer, 1 Cor., p. 396; Theodor Zahn, Introduction to the New Testament, trans. J. M. Trout et al.; ed. M. W. Jacobus (3 vols.; 2d ed.; New York: Charles Scribner's Sons, 1917), I, 260; and Smith, St. Paul, p. 260.

Allo's statement (1 Cor., pp. 464-5) that this opinion is generally admitted is too optimistic, however. Joseph Barber Lightfoot, "The Mission of Titus to the Corinthians," Biblical Essays, ed. posthum. J. Rendel Harris (London: Macmillan and Co., 1893), pp. 271-84, originated the suggestion that "the brethren" of 16.11, 12 were the bearers of the letter and that Titus was one of their number. So, e.g., Alfred Plummer, A Critical and Exegetical Commentary on the Second Epistle of St. Paul to the Corinthians ("ICC"; Edinburgh: T. & T. Clark, 1915), p. xvii, as the best guess, and William Mitchell Ramsay, St. Paul the Traveller and the Roman Citizen (New York: G. P. Putnam's Sons, 1896), p. 284.

pleted from the point of view of the reader). But as Lightfoot said,

> The theory of a previous letter is rendered necessary by the words ἐν τῇ ἐπιστολῇ, which are quite meaningless, if applied to our extant Epistle. It is true that ἡ ἐπιστολή is a phrase used sometimes of the letter itself in which it occurs (Rom. xvi. 22, I Thess. v. 27, Col. iv. 16, and probably 2 Thess. iii. 14, . . .); but in all these cases the expression occurs in a postscript, when the Epistle is considered as already at an end. . . . The hypothesis of a previous letter is as old as the first Latin commentator Ambrosiaster, and is accepted by Calvin, Beza, Estius, Grotius, Bengel, Meyer and many others.[1]

Thus it is clear that before writing 1 Corinthians Paul had written to the Church in Corinth at least once.

Therefore, 1 Corinthians gives evidence of two events which preceded its composition: (a) a three-fold arrival of news from Corinth and (b) a previous letter from Paul to the Corinthians. In order to reconstruct the background to 1 Corinthians the relative order of these events must be determined. The clue lies in 1 Cor. 5.9–11. This passage is in effect a short dialogue between Paul and the Corinthians which can be outlined as follows:

Paul: Do not associate with immoral men.[2]

Corinthians: Do you mean that we should have *no* dealings with the world!

Paul: I meant that you should not associate with immoral *Christians.*

[1] *Notes,* p. 207. See also his essay, "The Mission of Titus to the Corinthians," *Biblical Essays,* p. 275, n. 1. On the decisive importance of this phrase see also Schmiedel, "Corr.," p. 94; and J. Weiss, *1 Cor.,* p. 138. That 1 Cor. 5.9 indicates that Paul had written to the Corinthians prior to the writing of 1 Corinthians is the position of all modern commentators known to the present writer.

An earlier point of view is represented by F. Blass, *Beiträge zur Förderung christlicher Theologie,* Vol. X, pt. 1, pp. 60ff (cited by Moffatt, *Intro. N. T.,* p. 111) who excised the phrase ἐν τῇ ἐπιστολῇ in the interest of the theological theory widely held at one time that nothing Paul wrote could have been lost. (For patristic ref. see Allo, *1 Cor.,* p. 128.) Among conservative Protestant scholars today the point is no longer defended. So, Grosheide, *1 Cor.,* p. 127, and Leon Morris, *The First Epistle of Paul to the Corinthians* ("Tynd."; London: The Tyndale Press, 1958), pp. 21, 24, 91. Modern Roman Catholic scholars also show no reluctance in taking 1 Cor. 5.9 to refer to a lost letter. So, Allo, *1 Cor.,* p. 128; and E. Osty, *Les Épîtres de Saint Paul aux Corinthiens* (3d ed.; "La Sainte Bible"; Paris: Les Éditions du Cerf, 1959), pp. 14, 35.

[2] The word πόρνος represented above (and by the RSV) as "immoral man" and the abstract noun πορνεία (RSV: "immorality") present a problem to the translator. Beare labels the RSV rendering an "intolerable bowdlerism" (*St. Paul,* p. 140n. Cf. pp. 68, 73). His comment as applied to 1 Cor. 6.9, where the term stands in a list of vices (including "adultery"), appears justified. But in 1 Cor. 5.9–11, summarized above, the term may be taken to apply to all non-Christians; "fornicators" seems too strong. Since the latter word strikes the modern ear as somewhat archaic, and since the expression "sexual immorality" is almost a tautology to-day, we propose to use the RSV renderings for the sake of uniformity, although the reader should remember that the terms have a range of meaning. Further, we believe that some of Paul's most important uses of these terms involve a meaning for which "fornification" and "fornicator" would be too narrow as renderings.

Paul's first statement was in the "Previous Letter" (as we may now call it) and his clarifying statement is in 1 Corinthians. Between these two points occurred both the Corinthians' misunderstanding of the Previous Letter and the communication of this misunderstanding to Paul.[1] Thus we may conclude that the Previous Letter arrived in Corinth before the departure of at least one of the groups of travellers who brought information to Paul. It is, of course, possible (considering only the evidence of 1 Cor. 5.9–11) that the Corinthians had dispatched their letter to Paul before receiving the Previous Letter and that Paul heard of their misunderstanding of his letter from Chloe's people. But since both groups of informants seem to have come to Paul at about the same time it is natural to assume that they left Corinth at about the same time also. At least Paul appears to treat all the information he received as reflecting the present mind of the Corinthian Church. At a later point we will examine more closely the relationship of the Previous Letter to the Corinthians' letter.[2] All that is necessary at this point is to assume the simplest sequence of events in the exchange or conversation between Paul and the Corinthians. Provisionally, therefore, we may place the Previous Letter before the departure from Corinth of both sets of travellers and adopt the following as the minimum number of stages:

	From Paul	*From Corinth*
1.	Previous Letter	
2.		Information partly oral and partly written carried by two groups
3.	1 Corinthians	

In defining these stages it does not matter (i) whether 1 Corinthians

---

[1] A few scholars, however, believe that Paul's enumeration in v. 10 of what he did not mean ("not at all meaning the immoral of this world . . .") is purely rhetorical and serves merely to emphasize what he did mean. So, Grosheide, *1 Cor.*, p. 128. In addition, Robertson and Plummer, *1 Cor.*, p. 104, and Evans, *Corr.*, p. 86, admit this possibility. This interpretation would paraphrase as follows: "I wrote you to avoid, not immoral men in general, but immoral Christians in particular." Thus no reaction from the Corinthians would be involved.

But this exegesis is improbable. We know (*a*) that Paul had received information from Corinth on other points. Moreover, (*b*) the above interpretation does not explain why Paul felt it necessary to protest that he *could* not have been referring to the "immoral of this world . . . since then you would need to go out of this world". Neither (*c*) does this interpretation explain v. 12, "For what have I to do with judging *outsiders*? Is it not those *inside* the Church whom you are to judge?" These three considerations make it almost certain (as most scholars hold) that Paul's original statement had been misunderstood by the Corinthians to apply primarily to those outside the Church. This opinion Paul firmly rejects in 5.10–12.

[2] See pp. 213–20 below (especially p. 216).

is a single letter or two letters written in succession (Letters "B" and "C" in Table 4 above). There is no evidence, nor do those who subdivide I Corinthians claim, that "Letter C" reflects knowledge by Paul of a response from the Corinthians to "Letter B". The theory of two letters merely results from the dual occasion for I Corinthians; the hypothesis does not imply additional stages in Paul's conversation with Corinth.

Nor does it matter (ii) whether all the information from Corinth was exactly simultaneous. This information arrived by various channels, but since in I Corinthians Paul treats it all as new and fresh we may consider, therefore, that it all belongs to a single stage. What is important to notice is that there is no real possibility that an exchange of information between Paul and Corinth intervened between the arrival of these two groups of travellers. Thus it is not necessary to decide now which items of information came from which traveller, or which were written and which oral.[1]

And (iii) although strictly speaking it is possible that the Previous Letter did not arrive in Corinth before the departure of both parties of travellers, yet the fact that even one item from the Previous Letter received a reply in the intermediate stage above puts the Previous Letter in the preceding stage.

There is at least one other stage in this exchange which preceded I Corinthians to be considered.

PAUL'S ORIGINAL VISIT TO CORINTH

There is no doubt but that the Church in Corinth was founded by Paul. Although this fact has always and everywhere been assumed on the combined evidence of Acts and Paul's letters, there is more than sufficient evidence in I Corinthians alone. In I Cor. 3.5-15, where he discussed the relationship between Apollos and himself, Paul used two metaphors:

(i) Agricultural: "I planted, Apollos watered, but God gave the growth" (3.6).

Then he made the translation to the second image by means of 3.9, "You are God's field, God's building".

---

[1] As we shall see later, however, it will be helpful to distinguish between information which takes the form of a description of the situation in Corinth, and information in the form of questions put to Paul by the Corinthian Church. It is a reasonable assumption that the former originated with Chloe's people, and that the latter was contained in the letter from Corinth. See further, pp. 61-5 below.

(ii) Architectural: "Like a skilled master builder I laid a foundation . . ." (3.10).

Paul's argument here concerning the relationship between his ministry and that of Apollos would have had no force if any evangelist had preceded him in Corinth. Moreover, 1 Cor. 4.15 confirms the point: "For I became your father in Christ Jesus through the gospel." The same is implied by 1 Cor. 9.1, 2: "Are you not my workmanship in the Lord? . . . You are the seal of my apostleship in the Lord." But most decisive of all is Paul's specific statement that he himself had baptized Stephanas and his household (1.16), the group which he designated as "the first converts (ἀπαρχή) in Achaia" (16.15).

Paul's evangelization of Corinth and founding of the Corinthian Church is, therefore, the earliest stage in this conversation between Paul and the Corinthians with which we are concerned.

OTHER STAGES?

Having identified, on the one hand, the two stages in the exchange between Paul and Corinth which immediately preceded the writing of 1 Corinthians, and, on the other hand, having determined the earliest stage of all in this series, the question must now be asked whether any stages intervened. Is there any evidence to suggest that other letters or visits preceded Paul's Previous Letter?

Other Letters? There are no further indications in 1 Corinthians of any previous correspondence between Paul and the Corinthians besides the two letters already discussed. 2 Corinthians, however—a letter (or letters) universally considered to be subsequent to 1 Corinthians[1]—makes two-fold reference to an earlier letter:

> And I wrote as I did, so that when I came I might not be pained by those who should have made me rejoice. . . . For I wrote you out of much affliction and anguish of heart and with many tears, not to cause you pain but to let you know the abundant love that I have for you (2.3, 4).

> For even if I made you sorry with my letter, I do not regret it (though I did regret it), for I see that that letter grieved you, though only for a while (7.8).

From these two passages and their contexts it can be seen that the letter in question was extremely severe (2.4), so severe that Paul

---

[1] Traditionally the canonical order of the Corinthian (and Thessalonian) letters was taken to be the order of their composition. But for critical scholars there is enough evidence that this order is correct for 1 and 2 Corinthians (taken as a whole) that the reverse order has not been suggested. See, e.g., Paul's references to the collection which in 1 Cor. 16.1–4 are introductory and in 2 Cor. 8 and 9 are clearly later in date, and his emphatic statements in 2 Cor. 12.14 and 13.1 that his next visit will be his third.

regretted sending it (7.8) until he heard from Titus that the letter had grieved the Corinthians into repentance (7.9).

Concerning this letter (the "Severe Letter") there are five possibilities; it can be identified with:

(i) 2 Corinthians.
(ii) A letter between 1 and 2 Corinthians.
(iii) 1 Corinthians.
(iv) The Previous Letter.
(v) An otherwise unknown letter before 1 Corinthians.

The first position is so unlikely as to be not worth considering.[1] The second is the view of the overwhelming majority of critical scholars.[2] The third is the traditional view which avoids the necessity of assuming that a letter of Paul's could have been lost.[3]

Only the two remaining possibilities affect the question at hand, however. At least one scholar has identified the Severe Letter with the Previous Letter.[4] This theory, while it does avoid a multiplication of lost letters, involves the unlikely assumption that Paul had heard about the Corinthians' misunderstanding of one part of his letter, but that after Paul's informants had left Corinth the letter began to grieve the Corinthians to the point of repentance. News of this change of heart did not reach Paul until the time of writing 2 Corinthians. One must also assume, again against the vast majority of modern scholars, that Paul's second visit to Corinth (see below) preceded the Previous (Severe) Letter. Otherwise Paul's evident surprise and joy in 2 Corinthians over the effect of the Severe Letter cannot be accounted for.

The fifth possibility is actually not a real possibility at all. The Severe Letter cannot have been sent before the Previous Letter, since neither the visitors from Corinth nor Paul know of its effect at the time 1 Corinthians was written. Neither can the Severe Letter have been

---

[1] However, Heinrich August Wilhelm Meyer (*Critical and Exegetical Handbook to the Epistles to the Corinthians*, trans. D. D. Bannerman and D. Hunter; ed. W. P. Dickson [2 vols.; "Meyer"; Edinburgh: T. & T. Clark, 1881–3], II, 166) reported that such was the opinion of Chrysostom, Grotius, and Oldhausen, an opinion resulting, no doubt, from the severity of 2 Cor. 10—13.

[2] Friedrich Bleek, "Erörterungen in Beziehung auf die Briefe Pauli an die Korinther," *Theologische Studien und Kritiken*, III (1830), 614–32, was the first scholar to argue that 2 Cor. 2.3, 4 and 7.8 refer to a letter written after 1 Cor. He believed this letter to be lost. However, Adolf Hausrath, *Der Vier-Capitelbrief des Paulus an die Korinther* (Heidelberg: Bassermann, 1870) added to this theory the hypothesis that the intermediate letter was partially preserved in 2 Cor. 10—13. Bleek's theory with or without Hausrath's contribution is by far the most popular among modern scholars.

[3] So, e.g., Paley, *Horae Paulinae*, Ch. 4, sec. 4; H. A. W. Meyer, *Corr.*, II, 127, 166; and Zahn, *Intro. N. T.*, I, 330.

[4] Wieseler, cited by Plummer, *2 Cor.*, p. 49 n.

written after the arrival of Paul's informants, but before 1 Corinthians, for 1 Corinthians is clearly Paul's immediate response to their information. The only theoretically possible opportunity for the writing of the Severe Letter before 1 Corinthians is the time during which the Previous Letter was in transit. 1 Corinthians, however, gives not the slightest hint that Paul had received information from Corinth not long before which had caused him to write a letter so severe that he later went anxiously first to Troas and then to Macedonia to find out from Titus what its effect had been (2 Cor. 2.12, 13; 7.5–8).

Therefore, there is neither historical evidence nor any real possibility that Paul wrote the Severe Letter before writing 1 Corinthians. And there is no indication in Paul's letters of any further correspondence with Corinth in this period.

Other Visits? Is it possible that Paul visited Corinth between his founding visit and 1 Corinthians? Twice in 2 Corinthians Paul spoke of the visit which he anticipated making to Corinth as his *third* visit (2 Cor. 12.14; 13.1). Before the writing of these statements, therefore, Paul had visited Corinth twice. His first visit is definitely fixed. Clearly it is the visit during which he founded the Corinthian Church. The "painful" visit referred to in 2 Cor. 2.1 ("For I made up my mind not to make you another painful visit") must be his second. But the relative dating of this visit is uncertain. It occurred sometimes before 2 Cor. 2 was written. Is it possible that it also antedated the writing of 1 Corinthians, and thus falls within the period under consideration?

Since there is no mention in 1 Corinthians of such a visit, a visit so painful that Paul was reluctant to return to Corinth (2 Cor. 2.1), it is more natural to suppose that the visit occurred after this letter had been written than before. Further, the simplicity of Paul's statements in 1 Cor. 2.1 ("When I came to you brethren, . . ."), 3.2 ("I fed you with milk . . ."), and 11.2 ("I commend you because . . . you maintain the traditions even as I have delivered [παρέδωκα] them to you") all imply a single previous campaign in Corinth. Moreover, 1 Cor. 4.19; 11.34; and 16.5–9 all indicate that when Paul wrote 1 Corinthians he intended to visit Corinth in the near future. That Paul's second visit to Corinth took place after the writing of 1 Corinthians is the opinion of the great majority of modern scholars.[1] The matter is not, however, settled

[1] The theory originated with Ewald in 1850, and was incorporated by him in his *Sendschrieben*, pp. 223–34, 256. Having accepted Bleek's position for the Severe Letter, he hypothesized that the "painful" visit immediately preceded and was the cause of the Severe Letter. The close connection between these two events is now almost universally accepted by Pauline scholars. E.g., J. Weiss, *Primitive Christianity*, pp. 341–5; Moffatt,

beyond all shadow of doubt. A number of great scholars of the past generation held that there is no room between 1 and 2 Corinthians for a visit by Paul to Corinth. They therefore placed the second visit before the Previous Letter, even though the visit is not specifically mentioned until 2 Cor. 2.1.[1] But the complicated problems which surround 2 Corinthians and Paul's second visit to Corinth need not detain us further. For our purposes the following points are all that need to be noted here:

(i) If it be supposed that Paul visited Corinth a second time before writing 1 Corinthians, his visit must almost without doubt antedate the Previous Letter. A date between the Previous Letter and 1 Corinthians is exceedingly unlikely for two reasons. (a) There is almost no possibility that the visit could have fallen between the Previous Letter and the return letter from Corinth. Paul wrote because he could not go to Corinth; the Corinthians wrote because he was not there, and was not expected in the near future. And obviously (b) Paul did not visit Corinth after receiving the letter from the Corinthians; 1 Corinthians, not a visit, was his response.

(ii) But if, therefore, the only real possibility (however remote) for an extra visit is before the Previous Letter, then for the purposes of the present study the visit becomes part of the earliest stage—Paul's mission to Corinth. If such a visit occurred in this period, there is no evidence that it received a response from the Corinthians which was distinct from their total response to his first missionary work. Thus even if the somewhat unlikely hypothesis of an early return visit to Corinth should be allowed, it does not add to the number of stages in the exchange between Paul and the Corinthian Church.

CONCLUSION

It can now be said that there is clear evidence that 1 Corinthians is the fourth stage in an exchange which took place between Paul and the Corinthian Church. These stages then are as follows:

Intro. N. T., pp. 116–19; Windisch, *2 Cor.*, pp. 10–11; Evans, *Corr.*, p. 22; Enslin, *Beginnings*, pp. 255, 258; Allo, *2 Cor.*, p. ix; Lietzmann, *Corr.*, pp. 102–3; Craig, "1 Cor.," p. 13; Wendland, *Corr.*, p. 2; Jean Héring, *La Seconde Épître de Saint Paul aux Corinthiens* ("CNT," VIII; Neuchâtel: Delachaux & Niestlé S. A., 1958), p. 13. Schmithals, *Gnosis*, pp. 24–5, does not bother to discuss the problem, for as he says, "Dass dieser Besuch zwischen dem 'I Kor' und dem 'II Kor' . . . stattgefunden hat, wird von den modernen Exegeten fast einmütig anerkannt."

[1] So Lightfoot, *Biblical Essays*, pp. 222, 274; Schmiedel, "Corr.," pp. xii–xiii, 41, 54; Findlay, "I Cor.," pp. 736–7; Robertson and Plummer, *1 Cor.*, p. xxiv; and Zahn, *Intro. N. T.*, I, 272, n. 14; 316, n. 2. All of these opinions were written before 1918.

Stage 1. Paul's first preaching in Corinth and the founding of the
          Corinthian Church.

Stage 2. Paul's Previous Letter to the Corinthians.

Stage 3. Information in reply, partly oral and partly written,
          brought to Paul from Corinth by Stephanas, Fortunatus,
          and Achaicus, and by Chloe's people. Some of this infor-
          mation was in the form of questions addressed to Paul by
          the Church; some in the form of comments on the situa-
          tion at Corinth by some or all of the travellers.

Stage 4. 1 Corinthians, Paul's response both to questions he had
          been asked, and to news about situations in Corinth
          which he believed needed correcting.

There is no evidence and small probability that any other letter or visit
occurred in this period. The only possible addition to this list would be
the reception by Paul of news about the Corinthian Church just before
the writing of the Previous Letter, as B. W. Bacon and W. L. Knox,
for example, suggest.[1] This possibility must be left open until the
contents of the Previous Letter have been reconstructed.[2]

Having now established in these first two chapters both what is
not and what is the historical framework for this investigation, we
shall in the chapters that follow proceed stage by stage from the latest
to the earliest, attempting from each stage to reconstruct its predecessor.
Thus we shall try to learn from 1 Corinthians the contents of the information from Corinth. From this material together with Paul's statement in 1 Cor. 5.9 we shall try to outline the Previous Letter. And by a
comparison of these two stages we shall attempt to arrive at as clear an
idea as possible of what Paul with Silvanus and Timothy (2 Cor. 1.19)
preached at Corinth during the founding visit.

1 Corinthians is a manifold document, however, giving more
information than any other of Paul's letters about the problems of the
early Church. In order, therefore, adequately to fulfill our projected
task it will be necessary to pass by many interesting aspects of 1 Corinthians, of Hellenistic thought, and of Pauline theology, and to hold
as far as possible only to those items which found a place in the discussion between Paul and the Corinthian Christians. To the task of reconstructing this discussion we now turn.

----

[1] Bacon, *Story*, p. 272, n. 1; W. L. Knox, *Jerusalem*, p. 311.
[2] See below, pp. 259–62.

PART 2

Paul's Information from Corinth

CHAPTER 3

The Knowledge shown by 1 Corinthians of the Corinthian Church

TYPES OF INFORMATION

The situation of the Corinthian Christians to which Paul directed 1 Corinthians can, of course, only be partially reconstructed. 1 Corinthians presents a spectrum of evidence rather than discrete items of information. The evidence ranges from what appears certain to what is only a matter of bare inference. In the first place, although 1 Corinthians at times provides direct statements concerning Paul's knowledge of the state of affairs in Corinth,[1] more often this information can only be inferred from the things that Paul said, from the things he left unsaid, and from the tone of what he wrote. Secondly, 1 Corinthians is not based on the actual state of affairs in Corinth but on what Paul *believed* to have been the situation there. His understanding included both his presumably objective knowledge of the letter from Corinth and his somewhat emotional reactions to the unofficial oral reports he had received about the behaviour of the Corinthians. Thirdly, neither can the information Paul received be considered free of bias. On the one hand, the oral reports involved, of course, the interpretation of the reporters, who may well have had an unfavourable view of the situation at Corinth. At least, they seem to have made little effort to conceal information from Paul. The Corinthians' letter, on the other hand, could be expected to present as favourable a picture of the Church as possible, if only by a selection of material. And, finally, there is no real way of knowing the extent to which Paul's knowledge of and feelings about the Corinthians gained on his first stay in Corinth (Stage 1) affected his interpretation of the information brought to him by the travellers from Corinth (Stage 3). Thus, although we have an

[1] E.g., 1 Cor. 1.11; 5.1; and 6.6.

excellent knowledge of the text of 1 Corinthians (Stage 4), the information upon which the letter was based (Stage 3) appears to be a complicated tangle of truths, half-truths, and opinions. It becomes a real question whether Stage 3 can be reconstructed at all, to say nothing of Stages 2 and 1.

There are, however, two distinctions which, if they could be maintained, would bring some objectivity into these uncertainties. In the first place (a), there is the distinction between the material in 1 Corinthians written in response to the letter from Corinth, and the material which deals with word of mouth information concerning the Church in Corinth. If it is possible to find in 1 Corinthians sections which appear to be directly based upon the written communication from Corinth and to separate this material from those passages based on a hearsay knowledge of the Corinthian Church, then there is hope of reconstructing at least partially the Corinthians' letter and thus of gaining an entrance into the mind of the Corinthian Church itself. Clearly the greater objectivity attaches to the written portion of the information brought to Paul from Corinth; the greater subjectivity, to the oral reports received by him. In addition (b), another distinction might be sought in 1 Corinthians—the distinction between the passages where Paul appears more emotionally involved than usual and the passages where his manner is calmer and more detached. Clearly the latter type of material is a surer guide in the reconstruction of Stage 3 than the former.

Now there is considerable evidence to support two conclusions:

(i) That these two distinctions are in large measure the same distinction, and thus that a double measure of objectivity is provided by Paul's calmer treatment of his written information.

(ii) That Paul, for the most part, treated the oral information separately from the written, and thus that the separation suggested above can actually be made with a fair degree of probability.

Concerning the first point (i) it has already been suggested that the Corinthians' letter did not present an unfavourable picture of the Church in Corinth in the minds, at least, of its authors. Thus it seems probable that the official written information received by Paul would have been less likely to arouse his anger than the unofficial oral news, and thus that this material was both more objectively known to Paul (because written) and more objectively treated by him (because favourable to the Corinthian Church). At least at the point where Paul specifically mentions the Corinthians' letter ("Now concerning the matters about which you wrote . . ." [7.1]) his manner seems calm and analytical. On the other hand, at the points where Paul mentions his oral information his tone is noticeably more disturbed, particularly in connection with the case of incest:

> It is actually (ὅλως) reported that there is sexual immorality among you, and of a kind that is not found even among pagans; for a man is living with his father's wife. And you are arrogant! Ought you not rather to mourn? (5.1, 2)[1]

Concerning the second point (ii), that it is possible to separate out of I Corinthians the material based on the letter from Corinth, it has been noted by a number of scholars that the passage in which Paul refers directly to their letter (7.1) is introduced by a formula which recurs periodically in the second half of I Corinthians. The formula occurs as follows:

(i)   7.1   Now concerning (περὶ δέ) the matters about which you wrote, . . .

(ii)   7.25   Now concerning (περὶ δέ) the unmarried (or "celibate"), . . .

(iii) 8.1   Now concerning (περὶ δέ) food offered to idols: . . .

(iv)   12.1   Now concerning (περὶ δέ) spiritual gifts (or "men"), . . .

(v)   16.1   Now concerning (περὶ δέ) the contribution for the saints: . . .

(vi)   16.12 Now concerning (περὶ δέ) our brother Apollos, . . .

The fact that this formula occurs six times in the last ten chapters of I Corinthians but elsewhere in the Pauline corpus only at I Thess. 4.9 and 5.1 (and in the form περὶ γάρ in 2 Cor. 9.1) emphasizes its import-

---

[1] Some commentators take ὅλως in the sense of "generally" or "everywhere" and thus think of ἀκούεται as indicating a general rumour Paul had heard some time earlier. So the AV, "commonly". So also, e.g., Allo, *1 Cor.*, p. 117, "Ici Paul ne s'en rapporte plus aux 'gens de Chloé', ni à aucun informateur nommément désigné, mais à la voix publique, qui ne parlait que trop haut." J. Weiss, *1 Cor.*, p. 124, also translated ὅλως as "überall, allgemein = πανταχοῦ oder ἐν ὅλῳ τῷ κόσμῳ", and said that the news reached Paul "als anonymes Gerücht". And Héring, *1 Cor.*, p. 34, said confidently, "The word 'holōs' can only have a local sense = 'everywhere'. . . . The affair has gained notoriety in several Churches."

The more general opinion, however, seems to be that ὅλως indicates Paul's amazement and special disapproval. So the RV and RSV, "It is *actually* reported. . . ." So also Robertson and Plummer, *1 Cor.*, p. 95; Alexander Souter, *A Pocket Lexicon to the Greek New Testament* (Oxford: The Clarendon Press, 1917), p. 174; Moffatt, *1 Cor.*, p. 53; Arndt/Gingrich, p. 568, who also cite Anton Fridrichsen, *Symbolae Osloenses*, XIII (1934), 43f, "to say it all at once"; and Craig, "1 Cor.," pp. 59–60; and Morris, *1 Cor.*, p. 86. Both Lietzmann, *Corr.*, p. 22, and Wendland, *Corr.*, p. 38, translate ὅλως with "überhaupt" in the sense of "especially" (rather than "on the whole").

ance to the structure of 1 Corinthians.[1] Moreover it is significant that
in these last three passages, as in 1 Cor. 7.1, the phrase is associated
with the verb γράφω. A number of scholars go so far as to suggest that
the two Thessalonian occurrences refer in the manner of I Cor. 7.1
to a letter, in this case a letter to which Paul was responding when he
wrote the latter part of 1 Thessalonians.[2] As we shall see, each of the
passages thus introduced in 1 Corinthians appears to consist of an answer
to a question or questions asked Paul by the Corinthians. It is reasonable to suppose, therefore, that Paul's list of answers corresponds more
or less closely to a list of questions from the Corinthian Church. And
since Paul says (7.1) both that the first of these topics was contained in
the Corinthians' letter and that they had written him about more than
one matter, it is also reasonable to suppose that the rest of this list of
questions from the Corinthians was also contained in their letter to
Paul. As Kirsopp and Silva Lake say, for example, concerning the
letter from Corinth, "Paul's answer begins in vii. 1. As he takes up the
Corinthian letter, question by question, it is almost possible to reconstruct the Epistle which he received."[3] And Wendland expresses the

[1] The following scholars call attention to the significance of this repeated phrase:
Schmiedel, "Corr.," p. 42; Lightfoot, Notes, p. 219; J. Weiss, 1 Cor., p. 169; H. L. Goudge,
The First Epistle to the Corinthians (3d ed. rev.; "West."; London: Methuen & Co. Ltd.,
1911), p. 169; Findlay, "1 Cor.," p. 949; Robertson and Plummer, 1 Cor., p. xxv; Bousset,
"1 Cor.," p. 76; Zahn, Intro. N. T., I, 260; Evans, Corr., p. 21; Adolf Schlatter,
Paulus, der Bote Jesu: Eine Deutung seiner Briefe an die Korinther (Stuttgart: Calwer Vereinsbuchhandlung, 1934), pp. 208-9; Allo, 1 Cor., p. 152; Bachmann, 1 Cor., pp. 237, 253,
375, 473; McNeile, Intro. N. T., p. 137; Grosheide, 1 Cor., pp. 248, 278, 401; Craig,
"1 Cor.," p. 76; Wendland, Corr., pp. 92, 141; Jeremias, "Briefzitate," p. 151; W. G. H.
Simon, The First Epistle to the Corinthians: Introduction and Commentary ("Torch"; London:
SCM Press Ltd, 1959), p. 31; Manson, Studies, pp. 274-7 (who on p. 275 cites as "an exact
parallel" the Emperor Claudius' letter to the citizens of Alexandria published in H. I. Bell,
Jews and Christians in Egypt [1924], pp. 1-37); and C. S. C. Williams, "1 and 2 Corinthians," in Peake's Commentary on the Bible, ed. M. Black and H. H. Rowley (London:
Thomas Nelson and Sons Ltd, 1962), §834a.
  A. S. Geyser says expressly, "περὶ δέ ... (1 Cor. 8.1) is the usual formula used by Paul in
answering written questions" ("Paul, the Apostolic Decree and the Liberals in Corinth,"
p. 124, n. 2). And C. E. Faw is even more explicit. He surveyed the entire N. T. evidence
and concluded: "(1) that περὶ δέ is a formula of reply to specific questions or problems,
especially where there is a series of such; (2) in series of replies it is properly used to introduce those from the second point onward; (3) in Pauline usage it is confined to the answering of specific questions or problems brought up in letters from the churches to which he
is writing" ("On the Writing of First Thessalonians," JBL, LXXI [1952], 221).
[2] So J. Rendel Harris, "A Study in Letter-Writing," The Expositor, Ser. 5; VIII (1898),
161-80; Bacon, Story, pp. 235-7 (cf. his An Introduction to the New Testament [New York:
The Macmillan Company, 1900], pp. 73-4); Milligan, Thess., p. 126 (as a possibility);
Frame, Thess., pp. 9, 106, 157, 166, and 178; Lake, Earlier Epistles, pp. 86-7; Smith, St.
Paul, pp. 152, 156-66; Bicknell, Thess., pp. xvii, 40; Albert E. Barnett, The New Testament: Its Making and Meaning (New York: Abingdon Press, 1946), p. 37 (as a plausible
suggestion); Neil, Thess., p. 84 (possibly); Faw, "Writing of 1 Thess.," pp. 218-21; and
Masson, Thess., pp. 51, 66 (not improbable).
[3] An Introduction to the New Testament (London: Christophers, 1938), p. 112. See also
Lake, Earlier Epistles, pp. 136-9.

same conviction: "Es ist wahrscheinlich, dass er von Kap. 7 an bei seiner Behandlung der Gemeindenöte der Reihenfolge der Fragen in dem korinthischen Briefe folgt."[1] We have already seen that the letter from Corinth is the most objective element in Stage 3. Now it appears that there is special reason to hope that the material in I Corinthians which relates to this letter can be identified. To the separation of this material we now turn.

SECTIONS IN I CORINTHIANS DEALING WITH THE LETTER FROM CORINTH

The passages beginning περὶ δέ (particularly the first) are the starting point in the attempt to identify the sections in I Corinthians which deal with the letter from Corinth. In the process of analysing these passages we shall seek to establish a list of characteristics which mark answers to the Corinthians' letter so that we may then assess passages in I Corinthians without the introductory formula περὶ δέ.

1. *"Now concerning the matters about which you wrote"* (7.1)

The whole of 7.1–24 deals with problems concerning marriage. The abrupt shift in subject matter from the preceding sections is noticeable.[2] Paul specifically says that the new topic is one contained in the letter from Corinth. Clearly the Corinthian communication on this point was in the form of a question or questions concerning marriage. Paul responds calmly and systematically. The style is legal, or as Johannes Weiss says, "Die Behandlung ist überwiegend kasuistisch, alle einzelnen Fälle und Möglichkeiten werden erwogen".[3] Paul treats not only the present relationships to which his directions apply, but future contingencies as well. The section can be outlined as follows:

RULES CONCERNING MARRIAGE

1. General principles, 7.1–7.
2. Application to:

---

[1] *Corr.*, pp. 48–9. So also Bacon, "Paul gives his answers *seriatim.* . . . We can follow the letter of inquiry paragraph by paragraph in Paul's reply" (*Story*, p. 270). The correspondence in order of the topics introduced by περὶ δέ in I Cor. with the topics in the Corinthians' letter was also suggested by Lightfoot, *Notes*, p. 219; Robertson and Plummer, *I Cor.*, p. 163; and Lietzmann, *Corr.*, p. 29.

[2] Although as Schmiedel, e.g., noted ("Corr.," p. 100), the concern about πορνεία continues from the preceding section, 6.12–20, a section whose possible connection with the letter from Corinth will be discussed below, pp. 87–9.

[3] *I Cor.*, p. 169.

(a) Case of unmarried and widows:
    (i) General case, 7.8.
    (ii) Case of the incontinent, 7.9.
(b) Case of those already married:
    (i) General case, 7.10.
    (ii) Case of those who separate, 7.11.
(c) Other cases:
    (i) Man with pagan wife, 7.12, 14a.
    (ii) Woman with pagan husband, 7.13, 14b.
    (iii) Divorce initiated by pagan spouse, 7.15, 16.
3. Generalizing conclusion, 7.17–24.

It is to be noted that there is in this passage no reference to the past behaviour of the Corinthians. If Paul knew, for example, that some Corinthians had been divorced, he made no mention of it. Paul dealt with the future. Thus it was inevitable that he should make frequent use of the conjunction ἐάν (7.8, 11) and the conditional particle εἰ (7.15, 16a, 16b, 21). Without analysing the temporal reference of each occurrence it is certainly worth noticing that the two occur in 1 Corinthians as follows:

1 Cor. 1—6	1 Cor. 7—16
(9 Nestle pages)	(22 pages)
ἐάν 5	44
εἰ 9	45

There appears, therefore, to be a distinct difference between 1 Cor. 1—6 and 7—16 as far as the definiteness of Paul's statements is concerned.

A further characteristic of 1 Cor. 7.1–24 is Paul's apparent desire to establish as strong an authority as possible for his directions to the Corinthians. At one point in this passage he appeals directly to Jesus' teachings, "To the married I give charge, not I but the Lord, that the wife should not separate from her husband" (7.10). That this reference to "the Lord" is not simply a happy coincidence occasioned by the fact that tradition had preserved for Paul Jesus' pronouncement forbidding divorce is shown by two succeeding passages:

7.12 To the rest I say, not the Lord. . . .
7.25 Now concerning the unmarried, I have no command of the Lord, but I give my opinion as one who by the Lord's mercy is trustworthy.

Clearly Paul intended to bring to bear on the Corinthians' question the best authority he could muster.

A somewhat more subtle feature of Paul's answer is his opening statement, "It is well for a man not to touch a woman" (7.1). We shall examine this statement in some detail in Chapter 5. Here it is only necessary to say that the principle contained in this statement does not serve to further Paul's argument in 1 Cor. 7.1–24, and that if the saying were unattached it might well be assigned to the position *against* which Paul directs his own calm and balanced statement. In fact, a number of scholars have suggested that this and similar passages elsewhere are quotations from the letter of the Corinthians. The passages in question are as follows:[1]

6.12, 10.23   All things are lawful.
6.13   Food is meant for the stomach and the stomach for food.
7.1   It is well for a man not to touch a woman.
8.1   All of us possess knowledge.
8.4   An idol has no real existence. There is no God but one.
8.5, 6   For although there may be so-called gods in heaven or on earth (as indeed there are many "gods" and many "lords") yet for us there is one God, the Father, from whom we exist, and one Lord, Jesus Christ, through whom are all things and through whom we exist.
8.8   Food will not commend us to God. We are no worse off if we do not eat, and no better off if we do.
11.2   We remember you in everything and maintain the traditions even as you delivered them to us [reversing the pronouns].

Table 5 lists scholars who single out three or more of these passages as quotations of the letter from Corinth.[2] Whatever is finally decided about 7.1 it is to be noticed that, having stated the general principle, "It is well for a man not to touch a woman", Paul immediately qualified it, "But because of immorality. . . ." We shall want to see whether similar qualifications of general principles appear elsewhere in 1 Corinthians.

Having discussed some of the characteristics of this section known to have been written in answer to a question from Corinth, let us now examine the other sections introduced by the formula περὶ δέ.

[1] One additional passage is sometimes cited: 6.18, "Every sin which a man commits is outside the body." So W. J. Conybeare and J. S. Howson, *The Life and Epistles of St. Paul* (2 vols. in 1; New York: Scribner, Armstrong & Co., 1874), II, 43; Robert McQueen Grant, "Hellenistic Elements in I Corinthians," in *Early Christian Origins: Studies in Honor of Harold R. Willoughby*, ed. A. Wikgren (Chicago: Quadrangle Books, 1961), p. 64, n. 19; C. F. D. Moule, *An Idiom Book of New Testament Greek* (2d ed.; Cambridge: The University Press, 1959), pp. 196–7; Morris, *1 Cor.*, p. 103; and F. C. Grant, *N. T.*, p. 86.

[2] Scholars whose works have not previously been cited are C. F. Georg Heinrici, *Das erste Sendschreiben des Apostel Paulus an die Korinther* (Berlin: Wilhelm Hertz, 1880); and Walter Lock, "I Cor. 8.1–9. A Suggestion," *The Expositor*, Ser. 5; VI (1897), 65–74.

TABLE 5

Scholarly Opinion Affirming the Presence in 1 Corinthians of Quotations from the Corinthians' Letter

	6.12	6.13	7.1	8.1	8.4	8.5f	8.8	11.2
Conybeare & Howson, *Paul*, II,	43	43		47				52
Farrar, *Paul*,	379	389	390	379	379			378
Heinrici, *1 Cor.* (1880),				224	....	....	229	
Lock, *Expos.* (1897),	73	73	73	67	67	67	67	74
Findlay, "Letter,"	405			404	404	404		
Bacon, *Story*,	278			278	278	278	278	279
J. Weiss, *1 Cor.*,	157	159		214	219			
Goudge, *1 Cor.*,	47	47	53	69	70			94
Robertson & Plummer, *1 Cor.*,	xxv	123	xxv	xxv	166			228
Bousset, "1 Cor.," II,	99	99		110	111	111		128
Zahn, *Intro. N.T.*, I,	260		260	260				261
Parry, *1 Cor.* ("Camb."),	63	64	70	86	87	87	90	111
D. Smith, *Paul*,			262	270	271	271	271	282
Evans, *Corr.*,	88	89		104	104		104	117
Allo, *1 Cor.*,	142	143		197	199			255
Moffatt, *1 Cor.*,	68	68	75	104	104			148
Lietzmann, *Corr.*,	27			37	37			53
Héring, *1 Cor.*,	45	46		67				
Grosheide, *1 Cor.*,	144			188	188	192	194	
Craig, "1 Cor.,"	73	73		90	92			
Jeremias, "Briefzitate,"	152		151	151	151		152	
Wendland, "Corr.,"	59			59	60			
Morris, *1 Cor.*,	99	99	124	125			128	
F. C. Grant, *N.T.*,	63	63		63	63	(86)	(86)	

2. *"Now concerning the celibate"* (7.25)

Who these παρθένοι, "virgins", were will be discussed in the next chapter. Apparently they were male[1] as well as female.[2] Clearly Paul in this section (7.25–38) took up a problem related to the preceding yet distinct from it. As we noted above, he began with another reference to authority, this time to the Lord's support of his own: "I have no command of the Lord, but I give my opinion as one who by the Lord's mercy is trustworthy" (7.25). This section like the preceding is not a commentary on the past behaviour of the Corinthians but deals in a systematic way with types of future behaviour. Paul stated his highest hope for them, but added a concession to possible future weakness on

[1] 7.27, 28a, 32–4a, 36–8.   [2] 7.28b, 34b.

the part of the celibate. All the evidence points toward the conclusion that here Paul answered yet another question of the Corinthians.

I Cor. 7.39, 40 appears to be an afterthought to the first question (7.1–24; in particular, vv. 8–10).[1]

3. "Now concerning meat offered to idols" (8.1)

In I Cor. 8.1 Paul abruptly took up a new topic. Table 5 shows how widespread is the opinion that Paul opened this section by quoting a slogan of the Corinthians, "All of us possess knowledge" (8.1a). This sentiment he immediately qualified (8.1b–3). Further quotations appear in 8.4 (and perhaps also vv. 5–6). Paul qualified these slogans as well (8.7). The introductory formula, the abrupt change of subject matter, the slogans and their qualification, all indicate that here Paul began to answer another of the Corinthians' questions.

In this answer, however, a new characteristic previously implicit becomes explicit: Paul appealed directly to Christian love as the highest ethical principle of all. In contrast to the Corinthians' boasted "knowledge" Paul exalted love: "knowledge puffs up, but love ($\dot{a}\gamma\dot{a}\pi\eta$) builds up" (8.1; in addition, the verb $\dot{a}\gamma a\pi\hat{\omega}$ appears in 8.3). And in contrast to their confident scorn of idols Paul reminded them of the love they owe their weaker brothers (8.7–13). If a weaker brother should happen to see a knowledgeable brother eating meat in a temple, then he might try to emulate his brother and might possibly fall away from Christ. Therefore, in loving regard for his fellow Christians each Christian should avoid idol meat. As we shall see, this principle will be important in connection with answers to other questions from Corinth.

If Paul's answer to the problem of idol meat begins in 8.1, the question remains: where does it end? In 9.1 without the usual introductory formula Paul suddenly began to assert his apostolic authority. But in 10.1, again with apparent suddenness, he returned to the subject of idolatry, although in somewhat different terms. Finally, in 10.23—11.1 he seems to have reasserted his general principle of 8.8 ("Food will not commend us to God"), and once again qualified it with concern for the hypothetical weaker brother. In fact, "Not all things build up" (10.23, $o\dot{i}\kappa o\delta o\mu\epsilon\hat{i}$) echoes "Love builds up" (8.1, $o\dot{i}\kappa o\delta o\mu\epsilon\hat{i}$). I Cor. 8.1–13 and 10.23—11.1, therefore, belong together. Those scholars who partition I Corinthians, however, believe 10.1–22 to be so different in its treatment of the problem of idol meat that it must come from

---

[1] So, e.g., Moffatt, 1 Cor., pp. 100–1; Lietzmann, Corr., p. 37; and Wendland, Corr., p. 58.

the earlier, stricter Previous Letter. Whether this rearrangement is probable will be examined in Chapter 5 when we discuss Paul's motivation in this section. Here we need only note that 10.1–22 does not give any more evidence than do 8.1–13 and 10.23—11.1 that Paul had been told that some Corinthians had actually joined in pagan sacramental meals. In this passage as well as the other two Paul laid down rules for the future conduct of the Corinthians. This section, since it is not descriptive but proscriptive, and since it deals with a topic which has already been designated as a question from Corinth, must be considered as part of the "answer" material of 1 Corinthians (subject to an investigation of the integrity of these chapters[1]).

1 Cor. 9, on the other hand, appears to have no connection with the Corinthians' question about idol meat. Neither idolatry nor idol meat is mentioned in this section. Instead the chapter begins with a vigorous assertion by Paul of his apostolic authority. But as Paul's treatment of the questions on marriage shows, the problem of authority was important for Paul when answering the Corinthians' questions. Where possible he cited the authority of Jesus. Where he could not he twice buttressed his authority by a reference to his own relationship with God:

> 7.25 I give my opinion as one who by the Lord's mercy is trustworthy.
> 7.40 And I suppose that I have the Spirit of God, too.

1 Cor. 9.1, 2, then, may be considered to serve the same function for Paul's treatment of the problem of idol meat that the above verses serve in his discussion of marriage.

1 Cor. 9.3–27, however, contains information on another level about the Corinthians' thoughts. Paul's statement, "This is my defence to those who would examine me" (9.3), indicates that he believed that in some measure his authority had been challenged (9.1, 2, 5). Apparently he had been criticized by some of the Corinthians concerning his use of money. His angry questions, "Do we not have the right to our food and drink? Do we not have the right to be accompanied by a wife...?" (9.4, 5) are referred by most commentators solely to the claim made in 9.6–18 for Paul's right to be supported financially by the Churches.[2]

---

1 See below, pp. 131–42.

2 So, e.g., Schmiedel, "Corr.," p. 112; J. Weiss, 1 Cor., p. 234; Robertson and Plummer, 1 Cor., pp. 175, 179; Bousset, "1 Cor.," p. 114; Allo, 1 Cor., p. 211; Bachmann, 1 Cor., p. 311; Moffatt, 1 Cor., p. 116; Lietzmann, Corr., p. 40; Jacques Dupont, Gnosis: La Connaissance Religieuse dans les Épîtres de Saint Paul (2d ed.; "Universitas Catholica Lovaniensis Dissertationes," Ser. 2, Vol. XL; Louvain: E. Nauwelaerts, 1960), p. 316; Héring, 1 Cor., p. 76; Craig, "1 Cor.," p. 99; Wendland, Corr., p. 64; and Morris, 1 Cor., p. 132.

This interest surely is basic, but it is certainly worth noting that the items Paul chose to defend here are two matters which were at issue between the Corinthians and himself, the two matters that he had just discussed—regulations concerning marriage and diet. On the latter point he says specifically, "If I partake with thankfulness, why am I denounced because of that for which I give thanks?" (10.30). Both of these problems relate to the whole question of the extent to which the Torah was binding for Christians, a question discussed in 9.19–23. Furthermore, Paul's use of money directly concerns the anticipated collection which, as we shall see, is the topic of another of the Corinthians' questions. Since, therefore, each of the three additional points on which Paul appears to be informed in 9.1–27 concerns one of the questions from Corinth, it is probable that this chapter functions as part of Paul's answer to the problem of idol meat, but that it has been expanded because of what Paul takes to be the critical thrust of the three questions concerning marriage, concerning idol meat, and concerning the collection. Thus, the probability is that the whole of 1 Cor. 8.1—11.1 should be classified as part of Paul's answer to the Corinthians' letter.

4. "Now concerning spiritual gifts" (12.1)

1 Cor. 12.1 begins a long discussion περὶ τῶν πνευματικῶν, concerning "spiritual things" or "spiritual persons". This discussion occupies 1 Cor. 12, 13, and 14. The whole section is a plea for love as the highest gift of the Spirit with rational preaching as its expression, as contrasted with the dissension and individualism expressed by the glossolalia at Corinth. Clearly these chapters show more knowledge about the Corinthians than would have been contained in a simple request for information. In fact, it is difficult to know whether this section was occasioned by a question from the Corinthian church at all, for, as Robertson and Plummer said, "There is a possible reference to the letter of the Corinthians to the Apostle; but he would no doubt have treated a number of the topics which are handled, even if they had not mentioned them."[1] Paul speaks as though he were sure of the situation he addressed, and his confidence implies that he had information descriptive of the glossolalia at Corinth. The source of what Paul knew is hard to determine, however. Clearly he knew the manner of worship which the Corinthians came to use during his first visit to Corinth (Stage 1). Comments by the bearers of the letter from Corinth or by

---

[1] 1 Cor., p. 257.

"those of Chloe" may have brought him up to date on this aspect of the Corinthians' worship as on the matter of divisions at the Lord's Supper. But, whatever the source, the whole argument of 1 Cor. 12—14 is carefully directed toward a problem Paul obviously considered not only important but real: the problem of glossolalia. And yet, at the points where Paul actually speaks of the Corinthians' worship, his references become hypothetical:

> He who speaks in a tongue edifies himself (14.4).
>
> If you in a tongue utter speech that is not intelligible, how will anyone know what is said (14.9)?
>
> He who speaks in a tongue should pray for the power to interpret (14.13).
>
> If you bless with the spirit, how can any one in the position of an outsider say the "Amen" to your thanksgiving when he does not know what you are saying (14.16)?
>
> If, therefore, the whole church assembles and all speak in tongues, and outsiders or unbelievers enter, will they not say that you are mad (14.23)?

These hypothetical references are particularly reminiscent of Paul's arguments concerning idol meat and the weaker brother (8.7–13; 10.28, 29). As in 1 Cor. 8—10, so here, Paul does not refer directly to the Corinthians' customs; he does not criticize and condemn past behaviour. This fact together with the opening formula περὶ δέ, and Paul's persuasive, instructive tone are all evidence that a question from Corinth occasioned these chapters. Such is the opinion of a large number of scholars.[1] Moreover, two further points confirm this opinion:

(a) Paul, as Johannes Weiss said, plunged *in medias res*.[2] He did not stop as in 5.1 to remind his readers of some situation which he wanted to correct. Instead, he informed them ("I do not want you to be uninformed . . ." [12.1]; "I want you to understand . . ." [12.3]), rather than warning, exhorting, cajoling, or threatening them. These opening verses remain enigmatic to us because the relevance of the information Paul supplied was already known by the Corinthians. Paul had only to say "now concerning spiritual things" to bring the question they had asked into their minds again.

---

[1] So, with greater or less definiteness, Schmiedel, "Corr.," p. 135; J. Weiss, *1 Cor.*, p. 294; Goudge, *1 Cor.*, p. 108; Findlay, "1 Cor.," p. 822; Bousset, "1 Cor.," p. 134; Smith, *St. Paul*, p. 289; Evans, *Corr.*, p. 60; Grosheide, *1 Cor.*, p. 278; Craig, "1 Cor.," p. 146; Wendland, *Corr.*, p. 92; Morris, *1 Cor.*, p. 166.

Moffatt and Héring, however, ignore the περὶ δέ and do not mention the letter from Corinth at this point.

[2] *1 Cor.*, p. 294.

(*b*) Paul's concern that love be shown to the morally or spiritually weak has already appeared in three sections which are most probably answers to questions from Corinth. In 1 Cor. 7.1–11 the motive to which Paul appeals in order to qualify the absolute motto, "It is well for a man not to touch a woman", is concern for those who are morally less robust. The same is true of 1 Cor. 7.36–8, concerning the celibate. In 1 Cor. 8.1, 2 he specifically appeals to love in contrast to knowledge. Then in 8.7–13 and 10.28, 29 he discusses in detail the spiritually weaker brother with reference to the eating of idol meat.[1] 1 Cor. 12—14 in its entirety, however, deal with the loving concern which Christians should show toward each other. 1 Cor. 13 is, of course, the focus of this concern. Paul used the noun ἀγάπη fourteen times in 1 Corinthians; ten of these occurrences fall in the single chapter, 13.1—14.1. Clearly this concept, which was only referred to implicitly in connection with the problems of the married and of the celibate, and which was given increased prominence over the matter of idol meat, has now become the governing principle of Christian life. 1 Cor. 13, therefore, is a flower which has its roots in the answers Paul had already written to questions from the Corinthian Church.

Both these observations point in the same direction; they lend strength to the conclusion that here again περὶ δέ marks the answer to a question from Corinth.

5. *"Now concerning the collection" (16.1)*

In 1 Cor. 16.1 Paul turned abruptly to the matter of "*the* collection for *the* saints", and from his manner it is clear that the Corinthians had already been told what this collection was and who these saints were. The passage is informative; it deals with the future. Paul says nothing by way of condemnation or praise for any past action or inaction of the Corinthians in this project. The passage is easily explained by some question from Corinth as to the mechanics of the collection. Thus almost all commentators believe that this topic appeared in the Corinthians' letter to Paul.[2]

If Paul's answer begins in 16.1, where does it end? The matter of the

---

[1] Hans von Soden notes the identity of the motivations to which Paul appealed in 1 Cor. 8 and in 1 Cor. 13. See his essay, "Sakrament und Ethik bei Paulus: Zur Frage der literarischen und theologischen Einheitlichkeit von 1 Kor. 8–10," in *Urchristentum und Geschichte: Gesammelte Aufsätze und Vorträge*, hrsg. Hans von Campenhausen (2 Bde.; Tübingen: J. C. B. Mohr [Paul Siebeck], 1951–6), I, 241, 244.

[2] So Schmiedel, "Corr.," p. 171; J. Weiss, *1 Cor.*, pp. 380–1; Goudge, *1 Cor.*, p. 167; Findlay, "1 Cor.," p. 945; Robertson and Plummer, *1 Cor.*, p. 383; Bousset, "1 Cor.," p. 76; Evans, *Corr.*, p. 149; Allo, *1 Cor.*, p. 455; Bachmann, *1 Cor.*, pp. 472–3; Craig, "1 Cor.," p. 255; and Morris, *1 Cor.*, p. 237.

collection, as 16.3, 4 shows, involved Paul's future plans: "And when I arrive, I will send those whom you accredit by letter to carry your gift to Jerusalem. If it seems advisable that I should go also, they will accompany me." Perhaps the Corinthians had inquired how the money was to reach Jerusalem. Was Paul to receive this money himself? In any case, it is probable that a question from Corinth stands behind the whole of 16.1–9.

6. "*Now concerning Apollos*" (*16.12*)

The reference to Apollos' plans in 16.12 is abrupt, informative, and can easily be thought of as an answer to a question from Corinth. Certainly there are no indications to the contrary. In general commentators assume this to be the case.[1]

We conclude, therefore, that in each of its six occurrences περὶ δέ serves to introduce an answer by Paul to a question from the Corinthians.[2]

Summary

In examining the above six passages we have noted the following characteristics which collectively mark Paul's answers to these six topics from the Corinthians' letter:

(*a*) The new topic appears abruptly, introduced only by the common formula, περὶ δέ.

(*b*) The treatment is systematic and the tone calm.

(*c*) The reply looks toward the future; there is no criticism of the past behaviour of the Corinthians.

(*d*) Paul seeks to be as persuasive as possible, appealing to the authority of Jesus, scripture, common sense, custom, and his own apostolic commission.

(*e*) Often he quotes slogans from the Corinthians' letter in order to qualify their statements.

(*f*) Paul seems much aware of the weakness of human nature and appeals for sympathetic, loving concern for the "weaker brother".

Let us now examine the passages which clearly were written in response to oral information received by Paul to see if a different set of characteristics emerges.

---

[1] So all the scholars mentioned in the preceding note (except Craig).

[2] Scholars who refer all six occurrences to the Corinthians' letter include Farrar, *St. Paul*, pp. 378–9; Findlay, "1 Cor.," pp. 822, 949; Lake, *Earlier Epistles*, pp. 136–9; Allo, *1 Cor.*, pp. 152–3; Moffatt, *1 Cor.*, pp. xv–xvi; and McNeile, *Intro. N. T.*, p. 137.

SECTIONS DEALING WITH THE ORAL
INFORMATION FROM CORINTH

Having located the passages in I Corinthians which have the highest probability of constituting answers to written questions from Corinth, it is necessary to locate the passages which were most probably written on the basis of oral information. When the characteristics of both types of material in I Corinthians have been noted, it will be possible to examine the remaining sections of I Corinthians to see whether the type of information they presuppose can be determined. Paul referred three times to information which he had "heard" about the Corinthians: I Cor. 1.11; 5.1; and 11.17.

1. *1 Corinthians 1.10—4.21*

(a) *The party divisions.* The topic uppermost in Paul's mind when he began to write I Corinthians was the report of Chloe's people concerning party strife within the church at Corinth:

> I appeal to you, brethren, by the name of our Lord Jesus Christ, that all of you agree and that there be no dissensions (σχίσματα) among you, but that you be united in the same mind and the same judgement. For it has been reported to me by Chloe's people that there is quarrelling among you, my brethren. What I mean is that each one of you says, "I belong to Paul," or "I belong to Apollos," or "I belong to Cephas," or "I belong to Christ" (1.10–12).

Undoubtedly the Corinthians knew the situation to which Paul referred, but these verses remain enigmatic to-day. They have occasioned numerous scholarly hypotheses as we shall see in the next chapter. Whatever the situation may have been, however, it is a problem which stands behind the whole of I Cor. 1.10—4.21. Paul mentions their "jealousy and strife" in 3.3. The names of the leaders of the Corinthian "parties" (as they are usually called) appear in 3.4,5 (Paul and Apollos), 3.22 (Paul, Apollos, and Cephas), and 4.6 (Paul and Apollos).

At no point in this discussion, however, does Paul sound as though he were answering a question from the Corinthians. He had learned of a situation about which the Corinthians either did not concern themselves, or did not intend him to know. We note that Paul's information is descriptive of the present or past behaviour of the Corinthians and that it is generally unfavourable to them. He writes to condemn and correct their past actions. Here Paul discusses no ethical subtleties concerning problems to which there are two sides. Here all is black and white. In Paul's mind there are no principles which might partially justify the attitude of the Corinthians, as there were in the case of the idol meat problem, for example. He quotes no slogans in order to qualify them. His comments are more in the nature of a directive to the Corinthians than a discussion with them. His tone is stern, vigorous, and, at times, angry. As many a father has said in one way or another to many a child, "What do you wish? Shall I come to you with a rod, or with love in a spirit of gentleness?" (4.21).

(b) *Wisdom.* Not only was Paul disturbed about the quarrelling at Corinth, he was also much concerned over some at Corinth who appear to have thought themselves wise beyond the ordinary. In fact, Paul seems to have considered these two problems as one problem. His discussion of the parties in 1.10–16 suddenly changes in 1.17 into a discussion about wisdom:

> For Christ did not send me to baptize [which would have given occasion for *divisions*] but to preach the gospel, and not with eloquent *wisdom*, lest the cross of Christ be emptied of its power.

After urging the superiority of the cross of Christ to the "wisdom of the wise" (1.18—2.5), Paul indicated his conviction that mature Christians possess a higher than human wisdom through the Spirit of God (2.6–16). Then in 3.2, 3 he made the reverse transition to that in 1.17 and returned to the problem of party divisions:

> I fed you with milk, not solid food; for you were not ready for it [i.e., the strong meat of the secret and hidden *wisdom* of God, 2.7]; and even yet you are not ready, for you are still of the flesh. For while there is *jealousy and strife* among you, are you not of the flesh, and behaving like ordinary men?

And in 3.18–23 the two themes are completely interwoven and remain so to the end of the discussion in 4.21.

Clues to Paul's attitude toward the Corinthians are found in his statements,

> We are fools for Christ's sake, but you are wise in Christ. We are weak, but you are strong. You are held in honor, but we in disrepute (4.10).
> Some are arrogant ($\dot{\epsilon}\phi\upsilon\sigma\iota\dot{\omega}\theta\eta\sigma\alpha\nu$) as though I were not coming to you. But I will come to you soon, if the Lord wills, and I will find out not the talk of these arrogant people ($\pi\epsilon\phi\upsilon\sigma\iota\omega\mu\acute{\epsilon}\nu\omega\nu$) but their power (4.18, 19).

It is significant that the verb $\phi\upsilon\sigma\iota\acute{o}\omega$ which occurs nowhere in the New Testament but in Paul's letters, occurs only once outside 1 Corinthians (i.e., Col. 2.18), but in 1 Corinthians six times. The first three occurrences are contained in the passage under discussion: 4.6, 18, 19. The next, in 5.2, also reflects Paul's knowledge of the Corinthians' mis-behaviour. In 8.1 the Corinthians' proud slogan, "We all have know-ledge", causes Paul to use the word once more: "Knowledge puffs up". And the final occurrence, 13.4, is also significant as we shall see in the next chapter. Clearly, therefore, this word expresses Paul's strong disapproval of the attitude of these too wise Corinthians.[1] On the subject of the Corinthians' "wisdom" Paul was as disturbed and angry as he had been concerning their divisions.

Both Paul's oscillating manner of dealing with these two aberrations in the Corinthian Church and his common attitude of disapproval toward them show that these problems were closely related in his mind. 1 Cor. 1—4, therefore, deals in effect with a single problem having two aspects. For these chapters only a single item of information need be presupposed. Thus the single mention of a report by Chloe's people in 1.11 fully provides the occasion for these four chapters.

2. 1 Corinthians 5: The incestuous man

Concerning the incestuous man Paul again stated explicitly that he had received information from Corinth: "It is actually reported that there is immorality among you . . ." (5.1), although this time his informants are not named. The vague "it is . . . reported" may point to Chloe's people again,[2] or it may tactfully conceal Stephanas, Fortunatus, and Achaicus.[3] But, whatever the source of this information, Paul con-sidered the situation shocking, and he angrily pronounced sentence on the offender: he was to be delivered to Satan (5.5). Moreover, he deplored the attitude of the other Corinthians: "Your boasting (καύχημα) is not good" (5.6). καύχημα and καυχάομαι are terms which Paul had already used to express his unfavourable opinion of the "wise" and divided Corinthians (1.26, 31 bis; 3.21; and 4.7).[4]

---

[1] The importance of this word in 1 Corinthians is noted by Moffatt, 1 Cor., p. 196, and Craig, "1 Cor.," p. 175. Dupont, Gnosis, p. 377, n. 1, discusses the gnostic associations of the term.

[2] As Bousset, "1 Cor.," p. 75; and Lake, Earlier Epistles, p. 135, tentatively suggest.

[3] So, e.g., Lightfoot, Notes, p. 202: "Who then was St. Paul's informant? Possibly the household of Chloe (i. 11), but more probably Stephanas and his household mentioned in xvi. 15 sq. For we notice an evident anxiety to shield them from the displeasure of the Corinthians. Hence the suppression of the informants' names here. But this is pure con-jecture."

[4] The only other occurrences of these words are in 9.15, 16, Paul's apostolic "boast" to preach the gospel free of charge. In 13.3 καυχήσομαι (so P46, ℵ, A, B, 048, 33, 1739*, etc.) seems clearly an early corruption of καυθήσομαι. See Zuntz, Text, pp. 35-7 (although he cites Hort, Harnack, and Benoit for the contrary opinion); Robertson and Plummer, 1 Cor., p. 291; Deissmann, Paul, p. 95, n. 9; J. Weiss, 1 Cor., p. 314, n. 1; E. Preuschen, " 'Und liesse meinen Leib brennen' I Kor. 13,3," ZNW, XVI (1915), 127-38; Lietzmann, Corr., p. 65; and Craig, "1 Cor.," pp. 170-2.

Thus we can say that this passage exhibits none of the characteristics of Paul's answers to questions from Corinth. On the contrary, Paul was upset and angry. He was not persuasive but dictatorial. He dealt with the past behaviour of the Corinthians, not with future contingencies. He made no appeal for loving concern toward the wrong doer(s). Clearly the occasion for this passage was not a question from Corinth, but oral information unfavourable to the Corinthians to which Paul reacted with considerable heat.

In 1 Cor. 5.9–13a, however, occurs a reference to Paul's Previous Letter and its reception among the Corinthians. This passage was used in Chapter 2 to identify the stages in the exchange between Paul and Corinth which preceded 1 Corinthians. Paul here shows that he had knowledge (Stage 3) of the Corinthians' interpretation of the Previous Letter (Stage 2). The question whether Paul's knowledge rested on written or oral information will have to be considered in the next section below. Here we need only note that according to Paul's own testimony the Corinthians had been unconcerned about the marital irregularities of the man under discussion in 5.1–8. Therefore, it must have been Paul himself who made the connection between what had been said in the Previous Letter about immorality in general and the specific case at hand. He said in effect that they had misunderstood his earlier pronouncement on the subject of immorality and that their attitude toward this man was a perfect example of their misunderstanding. Thus 5.9–13a, which does involve some conversation between Paul and the Corinthians, was not a topic attached to the case of the incestuous man prior to Stage 4, 1 Corinthians.[1] The two items are distinct: (a) the unfavourable oral report about the Corinthians' behaviour, and (b) the Corinthians' interpretation of the Previous Letter. After his reference to the latter, Paul returns to the former and urges once more that the Corinthians drive the offender out (5.13b). By itself then, 1 Cor. 5.1–8, 13b does not involve a discussion with the Corinthians. No slogans of theirs are quoted. Paul simply passes judgement.

3. 1 Corinthians 11.17–34

At 1 Cor. 11.18 occurs the third of Paul's explicit references to this oral and unofficial information:

---

[1] *Pace* Hermann von Soden, *The History of the Early Christian Literature: The Writings of the New Testament*, trans. J. R. Wilkinson, ed. W. D. Morrison ("Crown Theological Library," Vol. XIII; London: Williams & Norgate, 1906), p. 38, who appears to be alone in his opinion that the Previous Letter was directed at this scandal.

For, in the first place (πρῶτον μέν), when you assemble as a church, I hear that there are divisions (σχίσματα) among you; and I partly believe it.

The content of Paul's information is plainly indicated, at least in part, by the following statements:

I hear that there are divisions among you (11.18).
One goes ahead with his own meal, and one is hungry, and another is drunk (11.21).
Many of you are weak and ill, and some have died (11.30).

Although 1 Cor. 11.17–34 is separated from the above-mentioned items of oral information by the answers to several questions from the Corinthians' letter, the passage has many similarities with 1 Cor. 1—5. Paul comments unfavourably on the past behaviour of the Corinthians. He is direct and dogmatic; his questions are angry and barbed:

What! Do you not have houses to eat and drink in? Or do you despise the church of God and humiliate those who have nothing? What shall I say to you? Shall I commend you in this? No, I will not (11.22).

The only item in 11.17–34 which could be taken as characteristic of Paul's answers to the Corinthians' questions is his appeal to the Lord's authority in 11.23–6. But the purpose of this section seems to be the correction of abuses in the observance of the Lord's Supper rather than the answering of some uncertainty on the part of the Corinthians concerning the manner of celebrating the Eucharist.

It is noticeable that Paul's rehearsal of the Lord's teaching here does not seem intended to give the Corinthians new information to settle a new problem, but seems intended rather to recall them to earlier behaviour from which they had strayed. The Corinthians' present behaviour was all the more reprehensible to Paul because they already knew what the Lord had said about the proper celebration of the Lord's Supper. All in all there is no doubt but that 11.17–34 is a treatment of oral information disturbing to Paul.

There are two related problems to discuss concerning this passage:

(a) πρῶτον μέν. Strictly speaking the πρῶτον μέν, "first of all", in 11.18 implies that the "divisions" are but the first of a series of abuses to be discussed. The opinion of some older scholars (cited by Meyer) that the second member of the series begins in v. 20 is now no longer current. It is firmly rejected by more recent commentators.[1] A number of scholars suggest that 11.34b ("About the other things I will give

---

[1] H. A. W. Meyer, Corr., I, 332–3; Schmiedel, "Corr.," p. 130; J. Weiss, 1 Cor., pp. 278–9; Goudge, 1 Cor., p. 98; Allo, 1 Cor., p. 271; Bachmann, 1 Cor., p. 362; Moffatt, 1 Cor., p. 160; Lietzmann, Corr., p. 56; Héring, 1 Cor., p. 112; Grosheide, 1 Cor., p. 265; and Morris, 1 Cor., p. 157.

directions when I come") indicates that Paul broke off the series begun in 11.18 at this point.[1] The most popular position, however, is that 11.18 looks ahead to 12.1, "Now concerning spiritual gifts. . . ."[2] This last suggestion probably should not be accepted, however. In the first place, it may well be that Paul did not intend to begin a series in 11.18. If it is argued that strict grammatical usage requires that $\pi\rho\hat{\omega}\tau o\nu$ $\mu\acute{\epsilon}\nu$ be considered the first member of a series, then it should be noted that grammatically speaking there is no second member. The expected $\delta\epsilon\acute{\upsilon}\tau\epsilon\rho o\nu$ $\delta\acute{\epsilon}$ or $\ddot{\epsilon}\pi\epsilon\iota\tau\alpha$ $\delta\acute{\epsilon}$ does not appear. Moreover, a second member is not actually required either by Greek usage in general or by Paul's style in particular.[3] But secondly, even if it is supposed that 11.18 begins a series, it should be noted that 11.34b is a definite break in the sequence. Paul indicated that he had omitted an indefinite number of items at this point. The series, if such was intended, may well end here. And, thirdly, our discussion above of 12.1ff reached the conclusion that the $\pi\epsilon\rho\grave{\iota}$ $\delta\acute{\epsilon}$ was most probably a reference to a new subject in the Corinthians' letter. The general tone of disapproval may carry over from 11.17–34 into chapter 12, but it is unlikely that the question behind 12.1ff is logically coordinate with the abuse dealt with in 11.17–34. Thus it is probable that $\pi\rho\hat{\omega}\tau o\nu$ $\mu\acute{\epsilon}\nu$ and the oral information it introduces does not look further ahead than 11.34. The phrase cannot be counted as evidence that the oral report referred to in 11.18 connects in any way with chapters 12—14.

(b) *The divisions.* Scholars disagree sharply over the identification or separation of the two references to $\sigma\chi\acute{\iota}\sigma\mu\alpha\tau\alpha$, "divisions", in 1.10 and 11.18.[4] In part the problem of relating these references is bound up

---

[1] So definitely Grosheide, *1 Cor.*, p. 265, and, as an alternative of more or less the same probability as the next considered below, J. Weiss, *1 Cor.*, p. 279; Allo, *1 Cor.*, p. 271; Moffatt, *1 Cor.*, p. 175; and Lietzmann, *Corr.*, p. 56. The reference to 11.34b is, however, specifically rejected by Schmiedel, "Corr.," p. 130; and Findlay, "1 Cor.," p. 877.

[2] So H. A. W. Meyer, *Corr.*, I, 333; Schmiedel, "Corr.," p. 130; J. Weiss, *1 Cor.*, pp. 278–9; Goudge, *1 Cor.*, p. 98; Findlay, "1 Cor.," p. 877; Robertson and Plummer, *1 Cor.*, p. 239 ("possibly"); Allo, *1 Cor.*, p. 271; Bachmann, *1 Cor.*, p. 362; Moffatt, *1 Cor.*, p. 175; Lietzmann, *Corr.*, p. 56; and Héring, *1 Cor.*, p. 112.

[3] So Blass/Debrunner, §447(4). Robertson and Plummer cite Rom. 1.8; 3.2; 10.1; 11.13; and 2 Cor. 12.12 as parallels (*1 Cor.*, p. 239).

[4] H. A. W. Meyer, *Corr.*, I, 333; Schmiedel, "Corr.," p. 130; J. Weiss, *1 Cor.*, pp. 279–80; and Grosheide, *1 Cor.*, p. 265, deny the connection between these passages. It is noticeable that, in addition to Weiss, all of the scholars discussed in the preceding chapter who partition 1 Cor. place 1.10 and 11.18 in different letters. But Goudge, *1 Cor.*, p. 98; Findlay, "1 Cor.," p. 877; Bousset, "1 Cor.," p. 130; Zahn, *Intro. N. T.*, I, 284; Allo *1 Cor.*, pp. 270–1; Lietzmann, *Corr.*, pp. 55–6; Craig, "1 Cor.," p. 132; Morris, *1 Cor.*, p. 157; and F. C. Grant, *N.T.*, p. 94, equate the two references. Wendland, *Corr.*, pp. 83–4, believes that they are the same divisions but is puzzled to know why the divisions of 1.10 would have affected the celebration of the Lord's Supper in the manner described by Paul in 11.20–2.

with the problem of the nature of the parties described in 1 Cor. 1—4. Thus Hans Lietzmann, for example, having distinguished two types of ritual meal in the early Church (the joyful Jerusalem type and the sombre Pauline type), is able to think of the Cephas party (1.12) as agitating for the practices of Jerusalem and thereby disrupting the Lord's Supper (11.18).[1] Johannes Weiss, on the other hand, who has an equally high view of the radical nature of the divisions of 1 Cor. 1—4, argues from Paul's uncertain reference to the divisions in 11.18 ("I partly believe it"),

> either that it is not a question of those same parties which he deals with so sharply and so seriously in the section 1.10—4.21, or, if they are the same, that he has at this point only received an incomplete report of them. The "I hear" of 11.17 can hardly be identified with the account which he received from the household of Chloe (1.11). For this reason, we consider, only tentatively of course, the section 11.17–34 as a piece of the first letter.[2]

A third position is represented by Johannes Munck, who desires to minimize the rigidity of the divisions in the Corinthian Church. He argues that Paul's use of the same word, σχίσματα, in 1.10, 11.18, and 12.25 indicates that these divisions are all of the same type, and therefore that the groups in 1 Cor. 1—4 are not so much "parties" but cliques as in 11.17–22.[3]

Of the three suggestions, that of Weiss seems the least satisfactory. He is very probably correct in connecting the "divisions" of 11.18 closely with the observance of the Lord's Supper,[4] and in saying that Paul's description of these groups in 11.17–34 purely in terms of the Lord's Supper appears strange if he had known of the serious party divisions caused by the issues described in 1.10—4.21. But the alternative is not a partition of the letter. The strangeness of Paul's reference here in 11.17–34 is explained either by Munck's hypothesis that 1.10—4.21 does not describe serious party divisions, or by Lietzmann's suggestion that the rationale behind the divisions of 1.10—4.21 involves the manner of observance of the Lord's Supper. The phrase "I partly believe" (1.18) which Weiss contrasts with the assurance of Paul's statements in 1.10–12 is actually no real objection to the identification of these two references. As Allo says, the expression may well be an

---

[1] *Mass and Lord's Supper: A Study in the History of the Liturgy*, trans. D. H. G. Reeve (Leiden: E. J. Brill, 1953–5), pp. 249–55 (author's pagination).

[2] J. Weiss, *Primitive Christianity*, p. 332.

[3] "The Church Without Factions: Studies in 1 Corinthians 1–4," chap. v of *Paul and the Salvation of Mankind*.

[4] See above on πρῶτον μέν, pp. 79–80.

example of litotes.[1] Certainly Paul does not sound any less sure of the ground of his criticisms in 11.17-34 than in 1.10—4.21. Between the views of Lietzmann and Munck, however, both of whom relate 11.18 to 1.11, although in different ways, we cannot decide as yet. (See Chapter 7 below.)[2] All that can be said at this point is that 11.18 indicates either that Paul is discussing another facet of the same information which lies behind 1.10—4.21, this time in relation to the conduct of worship (11.1-16; 12.1—14.40), or that Paul discusses here another example of the Corinthians' general tendency toward factiousness. In either case we may say that the information which 11.17-34 presupposes is simply another aspect of the news which Paul explicitly said he had heard from "Chloe's people".

Summary

In contrast to Paul's answers to the Corinthians' questions, his treatment of the oral information supplied to him can be characterized as follows:

(a) His tone is aroused, even angry.

(b) The treatment is direct and one-sided; all is black and white.

(c) He condemns the past behaviour of the Corinthians; his only concern for the future is the correction and prevention of the abuse in question.

(d) In general he does not appeal to supporting authorities, but speaks for himself.

(e) He does not discuss or seek to persuade; instead he speaks authoritatively.

(f) He makes no appeal for a compassionate understanding of the point of view of those who err. On the contrary, he is unsympathetic and censorious.

We have now dealt with 1 Cor. 1.11—5.8, 13b, and 11.17-34 on the one hand, and with 7.1—11.1; 12.1—14.40; and 16.1-12 on the other hand, and we have seen that there is sufficient difference in style and method of argument between these two groups of passages to make it possible to separate them according to their origin in oral report or written questions. Now we must examine the remaining sections of 1 Corinthians to see whether this material is also separable into these two categories.

---

[1] 1 Cor., p. 270.   [2] In particular, pp. 269-70.

THE REMAINING SECTIONS OF
I CORINTHIANS

1. *1 Corinthians 5.9–13a*

In 1 Cor. 5.9 Paul referred directly to what we have labelled his Previous Letter: "I wrote to you in my letter not to associate with immoral men. . . ." Some time after writing the Previous Letter Paul heard that his words had been interpreted in a way which he desired here to disclaim. The information about the Corinthians' misunderstanding must have reached Paul either through the letter from Corinth or by word of mouth. A considerable amount of ink has been spilled in an attempt to decide between these two possibilities.[1] Since this passage occurs in the context of Paul's discussion of oral information (5.1–8, 13b), and is considerably removed from Paul's explicit answers to the Corinthians' questions (7.1ff), probability might seem to favour including this item with those sections occasioned by oral information. On the other hand, it has already been noted that this item was not based on an item of information connected with the news concerning the incestuous man and is thus free of its present context. Certainty is obviously not possible here, nor is it really necessary. What is important is that Paul had received news of the Corinthians' reaction to something he had said to them in the Previous Letter, and that their reaction received a reply in 1 Corinthians. Thus whether Paul's information was actually written or oral, the problem is to be included for our purposes with the written material, since we have found other instances of dialogue reflected only in the written exchanges between Paul and the Corinthians. The passage gives a unique insight into the tenor of the Previous Letter and the manner of its reception in Corinth. 1 Cor. 5.9–13a is, therefore, evidence of the highest importance concerning the conversation between Paul and Corinth.

2. *1 Corinthians 6*

This chapter may be considered in two parts. Lukas Vischer strongly defends the exegetical unity of 6.1–11.[2] 1 Cor. 6.12 begins a new

---

[1] E.g., Robertson and Plummer, *1 Cor.*, p. 131; Bachmann, *1 Cor.*, p. 237; J. Weiss, *1 Cor.*, p. 157; and Moffatt, *1 Cor.*, p. xvi, insist that Paul did not take up (or even receive) the Corinthians' letter until the time of writing 1 Cor. 7.1. Zahn, *Intro. N. T.*, I, 261, and Lietzmann, *Corr.*, pp. 25, 27, on the other hand, believe that both this passage and 6.12–20 were occasioned by the letter from Corinth.

[2] *Die Auslegungsgeschichte von I. Kor. 6, 1–11: Rechtsverzicht und Schlichtung* ("Beiträge zur Geschichte der neutestamentlichen Exegese," No. 1; Tübingen: J. C. B. Mohr [Paul Siebeck], 1955), p. 6.

section which involves quoted slogans from the Corinthian Church.

(a) *1 Corinthians 6.1–11: Civil magistrates.* 1 Cor. 6.1–11 is a passage which clearly reflects Paul's knowledge that some Corinthians had gone before a civil magistrate to settle their dispute(s). Paul refers to a situation familiar to the Corinthians but puzzling to moderns. J. H. Bernard has argued at some length that 1 Cor. 5 and 6 together concern the same matter and that the injured father (5.1) had taken his refractory son to court (6.1).[1] Ernest Evans gave his suggestion thoughtful and sympathetic consideration but concluded that, "if we so regarded the matter, we should involve ourselves in what seems to be an insuperable difficulty, namely that St. Paul treats as practically on a level with the enormity of the son's crime the at worst misguided act of the father in bringing the case into court".[2] No commentator seems to have accepted Bernard's suggestion.[3] And the probability is that Paul alludes to a piece of information from Corinth separate from the oral report which lies behind 1 Cor. 5.1–8, 13b.

Was the information on which 1 Cor. 6.1–11 is based oral or written? It is clear that Paul comments in this passage upon the past behaviour of the Corinthians and with obvious disapproval. As Robertson and Plummer say of the opening word of his question, τολμᾷ τις ὑμῶν. . . (6.1), "The word is an argument in itself; 'How can you dare, endure, bring yourself to?' "[4] Moreover, Paul comments with biting irony that their conduct implies not that *all* of them are wise, as they boast (1.17—3.2; 8.1), but that *not one* of them is wise (6.5). Further, Paul does not discuss the issue pro and con, but condemns their action(s) without reservation or qualification. It is true that he suggests hypothetical future behaviour ("Why not rather suffer wrong? Why not rather be defrauded?" [6.7]), but his suggestions are polemical and not part of a reasoned programme of ethical action. Thus there seems to be no reason for denying, and every reason for

---

[1] *Studia Sacra* (London: Hodder and Stoughton, 1917), pp. 232–47. It is interesting to notice that he arrived at this suggestion by somewhat the same path that we are following —a concern for the occasion of each section of 1 Corinthians. Thus he says, "To understand I Corinthians it is necessary to remember its structure. . . . [Paul] devotes chapters i.–iv. to the matter of schism and faction, and chapters v., vi. to the discussion of sins of the flesh and the proper way to deal with them" (p. 233).

[2] *Corr.*, p. 83.

[3] Goudge, *1 Cor.* (1911), p. 43, allows a possible connection. But the commentators listed in previous footnotes to this chapter unanimously reject the idea. E.g., Lietzmann *Corr.*, p. 25, "ein weiterer Fall". Vischer, *Ausgelegungsgeschichte*, p. 6, does not cite Bernard and categorically rejects any connection between the two difficulties.

[4] *1 Cor.*, p. 110.

supposing, that 6.1–11 was occasioned by oral information brought to Paul.

In connection with this passage, however, two observations should be made:

(i) As a means of discomfiting his opponents on this issue Paul adopted the tactic of bombarding them with questions which implied that they lacked a knowledge of the basic facts of their Christian faith. The phrase οὐκ οἴδατε ὅτι occurs ten times in I Corinthians; elsewhere in Paul's writings only at Rom. 6.16. The passages in I Corinthians are as follows:

3.16 Do you not know that you are God's temple and that God's Spirit dwells in you?

5.6   Do you not know that a little leaven ferments the whole lump of dough?

6.2   Do you not know that the saints will judge the world?

6.3   Do you not know that we are to judge angels?

6.9   Do you not know that the unrighteous will not inherit the kingdom of God?

6.15 Do you not know that our bodies are members of Christ?

6.16 Do you not know that he who joins himself to a prostitute becomes one body with her?

6.17 Do you not know that your body is a temple of the Holy Spirit within you, which you have from God?

9.13 Do you not know that those who are employed in the temple service get their food from the temple?

9.24 Do you not know that in a race all the runners compete, but only one receives the prize?

Some of these questions relate more to a general knowledge about the world; some more to Christian faith in particular.[1] It appears, however, that to a greater or lesser extent all these questions are thrusts aimed at the Corinthians.[2] The first two occur in Paul's treatment of the scandals at Corinth of which he had heard orally. The last two occur in I Cor. 9 concerning which it has already been suggested that Paul digressed

[1] Cf. R. M. Grant, "Hellenistic Elements," pp. 60–1. He cites as further examples of Paul's appeal to the Corinthians' common sense I Cor. 10.15 ("I speak as to sensible men; judge for yourselves what I say.") and 11.13 ("judge for yourselves"), and he concludes: "Paul can build his arguments on data both Christian and non-Christian."

[2] Evans, e.g., says that these questions refer "to points of Christian teaching already accepted, or to matters of fact which the readers ought to have noted and acted upon" (*Corr.*, p. 87). Cf. I Cor. 11.23–6 discussed above, another embarrassing rehearsal of teachings which they should have honoured.

from his argument about idol meat to meet the hostile implications of some of the Corinthians' questions to him. The three in 1 Cor. 6.1–11 can hardly be considered flattering to the Corinthians. Paul asks, in effect, "Can it be that you do not know . . . ?" The three in 1 Cor. 6.12–20 remain to be discussed below, but they also appear to be none too complimentary to the Corinthians.

(ii) There is no pressing reason to suppose that Paul's information about the Corinthians' use of the civil magistrate concerns more than one case of this practice. The τις in 6.1 may well be as definite in its reference as the τινα in 5.1.[1] Just as 5.1 is translated, "A man is living with his father's wife," so 6.1 may be translated, "Does a man with a grievance against a brother *dare* to go to court . . . ?" In 5.1–5 Paul clearly has a definite case in mind; in 6.1–7 the same may be true. In 6.1–7, however, Paul passes no judgement upon those involved but is primarily concerned lest this recourse to the civil magistrate become a practice among them: hence the plurals in vv. 2–4 and v. 7. In vv. 8–11 Paul adds a general condemnation of this and other sins which should find no place in the Church, just as he had followed his discussion of the single case of incest (5.1–5) with a general exhortation to the whole Church (5.6–8).[2] It seems hardly probable that in a small community they would have had an opportunity to use the civil law courts repeatedly.[3] The simplest hypothesis is that one scandal provoked 5.1–13 and a second, 6.1–11.

(*b*) *1 Corinthians 6.12–20: Immorality.* In a number of ways 1 Cor. 6.12–20 is similar to those of Paul's answers to the Corinthians' questions which we have discussed. In 6.12, 13 Paul appears to quote two of the Corinthians' slogans: "All things are lawful", and "Food is meant for the stomach and the stomach for food".[4] Although in the preceding sections of 1 Corinthians he had been referring to a number of abuses in the Corinthian Church which he desired to correct, in this passage he does not refer to any specific action of the Corinthians.[5] As

---

[1] Cf. also 2 Cor. 10.7 and 12.1.

[2] It is 6.8 in particular that commentators use as evidence that Paul was dealing with a habitual practice of the Corinthians. E.g., Robertson and Plummer, *1 Cor.*, p. 110; Allo, *1 Cor.*, p. 132; and Craig, "1 Cor.," p. 71.

[3] Ewald, *Sendschreiben*, p. 154, suggested that the case concerned a rich and powerful man whom the Corinthians hesitated to criticize (6.5). The following commentators also suggest that only one lawsuit had occurred: Goudge, *1 Cor.*, p. 43; Bernard, *Studia Sacra*, pp. 232–47; Evans, *Corr.*, p. 87; Manson, *Studies*, p. 198; and Werner Meyer, *Der erste Korintherbrief* (2 Bde.; "Prophezei: Schweizerisches Bibelwerk für die Gemeinde"; Zürich: Zwingli Verlag, 1947, 1945), I, 194.

[4] See Table 5 above, p. 68.

[5] Quite artificially Robertson and Plummer, *1 Cor.*, p. 121, call the subject of this passage "a fourth matter for censure". There is no new subject here, however.

Clarence T. Craig says, "In the style of a diatribe, Paul argues with an imaginary opponent."[1] Furthermore, Paul's reference to Gen. 2.24 (in 6.16) may be considered the appeal to authority which we have noted in Paul's answers to the Corinthians' questions.[2]

On the other hand, however, there are also many similarities with Paul's treatment of his oral information. Paul was clearly aroused, even angry, when he wrote this passage. His conjunction of the words "Christ" and "prostitute" ("Shall I therefore take the members of Christ and make them members of a prostitute?! Never!" [6.15]) tends to make the same kind of impression as the excessive language of Gal. 5.12, "I wish those who unsettle you would mutilate themselves!" His thrice repeated question, "Do you not know . . . ? (v. 15), Do you not know . . . ? (v. 16), Do you not know . . . ?" (v. 19), is jarring and aggressive. In general these questions elsewhere have marked oral information (except 9.13 and 24). The evidence is thus evenly divided, and it seems impossible to assign 6.12–20 to one class of material or the other with any degree of certainty.

Because of the tone, the contents, and the general freedom of 1 Cor. 6.12–20 from its context, a number of scholars believe that this passage is a fragment of the Previous Letter.[3] We can now see that this suggestion is improbable, however. Our examination of the types of information on which Paul based 1 Corinthians has led us to identify 1.11— 6.11 (except 5.9–13a) as based on oral reports and at least 7.1—11.1 as based on the Corinthians' letter. Here at the juncture of these two types of material stands a section (6.12–20) which continues the emotional tone of the preceding sections while setting the stage for the topics which are to follow. It is well known that the opening "Thanksgiving" sections of Paul's letters serve to introduce the major concerns of each letter.[4] In the same way 1 Cor. 6.12–20 touches on the main motifs of 1 Cor. 7—15. The most striking points of contact are as follows:

> (i) "All things are lawful for me," but not all things are helpful. "All things are lawful for me," but I will not be enslaved by anything. "Food is meant for the stomach and the stomach for food" (6.12, 13a).

Paul quotes these slogans here in connection with his condemnation of immorality. The first maxim, however, reappears in 10.23 in his discussion of the eating of idol meat. And the second slogan above is

---

[1] "1 Cor.," p. 73.
[2] Cf. Paul's appeal to Exodus and Numbers in 1 Cor. 10.1–10 on the subject of idol meat.
[3] See Table 4 above, p. 45.   [4] See Schubert, *Pauline Thanksgivings*.

actually more appropriate to the idol meat problem than to its present context. There is a connection, of course, between gastronomic indulgence and sexual licence, but the obvious reference of such a slogan is to a matter involving diet. "After all, what does it matter what we eat or do not eat?" they argue. "Food is meant for the stomach and the stomach for food." It is as though Paul had used ahead of time one of the points he intended to make in connection with the problem of idol meat (I Cor. 8—10).

(ii) God raised the Lord and will also raise us up by his power (6.14).

This verse is the first reference to resurrection in I Corinthians. The only other occurrences of the verb to "raise" (ἐγείρω) are the nineteen appearances of the word in I Cor. 15.

(iii) Do you not know that your bodies are members of Christ (6.15)?

The concept of the Christian as a member of Christ does not appear earlier in I Corinthians. The only other occurrences of the word "member" (μέλος) are the thirteen in I Cor. 12.

(iv) Do you not know that he who joins himself to a prostitute becomes one body with her? For it is written, "The two shall become one" (6.16; Gen. 2.24).

Paul's quotation from the Garden of Eden story is exceedingly interesting because Mark's Gospel preserves the tradition that Jesus also quoted these words (Mark 10.8) as grounds for his prohibition of divorce (Mark 10.1–10). Paul also discussed divorce, not here but in I Cor. 7.10–16, and said specifically, "To the married I give charge, *not I but the Lord*, that the wife should not separate from her husband" (I Cor. 7.10). But "the Lord's" words on the subject do not follow in 7.10; they had already appeared in 6.16. It appears that Paul had once more anticipated himself (as in 6.13) and used material ahead of the point where it logically belonged in his argument.

These are some of the links which connect I Cor. 6.12–20 with the chapters which follow.[1] It would be exceedingly improbable to expect that such an appropriate fragment could have been found in Paul's Previous Letter, and it would require an exceedingly perceptive editor

---

[1] Cf. also 6.17 ("He who is united to the Lord becomes one Spirit with him.") with 15.45–8 ("The last Adam became a life-giving spirit. . . . As is the man of heaven, so are those who are of heaven."); and 6.19, 20 ("You are not your own; you were bought with a price.") with 7.22, 23 ("He who was free when called is a slave of Christ. You were bought with a price.").

to place the fragment in its present position. It is far more probable that 6.12–20 was intended by Paul as a transitional passage to conclude his treatment of the oral information and to introduce his answers to the Corinthians' questions. In particular he referred in this passage to the danger of immorality, an example of which was actually to be found among the Corinthians (5.1–13), in order to prepare for his discussion of marriage, a discussion in which he repeatedly warned them of the dangers of immorality (7.2, 5, 9, 36).[1]

[1] Paul's fondness for transitional passages (i.e., his reluctance to make a sharp break in the continuity of his writing) appears from an examination of the other περὶ δέ passages in I Corinthians.

(i) The most obvious example is 12.1ff. Here for the first time Paul takes up the problem of spiritual gifts, but although he praises the numerous gifts of the spirit, it is clear that in this section (I Cor. 12—14) he is primarily concerned to discourage the Corinthians' over-dependence on the single gift of "tongues", i.e., he is concerned about the conduct of worship among the Corinthians. But 11.2–34 is also concerned about the proper manner of Christian worship. Paul even outlines briefly the liturgy of the Church (11.23–6). It is probable, however, as we have seen, that 11.12–20 is based on unfavourable reports about the situation in Corinth. This passage, then, is evidence that Paul could deal with disciplinary matters in such a way as to introduce an answer to a question raised by the Corinthian Church.

(ii) The question of the celibate in 7.25–38 is preceded by 7. 17–24, an appeal for maintenance of the *status quo*. This appeal serves equally well as a final general argument to support Paul's rulings in 7.1–16 and as an introduction to 7.25–38, where Paul again wished the situation to remain unchanged.

(iii) In 16.11 the reference to Timothy's movements and, in particular, to the mysterious "brethren" serves as a brief but definite introduction to 16.12, "concerning Apollos" and his relationship to the same "brethren".

(iv) In the same manner 15.58 functions as an introduction to 16.1 and the collection. Concerning the "collection for the saints" (16.1) Paul hoped that their "labour" would not be "in vain" (15.58).

(v) At first glance 8.1 seems an exception, since it immediately follows 7.39, 40, Paul's opinion on the remarriage of widows. Yet even so a token introduction is present. Paul mentioned the new topic at 8.1, but 8.1–3 does not concern idols or meat directly. Thus 8.4 is, as it were, a second beginning, or a beginning after an introduction.

Four other transitions in I Corinthians are also smoothed by means of brief passages each of which concludes the previous discussion and at the same time introduces the succeeding topic:

(i) I Cor. 4.18–21 serves as a final summary to Paul's sustained protest against the Corinthians' divisions and their boasted wisdom. But at the same time the repeated reference to the "arrogant" (4.18, 19) anticipates 5.2: "And you are arrogant!" His repeated mention of "power" (4.19, 20) is reflected in 5.4, "the power of our Lord Jesus". And his final threat, "Shall I come to you with a rod, or with love in a spirit of gentleness?", applies equally well to what he has discussed and the serious matter with which he is about to deal.

(ii) I Cor. 5.12, 13 closes Paul's protest that in the Previous Letter he had meant only to forbid association with the immoral within the Church: "For what have I to do with judging outsiders? Is it not those inside the Church whom *you* are to judge?" (5.12; note the change from "I" to "you"). In 6.1–11 he continues to deal with the problem of "judging" and asks, "Can it be that there is no man among you wise enough to decide between members of the brotherhood . . . ?" (6.5).

(iii) A notable confusion surrounds 11.1. The verse logically belongs with 10.23–33 as the climax of Paul's argument, yet it clearly serves to introduce 11.2. The majority of Greek MSS., followed by Stephen Langton (13th century) and thus by the modern versions, begin the new chapter with 11.1. However, the codices Vaticanus (B) and Zacynthius (Ξ),

3. *1 Corinthians 11.2–16*

A number of scholars believe that 1 Cor. 11.2 is an indirect quotation from the Corinthians' letter:

> I commend you because you remember me in everything and maintain the traditions even as I have delivered them to you.[1]

This allusion immediately suggests that Paul is still dealing with the Corinthians' letter although the introductory περὶ δέ is absent.[2] Further, the section has a number of the characteristics which we have already noted in Paul's answers. He is systematic and calm. The topic is introduced without explanation. He seems to assume that the Corinthians will find his discussion relevant. He does not refer to any particular abuse in the past which he desires to correct; the reference is to the future conduct of the Corinthians. He appeals to authority, in this case to their own common sense ("Judge for yourselves . . ." [11.13]), to the laws of nature ("Does not nature itself teach you . . . ?" [11.14]),[3] to the custom of the "Churches of God" (11.16), and to his own policy ("We recognize no other practice." [11.16]). In view of the

and the minuscule 97 use a system of Chapters which makes the division after 11.1. The second and later system in B even divides after 11.2. See *Novum Testamentum Graece*, ed. E. Nestle and K. Aland (25th ed.; Stuttgart: Würtembergische Bibelanstalt, 1963), pp. 82*, 443–4; Alexander Souter, *The Text and Canon of the New Testament*, rev. C. S. C. Williams ("Studies in Theology"; London: Gerald Duckworth and Co., 1954), p. 48; and Philip Carrington, *The Primitive Christian Calendar: A Study in the Making of the Marcan Gospel*, Vol. 1: *Introduction and Text* (Cambridge: The University Press, 1952), pp. 23–4.

(iv) Precisely the same confusion attends the opening of 1 Cor. 13 where the three systems of chapter division fail once more to agree. "But earnestly desire the higher gifts. And I will show you a still more excellent way" (12.31) concludes and introduces at one and the same time. (On the text see Zuntz, *Text*, pp. 90–1.)

Thus we conclude that it was characteristic of Paul to think ahead as he wrote and to prepare the minds of his readers at each turning-point in his letter for what was to follow. 1 Cor. 6.12–20 then can legitimately be thought of as serving the double function of concluding 1 Cor. 1.11—6.11 and introducing 1 Cor. 7.1ff.

[1] See Table 5 above, p. 68.

[2] Faw, "Writing of 1 Thess.," p. 221, considers, however, that the δέ in 11.2 is an abbreviated form of the περὶ δέ formula. His suggestion becomes more attractive when it is noticed that, while δέ occurs several times at the turning points of 1 Corinthians (the paragraphs in the Nestle text, for example), it usually carries an adversative sense: 1.10; 2.6; 11.17; and 15.12, 20. At 7.8; 11.2; and 15.1, however, the sense is consecutive, as in the περὶ δέ formula. Faw believes that each of these last instances introduces a new topic or sub-topic from the Corinthians' letter.

Of the scholars listed in Table 5 the following believe that a question from the Corinthians motivated 11.2–16: Robertson and Plummer, *1 Cor.*, p. 228; Bousset, "1 Cor.," p.128; Zahn, *Intro. N. T.*, I, 261; Parry, *1 Cor.* ("Camb."), p. 111; Evans, *Corr.*, p. 117; Moffatt, *1 Cor.*, p. xv; and Lietzmann, *Corr.*, p. 53. To these scholars should be added Lake, *Earlier Epistles*, p. 137.

[3] On the appeal to "nature" see R. M. Grant, "Hellenistic Elements," p. 62.

evidence then, both of 11.2 and of 11.3–16, it seems highly probable that here Paul answered yet another of the Corinthians' questions.

4. 1 Corinthians 15

Concerning 1 Cor. 15 scholars are sharply divided between those who take the problem of resurrection to be an issue raised by the Corinthians' letter[1] and those who believe that Paul had already finished with their letter (except, perhaps, for the matters of the collection and of Apollos).[2] James Moffatt states this latter position succinctly:

> From what he had learned about the inside situation, he was able not only to handle the four questions put to him by the church (vii, viii, xii, xvi. 1), but to drive some other matters home to their conscience with apostolic authority and affectionate remonstrances. In fact the opening section (i.-iv., v.-vi.) is entirely devoted to very serious subjects on which the Corinthians had not asked his opinion; so is the final counsel on the resurrection. The bulk of his reply to their actual letter lies between these.[3]

It may be that the problem of the occasion for 1 Cor. 15 will never be satisfactorily solved, but against Moffatt two points should be observed.

(i) 1 Cor. 15 has the characteristics of those answers to Corinthian questions we have previously discussed. Paul introduces the topic suddenly without indicating the situation which he addressed. He does not condemn past behaviour of the Corinthians. He is calm, persuasive, instructive, logical, and systematic. For added authority he appeals to five witnesses (or groups of witnesses) to Christ's Resurrection besides himself in the famous passage 1 Cor. 15.3–8. And he explicitly refers to at least one question that the Corinthians were asking: "How can some of you say there is no resurrection of the dead?" (15.12).

(ii) Paul deals here with a belief held (or disputed) by the Corinthians, not with their behaviour. Since the matter is not disciplinary, but a subject for intellectual discussion between Paul and the Corinthians, we must consider 1 Cor. 15 as a part of "answer" material in 1 Corinthians whether or not its occasion was oral or written information. That Paul, at least, believed that questions about the resurrection of believers

---

[1] So Schmiedel, "Corr.," p. 42; Lake, Earlier Epistles, p. 138 ("probable"); Bousset, "1 Cor.," p. 76; Lietzmann, Corr., p. 76 (probable); and Faw, "Writing of 1 Thess.," p. 221.

[2] So J. Weiss, 1 Cor., p. 343; Findlay, "1 Cor.," p. 917; Robertson and Plummer, 1 Cor., p. 329; Evans, Corr., p. 136; Zahn, Intro. N. T., I, 261; Allo, 1 Cor., p. 387; Schlatter, Bote Jesu, p. 209; Craig, "1 Cor.," p. 214; and C. S. C. Williams, "Corr.," §841a.

[3] 1 Cor., p. xvi.

existed in the mind of the Corinthians cannot be doubted. He knew that some of them had died since they became Christians (11.30). He had ample opportunity to inform himself as to the state of mind of the Corinthians. Clearly 1 Cor. 15 is a most important part of the conversation between Paul and Corinth, whatever the particular source of Paul's information at this point.

CONCLUSION

It has been the purpose of this Chapter to inquire whether it is possible to separate the sections of 1 Corinthians in which Paul dealt with the written questions of the Corinthians from those sections where Paul dealt with his hearsay knowledge. Our conclusion is that this separation can be made to a surprising extent and with surprising clarity. For almost three quarters of the text of 1 Corinthians (that is, for 1 Cor. 1—5; 11.17–34 and 7.1—11.1; 12—14; 16.1–9, 12) the source of Paul's information is clearly indicated, on the one hand, by his direct references to what he had "heard" or, on the other hand, by the formula περὶ δέ. Most of the remaining passages may be classified more or less definitely. Moreover, except in 6.12–20 Paul seems never to use these two types of information simultaneously. Two apparent exceptions are (a) 1 Cor. 5.1–8, 13b into which is inserted 5.9–13a, and (b) 11.17–34, which stands in a context of answer material. But in each of these instances the two types of information are treated successively, not simultaneously. Paul appears to have shifted deliberately from one type to the other and back. The sections dealing with each are clearly separable. That competent scholars can believe that 1 Cor. 1—4 was a separate letter, composed after the rest of 1 Corinthians had been written and sent, shows that it is certainly not evident that any knowledge of the parties at Corinth affected Paul's treatment of the Corinthians' questions.[1] For example, it may well have been part of Paul's purpose in writing 1 Cor. 12 and 13 to encourage the reunion of the Corinthians on the basis of their membership in Christ and in Christian love for one another, but Paul nowhere in this section referred to their dissensions directly. This purpose has to be read into these chapters from 1 Cor. 1—4. Again, 1 Cor. 14, part of an answer to a Corinthian question, betrays an obvious knowledge of the manner of worship of the Corinthians, yet Paul did not here condemn the Church for its prac-

[1] See Table 4 above, p. 45.

tices. He did not both discipline and instruct at the same time, even at the points where his two types of information were related.

The separation of these two classes of material is as follows:

Material dealing with oral information	Material dealing with written questions
1.10—5.8	
	(5.9-13a)
5.13b—6.11	
(6.12-20)	
	7.1—11.16
11.17-34	
	12.1—14.40
	(15.1-58)
	16.1-9,12

The subjects of these two groups of material can be outlined thus:

A. *Oral information from Corinth*

   1. Boasting and quarrelling
      (*a*) Party divisions which divide even   1.11–17; 3.3—4.21;
           the Lord's table   11.17–34
      (*b*) False wisdom   1.17—3.2, 18–23;
           4.1–21
   2. A case of incest   5.1–8, 13b
   3. A case of litigation   6.1–11

B. *Written questions contained in the Corinthians' letter to Paul*

   1. (Immorality)   (5.9–13a)
   2. Marriage   7.1–24, 39–40
   3. The celibate   7.25–38
   4. Idol meat   8.1—11.1
   5. The veiling of women   11.2–16
   6. Spiritual gifts (or "men")   12—14
   7. (Bodily resurrection of the dead)   (15)
   8. The collection   16.1–9
   9. Apollos   16.12

The pattern of I Corinthians, therefore, appears to be as follows: (i) Paul dealt first with his oral information inserting at the relevant point a comment upon a single item in the Corinthians' letter, and (ii) he then responded to the rest of their letter inserting, again at the relevant point, a comment upon a matter about which he had been informed orally. Paul's oral information will be the subject of Chapter 4; the Corinthians' written questions will be discussed in Chapter 5.

CHAPTER 4

The General Background to the Corinthian Correspondence

The course which we have now determined for the investigation of Paul's early Corinthian mission consists primarily in a reconstruction of the written exchanges—the questions and the answers—which passed between Paul and Corinth culminating in the writing of 1 Corinthians. Not only is it possible to isolate the sections of 1 Corinthians which deal with these written communications, but this written material provides by far the most objective basis for the reconstruction of Paul's Corinthian mission. It is, of course, impossible to separate completely the written dialogue from the background situation at Corinth about which Paul had received oral information; the two are mutually illuminating. But the priority of importance clearly belongs to the written material.

In the literature of Pauline scholarship, however, there are a substantial number of studies dealing with what we have labelled the oral reports or descriptive information, as well as countless opinions expressed by scholars within larger works. Before attempting to reconstruct the Corinthians' letter to Paul, therefore, it will be useful (1) to summarize the state of scholarly opinion concerning the general situation in Corinth out of which the Corinthians' letter came, and (2) to see whether 1 Corinthians affords evidence as to the general attitude of Paul toward the Corinthians and of the Corinthians toward Paul. This general background may help to illuminate our primary investigation. In any case, it will be well to clarify the general assumptions with which we read that part of 1 Corinthians which dealt with the Corinthians' questions.

SCHOLARLY OPINION CONCERNING
THE SITUATION AT CORINTH

In their estimate of the situation in the Corinthian Church during the period before the writing of 1 Corinthians scholars rely mainly on the descriptive (oral) information reflected in the letter, together with their general understanding of the religiosity of the period. The sub-title of Ulrich Wilckens' recent book illustrates both aspects of this approach to 1 Corinthians: *Weisheit und Torheit: Eine exegetisch-religionsgeschichtliche Untersuchung zu 1. Kor. 1 und 2*.[1] The fact that in 1 Corinthians Paul dealt first with the descriptive information at his disposal makes the conclusions of these scholars doubly important. Certainly one would expect Paul to have taken up first the matters which were most important to him, so that the first chapters of 1 Corinthians should be the key to the interpretation of the whole letter. Paul began 1 Corinthians by denouncing the fact that the Church at Corinth had fallen into discord because four names had become watchwords for various groups among them: Paul, Apollos, Cephas, and Christ (1.12). Now the perplexing fact is that the remainder of 1 Corinthians does not seem to give any information about the issues which separated these four parties about which Paul was so concerned when he began to write. 1 Corinthians apparently was addressed by Paul to a single, more or less unified, opposing point of view. Scholars explain this paradox in various ways. Some suggest that Paul knew the issues which were in dispute among the Corinthians, but that he rose above these details and dealt solely with the painful fact of their divisiveness and dissensions. Thus, for example, Moffatt says, "Paul does not analyse the opinions of the various parties. He was concerned not so much with them in whole or part as with the quarrelsome spirit which they bred."[2] Others explain the fact that Paul does not address various theological points of view by saying that the parties did not differ doctrinally. As Grosheide puts it,

> Paul does not say in I Cor. 1 that the members of the Church with their slogans adhered to a definite doctrine, i.e., a false doctrine. . . . The one thing we find here is that each Corinthian has his slogan. No other difference is mentioned but these slogans. . . . And when in the following chapters Paul

---

[1] "Beiträge zur historischen Theologie," hrsg. Gerhard Ebeling, 26. Hft.; Tübingen: J. C. B. Mohr (Paul Siebeck), 1959.
[2] *1 Cor.*, p. 9. So also von Dobschütz, *Primitive Church*, pp. 72–3.

reprimands several sins it is not one group but the whole church which is reprimanded. Therefore we conclude that there was no essential or doctrinal difference between the four groups.[1]

Even Johannes Weiss, who tries his utmost to differentiate these groups, is forced to say,[2]

> The difficulty of forming a judgment about the Cephas party is . . . due to the fact that they do not stand out in clear distinction from the Apollos party. After Paul has spoken about the leaders in 3:5–9 and 3:10–17, he includes both together under one verdict, and this continues up to 4:13. It is as though in this section both parties combined in his mind into one perverse, insubordinate, arrogant and hostile group. Even the intellectual conceit which we have hitherto expected to find only among the adherents of Apollos is rebuked in 3:18ff in direct connection with the outburst against the leaders of the Cephas Party.[3]

But most other scholars begin by reconstructing the single point of view which was opposed to Paul's and then seek to identify this position with one of the parties mentioned in 1 Cor. 1.12. By implication the other parties are to be considered of minor importance. Kirsopp Lake assumes that this approach is the only one possible, but he wisely points out its limitations:

> If it be conceded that the opponents of St. Paul were πνευματικοί, it is impossible not to think that they were identical with the persons to whom he refers in the opening chapters of 1 Corinthians. But, if one goes further, and asks if this enables us to identify these persons with the parties of Apollos, or Cephas, or Christ (if there was such a party), the answer must be indeterminate. Everything is possible. . . . More or less imaginative sketches can be found in almost all the books cited [above]. . . . Personally, I do not see how it can ever be possible to say more than that the general tone of 1 Cor. i.–iv., coupled with the Alexandrian history of Apollos, makes the party of Apollos not improbable as a "spiritual" party.[4]

Other scholars, while adopting this procedure, show less restraint than Lake. Although no scholar appears to have suggested that the Pauline party represented Paul's chief opposition, each of the other three parties has been given this honour at one time or another.

(a) *Apollos.* The Apollos party has the advantage with scholars over the other two parties in that both 1 Corinthians and Acts agree in saying that Apollos had actually visited Corinth and worked there.

---

[1] *1 Cor.*, p. 37. On this point Héring agrees: "It is not in fact said that the boundaries of these personal cliques were also the boundaries of theological groups" (*1 Cor.*, p. 44).

[2] Weiss, as we shall see below, rejected the reference to the "Christ party" as a gloss (*1 Cor.*, pp. xxxvi–xxxviii). "Those of Paul" he considered to be Corinthians faithful to Paul and therefore not to be counted among the opposition (*1 Cor.*, p. xxxi).

[3] *Primitive Christianity*, p. 339. [4] *Earlier Epistles*, pp. 231–2.

Further, it is obvious from 1 Corinthians that this visit occurred after Paul's original visit (Stage 1) and before the writing of this letter (Stage 4): as Paul says, "I planted, Apollos watered . . ." (3.6). Moreover, it is Apollos who receives the most attention from Paul in Cor. 1—4, his name appearing six times. Thus Robert M. Grant says,

> The conflict really seems to be between Paul and Apollos, or rather between adherents of each who misinterpret the views of both. Paul and Apollos are, or are made to appear, the principal antagonists (3.4–9). Apollos was a Jew of Alexandria, eloquent and well versed in the scriptures (Acts 18.24). His knowing "only the baptism of John" (Acts 18.25) might suggest that he understood John's baptism as Josephus did, as a ritual purification of the body (*Ant.*, xviii. 117) like that of Essenes (*Bell.* ii. 138). Paul's view of baptism is of course completely different.
>
> We may suggest that it was Apollos who permitted the Corinthians to interpret their religion as a form of popular philosophy [i.e., Stoicism].[1]

With this suggestion Eric L. Titus is in full agreement, and he says,

> It is to be noted that Paul in 1 Corinthians reduces the problem under consideration to himself and Apollos (4.6). If Apollos is the real "thorn in the flesh" so far as the Corinthian situation is concerned, then the "wisdom" and "mystery" of which Paul speaks would be an Alexandrian allegorical interpretation of the gospel. But may we allow this kind of opposition to exist between two great personalities of early Christian history? Certainly it is not explicit in Paul's letters, but then it might not have been prudent for it to be made explicit. Apollos may have been much more influential than the extant literature portrays; certainly there are hints of it present both in Paul's letters and in Acts.[2]

E. Evans also belongs to this school of scholarly opinion: "Perhaps the fact that the 'Cephas' faction is not mentioned at iii. 4, iv. 6, as might have been expected, signifies that it was neither important nor very dangerous, and that the self-styled partisans of Paul and Apollos were causing most of the trouble."[3] This position is attractive. There is considerable evidence in the text to support it. And the connection in Acts 18.24 between Apollos and Alexandria opens many inviting fields of speculation.[4]

---

[1] "The Wisdom of the Corinthians," in *The Joy of Study: Papers on New Testament and Related Subjects Presented to Honor Frederick Clifton Grant*, ed. Sherman E. Johnson (New York: The Macmillan Company, 1951), p. 55.

[2] *Essentials of New Testament Study* (New York: The Roland Press Company, 1958), p. 131, n. 1.

[3] *Corr.*, p. 66.

[4] J. H. A. Hart speculated elaborately on Apollos' Alexandrian (and therefore Philonic) theology in his article, "Apollos," *JTS*, VII (1906), 16–28.

Since then fashions have changed. Martin H. Scharlemann in a critical review of Wilckens, *Weisheit und Torheit*, writes, "It is evident from the epistle itself that Apollos

Other scholars, however, dissent. Concerning the Apollos party T. W. Manson, for example, confidently asserts,

> One party division can, I think, be disposed of fairly easily. The Apollos party does not represent a real split in the community. No doubt there were members of the Corinthian Church who looked to Apollos as their father in the Gospel in the sense that they owed their conversion to Christianity to his preaching. But that did not in any way trench on the authority of Paul. On the contrary, Paul himself recognizes Apollos as a useful and valued colleague. "I planted, Apollos watered." Here there is no rivalry or jealousy: Paul and Apollos collaborate in the work.[1]

In saying the above, Manson echoes the sentiments of Wilfred L. Knox: "The last group [the "party of Apollos"], however, can hardly have constituted a serious danger in view of the fact that the leader to whom they appeal is at the moment in S. Paul's company and on the friendliest possible terms with him (1 xvi. 12)."[2] And Kirsopp Lake also speaks of "the obviously friendly relationship between St. Paul and Apollos (cf. 1 Cor. xvi. 12)".[3] Leon Morris says sweepingly, "From the general tone of Paul's references to Apollos, and from all that we know of this disciple from other passages, it is clear that there was no difference in their teaching."[4] Thus on the subject of the Apollos party scholarly opinion runs the gamut.

(b) *Peter.* Some scholars have singled out Peter as the chief source of Paul's difficulties with the Corinthians. Much of the evidence used by these scholars is found in 2 Corinthians where Paul is clearly combating

---

was something of a key to this whole problem. Since Apollos had been trained in Alexandria, where he had come into contact with a distinctive movement that had its origins with John the Baptist, our whole interpretation of the Corinthian philosophy ought possibly to hinge on him as a possible, and even a probable, link with certain views of the Qumran community" (*JBL*, LXXIX [1960], 190). Scharlemann repeats this suggestion in his more general study, *Qumran and Corinth* (New York: Bookman Associates, 1962), pp. 45, 68.

[1] *Studies*, p. 194.

[2] *Jerusalem*, p. 321, n. 8. So also Goudge, *1 Cor.*, p. xxi; and R. St. John Parry, who wrote, "It is quite clear that Apollos was not one of these [party leaders], nor even implicated in their proceedings. The way in which S. Paul names him and associates him with himself throughout this section is decisive: and the reference in c. xvi. confirms this conclusion" (*The First Epistle of Paul the Apostle to the Corinthians* ["Camb."; Cambridge: The University Press, 1916], p. xxvii).
The view that the Apollos party may be eliminated is, of course, to be found in the influential work of Ferdinand Christian Baur, *Paul, the Apostle of Jesus Christ: His Life and Work, His Epistles and His Doctrine*, rev. Eduard Zeller; trans. A. Menzies (2 vols.; 2d ed.; London: Williams and Norgate, 1875–76), I, 263–4.

[3] *Earlier Epistles*, p. 129. So also Lightfoot, *Notes*, p. 154; Héring, *1 Cor.*, p. 5; Craig, "1 Cor.," p. 21; and Simon, *1 Cor.*, pp. 63–4.

[4] *1 Cor.*, pp. 39–40.

Jewish Christians at Corinth: "Are they Hebrews? So am I. Are they Israelites? So am I. Are they the descendants of Abraham? So am I" (2 Cor. 11.22). These scholars begin by showing that the difficulties reflected in 2 Corinthians are not different from those in 1 Corinthians. Jacques Dupont, for example, says, "Il y a parfaite homogénéité entre la *gnosis* charismatique de la Ire aux Corinthiens et la *gnosis* dont il est question en *II Cor.*, VIII, 7 et XI, 6."[1] And W. L. Knox asserts that the "false apostles" of 2 Cor. 11.13 are responsible for the opposition to Paul reflected in 1 Corinthians.[2] Hans-Joachim Schoeps also discusses 2 Corinthians first in order to explain the situation in Corinth to which Paul addressed 1 Corinthians.[3] With this identification made, the way is clear to say as W. L. Knox does,

> It is hardly possible to suppose that the "party of Cephas" is not due to the activity of Jewish emissaries who regard S. Peter as their natural leader. . . . The Corinthians have been visited by certain Jewish teachers who have been shocked at the scandals they have witnessed. They have urged the Corinthians to appeal to S. Peter, whom they regard as the chief of the Apostles and therefore responsible for supervising the development of all Christian Churches, to set matters right.[4]

Other scholars go further and assert that Peter himself had visited Corinth, winning converts who designated themselves by his name.[5] But an equally distinguished group of scholars denies that Peter had ever been in Corinth.[6] Some scholars emphasize the Jewishness of the Petrine party, identifying it with the Judaizers with whom Paul had had so much difficulty in Jerusalem, Antioch, and Galatia. Thus, for example, Goguel says of them, "Their tactics were not the same in each case. While they worked by gradually worming themselves in

[1] *Gnosis*, p. 258.   [2] *Jerusalem*, pp. 311, 320–2.
[3] *Paul*, pp. 78–82.   [4] *Jerusalem*, p. 321.
[5] Although not in favour of this position himself, Oscar Cullmann, *Peter: Disciple—Apostle—Martyr: A Historical Study*, trans. F. V. Filson (2d ed. rev.; "The Library of History and Doctrine"; London: SCM Press Ltd, 1962), p. 55, n. 64, listed the following scholars for this view: Eduard Meyer, A. Harnack, H. Lietzmann, J. Zeiller, and H. Katzenmayer. Similarly M. Goguel, *The Birth of Christianity*, trans. H. C. Snape (London: George Allen & Unwin Ltd, 1953), p. 309, n. 2, cited the names of B. Weiss, Link, and Ed. Schwartz. To these lists should be added Bousset, "1 Cor.," pp. 75, 79 ("vielleicht"); Moffatt, *1 Cor.*, p. 10; Nock, *St. Paul*, p. 111; and Craig, "1 Cor.," p. 21. Lake goes so far as to say, "Probably, then, St. Peter ought to be regarded, along with St. Paul and Apollos, as one of the founders of the Church at Corinth" (*Earlier Epistles*, p. 116).
[6] Goguel himself rejected such a visit (*Birth*, p. 309), and cited in his support E. Renan; Reuss; A. Jülicher; Belser; and W. Bauer, *Rechtglaubigkeit und Ketzerei im ältesten Christentum* (1934). So also Schmiedel, "Corr.," pp. 41–2; Lightfoot, *Notes*, pp. 153–4; J. Weiss, *1 Cor.*, p. xxxiv; Robertson and Plummer, *1 Cor.*, p. 12; Zahn, *Intro. N. T.*, I, 287, 302–3; Evans, *Corr.*, p. 66; Allo, *1 Cor.*, p. 9; Héring, *1 Cor.*, p. 5; Cullmann, *Peter*, p. 56; and Wendland, *Corr.*, p. 14.

secretly in Greece, in Galatia they attacked directly."[1] Other scholars deny that the Torah and circumcision were even secretly an issue at Corinth.[2] And some, going further, reject the view that the Cephas party was a "Judaizing" faction which represented the Pharisaic-Rabbinic wing of the Jewish-Christian Church. For example, Kirsopp Lake speaks of "the existence of opponents of St. Paul, who were Jews, but πνευματικοί, not Judaizers",[3] and says that "the figure of a Judaizing St. Peter is a figment of the Tübingen critics with no basis in history."[4] More recently T. W. Manson has ascribed the excesses of the Corinthians' worship reflected in 1 Cor. 12—14 (which are usually considered the result of Hellenistic influence) to a demand from the Cephas party that glossolalia be encouraged as the true sign of the Spirit.[5] And, finally, the independent existence of the Cephas party is denied by F. C. Baur and his followers.[6] These scholars identify the Cephas party with the Christ party. Thus the Cephas party disappears altogether as a distinct point of view.

(c) *Christ*. The motives which may have led some Corinthians to designate themselves in a special way as "those of Christ" can only be guessed at. Therefore this group has been the object of the widest range of speculation. The situation in 1935 is well summarized by Allo (with the more important references added to his statement):

Parmi ceux qui reconnaissent l'existence d'un "parti du Christ" bien tranché, les uns l'ont cherché *parmi les judaïsants*. Ainsi *Baur* les mettait avec les gens de Céphas, les *pètro-christins* opposés aux *paulino-apolloniens*.[7] Pour *Holsten*, *Schmiedel*,[8] *Heinrici* (celui-ci à condition qu'il ne vaille pas mieux supprimer ἐγὼ δὲ Χρ.), ce sont des judéo-chrétiens extrémistes, "ceux de Céphas" étant plus modérés; pour *Weizsäcker* et d'autres, des émissaires de Jacques. Des théories d'école ont influé sur toutes ces vues. *Rob.-Pl.*[9] y voient des judaïsants qui se vantaient d'avoir "connu le Christ dans le chair" (cfr.

---

[1] *Birth*, p. 307. Goudge states the same opinion: "The real hostility [in Corinth] probably lay, as in the churches of Galatia, between those who were faithful to S. Paul's teaching and the followers of teachers who desired to subject the Gentile converts to the burden of the Jewish law" (*1 Cor.*, p. xxi). According to Héring the Cephas party "must have been made up of Jewish Christians from Palestine" (*1 Cor.*, p. 5).

[2] So, e.g., Parry, *1 Cor.*, ("Camb."), p. xxx ("There is no evidence in either Epistle of such an attempt [to impose the Jewish law] being made at Corinth."); W. L. Knox, *Jerusalem*, pp. 320–1; Evans, *Corr.*, p. 66 ("unlikely"); Allo, *1 Cor.*, p. 82; and Craig "1 Cor.," p. 21 ("The Judaizing problem is not faced until II Corinthians.").

[3] *Earlier Epistles*, p. 227.

[4] *Ibid.*, p. 116. Cf. also pp. 128–9. So also J. Weiss, *Primitive Christianity*, p. 338 ("The real opposition of the Cephas party was confined to personal grounds."). Lake's suspicions of the Tübingen school sound particularly modern: cf. Munck, "The Tübingen School and Paul," *Paul and the Salvation of Mankind*, pp. 69–86.

[5] *Studies*, pp. 204–5. [6] *Paul*, I, 258–95. [7] Ibid. [8] "*Corr.*," pp. 41–2, 46–50.

[9] Robertson and Plummer, *1 Cor.*, p. 12.

II *Cor.* v, 16); *Hilgenfeld* et *Holsten*, à peu près de même; *Osiander, Reuss, Klöpper, B. W. Bacon* (Expositor 1914[1]) des docteurs judaïsants soumis à la Loi "comme le Christ"; *Beyschlag* et *Godet*, une faction soumise à d'anciens prêtres ou pharisiens méfiants à la fois des Douze et de Paul (*Godet* admettrait aussi des gnostiques ou théosophes[2]); *Lemonnyer*, des judaïsants extrêmes, originaires de Palestine, qui avaient pu voir le Christ et prétendaient détenir sa vraie pensée, et qu'on retrouvera *II Corinthiens*.—D'autre part, tous ces "indépendants", qui se mettent au-dessus de Céphas lui-même et de toute autorité apostolique (*Giustiniani, Messmer, Schäfer, Zahn,*[3] *Jülicher,*[4] *Lietzmann,*[5] al.) seraient des "pneumatiques" anarchistes (*Schenkel, De Wette, Grimme*) ou des rationalistes (*Neander*[6]); *Lütgert*[7] les tient aussi pour des "spirituels" antinomistes, libertins et gnostiques, venus de paganisme, tandis que *Schlatter* les croirait sortis d'entre les Juifs. *Toussaint* y voit le germe du parti rebelle de II *Cor.*, celui-ci s'étant formé plus tard par leur alliance avec des intrus d'origine judéo-chrétienne pour combattre Paul. C'est bien dans ce dernier sens que le problème nous paraît pourvoir être tranché.[8]

The situation is further complicated by the fact that a number of scholars reject the existence of the Christ party altogether. Georg Heinrici and Johannes Weiss considered the phrase a gloss, perhaps the

---

[1] "The Christ-Party in Corinth," *The Expositor*, Ser. 8; VIII (1914), 399–415.

[2] Godet attributed to the Christ party the cry, "Jesus is accursed!" (12.3), commenting, "Such a fact may . . . be explained when we call to mind a doctrine like that professed by the Judaizing Christian Cerinthus, according to which the true Christ was a celestial virtue which had united itself to a pious Jew called Jesus. . . . It is known that Cerinthus was the adversary of the Apostle John at Ephesus; Epiphanius—on what authority we know not—asserts that the First Epistle to the Corinthians was written to combat this heresy. . . . We adopt fully, therefore, the words of Kniewel (*Eccl. Cor. vetustiss, dissentiones*, 1842), who has designated *those of Christ* as 'the Gnostics before Gnosticism' " (*Commentary on St. Paul's First Epistle to the Corinthians*, trans. A. Cusin [2 vols.; "Clark's Foreign Theological Library," N.S., Vols. XXVII, XXX; Edinburgh: T. & T. Clark, 1893], I, 76–7).

Bacon referred to and accepted Godet's interpretation of 1 Cor. 12.3 (*Intro. N. T.*, p. 92, n. 2), and was himself referred to by Robertson and Plummer (*1 Cor.*, p. 284) as holding a plausible point of view.

Quite independently the same suggestion has recently been made by Schmithals, *Gnosis*, who says at the end of his discussion of ἀνάθεμα Ἰησοῦς, "Ich war einigermassen überrascht, als ich lange nach Vollendung der vorliegenden Untersuchung in dem alten Kommentar von FGodet (1886) eine Auslegung von I 12, 3 fand, die bis in die Einzelheiten hinein der oben gegebenen entspricht" (p. 50, n. 1). On this particular slogan see p. 193 below.

[3] *Intro. N. T.*, I, 293.

[4] Adolf Jülicher, *An Introduction to the New Testament*, trans. Janet P. Ward (New York: G. P. Putnam's Sons, 1904), p. 83.

[5] *Corr.*, pp. 6–7.

[6] Cf. more recently Manson, *Studies*, p. 207, who characterizes the Christ party as Hellenistic intellectuals, "the opposite extreme to the Cephas party".

[7] Wilhelm Lütgert, *Freiheitspredigt und Schwarmgeister in Korinth: ein Beitrag zur Charakteristik der Christus Partei* ("Beiträge zur Förderung christlicher Theologie," XII, 3; Gütersloh: C. Bertelsmann, 1908).

[8] Allo, *1 Cor.*, p. 86. In agreement with Allo are Moffatt, *1 Cor.*, p. 10; Wendland, *Corr.*, pp. 14–15; and Osty, *Corr.*, p. 15.

marginal addition of a pious scribe.[1] Räbiger suggested that the slogan, "I am of Christ", was not the cry of a special "Christ party" but was the common claim of each of the three parties in Corinth: "I am of Christ!" "No, I am of Christ!!" "No, I am of Christ!!!"[2] Kirsopp Lake adopted but reapplied Räbiger's suggestion that the fourth party cry was not co-ordinate with the first three. Lake's theory is that Paul added the last slogan to characterize his own position. He punctuates I Cor. 1.12, 13, therefore, as follows:

> I mean that each says "I am of Paul, and I of Apollos, and I of Cephas,"— but I am of Christ! Is Christ divided? was Paul crucified for you? or were ye baptized into the name of Paul?[3]

This interpretation is indeed very similar to that of Chrysostom who understood "I am of Christ" to be Paul's statement of the slogan which all the Corinthians should have adopted: "I am of *Christ* (you should say)". Thus Chrysostom wrote, "This was not his charge, that they called themselves by the Name of Christ, but that they did not all call themselves by that Name alone. And I think that he added this of himself, wishing to make the accusation more grievous, and to point out that by this rule Christ must be considered as belonging to one party

---

[1] C. F. Georg Heinrici, *Der erste Korintherbrief* ("Meyer," 5. Abt., 8. Aufl.; Göttingen: Vandenhoeck und Ruprecht, 1896), pp. 56ff.; J. Weiss, *1 Cor.*, pp. xxxvi–xxxviii. So also Goguel, *Intro. N. T.*, IV.2, pp. 118–25; Richard Reitzenstein, *Die hellenistischen Mysterien-religionen nach ihren Grundgedanken und Wirkungen* (3d ed. of 1927 reprinted; Stuttgart: B. G. Teubner Verlagsgesellschaft, 1956), pp. 333–4; W. Michaelis, *Intro. N. T.*, pp. 172–3; and Héring, *1 Cor.*, p. 6.

This position is specifically rejected by Lietzmann, *Corr.*, p. 7; and Grosheide, *1 Cor.*, p. 36.

Allo cites and rejects the opinion of R. Perdelwitz (*Die sogenannte Christuspartei in Korinth* [1911]) that χριστοῦ should be emended to κρίσπου (1.14) as "fantaisiste et désespérée" (*1 Cor.*, p. 82, n. 1). More in perversity than desperation A. Powell Davies emends the text to read "Chrestos" whom he identifies tentatively with the Righteous Teacher of the Qumrân community (*The First Christian: A Study of St. Paul and Christian Origins* [New York: Farrar, Straus and Cudahy, 1957], p. 193)! Thomas Charles Edwards *A Commentary on the First Epistle to the Corinthians* (3d ed.; London: Hodder and Stoughton, 1897), p. 19, seventy years earlier had rejected the same emendation which, he reported, had been suggested previously by Grätz.

[2] Julius Ferdinand Räbiger, *Kritische Untersuchungen über den Inhalt der beiden Briefen an die korinthische Gemeinde* (2d ed.; 1886), cited by Lake, *Earlier Epistles*, p. 127.

[3] Ibid. So also, at about the same time, von Dobschütz, *Primitive Church*, pp. 72, 75; and Bousset, "1 Cor.," p. 79 (tentatively). Later also Evans, *Corr.*, p. 66 ("perhaps preferable"); Heard, *Intro. N. T.*, p. 190 (as a suggestion); William Barclay, *The Letters to the Corinthians* (2d ed.; Philadelphia: The Westminster Press, 1956), p. 17 (as one of two suggestions); and C. S. C. Williams, "Corr.," §830b ("unless the words 'And I am of Christ' are a gloss").

This position is specifically rejected by Robinson and Plummer, *1 Cor.*, p. 12; and by Morris, *1 Cor.*, p. 40.

Craig, "1 Cor.," pp. 21–2, does not decide between Lake and Weiss but doubts the existence of the Christ party.

only: Although they were not so using the name themselves."[1]

These theories are based on the fact that the Christ party enjoys only a shadowy existence in 1 Corinthians. The names of the parties appear as follows:

1.12	Paul	Apollos	Cephas	Christ
3.4, 5	Paul	Apollos		
3.22	Paul	Apollos	Cephas	
4.6	Paul	Apollos		

Thus the Christ party stands apart from the other three as an anomaly. There is no evidence in 1 Corinthians beyond the single reference in 1.12 that those whose allegiance is to Christ are to be distinguished from the rest of the Corinthian Church as a special point of view or party.

There is, in fact, evidence to the contrary. In 1 Cor. 1.13 commences a series of four items each of which is favourable to the position of a "Christ party" and therefore unfavourable to the theory of the existence of such a party.

(i) Is Christ divided?
(ii) Was Paul crucified for you?
(iii) Were you baptized in the name of Paul? (1.13)
(iv) I am thankful that I baptized none of you except Crispus and Gaius; lest any one should say that you were baptized in my name (1.14, 15).

To the first question the Christ party would only have answered, "Of course Christ is *not* divided. *We* are the only ones who are of Christ". It is axiomatic that Christ is a unity (cf. 12.4–27). Thus the question is no challenge to a group who claimed Christ as their sole possession.[2]

---

[1] *The Homilies of Saint John Chrysostom on the Epistles of Paul to the Corinthians*, trans. H. K. Cornish, J. Medley, and J. Ashworth; rev. Talbot W. Chambers ("A Select Library of the Nicene and Post-Nicene Fathers of the Christian Church," ed. Philip Schaff, 1st Ser., Vol. XII; New York: The Christian Literature Company, 1889), p. 12.

[2] Another interpretation of μερίζω has been proposed to smooth out the difficulty. Robertson and Plummer, *1 Cor.*, p. 13; and Grosheide, *1 Cor.*, p. 38, translate the question thus: "Is Christ assigned (i.e., to one party)?" It is true that μερίζω can sometimes be translated "to assign", as at 1 Cor. 7.17, "Let everyone lead the life which the Lord has assigned to him". But even here the basic meaning of the verb remains: to divide from a larger whole in order to assign to an individual. The other examples listed by Arndt/Gingrich under the meaning, "to assign", clearly speak of the division of a whole into parts: e.g., Rom. 12.3; 2 Cor. 10.13 (both with μέτρον); and most clearly, Heb. 7.2, "And to him Abraham assigned a tenth of everything". The same is true of the examples cited by Moulton/Milligan. It seems highly unlikely that in 1.13 the verb can mean, "Has Christ been assigned (without division) to one party?" since the verb properly implies some sort of division. But if a division is allowed, then it is easiest to translate (as almost all scholars do), "Has Christ been divided up among you?"

The following pair of questions as well, (ii) and (iii), are without meaning if considered as addressed to a "Christ party". The expected answer to the first question is clearly, "No, *Christ* was crucified for us", and, to the second, "No, we were baptized into *Christ*". These questions simply further the claims of the supposed Christ party. Paul's final statement (iv) carries the same implication. Paul goes out of his way to renounce any personal stake he might have been considered to have in the baptism of the Corinthians. What is important about their baptism, he is saying, is that they were all baptized into *Christ* (cf. 10.1–4). Again he does not seem to have the existence of a "Christ party" in mind. And a fifth passage should be counted with the above:

> (v) For all things are yours, whether Paul or Apollos or Cephas or the world or life or death or the present or the future, all are yours, and you are Christ's and Christ is God's (3.21b–23).

Johannes Weiss succinctly restated the argument of this passage as follows: "How can you say, I am of Paul or of Apollos or of Cephas, whereas ye are really of Christ?"[1] The whole thrust of Paul's argument wherever he mentions the names of the parties is that the separate designations, "Paul", "Apollos", and "Cephas", ought to be replaced by the single affirmation, "I am of Christ". Thus the existence of a Christ party in Corinth is extremely doubtful.

Walter Schmithals, whose elaborate theories about the influences of gnosticism on the Corinthian Church are centred on the Christ party, takes the question, "Is Christ divided?", to be one of the slogans of the Christ party itself. In effect he would paraphrase the claim of the Christ party as follows: "We only are the spiritual followers of Christ. Is Christ divided into pieces and distributed among mere apostles (as the rival claims of the parties of Paul, Apollos, and Cephas imply)?"[2] Schmithals has correctly seen that the question, "Is Christ divided?", is favourable to the position of a "Christ party". But if this question is to be assigned to such a party, then why not also questions (ii) and (iii) above? However, (iv) cannot belong to anyone but Paul, since he speaks of himself in the first person. Yet (iv) is the equivalent of (iii), and if (iii) and (iv) are Paul's, then (i) and (ii) undoubtedly are also his. Moreover, if the traditional speakers are to be reassigned in this section, it is certainly more plausible to attribute the statement, "I am of Christ", to Paul (as Lake suggested), than to consider the question, "Is Christ

---

[1] *Primitive Christianity*, p. 340. The above points are forcefully argued by him at greater length in *1 Cor.*, pp. 17–18; and by Wilckens, *Weisheit*, p. 12.
[2] *Gnosis*, p. 166.

divided?'', as the words of a "Christ party". Thus it appears that those scholars who build their reconstructions of the situation in Corinth upon the "Christ party" have built upon sand (whether we adopt the theory of J. Weiss, of Chrysostom, or of Lake).

To complete the circle of opinion we may note that there are scholars who, instead of attaching their theories to one or another of the parties, are primarily interested in minimizing or eliminating the whole idea of such divisions within the Corinthian Church. So, for example, Sir William M. Ramsay, quoting Dean Alford before him, commented on 1 Cor. 1.12 as follows:

> The attempt has been made by many commentators to specify the character of four supposed parties which used these four expressions as signs and badges of their respective views; but it may be doubted if the attempt has been made on the proper lines or if it can be successful. Especially, as Alford says, "the German commentators are misled by too *definite* a view of the Corinthian parties," p. 464; and "much ingenuity and labour have been spent in Germany on the four supposed distinct parties at Corinth, and the eminent theologians have endeavoured, with very different results, to allot to each its definite place in tenets and practice," p. [45]. Such attempts are on a radically false principle.[1]

Simultaneously Theodor Zahn, himself a "German commentator", wrote, "Nothing could be more erroneous than to suppose that either in Paul's thought, or in fact, the Church was divided into four factions or even sects."[2] And Morton Enslin grumbled,

> From 1 Cor. 1.10–17 it has often been argued that there were at least three, perhaps four, separate cliques or parties in Corinth, and that it is against them and the wrangling thus engendered that Paul is writing. Much has been written about the nature of the "party of Paul," "of Apollos," "of Cephas," and "of Christ." Since there is no scintilla of evidence, one's imagination could and did run riot. . . . My own impression is that not only is this type of reconstruction sheer nonsense, but that these parties are far less important than has often been assumed.[3]

More recently Johannes Munck entitled the fifth chapter of *Paul and the Salvation of Mankind*, "The Church Without Factions: Studies in 1 Corinthians 1—4". And he concluded, "If the interpretation here is correct, then not only were there no factions, but there was also no Judaizing in the Church at Corinth at the time Paul wrote his first letter to the Corinthians."[4]

---

[1] "Historical Commentary on the Epistles to the Corinthians," *The Expositor*, Ser. 6; I (1900), 28. The sixth edition of Henry Alford's commentary on 1 Corinthians was published by Rivingtons in 1871.

[2] *Intro. N. T.*, I, 283.   [3] *Beginnings*, p. 249.   [4] P. 167.

In the face of the critical difficulties which surround the attempt to put flesh on the bare references in 1 Cor. 1.12 a number of scholars prefer to discuss the point of view of Paul's opponents without fixing on any particular party by name. Thus K. Lake and Enslin characterize them simply as the "spirituals", denying that they were Judaizers.[1] And Bultmann, Käsemann, and Dinkler deal with the situation in terms of a Hellenistic and mystic "pre-Christian Gnosis".[2] Jacques Dupont, on the other hand, understands the "wisdom" of the Corinthians to derive mainly from charismatic Jewish-Christians from Palestine.[3] And Schoeps, too, emphasizes the Jewishness of Paul's opposition at Corinth in conscious opposition to Lütgert and his followers.[4]

What does the oral information describing the situation in Corinth mean? Perhaps it is not too harsh a judgement to say that more often than not the answer which scholars have given to this question has been determined more by what each scholar has brought to 1 Corinthians than by what he has learned from this letter. To seek, for example, the nature and source of the superior knowledge and wisdom of the Corinthians leads the scholar away from 1 Corinthians down various paths of investigation affording a variety of answers. At present scholarly opinion appears to be at something of a stalemate on the subject of the larger background of the Corinthian situation. Since this is the case it seems wise to pass over the smaller issues contained in the oral information—the case of incest, the case of litigation, and the irregularities in the Corinthians' worship—fascinating though they are, and to prefer the evidence obtained from an investigation of the written dialogue between Paul and the Corinthians.

There is, however, one general problem which may profitably be discussed at this point, since it will affect the reconstruction of the stages prior to 1 Corinthians.

---

[1] Lake, *Earlier Epistles*, p. 230; Enslin, *Beginnings*, p. 249.

[2] Rudolf Bultmann, *Exegetische Probleme des zweiten Korintherbriefes* ("Symbolae Biblicae Upsalienses," 9; Uppsala: Wretmans Boktryckeri, A.-B., 1947), *Theology of the N. T.*, I, 180–1; Ernst Käsemann, "Die Legitimität des Apostels. Eine Untersuchung zu II Kor. 10—13," *ZNW*, XLI (1942), 33–71; Erich Dinkler, "Zum Problem der Ethik bei Paulus. Rechtsnahme und Rechtsverzicht (1 Kor. 6, 1–11)," *ZThK*, XLIX (1952), 167–200. Schmithals, discussed above, is an extreme example of this gnosticizing tendency. His description of the Christ party is largely based on second century documents.

[3] Dupont, *Gnosis*, pp. 371–5. [4] Schoeps, *Paul*, pp. 74–6.

THE RELATIONSHIP BETWEEN PAUL
AND THE CORINTHIAN CHURCH

In attempting to recover the substance of the Corinthians' letter to Paul
(Stage 3) it would be useful to know as much as possible about the
relationship between Paul and the Corinthians. We would like to
know, for example, whether this relationship was friendly or stormy,
frank and open, or secretive and suspicious. Did the Corinthians think
of themselves as Paul's equals in a discussion or perhaps an argument
with Paul? Or did they cast themselves in the role of pupils inquiring
of their teacher? There are numerous possibilities. 1 Corinthians, of
course, provides primary evidence only for Paul's attitude toward the
Corinthians. But undoubtedly Paul's attitude is not unrelated to that
of the Corinthians toward him.

The first impression that a reading of 1 Corinthians gives is that the
bond between Paul and the Corinthians is strong, although certain
irregularities have arisen. Upon these irregularities, however, Paul
feels free to speak his mind in full confidence that his voice carries
authority. Concerning the case of incest he says,

> For although absent in body I am present in spirit, and as if present, I have
> already pronounced judgment in the name of our Lord Jesus on the man
> who has done such a thing. When you are assembled, and my spirit is
> present, with the power of our Lord Jesus, you are to deliver this man to
> Satan for the destruction of the flesh, that his spirit may be saved in the day of
> the Lord Jesus (5.3–5).

Whatever the precise meaning of this interesting passage, Paul's tone
of authority is clear. It is an authority like that of a father over his
children.

> I do not write this to make you ashamed, but to admonish you as my beloved
> children. For though you have countless guides in Christ, you do not have
> many fathers. For I became your father in Christ Jesus through the gospel
> (4.14, 15).

The Corinthians, on their part, have not broken this relationship. It is
to Paul that they have directed their questions. Although some have
said of themselves, "I belong to Apollos", it is to Paul that they have
addressed their question concerning a possible return visit of Apollos to
Corinth (16.12). The Corinthians may have tended to be somewhat
factious, but there is no evidence of any move to secede from Paul's

sphere of authority. Although 1 Cor. 9.1–3 has often been interpreted as implying that the Corinthians had questioned Paul's apostleship,[1] it is doubtful whether this was the case.

> Am I not free? Am I not an apostle? Have I not seen Jesus our Lord? Are you not my workmanship in the Lord? If to others I am not an apostle, at least I am to you; for you are the seal of my apostleship in the Lord. This is my defense to those who would examine me.

This last verse (9.3) makes it clear that Paul believed himself challenged directly or indirectly on some point or points. The problem is whether this verse refers back to what Paul had just said, or ahead to what he was about to say. Does Paul's "defense" concern his apostleship (9.1, 2), or does it concern his right to be supported by the Churches, his general use of money in connection with the Collection, and his personal dietary habits in connection with the problem of idol meat (9.4–27)?[2] Clearly Paul's apostleship and his right to support from the Churches are related topics. The question is whether Paul is arguing that his right to be supported proceeds from his apostolic office, or that his apostolic status is not prejudiced by the fact that he has not depended on the Corinthians financially. The latter is the choice of W. L. Knox,[3] Moffatt,[4] and Héring,[5] who theorize that the same problem is reflected in 2 Cor. 10—13, particularly in 12.12, 13,

> The signs of a true apostle were performed among you in all patience, with signs and wonders and mighty works. For in what were you less favored than the rest of the churches except that I myself did not burden you? Forgive me this wrong!

But for two reasons it is unlikely that this interpretation is correct.

(i) The simplest defence that Paul could have made against the charge that he was not a real apostle because he did not receive support from his Churches would have been the plain statement that he *did* receive such support, but from other congregations. 2 Cor. 11.9 is precisely such a statement:

> When I was with you and was in want, I did not burden any one, for my needs were supplied by the brethren who came from Macedonia. So I refrained and will refrain from burdening you in any way.

[1] So Schmiedel, "Corr.," p. 112; Goudge, *1 Cor.*, p. 73; Findlay, "1 Cor.," pp. 845–6; Robertson and Plummer, *1 Cor.*, p. 179; Bousset, "1 Cor.," p. 114; Moffatt, *1 Cor.*, pp. 114–19; Manson, *Studies*, pp. 200–1; Lietzmann, *Corr.*, p. 39; Héring, *1 Cor.*, pp. xiii, 75; and Morris, *1 Cor.*, pp. 131–2. Findlay and Lietzmann single out the Cephas party as the source of this challenge.

[2] On the connection between these items and the Corinthians' questions to Paul see pp. 70–1 above.

[3] *Jerusalem*, p. 314.   [4] *1 Cor.*, pp. 114–19.   [5] *1 Cor.*, p. 76.

No such statement appears in 1 Corinthians, although the financial support from Macedonia dated back to "the beginning of the gospel" (Phil. 4.15). If Paul was willing to inform the Corinthians of such support when writing 2 Cor. 10—13, we should expect him to make the same sort of statement in 1 Cor. 9. Yet in 1 Cor. 9.15–18 we find Paul arguing exactly the opposite case: his boast is that he makes it a matter of principle to preach the gospel "free of charge" (v. 18). Since Paul's defence here is the opposite of that in 2 Cor. 10—13, it is unlikely that the accusations behind both passages were the same.

(ii) If Paul's apostleship had been challenged on the grounds suggested by the above group of scholars, then they are probably correct in assuming that such a challenge betrays outside influence in the Corinthian Church. The Corinthians themselves do not impress us with their liberality. 1 Cor. 16.1 is at least the second announcement to them of the "Collection for the Saints", yet in 2 Cor. 8 and 9 Paul is still trying to persuade them to take part in this enterprise. It would certainly have been highly perverse (though, of course, possible) for them to have criticized Paul for not accepting the support they seem unwilling to give. It appears probable that the subject of payment for the ministry would only have been brought up by outsiders, i.e., by the "apostles" who figure in 2 Cor. 10—13, and who presumably would not have been adverse to payment themselves. Yet if outsiders were responsible for a challenge to Paul's apostleship, it is strange that 1 Corinthians is free of the extreme language which Paul uses elsewhere to castigate his rivals. There is nothing in 1 Corinthians to correspond to such passages as 2 Cor. 11.13, 14

> Such men are false apostles, deceitful workmen, disguising themselves as apostles of Christ. And no wonder, for even Satan disguises himself as an angel of light.

In writing to the Galatians (Gal. 5.12) he even goes so far as to say, "I wish those who unsettle you would mutilate themselves!" But since the violent attacks against outsiders found in 2 Cor. 10—13 are absent from 1 Corinthians, it seems probable that the "apostles" in question arrived in Corinth some time after 1 Corinthians had been sent, and that the problems of 2 Cor. 10—13 do not underlie 1 Corinthians.

For these two reasons, therefore, it is probable that 1 Cor. 9 is not a defence against an attack on Paul's apostleship, but is his defence against a challenge, real or imagined, to what he considers his rights as an apostle. Thus as Evans said of 1 Cor. 9, "This chapter is not primarily a defence of St. Paul's status and privileges as an apostle, such as he was forced to make at Gal. i and II Cor. x, xi, but a demonstration of the fact that in spite of his admitted possession of such privileges he has refrained from using them."[1] And concerning Paul's relationship with the Corinthians Grosheide says in commenting on 1 Cor. 9.1, 2, "He does not defend his apostleship but he explains what his rights are as an apostle and states that he does not use those rights. . . . Paul knows that there are some who do not regard him as an apostle. This is not the case at Corinth for there everyone honored him as an apostle."[2]

We conclude, therefore, that in 1 Corinthians Paul liked to picture the relationship between himself and the Corinthian Church as that between a teacher and his pupils, or between a father and his children. No communication from the Corinthians seems to have disturbed this picture in any direct or open way. Apparently the Corinthians have not, for example, challenged Paul's authority as an apostle.

There is evidence, however, that on a deeper level relations between Paul and the Corinthians were somewhat strained. Some of Paul's remarks to them hardly sound affectionate:

> Your boasting is not good (5.6).
>
> What! Did the word of God originate with you, or are you the only ones it has reached (14.36)?
>
> Already you are filled! Already you have become rich! Without us you have become kings! And would that you did reign, so that we might share the rule with you! . . . We are fools for Christ's sake, but you are wise in Christ. We are weak, but you are strong. You are held in honor, but we in disrepute (4.8, 10).

That Paul himself was conscious that this last passage did not harmonize with the relationship which he was supposed to have with the Corinthians may well have been the motivation of his protest, "I do not write this to make you ashamed, but to admonish you as my beloved children" (4.14). Paul's frequent use of the verb φυσιόω to describe them has already been noted;[3] so too has his barrage of pointedly elementary questions, "Do you not know . . . ?", "Do you not know . . . ?"[4] Moreover, Paul not only calls them his children; he often, in effect, calls them childish:

> But I, brethren, could not address you as spiritual men, but as men of the flesh, as babes in Christ. I fed you with milk, not solid food; for you were

---

[1] *Corr.*, p. 105.
[2] *1 Cor.*, pp. 200–1. This conclusion is supported by Allo, *1 Cor.*, pp. 208–11.
[3] See above, pp. 76–7.   [4] See above, pp. 85–6.

not ready for it; and even yet you are not ready, for you are still of the flesh (3.1–3).

Brethren, do not be children in your thinking; be babes in evil, but in thinking be mature (14.20).

Furthermore, as a number of scholars have suggested, the famous "Hymn to Love" in 1 Cor. 13 has clear, yet often overlooked, implications concerning Paul's opinion of the Corinthians. Writing about Paul's relationship with the Galatians, Olof Linton in his important article, "The Third Aspect: A Neglected Point of View," derives from Gal. 1.11—2.10 the claims and charges of Paul's opponents by the simple expedient of omitting the emphasized negatives in the passage.[1] The same method applied to 1 Cor. 13.4–6 produces the following striking result:

Description of Love	*Description of the Corinthians*
Love is patient and kind;	They are impatient and unkind;
love is not jealous or boastful;	they are jealous[2] and boastful;
It is not arrogant or rude.	they are arrogant[3] and rude.
Love does not insist on its own way;	They insist on their own way;[4]
it is not irritable or resentful;	they are irritable and resentful;
it does not rejoice at wrong, but rejoices in the right.	they rejoice in doing wrong rather than right.

As Bousset said, "Jedes Wort ist . . . eine Mahnung an die Adresse der Korinther und ihren aufgeblasenen Weisheitsstolz."[5] And Moffatt agreed: "The lyric is thus a lancet. Paul is probing for some of the diseases that were weakening the body spiritual at Corinth."[6]

Fewer scholars, however, have noticed that Paul made a second thinly disguised allusion to the Corinthians in this same chapter:

When I was a child, I spoke ($\dot{\epsilon}\lambda\dot{\alpha}\lambda o\upsilon\nu$) like a child, I thought like a child, I reasoned like a child; when I became a man, I gave up childish ways (13.11).

[1] "The Third Aspect: A Neglected Point of View: A Study in Gal. i–ii and Acts ix and xv," *Studia Theologica*, III (1950), 79–95.

[2] Cf. 3.3 and 14.12.   [3] On $\phi\upsilon\sigma\iota\dot{o}\omega$ see above, pp. 76–7.

[4] For $\zeta\eta\tau\dot{\epsilon}\omega$, cf. 1.22; 10.24, 33.   [5] "1 Cor.," p. 141.

[6] Moffatt, *1 Cor.*, p. 198. So also Schmiedel, "Corr.," p. 141; Goudge, *1 Cor.*, p. 117; Robertson and Plummer, *1 Cor.*, p. 292 ("aimed at the special faults exhibited by the Corinthians"); Allo, *1 Cor.*, p. 345; Grosheide, *1 Cor.*, pp. 306–7; Craig, "1 Cor.," pp. 174–8; and Wendland, *Corr.*, p. 105.

The above analysis does not allow the hypothesis of a few scholars that 1 Cor. 13 was composed previously (whether by Paul or someone else) and inserted into 1 Corinthians. Such a theory is held by J. Weiss, *1 Cor.*, pp. 309–12; Loisy, *Origins*, p. 269; and Héring, *1 Cor.*, pp. xiv, 134.

Since the verb λαλέω is connected with the noun γλῶσσαι, "tongues", in 12.30; 13.1, and eleven times from 14.2 to 14.39, it seems most probable that Paul meant to imply that the ecstatic babblings (glosso-lalia) of the Corinthians were like those of babies. In addition, it is probable that Paul also intended to imply that the Corinthians were equally childish in their "wise" thoughts and reasonings.[1]

Thus it would seem that Paul's attitude toward the Corinthians con-tained a substantial measure of veiled hostility. To use the modern jargon, he was ambivalent toward them. We have in 1 Corinthians, therefore, a foreshadowing of the "painful" visit of 2 Cor. 2.1, and of the open hostility of 2 Cor. 10—13. However, since Paul's criticisms of the Corinthians discussed above never quite come out into the open, it can reasonably be inferred that the obstinacy or rebelliousness of the Corinthians was similarly veiled. Paul knew from his oral information that the Corinthians had not been altogether candid with him in the letter they addressed to him. Yet his answers to their questions do not show the anger which would certainly have been his response to any open expression of insubordination on their part. However, as 1 Cor. 9 indicates, Paul detected in their seemingly polite questions a hostility directed toward him which made him feel that their inquiries were some sort of examination against which he had to defend himself (9.3). Thus we shall have to allow and even expect that the questions in the Corinthians' letter were not simple requests for information on topics concerning which the Corinthians were uncertain, but that they were objections put in the form of questions concerning topics over which the Church in Corinth disagreed with Paul. The reconstruction of these questions, therefore, must reflect this undercurrent of hostility and obstinacy in the relationship between Paul and the Corinthian Christians. Chapter 5 is the attempt to make such a reconstruction of the Corinthians' letter to Paul.

[1] So Goudge, *1 Cor.*, p. 121; Findlay, "1 Cor.," p. 900; Moffatt, *1 Cor.*, p. 200; and Lietzmann, *Corr.*, p. 66 (only with reference to the boasted "knowledge" of the Corinth-ians).

CHAPTER 5

The Corinthians' Letter to Paul

In Chapter 3 reasons were given for believing that most of the material in 1 Cor. 7—16 was written in answer to a series of questions contained in the letter of the Corinthians to Paul mentioned in 1 Cor. 7.1. The topics of Paul's answers were identified and listed at the conclusion of that chapter. In Chapter 4 the general situation of the Corinthian Church was examined. It was concluded that the confused state of scholarly opinion indicated that it would be precarious to approach the reconstruction of Paul's written conversation with the Corinthians with preconceptions any more definite than the following:

(*a*) That the Corinthians were confident (or too confident) of their "knowledge".

(*b*) That they had made no overt move to challenge Paul's authority.

(*c*) That they were, however, somewhat antagonistic and rebellious toward Paul.

Without attempting to define these preconceptions further we turn now to the more objective task of seeking to recover the substance of the written questions which the Corinthians addressed to Paul in their letter.

It has already been noted that a number of scholars believe that the order of Paul's answers in 1 Corinthians is quite probably the same as the order of the topics in the letter from Corinth.[1] There is a certain amount of plausibility to this suggestion, although by the nature of the case it can never be proved. However, for the purposes of the present chapter it will be more convenient to deal first with the problem of idol meat before taking up the remaining topics in order.

[1] See above, pp. 64–5, and especially n. 1, p. 65.

CONCERNING IDOL MEAT (I COR. 8.1—II.1)

It is important to begin by discussing Paul's treatment of the problem of idol meat (I Cor. 8.1—11.1), because this section is the keystone of the various attempts to divide I Corinthians into two or more letters.[1] Suspicions about the integrity of I Corinthians focus on I Cor. 10.1–22 (23), which is held to reflect a different theology from that of Paul's comments on the problem of idol meat in I Cor. 8.1–13 and 10.23—11.1. Moreover, the apparent lack of connection between I Cor. 9 and its context is often regarded as corroborating evidence that I Cor. 8.1—11.1 is an editorial compilation. It is fair to say that if it can be shown that this section is most probably a unity, then the more radical of the compilation theories (summarized in Table 4) may be set aside.[2] We begin by discussing the situation and the questions implied by I Cor. 8 in order to reach some preliminary conclusions which will be of importance to the problem of the integrity of I Corinthians.

I. *Earlier reconstructions of the Corinthians' position*

The most elaborate attempt to reconstruct the questions from Corinth is that of George G. Findlay.[3] On the topic of idol meat he suggests the following as a quotation from the Corinthians' letter:

> We are perplexed about the eating of *idolothyta* (viii, etc.). We all have knowledge in this matter, understanding since we have turned to the living God, that the idol is a vain thing and cannot pollute the creatures offered to it. For us, as thou hast taught us to say, 'There is one God, the Father, of whom are all things and we for Him; one Lord, even Jesus Christ, through whom are all things and we through Him.' And in this knowledge some of the brethren are so strong that they dare even to sit and eat in the house of the idol. To others this kind of freedom is a sore offence and scandal. They shudder at the thought of touching that which has been in contact with the idol; if they go to market they inquire anxiously whether the meat on sale is consecrated flesh; if they dine in the house of an unbeliever, they are in embarrassment and fear (x. 25ff.). Thus, thou seest, we are divided in opinion, and many times annoyed and vexed with each other. We remember thee saying in regard to the like matters, 'All things are within my right.' From

---

[1] See above, p. 47, item ii.

[2] I Cor. 6.12–20 has already been discussed. On pp. 87–9 above it was argued that this passage was almost certainly composed by Paul to occupy its present position in I Corinthians.

[3] "Letter of the Corinthian Church." Two earlier reconstructions along the same lines are those of Thomas Lewin, *The Life and Letters of St. Paul* (2 vols.; 5th ed.; London: George Bell & Sons, 1890), I, 266–8; and Farrar, *St. Paul*, pp. 378–9.

this is would seem that those are justified who use an unshackled liberty; and most of us incline to this way of thinking. But again we ask, what is thy judgement touching this thing, and how wouldst thou have us act?"[1]

This somewhat flowery reconstruction conceals a considerable amount of learning. Findlay's opinion, accepted by most scholars, is that in the time since Paul's departure from Corinth a disagreement had developed between two groups within the Corinthian Church over the suitability or advisability of Christians eating meat previously dedicated to a pagan deity. As Kirsopp Lake said,

> Apparently there were two opinions on the matter in Corinth: one party maintained that an idol was nothing, and that therefore things offered to idols had no importance: they thought that the whole matter was indifferent, and that Christian freedom justified them in doing as they wished. Another party held the opposite opinion and thought that, cost what it might, Christians ought to abstain absolutely from the contamination of things offered to idols.[2]

And he added confidently, "This much is clear from 1 Corinthians on any hypothesis."[3] And, more recently, Wendland put it, "So teilt sie sich in zwei Gruppen, die 'Starken' und die 'Schwachen'. Diese Bezeichnungen werden in Korinth entstandene Schlagworte sein."[4]

A similar though less well defined position is held by a number of scholars who phrase the Corinthians' question in some such manner as, "May Christians eat idol meat or not?"[5] Although such a proposal for the Corinthians' question may appear to be the simplest possible, this suggestion actually involves the additional assumption that there were two points of view in Corinth on the subject of idol meat. Thus, whether scholars picture the Corinthians as being of two minds or of

---

[1] "Letter of the Corinthian Church," pp. 404–5.
[2] *Earlier Epistles*, pp. 199–200.   [3] Ibid., p. 200, n. 1.
[4] Wendland, *Corr.*, p. 62. Other scholars who hypothesize a division over this issue among the Corinthians are Godet, *1 Cor.*, I, 402; von Dobschütz, *Primitive Church*, p. 67–9; Bacon, *Story*, p. 278; J. Weiss, *1 Cor.*, pp. 211–12; Parry, *1 Cor.* ("Camb."), p. 83; Zahn, *Intro. N. T.*, I, 274; W. L. Knox, *Jerusalem*, p. 316; Deissmann, *Paul*, p. 72; Joseph Sickenberger, *Die Briefe des heiligen Paulus an die Korinther und Römer* (4. Aufl., "HSNT"; Bonn: Peter Hanstein, Verlagsbuchhandlung, 1932), pp. 39–40; Gustav Stählin, art. ἀσθενής, *TWNT*, I, 490; Allo, *1 Cor.*, p. 195; Nock, *St. Paul*, pp. 180–6; Enslin, *Beginnings*, p. 251; Moffatt, *1 Cor.*, pp. 102–3; Goodspeed, *Paul*, p. 120; Héring, *1 Cor.*, p. 66 (quoting Godet at length); Heard, *Intro. N. T.*, p. 190; Dibelius, *Paul*, p. 97; Grosheide, *1 Cor.*, p. 188; Craig, "1 Cor.," p. 94; Geyser, "Paul, the Apostolic Decree and the Liberals in Corinth," p. 124; C. A. Pierce, *Conscience in the New Testament* ("Studies in Biblical Theology," No. 15; London: SCM Press Ltd, 1955), p. 80; Carrington, *Early Christian Church*, I, 136; Howard C. Kee and Franklin W. Young, *Understanding the New Testament* (Englewood Cliffs, N. J.: Prentice-Hall, Inc., 1957), p. 259; Morris, *1 Cor.*, p. 128; Simon, *1 Cor.*, p. 96; and C. S. C. Williams, "Corr.," §835a.
[5] So Goudge, *1 Cor.*, p. 69; Robertson and Plummer, *1 Cor.*, p. 166; Bousset, "1 Cor.," pp. 110–12; and Caird, *Apostolic Age*, p. 139.

two parties, the assumption is that the difficulty developed and flowered within the Corinthian Church, and Paul is cast in the rôle of arbitrator to whom the congregation has appealed.

2. *Two groups or one?*

It is most important to determine whether or not the Corinthians' question concerning idol meat represented a division of opinion within the Corinthian Church. The reconstruction of the Corinthians' inquiries on this topic and on the other topics to be discussed later in the chapter depends on this point. There are four lines of argument which have been advanced to support the widely held view that the Corinthians were divided or at least of two minds on the subject of idol meat.

(*a*) It is generally assumed that the party names listed in 1 Cor. 1—4 indicate that there were serious cleavages within the Corinthian Church.

(*b*) It has been held that to dissuade the Corinthians from eating idol meat Paul used one line of argument in 1 Cor. 8.1–13; 10.23—11.1, and a different line in 10.1–22, and that the duality of his argument resulted from his desire to persuade two different points of view within the Corinthian Church.

(*c*) It has also been held that even within 1 Cor. 8.1–13; 10.23—11.1 there are statements which do not seem consonant with Paul's general purpose to contest the position of the too wise Corinthians. These statements are taken as intended to educate a second group or point of view which could be described as too scrupulous.

(*d*) Finally, it is widely believed that Paul's explicit mention of the weaker brother (ὁ ἀσθενῶν) in 1 Cor. 8.7–13 and 10.28, 29 is evidence of the existence of a group of men at Corinth with a viewpoint different from that of the knowledgeable majority.

(*a*) *1 Cor. 1—4.* 1 Cor. 1—4 can be used as evidence of a division among the Corinthians concerning idol meat only if it is assumed (i) that these chapters reflect at least one serious division within the Corinthian Church and (ii) that this division concerns issues which would involve the problem of idol meat. The first assumption (i) is problematical. As Chapter 4 showed, scholars have difficulty in characterizing the position of more than one party (however it be conceived or named) in opposition to Paul. Thus although these scholars differ widely in their conclusions, their work taken as a whole implies that the major division lay not between two (or more) Corinthian parties, but between Paul and the Corinthian Church. Concerning the second assumption (ii), it is reasonable to identify the knowledgeable Corinthians whom Paul addressed in 1 Cor. 8.1 with those rebuked in 1 Cor. 1—4. But in order to find in 1 Cor. 1—4 a second party holding the scrupulous position concerning idol meat one must either read this information from 8.1—11.1 back into 1 Cor. 1—4, or rely solely on the names of the leaders listed in 1.12. In the first case it is clear that 8.1—11.1 is the primary passage to be examined. As for the second approach, it is hoped that Chapter 4 showed the precariousness of this method. The best that can be said on the basis of 1.12 is that there is a bare possibility that the Cephas party, if it existed as a party, contested the freedom of other Corinthians in their use of idol meat.[1]

(b) *1 Cor. 10.1–22.* The argument that 1 Cor. 10.1–22 differs in point of view from that of 8.1–13 and 10.23—11.1 is more complicated. Concerning 1 Cor. 10.1–22, Johannes Weiss wrote,

> Here Paul comes very close to the standpoint of the Jewish dread of demons. No doubt the heathen idols are for him no longer gods but demons, yet these are still present and powerful and all too readily lay hold of unarmed and careless brethren. . . . Does not this sound like an echo of Jewish or Jewish Christian remonstrances? . . . We cannot get rid of the idea that Paul has at this point allowed a greater weight to Jewish Christian scruples than he felt justified in granting at other times. . . .
>
> The section I Cor. 10.1–23 was written at a time when Paul was still firmly convinced that the reins of discipline must be drawn tighter in order to meet the criticisms of the Jewish Christians, that the quite harmless and unobjectionable intercourse of the Gentile Christians with their fellow-countrymen must be checked.[2]

Yet what Weiss has really argued here is that Paul wrote this section *from* a viewpoint different from that of 8.1–13 and 10.23—11.1, not that he wrote *to* a second point of view. Weiss assumed that these Jewish Christians constituted a party at Corinth. He hypothesized their existence at this time solely to explain the fact and manner of Paul's arguments in 1 Cor. 10.1–22 against eating idol meat, for according to his reconstruction of Paul's Corinthian correspondence 1 Cor. 1—4; 5—6.11; 7—9; and 10.23—15 all belong to later letters.[3] But it is hardly necessary to hypothesize a special party in Corinth to explain the origin of Jewish elements in Paul's thought. The weakness of the argument which finds a second party reflected in 1 Cor. 10.1–22 is shown by Kirsopp Lake's presentation of it. Having said that Paul's

---

[1] Cf. Gal. 2.11–14. See further pp. 269–70 below.
[2] *Primitive Christianity*, p. 326.   [3] See Table 4 above, p. 45.

references to the Exodus event in 1 Cor. 10 suggest the presence of a "strict school" in Corinth, he has to admit that,

> the whole of this section in its context is only intelligible as directed against the argument that those who have been initiated into the Christian Mysteries may safely do anything they like [i.e., against what he calls "the party of freedom"]. . . .
>
> This difference of opinion between two parties in Corinth is clearly reflected in St. Paul's advice, and explains its strange turns and apparent inconsistencies. This is especially marked in I Cor. x. 14ff. Here St. Paul is conceding to the scrupulous party the correctness of their objection to idolatry; but he is thinking all the time of the effect his words will have on the party of freedom, and therefore he turns to them and invites them to consider accurately the exact force of his admission.[1]

Lake does not challenge the general agreement among scholars (including J. Weiss) that 1 Cor. 8.1—11.1 in its entirety was aimed at more or less the same over-enlightened point of view. He maintains, however, that the argument in 10.1–22 concerning demons is not Paul's, but is his concession to the position of a scrupulous party in Corinth. This conclusion he deduces from the verb $\phi\eta\mu\iota$ found in 10.15 and 19. As he says, "Of course $\phi\eta\sigma\iota$ and $\phi\alpha\sigma\iota$ are neutral expressions, but I suggest that $\phi\eta\mu\iota$ always implies some degree of assent to a proposition, explicit or implicit, and so often comes to mean 'I admit.'"[2] But "often" is far from "usually". Moreover, one can hardly distinguish from the word $\phi\eta\mu\iota$ alone the difference between assent to a proposition because it is congenial (i.e., because it is Paul's own opinion), and assent to a proposition one dislikes (i.e., a concession by Paul to the viewpoint of a stricter party). Furthermore, the context does not support such a distinction. The danger from demons is the premise of Paul's argument in this section; it does not appear to be a point which Paul had reluctantly conceded, and with which he was not in full agreement. Thus it appears probable that Lake has added the scrupulous party to 1 Cor. 10.1–22. Clearly the whole passage was designed to discourage the eating of idol meat and thus, by definition, was not directed at the hypothetical scrupulous party. Nor, if such a party existed, is there any reason why Paul would have adopted their arguments and thus increased the discord at Corinth. There is no real evidence in this section for a second point of view in Corinth on this matter.

(c) *Slogans in 1 Cor. 8.1–13 and 10.23—11.1.* Do 1 Cor. 8 1–13 and

---

[1] *Earlier Epistles*, p. 201.   [2] Ibid., n. 1.

10.23—11.1, however, give evidence of two parties at Corinth dis-
agreeing over the problem of idol meat? Scholars generally agree that
Paul's principal object in these sections was to dissuade the over-wise
Corinthians from the flagrant eating of idol meat. But in his argument
he included a number of items which appear to favour his enlightened
questioners, and seem intended to persuade a second, over-scrupulous
point of view:

1. We all possess knowledge (8.1).
2. An idol has no real existence (8.4).
3. There is no God but one (8.4).
4. For although there may be so-called gods in heaven or on earth, . . . yet
for us there is one God, the Father, from whom are all things and for whom
we exist, and one Lord, Jesus Christ, through whom are all things and
through whom we exist (8.5, 6).
5. Food will not commend us to God. We are no worse off if we do not eat,
and no better off if we do (8.8).
6. All things are lawful (10.23; 6.12).

It will be recognized immediately that all of these propositions were
cited in Chapter 3 [1] as being, in the opinion of a number of scholars, [2]
Paul's quotations of the Corinthians' slogans. These scholars explain
the fact that the above statements favour the enlightened Corinthians'
position by suggesting that they are in fact the Corinthians' own words.
If upon examination this position proves to be probable, then these
passages cannot be used as evidence for the existence of a scrupulous
party at Corinth.

There are two main reasons for supposing that at least some of these
statements are quotations from the Corinthians' letter to Paul.

(i) In 8.1 the double "we" is awkward, "*We* know that *we* all have
knowledge". The subjects of the two verbs do not appear identical.
The first verb is best referred to the author(s) of 1 Corinthians. Recognizing this fact a number of older scholars [3] suggested reading οἶδα μέν
for οἴδαμεν, thereby removing one of the awkward "we's" but introducing a still more awkward μέν. The clue, however, lies in Arndt
and Gingrich's observation that "the formula οἴδαμεν ὅτι is freq. used
to introduce a well-known fact that is generally accepted". [4] And they
draw attention to the similar function of the negative phrase οὐκ
οἴδατε ὅτι, "Do you not know?", whose ten occurrences in 1 Corinthians were listed in Chapter 3. [5] The ὅτι, therefore, has a function similar

---

[1] See above, p. 67.   [2] See Table 5, p. 68 above.
[3] J. Weiss (*1 Cor.*, p. 214, n. 4) lists Semler, Hofmann, and Bachmann (without, however, accepting this opinion). More recently, Jeremias, "Briefzitate," p. 151.
[4] Arndt/Gingrich, p. 558b.   [5] See p. 85 above.

to the ὅτι *recitativum* and frees the material which it introduces from its grammatical context. Thus the statement, "We all possess knowledge", was not composed by Paul as he dictated 1 Corinthians but was quoted by him at this point (whatever its source).

With this quotation in 8.1, however, is to be associated the pair of statements in 8.4. The connection is indicated by the οἴδαμεν ὅτι ... ὅτι, as Lietzmann emphasized.[1] Thus statements (1), (2), and (3) above are all most probably slogans quoted by Paul from a source we have not as yet specified. A second line of argument confirms the above conclusion and helps to identify the source of these quotations.

(ii) It is noticeable that items (1) and (6) are statements which Paul did not wholly accept. To each he added immediate and definite qualification:

1. "We all possess knowledge." "Knowledge" puffs up, but love builds up (οἰκοδομεῖ).
6. "All things are lawful," but not all things are helpful. "All things are lawful," but not all things build up (οἰκοδομεῖ).

Paul's counterstatements are evidence that the initial statements, (1) and (6), were not Paul's own composition here in 1 Corinthians, but were quotations which he used in order to modify them.

It is probable also that statements (2) and (3) are similarly modified, although this possibility is less often recognized by commentators. In fact, as Table 5 indicates, a number of scholars have suggested that the somewhat polytheistic section (8.5, 6) which immediately follows this pair of slogans (8.4) is itself a quotation from the Corinthians' letter. These two verses have been quoted above as (4), omitting the parenthesis in 8.5 ("as indeed there are many 'gods' and many 'lords'") as Bousset suggested.[2] There seem to be two reasons why vv. 5 and 6 often are not attributed to Paul. On the one hand there seems to be a hesitancy among some commentators to admit that Paul, like Jesus, could have believed in the real existence of a variety of spiritual powers, some of them good but most of them evil.[3] And, on the other hand, as Craig says of 8.6, "Some interpreters have sought to exclude the idea of the cosmic mediation of Christ by assigning the whole verse to the Gnostics whom Paul has been quoting. That is unlikely, for it is

---

[1] *Corr.*, p. 37. So too W. L. Knox, *Jerusalem*, p. 325, n. 29.　　[2] "1 Cor.," p. 111.
[3] E.g., Findlay says emphatically that these verses are "foreign to Pauline ... phraseology, but natural *on the lips of old polytheists*" ("1 Cor.," p. 840). Moffatt, who believes that Paul was ironically quoting formulas from Greek philosophy, comments concerning these "gods": "Now, as at Athens (Acts xvii. 16), he scornfully dismisses them as the phenomena of polytheism" (*1 Cor.*, p. 106).

impossible to deny successfully that Paul believed in the pre-existence of Christ."[1] Thus on the whole, it seems best to understand 8.5, 6 as neither too primitive and naïve nor too sophisticated and mature for Paul. Even with the parenthesis omitted, (4) is not really consonant with (2) and (3), and it is improbable to suppose that they came from the same source, or, at least, from the same source during the same discussion. As they stand, (2) and (3) might well be understood as part of an argument for freedom in the matter of eating idol meat. But the mention in (4) of the existence of other "gods" and "lords", and the henotheistic-sounding statement, "for *us* there is one God", support Paul's cautious argument and tell against the position of careless freedom with respect to idol meat. In fact, (4) is as emphatic a qualification of the monotheism of (3) as Paul could have made as a Christian. As Wendland says, "Er erkennt das *Dasein* vieler Götter und Herren an, aber sie sind 'kosmische' Realitäten, die Himmel und Erde erfüllen, nicht wirkliche Götter, da es ja nur den einen Gott gibt, sondern Dämonen."[2] Thus I Cor. 8.5, 6 is probably Paul's expansion and qualification of the statements in 8.4. As Goudge said of 8.5, "S. Paul explains and limits the assertions of the previous verse."[3] Paul certainly agreed with the twin principles (2) and (3), yet by mentioning other "gods" and "lords" he modified and limited their absolute application.

This conclusion removes (4) from the above list, but it adds a second point to the mutual similarity of (1), (2), (3), and (6): not only are these four passages favourable to the argument of the wise Corinthians but they are also qualified by Paul in a way which indicates that he cannot accept them without severe reservations.

These two lines of argument, the first (i) based on grammatical indications of quotation and the second (ii) on the nature of Paul's argument, reinforce each other. Together they create a high probability that (1), (2), (3), and (6) are not Paul's composition but are slogans quoted by him for the purposes of his argument in I Corinthians.[4] Once this conclusion has been reached the source of these quotations becomes obvious. These slogans favour the Corinthians' position. Paul would hardly have inserted quotations such as these if they were

---

[1] Craig, "I Cor.," p. 94, probably with reference to Heinrici and the scholars cited by him, *I Cor.*, p. 64, n. 1.

[2] Wendland, *Corr.*, p. 60. So also Bachmann, *I Cor.*, pp. 299–300; and Lietzmann, *Corr.*, p. 37.

[3] *I Cor.*, p. 70. So also Jeremias, "Briefzitate," p. 152.

[4] Table 5 (p. 68 above) shows how widely this conclusion is shared by commentators.

not in fact the principles by which the Corinthians justified their boasted freedom. Paul was unable flatly to reject their slogans, but he did his best to show the Corinthians the limitations of their position.

Item (5) is more difficult. It is certainly possible to punctuate the passages as follows, and to understand the succeeding verse (8.9) as a qualification of the proposed slogan (8.8):

> "Food will not commend us to God. We are no worse off if we do not eat, and no better off if we do." Only take care lest this liberty of yours somehow become a stumbling-block to the weak.

Paul's reference to "the weak" makes it clear that he is addressing a strong position. But, as Lietzmann and Allo point out,[1] in order for the statement in 8.8 to be considered a slogan of the over-wise, the negative would have to be shifted from the first clause to the second: "We are no worse off if we *do* eat, and no better off if we do *not*."[2] Moreover, the above (RSV) translation of 8.8, 9 ignores the δέ in 8.8 while translating the one in 8.9 as "only". Both the RV and the ASV, however, translate the repeated δέ in 8.7, 8, and 9, "but . . . but . . . but. . . ." As 8.8 stands, therefore, it is probably preferable to take it as one item in a series of criticisms of the liberal position and thus as originating from Paul.

We conclude, therefore, that (1), (2), (3), and (6), which might be taken as directed by Paul against a superstitious or scrupulous group of Corinthians, are more probably quotations from the Corinthians' letter to Paul. The other two passages, (4) and (5), appear to be part of Paul's own argument against the liberals in Corinth. Thus these six passages do not provide evidence for the existence at Corinth of a conservative group to which Paul supposedly directed a portion of his argument. On the contrary, these slogans give valuable information about the enlightened position opposed to Paul's.

(d) *The weaker brother.* In 1 Cor. 8.7–13 and 10.28, 29 Paul appealed to each of the liberal Corinthians to show concern for his "weaker brother". Does not his appeal imply the presence in Corinth of a group of such men? Scholars who believe that two parties at Corinth have

---

[1] Lietzmann, *Corr.*, p. 38; and Allo, *1 Cor.*, p. 204.

[2] The confusion in the manuscripts over the order of the last two phrases of 8.8 does not affect the meaning. The order given above in (5) is that of P46, B, A*, 1739 pc; Nestle and the RSV. However, Zuntz considers the more widely attested order superior (*Text*, pp. 161–2).

A few MS. authorities, including the corrector of A, move the μή from the first clause to the second thereby producing the reading favourable to the wise Corinthians. There seems to be no real possibility that this reading is original, however.

differed over the issue of idol meat assume that Paul is here asking the wise or "strong" party to show Christian charity ($\dot{a}\gamma\dot{a}\pi\eta$) for the "weak" party. Some scholars even believe that the terms "weak" and "strong" were labels used by the Corinthians themselves.[1] But in either form this assumption involves a number of difficulties.

In the first place, at the three points in 1 Corinthians where the two terms occur in direct opposition to each other they do not refer to two parties within the church at Corinth.

> For the foolishness of God is wiser than men, and the *weakness* of God is *stronger* than men (1.25).

> For consider your call, brethren; not many of you were wise according to worldly standards, not many were powerful, . . . but God chose what is foolish in the world to shame the wise, God chose what is *weak* in the world to shame the *strong* . . . (1.26, 27).

> We are fools for Christ's sake, but you are wise in Christ. We are *weak*, but you are *strong* (4.10).

Clearly Paul was attempting to deflate those whom he considered overwise. Of a "weak" party there is no hint. In fact Paul's very use of the term "weak" in the above passages implies that "weak" was not the designation of a particular Corinthian group either in his mind or in the Corinthians' usage.

Nor do the other occurrences of the word "weak" outside 1 Cor. 8 reveal any consistent usage. In 12.22 the comparative appears. Paul was comparing the variety of spiritual gifts to the parts of the body, some of which are "weaker" or less presentable than others. In 11.30 the "weak" do form a group within the Corinthian Church, but they are those who are "weak and ill". And in 9.22 ("To the weak I became weak . . .") Paul was speaking generally of his missionary practice, not specifically of the Corinthians.[2] Again the variety of usage tells against the assumption that the term carried a special connotation either for Paul or at Corinth.

[1] Stählin, *TWNT*, I, 490; Wendland, *Corr.*, p. 62; and Geyser, "Paul, the Apostolic Decree and the Liberals in Corinth," p. 124.

[2] A number of scholars, however, do connect the reference to "the weak" in 9.22 with Paul's argument in 8.7–13. So Parry, *1 Cor.* ("Camb."), p. 98; Lietzmann, *Corr.*, p. 43; Craig, "1 Cor.," p. 104; and Wendland, *Corr.*, p. 68. Grosheide, *1 Cor.*, pp. 213–14, adopts this position, but shows by the difficulty which he has with 9.22 that the weak party must be read into the passage from 8.7–13 in order to be found there. Paul speaks four times of "winning" various groups for Christ, but the fifth time, although the construction is entirely parallel, the verb "winning" must be understood to mean "seeking the spiritual welfare of a person" (Grosheide, *1 Cor.*, p. 214) if "the weak" are identified with "weak" Corinthians who are already Christians. The fact that all five occurrences of $\kappa\epsilon\rho\delta\dot{\eta}\sigma\omega$ are summed up with the $\sigma\dot{\omega}\sigma\omega$ of 9.22 makes this special interpretation of the fifth $\kappa\epsilon\rho\delta\dot{\eta}\sigma\omega$ still more improbable.

Moreover, the passages dealing specifically with the "weaker brother" do not really provide more evidence. As Craig said of 8.7–13 (on the assumption that two parties existed at Corinth), "It is striking that Paul did not attempt to educate those who lacked . . . knowledge, but accused those who were not showing love toward the brethren."[1] Paul's discussion would be less "striking", and therefore more natural, if it were understood as directed against a single, liberal, opposing position. The really striking fact is that in 8.10–13 and 10.28, 29 the "weaker brother" is completely hypothetical and indefinite:

> *If some one* should see you, a man of knowledge, at table in an idol's temple, *might* he not be encouraged, *if* his conscience is weak, to eat food offered to idols (8.10)?
>
> *If some one* of the unbelievers invites you to dinner . . . and *if some one* says to you, "This has been offered in sacrifice," then . . . do not eat it (10.27, 29).[2]

Only in 8.7–9 is there any slight degree of definiteness: "Not all possess this knowledge." These persons Paul characterized as having "weak" consciences. But the reference is general and leads into the hypothetical discussion in 8.10–13. All in all, it appears that Paul created two hypothetical situations involving a pair of hypothetical "weak" Christians solely as a way of dissuading the Corinthians from eating idol meat.[3]

Conclusion. Therefore, we conclude that the four lines of argument discussed above make improbable the theory that two groups in Corinth had disagreed over the matter of eating idol meat, and had appealed to Paul for his advice. The scholars listed above who make this assumption have hypothesized a more complicated theory than necessary. We may presume, as Paul presumed (8.7), that some Corinthians were less secure in their new faith than others. But nowhere is there evidence that they formed a group, or that their point of view had been communicated to Paul. In 1 Corinthians Paul appears solely concerned with those who are wise, knowledgeable, and boasted of their freedom.

[1] "1 Cor.," p. 94.

[2] On 10.28 Robertson and Plummer comment, "A pure hypothesis, and not so very probable" (*1 Cor.*, p. 221).

[3] It may be noted in passing that the "weaker brother" argument is particularly well adapted to Paul's needs here, because (i) it avoids the essential ethical issue of whether, or in what sense, the action is right or wrong in itself, and (ii) it is exceedingly flexible. Paul could for example, argue to the opposite conclusion by stressing the duty of the stronger members of the congregation to educate by example and by precept those who were less wise.

3. *The questions behind 1 Corinthians 8 and 9*

Three of the conclusions discussed above focus on the problem of reconstructing the Corinthians' question to Paul which received an answer in 1 Cor. 8 and 9.

(i) It is most probable, as we have just seen, that the difference of opinion over the question of idol meat is a disagreement which lies not in Corinth, but between Paul, on the one hand, and the Corinthian Church, on the other.

(ii) It is also probable that slogans (1), (2), (3), and (6) listed above are quotations from the Corinthians' letter to Paul.

(iii) Evidence was presented in Chapter 4 to indicate that a substantial amount of veiled hostility appears to have existed between Paul and the Corinthian Church.[1] Although conclusions (i) and (ii) were not arrived at in complete independence from each other, it is important to notice the extent to which these three conclusions are consistent with one another, and thus strengthen one another. They all point in the same direction. The slogans from the Corinthians' letter (ii) indicate that the Corinthians were not merely asking for information, but that they were aggressively defending their enlightened position (iii). Both the slogans (ii) and the antagonism (iii) are best understood as coming from a single rather than a plural source (i).

1 Corinthians 8. The evidence in 1 Cor. 8 points to some such question from Corinth as that suggested by Lietzmann: "Wir finden nichts Anstössiges darin, Opferfleisch zu geniessen, denn πάντες γνῶσιν ἔχομεν· οἴδαμεν γάρ, ὅτι οὐδὲν εἴδωλον ἐν κόσμῳ καὶ ὅτι οὐδεὶς θεὸς εἰ μὴ εἷς."[2] In effect the Corinthians' question is not "may we?" or "should we?" but "why can't we?"

> We see nothing scandalous about eating idol meat, because all of us possess knowledge. We know that an idol has no real existence and that there is no God but one.

1 Corinthians 9. To Lietzmann's suggestion we are probably justified in adding a comment concerning Paul's own behaviour as reflected by his protest in 9.4, "Do we not have the right to eat and drink?" A reminder from the Corinthians to Paul that he had himself eaten meat with them without inquiring as to its origin may well have been part

---

[1] See pp. 108–13 above.
[2] Lietzmann, *Corr.*, p. 37. So also Wendland, *Corr.*, p. 60, "Da es keine Götzen gibt, sondern nur den einen Gott, so finden wir auch nichts dabei, Götzenopfer-Fleisch zu essen." (For Wendland this is the expression of the "strong" party only, however.)

of the occasion for the defensive outburst which forms chapter 9. Certainly commentators have not suggested a more probable reason for Paul's abrupt change of tone in 9.1. As Table 4 shows, a number of scholars have even suggested that this chapter is not in its original context.[1] Other commentators simply give no reason why chapter 9 should follow chapter 8.[2] Craig says of the chapter that "it does not directly advance the discussion of the immediate issue".[3] Bousset called it "im Rahmen des ganzen Teils (Kap. 8–10) eine Einlage".[4] Those scholars who do make a connection between chapters 8 and 9 usually suggest that chapter 9 is a long expansion of 8.13: "If food is a cause of my brother's falling, I will never eat meat, lest I cause my brother to fall."[5] These scholars point to the fact that Paul alluded to his own ethical principles in 8.13, and that 1 Cor. 9 exhibits the same concern. But this observation suggests a consequence which does not seem to have been developed by commentators. It is Paul's conduct specifically with reference to eating idol meat which is the subject of 8.13. It may well be that chapter 9, which also concerns Paul's conduct, relates to the same problem, as well as to the question of the financial support of his ministry.

Certainly the defensive tone of chapter 9 is obvious. Paul said in fact, "This is my defence (ἀπολογία) to those who would examine me" (9.3). The chapter opens with a barrage of questions (fifteen in vv. 1–12 according to Nestle's punctuation) by which Paul attempted to justify himself. That he was deeply and personally involved in his argument is shown by his outburst in 9.15, "For a happy thing (it were) for me rather to die than—No one shall make void my glorying!"[6]

At the climax of the chapter stands the following:

For though I am free from all men, I have made myself a slave to all, that I might win the more. To the Jews I became as a Jew,[7] in order to win Jews; to those under the law I became as one under the law—though not being

[1] See p. 45 above. To these scholars should be added Héring, cited above p. 47, n. 2. Moreover, Schmiedel, "Corr.," p. 112; and J. Weiss, 1 Cor., p. 231, although they do not refer 1 Cor. 9 to another letter, believe that its present position is due to a later editor.

[2] E.g., Evans, Corr., p. 105; Moffatt, 1 Cor., p. 114; and Grosheide, 1 Cor., p. 200.

[3] "1 Cor.," p. 97.   [4] "1 Cor.," p. 113.

[5] So, explicitly, H. A. W. Meyer, Corr., I, 251; Goudge, 1 Cor., p. 73; Findlay, "1 Cor.," p. 845; Allo, 1 Cor., pp. 208–9; Bachmann, 1 Cor., p. 307; Lietzmann, Corr., p. 39; Grosheide, 1 Cor., p. 214; Wendland, Corr., p. 63; and, implicitly, Robertson and Plummer, 1 Cor., p. 176–7; Hans von Soden, "Sakrament und Ethik," p. 244; Morris, 1 Cor., p. 131, and Simon, 1 Cor., p. 98.

[6] According to Robertson and Plummer's translation (1 Cor., p. 188). The English versions smooth out the aposiopesis which most modern commentators believe to be present. E.g., Allo, 1 Cor., p. 220; Lietzmann, Corr., pp. 42–3; and Héring, 1 Cor., pp. 79, and 80, n. 13.

[7] Contrast 2 Cor. 11.22; Phil. 3.5, 6; and Rom. 11.1!

myself under the law—that I might win those under the law. To those outside the law I became as one outside the law—not being without law toward
God but under the law of Christ—that I might win those outside the law. To
the weak I became weak, that I might win the weak. I have become all
things to all men, that I might by all means save some (9.19–22).

Nils Lund has ably analysed the careful, chiastic structure of the passage.[1] Commentators never tire of extolling the nobility of the sentiments expressed here. But the practical purpose of the passage usually
goes unnoticed. Moffatt, while speaking with admiration of Paul's
"high principle of accomodation", notes that the principle may be
"readily caricatured", and that "suspicious people probably thought
and said that no one knew where Paul was".[2] To put it more directly,
the passage seems intended by Paul as a defence against the charge of
inconsistency. Like the lyric chapter 13 analysed above,[3] the main
elements of this passage arise directly from Paul's immediate situation.
Paul's insistence that a single policy guided his diverse actions clearly
implies that some have accused him of being without a single, consistent policy. The principal issue here seems to involve Judaism and the
law. Just what aspect of the law Paul had in mind may be surmised
from the connection of this chapter with 8.13 and from Paul's angry
question, "Do we not have the right to eat and drink?" (9.4). Thus it
seems probable that the Corinthians have criticized Paul for being
indifferent to the dangers of eating idol meat at some times, and at
other times forbidding its use.

There is additional evidence to support this conclusion. Although
many scholars have noted the similarity of 1 Cor. 8.7–13 and 10.28, 29,
sections which both express concern for the (hypothetical) weaker
brother,[4] the full extent of this similarity does not seem to have been
noticed. Closer comparison reveals that the whole of 1 Cor. 10.23—
11.1 is a point by point restatement and summary of the argument of
1 Cor. 8 and 9.[5] The parallel points are as follows:

[1] *Chiasmus*, p. 147.
[2] *1 Cor.*, pp. 123–4. To the same effect but in much greater detail see the excellent article
by Henry Chadwick, " 'All Things to All Men' (I Cor. ix.22)," *NTS*, I (1954/55), 261–75.
He sees the same type of criticism reflected in Gal. 1.10; 5.11; and 2 Cor. 1.13–24; 5.11.
[3] See pp. 112–13.
[4] So, e.g., Schmiedel, "Corr.," p. 123; J. Weiss, *1 Cor.*, p. 263 ("Schon der erste Satz
versetzt uns in die Atmosphäre des 8. Kapitels; das Leitmotiv ist nicht die Gefahr der
Anteilnahme an heidn. Mahlen, sondern die liebevolle Rücksicht auf andre."); Goudge,
1 Cor., p. 91; Moffatt, *1 Cor.*, p. 144 ("The argument is substantially the same as in viii.
7–13."); Héring, *1 Cor.*, p. 98 (with a reference to J. Weiss); Craig, "1 Cor.," p. 117; and
C. S. C. Williams, "Corr.," §837f. Those scholars who partition 1 Corinthians (see Table 4
above) presume a close similarity in the points of view of 8.1–13 and 10.23—11.1.
[5] That the pattern of Paul's argument on this point was an important part of his ethical
thought is shown by the repetition of this argument in Rom. 14.2—15.2.

1 Cor. 8–9

(8.1) "All of us possess knowledge." "Knowledge" puffs up, but love builds up (οἰκοδομεῖ).

(8.3) If anyone loves, he has reached knowledge.[1]

(8.4) Hence as to the eating of food offered to idols, we know that "an idol has no existence".

(8.6) For us there is one God, the Father, from whom are all things and for whom we exist.

(8.8) Food will not commend us to God. We are no worse off if we do not eat, and no better off if we do.

(8.10) For if anyone sees you, a man of knowledge, at table in an idol's temple, might he not be encouraged, if his conscience is weak, to eat food offered to idols?

(8.13) I will never eat meat, lest I cause my brother to fall.

(9.1) Am I not free (ἐλεύθερος)? Am I not an apostle?

(9.3, 4) This is my defense to those who would examine me. Do we not have the right to eat and drink?

1 Cor. 10.23—11.1

(10.23) "All things are lawful," . . . but not all things build up (οἰκοδομεῖ).

(10.24) Let no one seek his own good, but the good of his neighbor.

(10.25) Eat whatever is sold in the market without raising any question on the ground of conscience.

(10.26) For "the earth is the Lord's, and everything in it."

(10.27) If anyone invites you to dinner and you are disposed to go, eat whatever is set before you without raising any question on the ground of conscience.[2]

(10.28) But if some one says to you, "This has been offered in sacrifice", then out of consideration for the man who informed you, and for conscience' sake

do not eat it.
(10.29) I mean his conscience, not yours.

For why should my freedom (ἐλευθερία) be determined by another man's scruples?

(10.30) If I partake with thankfulness, why am I denounced because of that for which I give thanks?

---

[1] P⁴⁶ omits τὸν θεόν and ὑπ' αὐτοῦ as does Clement. The latter phrase is also omitted by ℵ* and 33. In spite of Kümmel's suggestion (in Lietzmann, *Corr.*, p. 179) that the shorter text is the result of attraction to the form of 8.2, Zuntz's support of the shorter text seems preferable (*Text*, pp. 31–2). Zuntz's discussion is based on Reitzenstein, *Die hellenistischen Mysterienreligionen*, pp. 299–300.

[2] The parallelism between 10.27–29a and 8.8–13 means that we should probably reject the suggestion of the following scholars that 10.27 refers to an invitation to a pagan home in contrast to participation in meals at a pagan temple (8.10 and perhaps 10.19–21): Schmiedel, "Corr.," p. 124; Findlay, "1 Cor.," pp. 867–8; Robertson and Plummer, *1 Cor.*, p. 219; Bousset, "1 Cor.," pp. 126–7; Evans, *Corr.*, p. 102; Allo, *1 Cor.*, p. 247 (firmly); Héring, *1 Cor.*, p. 98; Craig, "1 Cor.," p. 117; Wendland, *Corr.*, p. 75; Morris, *1 Cor.*, p. 149. Instead we should adopt the position that the invitation in question may well be similar to those extended in P. Oxy. I, 110 and III, 523, to dine "at the table of the lord Saraphis". So Lietzmann, *Corr.*, p. 49; Deissmann, *Light from the Ancient East*, p. 351, n. 2; and Hans von Soden, "Sakrament und Ethik," p. 268, n. 42.

1 Cor. 8–9	*1 Cor. 10.23—11.1*
(9.19–23) I do it all for the sake of the gospel . . .	(10.31) So, whether you eat or drink, or whatever you do, do all to the glory of God.
(9.20) To the Jews I became as a Jew . . .	(10.32) Give no offense to Jews
(9.21) To those outside the law I became as one outside the law . . .	or to Greeks
(9.22) To the weak I became weak . . .	or to the church of God,[1]
I have become all things to all men, that I might by all means save some.	(10.33) just as I try to please all men in everything I do, not seeking my own advantage, but that of many, that they may be saved.
(9.26, 27) I do not run aimlessly, I do not box as one beating air, but I pommel my body and subdue it. . . .	(11.1) Be imitators of me as I am of Christ.

The parallelism of these two passages and, in particular, of 9.3, 4 with 10.30 is strong evidence (i) for the continuity of thought between 1 Cor. 8 and 9, and (ii) for understanding 9.3, 4 ("Do we not have the right to eat and drink?") in the light of 10.30 ("Why am I denounced because of that for which I give thanks?"). Thus the clear implication of these three chapters is that Paul believed that he had been "denounced" for having eaten meat offered to idols.[2] If, as seems probable,

---

[1] Cf. 1 Cor. 1.27 ("God chose what is weak in the world to shame the strong").

[2] Among the commentators who have been cited in this chapter none suggests that 10.29, 30 is Paul's defence against an actual criticism. But the interpretations which they have proposed are not particularly satisfactory. As Héring says, a sea of ink has been spilled concerning these two verses (*1 Cor.*, p. 99, n. 52). Schmiedel, "Corr.," p. 125; and J. Weiss, *1 Cor.*, pp. 265–6, cite and adopt the suggestion of Hitzig, *Monatsschrift des wissenschaftlichen Vereins in Zürich*, I (1856), 66, that the verses are a gloss to v. 27. Wendland, *Corr.*, p. 75, says at the onset, "Schwer verständlich sind nun die beiden . . . Fragen." Lietzmann, *Corr.*, p. 52, suggests that Paul is raising hypothetical or rhetorical questions from the point of view of the "strong" party in the manner of a diatribe. So also Grosheide, *1 Cor.*, p. 243; Craig, "1 Cor.," pp. 120–1; and Wendland, *Corr.*, p. 75. Bousset, "1 Cor.," p. 127; and Héring, *1 Cor.*, p. 99, consider these questions to be directed by Paul at the "weak" party to limit their claims. Evans, *Corr.*, pp. 110–11, and the RSV treat 10.28, 29a as a parenthesis so that 10.29b, 30 is made to continue the "strong" provisions of 10.25–7. The above commentators, although they do not refer these verses to a concrete situation, and although they do not cite 9.1–4 as a parallel, at least understand the questions in 10.29b, 30 to express a "strong" position. We have argued that Paul was attempting to defend his own liberal behaviour in the past, while at the same time trying to persuade the Corinthians to avoid idol meat.

Many scholars, however, in a somewhat strained effort to make the questions in 10.29b, 30 continue the theme of consideration for the weak in 10.28, 29a invert the sense and interpret as follows: "Why should I act in such a way that my liberty will be con-

Paul's conduct was inconsistent to the extent that at certain times he had eaten idol meat, then

(i) The defensive tone of 1 Cor. 9 is entirely understandable.

(ii) Paul's statement in 9.21 becomes particularly apposite: "To those outside the law I became as one outside the law—not being without law toward God but under the law of Christ—that I might win those outside the law."

(iii) The difficulty of Paul's situation appears. He had to argue, in part, against his own practice. He could not, therefore, argue against idol meat on the level of absolute principle without condemning some aspects of his own past behaviour. Even his appeal for concern toward the "weaker brother" left him open to the charge of having been previously unconcerned for such a person. It is surely significant that each of Paul's expositions of the "weaker brother" argument (8.7–12 and 10.24, 28–29a) is followed by a vigorous self-defence (8.13—9.27 and 10.29b—11.1).

We conclude, therefore, that Paul's own inconsistencies in this matter produced some sort of criticism from the Corinthians.

The comparison given above between 1 Cor. 8.1—9.27 and 10.23—11.1 goes a long way toward establishing the integral relationship of these passages. But this comparison does not include 10.1–22, which is the focus of attacks on the integrity of 1 Corinthians. Therefore, before we can complete the reconstruction of the Corinthians' questions on the subject of idol meat, we must now discuss the problem of the literary integrity of 1 Cor. 8.1—11.1.

4. *The integrity of 1 Cor. 8.1—11.1*

As Table 4 and its explanation in Chapter 2 indicate, theories for the partition of 1 Corinthians are primarily based on the separation of 10.1–22(23) from its context. In this section Paul's arguments against eating idol meat appear somewhat different from the arguments used by him in 8.1–13 and 10.23—11.1. Hans von Soden in his article, "Sakrament und Ethik bei Paulus", gives a convenient summary of those differences between 10.1–22 (which he labels "B") and 8.1–13 ("A") plus 10.23–33 ("C"), which scholars have used to separate "B" from "AC", placing "B" in an earlier, stricter letter:[1]

demned by another's conscience? Why should I put myself in the false position of saying grace over meat for the eating of which I shall be denounced?" So Findlay, "1 Cor.," pp. 868–9; Robertson and Plummer, *1 Cor.*, pp. 222–3; Allo, *1 Cor.*, pp. 249–51; Bachmann, *1 Cor.*, p. 343; and Morris, *1 Cor.*, p. 150 (with a reference to Godet, *1 Cor.*, II, 98–9).

[1] "Sakrament und Ethik," pp. 254–5.

(*a*) In "AC" Paul accepts the arguments of the strong party and deals with these Corinthians on their own terms, urging love for the weaker party but not an acceptance of its scruples. In "B", however, Paul accepts the arguments of the weaker party including their proofs from scripture.

(*b*) In "AC" the act of eating or of abstinence is in itself a matter of indifference (8.8; 10.26), but in "B" eating at the table of demons is held to be an impossibility for a Christian.

(*c*) In "AC" the argument takes place on a high ethical plane in terms of συνείδησις, with all superstition rejected (8.4–6), but in "B" a superstitious belief in demons forms the basis for the argument, together with a magical, automatic concept of the sacrament of the Lord's Supper.

Concerning all these differences it should be noted first of all that the scholars who subdivide 1 Corinthians consider the discrepancies between "AC" and "B" great enough to show that "B" was not written at the same time as "AC", but small enough to allow "B" to have been written by the same author, to the same group, and on the same topic as "AC". These scholars allow Paul to be inconsistent with himself concerning the Corinthians' use of idol meat from one letter to the next, but they do not allow this inconsistency in the course of a single letter. This distinction is, therefore, possible but somewhat subtle. Against it must be balanced the fact that there is no hint either in the evidence of the manuscripts or in the patristic literature that 1 Corinthians ever circulated in any arrangement except the one which is traditional. By contrast, for example, the last chapters of Romans invite theories of compilation, because different manuscripts give different sequences of material. But the same cannot be said of 1 Corinthians. Thus any compilation theory for this letter must bear a substantial burden of proof. It is a real question, however, whether the simple expectation that Paul should have been more consistent over the issue of idol meat is sufficient to bear this burden. Moreover, it may be that the inconsistencies have been somewhat magnified by scholars. Let us examine each of these inconsistencies or differences in turn.

(*a*) *Different premises?* Since we have concluded that there is no evidence to support the theory of the existence of two groups in Corinth at odds with each other over the question of idol meat, the first inconsistency listed above must be restated. In "AC", we may say, Paul appears to accept the premises of the wise Corinthians; in "B" he appears to accept premises and a proof-text manner of argument which seem Jewish or Jewish-Christian. With respect to "AC", however, we have already argued that Paul's acceptance here of the Corinthians' position as represented by their slogans was neither complete nor wholehearted. True he did not flatly reject their principles. But neither did he commend them. Rather he set aside the complicated problem of the exact sense in which these slogans were acceptable and attacked on the ground of Christian love the conclusions which the Corinthians had reached. Thus the extent of Paul's own acceptance of the Corinthians' assumptions should not be overestimated on the basis of these passages.

On the other hand, the Jewishness of Paul's argument in "B" can also be easily exaggerated. Those scholars who have made a special study of Paul's use of the Old Testament do not suggest that 1 Cor. 10.1–22 is somehow non-Pauline in its treatment of the Old Testament.[1] Actually, one may suspect, it is not the manner of Paul's use of the Old Testament which causes some scholars to partition these chapters; it is the present position of these references which makes them seem awkward and superfluous. Paul, having used the "weaker brother" argument which appeals powerfully to many modern Christians, then resorted to proofs from scripture which seem less satisfactory to moderns. Yet, as Hans von Soden has pointed out, precisely the same double argument is found in Rom. 14—15.[2] The argument concerning the "weaker brother" appears in Rom. 14 with striking similarities in language to 1 Cor. 8.7–13. Thus, for example, Paul wrote to the Romans,

> If your brother is being injured by what you eat, you are no longer walking in love. Do not let what you eat cause the ruin of one for whom Christ died. . . . It is right not to eat meat or drink wine or do anything that makes your brother stumble (14.15, 21).

Then in Romans Paul justified this concern for the weak with a quotation of Psalm 69.9 (in Rom. 15.3), explaining that

> Whatever was written in former days was written for our instruction, that by steadfastness and by encouragement of the scriptures we might have hope (15.4).

In exactly the same manner Paul turned from his discussion of the

---

[1] E.g., Joseph Bonsirven, *Exégèse Rabbinique et Exégèse Paulinienne* ("Bibliothèque de Théologie Historique"; Paris: Beauchesne et ses fils, 1939); W. D. Davies, *Paul and Rabbinic Judaism*; and E. Earle Ellis, *Paul's Use of the Old Testament* (Grand Rapids, Mich.: Wm. B. Eerdmans Publishing Company, 1957).

[2] "Sakrament und Ethik," p. 257.

"weaker brother" in 1 Corinthians (8.7–13) to make quotations from Exodus and Numbers (in 1 Cor. 10.1–10), adding as in the letter to the Romans:

> These things are warnings (τύποι) for us (10.6).
>
> These things happened to them as a warning (τυπικῶς) and they were written for our instruction upon whom the end of the ages has come (10.11).

Moreover, the same eschatological note is sounded here as in Rom. 15.4 above. Thus the parallelism between these two letters removes any force from the argument that Paul would not have resorted to proof texts (in "B") after his lofty appeal for love toward weaker Christians (in "A").

Principally, however, it is Paul's references to demons represented by idols (in "B") which are held to be inconsistent with the statement (in "A"), "an idol has no real existence" (8.4). The former is considered a Jewish theory; the latter, an enlightened Gentile conviction. Actually both theories (as well as several others) were current in Judaism.[1] Probably there was as little consciousness of the inconsistency between the two as is shown, for example, by the Synoptic Gospels concerning the two theories of disease: sickness considered the result of sin or of demon possession. We have already argued for the probability, however, that the above slogan (8.4) is a quotation from the Corinthians' letter. Furthermore, as a number of scholars have seen, Paul qualified the Corinthians' statement in a manner which is wholly consistent with his discussion of demons in 10.19–21.[2] Thus Paul's mention of various "gods" and "lords" in 8.5 may be considered a preparation for his argument in "B". Conversely his rhetorical question in 10.19 ("What do I imply then . . . that an idol is anything?") may well be an indication that he was consciously attempting to avoid contradicting his statement (in "A") that "for us there is one God, the Father" (8.6).[3] Thus on this point "A" and "B" are not only consistent, but also give signs of being mutually informed, and thus of having been composed on a single occasion.

(b) *Different conclusions?* Is it true that Paul concluded in "AC" that

[1] See Paul Billerbeck, *Die Briefe des Neuen Testaments und die Offenbarung Johannis erläutert aus Talmud und Midrasch*, Vol. III of *Kommentar zum Neuen Testament aus Talmud und Midrasch* by Hermann L. Strack and Paul Billerbeck (München: C. H. Beck'sche Verlagsbuchhandlung, 1926), pp. 48–60.

[2] So, e.g., Schmiedel, "Corr.," pp. 110, 123; Robertson and Plummer, *1 Cor.*, p. 167; Moffatt, *1 Cor.*, p. 106; Lietzmann, *Corr.*, p. 37 (commenting on 8.5 he said, "Die tatsächliche Existenz von Dämonen setzt Pls auch 10.18ff. voraus."); Hans von Soden, "Sakrament und Ethik," p. 241; and Wendland, *Corr.*, p. 60.

[3] So Hans von Soden, "Sakrament und Ethik," pp. 246–7, 257.

eating idol meat was a matter of indifference, but in "B" that such an act was an impossibility for a Christian? It is doubtful whether this position can be defended. As von Soden pointed out, in both "AC" and "B" the simple act of eating is a matter of indifference (8.8; 10.19).[1] In "AC" it is the kind of eating which destroys fellowship with a brother Christian (and endangers his fellowship with God) which is forbidden; in "B" it is eating which establishes fellowship with demons (10.20) and thereby destroys fellowship with God (10.21) which Paul attacked. Idolatry and disregard for the "brother for whom Christ died" (8.11) are co-ordinate sins against God (8.12; 10.22). On this point as on the previous, therefore, not only are Paul's arguments consonant, but to a certain extent they complement one another.

(c) *Different world views?* The third difference listed above is really a double objection: section "B" is alleged to show Paul's superstitious belief (i) in demons, by contrast to his enlightened statements in 8.4–6 and 10.26, and (ii) in a magical view of sacraments, by contrast to his thoughts on this subject elsewhere in 1 Corinthians. We have already dealt with (i) above. To meet the second half of the objection (ii) von Soden argues that in "B" Paul presents a sacrament as powerfully effective, not, however, *ex opere operato*, but *ex opere operantis*.[2] It is not the meat by and of itself, but the idolatrous eating of it which effectually produces fellowship with demons: "Für Paulus ist das Sakrament Pflichtzeichen, mit Zwingli zu reden, aber freilich nicht im Sinn eines Symbols, sondern einer dynamischen Realität, die jedoch nicht mechanisch, sondern kritisch wirksam ist. . . . Es bindet den Menschen an Gott, aber nicht Gott an den Menschen."[3]

Having argued that the view of sacraments in "B" is not as magical as some have supposed, von Soden, however, does not discuss the sacramental theology expressed in other sections of 1 Corinthians. There are three related passages: (i) 11.29, 30; (ii) 15.29; and (iii) 5.1–5.

(i) The first passage is a comment on the abuse of the Lord's Supper:

> For any one who eats and drinks without discerning the body eats and drinks judgment upon himself. That is why many of you are weak and ill, and some have died (11.29, 30).

A number of commentators assume that Paul believed that God was directly responsible for the sickness and death of the Corinthians in question.[4] These commentators give no other cause for the Corinthians'

---

[1] Ibid., pp. 262–6.   [2] Ibid., p. 259.   [3] Ibid., p. 260.
[4] So, e.g., Goudge, *1 Cor.*, p. 102; Parry, *1 Cor.* ("Camb."), p. 125; Moffatt, *1 Cor.*, pp. 173–4; Evans, *Corr.*, p. 124; Grosheide, *1 Cor.*, p. 275; and Simon, *1 Cor.*, pp. 119–20.

misfortunes. But the view of some other scholars is defensible and perhaps preferable. They attribute the immediate cause of this sickness and death to the power of the sacrament itself. Thus Allo maintains that these verses show Paul's belief in the "Présence Réelle" which explains the "réalisme terrible" of Paul's description of the results following the improper reception of the sacrament.[1] Without, of course, subscribing to the doctrine of the Mass, Lietzmann bluntly says, "v. 30 zeigt die Realität der Vorstellung: das φάρμακον ἀθανασίας (Ignatius Eph. 20, 2) wird bei unwürdigem Gebrauch zum φάρμακον θανάτου".[2] Thus here in 1 Cor. 11 may be a view of the sacraments which is more magical than von Soden allows in "B"! Since, however, the commentators who separate "B" from "AC" generally place 1 Cor. 11.2–34 at the time of "B", it is necessary for us to examine the other two passages cited above, which are almost without exception placed at least as late as the letter containing "AC".[3]

(ii) Paul's reference to persons who are "baptized on behalf of the dead" (15.29) has occasioned numerous conjectures. Bernard M. Foschini in a series of articles surveying the problem lists more than forty different classes of proposed solutions.[4] The most common opinion among critical scholars is that Paul was referring to the practice of vicarious baptism on behalf of dead persons. Bultmann is but one representative of this opinion:

> It is clear that in earliest Christianity the sacrament was by no means a symbol, but a miracle-working rite—most strikingly shown for the sacrament of the Eucharist in 1 Cor. 11.29ff . . . and for baptism in 1 Cor. 15.29. When people have themselves baptized for the dead, as they did in Corinth— i.e., when their intention is to have the supernatural powers that the sacrament bestows made effective for the dead—then no distinction is made between the sacrament and a magical act. . . . It is significant that Paul mentions the custom without any criticism whatever; for the mode of thought behind it is precisely his own.[5]

Some scholars agree with all but the last point. They suggest that Paul's argument was *ad hominem* and that he himself did not approve of

---

[1] *1 Cor.*, pp. 282–3. Allo is quoted with approval (on the latter point) by Héring, *1 Cor.*, p. 120.

[2] *Corr.*, p. 59.

[3] See Table 4, p. 45.

[4] " 'Those who are baptized for the Dead.' I Cor. 15:29," *The Catholic Biblical Quarterly*, XII (1950), 260–76, 379–88; XIII (1951), 46–78, 172–98, and 276–83.

[5] *Theology of the N. T.*, I, 135–6. So also Bousset, "1 Cor.," pp. 157–8; J. Weiss, *1 Cor.*, p. 363; Schweitzer, *Mysticism of Paul*, pp. 283–6; Moffatt, *1 Cor.*, pp. 252–3; Lietzmann, *Corr.*, p. 82; and Schoeps, *Paul*, pp. 113–14.

the practice.[1] But there is no hint in the context that such is the case. Moreover, as Bultmann notes, the sacramental theology expressed by this passage with respect to baptism corresponds with the point of view of 1 Cor. 11.29, 30 concerning the Eucharist. Thus it is a precarious procedure to date "B" on the basis of its view of sacraments.

(iii) A third passage combines the points of view of the two passages already mentioned. In 1 Cor. 5.1–5 Paul pronounced a solemn judgement upon the incestuous man and directed the Corinthians: "You are to deliver this man to Satan for the destruction of the flesh, that his spirit may be saved in the day of the Lord Jesus" (5.5). In the light of 1 Cor. 11.29, 30 it appears that Paul expected that exclusion from the Eucharist would produce the sickness and death of the man in question. Why then should his spirit be "saved in the day of the Lord Jesus"? Certainly not because of his Christian manner of life. There is no hint that he had some hidden faith not represented in his behaviour which would save him. Apparently we meet here as in 1 Cor. 15.29 the opinion that baptism in and of itself produces salvation. He had been baptized; he would be saved. Exclusion from the Lord's Supper would not only save the Church from contamination, but would also result in the destruction of this man's flesh and thus put an end to his immorality.

These three passages then harmonize with one another and with "B" in a way which makes it unlikely that "B" can be considered to exhibit a sacramental theology more magical and more primitive than that found in Paul's later correspondence with the Corinthians. We shall return to Paul's views on baptism and the Eucharist when we discuss his original preaching in Corinth (in Chapter 8). But it is not hard now to set aside the last alleged difference between "AC" and "B".

---

[1] Thus, e.g., Parry, 1 Cor. ("Camb."), p. 175 ("The plain and necessary sense of the words implies the existence of a practice of vicarious baptism at Corinth. . . . Many attempts have been made to evade this conclusion, . . . but all at the cost of violence to the language: and all due to the unwillingness to admit such a practice; and still more such a reference to it without condemnation. . . . It is to be observed, however, that S. Paul expresses no view as to the propriety of the custom. . . . He is using an *argumentum ad hominem*."); William Frederick Flemington, *The New Testament Doctrine of Baptism* (London: S. P. C. K., 1948), p. 55; Craig, "1 Cor.," pp. 240–1; Morris, 1 Cor., pp. 218–19; Wendland, *Corr.*, pp. 130–1; C. S. C. Williams, "Corr.," §841j; F. C. Grant, *N. T.*, p. 106; and George Raymond Beasley-Murray, *Baptism in the New Testament* (London: Macmillan & Co Ltd, 1962), pp. 190–2. Beasley-Murray's approach is revealing. In presenting Paul's views on baptism he begins with a passage each from Romans and Galatians, then three from Colossians, before turning to 1 Corinthians. He then denies that Paul would have originated the practice of baptism for the dead, because Paul's other "baptismal utterances are permeated with the spiritual and ethical religion that we have observed in the foregoing pages" (p. 190). This harmonizing use of Paul's letters was discussed in Chapter 1, p. 5.

(d) *The lectionary argument.* To the above three arguments which lie in the area discussed by von Soden we may add a fourth, one which does not seem to have been previously applied to the problem of the integrity of 1 Cor. 8—10. A considerable number of scholars have suggested that the imagery of 1 Cor. 5.6b–8 is doubly significant:

> Do you know that a little leaven ferments the whole lump of dough? Cleanse out the old leaven that you may be fresh dough, as you really are unleavened. For Christ, our paschal lamb ($\tau\grave{o}$ $\pi\acute{a}\sigma\chi a$ $\grave{\eta}\mu\hat{\omega}\nu$), has been sacrificed. Let us, therefore, celebrate the festival, not with the old leaven, the leaven of malice and evil, but with the unleavened bread of sincerity and truth.

Clearly the metaphor of the leaven was appropriate to Paul's purpose in writing to condemn the influence of the immoral man of 1 Cor. 5.1. But it may also be that the particular imagery of this passage was suggested to him by the theme of the season of the year at which he wrote. The time of year for the composition of 1 Corinthians is suggested by 16.8, "I will stay in Ephesus until Pentecost". Strictly speaking this last statement could have been written at any time during the year, but Paul's threat in 4.19 ("I will come to you soon . . .") indicates that his anticipated trip to Corinth lay in the not too distant future.[1] Moreover, when Paul wrote 1 Corinthians Timothy had been, or was at the moment being, dispatched to Corinth: $\check{\epsilon}\pi\epsilon\mu\psi a$ $\grave{\upsilon}\mu\hat{\iota}\nu$ $T\iota\mu\acute{o}\theta\epsilon o\nu$ (the time depending on whether the verb is understood as a simple aorist or an epistolary aorist). Yet Paul expected his letter to arrive in Corinth before Timothy, as 16.10 indicates: "*If* Timothy should come, see that you put him at ease among you. . . ." The "if" (with the subjunctive verb) shows that the letter was not entrusted to Timothy, and that Paul was not sure whether Timothy would reach Corinth or not.[2] Corinth, therefore, was not Timothy's principal destination. This fact suggests that Timothy had travelled north from Ephesus to visit the Churches in Macedonia, and that the letter was to travel a faster route. It is possible, of course, that the bearers of the letter planned to use the overland route but did not intend to visit along the way. It is more probable, however, that the faster route was a shorter route, namely

---

[1] Cf. also 11.34, which implies that Paul planned to visit Corinth soon enough that "the other things", which he believed to be important enough for him to deal with, could wait until he arrived.

[2] The "when Timothy comes" of the RSV is misleading. Héring comments: " 'Ean' = 'if' (conditional) instead of 'hotan' = 'when' (temporal) is surprising. He may not be quite sure that Timothy will travel as far as Corinth" (*1 Cor.*, p. 184).

the route by sea.[1] If this was in fact the case, then presumably the winter storms were by this time over and the direct sea route from Asia to Corinth once again safe.[2] Thus the probability is that 1 Corinthians was written a month or two before Pentecost, or about the time of Passover. Therefore, whether or not the Corinthians were themselves celebrating a Christian Passover, the theme of 1 Cor. 5.6–8 may well have been suggested to Paul by the season.[3]

Archbishop Carrington, however, goes beyond a consideration simply of this passage and of 16.8 when he says,

> I Corinthians is a Paschal letter, a fact which is made particularly clear in its use [in 1 Cor. 10.1–10] of Exodus-Numbers, or, more likely, a "midrash" upon it. . . . These events of the Exodus formed the historical background of the seven weeks from Pascha to Pentecost. . . . The rich liturgical material of the Corinthian epistles . . . makes it perfectly evident that a Christianized form of the Hebrew Calendar was even then in existence.[4]

Carrington's hypothesis has been subjected to careful analysis by W. D. Davies, who says of it,

> Paschal imagery does invade 1 Corinthians, and so too 2 Corinthians may well reflect Pentecostal and Tabernacle motifs, as Carrington and T. W. Manson have affirmed. . . . But it is quite another thing to ascribe to such imagery as we have referred to any strictly calendrical intention. Thus to take 1 Cor. 5:7 as implying a deliberate calendrical adherence to the Jewish Passover in a new Christian dress is to press the imagery too far. . . . Again

[1] So Zahn, *Intro. N. T.*, I, 259; and Héring, *1 Cor.*, p. 184 ("Paul's letter was naturally to go by the shortest route and to arrive in Corinth before Timothy."). For a map of the Aegean area see above, p. xiv.
[2] On the difficulties of winter travel by ship in this period see J. Rouge, "La Navigation hivernale sous l'Empire Romain," *Revue des Études Anciennes*, LIV (1952), 316–25; Manson, *Studies*, p. 225; and Otto Michel, *Der Brief an die Römer* ("Meyer," 4. Abt., 12. Aufl.; Göttingen: Vandenhoeck & Ruprecht, 1963), p. 1, n. 4.
[3] So John David Michaelis, *Introduction to the New Testament*, trans. and ed. from the 4th German ed. of 1788 by Herbert Marsh (6 vols.; Cambridge: John Burges, Printer to the University, 1801), IV, 42; Paley, *Horae Paulinae*, Ch. 3, sec. 12; Conybeare and Howson, *St. Paul*, II, 33, n. 1; H. A. W. Meyer, *Corr.*, I, 152; Schmiedel, "Corr.," p. 93; Lightfoot, *Notes*, p. 206; J. Weiss, *1 Cor.*, p. 137; Findlay, "1 Cor.," p. 811; Robertson and Plummer, *1 Cor.*, p. 102; Zahn, *Intro. N. T.*, I, 260; Smith, *St. Paul*, p. 654; W. L. Knox, *Jerusalem*, pp. 316; 327, n. 33; Oskar Holtzmann, *Das Neue Testament nacht dem Stuttgarter Griechischen Text übersetzt und erklärt* (2 Bde.; Giessen: A. Töpelmann, 1926), p. 570; Evans, *Corr.*, p. 85 ("possibly"); Allo, *1 Cor.*, pp. 125–7; Bachmann, *1 Cor.*, pp. 217–18; Moffatt, *1 Cor.*, p. 58; T. W. Manson, "*ΙΛΑϹΤΗΡΙΟΝ*," *JTS*, XLVI (1945), 8–9; Craig, "1 Cor.," p. 64 ("probably"); Osty, *Corr.*, p. 35 ("possible"); Simon, *1 Cor.*, p. 80; and F. C. Grant, *N. T.*, p. 77.
[4] *Primitive Calendar*, pp. 42–3. The connection between the Corinthian letters and such a midrash was earlier proposed in his *The Primitive Christian Catechism: A Study in the Epistles* (Cambridge: The University Press, 1940), pp. 6; 61, n. 2. Carrington restated his position in his *Early Christian Church*, I, 137, and with comments in response to his principal critic, W. D. Davies, in *According to Mark: A Running Commentary on the Oldest Gospel* (Cambridge: The University Press, 1960), pp. 1–29.

... the Pentecostal imagery in 2 Cor. 1–5 must not too certainly be taken to indicate the Pentecostal dating of that section.[1]

Evidence, however, for a special connection between 1 Corinthians and the Passover season is provided by Davies' own book, *Paul and Rabbinic Judaism*. Here, he says sweepingly, "It is highly significant that in *several places in the Epistles*, once explicitly and elsewhere by implication, the Apostle compares the Christian life to the Passover Festival."[2] But the examples which he cites to support this statement all come from 1 Corinthians: (i) 1 Cor. 5.6–8; (ii) 1 Cor. 10.1–5; and (iii) 1 Cor. 15.20.[3] Moreover, it is important to notice that these three passages appear to be completely independent of one another. The first (i) is the explicit reference mentioned by Davies: "Christ, our paschal lamb, has been sacrificed." The second (ii) is a midrashic retelling of certain events in Exodus 13—32 and Numbers 11—25. The third (iii) is a single word, "firstfruits" (ἀπαρχή). Since there is no reason to suppose that any one of these allusions would have suggested either of the others, it may well be that Davies underestimates the calendrical significance of these references.

In addition, Davies' rejection of Carrington's suggestions is weakened by his exaggeration of Carrington's claims. He apparently assumes that Carrington holds that the *Corinthians* were actually using a more or less full lectionary system based on what Carrington called "a Christianized form of the Hebrew calendar". This assumption lies behind his rejection of Carrington's interpretation of 1 Cor. 5.7 in the passage quoted above, especially in the phrases, "strictly calendrical intention" and "deliberate calendrical adherence". His use of the words "intention" and "deliberate" implies that he takes Carrington to mean that the Corinthians would have recognized Paul's imagery as calendrical, and thus that the Corinthians were using a liturgical lectionary themselves. This assumption appears even more clearly in his comments on Carrington's treatment[4] of 1 Cor. 15.1–5 and 11.23:

> 1 Cor. 15:1–5 and 1 Cor. 11:23 are not strictly concerned with lections as such. The first, 1 Cor. 15:1–5, presents the Gospel in what is probably a kind of "credal" summary of it; 1 Cor. 11:26 refers to the *recital* not the reading of the Passion narrative. . . . Carrington goes too far in thinking of the recital in

---

[1] "Reflections on Archbishop Carrington's 'The Primitive Christian Calendar' ", chap. iv of his *Christian Origins and Judaism*, p. 75.

[2] Pp. 104–5, emphasis added.

[3] A fourth passage which Davies lists in the same group, 2 Cor. 3.1–11, shows Pentecostal, not Paschal, imagery, as Davies himself says in the passage quoted above.

[4] *Primitive Calendar*, pp. 18–20.

lectionary terms. . . . Neither 1 Cor. 15:1–5 nor 1 Cor. 11:23f. can be urged as evidence for an early lectionary or for early lectionary units.[1]

But Carrington, for example, does not say that 1 Cor. 15.1–5 was a lection from an early Christian lectionary. He merely says that with such a passage, "we are in the realm of fixed oral documents of an authoritative character",[2] a statement which is exactly equivalent to saying that the passage is "a kind of 'credal' summary". Carrington nowhere claims that a lectionary was in use at Corinth. Instead he is contending that by the time Mark was written a lectionary could have developed from such short units of tradition as those with which Form Criticism deals, or analogous to those indicated in 1 Cor. 15.1–5 and 11.23. Carrington is, in fact, quite indefinite as to Paul's relationship to the lectionary tradition of Judaism and the extent to which the primitive Church had made use of it. Thus it does not appear that Davies' arguments have made improbable the conviction of Carrington (and other scholars) that Paul was influenced by the season of the year in the imagery which he used while writing 1 Corinthians.

It is important to notice what Carrington's view of 1 Cor. 10.1–5 implies. Both Carrington and Davies agree in pointing out the Paschal imagery of this passage, and Carrington considers this imagery to have calendrical significance. If after our analysis of Davies' objections we are allowed to take this imagery as a conscious or unconscious reflection of the time of year at which the passage was written, we have an additional argument in favour of the integrity of 1 Corinthians. If this passage was written at the same season of the year as 1 Cor. 5.6b–8; 15.20; and 16.8, then it is hard not to believe that they all were written in the same season of the same year, that is, on one occasion. None of the scholars whose partitions of 1 Corinthians were listed in Table 4 places 1 Cor. 10.1–22 and 1 Cor. 5.1—6.11 in the same letter. Yet both sections contain definite Paschal allusions, which are evidence of their simultaneous composition. These observations constitute a fourth line of argument favouring the integrity of 1 Corinthians.

Conclusion. Concerning the problem of the integrity or non-integrity of 1 Corinthians raised at the beginning of Chapter 2,[3] we can now say that our analysis of 1 Cor. 8.1—11.1 does not support a

---

[1] *Christian Origins and Judaism*, pp. 86–7.
[2] *Primitive Calendar*, p. 19. Carrington reiterated his point in *According to Mark*, pp. 15–16, with an apology for not making himself unmistakably clear.
[3] See pp. 43–7 above.

division of the letter. The same was true of our discussions of 1 Cor.
9.1–23[1] and of 6.12–20.[2] The only point still undiscussed is the problem
of the double occasion for 1 Corinthians. Part of 1 Corinthians was
written in answer to the Corinthians' letter; part in response to oral
reports concerning the Corinthians' conduct. Is it more probable that
each occasion produced a letter from Paul, or that the two sets of
information happened to reach Paul at the same time? We are now at
the point where we can assemble the pieces of the argument on this
issue. Our identification in Chapter 3 of the sections resulting from each
type of news indicates that these two types of material are now interwoven in 1 Corinthians.[3] But this interweaving is both subtle and
appropriate. 1 Cor. 5 contains a reference to the written correspondence
between Paul and Corinth at a point suggested by the disciplinary
problem under discussion; 1 Cor. 11 includes Paul's treatment of a
portion of his oral information in a context dealing with one of the
Corinthians' written questions on a similar subject. It is difficult to
believe that any editor could have taken a number of letter fragments,
perceived the type of information on which each was based, and pieced
them together to form the pattern which we have found in 1 Corinthians. It is also difficult to believe that an editor could have found a piece
(1 Cor. 6.12–20) with a special relationship to both types of his material,
noticed this fact, and thus produced such an appropriate transition
between the two. Finally, we should remember that, as we said when
the problem was first posed, any theory of compilation based solely on
internal evidence must bear the burden of proof. We believe that we
are now justified in setting aside the partition theories outlined in
Chapter 2. The somewhat slim evidence on which they are based is
more than counterbalanced by the evidence which ties the suspected
sections to the rest of 1 Corinthians. We can, therefore, return to the
problem at hand—the full formulation of the questions from Corinth
concerning idol meat.

5. The Questions behind 1 Cor. 10.1—11.1

1 Cor. 10.1–22. Having concluded that 1 Cor. 10.1–22 is an integral part
of Paul's treatment of the Corinthians' questions concerning idol meat,
we may consider the section as apparently a second and somewhat
stronger attempt by Paul to persuade them not to eat such meat. After
his appeal for consideration of the (hypothetical) "weaker brother",

[1] See pp. 70–1 and pp. 126–31 above.   [2] See pp. 86–9 above.
[3] See p. 93 above for an analytical outline of 1 Corinthians.

Paul portrayed for the benefit of the Corinthians the lurid punishments assigned in the Old Testament to those who worship idols (particularly the unfortunate twenty-three thousand mentioned in 1 Cor. 10.8). It is important to notice that Paul's condemnation of idolatry is equally as hypothetical as his argument concerning the "weaker brother". There is nothing in 10.1–22 to suggest either that Paul had heard of idolatrous worship by the Corinthians, or that they had specifically asked whether participation in pagan worship was permissible for Christians. Paul was against idolatry in the same way that he was against creating causes of offence for weaker Christians. In each case he fixed on an abuse of Christian freedom so obvious that the Corinthians would surely agree with him. In each case he sought to generalize the particular occasion on which idol meat should be avoided to include all occasions. In the first case the possibility of the presence of a newborn Christian which made it wiser, Paul argued, to avoid idol meat altogether. Thus Paul concluded, "If food is the cause of my brother's falling, I will *never* eat meat, lest I cause my brother to fall" (8.13). In the second case it is the terrible danger that God's well-known anger against idolatry might be aroused which makes it safer, according to Paul, to avoid any association with idol meat. Paul vehemently denounced the worship of idols and any act of ritual eating which might produce fellowship with demons. But he carefully did not specify whether the danger from demons attaches itself to the intention of the one who eats or to the actual meat wherever it is eaten. Thus he allowed the latter to be associated with the former. And he concluded (in 10.22) by demanding, "Shall we provoke the Lord to jealousy? Are we stronger than he?" The parallels between Paul's argument in 8.1–13 and that in 10.1–22 probably indicate that no new question from the Corinthians lay behind the latter section. The two passages were two similar attempts to dissuade the Corinthians from eating idol meat.

1 Cor. 10.23—11.1. The situation to which 1 Cor. 10.23—11.1 was directed seems more concrete than that of the preceding sections. Paul dealt here with two real problems concerning the relationship between the Corinthian Church and the world.

(i) It appears to be a fact that much, and perhaps most, of the meat offered for sale in the meat market (ἐν μακέλλῳ)[1] had been

---

[1] The gender and origin of this noun are disputed. Henry J. Cadbury, "The Macellum of Corinth," *JBL*, LIII (1934), 134–6, believes the word to be masculine and a Latin loan word. Arndt/Gingrich, p. 488, cites an early Greek occurrence of the word in the neuter. Moulton/Milligan, p. 368 (cited by Allo, *1 Cor.*, p. 246), refers to the Semitic root מכל.

offered to a deity at least by symbolic burning of a few hairs.[1]

[1] See, e.g., Lietzmann, *Corr.*, pp. 49–51, who devoted an excursus to "Kultmahle" in which he said (p. 49), "So soll auch der normale Fleischlieferant des Bürgers, der berufsmässigne Metzger, eigentlich verfahren: zum wenigsten wird er einige Stirnhaare des Tieres in die Flamme werfen—falls der Drang des gutgehenden Geschäftes ihn nicht diese Formalität übersehen heisst (vgl. Stengel Griech. Sakralaltertümer[3] 105ff., Wissowa Rel. u. Kult. d. Römer[2] S. 411.418)." This important statement was quoted by J. Weiss, 1 *Cor.*, p. 211, who added that 1 Cor. 10.27 implies that meat not offered to an idol could be found upon inquiry. Lietzmann also reproduced the ground plan of the macellum in Pompeii as evidence of the close connection between pagan worship (note the "chapel") and the sale of meat. Cadbury, however, doubts that such physical proximity was the rule elsewhere, although he points out that any market near the centre of a city of this period would be close to numerous temples ("Macellum," p. 141).
    When Cadbury wrote, a macellum at Corinth had not been identified. In 1937, however, Oscar Broneer published an article, "Studies in the Topography of Corinth at the Time of St. Paul," *ΑΡΧΑΙΟΛΟΓΙΚΗ ΕΦΗΜΕΡΙΣ*, CIV (1937), 125–33, in which he concluded: "There were probably more than one meat-market in Corinth in the second century A.D., when the city seems to have reached its greatest extent. However that may be, at the time of St. Paul's sojourn in Corinth the shops in the south half of the South Stoa were unquestionably used for the purpose usually designated by the term *macellum*" (p. 133). His conclusion was based on his interpretation of certain inscriptions, and the presence of inter-connecting wells which were used for cooling perishables. These wells are indicated on his plan by small circles in the centre of each of the shops in question. But, as his plan also indicates, most of the shops at the south-west end of the South Stoa had not been excavated when he wrote. Thus it is not surprising that subsequent work produced new evidence. In 1954 he had to say, "When the graffito was first discovered I suggested that the second line should be read as *Λάν[ι]ος*, a Greek transliteration of the Latin word *lanius*, butcher. . . . The incorrectness of my original reading was first pointed out by F. W. Householder. . . . The suggestion that the Stoa was used as a food market should in any case be discarded, since most of the wells had by that time been filled up and covered over" (Oscar Broneer, *The South Stoa and its Roman Successors*, Vol. I, Pt. 4 of *Corinth: Results of Excavations Conducted by the American School of Classical Studies at Athens* [Princeton, N. J.: The American School of Classical Studies, 1954], p. 101, n. 1). Broneer's colleague Robert L. Scranton, however, working on the "North Market" north of the archaic Apollo temple said, "The building was erected no later than the middle of the first century after Christ, and so far as the evidence now available is concerned, it could date from the first quarter of that century. . . . Its plan . . . is obviously similar to that of the Roman macellum as it appears . . . throughout the Roman world: a peristyle court surrounded by shops . . . [He also cites as an example the macellum of Pompeii.] The North Market, completely enclosed and off the line of monumental construction and the main highways and centres, but conveniently located nevertheless, would be well located for the purveyance of food stuffs" (Robert L. Scranton, *Monuments in the Lower Agora and North of the Archaic Temple*, Vol. I, Pt. 3 of *Corinth* [1951], pp. 191–3). Thus it may well be that this market was newly erected when Paul visited Corinth and that it is to this market (among others) that Paul referred in using the term "macellum".
    Other scholars who share Lietzmann's convictions about the symbolic sacrifice of a large portion of meat offered on the open market are Goudge, 1 *Cor.*, p. 69; Robertson and Plummer, 1 *Cor.*, p. 220 ("Probably a great deal of the meat offered for sale . . . came from the sacrifices, especially what was sold to the poor."); Lake, *Earlier Epistles*, pp. 198–9; R. St. John Parry, *The First Epistle of Paul the Apostle to the Corinthians* (2d ed.; "CambGk."; Cambridge: The University Press, 1926), p. 127 ("A sacrificial element was commonly present in all slaying of beasts for the market."); Deissmann, *Paul*, p. 72; Allo, 1 *Cor.*, p. 195 ("Une grande part des viandes de boucherie, surtout celles que pouvaient acheter les pauvres n'était que le déchet des victimes, ce que ne s'étaient pas réservé les dieux, le prêtres et les offrants."); Moffatt, 1 *Cor.*, p. 143 ("Such a store [i.e., macellum] offered for sale carcasses from an adjoining temple, which had been formally dedicated to a deity of the cults; as this meat was not only good but cheap, it was frequently bought even by poor folk."); Enslin, *Beginnings*, p. 251; Nock, *St. Paul*, pp. 180–1; Goodspeed, *Paul*, p. 120; Heard, *Intro. N. T.*, p. 190; Hans von Soden, "Sakrament und Ethik,"

(ii) Moreover, if idol meat were completely forbidden, table fellow-ship of the Corinthian Christians with their non-Christian neighbours would be almost impossible. Thus the Christians would have become a socially segregated group like the Jews.[1]

Clearly each of these problems represented an obstacle to Paul's attempt to persuade the Corinthians to avoid idol meat. It is certainly possible that Paul in writing 1 Corinthians anticipated the practical difficulties which his directions would produce, and that he discussed these problems ahead of time.[2] But it seems more likely that it was the Corinthians who had raised this double issue. On the one hand, it is not probable that Paul would have, in effect, argued against himself by suggesting these difficulties to the Corinthians. On the other hand, the Corinthians' questions as they are reflected in the preceding sections are all more or less objections to the point of view which would deny Christians the use of idol meat. Against such a position the following statements read naturally as protests:

(a) But we all possess knowledge.
(b) But an idol is nothing.
(c) But there is no God but one.
(d) But you yourself were accustomed to eat idol meat.

With these protests the following objections are entirely consonant:

(e) But most of the meat in the market can be called idol meat.
(f) But we shall be unable to eat with our non-Christian friends.

The probability that these last were objections originating from Corinth becomes a virtual certainty when it is remembered that this pair of difficulties reflects the normal, day-to-day life of the Gentile Christian. Thus it was not Paul, but the Corinthians, who by their letter posed the problem of the Christian use of idol meat. These twin issues cannot fail to have been raised by even the mere consideration of

p. 243 ("Nach antiker Sitte [war] jede Schlachtung mit einem Opfer verbunden."); Grosheide, 1 Cor., p. 240 ("Every animal that was killed was a sacrifice inasmuch as the butchers burnt at least a few hairs of every animal they slaughtered by way of a sacrifice to the gods."); Dibelius, Paul, p. 97; Craig, "1 Cor.," p. 118 ("Certainly most of the meat would have been sacrificed in a temple."); Barclay, Corr., p. 80; Morris, 1 Cor., p. 124; Osty, Corr., p. 43; and Simon, 1 Cor., p. 95.

[1] On the position of Jews see Lietzmann, Corr., p. 51 ("Dem Juden ist der Genuss von Fleisch aus dem Macellum verboten"). He refers also to Billerbeck, Kommentar, III, 420–1. In his book The Beginnings of the Christian Church, trans. B. L. Woolf (3d ed., rev.; London: Lutterworth Press, 1953), p. 139, Lietzmann says that to avoid idol meat Christians would have had either to patronize a Jewish slaughterer or to set up their own slaughterhouse.

[2] Thus as Héring says, "In practical terms the Apostle envisages two cases" (1 Cor., p. 98). So also, e.g., Findlay, "1 Cor.," p. 867 ("The above rule [v. 24] is now applied in the concrete."); Evans, Corr., p. 110; and Grosheide, 1 Cor., p. 240.

Loc

the avoidance of idol meat, and it is clear that the Corinthians have had at least this much contact with the subject.

To the above list of Corinthian objections should be added the slogan contained in 1 Cor. 10.23, "All things are lawful".[1] The reasons for considering this statement to be a quotation from the Corinthians' letter are largely the same as for the slogans in 1 Cor. 8.1 and 4, together with the fact that this slogan appears four times in 1 Corinthians (i.e., twice in 10.23 and twice in 6.12). Moreover, it was suggested in Chapter 3[2] that because the slogan occurred at 10.23 in direct connection with Paul's response to the problem of idol meat, its function in 6.12 was to prepare the reader for the argument of 1 Cor. 8—10. A number of other items in 6.12-20 appear to serve a similar purpose for others of Paul's answers. If this suggestion is allowed, then it may be that the slogan in 6.13, "Food is meant for the stomach and the stomach for food", is also to be connected with the idol meat issue, although it does not reappear in 8.1—11.1. As we noted in Chapter 3, the subject matter of this slogan makes such a connection attractive, although, of course, this suggestion can be only tentative. The two additional objections, therefore, would be as follows:

(g) But all things are lawful for us.
(h) But food is meant for the stomach and the stomach for food.

6. The Corinthians' question concerning idol meat

The question from Corinth. We are now in a position to summarize the preceding discussions by suggesting the content of the Corinthians' question concerning idol meat:

> We find nothing wrong with eating idol meat. After all, we all have knowledge. We know that an idol has no real existence. We know that there is no God but one. For those in Christ all things are lawful, and as far as food is concerned everyone knows that "food is meant for the stomach and the stomach for food". We fail to see what is to be gained by the avoidance of idol meat. You know yourself that when you were with us you never questioned what you ate and drank. Moreover, what of the markets? Are we to be required to inquire as to the history of each piece of meat we buy? And what of our friends? Are we to decline their invitations to banquets because of possible contamination by idol meat?

This reconstruction agrees at many points with that of George G. Findlay quoted at the beginning of this chapter.[3] However, there are

---

[1] See Table 5, p. 68 above, for the widespread scholarly support of this suggestion.
[2] See pp. 87–8 above.   [3] See above, pp. 115–16.

two important differences which separate Findlay's version from ours. For reasons which have been discussed above we hold that:

(i) The Corinthians were primarily voicing an objection to the subject to Paul, and were not asking for guidance from him.

(ii) The Corinthians' objections stem from a single point of view at Corinth opposed in some degree to Paul's. There was no "weak" or "scandalized" second party.

While the first point has been suggested by some scholars,[1] the second does not seem to have been defended before. We hold that, taken together, these two conclusions afford new possibilities for understanding the conversation between Paul and the Corinthians. The above reconstruction may serve as a model for the recovery of the Corinthians' other questions, and together with them will form the basis for an investigation of the Previous Letter.

The nature of Paul's reply. Every care has been exercised to make the above reconstruction of the Corinthians' question as objective and accurate as possible. Yet when their question is compared with Paul's answering statement a number of peculiarities appear. For one thing, it is noticeable that Paul does not directly attack any of the Corinthians' objections. He does not deny that Christians have "knowledge", that "an idol is nothing", and, of course, that "there is no God but one". Properly defined, he accepts the principle that "all things are lawful". He defends his past personal conduct; he does not claim, for example, never to have eaten idol meat. How different in this respect is his letter to the Galatians. In that letter Paul carefully set the record straight concerning his own actions,[2] and he vehemently denounced some of the current beliefs and practices of the Galatians as the result of religious seduction at the hands of outsiders.[3] In 1 Corinthians, however, Paul does not attack any of the principles of the Corinthians as being, for example, the result of gnostic influence, an intrusion into the gospel he preached at Corinth. In Chapter 6 we shall have an opportunity to seek the reasons for Paul's oblique manner of argument concerning idol meat.

Secondly, it is important to notice that, in spite of his vehemence, Paul limited the conduct of the Corinthians only slightly, if at all:

Eat whatever is sold in the meat market without raising any question on the ground of conscience. For "the earth is the Lord's, and everything in it." If

[1] E.g., Zahn, who calls the Corinthians' communication on this point "caustic questions" (*Intro. N. T.*, I, 276).
[2] Gal. 1.13—2.14.   [3] Gal. 1.9; 3.1; 5.12; 6.12, 13.

one of the unbelievers invites you to dinner and you are disposed to go, eat whatever is set before you without raising any question on the ground of conscience (10.25–7).

The only limitations Paul set on their freedom was that they (i) must not offend a weaker Christian, and (ii) must not commit an act of idolatry. The exposition of these limitations occupies the major part of Paul's reply, yet it is interesting to note that from the point of view of the Corinthians he had restricted their actual behaviour almost not at all. In the first place, the "weaker brother" appears to have been a hypothetical construction of Paul's, created for the purposes of his argument. There is no evidence that such persons constituted a significant group at Corinth. Moreover, Paul's principle of loving concern for others is an argument which may be applied in many ways. The Corinthians could well argue that radical behaviour could be lovingly calculated to educate and strengthen newer Christians! It does not seem, therefore, that this first limitation would have been understood by the Corinthians as requiring much real change in their practice concerning idol meat. Secondly, it is clear that the Corinthians did not consider their eating of idol meat as an act of idolatry. They could wholeheartedly agree with Paul that to ascribe real worship to pagan deities would be a complete denial of their new-found Lord. But since they did not consider themselves to be worshipping idols by eating idol meat (wherever it was served), Paul's vigorous condemnation of idolatry could not have been viewed as a serious limitation by the Corinthians. Paul, in fact, gives evidence that he was conscious that his denunciation of idolatry might be deemed irrelevant by the Corinthians. Thus he warned them, "Let any one who thinks that he stands take care lest he fall" (10.12).

Therefore, we reach the somewhat strange conclusion that Paul appears to have permitted the Corinthians to continue their current practices concerning idol meat virtually unchanged, that he had himself eaten such meat when he was in Corinth, and thus that he accepted to some extent the principles concerning Christian freedom which they expressed in their letter. Yet instead of immediately stating his large measure of agreement with the Corinthians, adding only a word or two of warning as to possible dangers in this matter, Paul devoted the major part of his reply to vigorous disagreement with them, and only at the close did he give them permission to behave as in fact they had been behaving. Paul accepted at least partially the Corinthians' principles and practices, yet he felt compelled to disagree with their letter.

Possibly, as Henry J. Cadbury said, "Paul himself is somewhat of two minds on the question".[1] Possibly other factors played a rôle. We shall want to probe more deeply Paul's motivations on this subject when we return to the problem of idol meat in Chapter 6.

CONCERNING IMMORAL MEN (I COR. 5.9–11)

As we noted in Chapter 2,[2] 1 Cor. 5.9–11 gives first-hand evidence of the dialogue between Paul and the Corinthian Church:

> I wrote you in my letter not to associate with immoral men (πόρνοι); not at all meaning (οὐ πάντως) the immoral of this world, or the greedy and robbers, or idolaters, since then you would need to go out of the world. But rather I wrote to you not to associate with any one who bears the name of brother if he is guilty of immorality or greed, or is an idolater, reviler, drunkard, or robber—not even to eat with such a one.

On the point at issue here, however, our knowledge of the Previous Letter (Stage 2) is better than of the Corinthians' question (Stage 3). As Paul himself says, he had written (in the Previous Letter), "Do not associate with immoral men" (5.9). To this statement the Corinthians have responded.

1. *The origin of the Corinthians' question*

There are three possibilities concerning the origin of the Corinthians' response to Paul:

(i) Paul's statement may have been phrased ambiguously, and the Corinthians may therefore have written to him for clarification.

(ii) The Corinthians may not have considered Paul's statement ambiguous, but their interpretation of it may not have been the one intended by Paul. Some question from the Corinthians concerning procedure in this matter may have revealed to Paul their misunderstanding and caused him to write 1 Cor. 5.9–11.

(iii) The Corinthians may have intentionally over-interpreted or misrepresented Paul's position, perhaps in order to evade his meaning, perhaps to have yet another ground for objection to his directions to them.

(i) *Request for clarification?* That the Corinthians have argued among themselves over the meaning of Paul's statement and have finally written for clarification is the position of George G. Findlay. He reconstructs the Corinthians' request as follows:

---

[1] Cadbury, "Macellum," p. 134.   [2] See pp. 50–3 above.

We received thy letter of admonition (v. 9) with heedfulness and godly fear. Seeking to obey thy behests as the command of Christ, we desire to know more clearly their intent, concerning which there is debate amongst us. Thou biddest us separate ourselves from the unclean and have no fellowship with those who live in the sins of the Gentiles. Are we to take this injunction in its unrestricted sense? Our city, as thou well knowest, teems with impurities. If we may not in any wise mix with transgressors, we must depart from Corinth—nay, we doubt whether in the whole world we should find any spot where men dwell that is clear of defilement. We stand in doubt therefore, and beg thee to write once more (unless thou wilt thyself come forthwith), giving us instructions that none can mistake; for it is our wish to be ruled by thee and to please thee in whatsoever is possible.[1]

This theory provides a clear and easy motive for the Corinthians' question to Paul, but it reflects the same somewhat dubious assumptions concerning the Corinthians' general obtuseness and exaggerated subservience to Paul which we noted in Findlay's treatment of the question concerning idol meat. His suggestion that Paul sent directions to the Corinthians which they received with the friendliest and best intentions in the world but were unable to decipher seems unlikely in view of the antagonism which appears to have existed between Paul and the Corinthian Church. That Paul's original statement afforded some grounds for misinterpretation seems likely; that the ambiguity was complete is improbable.

(ii) *Unintentional misunderstanding?* A number of scholars have suggested that the Corinthians, with innocence equal to that ascribed to them by Findlay, had misread Paul's directions at this point.[2] There are, however, two principal difficulties with this theory. In the first place, Paul's reply makes it clear that some at least of the Corinthians had interpreted Paul to mean that Christians should avoid immoral men wherever they are found. If this interpretation was being held sincerely by the Corinthians, then from Paul's point of view they would have adopted a more rigorous standard of behaviour than he had intended. Yet Paul's purpose in referring to their misunderstanding of his Previous Letter in the context of his discussion of the incestuous Corinthian was to rebuke them for the laxity of their behaviour and attitudes. Secondly, this theory affords no real explanation of Paul's knowledge of the Corinthians' misinterpretation of his directions to

---

[1] "Letter of the Corinthian Church," p. 403.

[2] So Moffatt, *1 Cor.*, p. 60 (who paraphrases Paul as saying, "Do not misunderstand me, as you misunderstood my previous letter."); Grosheide, *1 Cor.*, p. 128; and Barclay, *Corr.*, p. 52. This view is considered a good possibility by Evans, *Corr.*, p. 86; and Morris, *1 Cor.*, p. 91.

them. If the Corinthians believed that they had understood Paul, then they had no particular reason to communicate with him on the subject. Paul's knowledge of their misunderstanding must have come to him accidentally, either by word of mouth or in connection with some procedural question about avoiding immoral men—a question unanswered, however, in 1 Corinthians. Since this theory must appeal to chance at this point, it becomes less probable than either the one discussed above or the one next to be examined, both of which provide the Corinthians with a clear motive for raising the issue with Paul. This consideration together with the one discussed above combine to make this theory the least likely of the three.

(iii) *Deliberate misinterpretation?* That the Corinthians had deliberately seized on some ambiguity in Paul's earlier statement, in order perhaps to turn attention away from their own behaviour, or simply to have another subject about which to argue, is the position of many scholars. W. L. Knox, for example, says,

> It appears that S. Paul wrote ordering the Corinthians to have no communication with fornicators, that the wording of the letter was such that it might be interpreted as meaning that they were to cut themselves off from all persons guilty of fornication, whether Christian or not, and that the letter in fact proved ineffective. Such a result is intelligible if the advocates of license seized on the ambiguity of the wording, of which S. Paul himself has grown conscious when he writes I Cor. v. 9, in order to discredit his whole authority by pointing out that what he advocates is in any case impracticable.[1]

This theory combines the virtues of the two preceding theories but avoids their faults. With the first it gives occasion for a written question from the Corinthians to Paul on this precise subject, thus providing a natural explanation of Paul's knowledge of the Corinthians' misunderstanding. With the second it takes the position that the Corinthians had placed a definite interpretation on Paul's directions. In addition, it helps to explain the accusation of laxity which Paul directed

---

[1] *Jerusalem*, p. 320, n. 9. So also H. A. W. Meyer, *Corr.*, I, 152 ("misinterpreted in Corinth by his malevolent adversaries"); Schmiedel, "Corr.," p. 94; von Dobschütz, *Primitive Church*, p. 45; J. Weiss, *1 Cor.*, p. 139 ("Man hatte sie in K. abschütteln zu können geglaubt, weil man sie in einem radikalen Sinne verstehen zu müssen vorgab, als habe P. etwas Unmögliches verlangt."); Findlay, "1 Cor," p. 811; Allo, *1 Cor.*, p. 128; Lietzmann, *Corr.*, p. 25 ("Pls korrigiert ihre Wortklauberei."); Craig, "1 Cor.," p. 65 ("It would almost appear as if the Corinthians had purposely misunderstood the meaning of Paul's injunction."); and Simon, *1 Cor.*, p. 80 ("evasive action"). Robertson and Plummer, *1 Cor.*, p. 104; and Morris, *1 Cor.*, p. 91, suggest this interpretation together with one of the preceding theories. Zahn, *Intro. N. T.*, I, 276, finds a clue to Paul's opinion of the Corinthians on this point reflected in the contrast Paul had just made between "the leaven of malice" and "the unleavened bread of sincerity" (1 Cor. 5.8).

at the Corinthians in the face of their apparently overstrict interpretation of his words. Finally, it makes Paul's sharp tone all the more
natural. Paul's vehemence appears in 5.10 ("*not at all* meaning the
immoral of this world . . . since then you would need go out of this
world") and 5.12 ("What have I to do with judging outsiders?"). The
Corinthians had, Paul maintained, attributed to him an impossible idea,
not out of innocence, but, as their own actions indicated (5.1, 2), out
of a deliberate desire to make him appear ridiculous.

2. *The content of the Corinthians' question*

We conclude from the above discussion that the Corinthians had interpreted Paul to mean that the Christian should avoid immorality wherever it is found and that their interpretation was a deliberate attempt to
caricature his position. "The world is full of immoral men", they
objected. "How is it possible to 'avoid immoral men'?"

Was there any further content to their objection? Considering the
number of slogans by which they defended their actions concerning
idol meat, it seems reasonable to suppose that the immoral situation
reflected in 1 Cor. 5.1, 2 was not from the point of view of the Corinthians a matter of pure license, but involved, in part at least, conscious
principles of ethical action.[1] Certainly Paul implies that such was the
case when he calls them "arrogant" (5.2) and denounces them for
their "boasting" (5.6). It is not necessary to suppose, nor is it probable,
that the Corinthians would have entirely defended the conduct of the
incestuous man. What is probable is that they have adopted a studied
indifference toward the dangers of contagion from the immorality of
the world around them, and that this indifference has made them less
sensitive to moral problems within the Church. We may suppose,
therefore, that their question contained some assertion of freedom:
"You write us to avoid immoral men. Why is this necessary? Are we
not protected from the world by the fact of our new life?"

The similarities between the above assessment of the Corinthians'
position on the matter of immorality and the reconstruction in the
preceding section of their attitude toward idol meat are obvious. In
both cases the Corinthians have rejected a cautious, scrupulous form of
ethical behaviour in favour of a bold, free line of action. In both cases
they have asserted their position against Paul's by asking him aggressive
and pointed questions. In both cases there is the same implication of

---

[1] The possibility will be suggested below, pp. 277–8, that the problem of 1 Cor. 5.1, 2
may have resulted from the custom of "spiritual marriages" reflected in 7.36–8.

antagonism between Paul and the Corinthians which was discussed in Chapter 4.[1] Paul's reference to the problem of immorality probably occurs in 1 Corinthians ahead of its relative position in the Corinthians' letter, because Paul dealt with this topic in connection with the scandal of the incestuous man. If this suggestion is accepted, then the question of the original context of the Corinthians' objections concerning contact with immoral men remains open. Obviously an answer to this question can never be more than tentative, but it is interesting that there are four links which connect this topic to that of idol meat.

(i) Although it is not clear whether or not the list of vices in 1 Cor. 5.10, which is repeated and slightly expanded in 5.11, was contained in the Corinthians' letter, it is noticeable that in both lists the idolater appears along with the immoral man. Thus immorality and idolatry are associated at two points in this passage, a fact which affords some support to the suggestion that these problems were connected in Paul's mind at least, and perhaps for the Corinthians also.

(ii) Moreover, not only did Paul direct the Corinthians to refrain from associating with immoral Christians, he also specified that they were not to *eat* with such men (5.11). His command is reminiscent of 1 Cor. 10.21, "You cannot partake of the table of the Lord and the table of demons."

(iii) The slogan, "all things are lawful" (6.12), provides an excellent summary of the principles which appear to have governed the Corinthians' attitude toward immorality. And it is significant that Paul's graphic description of the depravity into which this principle could lead a man is solely concerned with sexual immorality (6.12–20). The same slogan, however, appears, as we have noted, in 10.23 and was probably one of the principles by which the Corinthians justified their attitude toward idol meat. Here then is another connection between the problems of immorality and of idol meat.

(iv) In general we can note that the two problems, as the Corinthians presented them, both concerned the relation of the Christian to the world around him. All the other topics which we have identified in the Corinthians' letter concerned problems within the church. There is thus a topical reason for associating these two items.

Perhaps these four considerations are strong enough to allow us (a) to connect the slogan, "all things are lawful", with the topic at hand and (b) to associate this topic with that of idol meat when we assemble the reconstructed pieces of the Corinthians' letter.

[1] See pp. 108–13 above.

In conclusion we can suggest the following as the substance of the Corinthians' question concerning immoral men:

> You write us to avoid immoral men. How is this possible? The world is full of immoral men. We are surrounded by immoral men. Moreover, why is this necessary? We have nothing to fear from the world. All things are lawful for us.

CONCERNING MARRIAGE (I COR. 7.1–24, 39–40)

Problems connected with marriage form the subject of the first of the main series of responses by Paul to the Corinthians' questions. Probably an inquiry concerning marriage stood at the head of the list of questions in the Corinthians' letter to Paul, although it is, of course, possible that their first topic happened to be the problem of the immoral, which Paul took up ahead of time (1 Cor. 5.9–13a) among the disciplinary matters. Paul opened his first formal reply to the Corinthians' inquiries with a specific reference to their letter: "Now concerning the matters about which you wrote . . ." (7.1). This reference is the reason that more scholars have attempted the reconstruction of the Corinthians' questions concerning marriage than have attempted the formulation of their inquiries on any other topic.

Scholarly opinion differs, however, concerning the extent of Paul's reply. As we shall see, many commentators who mention the Corinthians' letter when dealing with 7.1–7 fail to specify whether the material in 7.8–9, 10–11, 12–24, and 25–40 was also written in reply to questions from Corinth. Tentatively we may observe that, in spite of the new beginning in 7.25 ("Now concerning 'virgins' . . ."), the whole of chapter 7 seems to have formed a unit in Paul's response to the Corinthians' letter. Not only is the subject matter of 7.1–24 closely related to that of 7.25–38, but 7.39, 40, concerning widows, appears to be an afterthought to 7.8, 9. Paul, having given (in 7.8, 9) general permission to "the unmarried and widows" to marry (if necessary), added (in 7.39, 40) a special word to widows: they more than the rest should try not to remarry, but if they should marry again, then it must be "only in the Lord" (whatever the precise meaning of this expression). Thus it appears that Paul thought of this whole section (7.1–40) as forming a unit in itself, although the repeated περὶ δέ indicates that the single unit consisted of two parts. We shall deal with these two parts separately, since Paul indicated a separation, but in discussing the second we shall need to refer back to the first.

1. Previous reconstructions

Is marriage desirable? The opinion held by a number of commentators is that the basic question asked by the Corinthians was, "Is marriage desirable?" Paul's answer, they believe, consists of 1 Cor. 7.1–9. To this question some scholars add others derived from 1 Cor. 7.10–24. Thus in 1788 J. D. Michaelis said concerning the Corinthians' inquiries, "These questions were: (1) Whether it were, in general, good and commendable to marry. (2) Whether it were necessary to separate from an unbelieving consort. The former of these questions was divisible into two, each of which required distinct answers, the one relative to virgins, the other to widows. . . ."[1] G. G. Findlay in his archaizing style gives an elaborate reconstruction along the same lines:

> Is the single or married state worthiest and fittest for a Christian,—especially for ourselves situated as we are in Corinth? (vii). It is gravely doubted whether a fixed condition of celibacy is right in itself and according to God's will for man. Thou knowest, moreover, the perils and suspicions to which the unwedded are here exposed. . . . There are not a few of the married, both men and women, whose spouses are still unbelieving. To such the yoke of wedlock is often grevous; the Christian partner is much hindered in the service of the Lord, and exposed to bitter trials. Sometimes a separation is wished for by the unbeliever; often it is refused. Several of our members judge that earlier marriage ties are dissolved by union with Christ, and thou hast bidden us 'not to be unequally yoked'; others hold marriage to be indissoluble by the law of the Creator. What sayest thou concerning this?[2]

And William M. Ramsay summed up the consensus of scholarly opinion in his day (with which, however, he was in disagreement) as follows: "It is commonly said that the section of the Church in Corinth which 'was of Cephas' upheld marriage because Cephas was married, while the section which 'was of Paul' argued that the single life was better, because Paul was either unmarried or a widower; and their dispute was referred to the Apostle for decision."[3]

Ramsay himself was one of a small group of scholars who supposed that the Corinthians' communication had not questioned the desirability of marriage for Christians, but, on the contrary, was a strong demand by them that marriage be made the rule: "Make marriage

---

[1] *Intro. N. T.*, IV, 64.   [2] "Letter of the Corinthian Church," p. 404.
[3] "Corr.," *The Expositor*, Ser. 6; I (1900), 288. H. A. W. Meyer, *Corr.*, I, 192, lists a number of older scholars who held this position. So Zahn, *Intro. N. T.*, I, 277, "Some . . . treated marriage contemptuously, possibly on the strength of what Paul had said. . . ." Also, more recently, Moffatt, *1 Cor.*, p. 74; and Craig, "I Cor.," p. 76, "Paul's own point of view inevitably lent encouragement to those who felt that marriage should be repudiated entirely."

universal and vice will disappear."[1] His suggestion was immediately and vigorously rebutted by John Massie, who defended the traditional position:

> St. Paul's Corinthian correspondents had in their letter consulted him on the question—answered in the affirmative by some among them—"Is not celibacy a duty?", and . . . the Apostle in his reply justifies marriage, at the same time pointing out where and when celibacy had its place. . . .
> In spite . . . of Professor Ramsay's interesting ingenuity there seems no sound reason why the old interpretation should not hold the field.[2]

Robinson and Plummer cited Massie's work and adopted his conclusion. Thus they suggested that the Corinthians had asked, "Is marriage to be allowed?"[3] And a number of scholars agree with this opinion, differing only as to the force and extent which they attribute to this ascetic tendency within the Corinthian Church.[4]

Is marital intercourse desirable? A second group of commentators, however, believes that the Corinthians' inquiry also concerned (or mainly concerned) the question whether intercourse between married persons was desirable for Christians. Thus, for example, Tertullian (when a Montanist) commented on 1 Cor. 7.1, 2 as follows: "He shows that there were who, having been 'apprehended by the faith' in (the state of) marriage, were apprehensive that it might not be lawful for them thenceforward to enjoy their marriage, because they had believed on the holy flesh of Christ."[5] In the same vein Chrysostom in his homily on 1 Cor. 7.1, 2 said of the Corinthians, "They had written to him, 'Whether it was right [$\delta\epsilon\hat{\iota}$] to abstain from one's wife, or not'."[6] Following in the same tradition, but suggesting more conviction on the part of the Christians, Lietzmann wrote,

> There were some Christians in Corinth who regarded all sexual intercourse as improper—even within marriage. This was an entirely un-Jewish point of view, although it was frequent in later antiquity as a consequence of dualistic philosophy. It was to be met among the Essenes, the Therapeutae, and also in

---

1 "Corr.," *The Expositor*, Ser. 6; I (1900), 381. Ramsay was anticipated on this point by Godet, *1 Cor.*, I, 320–1; and followed, in part, by Findlay, "1 Cor.," p. 822, who believed that some at Corinth thought celibacy to be "inhuman".

2 "Did the Corinthian Church Advocate Universal Marriage? A Study in Interpretation," *JTS*, II (1901), 527, 538.

3 *1 Cor.*, p. 132.

4 So J. Weiss, *1 Cor.*, pp. 169, 172–3; Bousset, "1 Cor.," p. 102; Allo, *1 Cor.*, pp. 153–4; W. Meyer, *1 Cor.*, I, 231–2; and Morris, *1 Cor.*, p. 105.

5 "On Monogamy," trans. S. Thelwall, *Fathers of the Third Century*, Vol. IV of *The Ante-Nicene Fathers: Translations of the Fathers down to A.D. 325*, ed. A. Roberts and J. Donaldson, American reprint rev. A. C. Coxe (10 vols.; Buffalo: The Christian Literature Publishing Company, 1885), p. 68.

6 *Corr. Homilies*, Homily XIX, p. 105.

Hellenistic Judaism. . . . The fundamental feeling was that sexual intercourse was in itself of lower moral value and unclean.[1]

And Héring takes almost exactly the same position: "The Apostle's argument shows that some Christians (probably of a gnostic tendency, but at the opposite pole from the libertines) were asking whether complete continence was not required by the nearness of the Parousia, or from the general circumstance of belonging to the body of Christ."[2]

Four questions. The most popular position among modern commentators, however, combines both the above suggestions and explains I Cor. 7.1–24 as the result of four distinct questions from the Corinthians. W. G. H. Simon is the most recent exponent of this approach:

> *1–9.* Here there are two problems on which the Apostle has been consulted; in the case of married people ought sexual relations to be abandoned, and in the case of those who are not married, ought they to aim at the celibate life, and not marry at all? . . .
>
> *10f.* The third Corinthian question concerned the possibility of divorce. . . .
>
> *12–16.* The fourth question now follows: what about a marriage in which one partner is converted to Christianity while the other remains heathen?[3]

These scholars, in turn, fall into two groups: (*a*) those who, like Simon, believe that Paul answered the first two questions simultaneously in vv. 1–9;[4] and (*b*) those who consider vv. 1–7 as solely directed to the first question, the answer to the second comprising vv. 8, 9.[5] As an example of the latter group the rather neutral reconstruction of Evans may be quoted:

> (1) vii. 1–7: whether it is desirable for those already married to continue or to abstain from intimate relations with each other:
> (2) vii. 8, 9: whether it is desirable for persons not yet married to remain as they are:
> (3) vii. 10–24: what is to be done if one of the partners is a believer and the other is a pagan.[6]

---

[1] *Beginnings,* p. 135 (and, similarly, *Corr.,* p. 29). So also Lake, *Earlier Epistles,* p. 180: "Some of the Corinthians were opposed altogether to marriage (cf. I Cor. vii, 1, 2); and some were anxious to deprive it of any sexual significance (cf. I Cor. vii, 3–7)"; Craig, "I Cor.," p. 76: "Probably some zealots were insisting upon abstention from marital intercourse"; Chadwick, " 'All Things' ", p. 265: "Evidently at Corinth Christian husbands and wives are understanding the pneumatic life to imply an elevation above carnal things"; and Else Kähler, *Die Frau in den paulinischen Briefen (unter besonderer Berücksichtigung des Begriffes der Unterordnung)* (Zürich: Gotthelf-Verlag, 1960), p. 23.

[2] *1 Cor.,* p. 48.   [3] *1 Cor.,* pp. 88–90.

[4] So Lightfoot, *Notes,* pp. 219, 225; and Zahn, *Intro. N. T.,* I, 276–7.

[5] So Schmiedel, "Corr.," p. 107; Goudge, *1 Cor.,* pp. 53–5, and Moffatt, *1 Cor.,* pp. 74–6.

[6] *Corr.,* p. 90. Note that Evans combines the last two questions.

But in general both groups agree that there was an ascetic tendency or group in Corinth which was suspicious of all sexual relations.

2. The meaning of 1 Cor. 7.1b

The variety which exists in the reconstructions of the Corinthians' question(s) to Paul arises in large part from the even larger variety of interpretations placed by scholars upon 1 Cor. 7.1b, καλὸν ἀνθρώπῳ γυναικὸς μὴ ἅπτεσθαι: "It is well for a man not to touch a woman." This statement poses a double problem: (a) the meaning of ἅπτεσθαι and (b) the implications of καλόν.

(a) "To touch a woman." Scholars are sharply divided into two groups over the intention behind the verb ἅπτεσθαι, "to touch". Most begin by noting that the expression is a euphemism for sexual relations, as in Gen. 20.6, Abimelech's dream, or in Prov. 6.29,

> So is he who goes in to his neighbor's wife;
> None who touches her will go unpunished.

But here opinions divide. Some maintain that the term was intended to refer specifically to sexual intercourse, and thus, since extramarital intercourse was obviously not the issue under debate here, to intercourse between married persons.[1] Others believe this interpretation to be at once too general (as referring to all sexual intercourse) and too specific (as dealing with only one aspect of the relations between man and woman). They understand Paul to refer to the relationship based upon sexual intercourse, that is, to marriage. Thus Grosheide declares: "The general nature of this expression shows that Paul does not speak about what should happen in marriage but about the question whether or not one should marry. Nor does he say: no woman, or: his wife, but: a *woman*."[2]

(b) "It is well." The connotations of the word καλόν, "good" or "well", are variously estimated. Although a certain confusion of terminology reigns, generally scholars may be divided into four groups:

---

[1] So Tertullian, Chrysostom, Schmiedel, Goudge, Evans, Lietzmann, Héring, and Craig as noted above.

[2] 1 Cor., p. 155. So, explicitly, H. A. W. Meyer, Corr., I, 193 ("Marriage is the particular case. . . ."); Godet, 1 Cor., I, 321 ("The expression . . . does not refer . . . to the conduct of those united in marriage."); E. Fascher, "Zur Witwerschaft des Paulus und der Auslegung von I Cor. 7," ZNW, XXVIII (1929), 64 ("Der Satz 7.1 spricht ganz allgemein von der Ehelosigkeit."); and Morris, 1 Cor., p. 105 ("In this context *touch* refers to marriage."). So, implicitly, J. D. Michaelis, Lightfoot, Findlay, Ramsay, Massie, Robertson and Plummer, Lake, Bousset, Zahn, Allo, W. Meyer, and Simon as cited above.

(i) Some give the term a purely utilitarian and pragmatic meaning.[1]

(ii) Others interpret the term to refer to a moral "good", but only as one "good" among several "goods" of more or less equal value.[2]

(iii) Still others consider the expression to be the goal of morality, the highest member of a series of lesser "goods".[3]

(iv) A few of the Fathers understood the term to mean here an absolute of ethical conduct beside which no other behaviour can be called "good".[4]

Without spelling out the eight possible interpretations of 1 Cor. 7.1b which result from the combination of the various views on καλόν

[1] So, e.g., Hermann Olshausen, *Biblical Commentary on St Paul's First and Second Epistles to the Corinthians*, trans. J. E. Cox ("Clark's Foreign Theological Library," Vol. XX; Edinburgh: T. & T. Clark, 1855), p. 116 ("καλόν has here no moral meaning; it merely signifies 'salutary.' "); Bachmann, *1 Cor.*, p. 254; Parry, *1 Cor.* ("Camb."), p. 69 ("It is not a question of a principle or of an ideal: there is no hint that S. Paul regards the celibate life as morally superior to the married life: it is throughout a question of 'what is well,' desirable, profitable, under present circumstances. . . ."); Héring, *1 Cor.*, p. 49 (" '*Kalon*' . . . cannot here mean 'good' or 'admirable' in a moral sense."); Grosheide, *1 Cor.*, pp. 154–5 ("It does not mean: morally good. . . . It rather denotes an attitude which is commendable. . . . It may be useful. . . ."); and Morris, *1 Cor.*, p. 105 ("*good* [not 'necessary', nor 'morally better' . . .]").

[2] So, e.g., H. A. W. Meyer, *Corr.*, I, 193–5; Godet, *1 Cor.*, I, 320–1 ("The apostle means simply to assert that there is nothing unbecoming in a man's living in celibacy."); Schmiedel, "*Corr.*," p. 100; Findlay, "1 Cor.," p. 822 ("*Honourable, morally befitting.* . . . Paul is not disparaging marriage . . . but defending *celibacy* against those who thought it inhuman."); Robertson and Plummer, *1 Cor.*, p. 100 ("laudable"); Zahn, *Intro. N. T.*, I, 276–7; Evans, *Corr.*, p. 91 ("The general principle of abstinence is unexceptionable. . . ."); Sickenberger, *Corr.*, pp. 30–1; and W. Meyer, *1 Cor.*, I, 231 (" 'Nicht Heiraten ist sehr gut, aber Heiraten ist unter Umständen besser.' ").

[3] So Lightfoot, *Notes*, pp. 220–1 (" 'good,' 'right,' . . . not 'convenient.' There is no qualification in the word itself."); Bousset, "1 Cor.," p. 102; Allo, *1 Cor.*, pp. 153–4; and Wendland, *Corr.*, p. 49. The following scholars accept this interpretation as Paul's but believe that the Corinthians may have used the word in sense (iv) below: Goudge, *1 Cor.*, p. 53; Moffatt, *1 Cor.*, pp. 73–6 ("Reluctantly but firmly he views marriage . . . as a lesser risk . . . than any overstrained attempt to practise the celibate life."); Lietzmann, *Corr.*, p. 29 ("Die Jungfräulichkeit ist das ethische Ideal." Lietzmann believes that Paul considered marriage "höchstens ein prinzipielles ἀδιάφορον."); and Craig, "1 Cor.," pp. 76–7 ("It is regrettable that Paul, the bachelor, should have ignored so completely all other aspects of the companionship of married couples and should have written as if marriage were little more than legalized cohabitation.").

[4] So Tertullian, "On Monogamy," *Ante-Nicene Fathers*, IV, 60 (" 'Good,' he says, '[it is] for a man not to have contact with a woman.' It follows that it is evil to have contact with her; for nothing is contrary to good except evil."); and Jerome, *Adversus Jovinianum*, I, 7 (*Patrologiae Cursus Completus*. . . . *Series Latina*, ed. J. -P. Migne [221 vols.; Paris: Garnier Brothers, 1844–1903], XXIII, col. 229 ("Si bonum est mulierem non tangere, malum est ergo tangere: nihil enim bono contrarium est nisi malum. Si autem malum est, et ignoscitur, ideo conceditur, ne malo quid deterius fiat.") When challenged on this opinion Jerome defended himself in a letter "To Pammachius" in which he grudgingly allowed some value to widowhood and to marriage, but said of the passage quoted above, "In what way does my meaning differ from that intended by the apostle? Except that where he speaks decidedly I do so with hesitation." ("Letter XLVIII," *The Principal Works of St. Jerome*, trans. W. H. Freemantle ["A Select Library of Nicene and Post-Nicene Fathers of the Christian Church," 2d Ser., Vol. VI; New York: The Christian Literature Company, 1893], p. 73).

and ἅπτεσθαι cited above, we may proceed directly to make some observations.

First of all, it seems best to take καλόν in sense (iii) above. The first two positions, (i) and (ii), result from an attempt to harmonize this passage with other passages in Paul's letters (e.g., with 1 Cor. 11.3; Col. 3.18, 19 and Eph. 5.21–33) in order to avoid ascribing to Paul a view of marriage different from that of the main stream of Christian tradition. Grosheide betrays this interest when he says, apologetically, "The question arises whether Paul's estimate of marriage is not rather low if he sees no other reason for marriage but to avoid fornication (7.2). . . . We must realize that Paul does not speak about the purpose of matrimony. His statement in vs. 1 does not contain an absolute, universally valid rule. In vs. 2 Paul indicates why his rule cannot be an absolute one, why it is only 'good.' "[1] And in just the same manner Héring betrays embarrassment at this point. He also refers to Col. 3.19 and Eph. 5.25, and rejects any moral connotation to καλόν. But he has to confess that "secular Greek lexicography affords little support for this translation".[2] These attempts to make Paul more consistent with himself and with later Christian thought are an example of the harmonization which we explicitly agreed to forego at the close of Chapter 1.[3] The word καλόν has had a long and honourable history as an ethical ideal of the highest rank. The phrase καλὸς κἀγαθός was so widely used, in fact, that it gave rise to the single word καλοκἀγαθία.[4] Thus general ethical usage points beyond interpretations (i) and (ii). But, on the other hand, it is hardly necessary to say that sense (iv) above is the result of special pleading on the part of two very unrepresentative individuals. In general, both Greek and Christian ethical

---

[1] 1 Cor., p. 155. So, more briefly but precisely to the same effect, Morris, 1 Cor., p. 106. So also Olshausen, Corr., p. 116; H. A. W. Meyer, Corr., 1, 194 ("Can it be true, then, that he, who looked upon the union with Christ itself as the analogue of wedded life, valued marriage only as a 'temperamentum continentiae'? No!" [Note the exclamation mark.]); Godet, 1 Cor., I, 322–3 ("Now as it is improbable that Paul modified his conception of marriage, and as the passages of our Epistle quoted above [7.14; 11.3] show that in fact there is nothing of the kind, it must be concluded that in this exposition the apostle desired to keep strictly within the limits traced out for him by the questions of the Corinthians on the subject."); Findlay, "1 Cor.," (Findlay prefaces his discussion of 7.1–9 with the statement, "The local impress and temporary aim of the directions here given on the subject of marriage must be borne in mind; otherwise Paul's treatment will appear narrow and unsympathetic, and out of keeping with the exalted sense of its spiritual import disclosed in Eph. v."); Robertson and Plummer, 1 Cor., p. 133 ("The man who wrote Eph. v. 22, 23, 32, 33 had no low view of marriage."); and W. Meyer, 1 Cor., I, 232 (with a reference to Eph. 5.22–33).

[2] 1 Cor., p. 49.   [3] See p. 42 above.

[4] For a brief history of the phrase see Walter Grundmann, art. καλός, TWNT, III, 540–5.

thought was wiser than to say that only what is perfect can be called καλός and that all else is κακός.

Secondly, ἅπτεσθαι probably refers specifically to sexual intercourse rather than to marriage in general. Paul made the divisions of his reply clear. In v. 8 begins his advice "to the unmarried and widows" on the problem of whether they should marry. Paul did not indicate by any division of his argument that vv. 1–7 concern more than one problem. Thus all of 7.1–7 most probably concerns the question of marital intercourse, as vv. 3–5 so clearly do:

> The husband should give to his wife her conjugal rights, and likewise the wife to her husband. For the wife does not rule over her own body, but the husband does; likewise the husband does not rule over his own body, but the wife does. Do not refuse one another except perhaps by agreement for a season, that you may devote yourselves to prayer; but then come together again lest Satan tempt you through lack of self-control (7.3–5).

Scholars who do not adopt the view suggested here rely on two points of evidence:

(i) Paul's next statement (v. 6), "I say this (τοῦτο) by way of concession, not of command", if understood as a reference to marital intercourse (vv. 3–5) and not to marriage, would make Paul appear exceedingly ascetic. It will be noticed that most of the scholars who adopt a weakened interpretation of καλόν also refer Paul's concession here to marriage (7.1, 2, as they interpret these verses), rather than to marital intercourse (7.5).[1] Thus concerning the reference of v. 6, Robertson and Plummer say without explanation or further evidence, "It is not clear how much the τοῦτο [of v. 6] covers; probably the whole of vv. 1–5. The least probable suggestion is that it refers solely to the resumption of married life, καὶ πάλιν κ.τ.λ. [v. 5b]."[2] Zahn achieves the same moderate end by referring Paul's concession in v. 6 to the next to the last clause of v. 5, "except perhaps by agreement for a season, that you may devote yourselves to prayer". He justifies this reference by saying that "vii. 6, . . . rightly understood, cannot refer to the positive commands in ver. 2 or vv. 3–5a, but only the concession (εἰ μήτι) in 5b."[3] But it is far more probable that v. 6 ("not of command") refers

---

[1] So H. A. W. Meyer, Godet, Findlay, Robertson and Plummer, Grosheide, and Morris as cited above.

[2] 1 Cor., p. 135. So also Godet, 1 Cor., I, 326 ("Vers. 3–5 have only been a digression. . . ."); Lightfoot, Notes, p. 223; Findlay, "1 Cor.," p. 824 ("τοῦτο δὲ λέγω points to . . . ver. 2, from which vv. 3–5 digressed."); Grosheide, 1 Cor., p. 158; and Morris, 1 Cor., p. 107 ("This will refer, not to the last provision, but to the whole of the foregoing, with its acceptance of marriage.").

[3] Intro. N. T., I, 296, n. 3. Grosheide uses the same line of reasoning to refer v. 6 to v. 2 (1 Cor., p. 158).

Moc

back to a section which sounded to Paul more like a command than a concession, i.e., to v. 5a ("Do not refuse one another.") rather than to v. 5b ("except perhaps for a season").[1] Thus Zahn's suggestion is most unlikely. The asceticism of this passage can only be avoided if v. 6 is made to refer back to v. 2, and then only if v. 2 is interpreted to refer to marriage rather than to intercourse.

(ii) This last reference is the second point upon which these scholars rely. They understand v. 2, "But because of the temptation to immorality, each man should have his own wife and each woman her own husband", to mean, "Every Christian (except perhaps those with the gift mentioned in v. 7) should enter a monogamous relationship". The idea of monogamy is unexpected, however. It seems probable that the redundancy of Paul's language ("his own wife . . . her own husband") has another reference. In 1 Cor. 5.1 ("a man *has* his father's wife") the verb ἔχειν refers primarily to the sexual side of the relationship. Since in 7.2 the contagion of sexual immorality is once again under discussion, it seems natural to understand ἐχέτω to imply "let him (or "her") have sexually". Thus 7.3 ("The husband should give to his wife her 'due' [τὴν ὀφειλήν], and likewise the wife to her husband.") is a slightly less euphemistic restatement of 7.2. Hans von Campenhausen comments forcefully,

> Die Frage des Eheschlusses für "die Unverheirateten und die Witwen" beginnt erst 7, 8; 7, 2–6 handelt vom Verhalten innerhalb der Ehe. Der ἀνήρ oder ἄνθρωπος ist hier also der Ehemann, das ἔχειν darf nicht im Sinne von 7, 9 als γαμεῖν verstanden werden, und die "Konzession" (συγγνώμη), von der Paulus 7, 6 spricht, bezieht sich somit nicht auf dem Eheschluss, sondern auf den Vollzug der ehelichen Pflichten, deren Ausübung . . . von Paulus nur gestattet wird. . . . Es ist mir aber nicht zweifelhaft, dass . . . [die] traditionelle Exegese falsch ist.[2]

The non-ascetical interpretation of 7.1–7, therefore, rests on three improbabilities: (i) that v. 6 refers to v. 2, but not to vv. 3–5; (ii) that v. 2 is simply an exhortation to marriage; and (iii) that ἅπτεσθαι in v. 1 also refers figuratively to marriage. It seems far more probable that "to touch" means "to touch sexually" and not "to marry"; that v. 2

---

[1] As H. A. W. Meyer, *Corr.*, I, 197, soundly pointed out.
[2] *Die Begründung kirchlicher Entscheidungen beim Apostel Paulus: zur Grundlegung des Kirchenrechts* ("Sitzungsberichte der Heidelberger Akademie der Wissenschaften: Philosophisch-historische Klasse," 1957, 2. Abhandlung; Heidelberg: Carl Winter, Universitätsverlag, 1957), p. 21, n. 38. He cites J. Weiss, *1 Cor.*, p. 175, and Jean-Jacques von Allmen, *Maris et femmes d'après saint Paul*, now translated as *Pauline Teaching on Marriage* ("Studies in Christian faith and Practice," VI; London: The Faith Press, 1963), pp. 13–14, 56–8.

concerns the same issue as vv. 1 and 3; and that the ambiguous reference of v. 6 ("I say *this*") is the result of the unity of purpose in vv. 2–5. It matters little whether Paul's "concession" be referred to v. 5, to vv. 3–5, or to vv. 2–5. In any case Paul's meaning is the same: marital intercourse is his concession but not his command.

Quotation? If the above analysis of 1 Cor. 7.1–7 is correct, then it appears that the whole passage is an appeal by Paul, in spite of his own personal inclinations and conduct, that the *physical side* of marriage should not be rejected. The implication of this conclusion is that the Corinthians had tried to discourage sexual intercourse within marriages. Now we may note that v. 1, as we have interpreted it, expresses a principle of sexual morality which exactly corresponds with the Corinthians' apparent attitude, but which, as it stands, only hinders Paul's argument. If we preserve what seems to be the natural force of 1 Cor. 7.1b, then we are left with the difficult picture of Paul opening his argument with a principle exactly opposed to the general practice which he felt it necessary to recommend. Thus we conclude that, as a number of scholars have suggested, the statement "It is well for a man not to touch a woman," was a quotation from the Corinthians' letter.[1] Our analysis of the opening of Paul's discussion of idol meat (8.1–4) increases the probability of this conclusion. There, it will be remembered, we argued that Paul began his long reply with quotations from the Corinthians' letter. He neither accepted nor rejected their slogans, but he immediately qualified them. Here in 7.1 the same type of qualification is present: "It is well . . . *but* because of immorality. . . ." Moreover, the probability that 7.1b is a quoted slogan is increased still further when it is noticed that there is no subject heading for Paul's discussion here. Paul said vaguely, "Now concerning the matters about which you wrote". To take 7.1b ("It is well for a man not to touch a woman") as a quotation would explain this omission, since the slogan would have been a direct reminder to the Corinthians of the particular "matter" Paul wished to discuss first. With this slogan then we have the beginnings of a reconstruction of the Corinthians' inquiry concerning marriage.

3. *The Corinthians' question concerning marriage*

(*a*) *1 Cor. 7.1–7.* Having concluded that 1 Cor. 7.1b is a quotation from

---

[1] See Table 5, p. 68 above. In agreement on this point are Allmen, *Pauline Teaching on Marriage*, p. 13; Chadwick, " 'All Things,' " p. 265; Campenhausen, *Begründung*, p. 20, n. 37 ("vielleicht"); and Simon, *1 Cor.*, p. 89 ("probably").

the Corinthians' letter, we can describe Paul as dealing first with the Corinthians' key argument. As in the case of the idol meat controversy Paul did not attack or deny their slogan; rather he added to it a further consideration which changed the ethical calculation and its conclusion. Here concerning marriage Paul stressed the prevalent danger of sexual immorality (7.2). And concerning idol meat Paul had warned of the danger both to the individual through idolatry and to a weaker Christian through lack of Christian love. The arguments, therefore, are parallel in this respect.

Moreover, the Corinthians' position, if it is fairly characterized by the slogan, "It is well for a man not to touch a woman", was clear-cut and unequivocal, as also on the problem of idol meat. Once again the Corinthians' position was in opposition to Paul's. Once again it appears probable that the Corinthians' letter expressed and therefore emanated from a single point of view. Thus those reconstructions of the Corinthians' question which take the form of a request for information, guidance, or arbitration between party viewpoints will have to be set aside.[1] More probable is the position held by most scholars, in spite of what they take to be the libertinism reflected in 1 Cor. 5, 6, and 8—10, that the Corinthians' question on the subject of marriage came solely from an ascetic point of view. The discrepancy between the Corinthians' freedom concerning marital irregularities (1 Cor. 5) and the eating of idol meat (1 Cor. 8—10) on one hand, and their asceticism on the subject of marital intercourse on the other, is solved by these scholars by means of the hypothesis of various parties at Corinth. This discrepancy, however, is more apparent than real. In Chapter 3 we suggested that 1 Cor. 6.12-20 is not an attack by Paul upon actual licentiousness at Corinth, but that this section serves rather (a) to contest the Corinthians' claim to freedom (6.12) by describing the depths to which such a principle might carry a man, and (b) to provide a background for the discussion of 1 Cor. 7 by demonstrating the theological seriousness of the problem of sexual morality.[2] In addition, the position held by the Corinthians concerning idol meat is, we believe, more correctly described as "strenuous" than as "unprincipled". The Corinthians have pictured themselves as rising above conventions and moral systems into a new freedom under Christ. It is in this sense that they have claimed that "all things are lawful" (6.12; 10.23). Thus understood, the Corinthians' attitudes toward idol meat and toward marital intercourse are entirely consistent. In each case they have claimed that, informed by

[1] E.g., those of Findlay, Lake, and Evans quoted above.   [2] See pp. 86–9 above.

their higher knowledge, they had chosen the superior, harder, and more dangerous course of action. Confident of their strength, they boasted that they were able to expose themselves safely to the temptations of idolatry and the lure of sexual immorality.

1 Cor. 5.1–8, 13b, however, which falls outside the reply material in 1 Corinthians, gives apparent evidence of a certain moral callousness on the part of the Corinthians. It is difficult and perhaps impossible to decide whether Paul has magnified a slight moral irregularity out of all proportion to its true seriousness (in irritation, perhaps, at the Corinthians' thinly disguised challenge of his authority), or whether the moral principles cited by the Corinthians were put forward to justify their behaviour and to embarrass Paul. In the first case we may assume that the Corinthians were honestly attempting to live up to the high principles which they professed in their letter; in the second, that their behaviour did not correspond to their published ideals. To this problem we shall return at a later point,[1] but in neither case is it probable that two (or more) parties were responsible for the Corinthians' letter to Paul, or that separate groups of libertines and ascetics existed at Corinth. 1 Cor. 5.1–8, 13b gives no evidence that Paul intended to criticize only a part of the Corinthian congregation. We conclude, therefore, that those principles contained in the Corinthians' letter which we have so far discussed are mutually consistent and that they express an enlightened position which Paul finds hard to meet on a theoretical level.

Thus on the particular issue under discussion the Corinthians appear to have advocated sexual abstinence for married couples, and to have defended their position with the general principle that "it is well for a man not to touch a woman".

(b) *1 Cor. 7.8, 9.* It was mentioned above that the structure of 1 Cor. 7.1–24 is carefully organized. The divisions are indicated by a series of datives:

v. 8   To the unmarried and widows I say . . .
v. 10 To the married I give charge . . .
v. 12 To the rest I say . . .

Thus 1 Cor. 7.8, 9 is a new sub-section. But here we reach a problem. Was 7.1–24 Paul's response to a single statement in the Corinthians' letter (as on the problem of idol meat), or did their letter contain a series of statements related to the topic of sexual morality? In Chapter 3

---

[1] See below, pp. 242–6, 277–8, and 287.

we pointed out that it was characteristic of Paul in answering the
Corinthians' questions to be systematic and complete. An outline of
1 Cor. 7 was given to emphasize the orderliness of Paul's answer.[1]
Now we must determine how many of the items in 7.8–24 were occasioned by questions from Corinth and how many were the result of
Paul's systematic treatment of the subject. That the Corinthians may
have made multiple statements about their position on marriage is
hinted by 7.25–40, which concerns another aspect of the marriage
problem, and which, as the opening περὶ δέ indicates, was a topic
mentioned in the Corinthians' letter. For the material in 7.8–24, the
criterion by which we can decide the origin of each section is whether
the item appears to be a logical extension and development of Paul's
argument, or whether it represents a difficulty to his position.

Paul began his argument, as we have characterized it above, by
maintaining that, because of the danger of sexual immorality, the
Corinthians should not discourage the physical side of the marriage
relationship (7.1–7). Then, having dealt with sexual relations within
marriage, Paul turned to the "unmarried and widows" (7.8, 9). To
them he said, "It is well for them to remain (single) as I do. But if they
cannot exercise self-control, they should marry." This pair of statements is closely parallel to the pair in 7.1, 2. Each opens with a statement beginning καλόν followed by the dative of the person(s) concerned. Each statement is immediately qualified with a counter-
statement. In each case the contrast is indicated by δέ. In each case the
first statement is in opposition to marriage and normal sexual relations,
and the second advocates both as a means of avoiding πορνεία:

> 7.1, 2 It is *well* for a man not to touch a woman. *But* because of immorality,
> each man should have (fully) his own wife. . . .

> 7.8, 9 It is *well* for them to remain (single) as I do. *But* if they cannot exercise
> self-control, they should marry.

It appears probable, therefore, as many scholars have suggested that the
Corinthians had made some statement indicating their general disapproval of marriage. And since on the preceding topic the Corinthians had not only stated but also attempted to justify their position, it
is probable that they had also undertaken to justify their position here.
Clearly the slogan of 7.1b could apply to marriage in general as well
as to marital intercourse. It may also be that the Corinthians had made
a direct reference to Paul's own marital status. Such a reference could

---

[1] See above, pp. 65–6.

well explain Paul's statement in 7.7 ("I wish all were as I myself am. But each has his own special gift from God, one of one kind and one of another"), and the form of his advice in 7.8 ("It is well for them to remain as I am"). It is unlikely that Paul would have independently reminded the Corinthians of his own celibacy, a topic that certainly did not further the practical goal which, we have suggested, Paul had in mind.

We conclude, therefore, that behind 1 Cor. 7.1–9 stand two topics from the Corinthians' letter: (i) the question of sexual intercourse for the married, and (ii) of marriage for the unmarried. Concerning the first (and probably the second as well) the Corinthians had said, "It is best for a man not to touch a woman". Concerning the second they may have said, "It is best that they remain as you are."

(c) *1 Cor. 7.10, 11 and 12–16.* It is difficult to see how Paul's emphatic rejection of divorce in 1 Cor. 7.10, 11 could be considered an extension of his argument in 7.1–9. On the other hand, the very fact that he rejects divorce with such emphasis implies that the Corinthians had made some statement in its favour. Certainly divorce could be justified by their slogan as quoted by Paul, and a number of scholars have suggested that Corinthians had carried their hostility to marriage to the point of advocating divorce.[1] But if Christian couples were willing to practice intramarital asceticism, then divorce would seem to serve no useful function. Thus some scholars connect this topic with the following one which concerns mixed marriages (vv. 12–16).[2] In this case, however, Paul's new beginning in v. 12 ("To the rest I say . . .") is difficult to explain. Probably, therefore, mixed marriages are but one class of a general problem raised by the Corinthians' views on sex—the problem which occurs when one partner is unwilling to forego his (or her) marital rights.[3] In this eventuality the Corinthians appear to have recommended separation or divorce. Paul's answer, therefore, falls naturally into two parts: (a) in the case of Christians who are married

---

[1] So Findlay, "1 Cor.," p. 825, who says, "In some cases, not so much incompatibility as ascetic aversion (cf. 3f) caused the wish to separate" (cited with approval by Robertson and Plummer, *1 Cor.*, p. 140); Zahn, *Intro. N. T.*, I, 277 ("Some in Corinth . . . treated marriage contemptuously . . . recommending or even insisting that married persons . . . dissolve their marriage relation altogether. . . ."); Lake, *Earlier Epistles*, p. 183 ("There was an ascetic tendency . . . which led some Christians to regard marriage as immoral, and therefore, to regard divorce as desirable for Christians."); and Moffatt, *1 Cor.*, p. 78 ("The feminist party in the local church had evidently claimed freedom to desert or divorce a husband. . . .").

[2] So, e.g., Evans, *Corr.*, p. 90 (as quoted above).

[3] We must defer until Chapter 6 a discussion of the possibility (suggested, e.g., by Findlay as quoted above) that the admonition to "avoid immoral men" in Paul's Previous letter had helped to make mixed marriages a separate topic. See pp. 223–4 below.

there is to be no talk of divorce; (b) in the case of a marriage between a Christian and a non-Christian there is to be no divorce as far as the as the Christian is concerned except by mutual consent.

(d) *Summary*. As a summary of the above discussions we may suggest the following as containing the substance of the Corinthians' communication to Paul:

> Concerning problems of sex and marriage: we believe that Christian couples should forego marital intercourse so that they may devote themselves more fully to things spiritual. After all, is it not true that it is well for a man not to touch a woman? For this reason we also think it best that the unmarried and widows among us remain unmarried, an attitude of which you must approve since you yourself remain unmarried.
>
> It sometimes occurs that the harmony of a marriage is threatened by the demands of the spiritual life. On the one hand, some of the brothers are unable to refrain completely from their wives; on the other hand, some of the marriages include one partner who is not a believer. In these cases we recommend separation so that the spiritual life of the more devout partner is not hampered.

These topics, we believe, were contained in the Corinthians' letter to Paul. Paul in 1 Corinthians then organized his response to these topics into the pattern which we noted in Chapter 3.

4. The nature of the Corinthians' question

As we suggested above, the Corinthians' question on subjects relating to marriage expressed a single, ascetic point of view, and therefore presumably came from a single group of the same point of view. The Corinthians' statements show no uncertainty, but are definite and even aggressive. Their slogan and their probable reference to Paul's own marital state betray a desire on their part to argue against what appears to have been a suggestion that normal marriage relationships should be made the rule. The whole problem of the origin of this and the rest of the Corinthians' questions will be discussed in Chapter 6.

The Corinthians' position on the relationship between the sexes is analogous to their position on idol meat and on immoral men. On all three topics the Corinthians have claimed a course of action free of cautious calculation, and aspired to behaviour which exposed them to dangers too severe for men of lesser knowledge. We cannot be sure how sincerely they held these principles of a strenuous morality, but on the assumption that at least a portion of the congregation were genuine supporters of these ideals, Henry J. Cadbury refers to their convictions by the happy designation, "overconversion".[1] And with the topics of marriage and idol meat Cadbury correlates the next topic, which we must now discuss.

CONCERNING "VIRGINS" (1 COR. 7.25-38)

In subject matter the topic to which Paul responded in 1 Cor. 7.25-38 is associated with that of the preceding section. Both concern sexual morality. The περὶ δέ in 7.25, however, implies that in some sense the problem thus introduced is separate from the preceding.

1. Previous reconstructions

Suggestions by scholars as to the Corinthians' question to Paul "concerning 'virgins' " fall into two widely separated categories.[2]

(a) *Fathers and daughters.* One group of commentators holds to the traditional opinion that Paul's cryptic remarks in 7.36-8 concern the problem of Christian fathers who are anxious to know what to do about their unmarried daughters. Thus Findlay included in his reconstruction of the Corinthians' letter the statement, "About our maiden daughters, who are asked in marriage, some of us know not how to decide for the best."[3] Goudge also suggests, "Ought Christian fathers to give their daughters in marriage?"[4] And Robertson and Plummer agree: "The Corinthians had asked him about the duty of a father with a daughter of age to marry."[5]

---

[1] "Overconversion in Paul's Churches," *The Joy of Study: Papers on New Testament and Related Subjects Presented to Honor Frederick Clifton Grant*, ed. Sherman E. Johnson (New York: The Macmillan Company, 1951), pp. 44-5.

[2] For *detailed* bibliographical study of the key passage in this section : Werner Georg Kümmel, "Verlobung und Heirat bei Paulus (I. Cor 7, 36-38)," *Neutestamentliche Studien für Rudolf Bultmann* ("Beihefte zur ZNW," Beiheft XXI; Berlin: Alfred Töpelmann, 1954), pp. 275-95. Further bibliography may be found in Alfred Juncker, *Die Ethik des Apostels Paulus* (2 Bde.; Halle a. S.: M. Niemeyer, 1904-1919), II, 191, n. 1; Allo, *1 Cor.*, pp. 189-94; Mervin Monroe Deems, "The Sources of Christian Asceticism," in *Environmental Factors in Christian History*, ed. J. T. McNeill, M. Spinka, and H. R. Willoughby (Chicago: The University of Chicago Press, 1939), p. 149, n. 1; and Arndt/Gingrich, p. 150b.

[3] "Letter of the Corinthian Church," p. 404. The section concerning marriage is quoted above, p. 155.

[4] *1 Cor.*, p. 60.

[5] *1 Cor.*, p. 158. The same question is proposed by Schmiedel, "Corr.," pp. 106-7; Lightfoot, *Notes*, p. 234; Parry, *1 Cor.* ("Camb."), p. 78; Bachmann, *1 Cor.*, p. 280; Allo, *1 Cor.*, p. 177; and Grosheide, *1 Cor.*, p. 184.

Scholars who fail to formulate the Corinthians' question on this subject but who defend the above interpretation of the passage against the view next to be considered include Joseph Sickenberger, "Syneisaktentum im ersten Korintherbrief?," *Biblische Zeitschrift*, III (1905), 44-69; Hugo Koch, "Vater und Tochter im ersten Korintherbrief," *Biblische Zeitschrift*, III (1905), 401-7; Schlatter, *Bote Jesu*, p. 246; Peter Ketter, "Syneisakten in

(b) Spiritual marriages. A second group of scholars believes that the "virgins" referred to (at least those in 7.36–8) are women who have entered into spiritual marriages with men who have vowed themselves to celibacy. Kirsopp Lake explained this point of view as follows: "The suggestion is that men and women had made a practice of living together under a vow of virginity, and that, in some cases, the situation was proving too great a strain for human nature. Under these circumstances, St. Paul's advice was sought."[1] This view has probably become the most popular among scholars to-day, although the issue is by no means beyond debate.[2] Most of these scholars, unfortunately, do not bother to formulate the Corinthians' request, believing it to be obvious in the situation. Evans is an exception, however. In his systematic manner he makes the following reconstruction:

> vii. 25–38: in the special case of persons legally married who had resolved not to consummate the marriage, are such persons precluded from changing their mind about that resolution [?][3]

Korinth? Zu I Cor. 7, 36–38," *Trierer Theologische Zeitschrift*, LVI (1947), 175–82; E. Alzas, "L' Apôtre Paul et le Célibat," *Revue de Théologie et de Philosophie*, N. S. XXXVIII (1950), 226–32; and with reluctance, Morris, *I Cor.*, pp. 120–2.

[1] *Earlier Epistles*, p. 190.

[2] This exegesis of 7.36–8 seems to have been suggested first by Carl von Weizsäcker, *The Apostolic Age of the Christian Church*, trans. James Millar (2 vols.; "Theological Translation Library," Vols. I, V; London: Williams and Norgate, 1894–1895), II, 371, 388, 396. His somewhat casual suggestion was picked up and elaborated by Eduard Grafe, "Geistliche Verlöbnisse bei Paulus," *Theologische Arbeiten aus dem rheinischen wissenschaftlichen Prediger-Verein*, N. F. III (1899), 57–69.
The best discussions of this position are to be found in Hans Achelis, *Virgines Subintroductae: ein Beitrag zum VII. Kapitel des I. Korintherbriefs* (Leipzig: J. C. Hinrichs'sche Buchhandlung, 1902); J. Weiss, *1 Cor.*, pp. 206–9; Lake, *Earlier Epistles*, pp. 184–91; Morton Scott Enslin, *The Ethics of Paul* (New York: Harper & Brothers, 1930), pp. 178–93; Gerhard Delling, *Paulus' Stellung zu Frau und Ehe* ("Beiträge zur Wissenschaft vom Alten und Neuen Testament," 4. Folge, Heft 5; Stuttgart: W. Kohlhammer Verlag, 1931), pp. 86ff.; Lietzmann, *Corr.*, pp. 35–7; and Héring, *1 Cor.*, pp. 62–4.
Scholars who hold this position include F. Fahnenbruch, "Zu I Cor. 7, 36–38," *Biblische Zeitschrift*, XII (1914), 391–401; Herbert Preisker, *Christentum und Ehe in den ersten drei Jahrhunderten: eine Studie zur Kulturgeschichte der alten Welt* ("Neue Studien zur Geschichte der Theologie und der Kirche," hrsg. Reinhold Seeberg, 23. Stück; Berlin: Trowitzsch & Sohn, 1927), pp. 133ff.; Karl Müller, *Kirchengeschichte* (1. Bd., 1. Halbbd.; 3. Aufl. in Gemeinschaft mit H. von Campenhausen; Tübingen: J. C. B. Mohr [Paul Siebeck], 1941), pp. 105–7; Heinrich Schlier, "Über das Hauptanliegen des I. Korintherbriefes," *Evangelische Theologie*, VIII (1948/49), 469; L.-A. Richard, "Sur I Corinthiens (VII, 36–38). Cas de Conscience d'un Père Chrétien ou 'Mariage Ascétique'? Une Essai d'Interprétation," *Mémorial J. Chaine* ("Bibliothèque de la Faculté Catholique de Théologie de Lyon," Vol. 5; Lyon: Facultés Catholiques, 1950), pp. 309–20; Bultmann, *Theology of the N. T.*, I, 103n., II, 224; Martin Albertz, *Die Botschaft des Neuen Testaments* (2 vols. in 4 pts.; Zollikon-Zürich: Evangelischer Verlag AG., 1947–1957), II, 185; and McNeile, *Intro. N. T.*, p. 137.

[3] *Corr.*, p. 90.

(c) *Engaged couples.* There is a third position held by a number of scholars which stands as a sort of half-way house between the two major theories summarized above. It was, in fact, the fore-runner of the "spiritual marriage" theory, having been suggested first (according to Kümmel) by W. C. van Manen in 1874.[1] The suggestion is that Paul was speaking to a group of engaged couples at Corinth who were wondering whether to go ahead with their wedding plans. Thus Wendland after outlining the above two theories says: "Daher ist die dritte Möglichkeit bei weitem vorzuziehen, dass hier nicht von einer geistlichen Asketen-Ehe, sondern von dem 'Vernältnis eines Mannes zu seiner Braut' die Rede ist (Kümmel[2]). Paulus antwortet dann auf die ganz einfache und klare Frage, wie es ein Mann halten soll, der Heiratsabsichten hat und schon ein Mädchen für die Ehe in Aussicht nahm."[3]

2. *The meaning of 1 Cor. 7.36–8*

It will be clear from the foregoing that the content of the Corinthians' inquiry cannot be determined until the meaning of 1 Cor. 7.36–8 is discussed. This passage is one of the most difficult and controversial in the New Testament, because a number of serious ambiguities occur in these three verses. It is not even possible to translate these verses without first adopting one of the theories outlined in the section above. For comparison, translations according to the two most divergent theories may be placed in parallel columns:

Fathers and Daughters	*Spiritual Marriages*
If any one thinks that he is behaving *dishonorably* toward his *virgin daughter*, if *she is past the flower of her age*, and if it *ought to be*, let him do what he will, he does not sin; *let them marry*. But whosoever is firmly estab-	If any one thinks that he is behaving *shamefully* toward his *virgin*, if *his passions are strong* and if it *has to be*, let him do what he will, he does not sin; *let them marry*. But whosoever is firmly established in

[1] Kümmel, "Verlobung," p. 277. Van Manen's suggestion was cited and adopted by J. M. S. Baljon, *De Tekst der Brieven van Paulus aan de Romeinen, de Corinthiërs en de Galatiërs als Voorwerp van de Conjecturaalkritiek Beschouwd* (Utrecht: Kemink & Zoon, 1885), pp. 65–6.

[2] The reference is to Kümmel's added note in Lietzmann, *Corr.*, p. 179 (S. 37, Z. 4).

[3] *Corr.*, p. 58. So also Adolf Jülicher, "Die Jungfrauen im ersten Korintherbrief," *Protestantische Monatshefte* XXII (1918), 97–119; Edgar J. Goodspeed, *The New Testament: An American Translation* (Chicago: The University of Chicago Press, 1923), where "his virgin" in 7.36 is translated "the girl to whom he is engaged" (see further his *Problems of New Testament Translation* [Chicago: The University of Chicago Press, 1945], pp. 158–9); Samuel Belkin, "The Problem of Paul's Background: III, Marrying One's Virgin," *JBL*, LIV (1935), 49–52 (on the basis of the Tannaitic literature); the RSV ("betrothed"); Kümmel, "Verlobung," pp. 286–95; Chadwick, "'All Things,'" pp. 267–8; and F. C. Grant, *N. T.*, p. 85.

lished in his heart, being under no necessity but having his *will* under control, and has determined this in his heart, to keep her as his *virgin daughter*, he will do well. So that he who *gives* his own *virgin daughter in marriage* does well; and he who does not *give her in marriage* will do better.

his heart, being under no necessity but having his *desire* under control, and has determined this in his heart, to keep her as his *virgin*, he will do well. So that he who *marries* his *virgin* does well; and he who does not *marry* will do better.

The points of disagreement between these two versions are as follows:

(i) *The subject.* According to the first theory the τις, "any one", refers to certain fathers at Corinth with marriageable daughters. According to the second theory it refers to men who have entered marriage relationships with vows of celibacy. Neither is specified by the context; both Paul and the Corinthians already knew the problem to which Paul referred. What type of man stood in a possessive relationship toward these "virgins" cannot be decided from the τις.

(ii) *"Dishonour".* The actions to which Paul refers by the word ἀσχημονέω are differently understood by these two theories. On the one hand the word is applied to the impaired honour of those fathers who fail to provide husbands for their daughters. On the other hand it is understood to designate the thoughts and actions of those men who find continued contact with their "spiritual brides" too great a strain for their original resolutions. Since Paul used the noun ἀσχημοσύνη (Rom. 1.27) with reference to homosexual acts, and the adjective (substantively) τὰ ἀσχήμονα as a euphemism for the genitalia (1 Cor. 12.23),[1] Pauline usage would favour taking the word in the stronger sense required by the "spiritual bride" theory. Furthermore, in the preceding section of his argument Paul had favoured celibacy, other things being equal. Only because of the danger of sexual immorality did he advocate normal marriage relationships. In view of this attitude of Paul's together with his conviction that "the appointed time has grown very short" (7.29), it would seem to require more than the embarrassment of a group of fathers to cause him to permit the marriage of these "virgins".[2]

---

[1] So also Rev. 16.15; and in the LXX, Ex. 20.26; Lev. 18.7; and Deut. 23.14 (the noun form).

[2] Morris' comment that "to withhold marriage from a girl of marriageable age, and anxious to marry, would have been to court disaster, especially in first-century Corinth" (*1 Cor.*, p. 120), not only involves assumptions about the "virgin's" desire to marry, and her lack of protection or of character, but is also beside the point. The dishonour is the result of the man's action, not the "virgin's".

(iii) *"His virgin"*. "His virgin", ἡ παρθένος αὐτοῦ (v. 36) or ἡ ἑαυτοῦ παρθένος (v. 38), is understood to mean "virgin daughter" on the one hand and "spiritual bride" on the other. Since there are far more direct ways of saying "daughter" or "unmarried daughter", the first meaning is not too probable. The lack of explanation in the context favours taking παρθένος as a technical term of some sort.

(iv) *Maturity*. The rare word ὑπέρακμος poses a problem. Arndt and Gingrich do not decide between the meaning, "past the bloom of youth" (of the girl), and the meaning "with strong passions" (of the man). There seems to be evidence in Greek literature that either meaning is possible. If the word was genuinely ambiguous, then the immediate context favours referring it to the man, since he is the subject of the preceding verb.

(v) *"Ought"*. Henry Chadwick has argued that the verb ὀφείλει suggests that "the pressure is external and is being imposed by the usages of society", and that the reference is not to the private desires of the man who is in danger of behaving dishonourably.[1] He uses this distinction to support the "spiritual engagements" theory (to be discussed below) and to oppose the "spiritual marriages" theory. The same line of reasoning would, of course, also favour the "fathers and daughters" theory. But it is not at all to be assumed that the "spiritual marriages" hypothesis should be taken to concern the private conduct of the persons involved. The arrangement is presumably based on the public profession of a vow. In any case the ὀφείλει indicates no more congregational interest than does the fact that this problem received special attention in the Corinthians' letter to Paul. Against Chadwick's distinction it should be noted that Paul had just used the cognate noun ὀφειλή as a euphemism for marital intercourse in the preceding section (7.3). Probably, therefore, the verb cannot be used to help in deducing the original situation at Corinth.

(vi) *"Let them marry"*. The most natural explanation of the plural verb γαμείτωσαν, occurring as it does after a series of singular nouns and verbs, is that the understood subjects are the only persons previously mentioned—the "virgin" and the man who possesses her. He is the one in danger of immorality, or of an uneasy conscience. Paul directs that the couple should marry ("if it has to be") and that they should not consider this action sinful. The "fathers and daughters" theory must

[1] " 'All things' ", p. 267.

now produce a hitherto unmentioned fiancé.[1] We should have expected, "Let *her* marry".[2]

(vii) *"Will"*. "Will", θέλημα, may mean both "purpose" and "desire". The latter meaning probably occurs at John 1.13 ("the will of the flesh"), for example. The word does not favour either theory against the other.

(viii) *"To give in marriage"*. Paul's final statement (7.38) twice employs the verb γαμίζω. But in 7.9 (*bis*), 10, 28 (*bis*), 33, 34, 36, and 39 he used the verb γαμέω, "to marry". It is natural to suppose that Paul intended a difference of meaning between these two verbs. Since the -ίζω ending (corresponding to the English -ise/-ize) is often causative in meaning, the usual translation of γαμίζω is "to cause to marry", that is, "to give in marriage".[3] Even Hans Achelis, the most thorough proponent of the "spiritual marriage" theory, rejected Eduard Grafe's suggestion that γαμίζω be translated as γαμέω.[4] Since the causative translation is generally favourable to the "fathers and daughters" theory,[5] scholars who favour this theory attach great importance to this verb. Robertson and Plummer, for example, say, "The γαμίζω is decisive: the Apostle is speaking of a father or guardian disposing of an unmarried daughter or ward."[6]

Undoubtedly, if it were not for the difficulties which the rest of this passage poses for the "fathers and daughters" theory, the causative translation of γαμίζω would never have been questioned. The two other occurrences of the verb in the New Testament (Mark 12.25 and Luke 17.27 with parallels) readily admit the causative sense. However, as W. F. Howard said, "It is significant that in the only other passages

---

[1] Thus, e.g., Goudge has to explain, "*let them marry.* i.e. his daughter and her lover" (*1 Cor.*, p. 62).

[2] The singular does, in fact, appear in a few mss.: D*, G, 1611, and sy[p]. The reading is clearly easier and therefore secondary.

[3] At this point it is customary to quote the opinion of Apollonius Dyscolus (a second-century A.D. grammarian) who wrote, "For there is, on the one hand, γαμέω, "I enter marriage," and, on the other, γαμίζω, "I give someone in marriage" (*De Syntaxi*, 280, 11 [Bekker ed]). So Moulton/Milligan, p. 121; Allo, *1 Cor.*, p. 193; and Arndt/Gingrich, p. 150. It should be remembered, however, that distinctions which grammarians have to define are those which are not obvious and, often, those which are passing (or have passed) out of the language. Apollonius' note, therefore, is evidence that these two verbs in particular were often confused in his time.

[4] *Virgines Subintroductae*, p. 22, n. 1. Grafe's suggestion appeared in his "Geistliche Verlöbnisse," p. 69.

[5] Some scholars of the other persuasion picture the spiritual bridegroom as giving his "virgin" in marriage to *another* man. So Achelis, *Virgines Subintroductae*, p. 26, who translates γαμίζω as "verheiraten". Lake allows this theory as a possibility (*Earlier Epistles*, p. 188). The idea is defended by Karl Holzhey, "Zur Exegese von I Co[r 7,] 36–37," *Theologie und Glaube*, XIX (1927), 307ff.

[6] *1 Cor.*, p. 159. This opinion is quoted with approval by Morris, *1 Cor*, p. 121.

where the word occurs...γαμίζεσθαι means no more than γαμεῖσθαι."[1] In fact, there is considerable evidence that this rare and post-classical verb may not need to carry a causative force at all. Moulton and Milligan say, "No instances of this verb have as yet been quoted outside the NT....[2] It may be noted, however, that many verbs in -ίζω are found used in the same way as verbs in -έω."[3] Both Howard and Lietzmann list examples of -ίζω verbs with intransitive meanings (for example, ἐλπίζω, ἐρίζω, παννυχίζω, etc.).[4] And David Smith argues: "On the analogy of similar formations (cf. πελεκίζειν, ἱματίζειν, σαββατίζειν, ἰουδαΐζειν) it [i.e., γαμίζειν] should denote, not 'give in marriage,' but rather 'practise marriage,' 'put to the marriage-use.'"[5] It appears, therefore, that the causative force of the -ίζω termination was waning in the Hellenistic period and that this suffix was often used simply as a convenient method of forming a verb. There are even several examples of pairs of verbs, each pair with the same stem and same meaning but with different terminations, one verb formed with -έω and one with -ίζω (for example, κομέω/κομίζω and ὑστερέω/ὑστερίζω).[6] We conclude, therefore, that although the verb is probably to be counted as evidence in favour of the "fathers and daughters" theory, its weight is not to be relied upon to any great extent.[7]

Conclusion. Of the seven points of exegesis listed above, the first and the sixth cannot be counted in favour of either theory. Of the rest only the last favours the "fathers and daughters" theory. It appears probable that this theory, therefore, should be set aside.

Kümmel defends this conclusion, but instead of accepting the

[1] James Hope Moulton and Wilbert Francis Howard, A Grammar of New Testament Greek: Vol. II, Accidence and Word-Formation (Edinburgh: T. & T. Clark, 1929), p. 410.
Clearly Morris begs the question and overstates his case when he says that γαμίζω is "a verb which elsewhere always means 'give a woman in marriage' " (1 Cor., p. 122).
[2] In 1954 Kümmel wrote that a friend in the Marburger Institut für Papyrusforschung still could report no extra-Biblical occurrence of this verb ("Verlobung," p. 287, n. 44.).
[3] Moulton/Milligan, p. 121.
[4] Moulton and Howard, Grammar, pp. 409-10; Lietzmann, Corr., p. 36.
[5] St. Paul, p. 268, n. 6.
[6] Cited by Moulton and Howard, Grammar, p. 409. Allo admits these facts but says of them, "On a deux verbes pour une même notion, ce qu'il n'est pas du tout la même chose que d'avoir deux notions, aussi différentes que 'épouser' et 'marier', pour un seul et même verbe" (1 Cor., p. 193). But even if we should grant Allo's premise that γαμίζω frequently meant "to give in marriage", it does not follow at all that the verb could not also have the meaning "to marry". Allo is the victim of the linguistic fallacy which supposes that a distinction in thought must result in a corresponding distinction in the vocabulary of a language. James Barr, for example, labels this type of assumption "self-evidently absurd" (Semantics, p. 35). One need look no further than the English verb "betroth" to find the range of meaning to which Allo objects.
[7] Kümmel even goes so far as to say that the linguistic evidence favours the "spiritual marriage" hypothesis ("Verlobung," p. 289).

"spiritual marriage" hypothesis, he goes on to argue that there are now no reasons why the persons in question may not simply have been engaged to each other.[1] Clearly this ordinary relationship and the extraordinary "spiritual marriages" involve many of the same elements: in both cases the woman may be referred to as a "virgin"; in both cases there is a binding agreement which enables the man to speak of "his own virgin"; in both cases celibacy is required unless and until the relationship changes; both situations are unstable and dangerous if prolonged; and in both cases the problem has arisen because of the new-found faith of the individuals involved. The key difference is whether or not the couple were actually living together. In order to decide this point it will be necessary to consider the context in which 1 Cor. 7.36–8 occurs.

3. The purpose of 1 Cor. 7.25–35

(a) 1 Cor. 7.25–8. The situation reflected in 1 Cor. 7.26–8 and, in particular, the meaning of the word παρθένος in 7.25 and 28 (as well as 7.34) are difficult to determine. Most scholars believe that in 7.25–35 παρθένος is used in a general sense to mean "those women who have never been married", and that the word takes on a narrower meaning in 7.36–8. Thus, for example, Grosheide says, "Vs. 36 introduces a new subject to the extent that the apostle begins to treat a special case relating to virgins."[2] The general reason for this conviction is that 7.26–8 appears to concern the larger problem of all those not yet married:

> Concerning "virgins," . . . I think . . . that it is well for a person to remain as he is. Are you bound to a wife? Do not seek to be free. Are you free from a wife? Do not seek marriage. But if you marry you do not sin, and if a "virgin" marries she does not sin.

A more particular reason for separating this passage from 7.36–8 affects those scholars who hold the "fathers and daughters" theory. According to this theory the man who is addressed in 7.36–8 is the girl's father; 7.26–8, on the other hand, obviously is directed at the man who himself contemplates marriage. Thus Lightfoot expressed what is the usual view of Paul's response as follows: "St Paul generalized, first stating the guiding principle (v. 27), then applying it to both sexes (vv. 28–35), and finally dealing with the special point which the Corinthians had put to him (vv. 36–38)."[3]

---

[1] Ibid., pp. 287–95.   [2] 1 Cor., p. 182.
[3] Notes, p. 231. So Goudge, 1 Cor., pp. 60, 62; and Simon, 1 Cor., p. 92.

There are a number of reasons, however, why, contrary to the opinion of these scholars, 1 Cor. 7.26–8 should be considered as directed to the same problem as 7.36–8.[1]

(i) If our conclusion is accepted that the "fathers and daughters" theory is improbable, then the special reason noted above for making a distinction between 7.26–8 and 7.36–8 disappears. In fact, when this theory is set aside (whether we decide finally that 7.36–8 concerns engaged couples or "spiritual" marriages), the two passages become similar in emphasis. In both the primary concern is the problem of the man and what his actions should be toward his "virgin."

(ii) The use of the word παρθένος is an additional reason for associating these two passages. We have already argued that the word in 7.36–8 was used in a technical sense familiar to Paul and to the Corinthians. Yet the word appears in 7.25 as the subject heading for the whole section, as well as at 7.28 and 7.34. There does not seem to be sufficient explanation in the whole passage to enable the Corinthians to know in which sense Paul used the word, if he varied its meaning. This lack of explanation, therefore, makes it probable that παρθένος, both in the Corinthians' question and in Paul's response, carried a single meaning.

(iii) In both 7.26–8 and 7.36–8 Paul went out of his way to assure the parties to whom he spoke that marriage was not a sin.

> v. 28 If you marry you do not sin, and if the virgin marries she does not sin.
> v. 36 If it has to be, let him do what he will, he does not sin; let them marry.

Paul in these passages and elsewhere (for example, 7.6–9) expressed his disapproval of marriage. But in 7.1–16 there is no indication that the Corinthians held that marriage was a sin. In discussing 7.1b we rejected the opinion that if "it is good for a man not to touch a woman", it is evil to touch her.[2] In the rest of that passage Paul recommended marriage as a defence against the sin of fornication; he did not present it as the lesser of two sins. But the verses quoted above do contest the idea that marriage is somehow sinful. The implication is that the Corinthians believed that for the particular individuals under discussion here (whatever their exact status) marriage was a sin. A special relationship

---

[1] Johannes Weiss is almost the only scholar who believes that the entire passage concerns a single problem (1 Cor., pp. 194–5). R. Steck, "Geistliche Ehen bei Paulus? (I Cor. 7.36–38)," Schweizer Theologische Zeitschrift, XXXIV (1917), 177–89, held the same view as Weiss but used the passage as evidence that 1 Corinthians was written in the second century. Enslin also adopts Weiss's position, Ethics, pp. 176–8. Chadwick, " 'All Things,' " p. 266, n. 3, considers the hypothesis "certainly probable".

[2] See above, pp. 159–61.

or vow appears to be involved, in 7.26–8 as well as in 7.36–8. Thus Johannes Weiss comments on v. 28, "Der Ausdruck οὐχ ἥμαρτες ist doch ganz unmöglich, wenn es sich nur darum handelt, dass Jemand zur Heirat geschritten ist."[1]

(iv) If 7.26–8 is taken to refer to the same situation as 7.36–8, then 7.29–35 becomes an explanatory digression between two similar passages. The pattern of Paul's response then would be, as Weiss put it, "a-b-a".[2] It is significant that the same pattern appears in Paul's discussion of idol meat (1 Cor. 8, 9, and 10) and, as we shall see, of spiritual gifts (1 Cor. 12, 13, and 14).[3] Moreover, the present chapter also has the same tripartite structure (7.1–16, 17–24, 25–40). In each case the middle section is a digression which sets the argument in a larger context; the first and last sections, however, have the same or similar subjects. Thus Paul's habits of argument lead us to expect that 7.26–8 and 7.36–8 are closely related.

We conclude, therefore, that in all probability 7.26–8 concerns the same problem as 7.36–8. This conclusion leads to two further observations.

(i) It appears that the rather special relationships which lie behind 7.36–8 are in fact the subject of the whole passage "concerning virgins" (7.25–38). Since Paul—and, presumably, the Corinthians as well—considered the problem posed by these persons important enough to form a special topic of discussion, it is probable that the "virgins" constituted a special category within the congregation at Corinth. In the previous section (7.1–24) Paul had dealt with the natural divisions of their congregation, that is, with the married, with the unmarried, with widows, and with those married to non-Christians. Then he turned (7.25) not to the unmarried again (as the RSV has it), but to those we might better call the "celibate".

(ii) 1 Cor. 7.26, which forms Paul's opening statement on this problem, contains an awkward repetition of the word καλόν ("I think it *well* . . . that it is *well* for a person to remain as he is."). Robertson and Plummer comment: "The construction of the verse is not regular, but quite intelligible."[4] In view (a) of the ὅτι before the second καλόν, (b) of the use of the term καλόν in the Corinthians' slogan quoted in 7.1, and (c) of Paul's habit of quoting the Corinthians' position at the opening of each new topic, we may be justified in suggesting that the

---

[1] *1 Cor.*, p. 194.   [2] Ibid., p. 192.
[3] Allo also has noted the structural similarity of 1 Cor. 8—10 to 12—14, an observation which he uses as an argument in favour of the integrity of these sections (*1 Cor.*, p. 319).
[4] *1 Cor.*, p. 152.

Corinthians had said it was "well" if these persons did not change their status. Possibly, therefore, Paul was here simply giving his approval to the position stated in the Corinthians' letter.

(b) *Engaged couples or spiritual marriages?* In view of the relationship between 7.36–8 and 7.26–8 we can now return to the problem of attempting to decide whether the main question in 7.25–38 concerned engaged couples or spiritual marriages. It should be said immediately that there is no evidence in this passage which decisively favours one rather than the other possibility. There are, however, three considerations which indicate a probable solution to the problem.

(i) In the first place, the ordinariness of the proposed engagement relationship cannot be used as an argument in favour of this suggestion and against the spiritual marriage hypothesis. The engagement theory actually involves three steps. It proposes that there were couples at Corinth (a) who had agreed to marry (i.e., become engaged), (b) who then had been converted to an ascetic point of view before marrying, and (c) who finally, instead of dissolving the relationship, had converted it into an ascetic discipline. We should speak of "spiritual" engagements to emphasize that the relationship included both an initial agreement to marry and a subsequent agreement not to marry. The spiritual marriage theory, on the other hand, supposes that unmarried members of the Corinthian congregation had entered directly into ascetic relationships; it does not suppose that each couple began with a pre-conversion intention of marrying. In this respect the spiritual marriage theory is simpler and therefore to this extent more probable.

(ii) Moreover, we have argued above that the whole of 7.25–38 concerns a single problem, and therefore that the "virgins" or the "celibate" represented a group of some size and importance in the Corinthian congregation. But, statistically speaking, it is unlikely that the moment of conversion (either to Christianity, or to asceticism within Christianity) would have found a significant proportion of the Corinthians engaged to be married.

(iii) Finally, the spiritual marriage relationship would seem to have more purpose and usefulness than an engagement. The couple would have all the social and legal advantages of marriage, that is, they would enjoy mutual encouragement and companionship in the faith, and they would enjoy the freedom and security of a Christian household by by contrast perhaps to the partly Christian or non-Christian homes from which they came. The care and burden of children in a world with only a brief future would be avoided. That the Corinthians could

favour (and Paul allow) intramarital asceticism is shown by 1 Cor.
7.1–7. On the other hand it is difficult to see what function spiritual
engagement would have served except as a special reminder to some
persons who had discontinued their plans to marry. Possibly it could
have provided an escape for a girl whose non-Christian father was
pressing her to marry. But such a suggestion seems rather special.

All in all, we conclude that the ascetical relationship which had arisen
in the Corinthian Church were probably marriages in every respect
save marital intercourse and the resulting parental responsibilities.

(c) 1 Cor. 7.29–35. Paul's justification for advising that "it is well for a
person to remain as he is" (7.26) is his assertion that "the appointed
time has grown very short" (7.29). But like the argument based on
concern for the weaker brother, the eschatological argument works
equally well in either direction. If things are not as they should be, then
rapid change is necessary. If impending changes are less satisfactory,
then no change should be made in view of the present crisis. Eschatological excitement adds urgency but not direction in ethical matters.
Clearly Paul favoured the *status quo* in Corinth, and thus he formulated
the eschatological argument in the manner in which it appears in
7.29–35. But if Paul felt it necessary to argue at such length in favour
of the *status quo*, it follows that some one had suggested or advocated a
change in the marital situation at Corinth since the time of Paul's first
visit there (Stage 1). But if 1 Cor. 7.1b, "It is well for a man not to
touch a woman", is, as we have argued, a slogan from the Corinthians'
letter, then it is probable that they are not the ones who had recommended a change in the status of these "spiritual" couples. The curious
result of our analysis is that we find Paul and the Corinthians arguing
in the same direction on this issue. The rather cautious advice that
spiritual marriages should be resolved into normal marriage relationships appear, therefore, to have arisen from another source sometime
between Stage 1 and Stage 4. In the next chapter we shall have an
opportunity to analyse the various Corinthian questions to see whether
we can discover their origin. And in the chapter following we shall
return to the problem of the source of the cautious influence in the
matter of spiritual marriages.

4. The Corinthians' question concerning "virgins"

Content of the question. To summarize the argument of the preceding
sections we may suggest the following as the substance of Corinthians'
question concerning "virgins":

Concerning our celibate couples it has been suggested that it would be safer for them to marry. With this advice we are in direct disagreement. We hold that it is well for them to continue in their spiritual state.

Nature of the exchange. Several observations should be made about the nature of the Corinthians' question and Paul's response to it. We note first of all that in this section Paul has put the weight of his argument in favour of an ascetic position, the reverse of his tendency in 7.1–24. Thus those couples who had previously enjoyed marital intercourse he advised to resume their former sexual relations lest they be tempted by Satan (7.5). But those who were spiritually married, and who had not lost their celibate status, he advised to avoid sexual relations. In the former case his advice seems to moderns to be full of common sense and moderation (especially if Paul's ascetic statement that his advice is "by way of concession" be forgotten). In the latter case, if we have correctly gauged the evidence, Paul took a more radically ascetic stand with a point of view not too different from that of the Corinthians. There seems to be a difference, therefore, between Paul's reluctance to recommend intramarital asceticism in the first case (although he allowed it for short periods), and his ascetic recommendations in the second case. Perhaps the distinction which he made between these parallel situations was governed by Jesus' command, "They are no longer two but one. What therefore God has joined together, let not man put asunder" (Mark 10.8, 9; 1 Cor. 6.16; 7.10). But perhaps, as we shall suggest, the situation was more complex.

Secondly, we may notice that Paul's response to the whole series of questions concerning marriage is similar to his reply concerning idol meat. In each case he accepted the Corinthians' slogan(s), or, at least, he did not directly reject their position. In each case he introduced special considerations which required or might have required a change in the Corinthians' behaviour. But in each case he ended by allowing the Corinthians to continue their behaviour with little or no change. Only in respect to divorce, where a command of the Lord applied, was Paul really vehement, and even on this topic Paul allowed the divorce of believers married to unsympathetic unbelievers. On marriage and its problems, just as on the matter of idol meat, Paul's advice when reduced to essentials would actually have required almost no change in the Corinthians' habits. In fact Paul's explicit principle concerning marriage was, "It is well for a person to remain as he is" (7.26, as well as 7.17–24). Why Paul's responses on these subjects appear so vehement and yet actually involve such slight practical demands is another problem to be deferred until Chapter 6.

We turn now to a second pair of questions put to Paul by the Corinthian Church.

CONCERNING THE VEILING OF WOMEN (I COR. 11.2–16)

The section of 1 Corinthians from 11.2 through 14.40 deals entirely with topics relating to the Corinthians' manner of worship. The analysis of 1 Corinthians given in Chapter 3 indicated the probability that 11.17–34 is a passage occasioned by oral information and inserted by Paul into the context of his answers to the Corinthians' written questions about worship, because the abuse which he wished to condemn also concerned their manner of worship.[1] Leaving this section aside, there remain two topics about which the Corinthians appear to have inquired: the veiling of women and spiritual gifts. The pattern of Paul's response to these two questions is parallel to his response to the two concerning sexual morality. In each case he added an afterthought about the first topic after he had dealt with the second. 1 Cor. 7.39, 40 on the remarriage of widows belongs with 7.1–24 rather than with 7.25–38. And 1 Cor. 14.33b–36 (the conduct of women in church) is more closely related to 11.2–16 (the veiling of women in church) than to 12.1—14.33a, 37–40 (the problem of glossolalia in church).[2] Paul opened his treatment of these two problems with a statement which many scholars[3] believe to be a reference to the Corinthians' letter, "I commend you because you remember me in everything and maintain the traditions (τὰς παραδόσεις) even as I have delivered them (παρέδωκα) to you" (11.2). Evans, for example, calls 11.2 "a reference, partly ironical, to expressions in the Corinthians' letter of inquiry, serving as introduction to the next four chapters".[4] This suggestion seems entirely probable for the following reasons:

(i) The statement presupposes some communication from Corinth—communication which must have occurred in Stage 3, unless we are to postulate some otherwise unrecorded occasion on which Paul received such information.

(ii) The communication was probably in written form, because it seems at variance with what we know of the oral information from

---

[1] See pp. 78–80, 92–4 above.   [2] So, e.g., Craig, "1 Cor.," p. 124.
[3] See Table 5 above, p. 68.   [4] *Corr.*, p. 117.

Corinth. In fact, Paul himself commented on the discrepancy when he turned to the item of oral information discussed in 11.17–34: "But in the following instructions I do *not* commend you" (11.17).

Not all commentators who accept 11.2 as a quotation believe that 11.3–16 was occasioned by a question from the Corinthians.[1] Our discussion of 11.3–16 in Chapter 3,[2] however, indicated the probability that this section was part of the answer material in 1 Corinthians, and a number of scholars take this position.[3]

According to most commentators who have hazarded a guess on the subject, the question asked by the Corinthians was a simple request for guidance. Thus Bousset proposed, "Soll die Frau beim Auftreten im öffentlichen Gottesdienst unverschleiert auftreten?"[4] And Lietzmann suggested, "Da wir allewege Deine Vorschriften zu befolgen bemüht sind, bitten wir Dich, uns Deine Ansicht über die Verschleierung der Frauen beim Gottesdienst zu sagen."[5] We shall return in Chapter 6 to his interesting mention of the Previous Letter; in other respects his version is the equivalent of Bousset's.

The reconstructions of these scholars, however, leave one major question unanswered. They do not explain what Moffatt called Paul's "curiously warm objection" to the Corinthians' communication.[6] If, as these scholars imply, the Corinthians had just assured Paul of their fidelity to his earlier directions (11.2) and had merely asked for further instruction, why did he not answer their question simply and directly? Instead, Paul's answer involves an appeal to custom, to Scripture (Gen. 1—2), to natural law, and to the practice of the other Churches. 1 Cor. 11.3–16 sounds far more like one side of an argument than a response to a simple request for guidance.

Therefore, it seems probable that in this section Paul was neither choosing between alternatives equally acceptable to the Corinthians nor replying to a polite request for his counsel, but instead was strongly urging his own point of view against the opposite opinion held by the Corinthians. Paul argued as persuasively as possible that women should be veiled during the worship of the Church. Apparently the Corinthians held the opposite view. Moffatt described their position as follows: "Why . . . should devout women be obliged to wear a covering veil on the head when men did not? Did not men and women worship bareheaded in Greek rites? As the Christian meetings were held in a large

---

[1] E.g., Findlay, "Letter of the Corinthian Church," p. 402, includes the former but omits the latter.

[2] See pp. 90–1 above.   [3] See above, p. 90, n. 2.   [4] "1 Cor.," p. 128.

[5] *Corr.*, p. 53.   [6] *1 Cor.*, p. 150.

room of some private house, it was felt that, while women's heads might be covered out of doors, there was no reason why the veil should be retained within the Household of the Lord."[1] It is not necessary to decide the difficult historical problem of the actual social *mores* which were current at the time.[2] Clearly Paul took a conservative position on the problem[3] and considered that the Corinthians were advocating an overenlightened, perhaps even dangerous,[4] practice.

Having concluded that Paul and the Corinthians were at odds over the question of the wearing of veils by women during worship, we can now see an interesting new possibility for the understanding of I Cor. 11.2. This verse, which reflects the Corinthians' fidelity to

---

[1] Ibid., p. 149.

[2] J. Weiss, *Primitive Christianity*, p. 332; and Dibelius, *Paul*, p. 38, maintain that Paul took the Jewish position on the veiling of women; Lake said that it was "remarkable" that Paul advocated the Greek practice (*Earlier Epistles*, p. 210); and Evans said that Paul followed a distinctively Christian tradition identical with neither (*Corr.*, pp. 115–17). J. A. Fitzmyer says, "Though many details about the wearing of the veil in antiquity, both by Jewish and Greek women, have been preserved for us, none of them bears directly on the problem of the Church in Corinth. We do not know the exact nature nor the origin of the abuse that Paul was trying to handle" ("A Feature of Qumrân Angelology and the Angels of I Cor. XI. 10," *NTS*, IV [1957/58], 48, n. 1).

[3] So Moffatt, *1 Cor.*, p. 155 ("He takes a conservative line on the issue."); and Simon *1 Cor.*, p. 111 ("He was conservative on the question of feminine liberty.").

[4] I Cor. 11.10 ("That is why a woman ought to have a veil [ἐξουσία] on her head, because of the *angels*.") is a *crux interpretum*. Fitzmyer, "Feature of Qumrân Angelology," pp. 48–58, provides a recent discussion of the problem. On the basis of rather distant parallels in the Qumrân scrolls he suggests that Paul believed that the "angels" were benevolent spirits which were actually present during the Church's worship and which merited respect and reverence. He rejects the opinion first suggested by Tertullian (in the treatise, *Concerning the Veiling of Virgins*, 7) that the "angels" were the fallen angels of Gen. 6.2 for the commonly adduced reason that "ἄγγελοι, used with the article, never designates bad or fallen angels in Pauline writings" (p. 54). Fitzmyer depends on Robertson and Plummer, *1 Cor.*, at this point. Cf. also Allo, *1 Cor.*, p. 266; and Morris, *1 Cor.*, p. 154). Since the only other such references to angels are I Cor. 13.1, which he cites, and Col. 2.18, which he does not, the "never" is unnecessarily impressive. The former reference is of neutral significance; the latter reference, in fact, may well be an exception to his rule. See, e.g., G. H. C. MacGregor, "Principalities and Powers: The Cosmic Background of Paul's Thought," *NTS*, I (1954/55), 18. For many scholars, however, references to good angels in Paul's letters are exceedingly infrequent. Héring, *1 Cor.*, p. 108, singles out Gal. 1.8 (which, in view of Gal. 3.19, is not too likely), and T. W. Manson, *On Paul and John* ("Studies in Biblical Theology," No. 38; London: SCM Press Ltd, 1963), p. 19, suggests 2 Thess. 1.7 (which, in view of the vengeance which these angels mete out, is only a partial possibility). Alan Richardson, *An Introduction to the Theology of the New Testament* (New York: Harper & Brothers, 1958), p. 209, even goes so far as to say, "There are no good angels in St Paul". For defence of the identification of "angels" with, e.g., the evil "rulers of this age" who crucified Jesus (I Cor. 2.6–8; 6.3) see Clinton D. Morrison, *The Powers That Be* ("Studies in Biblical Theology," No. 29; London: SCM Press Ltd, 1960), pp. 23–4; and Manson, *On Paul and John*, pp. 20–1. Thus Tertullian's opinion that these are hostile angels, an opinion accepted, e.g., by J. Weiss, *1 Cor.*, p. 274; Lietzmann, *Corr.*, pp. 54–5; Dibelius, *Paul*, p. 39; and G. B. Caird, *Principalities and Powers: A Study in Pauline Theology* (Oxford: The Clarendon Press, 1956), pp. 17–21, appears still to be the most probable. Therefore women without veils during worship expose themselves to an unnecessary danger.

Paul's teachings, does not seem consonant with the intensity of Paul's treatment of the problem of veils. Is it not more probable, in view of the antagonism between Paul and the Corinthians over this issue, that I Cor. 11.2 represents not an affectionate expression of loyalty by the Corinthians (as scholars assume), but an argument which they have used to defend their position. The conjunction of 11.2 with 11.3–16 implies that the Corinthians had written to Paul:

> Concerning the manner in which we worship: we have simply been follow-ing the traditions which you passed on to us. We have been doing nothing new. Our women from the very first have worshipped without veils. This was their practice when you were with us.

To this statement (if accepted) Paul replied in effect, "I am glad that you are following the traditions I delivered to you, but I want to explain that the head of every man is Christ. . . ." Thus Paul's multiple and somewhat incoherent argument is provided with an adequate occasion.

The probability of the above reconstruction is increased by three considerations:

(i) The discussion of I Cor. 9 above led to the conclusion that the Corinthians had probably referred to Paul's own eating habits during his stay with them (Stage 1) as one of their arguments for freedom in the matter of idol meat.[1]

(ii) On the subject of marriage as well it was suggested that Paul's own marital status had been used by the Corinthians as justification of their own attitude toward sexual relations.[2]

(iii) I Cor. 11.2, we have suggested, served to introduce both the problem of women's veils and that of spiritual gifts. On the latter subject, as we shall see more fully in the next section below, Paul admitted that he could speak in tongues more than all of them (14.18). Here again it seems probable that the Corinthians had used Paul's own conduct (Stage 1) as an argument to defend their own.

We shall return in Chapter 7 to the fascinating problem of the dis-crepancy between Paul's conduct in Stage 1 and his opinions expressed in I Corinthians (Stage 4) on these and other points. More generally, we may note the similarity between this reconstruction and those con-cerning the other topics in the Corinthians' letter which we have discussed. There is the same mood of antagonism. Paul once again began his reply by quoting from the Corinthians' letter and then modifying

---

[1] See pp. 126–31.   [2] See pp. 166–7.

or limiting the quotation. Once again he piled argument upon argument.

We turn now to the second of this pair of problems concerning the Corinthians' manner of worship.

CONCERNING SPIRITUAL GIFTS (1 COR. 12.1—14.40)

Paul's response to the Corinthians' inquiry concerning spiritual gifts (or spiritual men) is the longest of his answers, although it is only barely longer than his repetitious discussion of idol meat. Clearly the topic was an important one to Paul, to the Corinthians, or to both.

1. Previous reconstructions

A number of commentators who designate 1 Cor. 12.1 as the opening of an answer to yet another of the Corinthians' questions go no further and either make no suggestion about the import of the question,[1] or else barely hint as to its nature.[2] Other scholars, however, are more specific. As usual, Findlay's attempt is the most elaborate:

> Once more, we wish to inquire about *the workings of the Spirit*. We need some test to distinguish His genuine inspirations. Strange cries are raised, even in our assemblies as well as in other companies, that sound as divine and above nature and that confound our understanding (xii. 1–3). How may we discriminate these voices? Of the unquestioned gifts of the Spirit of Christ we have great variety and wealth. We need some means of regulating their use, so as to turn them to the best account. Some of us think more highly of this charism, some of that; and those who admire one gift are apt to disparage another. So there comes to be rivalry, and even wrangling and clamour in the assembly; and the exuberance of our spiritual powers, through the malice of Satan, is turned to confusion. The gift of Tongues, we know, is an eminent faculty, bestowed on the Church from the beginning; thou dost thyself excel in its exercise (xiv. 18). Should it therefore be practised in the meetings of the Church without restraint, and take precedence of other charisms, even of prophecy? Some of us venture to question its utility, and would forbid altogether its public display (xiv. 39); moreover, strangers who happen to witness the Glossolalia are unfavourably affected thereby, and give it out that we are demented rather than inspired of God (xiv. 23). We are much at a loss, and need the light of thy counsel concerning this also.[3]

Of these various suggestions the first ("We need some test to distinguish His genuine inspirations") is the one most often suggested by other

---

[1] E.g., Goudge, *1 Cor.*; Robertson and Plummer, *1 Cor.*; and Allo, *1 Cor.*
[2] So Parry, *1 Cor.* ("Camb."), p. 127; Craig, "1 Cor.," p. 148; and Morris, *1 Cor.*, p. 168.
[3] "Letter of the Corinthian Church," pp. 405–6.

scholars. Thus, for example, Bousset commented on 1 Cor. 12.1–3 as follows: "In der Gemeinde hatte man ihm die Frage gestellt, woran man denn die Wirkungen des Geistes sicher erkennen, wodurch man sie namentlich von den Wirkungen der Dämonen und des Teufels unterscheiden könne. . . . Wo ist das Unterscheidungs-Merkmal?"[1] Some scholars, however, also try as Findlay did to formulate questions which would provide the occasion for the whole content of these three chapters. Evans proceeds most directly: "The questions referred to St. Paul were four in number: (a) how to discern true from false spiritual expression; (b) what is the relative value of prophecy and speaking with tongues, and which of these gifts gives its possessor the prerogative in addressing the assembly; (c) what is to be the procedure when several speakers claim a hearing at once; and (d) are women under any circumstances to address the assembly[?]"[2] Thus Evans agrees with other scholars as to his first question (a), agrees with Findlay concerning questions (b) and (c), and adds a new inquiry (d) to explain Paul's silencing of women in church. Another aspect of Findlay's reconstruction finds support from Kirsopp Lake and Theodor Zahn. They suggest the usual question about testing the Spirit, but they both go on to propose with Findlay that the Corinthians' questions had arisen from a difference of opinion between two parties, one of which opposed glossolalia altogether.[3] Finally, Lake agrees with Evans concerning the latter's last point, the question of women speaking during worship.[4]

2. The purpose of 1 Corinthians 12—14.

Although previous reconstructions of the Corinthians' question to Paul concerning spiritual gifts differ widely in scope, they share the common assumption that 1 Cor. 12—14 is a collection of notes on subjects only partially related to one another. The shorter versions of the Corinthians' question are derived from 1 Cor. 12.1–3 and imply that Paul went on to talk of other matters suggested to him by the topic of the Corinthians' inquiry. The detailed reconstructions of Findlay and Evans consist of a series of requests, again with the assumption that no one topic lay behind these chapters. Thus it is assumed that

---

[1] "1 Cor.," p. 134. So, with great similarity, J. Weiss, *1 Cor.*, p. 295; Lietzmann, *Corr.*, p. 60; Wendland, *Corr.*, p. 92; Grosheide, *1 Cor.*, p. 280 (". . . whether everything spoken in the Spirit was good and to God's glory"); and Simon, *1 Cor.*, p. 122 (" 'What criterion have we for distinguishing between inspired persons?' ").
[2] *Corr.*, p. 128.
[3] Zahn, *Intro. N. T.*, I, 279; and Lake, *Earlier Epistles*, pp. 206–9.   [4] Ibid.,   209.

the Corinthians' question and Paul's answer must have been closely correlated in structure: a simple request should in all probability have produced a short and simple answer; a comprehensive request, a long and detailed response. If 1 Cor. 12.1–3 represents Paul's answer, then the request must have been brief. If 1 Cor. 12—14 is his response, then the Corinthians' inquiry must have consisted of a series of requests. A second assumption of these critics—one which we have met before in discussing others of the Corinthians' inquiries—is the belief that the Corinthians' question to Paul arose from some uncertainty or disagreement at Corinth concerning the gifts of the Spirit, and that therefore their inquiry was a polite request for information or arbitration.

There is evidence in 1 Cor. 12—14, however, that neither of these assumptions is well founded. The crux of the problem is the extent to which these chapters share a unity of purpose.

1 Corinthians 14. Clearly 1 Cor. 14 has as its topic the relative value of "speaking in tongues" and prophecy. Clearly in this chapter Paul expresses his preference for prophecy. What is important to notice, however, is that Paul's preference is so strong that the difference between the two gifts is more qualitative than quantitative: "I would rather speak five words with my mind . . . than ten thousand words in a tongue" (14.19). Since "ten thousand" is the largest number for which the Greek system of numeration had a symbol, we may better translate: ". . . rather five words with my mind . . . than an infinite number in a tongue."[1] The fact that in this chapter Paul never directly condemned the practice of glossolalia (for reasons which remain to be suggested) should not be allowed to conceal the fervour with which he sought to persuade the Corinthians to minimize or abandon the practice. Thus, although he said, "Now I want you all to speak in tongues" (14.5), and, "I thank God that I speak in tongues more than you all" (14.18), the context in each case shows how little he valued this "gift". The second statement is immediately followed by his strongest expression of preference for rational preaching quoted above; the first occurs as follows:

> He who speaks in a tongue edifies himself, but he who prophesies edifies the church. Now I want you all to speak in tongues, but even more to prophesy. He who prophesies is greater than he who speaks in tongues, unless someone interprets, so that the church may be edified (14.4, 5).

---

[1] Arndt/Gingrich does not even list "ten thousand" as a possible translation for μυρίος and gives instead "innumerable, countless" (p. 531).

Paul here "damned" glossolalia "with faint praise". He went on to give a long succession of arguments against the practice. He appealed to the concern which they ought to have for the edification of their fellow Church members (14.2–5) and interested visitors (14.16, 17). He invoked the authority of common sense ("If the bugle gives an indistinct sound, who will get ready for battle?" [14.8]) and of scripture (14.21, 22). He pleaded for decorum ("Will they not say that you are mad?" [14.23]) and decency ("All things should be done decently and in order" [14.40]). Such a piling up of arguments is evidence that Paul was not weighing a theoretical problem but was seeking to deal severely with the advocacy of glossolalia within the Corinthian Church. We are immediately reminded of the similar series of arguments in 1 Cor. 11.2–16 concerning the veiling of women, and of the longer sequence concerning idol meat (8.1—11.1). The two-fold appeal in behalf of the hypothetical weaker brother in the latter section is especially close to Paul's appeal here concerning the equally hypothetical outsider (14.16, 17, 23–5). On each of these issues it appears that Paul had a definite goal in mind toward which he bent every argument that came to hand.

1 Corinthians 13. 1 Cor. 13, moreover, manifests the same interest as chapter 14. Here is Paul's great description of the gift which is the source of active concern for others. As Chapter 4 suggested, however, the terms of Paul's description of love were not abstract, but reflected his opinion of the actual situation in the Corinthian Church.[1] The purpose of this portrayal of love was also practical. We have already noted his mention of the babbling of babies (13.11) in apparent reference to the glossolalia of the Corinthians.[2] Of himself Paul said, however, "When I became a man, I gave up childish ways" (13.11), an assertion which anticipates 14.20, "Brethren, do not be children in your thinking; be babes in evil, but in thinking be mature". The connection between these two chapters is further emphasized by the use Paul made of his panegyric on love. He concluded the passage: "Make love your aim, and earnestly desire the spiritual gifts, especially that you may *prophesy*" (14.1). Prophecy was inspired utterance which endeavoured to communicate, thus exhibiting in practice the loving concern for others (however hypothetical) which was the subject of chapter 13 and the basis of Paul's argument in chapter 14. Thus 1 Cor. 13, although it mentions speaking in tongues only obliquely (13.1, 8, 11), shares with 1 Cor. 14 the purpose which becomes explicit in the

[1] See pp. 108–13 above.   [2] See above, pp. 112–13.

latter chapter—Paul's desire to curtail speaking in tongues at Corinth.

1 Corinthians 12. We approach 1 Cor. 12 last of the three chapters under discussion because, as with 1 Cor. 13, its purpose appears most clearly in the material which succeeds it. In general, commentators have understood this chapter to be Paul's defence of the organic unity of the Church in spite of its apparent disunity: "Now there are varieties of gifts, but the *same* Spirit . . ." (12.4). Thus, for example, Robertson and Plummer say of this verse, "The Apostle goes on to point out the essential oneness of these very varied gifts [listed in verses 4–11]."[1] And Moffatt says of 12.4–11, "Within the Church the Spirit is the uniting power, which overcomes all differences of temperament and education and endowment, not obliterating them, but combining them in a common, co-operative service of the fellowship."[2]

There seem to be two factors which predispose scholars to take the above line of interpretation. In the first place, a memory of the divisiveness apparently expressed by 1 Cor. 1.12 and 11.18 lingers on, and it is assumed that Paul in 1 Cor. 12 was attempting to portray the basic ground of unity which the Corinthians shared despite their quarrels. Thus Simon says, "St. Paul faces once again two Corinthian weaknesses—pride and self-satisfaction, and a tendency to rivalries and jealousy. Consequently he emphasizes the truth that all the spiritual gifts they boast of come from one divine source, the Holy Spirit."[3] The second factor, less conscious than the first, is the widespread conviction among Christians to-day that the Church suffers grievously from its divisions and disunity both between and within Churches and denominations. Thus John A. T. Robinson says of the effect that our modern individualism has on our interpretation of this passage, "For us, starting as we do with our conception of the Body of Christ as a society, the most pressing problem is how the many can be one. The multiplicity is obvious, the unity problematic."[4]

It appears far more probable, however, that Paul was not primarily seeking to defend the unity of the Church in the face of its obvious multiplicity, but that his purpose was the reverse. He sought to encourage diversity within the Church. J. A. T. Robinson appears on the threshold of this insight when he writes,

---

[1] *1 Cor.*, p. 262.   [2] *1 Cor.*, p. 183.

[3] *1 Cor.*, p. 123. So also Goudge, *1 Cor.*, p. 108, who describes the Corinthians as "failing to recognise the unity of the Church"; Bousset, "1 Cor.," p. 134; Evans, *Corr.*, p. 128 ("no place for rivalry"); Allo, *1 Cor.*, p. 319; Héring, *1 Cor.*, p. 129 ("the menace of discord"); and Grosheide, *1 Cor.*, p. 290.

[4] *The Body: A Study in Pauline Theology* ("Studies in Biblical Theology," No. 5; London: SCM Press Ltd, 1952), p. 58.

The unity of Christ, as of the human body, is his starting point. He then proceeds to show that the body cannot in fact consist only of "one member", but must be "many" (v. 14). The point of the verses that follow (15–21) is *not* that the different members must be united among themselves (the question of schism does not enter till v. 25, and then it is quite incidental to the passage) but precisely that there must be more than one member if there is to be a body at all.[1]

Robinson rejects the usual interpretation of this chapter which has Paul say in effect, "Do not be blind to the unity of the Church because of the divisions which you see. The Church is like a body. . . ." Instead, Robinson believes that Paul intended to say, "Do not let your belief in the unity of Christ's body, the Church, be disturbed by the divisions which you see among you. A body must have many and differing members." As Robinson puts it, "Paul's argument is that the resurrection body of Christ *can* be articulated in diversity *without ceasing to be a unity*. All the members of a human body form one body *despite* their number. So it is with the person of Christ."[2] Thus for Robinson, as for other scholars, the basic issue is still the threat posed by the inner divisions of the Church.

By contrast, however, to previous scholarly interpretations of 1 Cor. 12 we hold that Paul did not take a negative view toward diversity within the Corinthian Church. Instead we suggest that Paul was disturbed over the narrowness and uniformity of the Corinthians' view of the operation of the Spirit. Paul stressed the variety of the gifts of the Spirit, not negatively, as though they represented a theological challenge to the doctrine of the unity of the Church, but positively, in order to persuade the Corinthians to broaden their viewpoint and to accept a variety of skills and ministries as actual evidence of the working of the Spirit.

> But there are *varieties* of gifts, and the same Spirit; and there are *varieties* of service, and the same Lord; and there are *varieties* of workings, and it is the same God who inspires them all in every one. To each is given the manifestation of the Spirit for the common good (12.4–7).

Paul then listed eight distinct gifts, each of which, he maintained, revealed the genuine inspiration of the Spirit. He next introduced the metaphor of the "body", which was used in antiquity to represent the

---

[1] Ibid., p. 59. So also C. S. C. Williams, "*Corr.*," §839e: "Paul starts from the one body and explains why it must have more than one member or else not be a body; he does not start from the many to reach the one."

[2] *Body*, p. 60.

interdependence of the "members" of a society.[1] Paul, however, adapted the image to serve his present purpose. In order to support his contention that the Spirit works through many ministries he argued,

> The body does not consist of one member but of many. . . . If the ear should say, "Because I am not an eye I do not belong to the body," that would not make it any less a part of the body. If the whole body were an eye, where would be the hearing? . . . If all were a single organ, where would the body be? . . . The eye cannot say to the hand, "I have no need of you." (12.14-20).

No part of the body can claim to be the true body; no single function of the body can be considered the only legitimate expression of the body's life. Similarly, numerous ministries of the Church are empowered and inspired by the Spirit; *all* the Corinthian Christians, in fact, are recipients of the Spirit: "By one Spirit we were *all* baptized into one body—Jews or Greeks, slaves or free—and *all* were made to drink of one Spirit" (12.13).

We do not have to look far to find the one manifestation of the Spirit which the Corinthians accepted as genuine. Each of the three lists of spiritual gifts which Paul gave (12.8-10; 12.28; and 12.29, 30) places speaking in tongues and its interpretation last of all. Since "the utterance of wisdom" heads the first series and "apostles" the other two, it appears that Paul put first the things most important and put last the things least important.[2] Thus, while he does not repudiate glossolalia entirely, he counts it the lowest of God's spiritual blessings. In this light his remark at the conclusion of the chapter becomes especially pointed: "But earnestly desire the *higher* gifts" (12.31).

Thus we conclude that Paul's heavy emphasis in 1 Cor. 12.4-31 on the variety of gifts and ministries within the Church served the same purpose as 1 Cor. 13—14. The three chapters form one long attack upon the notion that speaking in tongues was the single or the best manifestation of the Spirit at work in the Church. On the contrary, Paul maintained, glossolalia is the least gift of all (1 Cor. 12); the highest gift is love (1 Cor. 13); and, moreover, love, when it is present, leads to the suppression of the public practice of speaking in tongues (1 Cor. 14). There is, therefore, a striking unity of purpose in these

---

[1] For pre-Pauline references see Robinson, ibid., p. 59, n. 1, based on Lietzmann's collection of parallels, *Corr.*, p. 62.

[2] Cf. Robertson and Plummer, *1 Cor.*, p. 267 ("St. Paul placed last the gifts on which the Corinthians specially prided themselves. . . . Their enthusiasm for the gift of Tongues was exaggerated."); Allo, *1 Cor.*, p. 326; Héring, *1 Cor.*, p. 129; Craig, "1 Cor.," p. 163 ("The order . . . is deliberate."); Wendland, *Corr.*, p. 95 ("an letzter Stelle, wohl absichtlich"); and Simon, *1 Cor.*, p. 124 ("put by St. Paul, no doubt deliberately, at the end of his list").

three chapters, a unity which makes improbable the first assumption of the scholars noted above concerning the correlation in structure between the Corinthians' question and Paul's reply. A single, rather simple question may well have produced the whole of 1 Cor. 12—14.

3. The Corinthians' question

The length, the complexity, and the singleness of purpose of Paul's argument in 1 Cor. 12—14 indicate that he was attempting to persuade those who held a view contrary to his own, and that he was not answering a polite request for his opinion on the matter. The evidence, therefore, favours placing the difference of opinion between Paul and the Corinthians, rather than in the Corinthian congregation. Thus the second of the usual scholarly assumptions about this question is improbable. As in the case of the questions from Corinth already discussed, Paul stood on one side and the Corinthians on the other. On the matter at issue the Corinthians seem to have held a definite position, and presumably they have argued in its defence.

The content of the question. What the Corinthians' position was has already been suggested. They had maintained that glossolalia is the main (or only) evidence of possession by the Spirit. If an apostle, for example, speaks in tongues, then he can be known to be spiritual. In general, only those Christians who have this gift are to be classed as spiritual. How this position was expressed in the Corinthians' question is more difficult to decide, however. Paul began his reply as follows:

> You know that when you were heathen, you were led astray to dumb idols, however you may have been moved. Therefore I want you to understand that no one speaking by the Spirit of God ever says "Jesus be cursed!" and no one can say "Jesus is Lord" except by the Holy Spirit (12.2, 3).

As most of the reconstructions of the Corinthians' question noted above suggest, there seems to be some inquiry behind these verses about the manner by which the Spirit may be known. It seems hardly likely, however, that if cries of "Jesus be cursed!" had filled either the church or the synagogue, the Corinthians would have been at a loss to know whether such an utterance were the work of the Holy Spirit.[1] It appears more likely that "Jesus be cursed!" is the hypothetical opposite of the cry, "Jesus is Lord".[2] Paul intended to emphasize to the Corinthians

[1] Thus attempts to portray situations in which such a cry could have occurred seem unnecessary. See, e.g., the hypotheses of Moffatt, *1 Cor.*, p. 179; and of Schmithals, *Gnosis*, pp. 45-50 (on which see p. 102, n. 2, above).

[2] Cf. 1 Cor. 6.15, 16, where Paul seems to be describing the hypothetical extreme which might result from the Corinthians' principles of freedom. See above, pp. 86-9 and 164.

that before they became Christians they might have been deceived about spirits, but now they should know that the Spirit shows himself by the results he produces. This statement led Paul on to point out that there are many other products of the Spirit's action besides ejaculations of praise during worship: "Now there are varieties of gifts, but the same Spirit . . ." (12.4). Noticeable also is Paul's emphasis on the rationality of the Spirit's expression, a theme which he developed in 1 Cor. 14. Thus it appears that the Corinthians have asked, "Concerning spiritual men,[1] how can we test the Spirit when he speaks? How are we to distinguish between spiritual men?"

Whether the Corinthians' question included some defence of the practice of speaking in tongues, including perhaps an allusion to the fact that Paul himself was adept in this art (1 Cor. 14.18), is problematical. Paul certainly knew of their enthusiastic manner of worship from his original stay in Corinth (Stage 1) and perhaps also from the travellers from Corinth (Stage 3). On the other hand, Paul appears to have been made conscious of the fact that his original conduct was somewhat at variance with his present disparagement of glossolalia. Certainly his reminder to the Corinthians of his own facility in speaking with tongues (14.18; 13.11) did not serve to advance his argument. In fact, Paul's attitude toward glossolalia is similar to his attitude toward the slogans by which the Corinthians justified their behaviour at other points: he did not attack the gift directly, but he added to the discussion other considerations (for example, other gifts, particularly the gift of love) which enabled him to gain his objective without blatant self-contradiction. It may well be, therefore, that the Corinthians in their inquiry about testing for the Spirit had reminded Paul that he had not exercised notable powers of discrimination when he himself spoke with tongues.

This observation leads to the conclusion that on the matter of spiritual men, as on the other topics in their letter, the Corinthians had not asked for information or clarification; their inquiry was a defence of their position. Thus their mention of Paul's conduct was a justification

---

[1] The majority of commentators take πνευματικῶν as a neuter, "spiritual gifts", because of 14.1, for example. So Robertson and Plummer, 1 Cor., p. 259; Moffatt, 1 Cor., p. 177; Héring, 1 Cor., pp. 122–3; and Grosheide, 1 Cor., p. 278. But since it appears that it is Paul who has added the idea of a variety of spiritual gifts and that the Corinthians had thought only of the gift of glossolalia, it is probable that in the Corinthians' letter the term referred to "spiritual men" (masculine). So J. Weiss, 1 Cor., p. 294. Parry suggested, "It is possible that the ambiguity is due to the fact that the Corinthians used the word in the narrow sense, and St. Paul, without at first directly combating this view, so uses it that the wider sense becomes dominant" (1 Cor. ["Camb."], p. 127).

of their own behaviour. It seems, therefore, that they have not asked, "How can we test for the Spirit?" but, "How is it *possible* to test for the Spirit?" In summary then we may formulate their question as follows:

> Concerning spiritual men: How is it possible to test for the Spirit? How can we (or anyone else) distinguish between spiritual men? When you were with us and spoke with tongues you gave us no instruction on this point.

The nature of the question. Once again the Corinthians had advocated a single position opposed to that of Paul's. Once again Paul did not deny their principles ("Now I want you all to speak in tongues . . ." [14.5]) but appealed to a variety of arguments to dissuade them from their current practices. Especially close is the parallel between Paul's treatment of this topic and his previous discussion of idol meat. Both sections are long and complex. In each case Paul came closest to the Corinthians' question in the opening sentences of his discussion. In both cases his primary argument was based on the loving concern which a Christian ought to have for others. And in both cases, as well as on the subjects of marriage and the veiling of women, Paul seems to have been somewhat hampered in his argument by his earlier conduct or advice (Stage 1).

Having dealt with two questions concerning the Corinthians' worship (and an instance of reprehensible conduct during worship), Paul took up what was probably their next inquiry, a question more strictly doctrinal in nature.

CONCERNING THE RESURRECTION (1 COR. 15)

The discussion of 1 Cor. 15 in Chapter 3 concluded that, although it is not clear that the Corinthians had written Paul "concerning the resurrection", Paul at least was sure that a difference of opinion existed between the Corinthian Church and himself on this point.[1]

1. *Suggested reconstructions*
General consensus. Those scholars who do believe that a question from Corinth on this subject was a part of the Corinthians' letter make little attempt to reconstruct the wording of the inquiry. They are primarily concerned with the nature of the Corinthians' uncertainty. Thus Lake writes: "It is clear from I Cor. xv. that there was a party at Corinth which denied that there would ever be a resurrection of the

---

[1] See above, pp. 91–2.

dead. . . . The question was not whether there would be a future life, but whether a future life must be attained by means of a resurrection." [1] The same position is expressed by W. L. Knox, who says of Paul, "It would seem that he failed to allow for the extent to which the Jewish element in the Church [at Corinth] had declined; at any rate a considerable section of it was sufficiently acquainted with the outlook of popular philosophy to refuse to believe in the resurrection of the dead in the form in which he had presented it. That rejection was natural. No intelligent and educated person believed in a subterranean Hades." [2] In general scholars accept this position and adopt Paul's phrasing of the Corinthians' question (or objection), "There is no resurrection of the dead" (15.12). [3]

A Pauline misunderstanding? Scholars differ, however, as regards the manner in which they understand the intention of this objection. Rudolf Bultmann has suggested the theory that Paul had misunderstood the Corinthians on this point. According to Bultmann, Paul understood the Corinthians to mean by their statement that they rejected all belief in a life after death. Thus Paul was led to say, "If in this life only we have hoped in Christ, we are of all men most to be pitied" (15.19), and "If the dead are not raised, "Let us eat and drink for tomorrow we die' " (15.32). That Paul had misunderstood the Corinthians at this point is shown, Bultmann argues, by the practice among them of vicarious baptism for the dead (15.29). However, 2 Cor. 5.1–5 shows, Bultmann believes, that the Corinthians actually held "the Gnostic view that man's self at death will be released from the body (and from the 'soul') and will soar in the state of 'nakedness' into the heavenly world". [4] Thus he explains the difference between Paul's treatment of the Corinthians' beliefs in 1 Cor. 15 and his rather different argument in 2 Cor. 5.1–5 as the result of two rather different conceptions held by Paul of the Corinthians' single position. Since he believes the time interval to be short from Paul's first statement to his second, he

---

[1] *Earlier Epistles*, pp. 215–16.   [2] *Gentiles*, p. 125.

[3] So Schmiedel, "Corr.," p. 153; Bousset, "1 Cor.," pp. 149, 155; and Lietzmann, *Corr.*, p. 79.

The following scholars do not suppose that the subject was mentioned in the Corinthians' letter, but they postulate the same general situation in Corinth as the scholars mentioned above: H. A. W. Meyer, *Corr.*, II, 36–7; Godet, *1 Cor.*, II, 321–5; J. Weiss, *1 Cor.*, p. 344; Goudge, *1 Cor.*, p. 137; Findlay, "1 Cor.," p. 917; Robertson and Plummer, *1 Cor.*, pp. 346–7; Parry, *1 Cor.* ("Camb."), pp. lvii–lviii; Evans, *Corr.*, pp. 136–40; Sickenberger, *Corr.*, pp. 74–5; Allo, *1 Cor.*, pp. 387–8, 399; W. Meyer, *1 Cor.*, II, 228, 243–4; Héring, *1 Cor.*, pp. 162–3; Grosheide, *1 Cor.*, p. 356; Morris, *1 Cor.*, pp. 209–10; and Simon, *1 Cor.*, pp. 138–9.

[4] *Theology of the N. T.*, I, 169n. His exposition here is based on his earlier article, *Exegetische Probleme des II. Kor.*, pp. 3–12.

concludes that the earlier statement must have been the result of a misunderstanding.

Bultmann's position is basically similar to that of the scholars discussed in the preceding section. The main point of difference is Bultmann's conviction that 1 Cor. 15 was written to combat disbelief in life after death, rather than disbelief in bodily resurrection. But there are considerations to the contrary.

(i) It is *a priori* improbable that Paul would have attributed to the Corinthians a denial of life after death, especially since, as Bultmann's theory contends, Paul assumed that the Corinthians were still "baptizing on behalf of the dead". Moreover, such a denial would have been so unexpected and unusual that he presumably would have verified his interpretation of the Corinthians' statement. He had ample opportunity to do so since there were two groups of travellers whom he could question. With so much information available to him it is probable that he was correct in his estimate of the Corinthians' beliefs. We must begin by assuming, therefore, that Paul knew what he was talking about.

(ii) Bultmann finds evidence for his thesis that Paul was attempting to convince the Corinthians of life after death in 1 Cor. 15.19, 29–32. The text of v. 19 and the meaning of v. 29 are both problematic, but vv. 30–2 clearly argue for general survival after death, not for resurrection in particular. What Bultmann fails to allow for, however, is Paul's tendency to exaggerate his arguments. For example, Paul ended his appeal concerning the weaker brother with the statement: "If food is a cause of my brother's falling, I will never eat meat (οὐ μὴ φάγω κρέα εἰς τὸν αἰῶνα), lest I cause my brother to fall" (1 Cor. 8.13). Is Paul therefore a vegetarian? It appears that, in line with his manner of argument here (and elsewhere[1]), Paul has taken an objection to belief in bodily resurrection and declared it to be tantamount to a rejection of all belief in life after death. Compare the self-reference and the passion of the protests above with the similar protests in 15.30–32a:

> Why am I in peril every hour? I protest, brethren, by my pride in you which I have in Christ Jesus our Lord, I die every day! What do I gain if, humanly speaking, I fought with beasts at Ephesus?

It is doubtful that Paul believed that the Corinthians had really rejected all belief in life after death.

---

[1] Cf. 1 Cor. 6.12–20 and 10.21, 22 as examples of the same exaggeration. Note Paul's frequent use of the interrogative when his arguments become more vulnerable.

(iii) If indeed such was Paul's belief, then 1 Cor. 15 is not well constructed for his purposes. The whole of 15.35–57 concerns the manner by which it is possible for an early Christian to conceive of bodily resurrection. But heretofore we have found that Paul's treatment of the Corinthians' problems seemed to stay close to their questions. His long discussion of spiritual gifts was informed, we argued, by definite knowledge of the Corinthians' manner of worship. 1 Cor. 15.35–57 is evidence, therefore, that Paul believed that at least some of the Corinthians objected specifically to the idea of bodily resurrection. Thus it is unlikely that Paul had misunderstood the Corinthians' statement on this point.

Present resurrection? Hans von Soden has as high a view of the influence of gnosticism in Corinth as Bultmann, but he preserves an exegetical connection between 1 Cor. 15 and the Corinthians' theology: "Ebenso handelt es sich m. E. 1 Kor. 15 nicht um Leugnung der Auferstehung—so formuliert Paulus von seinem eschatologischen Verständnis der Auferstehung aus—, sondern um die Behauptung dass die Auferstehung schon erfolgt sei (in der γνῶσις, im πνεῦμα). Geleugnet wird in Korinth der somatische und eschatologische (beide gehört wesentlich zusammen) Charakter der Auferstehung."[1] This interesting suggestion is, of course, one of several possible elaborations of the generally held opinion (expressed by Lake above) that the Corinthians had reacted to the Jewish doctrine of resurrection on the basis of their own Hellenistic world view. It was argued in Chapter 4 that reconstructions of the Corinthians' beliefs which go too quickly beyond Paul's letters to rely on extra-Biblical evidence are somewhat precarious. We must first exhaust the evidence of the dialogue between Paul and the Corinthians. Thus at this point we shall have to defer von Soden's suggestion and others which are similarly specific until Chapter 8.[2]

---

[1] "Sakrament und Ethik," p. 259, n. 28. This view was held by a number of early critics on the assumption of the genuineness of the Pastoral Epistles: in 2 Tim. 2.18 Hymenaeus and Philetus are condemned for teaching that "the resurrection is past already". So Godet, *1 Cor.*, II, 323–4; and a number of earlier commentators listed by H. A. W. Meyer, *Corr.*, II, 38. More recently this suggestion has been accepted by Wendland, *Corr.*, p. 125, who cites von Soden and, in addition, Julius Daniel Schniewind, "Die Leugner der Auferstehung in Korinth," *Nachgelassene Reden und Aufsätze*, 1952.

Both Allo, *1 Cor.*, p. 399; and Craig, "1 Cor.," p. 215, suggest the view as one possibility among several.

The suggestion was specifically rejected by H. A. W. Meyer, *Corr.*, II, 38; and Robertson and Plummer, *1 Cor.*, p. 347.

[2] See pp. 284–6 below.

2. *The Corinthians' question*

Content. In 1 Cor. 15 Paul presented two main arguments:

(i) That the dead are resurrected bodily (15.1–34), and

(ii) That bodily resurrection, properly understood, is intellectually and spiritually not only a possible belief but a necessary one (15.35–57). Thus it seems probable that the generally accepted opinion of scholars is correct and that the Corinthians have said in some form, "There is no resurrection of the dead". Such a statement would certainly explain (i) above. In addition, there is some implication in (ii) that the Corinthians have reinforced their denial of bodily resurrection by attacking the physical aspects of the belief as absurd. Paul's introduction to this problem is impersonal, "But someone will ask, 'How are the dead raised? With what kind of body do they come?'" (15.35). He had, however, ample opportunity to inform himself of the beliefs of the Corinthians, and it seems probable that they had objected to the crudeness of the idea of resurrection.

It is usually suggested that the Corinthians' objections were the result of their participation in the "scientific" world view of their day. This is entirely possible. It may also be that the Corinthians had religious objections to the idea of resurrection. We noted in discussing 1 Cor. 12—14 the great emphasis placed by the Corinthians on possession by the Spirit. These chapters when taken with 15.35–57, a section in which Paul defended the spiritual nature of the resurrection body, imply that the Corinthians rejected resurrection in part, at least, because they considered it an unspiritual, grossly corporeal idea. Thus Héring says of the Corinthians' position, "The objection arises from the prejudice that there is only one sort of body, just as there is only one sort of matter. Consequently if there is such a thing as resurrection, the Kingdom of God is a grossly materialistic conception, according to which men live in heaven with fleshly bodies. That was indeed a notion common among the Greeks for whom ideas of materiality and of heavenly bliss were absolutely incompatible."[1]

Thus we conclude that the substance of the Corinthians' position was as follows:

Concerning resurrection: we maintain that there is no bodily resurrection

[1] *1 Cor.*, p. 173. So also Moffatt, *1 Cor.*, p. 240 ("So far from being rationalists, they were mystical enthusiasts of the Greek type who could not see anything relevant to spiritual Christianity in any doctrine which drew upon a Jewish belief about bodily resurrection after death as needful to immortal life"); and Allo, *1 Cor.*, p. 387 ("Un excès de spiritualisme mal compris.").

of the dead. The whole idea of such a thing is foreign to the Spirit which is the true gift of God.

The nature of the Corinthians' question. Once again it is evident that what we have called the Corinthians' question is actually more an objection than a question. The Corinthians have not asked for Paul's opinion; they have stated their position and made an attempt to defend it. The principal difference of opinion, therefore, lies between Paul and the Corinthians, and not between or among Corinthian parties.[1]

Secondly, it is interesting to notice that Paul used the Resurrection of Christ as evidence for the resurrection of believers. Paul rehearsed (15.3–8) the list of witnesses to Christ's Resurrection, not, however, to establish a new position from which to argue, but to remind the Corinthians of what they already believed (or once believed):

> Now I would remind you, brethren, in what terms I preached to you the gospel, which you received, in which you stand, by which you are saved, if you hold it fast—unless you believed in vain (15.1, 2).

Thus it appears that there was a distinction in the minds of the Corinthians between the Resurrection of Christ and the resurrection of Christians. The first they had accepted; the second they rejected. The reasons for this distinction and the whole question of the causes for the Corinthians' objection to a belief in the resurrection of the dead will be explored in Chapter 6 after the two remaining items in the Corinthians' letter have been discussed.

CONCERNING THE COLLECTION FOR THE SAINTS (1 COR. 16.1–9)

1. *Previous reconstructions*

Although, as we noted in Chapter 3,[2] a number of scholars suggest that 1 Cor. 16.1 (περὶ δέ . . .) begins Paul's answer to another of the Corinthians' questions, very few have made any attempt to reconstruct the content of that question. Allo is more thorough than most when he says, "L'église avait probablement consulté l'Apôtre sur la méthode à suivre".[3] The most complete attempt once again is that of Findlay:

---

[1] Lake, *Earlier Epistles*, p. 218, uses the φημί in 15.50 to argue here, as on the subject of idol meat (see p. 119 above), that there were two parties in Corinth, one Greek and one Jewish, and that Paul "admitted" his partial agreement with the Jewish party. Here again, however, it is not necessary or even probable to hypothesize a Jewish party to explain Jewish elements in Paul's thought.

[2] See p. 73, n. 2, above.   [3] *1 Cor.*, p. 455.

We received with all good will thy appeal touching the collection for the poor of the saints in Jerusalem (xvi); and Titus, when he came on this behalf, found us prepared to help according to our power (2 Cor. viii. 6). But the business halts through our uncertainty as to the best mode of gathering the money. Differing plans are proposed, and we are waiting for thy further advice, being wishful to do all things according to thy mind, and to collect a sum such as it will not shame thee to present (1 Cor. xvi. 4) as our contribution to this sacred necessity.[1]

Actually this reconstruction says little more than Allo's brief statement: the Corinthians agree to participate in the project, but are uncertain about procedure.

In attempting to amplify the work of these scholars we may note that in this section Paul dealt with two topics:

(i) The manner by which the money was to be accumulated (16.1, 2).

(ii) The manner by which the money was to reach Jerusalem (16.3–9).

2. *The manner of collection*

Two points in the previous reconstructions are clearly to be accepted:

(a) *Previous knowledge.* As we noted in Chapter 3,[2] Paul's manner of referring to "*the* collection for *the* saints" (16.1) indicates that the Corinthians had already been told what this collection was and for whom it was intended. In 1 Corinthians Paul did not explain the nature of this project; it is, for example, only incidentally from 16.3 that we learn that the money was to go to Jerusalem.

(b) *The Corinthians' consent.* Secondly, we may agree, that the Corinthians certainly have not rejected the undertaking. Paul would hardly have given directions concerning the procedures to be followed if the Corinthians had refused to take part in the project. They must have indicated to Paul their general willingness to participate, or, at least, they must have allowed Paul to assume that such was their attitude.

(c) *The Corinthians' reluctance.* That the Corinthians enthusiastically embraced the idea of the collection as Findlay believed may be doubted, however. Very probably it is with reference to this same collection that Paul wrote at a somewhat later date, "It is best for you now to complete what a year ago you began not only to do but to desire, so that your readiness in desiring it may be matched by your completing it out of what you have" (2 Cor. 8.10, 11). Paul understood their original intentions to be of the best, but, if we are to judge the Corinthians by

---

[1] "Letter of the Corinthian Church," p. 406.   [2] See p. 73 above.

their actions, we must conclude that their attitude toward the collection was somewhat halfhearted.

I Cor. 16.1, 2 provides further evidence of the same reluctance. Paul specified here a method for making the Corinthians' gift as large as possible: on the first day of the week each of them is to set some money aside. These directions imply that Paul was concerned about the size of the Corinthians' offering. Since the date for the final collection is still in the future ("When I arrive, . . ." [16.3]), Paul's concern must have been focused not on the Corinthians' past performance but on their resolution for the future. Moreover, since Paul did not believe that the Corinthians needed further persuasion about the merits of the collection, it is very probable that they had written Paul in effect as follows:

> We are glad to take part in this worthwhile project for the benefit of the saints in Jerusalem. We remind you of the limited nature of our resources, but we will certainly try to provide something when you come.

3. The manner of delivery

In I Cor. 16.3–9 Paul directed that the Corinthians' gift be sent to Jerusalem in the hands of their own representatives. He then dealt with his own plans for the coming summer and fall. It is possible, of course, that Paul's remarks about his own plans were casual and that the Corinthians had made no inquiries on the matter. It is also possible that the Corinthians had asked some question out of simple curiosity. But there are four points of evidence which make it probable that the Corinthians had intimated to Paul more or less directly their suspicions that his concern in the collection was not entirely disinterested.

(a) *Corinthian reluctance.* As we have noted, the Corinthians had agreed to participate in the collection, but Paul, at least, believed that they had not promised to give as much as they were capable of giving. Why were they reluctant? We might suppose that their attitude was simply an example of the normal human unwillingness to part with money were it not that there is considerable evidence that the Corinthians took their principles seriously even to the point, for example, of advocating an abandonment of the full marriage relationship. There is the implication, therefore, that some other factor limited their full acceptance of Paul's project. It may be that here, as on so many other points, it is their strained relationship with Paul which is involved.

(b) *Paul's plans.* Paul wrote as though he were entirely in command of the projected collection. *He* directed the manner of its gathering. *His* arrival in Corinth was to close the period of the collection. *He* was to dispatch those who were to carry the gift to Jerusalem. Yet it is remarkable that the arrangements he specified never gave him the least contact with the actual money. It was not to Paul that the money was to be delivered on his arrival, but to the accredited representatives of the Corinthians. With what may well be elaborate casualness he explained that he was not even sure that he would be going to Jerusalem at all. His rehearsal of his travel plans for the next year makes no mention of any interest in the collection. If, however, as most scholars believe, Rom. 15.25–32 refers to the same project at a later date,[1] it is noticeable (i) that at the time Paul wrote to the Romans he was resolved to go to Jerusalem in spite of his forebodings about the trip (15.30–2) and his desire to visit Spain (15.23, 24);[2] (ii) that Paul's projected visit to Macedonia, mentioned so casually in 1 Cor. 16.5, was actually for the purpose of promoting the collection there (Rom. 15.26); and (iii) that in Romans the undertaking seems uniquely Paul's ("*I* am going to Jerusalem with aid for the saints" [15.25]; "*my* service" [15.31]). It appears likely, therefore, that Paul in 1 Corinthians deliberately intended to minimize his connection with the collection money while generally remaining in charge of the project. The implication is that Paul wished to allay any suspicions on the part of the Corinthians that he had personal designs on the collection money.

(c) *Paul, the Corinthians, and money.* 1 Corinthians gives other evidence of Paul's financial relationship with the Corinthians. As we

---

[1] This identification is made both by those scholars who relate Paul's letters to one another primarily on the basis of Acts and those who do not. See, among many others, Paley, *Horae Paulinae*, Ch. 2, sec. 1; William Sandy and Arthur C. Headlam, *A Critical and Exegetical Commentary on the Epistle to the Romans* (5th ed.; "ICC"; Edinburgh: T. & T. Clark, 1902), p. 413; Lake, *Earlier Epistles*, p. 324; Robertson and Plummer, *1 Cor.*, p. 383; Valentin Weber, *Die antiochenische Kollekte, die übersehene Hauptorientierung für die Paulusforschung* (Würzburg: Buchhandlung Bauch, Echterhaus, 1917), p. 72; Moffatt, *1 Cor.*, p. 270; W. L. Knox, *Jerusalem*, pp. 292, n. 18; 317; and 345; Evans, *Corr.*, p. 149; C. H. Dodd, *The Epistle of Paul to the Romans* ("Moffatt"; New York: Harper and Brothers Publishers, 1932), pp. 228–32; Karl Holl, *Gesammelte Aufsätze zur Kirchengeschichte: Bd. II, Der Osten* (Tübingen: J. C. B. Mohr [Paul Siebeck], 1928), p. 59; Allo, *1 Cor.*, p. 455; J. Weiss, *Primitive Christianity*, p. 358; Minear, "Jerusalem Fund," p. 392; Clarence Tucker Craig, *The Beginning of Christianity* (New York: Abingdon Press, 1943), pp. 258–60; Manson, *Studies*, p. 225; Héring, *1 Cor.*, p. 183; Lietzmann, *Corr.*, p. 89; J. Knox, *Chapters*, p. 51; Buck "Collection," p. 10; Dibelius, *Paul*, pp. 94–5; Goguel, *Birth*, p. 317; C. K. Barrett, *A Commentary on the Epistle to the Romans* ("Black"; London: Adam & Charles Black, 1957), p. 3; Munck, *Paul and the Salvation of Mankind*, p. 289; Crownfield, *Historical Approach*, p. 270; Franz J. Leenhardt, *The Epistle to the Romans*, trans. H. Knight (London: Lutterworth Press, 1961), p. 374; Donald J. Selby, *Toward the Understanding of St. Paul* (Englewood Cliffs, N. J.: Prentice-Hall, Inc., 1962), pp. 224–6; F. C. Grant, *N. T.*, p. 109; and C. S. C. Williams, "Corr.," §842a.

[2] J. Knox (*Chapters*, p. 54) speaks of Paul as feeling a "great obligation" to make this trip, an opinion which makes the casualness of 1 Cor. 16.4, 6 still more significant.

noticed in discussing 1 Cor. 9 in Chapter 3,[1] Paul in 9.6–18 vehemently defended his right to be supported by his Churches and with equal vehemence declared that he had never accepted money from the Corinthians. Paul spoke of his conduct as being a matter of principle with him; it is his "reward" (9.18). The passion of 9.15 ("It were best for me rather to die than—No one shall deprive me of my ground of boasting!") has already been discussed.[2] Paul's sentiments at this point stand in odd contrast to those expressed in his affectionate farewell to the Philippians:

> You Philippians yourselves know that in the beginning of the gospel, when I left Macedonia, no church entered into partnership with me in giving and receiving except you only; for even in Thessalonica you sent me help once and again. . . . My God will supply every need of yours according to his riches in glory in Christ Jesus (Phil. 4.15, 16, 19).

Without reconstructing in detail the course of Paul's evangelization of Macedonia and Achaia, we may infer from this passage that Paul founded the Church at Philippi before preaching at Thessalonica, and, therefore, that when he left Macedonia he travelled southward. Both these moves agree with Paul's itinerary recorded in Acts 16.12—18.21, which, as was suggested in Chapter 1,[3] may have considerable historical value, being perhaps a source used by the author of Acts. The period, therefore, in which these gifts were made by the Philippians to Paul was probably close to that in which he founded the Corinthian Church. This impression is confirmed by 2 Cor. 11.7–10, a passage in which Paul speaking of his original evangelization of Corinth said, "I did not burden any one, for my needs were supplied by the brethren who came from Macedonia".[4] If these events were close in time, then Paul's renunciation of financial help in 1 Cor. 9.6–18 is especially strange. Even if the chronological reconstruction above is not accepted, it is clear that Paul was not constitutionally opposed to accepting money from his Churches. Why, therefore, did Paul not accept money from the Corinthians? The unavoidable answer is that they had not offered him financial support. Perhaps the arrival of gifts from Macedonia had aroused their suspicions. In any case, at a later date such suspicions formed the occasion for 1 Cor. 9.6–18. Presumably something in the Corinthians' letter had brought the subject up again. The only topic in their letter which we know involved money was that concerning the collection. Once again the implication is that the Corinthians had com-

---

[1] See pp. 70–1 above (especially, p. 70, n. 2).
[2] See p. 127 above.   [3] See pp. 28, 30 above.   [4] Cf. also 2 Cor. 12.13, 16.

municated their suspicion that part of this money might have been intended by Paul for himself. After all, from their point of view the project might well have looked suspicious. Perhaps, they may have thought, the "collection" is Paul's way of helping to pay for his travels. Thus Paul's defence in 1 Cor. 9.6–18 of his conduct regarding the Corinthians' money implies a suspicion on their part which was most probably focused on the projected collection.

(d) *2 Corinthians.* Without attempting to untangle the complex literary problems posed by 2 Corinthians, we may notice that several passages in that letter imply that the Corinthians had been and were suspicious about Paul's use of money. In 2 Cor. 8.16–19 Paul named Titus and "the brother who is famous among all the Churches" as agents for the collection,[1] the latter having been appointed "by the Churches" for this purpose. For, Paul explained, "We intend that no one should *blame* us about this liberal gift which we are administering, for we aim at what is *honorable* not only in the Lord's sight but also in the sight of men" (2 Cor. 8.20, 21). Since he was writing to the Corinthians it is not difficult to guess which men have questioned his honour and "blamed" him about the collection.

2 Cor. 12.16–18 is still more explicit:

> Granting that I myself did not burden you, I was crafty, you say, and got the better of you by guile. Did I take advantage of you through any of those whom I sent you? I urged Titus to go and sent the brother with him. Did Titus take advantage of you?

The issue again is money. Clearly Paul had been suspected by the Corinthians of obtaining, or of trying to obtain, money from them by guile. Notice that the fact that Paul had not received direct and open support from the Corinthians is assumed on both sides.[2] It is craftiness and guile of which Paul was accused. What could have seemed to the Corinthians like a plan contrived by Paul to enrich himself at their expense? Once again the collection for the saints is the obvious answer. As W. L. Knox said of the Corinthians' letter, "The suspicion was expressed that Paul's previous refusal to accept support from his converts at Corinth was a mere pretext for exacting larger sums at a later

---

[1] The usual scholarly assumption held, e.g., by those listed in the note above concerning Rom. 15.25–32 is that 2 Cor. 8, 9 refers to the same collection first mentioned in 1 Cor. 16.1.

[2] See also 2 Cor. 11.7–11 and 12.11–13, which show that the Corinthians perversely now maintain that if he were a true apostle he *ought* to have expected and received support from them (although, in fact, he had received none). Reasons for rejecting the opinion of some scholars that this problem lay behind 1 Cor. 9.6–18 were given above, pp. 109–10.

date on the score of the alleged collection, which, it was hinted, might very well fail to find its way to those for whom it was destined."[1]

These four independent observations make it probable that the Corinthians were sceptical of Paul's motives and, therefore, less than enthusiastic about "the collection for the saints".

4. The Corinthians' question

In summary we may formulate the Corinthians' question as follows (remembering that their letter to Paul was politely expressed):

> We shall be glad to make a contribution to your collection for the saints. We do not need to remind you, of course, of the limited nature of our resources. We shall, however, certainly try to provide something when you come. We would like more information on one point: will you be solely responsible for delivering this gift to Jerusalem. Perhaps some one of us should travel with you to share this responsibility.

Notice that on the subject of the collection as on so many other topics, relations between Paul and the Corinthians while outwardly smooth were actually somewhat strained. The evidence does not support the pleasant but somewhat vacuous version of the Corinthians' question reconstructed by Findlay.

CONCERNING APOLLOS (I COR. 16.12)

Paul's answer to the Corinthians' question "concerning Apollos" was the briefest of all his responses. Most probably the Corinthians had requested that Apollos return to Corinth.[2] His popularity with at least some of the Corinthians is indicated by the fact that a number had said of themselves, "I am of Apollos" (I Cor. 1.12). That they apparently had not similarly requested a visit from Paul is another indication of the strained relationship between Paul and the Corinthians.

Paul's attitude toward the Corinthians' request is a question not generally discussed by commentators. Certainly it is difficult to assess. On the one hand, Paul said that he had "strongly urged" Apollos to revisit Corinth. Thus Craig speaks of "the cordial relations between Paul and Apollos".[3] On the other hand, Paul's reply was almost brusque. He gave no explanation of Apollos' refusal to visit Corinth,

---

[1] *Jerusalem*, p. 328.
[2] So Findlay, "Letter of the Corinthian Church," p. 403; Robertson and Plummer, *1 Cor.*, p. 392; Bousset, "1 Cor.," p. 166; Allo, *1 Cor.*, p. 463; and Morris, *1 Cor.*, p. 242.
[3] "1 Cor.," p. 259. Cf. 1 Cor. 3.6.

saying only, "It was not at all his will to go now".[1] Certainly Paul did not go out of his way here to improve relations between Apollos and the Corinthian Church. He made no apologies for Apollos, and at the same time he made it perfectly clear that it was Apollos and not he who was at fault. Perhaps we are justified in saying that Paul's feelings toward Apollos were ambivalent, and that he somewhat resented the Corinthians' interest in Apollos.

SUMMARY

At the opening of this Chapter the problem of the integrity of 1 Corinthians raised in Chapter 2 reappeared in connection with Paul's treatment of idol meat. It was argued that 1 Cor. 8.1—11.1 is a literary unity and thus that doubts concerning the substantial integrity of 1 Corinthians have scant evidence to support them.

Secondly, evidence was given to show that the usually accepted scholarly assumption that two (or more) points of view were responsible for the letter of the Corinthians is ill-founded. The discussion of each of the problems raised by their letter gave evidence that Paul had not been called upon by the Corinthians to arbitrate a difference of opinion or to clear up a confusion. Instead, each reconstructed inquiry was found to reflect a single, well-defined point of view.

Thirdly, the suggestions made at the end of Chapter 4 concerning the underlying hostility and antagonism of the Corinthians toward Paul were amply confirmed. The Corinthians' "questions" (as they are usually called) proved to be objections which stated and defended the Corinthians' position on each of the several topics.

We concluded that in outline the substance of the Corinthians' letter was as follows:

1. *Problems of sexual morality*

(a) *Concerning marriage.* "We believe that Christian couples should forego marital intercourse so that they may devote themselves more fully to things spiritual. After all, is it not true that it is well for a man not to touch a woman? For this reason we also think it best that the unmarried and widows among us remain unmarried, an attitude of which you must approve since you yourself remain unmarried."

---

[1] Paul's manner is so blunt that a number of scholars have tried to soften his statement by translating, "It was not at all *God's* will for him to go now". So Moffatt, *1 Cor.*, p. 275; Héring, *1 Cor.*, p. 185; and the RSV.

"It sometimes occurs that the harmony of a marriage is threatened by the demands of the spiritual life. On the one hand, some of the brothers are unable to refrain completely from their wives; on the other hand, some of the marriages include one partner who is not a believer. In these cases we recommend separation so that the spiritual life of the more devout partner is not hampered."

(b) *Concerning the celibate.* "Concerning our celibate couples it has been suggested that it would be safer for them to marry. With this advice we are in direct disagreement. We hold that it is well for them to continue in their spiritual state."

2. *Problems relating to contact with the world*

(c) *Concerning immoral men.* "You write us to avoid immoral men. How is this possible? The world is full of immoral men. We are surrounded by immoral men. Moreover, why is this necessary? We have nothing to fear from the world. All things are lawful for us."

(d) *Concerning idol meat.* "We find nothing wrong with eating idol meat. After all, we all have knowledge. We know that an idol has no real existence. We know that there is no God but one. For those in Christ all things are lawful, and as far as food is concerned everyone knows that 'food is meant for the stomach and the stomach for food'. We fail to see what is to be gained by the avoidance of idol meat. You know yourself that when you were with us you never questioned what you ate and drank. Moreover, what of the markets? Are we to be required to inquire as to the history of each piece of meat we buy? And what of our friends? Are we to decline their invitations to banquets because of possible contamination by idol meat?"

3. *Problems connected with worship*

(e) *Concerning the veiling of women.* "We have simply been following the traditions which you passed on to us. We have been doing nothing new. Our women from the very first have worshipped without veils. This was their practice when you were with us."

(f) *Concerning spiritual men.* "How is it possible to test for the spirit? How can we (or anyone else) distinguish between spiritual men? When you were with us and spoke with tongues you gave us no instruction on this point."

4. *A problem of doctrine*

(g) *Concerning the resurrection.* "We maintain that there is no bodily resurrection of the dead. The whole idea of such a thing is foreign to the Spirit which is the true gift of God."

5. Problems of procedure

(h) *Concerning the collection.* "We shall be glad to make a contribution to your collection for the saints. We do not need to remind you, of course, of the limited nature of our resources. We shall, however, certainly try to provide something when you come. We would like more information on one point: will you be solely responsible for delivering this gift to Jerusalem? Perhaps some one of us should travel with you to share this responsibility."

(i) *Concerning Apollos.* "Will it be possible for Apollos to return to us and continue his ministry here?"

The Corinthians' communications to Paul when they are thus assembled show a coherence and general unity of point of view which helps to confirm the validity of the separate reconstructions, since, for the most part, they were arrived at independently. Noticeable also is an impression of incompleteness in the above outline which is only partially the result of the necessarily fragmentary nature of this reconstruction. The Corinthians' statements are definite, but they are definite in relation to something which is missing. They give the impression of being *counter*statements. We take up next the problem of the motivation and cause of the Corinthians' letter to Paul.

PART 3

Paul's Previous Letter to Corinth

CHAPTER 6

The Contents of Paul's Previous Letter

Having now discussed the contents and tenor of the Corinthians' letter to Paul (Stage 3), we are ready to try to penetrate behind this letter to seek the causes which produced it. Needless to say the further we venture from our text, 1 Corinthians (Stage 4), the more precarious becomes our investigation. Fortunately, however, there is direct evidence in 1 Cor. 5.9 and, as we shall see, related evidence in Acts and 1 Thessalonians which bear on our problem (Stage 2).

In discussing each of the questions posed by the Corinthians in their letter (with the exception of the inquiry concerning Apollos) we noted that their communication gave the definite impression of being an objection—polite, perhaps, yet firmly aggressive. We are now faced with two questions:

1. What is the origin of the ideas to which the Corinthians have objected?

2. What is the content of these ideas?

THE ORIGIN OF THE CORINTHIANS' OBJECTIONS

The first half of Chapter 4 summarized the various causes which have been suggested by scholars to explain the obvious tension reflected in 1 Corinthians between at least some of the Corinthians and Paul. These suggestions are for the most part of two types: (a) general religious and cultural influence (for example, the influence of Hellenistic ethical teaching or of gnosticism), and (b) the effect of travelling teachers at work in the Corinthian Church (for example, Apollos, Peter, or Judaizers). The first type of influence must have been present, but is difficult to assess. We have suggested that it is sounder historical method to pursue our literary reconstruction to the end before attributing ideas to such general outside influences. The second class of influence seems definitely excluded. Whenever Paul believed that his difficulties with a particular Church were the result of work by other teachers, he did not leave his hearers in doubt as to his feelings. In 2 Cor. 11.13–15 he said of his opponents,

> Such men are false apostles, deceitful workmen, disguising themselves as apostles of Christ. And no wonder, for even Satan disguises himself as an angel of light, so it is not strange if his servants also disguise themselves as servants of righteousness. Their end will correspond to their deeds.

Paul began his letter to the Philippians by mentioning those who "preach Christ from envy and rivalry" (1.15), and he warned, "Look out for dogs, look out for the evil-workers, look out for those who mutilate the flesh" (3.2). Of these persons he concluded, "Their end is destruction, their god is the belly, and they glory in their shame" (3.19). In Gal. 5.12 he exclaimed, "I wish those who unsettle you would mutilate themselves!" In 1 Corinthians, however, the passage which deals with other workers at Corinth (3.5–15) is quite different in tone. Paul represented himself as the "skilled architect" who laid the foundation (3.10). Others have built and are building on it.[1] Paul did not approve of all the work done on the building, but the responsibility for the defects was not yet assigned. The "Day" would disclose which workers would be rewarded and which would "suffer loss" (3.13–15). It is highly unlikely that any particular individuals known to Paul were the source of the teachings which resulted in the Corinthians' letter. Even if we suppose the friendliest possible relationship between Paul, and, for example, Apollos, it is highly unlikely that Paul would have refrained from mentioning Apollos' name in answering the Corinthians' objections.

Often, however, the theory of outside influence is presented in a less direct form. For example, as we noted in Chapter 4, a number of scholars suggest that the "Cephas party" was the result, not of an actual visit of Peter to Corinth, but of the immigration of Jewish Christians from Palestine.[2] But our investigation of the Corinthians' letter reached the conclusion that a single point of view was reflected in

---

[1] In 3.10 ἄλλος δὲ ἐποικοδομεῖ is translated by the RSV, "And another man is building", which gives the impression that a particular man was actively at work in Corinth (as Craig, "1 Cor.," p. 46, seems to believe). The indefiniteness of the passage, however, (e.g., the repeated τινος in vv. 14, 15) indicates that Paul merely meant that the superstructure was the work of others. So Lightfoot, Notes, p. 189; Robertson and Plummer, 1 Cor., p. 61; Moffatt, 1 Cor., pp. 39–40; Grosheide, 1 Cor., p. 84; and Morris, 1 Cor., p. 67. Most commentators, however, do not consider this phrase to be a problem: e.g., Bousset, Evans, Allo, Lietzmann, Wendland, and Simon.

[2] See above, pp. 99–100.

their letter. And what Paul wrote in response gives every indication that he intended to address the Corinthian Church as a whole. It is exceedingly improbable that the indirect influence of any outside teacher could have affected the entire Corinthian Church. Therefore we must look elsewhere for the origin of the ideas which caused the Corinthians' letter.

The single possibility which remains to be considered is Paul himself. A number of scholars in one way or another have made the suggestion that one or more of the items in the Corinthians' letter were written in reply to statements made by Paul. Many scholars adopt this position on the subject of immoral men, since we have in 1 Cor. 5.9–11 Paul's own word for the fact that his earlier statement on the subject had been misinterpreted by the Corinthians.[1] Most of these scholars, however, fail to connect this passage with the other topics of the Corinthians' letter and therefore make no suggestions about the origin of the rest of the Corinthians' questions. But since we have concluded that the problem of contact with immoral men was very probably a part of the Corinthians' letter,[2] the fact that the Corinthians' question on this subject was occasioned by Paul's "Previous Letter" leads us to ask whether others of the Corinthians' inquiries might have a connection with this earlier letter also. Several scholars say without explanation that the Corinthians' letter was written in reply to Paul's earlier letter.[3] Another group of scholars postulates that 2 Cor. 6.14–7.1 was originally part of the Previous Letter and gave rise to the Corinthians' objections reflected in 1 Cor. 5.9–11.[4] A few others also make the same type of suggestion for 1 Cor. 6.12–20, which they consider to be part of Paul's earlier letter.[5] And it should be noted that one of the motivations of those critics who subdivide 1 Corinthians into two or more letters is their desire to give such content to the Previous Letter that it would adequately explain the Corinthians'

---

[1] See above pp. 50–2.

[2] See above, pp. 50–3, 83, 92–4 and, particularly, pp. 149–54.

[3] So Parry, 1 Cor. ("Camb."), p. xiv ("apparently"); Zahn, Intro. N. T., I, 261; Allo, 1 Cor., p. 128 ("sans doute"); Goodspeed, Paul, pp. 122 ("without doubt"); and Albertz, Botschaft, I.2, p. 181.

[4] E.g., Bacon, Story, pp. 269–70; and Craig, "1 Cor.," p. 6. On this possibility see below, pp. 235–7.

[5] So Smith, St. Paul, p. 654. Interestingly Smith has used in the interests of his theory some of the links between 1 Cor. 6.12–20 and 1 Cor. 7–15 which we noted above, pp. 87–9. Thus he suggests that 6.13 produced a question from the Corinthians which Paul answered in 8.1–11.1 (idol meat), that 6.14 resulted in 15.35 ("How are the dead raised?"), and 6.20 in 7.21–4 (slavery). Examination of these passages will show that they do not bear the weight of his hypothesis.

letters.[1] There are other scattered references in the literature of Pauline scholarship concerning the occasion of one or another of the Corinthians' questions.[2] A few scholars have attempted to form a picture of the Corinthians' letter as a whole.[3] A few have noted the tone of opposition contained in the Corinthians' letter.[4] But to this writer's knowledge no scholar has called attention in a published work to the fact that, with the exception of the request concerning Apollos,

(i) *Every topic* in the Corinthians' letter may be considered a counter-statement to some earlier statement from Paul;

(ii) Every topic in their letter appears to have been an *immediate* reaction to something Paul had said;

(iii) And, therefore, it follows that their letter was very probably a topic-by-topic *reply* to Paul's Previous Letter.[5]

These points are of crucial importance. We should, therefore, discuss them separately.

1. *Counter-statement*

Instead of analysing the various topics in 1 Cor. 7—16 individually, tracing the history of each to its source, we have discussed each stage separately in order that the striking similarity of the Corinthians' various objections might be more readily apparent. Thus in abbreviated form we list below the contents of the Corinthians' letter (Stage 3) in one column and briefly the statements (Stage 2) which, we suggest, gave rise to this letter in a second column:

---

1 See Table 4, p. 45 above. J. Weiss, *Primitive Christianity*, pp. 324–34, gives the classic exposition of this argument. He suggests that 2 Cor. 6.14—7.1 produced the objection answered by Paul in 1 Cor. 5.9–13a (a possibility to be considered at the end of this chapter), that 1 Cor. 6.12–20 resulted in 1 Cor. 7, and that 1 Cor. 10.1–23 led to 1 Cor. 8; 10.24—11.1. His desire to find the motivation of Paul's responses is important, even though his conclusions are, we believe, improbable.

2 E.g., Findlay, "1 Cor.," p. 736, who includes a reference to the collection as a part of the Previous Letter; and Bachmann, *1 Cor.*, p. 482, who suggests that some plea for decency on Paul's part produced the protests reflected in 1 Cor. 7.1ff and 11.2ff.

3 E.g., sections of Findlay's attempt ("Letter of the Corinthian Church") have been quoted in the previous chapter. The works of Lewin and Farrar were cited above, p. 115, n. 3.

4 Zahn, *Intro. N. T.*, I, 274–7, is one of the few. He labelled the Corinthians' inquiries concerning idol meat, "caustic questions" (p. 276, as we noted above p. 147, n. 1), and said that on the subject of marriage they had in writing to Paul "taken him to task" for his views (ibid.). J. Weiss speaks of the "objections and scruples" contained in the Corinthians' letter (*Primitive Christianity*, pp. 330, 326).

5 But see the statement concerning the unpublished lectures of Buck, p. xii above.

Stage 3	Stage 2
(a) Concerning marriage:	
Married couples should forego marital intercourse. The unmarried should remain single. The spiritual life should be preserved by divorce, if necessary.	Christians should marry and lead normal married lives.
(b) Concerning the celibate:	
Our celibate couples should remain as they are.	(As above)
(c) Concerning immoral men:	
It is impossible to avoid immoral men in a world full of immoral men.	Do not associate with immoral men.
(d) Concerning idol meat:	
We see nothing dangerous or wrong in eating idol meat.	Do not eat meat offered to idols.
(e) Concerning the veiling of women:	
We have only followed the traditions you taught us. Our women have always worshipped without veils.	Women should be decently veiled during worship.
(f) Concerning spiritual men:	
How is it possible to test for the Spirit or to distinguish between spiritual men?	Test the Spirit and do not abandon ourselves to enthusiasm.
(g) Concerning the resurrection:	
There is no bodily resurrection; the idea is gross and unspiritual.	Do not mourn for the dead in Christ. They shall be resurrected when Christ comes.
(h) Concerning the collection:	
We will join in your collection. Will you be receiving the money in person?	I am making a collection for the poor in Jerusalem.

It is, therefore, highly probable that the Corinthians' letter consisted of a series of objections to a group of authoritative statements which they had received. The fact that their objections were directed to Paul and that he in 1 Cor. 7—16 mentioned no other party to this dispute indicates that Paul was the source of the statements to which the Corinthians had taken exception. In fact, in reconstructing the Corinthians' letter it has been difficult to avoid exploring prematurely Stage 2, so strong is the element of rebuttal in the Corinthians' statements. Indeed on the topic of "virgins" it was impossible to avoid suggesting the earlier statement. Paul in 1 Corinthians so completely took the Corinthians' side in this matter that the point of tension had to be indicated ahead of time. Naturally it will be necessary to discuss later each of these topics in order to recover Stage 2 as fully as possible. The suggested statements in the outline above should not be accepted or rejected at this point; the outline is only intended to show how completely and naturally each Corinthian statement can be understood as a counter-statement to something said earlier by Paul.

2. *Immediate reaction*

We consider it of the highest importance that a second point be recognized: that each of the above statements in the Corinthians' letter contains an element of immediacy. The above items give the strong impression that they were not a list of difficulties which had arisen with the passage of time as the Corinthians tried to live by their new faith. For example, their defence of the practice of eating idol meat strongly implies that they had *just* been directed to avoid this type of meat. Had this prohibition been given at some earlier stage, the obvious question whether meat sold in the public market was also forbidden would have been asked immediately and settled by the time Stage 2 was reached. The fact that this question is not settled until 1 Corinthians (Stage 4) indicates that, in all probability, the objection was raised in the Corinthians' letter (Stage 3) and that therefore the original prohibition occurred in Stage 2. The same immediacy is present in the Corinthians' objection concerning immoral men. From 1 Cor. 5.9 we know that Paul had told the Corinthians to "avoid immoral men". This statement immediately raised the question whether such a practice is possible for Christians. Paul's clarification of this matter in Stage 4 strongly implies, as we argued in Chapter 2, that the query came to Paul in Stage 3 as an immediate response to Paul's earlier statement in Stage 2.[1] A third example should suffice until these topics can be discussed in detail below. Concerning spiritual couples it does not seem likely that Paul had attacked the institution directly in Stage 2, since in 1 Corinthians he so strongly favoured a continuation of these relationships. It is more probable that Paul had made a statement advocating full and normal marriage relationships for Christians (as implied by the Corinthians' statements concerning marriage) and that the Corinthians had taken this recommendation to be a criticism of their celibate marriages. Paul in 1 Cor. 7.25–38 assured them that he thought it "well" that they thought it "well" that these couples remain as they were (7.26). Once again the immediacy of the Corinthians' response is evident. The passage of time had not produced second thoughts among the Corinthians about the feasibility of these relationships. On the contrary, the evidence in 1 Corinthians indicates that they were

[1] See above, pp. 51–3.

defending these relationships against what appeared to them to be adverse criticism. Therefore these three items and, as we shall see, the remaining items as well all imply that no great interval of time separated Paul's original statements and the Corinthians' objections to them. Their responses are all obvious, direct, and untempered by reflection or experience.

3. The Previous Letter

In the two sections above we have argued first that in 1 Corinthians Paul appears to have been defending or qualifying his own earlier statements, and secondly, that since the Corinthians' reactions (Stage 3) to these statements appear so direct and immediate, the statements themselves occurred in Stage 2. The question now arises: in what manner did Paul communicate these statements to the Corinthians? Chapter 2 presented evidence to show that the contact between Paul and the Corinthians which most closely preceded their letter (Stage 3) was Paul's Previous Letter.[1] We noted, however, that some older scholars placed Paul's second visit to Corinth immediately before the Previous Letter.[2] It is not difficult to choose which of these two possibilities was the occasion of the Corinthians' letter. Clearly if Paul had made the statements listed above in person, all of the Corinthians' questions would have been asked and answered face to face. It was, we submit, because Paul was *not* in Corinth when these statements reached the Corinthians that his directions were subject to the misinterpretations and objections which we found in the Corinthians' letter. The unavoidable conclusion is that Paul's earlier statements were contained in the Previous Letter. The Corinthians' letter, therefore, can now be designated the "Corinthian Reply".

The structure of the preceding argument should be noticed. We have argued that each topic in the Corinthians' letter implies a previous written statement in the recent past. Since these suppositions are independent of one another, the probability of the total argument is greater than that for any individual topic. We could have argued (*a*) that the topic of immoral men was contained in the Corinthians' letter, (*b*) that 1 Cor. 5.9 shows that this topic originally appeared in the Previous Letter, and therefore (*c*) that there is a probability that the other topics in the Corinthians' letter were also connected with the Previous Letter. But in this case the steps of the argument would appear in sequence and the probability of the whole would be less than

[1] See above, pp. 54–8.   [2] See p. 57, n. 1, above.

that for any single step. In fact, we can now reverse the above sequence and argue from (*c*), the probability of which we have established by the preceding discussion, back to (*a*). It will be remembered that in Chapter 3 we were not able to establish the connection between the topic of immoral men and the Corinthians' letter with the same probability as in the case of the topics marked by an introductory περὶ δέ.[1] At a later point we were able to point to the similarity of the Corinthians' objection on this subject with their position concerning idol meat.[2] Now, however, we can use the high probability that the topics contained in the Corinthians' letter also appeared in the Previous Letter to increase still further the likelihood that the Corinthians' objection to Paul's original statement concerning immoral men reached Paul in the Corinthian Reply. We may, therefore, consider our list of topics in the Corinthian Reply as established with all the probability which can reasonably be expected.

The importance of our conclusion that the Corinthians' letter was a point-by-point reply to Paul's Previous Letter can hardly be overestimated. The way is now clear to attempt the reconstruction of Paul's directions to the Corinthian church contained in his Previous Letter (Stage 2).

THE CONTENTS OF THE PREVIOUS LETTER

It is antecedently probable that Paul's argument in 1 Corinthians bore some relationship to his statements in the Previous Letter. Nowhere in 1 Corinthians did Paul indicate that he had changed his mind, or that he had been mistaken or shortsighted. Even at points where he may actually have revised his recommendations, we shall expect to find in 1 Corinthians at least some partial justification of his previous statements. And, conversely, we shall not expect to find in the Previous Letter directions which blatantly contradict Paul's somewhat complex position expressed in 1 Corinthians.

Although we spoke of the Corinthians' letter as being a point-by-point reply to the Previous Letter, we did not mean to imply the same relationship between these letters as that which existed between 1 Corinthians and the Corinthian Reply. In 1 Corinthians Paul carefully dealt with the topics in their Reply Letter one by one. But it is unlikely that the Corinthians had objected to every topic contained in the Previous Letter. Further, the Corinthians may have had several differ-

---

[1] See pp. 83–4 above.   [1] See above, p. 153.

ent objections to a single statement in the Previous Letter. Thus our reconstruction of the Previous Letter will necessarily be less complete than that of the Corinthian Reply. We may, however, hope that the apparently random order of the Corinthians' objections reflected in some measure the order of the Previous Letter.

1. Concerning immoral men

The starting point in a reconstruction of the Previous Letter is, of course, Paul's own statement in 1 Cor. 5.9, "I wrote you in my letter not to associate with immoral men" (μὴ συναναμίγνυσθαι πόρνοις). Obviously Paul had said more on the subject of immorality than these three words. His statement in 5.9 is merely a summary of what he had said before. We have already argued that the Corinthians had intentionally seized on Paul's earlier directive and overinterpreted it to make him appear ridiculous.[1] The question which now faces us is whether Paul had simply made an unguarded statement which by its ambiguity afforded the Corinthians an opportunity for their objection, or whether Paul had in fact been speaking of the relations of believers with unbelievers. In the first case it would have been the awareness of immorality (πορνεία) in general which had been foremost in Paul's mind; in the second, both the dangers of immorality and of unbelief. Either alternative is entirely possible. The answer to our question, therefore, is not to be found in 1 Cor. 5.9–13a, but rather in a consideration of others of the topics under dispute between Paul and the Corinthians. Does the Corinthian Reply give the impression that Paul had been primarily concerned with discipline within the Church, so that the Corinthians' objection on the subject of immoral men can probably be considered unjustified? Or is the relationship between the Church and the world also an issue with which Paul had been concerned? When the problem is put in these terms an interesting fact emerges. Both 1 Corinthians and the Corinthian Reply evince a special interest in the relation of the believer to the unbeliever (ἄπιστος). The word ἄπιστος itself occurs fourteen times in Paul's letters. Of these occurrences, eleven appear in 1 Corinthians; the remaining three are found at 2 Cor. 4.4; 6.14, 15. Significantly the latter two instances lie within the section 2 Cor. 6.14—7.1, which, as we have noted, a number of scholars believe to be a fragment of the Previous Letter. Regardless of the last point, however, (to which we shall return)[2] Paul showed in 1 Corinthians unusual interest in the unbeliever. It is particularly

---

[1] See above, pp. 151–2.   [2] See below, pp. 235–7.

significant that, immediately after scolding the Corinthians for their moral laxity (1 Cor. 5.1–8) in the face of what he had told them in the Previous Letter (5.9–13), he then condemned them (6.1–11) for taking a dispute before a magistrate who was an *unbeliever* (6.6). The implication is that here, as in the case of the incestuous man, they had disregarded his injunction, "Do not associate with immoral men".

In addition, the Corinthian Reply also reflects concern about the unbeliever at two other points:

(i) Concerning marriage: the case of believers married to unbelievers appears to have formed a special problem.

(ii) Concerning idol meat: the problem of the believer invited to the feast of an unbeliever also received special attention.

We shall examine these topics in their turn, but it is clear that both 1 Corinthians and the Corinthian Reply show unusual interest in the unbeliever. Therefore, we conclude that Paul probably had made a rather strong statement in the Previous Letter about the separation of the Church from the world of unbelievers. Undoubtedly Paul had been concerned primarily about the danger of πορνεία, and thus he later spoke of the unbelievers as πόρνοι (1 Cor. 5.9); but it appears that Paul had given the Corinthians grounds for their objection that to prohibit all association between Christians and unbelievers was unnecessary and impossible.

2. *Concerning marriage*

The Corinthians' objections concerning marriage clearly imply that Paul had strongly advocated normal marriage relationships for Christians. His statement had made the Corinthians wonder whether he intended that the practice of intramarital asceticism was to be abandoned and, further, whether he was suggesting that unmarried Christians should begin to search actively for a spouse. The latter uncertainty could have arisen from the simple statement, "Christians should be married". The former objection which deals with those already married might seem to require a different occasion. We may note, however, that the verb γαμέω, at least for Paul and the Corinthians, strongly connoted the sexual side of marriage. Concerning the spiritual couples, Paul directed that if the man's passions were strong they should "marry" (7.36). The above statement, therefore, might well have produced the objection that Paul appeared to have forbidden the spiritual practice of sexual abstinence within marriages.

The content of Paul's statement seems clear, but its motivation is less so. In 1 Cor. 7 Paul in the final analysis accepted the Corinthians' objections. Intramarital asceticism he allowed; the marriage of single persons he did not require. Yet in each instance he added a limitation. Abstinence within marriages, he said, is to be only for short periods "lest Satan tempt you through lack of self-control" (7.5). The unmarried are to remain single, unless they cannot "exercise self-control" (7.8). In each case the limitation may well be a partial justification of his advocacy of marriage in the Previous Letter; in each case he based his exception on the danger of the contagion of πορνεία. Immediately we are reminded of his argument on the subject of immoral men, which we have just discussed. The natural conclusion is that the basis of Paul's advocacy of marriage in the Previous Letter was his concern over the danger of πορνεία. He said, in effect, "Because of temptation to πορνεία Christians should be married." This suggestion gives new significance to 1 Cor. 7.1–9, especially to vv. 1 and 2:

> Now concerning the matters about which you wrote, "It is well for a man not to touch a woman." But because of the temptation to immorality (διὰ τὰς πορνείας), each man should have his own wife and each woman her own husband.

Moreover, 1 Corinthians as a whole exhibits a special interest in πορνεία. This word and those formed from the same stem, πόρνος, πόρνη, and πορνεύω, occur twenty times in Paul's letters. Of these, fourteen are in 1 Corinthians. Five of the remaining occurrences appear in lists of vices of three or more items. Outside 1 Corinthians Paul singled out this danger for special attention only once (1 Thess. 4.3). Clearly then 1 Corinthians shows a degree of interest in πορνεία which is unusual for Paul's letters. Particularly significant is the fact that in 1 Corinthians his strongest denunciation of πορνεία (6.12–20) occurs immediately before his treatment of the Corinthians' objections concerning marriage (7.1–40). We conclude, therefore, that Paul in the Previous Letter had not only forbidden association with immoral men (1 Cor. 5.9), but in addition he had probably advocated marriage as a bulwark against immorality (διὰ τὰς πορνείας).[1]

The second half of the Corinthians' objection concerning marriage

---

[1] There is a possibility, although of course only a possibility, that 1 Cor. 7.2 is Paul's own quotation (or summary) of his statement in the Previous Letter on this topic. We have already suggested that διὰ τὰς πορνείας appeared in this connection in the Previous Letter. We argued in Chapter 5 (pp. 162–3) that the verse as a whole referred in its present context to marital intercourse. Separated from 1 Cor. 7, however, it might well have been the general advocacy of marriage which the scholars listed above (p. 161, n. 1) believe it to have been even in its present position, and which we have suggested was the point of view of the Previous Letter.

seems to be of a somewhat different origin. We reconstructed their statement concerning divorce as follows:

> It sometimes occurs that the harmony of a marriage is threatened by the demands of the spiritual life. On the one hand, some of the brothers are unable to refrain completely from their wives; on the other hand, some of the marriages include one partner who is not a believer. In these cases we recommend separation so that the spiritual life of the more devout partner is not hampered.

From the evidence of 1 Cor. 7 and from our knowledge of the Corinthians' point of view such a reconstruction is entirely reasonable. However, now a new possibility presents itself. When compared with the rest of the contents of the Corinthian Reply, the above reconstruction is unique in that it is not an objection; it is a simple statement. But now having partially discussed the contents of the Previous Letter, we have a new point of view from which to approach this problem. We noted in discussing "immoral men" that the Corinthian Reply gave evidence of a special interest in the unbeliever, and that probably Paul had made a strong statement in the Previous Letter forbidding contact with unbelievers. Now it is possible to revise our understanding of the Corinthians' statement concerning divorce and to suggest that it too was an objection—an objection to Paul's prohibition of association with unbelievers. To Paul the Corinthians had protested, "What of those *married* to unbelievers? Do you mean that they should be divorced?" Paul's reply follows naturally: (*a*) there must be no talk of divorce among Christians (1 Cor. 7.10, 11), and (*b*) Christians married to unbelievers should not separate unless, that is, the "peace" of the marriage is threatened (7.12–16). The last exception may be seen as Paul's attempt to show that at times his earlier prohibition might be justified even in the case of Christians married to unbelievers. Thus here concerning marriage, Paul's commands in the Previous Letter to avoid πορνεία and to avoid ἄπιστοι, topics which on the basis of 1 Cor. 5.9–11 we argued were related in the Previous Letter, appear once again in close connection. We conclude, therefore, that 1 Cor. 7.1–16 shows that the Corinthians had protested against what they believed to be Paul's exaggeration in the Previous Letter of the dangers from πορνεία and from ἄπιστοι.

3. *Concerning the celibate*

At the opening of this chapter we suggested that the Corinthians' protest concerning their celibate couples was one of their immediate responses to Paul's advocacy of marriage in the Previous Letter. Thus this topic does not imply any addition to what has been postulated already as the contents of the Previous Letter. The fact that in 1 Corinthians the topic is separated from the section preceding it by an introduction of its own (περὶ δέ, 7.25) is probably to be explained as due to the unique status of these celibate persons and the special attitude which Paul appears to have held toward them. In 1 Cor. 7.1–24, 39, 40 Paul argued for his former advocacy of marriage, although he allowed the Corinthians' objections. In 7.25–38, however, Paul agreed with the Corinthians, although he contended that there was no "sin" (7.28, 36) in what he had directed earlier, and that in extreme circumstances his advocacy of marriage should still apply. Paul thought it "well" that they thought it "well" that these couples should remain celibate (7.26).[1]

4. Concerning idol meat

The Corinthians' protest that the eating of idol meat held no dangers for them clearly reflects a command in the Previous Letter that they avoid idol meat. This single prohibition explains naturally and fully the group of protesting slogans which the Corinthians sent to Paul in their Reply Letter. It remains to be determined, however, in what connection Paul had made this command. It was suggested above in our discussion of "immoral men" that the Corinthians' protest about eating with non-Christian friends was a second objection to Paul's demand that Christians avoid association with unbelievers (their objection concerning mixed marriages being the first). If, as we argued in Chapter 5, the invitations in question were to banquets held at a temple,[2] the connection between the avoidance of unbelievers and the avoidance of idol meat would have been a close one. This observation, however, does not mean that the whole subject of idol meat was the Corinthians' elaborate objection to Paul's prohibition of contact with unbelievers. Undoubtedly Paul had sent them two separate but related commands, "Avoid unbelievers" and "Avoid idol meat", in the same manner that he had, we have argued, issued the double command, "Avoid immorality" and "Encourage marriage". We conclude, therefore, that the Corinthians had objected to a command in the Previous Letter forbidding Christians to eat idol meat, and that they had made a further objection in this connection to Paul's prohibition of contact

[1] See above, p. 178.   [2] See above, p. 129, n. 2. Cf. also p. 144, n. 1.

with unbelievers. Thus we add one more item to our reconstruction of the Previous Letter: "Avoid idol meat."

Thus far we have postulated three prohibitions as the contents of the Previous Letter:

(i) Avoid immorality (and therefore encourage marriage).
(ii) Avoid unbelievers.
(iii) Avoid idol meat.

Further, we have suggested that the Corinthians had not only objected to each one of these commands in turn, but had also made objections which associated these prohibitions in pairs. Behind 1 Cor. 7.10–16 lay an objection, we argued, which involved both (i) and (ii), marriage and unbelievers. Behind 1 Cor. 10.27—11.1 stood a protest which connected (ii) and (iii), unbelievers and idol meat. It is certainly possible that these topics were also associated in the Previous Letter. To examine this hypothesis further we now inquire whether there was a connection between (i) and (iii). Had idol meat any connection with immorality? The answer is found in 1 Cor. 10.6–14. There Paul referred to the story which appears in Num. 25.1–9 of the "harlotry" of Israel in "bowing down" to the gods of Moab (Num. 25.1), and the resulting punishment in which twenty-four thousand (twenty-three, according to Paul) died. Paul sternly warned the Corinthians, "We must not indulge in immorality ($\mu\eta\delta\grave{\epsilon}\ \pi o\rho\nu\epsilon\acute{\upsilon}\omega\mu\epsilon\nu$) as some of them did, and twenty-three thousand fell in a single day" (10.8). In both the Numbers story and in 1 Cor. 10 immorality and idolatry are closely connected, and the two appear to have been associated in Paul's mind. Paul, therefore, argued against eating idol meat on two grounds: (i) that it brought Christians into contact with unbelievers (the private eating of meat sold in the market was not part of his concern; the Corinthians had raised that point), and (ii) that it involved Christians in idolatry, which was a form of immorality. It is in connection with this latter point that the Corinthians' protest that "an idol has no real existence" and "there is no God but one" (8.4) become especially significant. There is, therefore, an inner coherence among these three prohibitions; each is related to the other two. They are three foci of Paul's concern in the Previous Letter. We now pass to the remaining items in the Corinthian Reply.

5. Concerning spiritual men

For the purposes of the present discussion we take up the problem of spiritual men before that of the veiling of women. Concerning spiritual men the Corinthians had protested that it was impossible to "test" the spirit.[1] Clearly Paul in the Previous Letter had made some statement cautioning them against an uncritical acceptance of all manifestations of enthusiasm.[2] He expressed, that is, the same point of view which he later argued at much greater length in 1 Cor. 12—14. Since Paul had himself placed a high valuation on the evidences of the Spirit's power ("My speech and my message were not in plausible words of wisdom, but in demonstration of the Spirit and power" [1 Cor. 2.4].), the Corinthians had surmised, perhaps correctly, that he had confidence in his own spiritual experiences but not in theirs. In any case, they objected vigorously to his words of caution.

Once again the substance of Paul's statement is relatively clear, but the context of his admonition is obscure. What suggested the topic to Paul? Had he had news from Corinth of abuses in the manner of their worship? Or was the subject related to another topic in the Previous Letter in the same way, for example, that immorality and marriage were related? Either or both, of course, are possible, but it is certainly worth noticing the manner in which Paul opened his reply to the Corinthians' objection, "You know that when you were heathen, you were led astray to dumb idols, however, you may have been moved" (12.2). The meaning of this statement is clear enough, but commentators do not seem to have discussed its motivation. Why did Paul begin his treatment of the work of the Holy Spirit by mentioning first the enthusiasms of idol worshippers? Certainty is, of course, not possible, but we suggest that Paul's original cautious advice stood in the context of a condemnation of idolatry in the Previous Letter. The Corinthians' worship, he believed, was too similar to the enthusiastic worship of idolaters. In the Previous Letter he denounced this similarity and found that the Corinthians immediately objected that his distinction between enthusiasms was an impossible one. "How can we 'test' for the Spirit?" they asked.

In support of our suggestion that this topic was a second corollary to a general denunciation of idolatry in the Previous Letter (idol meat being the first corollary), we may note Paul's emphasis in 1 Cor.

---

[1] See above, pp. 193–5.

[2] It is interesting to notice that a statement which contains the substance of what Paul must have said to the Corinthians is to be found in 1 Thess. 5.19–22, "Do not quench the Spirit, do not despise prophesying, but test everything; hold fast to what is good, abstain from every form of evil." As we shall see below, 1 Thessalonians seem to have had a special relationship to the Previous Letter. See pp. 231–3.

12—14 on decency and proper order within the Church. The body has its divinely appointed structure, he argued, and so also has the body of Christ (1 Cor. 12). Acceptable worship is ordered and rational, he maintained (1 Cor. 14), "for God is not a God of confusion but of peace" (14.33). And he concluded his entire treatment of the subject with the statement, "All things should be done decently and in order" (14.40). Thus Paul's discussion of ideal worship appears set in contrast to a background of the indecency, shamefulness, and disorder which characterized pagan worship. In 1 Corinthians Paul did not develop the negative side of this comparison, but his brief mention of idolatrous worship at the very beginning of his discussion (12.2) strongly suggests that originally the topic had been connected more directly with a denunciation of idolatry.[1]

6. *Concerning the veiling of women*

The Corinthians in their letter of reply had strongly protested that their women had always gone without veils during worship. Clearly Paul had in the Previous Letter suggested that it would be more seemly if women covered their heads during public worship. Very probably the context of Paul's suggestion was also a condemnation of the influence of pagan worship. At least in 1 Corinthians Paul exhibited on this subject the same aversion to what is improper and shameful (11.5, 6) and the same consciousness of divine orderliness (11.3) that he evinced in his discussion of spiritual men (12—14). We noted above that Paul paired his answers concerning the veiling of women and concerning spiritual men in the same manner that he had paired the two concerning sexual morality.[2] It is therefore entirely probable that veils and spiritual men were associated topics in the Corinthians' letter, and that they were originally objections to two aspects of a single criticism by Paul directed against idolatrous influences in the Corinthians' worship.

The general consonance of Paul's statement on this point with the other topics which we have attributed to the Previous Letter is noticeable. As noted above, Bachmann suggested that the discussion over the problems of marriage and of women's veils originated from a plea for decency on Paul's part.[3] Developing his suggestion, we may include Paul's conviction that all association with unbelievers was indecent, and that unbridled, ecstatic worship was also indecent. The strongest

---

[1] Note that it was suggested above, p. 223, n. 1, that Paul's opening remark concerning marriage (7.2) also could be understood as a direct reference to his Previous Letter.
[2] See above, p. 182.   [3] *1 Cor.*, p. 482.

expression of indecency was, of course, πορνεία. Thus these three—fear of immorality, fear of unbelievers, and fear of idolatry—formed the burden of Paul's complaint in the Previous Letter, and eventuated in the painful discussions of 1 Cor. 7—14.

7. *Concerning bodily resurrection*

Each time that we have discussed 1 Cor. 15, the topic "concerning bodily resurrection" has appeared to stand apart from the other topics contained in 1 Cor. 7—16.[1] The problem here is doctrinal rather than disciplinary. Concerning the resurrection the Corinthians had protested (i) that they did not believe that Christians would be resurrected bodily, and (ii) that the notion was gross and unspiritual. It appears that Paul in the Previous Letter had for the first time told them that Christians who died before the Parousia would be resurrected bodily. In 1 Corinthians Paul reminded the Corinthians that he had preached to them the Resurrection of Christ (15.1–12), but he did not claim ever to have mentioned the resurrection of believers before. There is no suggestion in 1 Cor. 15 that Paul believed the Corinthians had misunderstood some original body of preaching concerning the future life of believers. Stage 4, therefore, is solely a defence of the doctrine; Stage 3 is an attack on the whole concept. It follows that Stage 2 contained Paul's initial statement on the subject. All that Paul could use from Stage 1 to defend the new teaching was the Corinthians' original acceptance of his preaching of the resurrected Christ. We conclude, therefore, that in the Previous Letter Paul had said in effect, "Do not mourn those who die before the Parousia. When Christ comes they will be resurrected as he was resurrected." The Corinthians in their protest seized upon the physical aspect of what Paul had intended as a comforting doctrine, so that Paul's rebuttal (1 Cor. 15) is primarily concerned with the possibility (15.1–34) and manner (15.35–58) of resurrection.

We suggest, therefore, that there was a point in Paul's Corinthian ministry before which he had not preached the doctrine of the resurrection of believers. Yet as 1 Cor. 6.2, 3 shows ("Do you not know that the saints will judge the world? . . . Do you not know that we are to judge angels?") he had instructed them about the Age to Come. Is it possible that he could have failed to mention the resurrection of believers? Or is it more probable that we have misread the evidence? Two passages afford the answer to this problem:

[1] See pp. 91–2, 195 above.

(i) The text of 1 Cor. 15.51 exists in manuscripts in a variety of forms: "All of us shall sleep, but not all of us shall be changed" (so ℵ, [A], C, F, G, 33, arm., aeth.); "All of us shall be resurrected, but not all of us shall be changed" (so D*, lat., Marcion); "Not all of us shall sleep and not all of us shall be changed" (so P⁴⁶); and "All of us shall not sleep, but all of us shall be changed" (so B, K, L, P, Dᶜ, sy., Tert.). Textual critics are agreed, however, that the last reading has the greatest claim to be original.[1] After the collection of Paul's

---

[1] So Westcott and Hort, N. T., II, 118; Hermann von Soden, *Die Schriften des Neuen Testaments in ihrer ältesten erreichbaren Textgestalt hergestellt auf Grund ihrer Textgeschichte* (2 Teile in 4 Abteilungen; Göttingen: Vandenhoeck und Ruprecht, 1902–1913), II, 725; Eberhard Nestle, *Einführung in das Griechische Neue Testament*, 4. Aufl. völlig umgearbeitet von Ernst von Dobschütz (Göttingen: Vandenhoeck & Ruprecht, 1923), p. 136; Moffatt, *1 Cor.*, p. 266; Zuntz, *Text*, p. 255 (who rejects the reading of P⁴⁶), and C. S. C. Williams, "Corr.," §841l.

The translation given above for the fourth and most probable variant is intentionally ambiguous. The Greek for the first clause reads πάντες οὐ κοιμηθησόμεθα. This is almost universally taken to mean, "Not all shall sleep". So AV, RV, RSV, Goodspeed; Schmiedel, "Corr.," p. 169; Godet, *1 Cor.*, II, 437; Robertson and Plummer, *1 Cor.*, p. 376; Parry, *1 Cor.* ("Camb."), p. 187; J. H. Burn, "1 Corinthians xv. 51," *ET*, XXXVII (1925/26), 236–7; Evans, *Corr.*, p. 147; Allo, *1 Cor.*, pp. 431–3; Moffatt, *1 Cor.*, p. 266; Lietzmann, *Corr.*, p. 86; C. F. D. Moule, *Idiom Book*, p. 168 (hesitatingly); Morris, *1 Cor.*, p. 233; and Wendland, *Corr.*, pp. 136–7. Westcott and Hort (just cited) accept the ingenious translation, "We all—I say not, shall sleep, but we shall be changed." So, to the same effect, Findlay, "1 Cor.," p. 941; Bachmann, *1 Cor.*, p. 470; and Grosheide, *1 Cor.*, p. 392. The difficulty which has produced this awkward translation is that πάντες οὐ should mean "none", and the sense adopted by the majority of critics should be derived from the opposite word order, οὐ πάντες, for which there is no manuscript evidence. In the Pauline Corpus the first sequence occurs at Rom. 3.20; Gal. 2.16; Eph. 4.29; 5.5. In every case the meaning is clearly "no one, none". The second order is found in Rom. 10.16; 1 Cor. 6.12; 10.23 (*bis*); 15.39. In 1 Cor. 6.12 and 10.23 the phrase cannot mean anything except "many, but not all". In Rom. 10.16 and 1 Cor. 15.39 this translation gives good sense, although the context does not absolutely exclude the meaning "a few" or "none". Occasionally in Greek literature when (*a*) the context makes the situation clear and (*b*) there is heavy emphasis on the word "all", the phrase πάντες οὐ . . . means "*all* did not . . .", i.e., "it is not true that everyone did . . .", i.e., "not everyone did. . . ." E.g., Herm. Sim., 8, 6, 2; Xenophon, *Anab.*, 2, 5, 35 (close to the text of A in 1 Cor. 15.51); and Num. 23.13 (presumably influenced by the Hebrew word order).

(*a*) Is the context clear? A number of scholars cite 1 Cor. 11.30, "That is why many of you are weak and ill and some have died", and assume, because of the reference to deaths among the Corinthians, that the obvious translation of 15.51, "None of us shall sleep", is impossible. But whether or not one accepts the suggestion made in Chapter 5 above (p. 136) that the sacrament of the Lord's Supper had become in a few instances a "medicine of death", Paul did connect the death of some Corinthians with the improper reception of the sacrament (11.28–30). The implication of this passage is that deaths were considered by Paul to be distinctly abnormal and the result of wrong-doing. (Cf. 5.1–5, discussed above, p. 137.) Thus this passage actually makes the majority opinion improbable, if the translation, "We shall not all sleep", is understood to mean "Most of us shall sleep, but not quite all of us". Instead, 11.30 favours translating 15.51, "None of us shall sleep".

(*b*) Is there a heavy emphasis on "all" which would account for the unusual word order? To place such emphasis would produce the meaning "Not quite all of us shall sleep", which we rejected above. It is highly improbable that Paul was here predicting that more deaths would take place but that at least a few Christians would survive to the Parousia.

On the other hand, it is also improbable that Paul intended to guarantee that no more

letters, some scribes found it impossible to imagine that Paul could have mistakenly believed that he and his fellow Christians would live to see the Parousia. Joachim Jeremias has argued convincingly that the whole of 1 Cor. 15.50–3 primarily concerns the change which those who live to the Parousia will undergo as they receive spirit bodies.[1] In our attempt to trace the earlier stages of thought behind 1 Corinthians, therefore, we appear to have reached a period (Stage 1) in which it was believed that all Christians would live to see Christ return to earth. Then in the Kingdom they would join with Christ in judging the world and the heavenly powers. A doctrine of resurrection for believers was unnecessary. Christ alone had been resurrected because he was to return in power. We shall discuss this obviously very early period in Paul's ministry later in Chapter 8. All that needs to be noted here is that, when 1 Corinthians was written, it was still believed that Christians would live to see Christ's return. Thus it is understandable that originally all had been expected to survive and that the death of the first Christian must have constituted a problem for Christian faith. To this problem Paul apparently devoted a section of the Previous Letter.

(ii) 1 Thess. 4.13–18 is a passage which exactly expresses what we have postulated as the statement in the Previous Letter on resurrection. In this section Paul was primarily concerned to assure the Thessalonians

deaths would take place. Probably therefore Paul was emphasizing, not the "all", but the change of natures to take place "at the last trumpet". Thus the verse could be paraphrased, "The general rule and normal expectation for us is that we shall not sleep but we shall be changed". Both J. Weiss, 1 Cor., p. 378; and Héring, 1 Cor., p. 181, n. 64, considered this interpretation "not impossible", although neither ended by accepting it. H. A. W. Meyer, however, was most emphatic that πάντες οὐ must mean "none" (Corr., II, 101–2). He maintained his exegesis by defining the "all" as "all those who with Paul survived to the Parousia". Thus in effect he rendered the verse, "At the time of the Parousia none of us (who survive) shall have to die to gain resurrection bodies, but all of us shall be changed". That "all" should mean "Paul and all the readers of his letter" Meyer considered absurd. There is considerable merit to this exegesis, for it allows the "all of us" in the first clause to have the same meaning as the "all of us" in the second clause, "All of us (who are alive) shall be changed". Further, Meyer's interpretation places v. 51 parallel to v. 52: "None shall die" (v. 51a) stands opposite "The dead shall be raised" (v. 52a), and "All of us (who are alive) shall be changed" (v. 51b) is then identical with "We (who are living) shall be changed" (v. 52b). But Meyer's position has the disadvantage that the more natural reference of "all of us" in v. 51a to Paul and his readers produces a meaning which Meyer's critics and even Meyer himself believed to be absurd. Yet it is not probable that Paul would make a statement which was on the face of it absurd and the truth of which could only be derived somewhat painfully from close attention to his subsequent statements. Thus Meyer's exegesis found few supporters. If, however, in the light of 11.30 we suggest that Paul in general expected his readers to be alive at the Parousia, then this difficulty disappears. Thus we would understand Paul to be saying, "We are, as you know, going to live to see the Parousia. When that Day comes none of us will have to pass through death to attain resurrection bodies. Instead, all of us will be transformed instantaneously at the last trumpet."

[1] " 'Flesh and Blood Cannot Inherit the Kingdom of God' (I Cor. XV. 50)," NTS, II (1955/56), 151–9.

that "we who are alive, who are left until the coming of the Lord, shall not precede those who have fallen asleep" (4.15). The implication is that this passage stood closer to the time at which the first Christian died than did 1 Corinthians. Paul's attention in 1 Thessalonians was focused on the conviction that the Christian dead would also enter the Kingdom. He assured the Thessalonians that "since we believe that Jesus died and rose again, even so, through Jesus, God will bring with him those who have fallen asleep" (4.14). Clearly such a statement could naturally result in an objection concerning the physical side of this miracle, and lead in turn to the discussion which we find in 1 Cor. 15. 1 Thess. 4.13–18 is evidence, therefore, that Paul did say to at least one other Church what we have reconstructed that he wrote to the Corinthians in the Previous Letter.

In spite of the general disfavour with which modern New Testament scholars view the idea of development within Paul's letters—a disfavour partly based, we suggested in Chapter 1, on exceedingly meagre chronological evidence[1]—a number of scholars have supported the above suggestion that 1 Thess. 4.13–18 represents an earlier stage in Paul's thought than 1 Cor. 15.[2] Thus C. H. Dodd said of 1 Thess. 4.13–17, "Evidently he had expressed himself at Thessalonica in such unqualified terms that his converts had been seriously shaken by the death of some of their number before the Advent, and he reassures them, and himself, that such exceptional cases will not be at a disadvantage because they have been thus temporarily separated from the main body of those who await the Lord from heaven."[3] Then Dodd makes a contrast between this statement and the point of view of 1 Corinthians: "Whereas in I Thessalonians it is distinctly exceptional for a Christian to die before the Advent, in I Corinthians he has to assure his readers that *not all* Christians will die. He himself, with others, will survive to the Advent."[4] C. K. Barrett echoes Dodd's opinion at this point, and says of 1 Cor. 15.51 ("We shall not all sleep . . ."), "A change of emphasis appears here in comparison with I Thess. 4.15; it is now the survivors who are treated as exceptional."[5] Jeremias notes development on a different point. Concerning the change of fleshly bodies into spiritual bodies he writes, "In I Thess. iv nothing is said

[1] See pp. 7–12, 19–42 above.   [2] See p. 8, n. 2(*b.c*), above.
[3] "Mind of Paul," p. 110.
[4] Ibid. However, see above, p. 230, n. 1, for an interpretation of 1 Cor. 15.51 which makes this passage seem earlier and closer to 1 Thess. 4.13–17.
[5] "New Testament Eschatology," *Scottish Journal of Theology*, VI (1953), 143. Barrett rejects, however, Dodd's hypothesis of further development in Paul's eschatology between, e.g., 1 Cor. 15 and 2 Cor. 5 (ibid., n. 2).

about the change. . . . This, then, seems to be the mystery [1 Cor. 15.51], the new revelation: the change of the living and the dead takes place immediately at the Parousia. This new idea . . . does not occur before I Cor. xv." [1] The opinion of these scholars about the developmental relationship between these two letters supports our contention that there was a brief period in Paul's ministry during which he simply taught that those few Christians who died before the Parousia would be resurrected as Christ was resurrected. This period we believe to be represented by 1 Thessalonians and the Previous Letter. [2] Not until later when the Corinthians had objected to the idea of resurrection did Paul face the problem of the nature of the resurrection body.

8. Concerning the collection

As a few commentators have noticed, the nature of the Corinthians' questions concerning the collection for the saints implies that they had been informed of this project only shortly before. The Previous Letter is the obvious occasion. [3] We have already indicated that money had been an issue between Paul and the Corinthians from the beginning. [4]

---

[1] " 'Flesh and Blood,' " p. 159. An earlier statement of precisely the same point was made by Thackery, *Relation of St. Paul*, p. 113 ("In I Thessalonians . . . no change was spoken of or apparently contemplated. St. Paul had now [in 1 Cor. 15] to answer to the direct question put to him by the Corinthians, 'How are the dead raised and with what body do they come?' "). Cf. also R. H. Charles, *Doctrine of a Future Life*, pp. 437–54 ("The two Epistles to the Thessalonians present us with the earliest form of the Pauline teaching and eschatology." [p. 438]; "The second stage in the development of the Pauline eschatology is to be found in the 1st Epistle to the Corinthians" [p. 445].).

[2] We have already noted two other links between 1 Thess. and the Previous Letter: (i) outside 1 Cor. it is only in 1 Thess. 4.3 that Paul made a special denunciation of πορνεία (see above, p. 223), a theme shared by the Previous Letter. Moreover, (ii) 1 Thess. 5.19–22 contains the statement about testing the Spirit which we postulated as the substance of Paul's directions on the subject in the Previous Letter (see above, p. 227, n. 2). That the Previous Letter was not written until shortly after 1 Thessalonians, however, is shown by the fact that the latter contains no mention of the collection for the saints.

[3] So Farrar, *St. Paul*, p. 378; and Findlay, "1 Cor.," p. 736 ("likely"). Less positive are Parry, *1 Cor.* ("Camb."), p. 190 ("perhaps"); and Moffatt, *Intro. N. T.*, p. 111n. The following mention the Previous Letter as a possible means of Paul's first announcement of the collection: Evans, *Corr.*, p. 149; Allo, *1 Cor.*, p. 455; and Grosheide, *1 Cor.*, p. 397. On the other hand, Duncan, *St. Paul's Ephesian Ministry*, p. 243, considers that "a matter of such significance and delicacy was not likely to have been dealt with merely by letter [i.e., the Previous Letter]." He suggests that Titus acted as Paul's deputy, although he thinks it probable, in view of the brevity of 1 Cor. 16.1–4, that Paul had also informed them of the collection "in a letter not now extant". Selby, *Understanding St. Paul*, pp. 224–6, refers to Duncan, rejects the Previous Letter as the source of the Corinthians' information, and says without explanation that Paul "had apparently started the collection while still in Corinth". The "apparently" results from Selby's conclusions regarding Acts. He locates Gal. 2.10, which he takes to be a reference to the collection, during the Council of Acts 15, a point in the Acts narrative well before Paul's founding visit to Corinth, Acts 18.1–18 (pp. 196–9, 225–6). But we have already given reasons for considering Paul's letters to be a higher authority. (See above, pp. 19–42) Selby has not noticed the element of immediacy in the Corinthians' questions about the collection.

[4] See above, pp. 202–6.

Thus it required no lapse of time for the Corinthians to have become suspicious of Paul's announcement of his new financial undertaking. It is the elementary nature of the questions by which they express their suspicions which indicates that they had just heard of the project. Paul had, therefore, announced in the Previous Letter that he was making this collection for the poor Christians in Jerusalem. Undoubtedly his announcement included a statement of the purpose and destination of this collection and an exposition of the reasons why the Corinthians ought to join in the undertaking. The line of argument which Paul may have used is suggested by 2 Cor. 8—9. There, in trying to revive the Corinthians' interest in the collection, Paul stressed both their need to develop generous habits and the need of the poor among the Jerusalem Christians:

> You will be enriched in every way for great generosity, which through us will produce thanksgiving to God; for the rendering of this service not only supplies the wants of the saints but also overflows in many thanksgivings to God (2 Cor. 9. 11, 12).

In addition to these twin arguments Paul may also have been rather direct in his approach, announcing that the collection was to be a fact among his Churches. Apparently the Corinthians received the impression that the collection was in some sense obligatory. When Paul believed that he had their agreement to participate, he spoke with authority: "As I directed (διέταξα) the church of Galatia, so you also are to do" (1 Cor. 16.1). A year or so later (2 Cor. 8.10) when Paul found it necessary to deal with the Corinthians' inaction, he stressed that their participation was not compulsory. Three times he used an emphatic negative:

> I say this *not* as a command ... (2 Cor. 8.8).

> I thought it necessary to urge the brethren to go on to you before me, and arrange in advance for this gift you have promised, so that it may be ready *not* as an exaction but as a willing gift (9.5).

> Each one must do as he has made up his mind, *not* reluctantly or under compulsion, for God loves a cheerful giver (9.7).

His emphatic statements that the collection was *not* compulsory seem to point to a belief among the Corinthians that it *was* to a certain extent compulsory.[1] Perhaps the note of coercion resulted from the increasing

---

1 Munck, *Paul and the Salvation of Mankind*, pp. 288–9, lays far too much stress on the literal meaning of these three passages from 2 Corinthians. He assumes because Paul said "not under compulsion" that therefore it was agreed by all parties from the very beginning that participation in the collection was entirely voluntary. On this point see further, p. 263, n. 1, below.

number of persons involved in the collection (Titus, "the brethren", "the brother who is famous among all the churches" [2 Cor. 8.18], and possibly "some Macedonians" [9.4]). But perhaps the sense of coercion dates from the beginning of the collection. In referring back to that point (i.e., in referring to the period of the Previous Letter and the Corinthian Reply), Paul said, "It is best for you now to complete what a year ago you began not only to do but to desire" (2 Cor. 8.10). On this verse Plummer comments, "Why is *doing* placed in this position, as if it were inferior to *willing?*"[1] Plummer rejects two solutions to this problem and proposes another, which itself is not too satisfactory. We suggest instead that what Paul was saying may be paraphrased as follows: "A year ago you not only obeyed me and began *to do* as I directed, but you obeyed *willingly*." The emphasis and value placed by Paul on "willing" implies that the Corinthians might have participated without "willing", that is, because they were directed to participate. The tone of authority is clear in 1 Cor. 16.1. Certainly there is no reason for Paul to speak more autocratically in 1 Corinthians than in the Previous Letter. At each point he had to get or to maintain the assent of the Corinthians. When the authoritative approach failed (after 1 Corinthians) Paul appears to have substituted persuasion (in 2 Cor. 8—9). But whatever his exact approach, it is clear that by means of the Previous Letter Paul was successful in winning from the Corinthians their cautious agreement to participate in the collection. Chapter 7 will suggest a possible chain of events which may have led to the announcement of the collection for the Jerusalem saints in the Previous Letter.

9. Concerning Apollos

The Corinthians' inquiry concerning Apollos does not appear to have been a protest against any statement of Paul's. It may well have stood among the greetings at the close of their letter. Or possibly Paul had said something about his future plans in connection with the collection which suggested the subject to the Corinthians. No probability can be established on this matter, however.

10. 2 Cor. 6.14—7.1

It was mentioned earlier that a number of scholars believe that 2 Cor. 6.14—7.1 is not an original part of 2 Corinthians but that it is a

---

[1] *2 Cor.*, p. 242 (emphasis added). Héring, *2 Cor.*, p. 69, comments on this problem: "Inutile d'énumérer les explications des commentateurs, en général assez embarrassées."

surviving fragment of the Previous Letter.[1] The passage exhibits the
two requirements necessary for a theory of interpolation: (i) the
subject matter of the passage has no real connection with its present
context, and (ii) when the section is removed the remaining material
reads more smoothly than before. In addition, most scholars believe
that 2 Corinthians 10—13 was originally a separate letter. Thus
there are other indications that the canonical 2 Corinthians was a
product of editorial compilation.

It is interesting to compare this brief fragment with our reconstruction of the Previous Letter. The following points of similarity are
noticeable:

(i) The passage contains a strong prohibition of contact with unbelievers (ἄπιστοι),

> Do not be mismated with *unbelievers*. For what partnership have righteous-
> ness and iniquity? Or what fellowship has light with darkness? What accord
> has Christ with Belial? Or what has a believer in common with an *unbeliever*?
> What agreement has the temple of God with idols (2 Cor. 6.14–16)?

We have already noted that two of the three occurrences of the word

---

[1] See p. 215 and, earlier, Table 4, p. 45. For bibliography see Goguel, *Intro. N. T.*,
IV.2, p. 29, n. 2 (on early scholarly opinion); Windisch, *2 Cor.*, pp. 18–19; and Allo,
2 Cor., pp. 190–3. Windisch and Allo, not themselves in favour of this hypothesis, list a
large number of scholars on both sides of the question. Additional scholars favouring the
suggestion include: Bacon, *Story*, pp. 268–70; Hermann von Soden, *Early Christian
Literature*, p. 38 ("probably"); Lake, *Earlier Epistles*, pp. 122–3, 162–3 ("attractive");
Smith, *St. Paul*, p. 654; Enslin, *Beginnings*, p. 248; Goodspeed, *Paul*, p. 231; McNeile,
Intro. N. T., p. 135; Titus, *N. T. Study*, p. 129; Crownfield, *Historical Approach*, p. 273
("probable"); Beare, *St Paul*, pp. 73–4 ("a quite reasonable conjecture"); Selby, *Under-
standing St. Paul*, pp. 258–9, 263–4; C. S. C. Williams, "Corr.," §843c; and F. C. Grant,
N. T., p. 64.

Plummer, *2 Cor.*, p. 204, gives reasons for rejecting the opinion of some that the passage
is non-Pauline. Recently this hypothesis has been revived, however. In 1954 Karl Georg
Kuhn in his article, "Les Rouleaux de Cuivre de Qumrân," *Revue Biblique*, LXI (1954),
203, nn.1,2, noted the similarities between 2 Cor. 6.14—7.1 and the Qumrân material
(principally the reference to Belial/Beliar, the sole occurrence of this word in the New
Testament). He suggested that Paul had adapted a piece of Essene material. Frank Moore
Cross, Jr, *The Ancient Library of Qumrân and Modern Biblical Studies* ("The Haskell Lectures," 1956–1957; Garden City, N. Y.: Doubleday & Company, Inc., 1958), p. 149, n. 6,
pronounced the suggestion "plausible". Fitzmyer, "Interpolated Paragraph," however,
has combined the similarities noticed by Kuhn, and the lack of connection between this
passage and its context noticed by many scholars, into a theory that the paragraph is
Essene in origin, Christianized by some unknown Christian, and accidentally included in
the Pauline Corpus. But since Fitzmyer does not examine the relationship between the
passage and Pauline thought (although he does admit that some of the elements common
to the passage and the Qumrân material also appear "in genuinely Pauline passages"
[p. 279]), he gives no reason against supposing that the anonymous Christian adapter was
Paul. We argue below that there are four significant points of contact between this
passage and our reconstruction of Paul's Previous Letter. If this argument carries conviction, then it is interesting to notice that Paul's similarities in style, theological method, and
vocabulary to the Qumrân tradition seem especially concentrated in this very early fragment. To this point we shall return in Chapter 8 (see pp. 276, n. 2, and 282–7 below).

ἄπιστος outside 1 Corinthians fall in this passage. Certainly the above fragment would have given the Corinthians ample justification for their protest that Paul had expected the impossible of them.

(ii) Paul's initial command, "Do not be mismated (ἑτεροζυγοῦντες) with unbelievers", might well have suggested to the Corinthians that he had intended to forbid mixed marriages.

(iii) The prohibition of idolatry here is equally as strong as the prohibition of contact with unbelievers. Idolatry, we have suggested, was a major concern of the Previous Letter. In fact, we noted that idolatry and association with unbelievers appeared to have been related topics in the Previous Letter. Here in this fragment the two subjects are interchangeable.

(iv) The quotation given above continues, "For we are the temple of the living God; as God said, 'I will live in them. . . . Therefore . . . touch nothing unclean . . .' " (2 Cor. 6.16, 17). At two points in 1 Corinthians Paul appears to refer to something the Corinthians had been told earlier,

> *Do you not know* that you are God's temple and that God's Spirit dwells in you? . . . God's temple is holy and that temple you are (3.16, 17).
>
> *Do you not know* that your body is a temple of the Holy Spirit within you which you have from God? You are not your own (6.19).

There is only one other occurrence of this metaphor in the Pauline Corpus (Eph. 2.21). Moreover, in 2 Cor. 6.16, 17 and in 1 Cor. 6.19 the contexts are identical: both concern the separation of Christians from the uncleanness of the world.

It is striking that four substantial points of contact exist between our reconstruction of the Previous Letter and these six verses from 2 Corinthians. We conclude, therefore, (*a*) that this fragment was originally a part of the Previous Letter, and (*b*) that, conversely, the presence of this floating fragment in Paul's letters affords confirmation that Paul had actually written to the Corinthians along the lines we have hypothesized in reconstructing the Previous Letter.

SUMMARY

In the light of our discussions in the preceding section it is now possible to revise the outlines of the Previous Letter and of the Corinthian Reply given earlier in this chapter.

Previous Letter	*Corinthian Reply*
1. *Avoid immorality.*	
(*a*) Christians should be married because of the danger of immorality.	But it is best for a man *not* to touch a woman. Do you mean that married couples should forego the discipline of continence? Do you mean that the unmarried should search for spouses? You yourself are unmarried. Do you mean that our spiritual couples should abandon their vows?
(*b*) Avoid all association with immoral men, i.e., unbelievers.	Do you mean that Christians married to unbelievers should obtain divorces? But it is neither possible nor necessary to avoid all contact with the world. All things are lawful for us.
2. *Avoid idolatry.*	But an idol is nothing. But there is no God but one.
(*a*) Do not eat idol meat.	But we have "knowledge." All things are lawful for us. We see nothing wrong or dangerous in eating idol meat. You yourself ate idol meat when you were with us. Do you mean that we may not even buy meat in the markets or eat with our friends?
(*b*) Do not let your worship be contaminated by the influence of idolatrous worship.	But we have been following the traditions you gave us.
(i) Women should wear veils.	But our women never have been required to wear veils in the household of the Church.
(ii) Do not quench the Spirit, but test everything. Do not abandon yourselves to mere enthusiasm as idolaters do.	But how is it possible to test for the Spirit or to distinguish between spiritual men? You yourself spoke freely in the Spirit without making such distinctions.
3. *Concerning the resurrection:* Do not mourn for those who have died. At the Parousia they shall be resurrected as Christ was resurrected, and join us in the Kingdom.	We do not believe in bodily, fleshly resurrection. The idea is gross and unspiritual.

Previous Letter	*Corinthian Reply*
4. *Concerning the collection:*	
I am making a collection for the poor of the saints in Jerusalem. Your generosity will be pleasing to God.	We shall be glad to join in your undertaking, although, of course, our resources are limited. One question however: Are you to receive this money in person? Perhaps others should share this responsibility.

This bare outline suggests the major emphases and essential structure of the Previous Letter. In addition, 2 Cor. 6.14—7.1 is, we believe, a fragment of the actual contents of this letter.

Now we must attempt to determine why Paul believed it necessary to send the Corinthians such a sternly moralistic letter.

CHAPTER 7

The Apostolic Decree and Paul's Previous Letter

In the preceding chapter we have reconstructed the contents of the Corinthian Reply as completely as we believe the evidence allows. Now we pose the further question: What circumstances led Paul to write the Previous Letter? To attempt to answer such a question about a document which is only a reconstruction, based in turn on another reconstruction, would appear speculative in the extreme. Yet it will be remembered that the various topics in the dialogue between Paul and the Corinthians were examined more or less independently, and each seemed to point in the same direction as the others. They therefore afford each other mutual support. Further support is provided by Paul's own reference to the Previous Letter (1 Cor. 5.9–12a), by parallel passages in 1 Thessalonians (4.3, 13–18; 5.19–22), and by the displaced fragment, 2 Cor. 6.14—7.1. In the present chapter we shall argue that additional support is available from still other sources. Thus we may hope that, exercising due caution, we shall be able to reach some useful conclusions about the events behind the Previous Letter. First, however, it is necessary to examine more closely the nature of the Previous Letter.

THE BACKGROUND OF THE PREVIOUS LETTER

The points at issue

We may safely assume that the reason Paul wrote the Previous Letter was that he wanted to direct the Corinthians about certain matters. The vigour of the Corinthian Reply confirms this supposition. At a number of points they indicated their sharp disagreement with Paul in matters of faith and discipline. Their disagreements imply that Paul's statements on these points were in the form of positive assertions or directives. In the Previous Letter Paul may have written many things now lost to us. The only topics which may be recovered are those which were at issue between Paul and the Corinthians. These topics, we have suggested were as follows:

1. Dangers of immorality:
   (a) Recommendation of marriage.
   (b) Avoidance of unbelievers.

2. Dangers of idolatry:
   (a) Avoidance of idol meat.
   (b) Veiling of women.
   (c) Control of "tongues".

3. Resurrection of believers.

4. Announcement of the Collection.

Of these topics the last can easily be understood as the result of a decision by Paul not long before the Previous Letter to undertake this project (for reasons which will be suggested at the end of this chapter). There is thus no reason to expect a relationship between this topic and Paul's original preaching in Corinth. Secondly, Paul's statements concerning the Resurrection may be understood most naturally as the result of the passage of time and the death of some believers. The problem had not existed when Paul evangelized Corinth. Once again the presence of this topic in the Previous Letter is no cause for surprise. But the other topics concern problems which certainly existed during Paul's first visit to Corinth.

It is reasonable to assume, as we shall argue shortly, that Paul and the Corinthians were in agreement on these matters at the time Paul founded the Church in Corinth. Yet when Paul wrote the Previous Letter an obvious difference of opinion existed between Paul and the Corinthians concerning, for example, the eating of idol meat. The Corinthians' protest indicates that they had had no scruples about eating such meat. Paul in the Previous Letter forbade the practice. What was the reason for this disagreement? Had the Corinthians grown lax in their adherence to principles taught them by Paul when he founded the Church? Or was the prohibition of idol meat a new idea which Paul announced to the Corinthians for the first time in the Previous Letter? Was it Paul or the Corinthians who had changed their attitude toward this and the other matters at issue between them?

Roc

Who had changed?

Strictly speaking there are four possible answers to the problem of which party had changed its point of view concerning these matters of Christian discipline and had produced the difference of opinion reflected in the dialogue between Paul and the Corinthians.

> (i) Neither party.
> (ii) The Corinthians.
> (iii) Paul.
> (iv) Both parties.

(i) That neither Paul nor the Corinthians had changed significantly since Paul's founding visit to Corinth is a possible solution. In other words, it is possible to suppose that Paul had always tried to persuade the Corinthians to avoid immorality and idolatry, and that the Corinthians had always objected to these attempts to limit their freedom. But this suggestion is improbable. Paul had founded the Church in Corinth. He had personally baptized its first members (1 Cor. 1.16; 16.15). Paul had become their "father in Christ Jesus through the gospel" (4.15). They were his "beloved children" (4.14). The implication of these passages is that the disagreement which existed at the time of the Previous Letter had once been non-existent. More decisive is the immediacy of the Corinthians' protests which we have already discussed. The nature of their objections strongly implies not only, as we argued in Chapter 6, that they had *just* received instruction on these points, but that they had just received this information *for the first time*. That they had to ask, for example, whether Paul had intended to prohibit the use of meat offered for sale in the public market indicates that the problem had not arisen before. Thus we may safely conclude that at one time (Stage 1) Paul and the Corinthians had been in agreement over these matters, and that some new factor caused one or both of them to change their point of view before the Previous Letter (Stage 2).

(ii) The usual assumption of scholars, as we noted at the beginning of Chapter 4, is that it was the Corinthians who had changed and become alienated in some measure from Paul, whether because of outside influences or as a result of the natural human tendency toward pride and sin. Thus, for example, Enslin writes,

> The real trouble-makers were these Christians who had arrogated to themselves the title "spiritual" because of the superior spiritual gifts which they

claimed. They could speak with tongues. They were free from the law, all law. . . . Some were even leading flagrantly immoral lives. They had the Spirit. Paul was preaching foolishness. "Yes," retorted Paul in substance, "it is foolishness to immature babes, but it is wisdom to mature men who have gained the true insight into the Christian mystery."[1]

But there are difficulties with this type of interpretation. Clearly 1 Cor. 1—4 indicates that the Corinthians thought of themselves as wise.[2] False wisdom is the theme of these opening chapters. But we must ask whether the Corinthians had boasted of their wisdom in contrast to Paul's original preaching or in reaction to the message of the Previous Letter. In general, commentators fail to distinguish Stage 1 from Stage 2 because they unconsciously assume that Paul's preaching had not changed. Further, the distinction may well seem hardly worth making. On the one hand, the slogans of the Corinthian Reply (for example, "All of us possess knowledge" [8.1]; "All things are lawful" [6.12; 10.23]) and Paul's criticism in 1 Corinthians of the Corinthians' "boasting" (5.6) indicate that at the time they wrote to Paul (Stage 3) they considered themselves mature and wise. And, on the other hand, Paul's description in 1 Corinthians of his first preaching in Corinth (Stage 1) seems intended to meet the criticism of those who had believed themselves wise and derided his early preaching as childish:

I *decided* to know nothing among you except Jesus Christ and him crucified (2.2).

I, brethren, *could not* address you as spiritual men, but as men of the flesh, as babes in Christ. I fed you with milk, not solid food; for you were not ready for it; and even yet you are not ready (3.1–3).

But these passages may equally well be understood to mean that only Paul and not the Corinthians had characterized his early preaching as childish, that is, as introductory and incomplete. Paul, according to this view, was not excusing his first preaching, but accusing the Corinthians of boasting in their knowledge of principles which actually were elementary. The theme of childhood and maturity reappears at several points in 1 Corinthians. Paul called the Corinthians his spiritual children (4.15); they were "babes in Christ" (3.1). Paul had put himself on their level, he said, when he came to them (2.1–3); he fed them

---

[1] *Beginnings*, pp. 249–50. Moffatt, *1 Cor.*, p. 34, also speaks of those in Corinth who had come to call Paul's preaching "folly". For the variety of ways in which scholars picture what they believe to be the Corinthians' apostasy see above, pp. 96–107.

[2] E.g., 1 Cor. 3.18 ("If any among you thinks that he is wise in this age, let him become a fool that he may become wise"); and 4.10 ("We are fools for Christ's sake, but you are wise in Christ").

milk (3.2). The Corinthians, however, had not matured, Paul complained; they were still children (3.2, 3). Paul urged them to grow out of their childishness:

> When I was a child, I spoke like a child, I thought like a child, I reasoned like a child; when I became a man I gave up childish ways (13.11).
>
> I urge you, then, be imitators of me (4.16).
>
> Brethren, do not be children in your thinking; be babes in evil, but in thinking be mature (14.20).

Once Paul had preached in simple terms; once he had relied on the "demonstration of the Spirit and power" (2.4); once he had spoken in tongues (13.11). Now, however, he sought to communicate mature doctrine (2.6, 7; 15.51, "a mystery"); now he preferred to speak in tongues no longer (13.11, "I gave up childish ways"; 14.19, "I would rather speak five words with my mind"; and 14.6). The impression these passages convey is that Paul had changed the level of his preaching and that the Corinthians had persisted in believing their original convictions to be the height of wisdom. Paul criticized them, not for their readiness to accept new doctrines for old, but for their failure to move beyond their earlier beliefs.

(iii) Three points confirm the above impression that it was Paul and not the Corinthians who had changed. In the first place, as we have already noted, Paul in 1 Corinthians neither accepted nor rejected the principles by which the Corinthians justified their behaviour. He quoted their slogans in order to qualify them with additional considerations. He did not attack their ideals as alien intrusions into the message he had preached.[1] The strong implication is that these principles bear a close relationship to Paul's earlier preaching.[2] By quoting these slogans the Corinthians placed Paul in a dilemma. He could not affirm these principles in 1 Corinthians, since they ran counter to his argument. Nor could he attack them, since then he would have been repudiating his own preaching. All that he could do was to qualify and limit them. Thus it appears that Paul was in the somewhat difficult position of having to adjust his earlier preaching to his newer positions. (We shall return to this point in Chapter 8.) Secondly, we have noticed at several

---

[1] Contrast in this respect Paul's attitude toward those in Galatia who sought to identify themselves more fully with the legal traditions of Israel: "I am astonished that you are so quickly deserting him who called you in the grace of Christ and turning to a different gospel" (Gal. 1.6).

[2] A number of scholars have noticed the similarity of the quoted slogans in 1 Corinthians to Paul's own point of view. See below, pp. 278–80.

points that there appears to have been a discrepancy between the commands of the Previous Letter and Paul's own behaviour at the time that he evangelized Corinth. We know that Paul had spoken in tongues frequently and forcefully (2.4; 14.18). It appears that he had made no distinctions among others who spoke in the Spirit. It also appears that Paul had eaten idol meat freely when in Corinth. There is the suggestion that the Corinthians' views on marriage had been formed in harmony with Paul's personal preference for celibacy. In defence of their unveiled women the Corinthians made the claim (11.2) that they had simply been following the traditions concerning worship which Paul had originally given them. The implication is that he had said nothing about the veiling of women when he was with them. Thus it appears once again that the Previous Letter contained regulations which were new to the Corinthians because Paul had changed his own view of these matters. Thirdly, the Corinthians' protests, as we have noted, have an inescapable immediacy to them. The elementary nature of these objections indicates that the Corinthians had never been faced before with the prohibitions and limitations which Paul laid upon them. If these issues had been part of a long-standing dispute between Paul and Corinth, the Corinthians might have used the same slogans that we found contained in the Corinthian Reply, but they would not have asked Paul whether he intended that Christians should avoid *all* unbelievers, whether mixed marriages should be dissolved, whether he meant that their celibate couples should abandon their vows, and whether he had commanded them to ascertain the history of meat sold in the public market. The fact that these elementary questions were very probably contained in the Corinthian Reply indicates that the disputed topics which form our reconstruction of the Previous Letter were each of them new to the Corinthians.

(iv) Is it possible that both Paul and the Corinthians had changed since Stage 1? Our discussion above may be taken as evidence that it was Paul who had made that change which led to the dispute between himself and the Corinthians. They, however, may well have changed in less significant ways. They may have increased in their own self-esteem during this period. Under the tutelage of Apollos and others they may have made general progress in the faith. Certainly the "parties" were a new phenomenon at Corinth. We shall return to this last problem at the end of this chapter. Here it is only necessary to emphasize that whatever development the Corinthians had achieved appears to have been along the lines of their original beliefs and practices. The change which gave rise to the dialogue between Paul and the Corinthians was a change in Paul's own views of Christian behaviour.

Therefore, in seeking the origin of the Previous Letter we may rephrase our question and ask: What circumstances led Paul to change his views on the topics we are discussing, and thus caused him to send to the Corinthians the Previous Letter?

THE APOSTOLIC DECREE

In searching for the historical situation which might have given rise to the Previous Letter we note that the only points in the New Testament outside 1 Cor. 8—10 where idol meat is mentioned are Rev. 2.14, 20 and Acts 15.29; 21.25. The references in Revelation may well depend on 1 Cor. 8—10. In any case they offer nothing for our problem. The references in Acts, however, occur in the repeated text of the so-called Apostolic Decree. According to Acts, the Decree was the decision of the Jerusalem Church regarding requirements for Gentile Christians:

> James replied, "Brethren, . . . my judgment is that we should not trouble those of the Gentiles who turn to God, but should write them to abstain from the pollutions of idols and from unchastity (and from what is strangled) and from blood" (Acts 15.13, 19, 20).

Since Acts connects this Decree with the problem of Gentile Christians in general (although only Syria and Cilicia appear in the salutation of the letter containing a copy of the Decree, 15.23–9),[1] it is obviously important that we examine the Decree further. We therefore digress to discuss briefly the historical problems connected with the Decree:

(*a*) The text of the Decree in Acts
(*b*) The original intention of the Decree

The text of the Apostolic Decree

The problem of the text of Acts is complicated and difficult; the problem of the text of the Apostolic Decree in Acts is one of the most complex afforded by the text of that book. The Decree appears at three places in Acts (Acts 15.20, 29; 21.25), each occurrence having a different set of textual variants. Moreover, several terms in the Decree

---

[1] Cf. also the speech of James, Acts 21.25 ("As for the Gentiles . . . we have sent a letter . . ."), and the delivery of the provisions of the Decree in South Galatia (Acts 16.4), an area beyond that specified in the letter.

are capable of more than one meaning. When the variant readings and ambiguous terms are combined, there are two almost completely different interpretations of the Decree. It can be understood either as a set of ritualistic regulations or as a group of moral provisions. The individual terms of the Decree are as follows:

(i) εἰδωλόθυτα, "idol meat". This term appears in Acts 15.29 and 21.25. In 15.20 the term is replaced by the phrase τὰ ἀλισγήματα τῶν εἰδώλων, "the pollutions of idols". In either wording the most natural reference of this provision would be cultic and dietary, but in a wider sense it could refer to idolatrous worship and even to general moral unfaithfulness toward God.

(ii) αἷμα, "blood". This term may be understood to refer to the meat of animals improperly slaughtered (e.g., Gen. 9.4, "You shall not eat flesh with its life, that is, its blood") or to crimes of violence (e.g., Gen. 9.6, "Whoever sheds the blood of man, by man shall his blood be shed").

(iii) πνικτός, "what is strangled". The word is the single unambiguous provision of the Decree. It can refer only to the meat of animals killed by strangulation, which because of the residual blood was forbidden by Jewish dietary laws.

(iv) πορνεία, "immorality". In the Jewish ethical vocabulary this word meant not only sexual immorality, but also (as in 1 Cor. 10.8) the infidelity to God expressed by idolatry. The Old Testament, for example, repeatedly uses the term זָנָה, "to commit fornication", to refer to idolatry.[1]

The manuscripts provide a complex variety of text forms for the Decree. For clarity we may separate the authorities for the text into two classes: Class 1, the main bulk of the manuscripts, particularly the Alexandrian and the Koine text traditions; and Class 2, those witnesses which contain readings that are present in some Western authorities. The more important variants in the text of the Decree are as follows:

---

1. *Acts 15.20.* απεχεσθαι των αλισγηματων των ειδωλων και της πορνειας και πνικτου και του αιματος.

Class 1	Class 2
(a) και της πορνειας:	
om. P⁴⁵; vgᵇ, aethʳᵒ; Or (C. Cels, viii, 29), Vigil, Gaudentius, Athan.	
text: P⁷⁴, B, ℵ, A, C, S, P, L, H, 81, etc.	

[1] E.g., Ex. 34.15, 16; Lev. 17.7; 20.5; Deut. 31.16; Judges 2.17; 8.27, 33; etc.

Class 1	Class 2

(b) του ante πνικτου:
　　P⁴⁵, ℵ, C, S, P, L, H, etc.　　　E
　　text: P⁷⁴, B, A, 33, 81

(c) και πνικτου:
　　　　　　　　　　om. D, 1739; d, gig; Ir, Ephr, Aug.

(d) post αιματος add: και οσα αν μη θελωσιν αυτοις γενεσθαι ετεροις μη
ποιειν

　　　　　　　　　　(D), 101ᵐᵍ, 322, 323, 385, 429, 464,
　　　　　　　　　　1739ᵐᵍ, 2298; d, sa, aeth; Irˡᵃᵗ
　　　　　　　　　　Porph. Eus.(D om. αν; leg. θελουσιν,
　　　　　　　　　　εαυτοις γεινεσθαι, ποιειτε)

2. *Acts 15.29.* απεχεσθαι ειδωλοθυτων και αιματος και πνικτων και πορνειας.

(a) πνικτου:
　　P⁷⁴, ℵᶜ, A², S, P, L, H; vgᶜˡ,　　　E; gig.
　　syᵖ, arm; Did, Chr.
　　text: ℵ*, A*, B, C, 81, 614; aeg;
　　Or, Cyril (Hier).

(b) και πνικτων:
　　　　　　　　　　om. D; d, aeth; Irˡᵃᵗ, Tert, Cypr,
　　　　　　　　　　Hier, Ambst, Aug, Pacianus, Fulg.

(c) post πορνειας add: και οσα μη θελετε εαυτοις γινεσθαι ετερω μη
ποιετε.

　　　　　　　　　　(D), 42, 51, 104, 234, 242, 322, 323,
　　　　　　　　　　429, 614, 1739; d, vgᶜᵒᵈᵈ, syʰ, sa,
　　　　　　　　　　aeth; Irˡᵃᵗ, Porph, Eus, Cypr (D:
　　　　　　　　　　αυτοις, ποιειν)

3. *Acts 21.25.* φυλασσεσθαι αυτοις το τε ειδωλοθυτον και αιμα και πνικτον
και πορνειαν.

(a) ante φυλασσεσθαι add: μηδεν τοιουτον τηρειν αυτοις ει μη
　　C, P, L, H,　　　　　　　　　D, E, 242, 322, 429; d.

(b) και πνικτον:
　　　　　　　　　　om. D; d, gig; (Ambst), Aug (Ep.
　　　　　　　　　　82, 9).

Manuscripts in Class 1, including as they do και (του) πνικτου (-των, -τον), represent an understanding of the decree in which the dietary aspect is unavoidable. If, however, this version of the Decree is interpreted solely as a set of food laws, then πορνειας seems somewhat unexpected. Probably a desire for greater consistency led some authorities to omit this provision.[1] Class 2 manuscripts reflect a tradition which regarded the Decree as purely ethical, omitting the unambiguous πνικτοῦ clause and adding (except at 21.25) the negative version of the Golden Rule. The latter addition is surely secondary. In 15.29 the Decree is followed by the suggestion: ἐξ ὧν διατηροῦντες ἑαυτοὺς εὖ πράξετε. Clearly the ἐξ ὧν refers to the several items which the Decree forbids. Only somewhat awkwardly could the phrase refer to these items together with the negative Golden Rule.[2] Since roughly the same manuscript authorities stand behind this longer reading in 15.20, there is no more reason to suppose it to be original there than in 15.29. Moreover, the Western text of Acts is characterized by a series of somewhat lengthy glosses which rarely commend themselves to textual critics. Thus, for example, Dibelius concludes after considering a number of Western additions, "These examples are enough to show that the Western text endeavours to smooth out roughnesses which resulted from the characteristic method by which Acts were composed."[3] In the case of the Decree the "roughness" is the reluctance of the later Church to believe that a group of Jewish dietary laws were or had been required of Gentile Christians.[4]

The rejection of the Western additions to the Decree does not solve the textual problem before us, however, because the omissions made by the Western text (for example, the πνικτοῦ clause in our passage) carry far greater weight than do its additions. Thus even Hort was

[1] O'Neill, Theology of Acts, p. 78, n. 1, says succinctly, "An omission of the unlike term". So also Vincent Taylor, The Text of the New Testament: A Short Introduction (London: Macmillan & Co Ltd, 1961), p. 100. But C. S. C. Williams, Alterations to the Text of the Synoptic Gospels and Acts (Oxford: Basil Blackwell, 1951), pp. 72–5, argued that P[45] (which omits και της πορνειας in 15.20 and which is not extant at 15.29 and 21.25) may have preserved the original text of the Decree. The supporting witnesses are scattered and few, however. It is noticeable that in his commentary on Acts (1957) he abandoned the idea in favour of the suggestion above (Acts, pp. 31, 183).

[2] So, e.g., William Sanday, "The Apostolic Decree (Acts XV. 20–29)," Theologische Studien Theodor Zahn zum 10. Oktober 1908 dargebracht (Leipzig: A. Deichert'sche Verlagsbuchhandlung Nachf. [Georg Böhme], 1908), p. 321.

[3] Studies in Acts, p. 87. Westcott and Hort's suspicion of the Western text is well known (see N. T., II, 120–6). James Hardy Ropes in his elaborate edition of the text of Acts printed both the texts of D and B, but decided almost wholly in favour of the latter (BC, III, ccxxiv–ccxxv).

[4] Among modern textual critics Albert C. Clark is almost alone in preferring the D-text to the B-text throughout Acts. He therefore includes the negative Golden Rule at 15.20 and 29 (The Acts of the Apostles: A Critical Edition with Introduction and Notes on Selected Passages [Oxford: The Clarendon Press, 1933], pp. 96–7, 361). An earlier attempt to establish the priority of the D-text was that of F. A. Bornemann, Acta Apostolorum ad Codicis Cantabrigiensis fedem recensuit (Grossenhain and London, 1848), cited ibid., p. xxiv, and Ropes, BC, III, lxxxiv. More recently the priority of the D-text has been defended by Henry Currie Snape, "The Composition of the Lukan Writings: A Re-assessment," HTR, LIII (1960), 34–46. He does not, however, believe the negative Golden Rule to be original (pp. 45–6).

forced to say: "A few . . . Western readings . . . we cannot doubt to be genuine in spite of the exclusively Western character of their attestation. They are all omissions, or, to speak more correctly, non-interpolations. . . . The doubtful words are superfluous, and in some cases intrinsically suspicious, to say the least; while the motive for their insertion is usually obvious."[1] The weight of the manuscript evidence is, therefore, very evenly divided between the four-clause version and the three-clause version with πνικτοῦ omitted. That the longer (and more widely attested) text was shortened by the removal of the single unambiguous item under the same moralizing tendency which later inserted the negative Golden Rule is as probable as that the shorter ambiguous version was lengthened by the addition of the gloss πνικτοῦ to specify the meaning of αἷμα. We must, therefore, leave the problem of the text open to this extent, and proceed to discuss various interpretations of the Decree which have been proposed.

The original intention of the Decree

The problem of the Decree has been much debated.[2] A number of scholars have held the opinion that originally the Decree was purely a set of moral precepts, and that the dietary aspect was added by the interpolation of the πνικτοῦ clause.[3] An increasing number of scholars, however, believe that the intention of the Decree was cultic, whether they hold to the traditional four-clause version,[4] or whether they

---

[1] Westcott and Hort, *N. T.* II, 175. Sanday, "Apostolic Decree," pp. 323–5, stated that it was his conviction that the passage was not an example of Western "non-interpolation". Werner Georg Kümmel, "Die älteste Form des Aposteldekrets," *Spiritus et Veritas*, ed. Auseklis (Eutin: Societas Theologorum Universitatis Latviensis [in exile], 1953), p. 92, ignores the point and uses the spuriousness of the negative Golden Rule to discredit the omission of πνικτου which marks some of the same authorities.

[2] For bibliographical surveys see Kümmel, "Die älteste Form des Aposteldekrets," p. 85, n. 4; Arndt/Gingrich, p. 686; and Haenchen, *Acts* ("Meyer," 13. Aufl.), pp. 390, n. 5, and 410–14.

[3] So, e.g., Adolf Harnack, *New Testament Studies, III: The Acts of the Apostles*, trans. J. R. Wilkinson ("Crown Theological Library," Vol. XXVII; London: Williams & Norgate, 1909), pp. 248–63 (his later position); Lake, *Earlier Epistles*, pp. 48–60; Smith, *St. Paul*, pp. 671–4; Blunt, *Acts*, pp. 203–6; Clark, *Acts*, pp. 360–1; Edward Gordon Selwyn, *The First Epistle of Peter: The Greek Text with Introduction, Notes and Essays* (2d ed.; London: Macmillan & Co. Ltd, 1955), p. 372, n. 1.

[4] So Harnack, "Das Aposteldekret (Act. 15,29) und die Blass'sche Hypothese," in his *Studien zur Geschichte des Neuen Testaments und der alten Kirche, I: Zur neutestamentlichen Textkritik* ("Arbeiten zur Kirchengeschichte," Bd. 19, hrsg. E. Hirsch und H. Lietzmann; Berlin: Walter de Gruyter & Co., 1931), pp. 1–32 (his earlier position); Wendt, *Acts*, pp. 232–4; J. Weiss, *Primitive Christianity*, p. 313, n. 46; Lyder Brun, "Apostelkoncil und Aposteldekret," *Paulus und die Urgemeinde* ("Beiheft I zu Norsk Teologisk Tidsskrift"; Giessen: Alfred Töpelmann Verlag, 1921), pp. 1–52; Windisch, *BC*, II, 324–5; Eduard Meyer, *Ursprung und Anfänge des Christentums* (3 Bde; Stuttgart: J. G. Gotta'sche Buchhandlung Nachfolger, 1921–1923), III, 189; Hans Lietzmann, "Der Sinn des Apostel-

prefer the three-clause version supported by the few authorities which omit both πνικτοῦ and the negative Golden Rule as well.[1] It appears probable that this trend is justified. Whatever be the final decision over the πνικτοῦ clause, it is arbitrary to deny a cultic meaning to εἰδωλόθυτα, for example. So, too, αἷμα is more naturally referred to meat than to murder, although, as Gen. 9.4–6 shows, the term might have carried both meanings at once. Those scholars who do deny the dietary aspect of the Decree appear to be influenced by special concerns. Thus, for example, Harnack said explicitly,

> The Apostolic Decree, if it contained a general declaration against eating sacrifices offered to idols, against partaking of blood or things strangled, and against fornication, is inconsistent with the account given by St. Paul in Gal. ii. 1–10, and with the corresponding passages in the First Epistle to the Corinthians. It is, accordingly, unhistorical. But if the Decree is unhistorical, it follows that it is the highest degree improbable that a companion of Silas and St. Paul either wrote or accepted from others what we read in Acts xv.[2]

By adopting the ethical interpretation of the Decree, Harnack was able to reaffirm the historicity of Acts 15, and retain his conviction that Luke, the companion of Paul, was the author-compiler of Acts. Kirsopp Lake also argued in favour of the ethical sense on the grounds that, "the absolute silence of St. Paul on the decrees in I Cor. x., when he is discussing 'things offered to idols,' . . . is almost unintelligible if we suppose that the decrees were a food law".[3] And Clark in his treatment of the passage is controlled by his desire to establish the D-text throughout Acts.[4] We conclude, therefore, that it is most unnatural to exclude the dietary sense of the Decree.

dekrets und seine Textwandlung," in his *Kleine Schriften, II: Studien zum Neuen Testament,* hrsg. K. Aland ("Texte und Untersuchungen zur Geschichte der altchristlichen Literatur," LXVIII; Berlin: Akademie Verlag, 1958), pp. 294–6; Craig, *Beginning,* p. 173; Klausner, *From Jesus to Paul,* p. 368, n. 18 (It appears that Stinespring has mistranslated, for the note reads, "The Western text . . . expunges the three latter things. . . ."); Goguel, *Birth,* p. 299; Cerfaux, "Chapitre XVᵉ des Actes," pp. 119, 124n; Dibelius, *Studies in Acts,* p. 98, n. 12; Kümmel, "Die älteste Form des Aposteldekrets," pp. 83–98; Snape, "Lukan Writings," p. 45; Haenchen, *Acts* ("Meyer," 13. Aufl.), p. 390; O'Neill, *Theology of Acts,* pp. 78, 101; Lampe, "Acts," in *Peake's Commentary on the Bible,* ed. M. Black and H. H. Rowley (London: Thomas Nelson and Sons Ltd, 1962), §792f; Stählin, *Acts,* p. 205; and R. M. Grant, *Historical Introduction,* p. 393.

[1] So Ropes, *BC,* III, 269; and Nock, *St. Paul,* pp. 113–14 ("possible").
[2] *Acts,* p. 249.
[3] *Earlier Epistles,* pp. 53–4. Similarly Blunt rejects the dietary interpretation in favour of the ethical, saying, "It is inexplicable, on the first alternative, that Paul never makes any reference to a Christian food-law in Galatians, Corinthians, or Romans" (*Acts,* p. 204).
[4] Smith also betrays a special concern when he writes, "It would be amazing had a Christian Council reckoned among the 'things necessary' to salvation a scrupulosity which our Lord had so emphatically condemned" (*St. Paul,* p. 674).

Some scholars, on the other hand, move in the opposite direction, and in the interests of consistency attempt to make of the Decree a set of purely ritualistic regulations. They deny the usual ethical sense of the word πορνεία, which they believe to be out of place beside the three (or two) dietary provisions. Instead they interpret πορνεία to refer to the Levitical proscription of marriage within certain degrees of consanguinity (Lev. 18.6–18).[1] The opinion of these scholars is based on Strack and Billerbeck's comment that the word could not have meant general sexual immorality, "denn in dem Sinne war die πορνεία ja jedermann verboten, so dass es eines besonderen Verbotes für die Christgläubigen aus der Heidenwelt nicht bedurft hätte".[2] This judgement, however, does not depend on these authors' special competence in the Rabbinic literature, but appears based on their assumption that the sexual behaviour of Gentile Christians was entirely acceptable to Jewish Christians, except for the need of a stricter definition of consanguinity. To begin by assuming a knowledge of the situation to which the Decree was directed is to beg the question. T. W. Manson provides still another example of pre-interpretation, when, having ridiculed the ethical interpretation of the Decree, he concludes: "But if the 'ethical' interpretation breaks down, the only real alternative is that which understands the prohibitions in connection with Jewish dietary practice. And in that case 'fornication' is quite out of place and should be removed from the text."[3] But the combination of ethical and dietary regulations is amply justified, however, by the parallels to the Decree in Jewish and Jewish Christian literature.[4] The Decree appears to be one example of a class of traditional formulations of conduct which no Jew might transgress even if his life were at stake,

[1] So Craig, Beginning, p. 173; Goguel, Birth, p. 299, n. 4; C. S. C. Williams, Acts, p. 183 (as a possibility); Trocmé, "Livre des Acts," p. 26; and Stählin, Acts, p. 205. In addition, Kümmel, "Die älteste Form des Aposteldekrets," p. 94, n. 27, cites Otto Bauernfeind, Die Apostelgeschichte ("ThHK"; 1939), p. 197; and H. Waitz, "Das Problem des sogenannten Aposteldekrets," Zeitschrift für Kirchengeschichte, 3. Folge, VI (1936), 227–63.

[2] Hermann L. Strack and Paul Billerbeck, Das Evangelium nach Markus, Lukas und Johannes und die Apostelgeschichte erläutert aus Talmud und Midrasch, Vol. II of Kommentar zum Neuen Testament aus Talmud und Midrasch by Hermann L. Strack and Paul Billerbeck (München: C. H. Becksche Verlagsbuchhandlung, 1924), p. 729.

[3] Studies, p. 184. From Kümmel's rebuttal ("Die älteste Form des Aposteldekrets," pp. 84, 89–90) it appears that Philippe H. Menoud, "The Western Text and the Theology of Acts," Studiorum Novi Testamenti Societas, Bulletin II (1951), 19ff., also argued on the same grounds that πορνεία should be dropped from the text.

[4] See, e.g., Lake, "The Apostolic Council of Jerusalem," Additional Notes to the Commentary: Vol. V of BC, pp. 206–9 (he refers to the Noachian Commands as found in Rabbinic literature, to the Sibylline Oracles and to the decision of the Rabbinic Council of Lydda (A.D. 132–5) concerning the three laws [idolatry, sexual immorality, and murder] which must not be broken even under persecution and the threat of death); and Bacon, Story, p. 134 (with references to the Clementine Homilies).

and which, conversely, each Gentile must obey if he is to enjoy social contact with Jews. Moreover, to distinguish rigidly between the ethical and the dietary sense is to introduce a decidedly modern emphasis.[1] Very probably, therefore, the Decree should be understood as a traditional group of requirements capable of interpretation to cover situations which modern ethical thought specifies variously as dietary, cultic, or moral. The εἰδωλόθυτα clause should not be made a moral provision, nor should πορνεία be eliminated or restricted to mean simply marriage within the Levitical degrees of consanguinity. Both the attempt to make the Decree purely ethical and the desire to interpret solely along Levitical lines spring from preconceptions about the purpose of the Decree; they are not implied by the text itself. At least Lake's method was sound—and we are not yet ready to deal with his conclusion—when he said, "The internal evidence of the decrees indicates that they, or the policy which they embody, belong to a different problem from that with which Luke has connected them."[2]

We have not solved the problem of the πνικτοῦ clause, but whether or not this provision is included, it seems clear that the Decree which the author of Acts incorporated into his book in two connections prohibited three main areas of conduct: idolatry, improper diet, and sexual immorality. These areas overlapped somewhat, since eating idol meat, for example, involved both idolatry and the eating of meat improperly killed. Moreover sexual immorality rendered a man unfit as a table companion, on the one hand,[3] and on the other, the term πορνεία often was used figuratively of idolatry. With these observations in mind, we may now return to the problem of the origin of the Previous Letter.

THE APOSTOLIC DECREE AND THE
PREVIOUS LETTER

We have seen that the Apostolic Decree considered by itself, and not as one part of a larger scholarly hypothesis, deals with conduct which is both moral and ritual in nature. Now we face the problem of the relationship of the Decree to the Corinthian correspondence. In this connection W. L. Knox wrote,

S. Paul's whole treatment of the subject of εἰδωλόθυτα and his failure to refer to the decrees of the Council of Jerusalem form of course one of the

[1] So, e.g., Lake, "Apostolic Council," BC, V, 207 ("a wrong antithesis").
[2] Ibid., p. 210.   [3] So Clementine Homilies, iii, 68, as quoted by Bacon, Story, p. 134.

main problems of Pauline history. Whatever text of those decrees is followed, and whether their original intention was to provide a food-law or a moral code for Gentile converts, it is clear that they prohibit the eating of meats offered to idols in the sense of I Cor. viii. 10 and x. 28, while to Jewish minds it would probably condemn the practice in the sense of I Cor. x. 25.[1]

Scholarly opinion

The majority of scholars, as we noted in Chapter 1,[2] date Paul's letters on the basis of the narrative of Acts. They are therefore squarely faced by the problem stated by Knox, for the promulgation of the Decree is described in Acts 15, and Paul wrote 1 Corinthians, according to the usual view, while at Ephesus in Acts 19.22. Why did not Paul, when dealing with the problem of idol meat, a problem specifically dealt with by the Decree, call upon the authority of this Apostolic decision? Two types of solution have been proposed to this dilemma. Most scholars have been content to suggest reasons for separating 1 Corinthians and the Decree; a few, on the other hand, have tried to deal positively with the problem by correlating the two.

Negative theories. A legion of theories have been propounded to excuse Paul's silence concerning the Decree in 1 Corinthians. Harnack's conversion of the Decree into a purely ethical instrument has been noted above. More frequently it is emphasized that the letter in Acts 15.23–9 containing the Decree is addressed only to "the Gentiles in Antioch and Syria and Cilicia" (15.23). Thus Conybeare and Howson comment: "The decrees were meant only to be of temporary application; and in their terms they applied originally only to the churches of Syria and Cilicia."[3] To the local nature of the Decree suggested by Acts is added here (quite gratuitously) a "temporary" quality as well.[4] The geographical limitation is also reflected by Carrington's comment on the problems Paul faced in Corinth: "We are here, for one short moment, on the grounds of the decision which had been made for

---

[1] *Jerusalem*, p. 326, n. 31.   [2] See pp. 12–19, and the appended notes, pp. 299–305.
[3] *St. Paul*, II, 47, n. 5. So also Sanday, "Apostolic Decree," pp. 331–2 ("The decree was only addressed in the first instance to a limited area: and I can well believe that it soon fell into comparative disuse even within that area." [quoted approvingly by Robertson and Plummer, *1 Cor.*, p. 174]); Bacon, "The Apostolic Decree against Πορνεία," *The Expositor*, Ser. 8; VII (1914), 42, ("It was never accepted . . . beyond the Cilician gates."); J. Weiss, *Primitive Christianity*, p. 314; and W. D. Davies, *Paul and Rabbinic Judaism*, p. 119. A recent defence of this point is that of A. S. Geyser, "Paul, the Apostolic Decree and the Liberals in Corinth." He concentrates on attacking the historicity of Acts 16.4, and thus is able to conclude that there is no evidence "that Paul handed the Apostolic Decree over to other churches besides those of Syria and Cilicia. At no time did he see himself and his Gentile churches under the obligation of the Apostolic Decree" (p. 138).
[4] This temporary aspect is emphasized, e.g., by H. A. W. Meyer, *Corr.*, I, 235, n. 1,

Gentile Christians in Syria by the Jerusalem council, five years before. . . . It would be interesting to know how it had fared during five years of history. Paul does not refer to it at all."[1] Some scholars suggest that the struggle in Corinth was not between Jew and Gentile, and, therefore, that the Decree was not relevant.[2] Others dismiss the Decree as a decision which was not as important as the author of Acts believed.[3] Other scholars break free of the Acts narrative and suggest that the Decree was not issued until sometime after the Council of Acts 15.[4] Thus they are able to free Paul from any connection with the Decree. Perhaps the most ingenious theory is that of Ethelbert Stauffer, who says,

> The so-called apostolic decree of which Acts says so much and Galatians nothing is, in my view, the draft of an agreement which James brought to

[1] *Early Christian Church*, I, 136.

[2] So, e.g., Lock, "I Cor. 8.1–9," pp. 70–1.

[3] So, e.g., Héring, *1 Cor.*, p. 98, n. 50.

[4] So Weizsäcker, *Apostolic Age*, I, 207; J. Weiss, *Primitive Christianity*, p. 260 ("The discussions in I Corinthians about eating meat offered to idols are unintelligible if Paul had been in a position of being able simply to appeal to the decree."); Foakes-Jackson and Lake, *BC*, II, 153–4 ("How could Paul treat of εἰδωλόθυτα as he does in I Corinthians, if an agreement on the subject had been reached by him and the Church of Jerusalem?" To which these scholars add the comment: "The more the present writers have considered this point, the more does this objection impress them."); Craig, *Beginning*, p. 176 ("When Paul later discussed with the Corinthians the problem of meat sacrificed to idols, . . . he nowhere indicated that he had been party to an official decision by the church at Jerusalem."); Porter, "Apostolic Decree," p. 172 ("Probably it [i.e., the Decree] represents the second thoughts of the Jerusalem church after the departure of Paul and Peter."); Dibelius, *Studies in Acts*, pp. 99–100 ("The events related in Gal. 2. 11f would have been quite impossible if a universal ruling on the question of food had been made at the same time as other problems came under consideration [Gal. 2.1–10]. . . . The Apostolic decree did not originate in this meeting."); Nock, *St. Paul*, pp. 115–17 ("Why does he not refer to the Decree in his lengthy discussion in I Corinthians of 'meats offered to idols'? . . . We are driven to accept the suggestion that the 'Decrees' are something formulated at Jerusalem *after* Paul had secured complete recognition for the freedom of Gentile Christians. . . . Paul regarded them as made in bad faith."); Beyer, *Acts*, p. 93 ("Umgekehrt hat Paulus das Aposteldekret nicht gekannt, wie seine ganz unbefangene Erörterung der Götzen-Opferfleisch-Frage 1. Kor. 8 und die Tatsache zeigen, dass Jakobus nach der eigenen Angabe der Apg. (21, 25) dem Paulus erst bei seinem letzten Aufenthalt in Jerusalem davon Mitteilung gemacht hat."); Kümmel in Dibelius-Kümmel, *Paul*, pp. 129–30 ("Paul, . . . on the question of eating meat offered to idols (1 Cor. 8—10), did not even mention that he had co-operated in reaching a decision which would, of course, have been binding for the Corinthians too. . . . It is probable that the 'apostles' decree' was issued at a later time (certainly without Paul's participation) and had nothing to do with the Council at Jerusalem."), and "Die älteste Form des Aposteldekrets," pp. 97–8; Goguel, *Birth*, pp. 298–300; J. N. Sanders, "Peter and Paul in the Acts," *NTS*, II (1955/56), 140 ("There is a passage later in the Acts [i.e., 21.18–25], and resting presumably on Luke's own testimony, which to me makes it very difficult to believe that Paul had any part in the Council or in publishing its decrees."); Trocmé, *"Livre des Actes,"* p. 157, n. 3, who also believes the author of Acts added the Decree to Acts 15 from Acts 21.25; Crownfield, *Historical Approach*, p. 270 ("Acts [15] . . . was honestly mistaken."); and Bornkamm, "Paulus," *RGG*[3], V, 172.

For the problems posed by Gal. 2.1–10 (especially 2.6) for the dating of the Decree, see pp. 265–9 below.

the Council of Five, but could not get accepted. . . . James somehow managed to keep the news of the defeat which he had suffered behind closed doors from his supporters outside. This gives a natural explanation why James' party could later engage in propaganda (*optima fide*) in Antioch, and awaken echoes with it—and above all why Acts itself could think of the abandoned draft as a decree signed by both sides.[1]

In these and other ways scholars have explained Paul's failure ever to mention the Apostolic Decree.

Positive theories. A far smaller number of scholars have tried to find a place for the Decree in the background of 1 Corinthians. In order to explain the difference of opinion between Paul and the Corinthians which is reflected in 1 Corinthians on the subject of idol meat, it can be argued either (i) that Paul had never accepted the Decree, but that his opponents had (or that he had accepted it for a while but abandoned it before writing 1 Corinthians), or (ii) that he had always stood by the principles of the Decree and that his opponents never had. From among the various theories discussed in Chapter 4[2] the proper type of opponent may be found to fit either type of theory. The most significant representative of the first position is Hans Lietzmann. Concerning the Decree he wrote: "This Decree of the Jerusalem church was known in Corinth about the year A.D. 52. We may well suppose that Peter brought it there, and thus to have occasioned the discussion into which Paul enters in his first epistle."[3] He did not believe that Paul was party to the Decree, and suggested that it was drawn up by the Jerusalem Church after Paul's departure.[4] On the contrary, Paul, according to Lietzmann, "pushed unruffled along the straight road of freedom from the Law".[5] Evidence that the Decree was known in Corinth he found in the fact that 1 Corinthians deals with the two major concerns of the Decree: immorality and idol meat.[6]

A modification of this position was held by T. W. Manson. He suggested that Paul had agreed to the Decree as "a working compromise", but that he angrily repudiated the agreement when Judaizers invaded

---

[1] *New Testament Theology*, trans. John Marsh (New York: The Macmillan Company, 1956), p. 262, n. 55.

[2] See pp. 96–107 above.

[3] *Beginnings*, p. 151. See in more detail his article, "Der Sinn des Aposteldekrets," pp. 297–8. So also Emanuel Hirsch, "Petrus und Paulus," *ZNW*, XXIX (1930), 72.

[4] *Beginnings*, p. 108.   [5] Ibid., p. 109.

[6] *Corr.*, p. 25; *Beginnings*, pp. 138–9. This last connection (concerning idol meat) was accepted by Massey H. Shepherd, "Source Analysis of Acts," p. 96, n. 18. Kümmel, on the other hand, in his note on Lietzmann's comment (*Corr.*, p. 174) rejected both the notion that Peter had visited Corinth and that the Decree was known there as "unbegründet und unwahrscheinlich".

the Galatian Churches.[1] Therefore, on the problem of idol meat in
1 Cor. 8.1—11.1 Manson wrote: "Why does Paul now discuss the
problem as if the Jerusalem Council had never met? I cannot help
thinking that the question was raised at Corinth by the Cephas party,
and that Paul's way of dealing with it is, and is meant to be, a snub."[2]
Paul, that is, did not lower himself to argue over, or even to mention,
an agreement broken by those of Peter's position. Like W. M.
Ramsay,[3] Manson believed that Paul's argument with Peter at Antioch
(Gal. 2.11ff) preceded the Apostolic Council (Gal. 2.1-10). Manson
placed the Previous Letter between these two episodes, and, concerning
this letter, made the following interesting suggestion:

> There is one remark [in the Previous Letter] that may be significant. It comes
> in [1 Cor.] v. 11, where Paul forbids association with Church members of
> bad character and will not saction even sitting down to a meal in their com-
> pany. Is it too hazardous to suggest that we may have here an echo of the
> controversy that shook the Church at Antioch a short time before and
> required a Council to settle it (Gal. ii. 11ff.; Acts xv. 28f.)? May it not be
> that Paul was giving in this letter *his* idea of what constituted a "kosher"
> table for Christians, with all the emphasis on the company rather than the
> viands?[4]

We shall arrive at a different conclusion below on this last point. Here
we need only notice that Manson did not allow any influence of the
Decree in the Previous Letter or before. What influence there was,
came, he believed, from the Cephas party at a later point. Although
Paul had agreed to the Decree at the Council, by the time of 1 Corinthians he had completely discarded the compromise. Thus neither
Manson nor Lietzmann believed that Paul ever favoured the Decree at
any stage in his relationship with the Corinthians.

Other scholars, however, believe that Paul's opponents in Corinth
distorted the Decree which Paul passed on to them, and that 1 Corinthians was written in part to correct this distortion. Thus Lake considered 1 Cor. 8.1—11.1 basically favourable to the Decree (in contrast
to Lietzmann and Manson), as indicated by the following cautious
statement concerning the provisions of the Decree: "I think it is quite
possible that they had been appealed to by the stricter party, and that
St. Paul's answer is intended as giving his view of the justification and
meaning of the decree so far as things offered to idols are concerned.

---

[1] *Studies*, p. 187.   [2] Ibid., p. 200.
[3] *St. Paul the Traveller*, pp. 157–60. See also Sanday, "Apostolic Decree," p. 333.
[4] *Studies*, p. 197.

Still this cannot be proved."[1] W. L. Knox also believed that Paul favoured the Decree as a compromise, but suggested that because the Corinthian Church was predominantly Gentile, he had waived all the provisions except that concerning idol meat, so that full table fellowship could be maintained. Knox suggested that an argument on this point among several parties had been referred to Paul in the Corinthians' letter.[2] Moffatt, however, believed that a single group may have objected to the Decree: "If at Corinth they were told of the Jerusalem decree against eating *eidolothuta*, they probably resented or scorned the idea that they should be hampered by any local edict of the Palestinian churches which enforced such irrelevant scruples."[3] Here, by contrast to Lake, the objectors are libertines. This last opinion is echoed by C. A. Pierce, who says of Paul's argument in 1 Corinthians on this matter: "St. Paul . . . recognises that it is useless to appeal to any pronouncement of authority. He had probably laid down the Jerusalem regulations at the onset of his Corinthian ministry: the present trouble would then have arisen partly from the Corinthians' defiance of them in the name of *gnosis*."[4]

This last group of scholars, as Pierce's statement shows, must face the problem of Paul's silence in 1 Corinthians concerning the Decree which he is supposed to be defending. Lake and Moffatt fail to pursue their suggestions. Knox suggested that Paul probably believed that an appeal to the authority of the Council would not only be useless but would weaken his own apostolic authority, which was being questioned at Corinth.[5] Thus we conclude that those scholars who have

---

[1] *Earlier Epistles*, p. 202. Smith (*St. Paul*, p. 673) held a similar position. He believed that Paul had given the Corinthians the Decree intending it ethically. The more scrupulous Christians misunderstood it to be dietary as well, a tendency which eventuated, he suggested, in the addition of the gloss πνικτοῦ. 1 Cor. 8—10 was, therefore, designed to define more precisely the intention of the Decree.

[2] *Jerusalem*, pp. 234, n. 41; 326, n. 31.

[3] *1 Cor.*, p. 102.   [4] *Conscience*, p. 76.

[5] *Jerusalem*, pp. 316, 326, n. 31; and *Acts*, p. 48. Cf. H. A. W. Meyer's suggestion that to have referred to the Decree would have been beneath Paul's apostolic dignity (*Corr.*, I, 235, n. 1).

To the above group of scholars should be added those who call attention to various points of similarity between the Decree and passages in Paul's letters: Carrington, *Primitive Catechism*, p. 19, who lists the parallels between the Decree and "1 Cor. v. 11, etc."; Selwyn, *1 Peter*, pp. 369–75, who does the same for the Decree, the Thessalonian letters, and 1 Peter, concluding that "a comparison of 1 and 2 Thessalonians with 1 Peter and certain other Epistles in the light of Acts xv. 29 points to a common catechetical pattern in the Church" (p. 374); and R. M. Grant, *Historical Introduction*, p. 395, who suggests that it may be accidental that Paul did not mention the Decree in the letters which survive. He finds the positions of the Decree advocated in 1 Thess. 4.3–7; 1 Cor. 5.1–5; 8–10; and Rom. 14. He believes that Paul brought the Decree to the western Churches as he founded them, and he concludes concerning Paul's later ministry, "It looks . . . as if Paul actually

tried to find a connection between the Decree and 1 Corinthians have been content to make a number of conjectures without pursuing the problem in any detail. Apparently there is only one scholar who has ever published the opinion which we are about to propose.

The occasion of the Previous Letter

Our reconstruction of the Previous Letter clearly rules out the suggestions of those scholars who believe that Paul was and remained hostile to the provisions of the Decree. It cannot escape our attention that the major concerns of the Decree and of the Previous Letter are strikingly similar:

Decree	Previous Letter[1]
1. Immorality	1. Immorality
	(a)Marriage
	(b) Immoral men
2. Idolatry	2. Idolatry
(a) Idol meat (blood; things strangled)	(a) Idol meat
(b) Pollutions of idols	(b) Idolatrous worship
	(i) Veils
	(ii) Tongues

In fact, if Paul had simply sent the Corinthians the provisions of the Decree, together with vigorous exhortation of the sort which we find in 2 Cor. 6.14—7.1, the nature and contents of the Corinthian Reply on these matters would be fully explained.[2] In Chapter 1 we argued that Acts 15 was the literary creation of the author of Acts, but that the Decree itself, as Dibelius suggested, may have been historical.[3] The Previous Letter, as we have reconstructed it, confirms this last point: the prohibitions which formed the Decree and which were among the traditions used by the author of Acts appear to be substantially the same prohibitions as those contained in the Previous Letter.

Of course, it is possible that this similarity was accidental. Perhaps Paul had heard reports concerning the Corinthians, and had decided

continued to teach the commandments of the apostolic decree, though he did so on grounds different from those advocated at Jerusalem." Cf. earlier Francis Crawford Burkitt, *Christian Beginnings* (London: University of London Press, Ltd., 1924), pp. 116–29.

[1] For the full outline of the Previous Letter see above, pp. 238–9.

[2] We had previously suggested that the Corinthians' inquiry concerning meat publicly sold was an objection which they had originated. Now the possibility appears that Paul had proscribed meat with blood (and πνικτοῦ?) as well as meat sacrificed to an idol, and therefore that the topic of the Corinthians' objection was contained in the Previous Letter.

[3] See pp. 35–41 above.

that stricter discipline was necessary in these matters. We argued in the preceding chapter, however, that the concerns of the Previous Letter represented a radically new emphasis in Paul's thought. Moreover, as we endeavoured to show in Chapter 5, Paul in 1 Corinthians returned to his former (Stage 1) position on almost every item of actual practice. The implication is that the prohibitions of the Previous Letter were an uncongenial intrusion into his thought. Thus, antecedently, we might expect to find their source outside the sphere of Paul's teaching and activity. Now, although there may possibly have been a number of similar ethical and ritualistic formulations in the early Church, we have argued that the Decree textually and linguistically referred to the same double area of concern as the Previous Letter. Moreover, the tradition which preserved the Decree until the writing of Acts appears to have connected it with Paul's name, since Paul is found in each of the two quite different stories in Acts concerning the Decree. Thirdly, both the occasion for the Previous Letter and the Decree were clearly of considerable importance. Paul's change of position in these matters was certainly not casual; the significance of the Decree is indicated by the fact of its preservation. It is, we submit, unlikely that there should have been two important formulations concerning the same areas of conduct both connected with Paul's name in the early Church. The simplest hypothesis is that we have in 1 Corinthians and Acts independent witnesses to a single formula of agreement in the early Church. It is enough that Paul in his extant letters should have been silent about one such agreement!

Therefore, in the light of the above parallelism between the Previous Letter and the Decree, we may conclude, not only that Paul originally accepted the Decree, but also that he attempted to enforce the Decree at Corinth by means of the Previous Letter. This opinion was suggested in passing by Wilhelm Erbt, an authority on Jewish and Teutonic folklore, in 1912, but to the present writer's knowledge the statement attracted no notice from New Testament scholars, other than a single scornful rejection by Bachmann.[1]

---

[1] Bachmann, *1 Cor.*, p. 219, n. 2. Erbt's book is *Von Jerusalem nach Rom: Untersuchungen zur Geschichte und Geschichtsdarstellung des Urchristentums* ("Mitteilungen der Vorderasiatischen Gesellschaft [E.V.]," 1912.2, 17. Jahrgang; Leipzig: J. C. Hinrichs'sche Buchhandlung, 1912). Erbt presented (pp. 25–8) the interesting and unorthodox theory that Mark (=John Mark) wrote a *two*-volume work: (1) his Gospel and (2) an account of early Christian history ending with the martyr death of Peter. Both volumes were later used by Luke, the second volume being represented by the material in Acts identified by Harnack as the Antiochean source (*Acts*, pp. 166–78, 199–202). In reconstructing the original sequence of events behind these sources, Erbt was led (p. 36) to the conclusion

At the end of the first section of this chapter we posed the question: What circumstances led Paul to change his views on the topics under discussion, and thus caused him to send to the Corinthians the Previous Letter? Having now discussed the Decree and its similarity to the Previous Letter, the following solution to this problem seems inescapable. The regulations contained in the Previous Letter were not a part of Paul's original preaching in Corinth (Stage 1), because they had not yet been formulated; later Paul adopted them and sent them to the Corinthians, not because they represented a logical development in his ethical principles, but, on the contrary, because they represented a compromise into which he had entered with a position quite different from his own. Paul, for example, had been unconcerned about dietary regulations when first in Corinth. Subsequently, he agreed to require a minimum observance among his Gentile converts in order to keep peace within the Church. For reasons yet to be discussed he did not inform the Corinthians of the nature of the agreement nor of the parties concerned. He merely fulfilled his part of the bargain by directing the Corinthians to conform on these points. The Corinthians immediately responded by challenging his lack of consistency. Paul's reply (1 Cor. 7—14), therefore, was a strained attempt to preserve the principles of his earliest preaching, and yet to give the impression that these principles implied at least a partial conformity (out of brotherly love) to the ethical and dietary requirements contained in the Previous Letter. It is no wonder that Paul's argument is obscure, tortuous, and repetitious, and that he appears to combat several points of view.[1] He was forced to

that the Apostolic Council took place during the visit of Acts 18.22. Support for his re-arrangement of Acts he found in 1 Cor. 5.9–11. He connected the reference there to "immoral men" with the "immorality" clause of the Apostolic Decree. He also suggested a connection between this topic and 1 Cor. 5—7. The "idol meat" clause he correlated with 1 Cor. 8—10, and the "blood" clause (interpreted to concern "Lieblosigkeit") with 1 Cor. 6.1–11. He theorized that the Corinthians had replied to Paul's earlier letter with a letter of their own on these subjects, which explains the presence of these topics in Paul's answering letter, 1 Corinthians. This sequence he took as evidence that the Council and the Decree occurred after the founding of the Corinthian church (Acts 18.1–18), but before the writing of 1 Corinthians (Acts 19). Since Erbt's comments on the Corinthian correspondence are not much longer than our summary of them, it appears that he had been led to these insights by his source analysis of Acts. Thus for a mixture of right and wrong reasons Erbt appears to be the first to suggest the connection between the Previous Letter and the Decree, a position supported by the present study.

[1] Chadwick, " 'All things,' " pp. 263–70, notices what he calls "the oscillating character of the argument" (p. 265) in 1 Cor. 6—14, especially chapter 7. This chapter, he comments, "oscillates between statements which surrender virtually everything to the ascetics, and qualifications which Paul subtly insinuates, which tell for the opposite standpoint. The consequence is without doubt a masterpiece of ingenuity" (pp. 264–5). While seconding Chadwick's estimate both of Paul's ability and of his method of argument, we maintain that Paul oscillated between two sets of opinions held by himself at two different times in the past.

try to justify his own earlier principles of freedom without repudiating the later limitations of conduct to which he had agreed. In this task he succeeded to an amazing degree, although, unfortunately, it appears that his troubles with the Corinthian Church did not end with the writing of 1 Corinthians.

Paul's silence concerning the Decree

The solution to the problem of the origin of the Previous Letter offered above raises a further problem, as we noted in passing: Why did Paul not mention the nature of the agreement which produced the Decree but only inform the Corinthians of the requirements of the Decree? The answer to this question is suggested by the single topic in the Previous Letter for which an occasion has not yet been suggested—the Collection. Apparently Paul changed his view on the items covered by the Decree, and more or less simultaneously decided to undertake the Collection for the Saints. It is noticeable that both these matters were of distinct benefit to the Jerusalem Church. On the other hand, neither was to Paul's advantage. The first severely endangered his hold over at least the Corinthian Church; the second involved him in a journey of perhaps several years' duration. That Paul should have undertaken both these endeavours at once, strongly implies both that he felt a great obligation toward the Jerusalem Church and, in addition, that he had received some consideration from that Church in return. The nature of this consideration is not far to seek. Paul became a witness to the Resurrection "last of all, as . . . one untimely born" (1 Cor. 15.8). He was unshakeable in his conviction that he was called to be *the* apostle to the Gentiles (Gal. 2.8, 9; Rom. 1.5, 6), and yet his references to the Jerusalem apostles frequently disclose an element of competition or antagonism:

> I worked harder than any of them, though it was not I, but the grace of God which is with me (1 Cor. 15.10).
>
> Those who were reputed to be something (what they were makes no difference to me; God shows no partiality) . . . added nothing to me (Gal. 2.6).
>
> When they perceived the grace that was given to me, James and Cephas and John, who were reputed to be pillars, gave to me . . . the right hand of fellowship (Gal. 2.9).
>
> When Cephas came to Antioch I opposed him to his face, because he stood condemned (Gal. 2.11).
>
> Do we not have the right to be accompanied by a wife, as the other apostles and the brothers of the Lord and Cephas? (1 Cor. 9.5).

There is even a hint of subservience both in Paul's rehearsal of his gospel before the Jerusalem apostles, "lest somehow" he "should be running or had run in vain" (Gal. 2.2), and in his prayers that after all his labour over the Collection his "service for Jerusalem may be acceptable to the saints" (Rom. 15.31). What Paul wanted and needed, therefore, was the recognition by the Jerusalem Church of his missionary work and the confirmation of his authority in the Churches he had founded. That Paul undertook the labours we have attributed to him indicates that he received this authority. The manner in which he attacked his two tasks implies that he, perhaps unwisely, put his newly-won authority to immediate use and approached the Corinthians with a series of commands rather than with persuasion. Table 6A presents a balance sheet for Paul's compromise with the Jerusalem Church.[1]

---

[1] The following argument by Munck challenges the suggestion above that a bargain lay behind the Collection, although Munck is discussing the meeting described in Gal. 2.1–10, a passage which we have not yet considered (*Paul and the Salvation of Mankind*, pp. 287–9). Munck contests the opinion of Karl Holl (*Gesammelte Aufsätze*, II, 58–60) that the recipients of the Collection, whom Paul refers to variously as "the saints" at Jerusalem (1 Cor. 16.1; 2 Cor. 8.4; 9.1, 12; Rom. 15.25, 31), "the poor" (Gal. 2.10), and "the poor among the saints" (Rom. 15.26) are corporately the entire membership of the Jerusalem Church, and that the Collection is a quasi-tax laid upon the Gentile Churches. Munck maintains on the contrary that the Collection is a response to the need of only a segment of the Jerusalem congregation (although he is at a loss to suggest why there should be so many "poor" Christians in Jerusalem or why Paul should be so anxious to help that particular group). He then argues, "It is impossible to hold to the assertion that the help for the poor of that church was a contribution that it forced on the Gentile churches at the meeting mentioned in Gal. 2.1–10. In such a case we should have to take into account that whenever Paul mentions the collection and emphasizes its voluntary character he is guilty of an untruth; and it seems to me more probable that Holl is mistaken in his assumption" (p. 288). Selby (*Understanding St. Paul*, p. 225) accepts Munck's contention and restates the position even more emphatically: "Paul's motive in this collection for Jerusalem has often been interpreted as a peace offering, which had been agreed upon at the Council (Galatians 2.10) and intended to heal the rift between him and the Jerusalem Church. Because it supposes that Paul would attempt to buy agreement on a basic religious principle and that Jerusalem might compromise such a principle for money, such an interpretation is unfair to both."

But Munck and Selby set up a false antithesis, because they do not recognize that an agreement concerning the Collection would actually involve three parties: the Jerusalem Church, Paul, and Paul's Churches. What Paul may have considered obligatory (see his remarks in Rom. 15.25–31) he seems to have presented to his Churches at first authoritatively (1 Cor. 16.1), but later more persuasively (2 Cor. 8—9). And when Paul was seeking to be especially persuasive he stressed the voluntary aspect of the Corinthians' participation (2 Cor. 8.8; 9.5, 7). (On this problem see pp. 233–5 above.) It is noticeable that while Paul speaks of the Collection *both* as a relief of the needy (2 Cor. 8.4; 9.12) *and* as a symbol of the gratitude of the Gentiles to the Jerusalem Church (Rom. 15.27), he emphasizes need when writing to those who are actually participating, and Jewish–Gentile unity when writing to those who are not. We infer, therefore, that the latter is the significance of the Collection for Paul, but that the former was the burden of his appeal to his Churches.

It is a moot question whether such an agreement as we have suggested would constitute truth or untruth, high principle or lack of principle on Paul's part. Apparently we have here what Chadwick described in another connection as "apostolic opportunism" (" 'All Things,' " p. 264), that is, not lack of scruple, but a subordination of lesser goods to a

TABLE 6A

Paul's Jerusalem Agreement
A Balance Sheet of Gains and Losses

Parties to the agreement	Collection	Decree	Comity
Paul	−	−	+
Jerusalem Church	+	+	−

An examination of the agreement between Paul and the Jerusalem Church which we have postulated will suggest the reasons for Paul's failure to mention its nature to the Corinthians. The Jerusalem Church had gained, we suggest, both Paul's agreement to require a minimum conformity to regulations about which Jewish Christians were particularly sensitive and his promise to raise money for them among his Churches. In return they had given him the authority to accomplish these ends and to administer his Churches with a more or less free hand. In addition, we may presume, they had promised to impose no further limitations (such as circumcision) upon the freedom of Paul's converts. When, however, we examine Paul's obligations a strange fact emerges. With respect to the Collection, Paul's obligation consisted only of the inconvenience of making the arrangements. The financial burden fell on his Churches. With respect to the Decree, Paul made little if any sacrifice. He declared himself always ready to be "all things to all men" in his manner of life (1 Cor. 9.22). But again his Churches (or at least their Gentile members) were obligated to a considerable extent in their conduct. We must correct Table 6A with Table 6B to show the interests of the Corinthian Church in this agreement. When the gains and losses are tabulated, the problem becomes, not to explain Paul's failure to mention the Decree, but to explain how he could have mentioned this arrangement to the habitually suspicious Corinthians. They were not a party to the agreement. They were obligated financi-

higher goal. There is no reason to suppose that Paul believed himself obligated to publish all his thoughts in the interest of "truth" if this action would have endangered the spread of the gospel. After all, Paul *did* believe himself to be entitled to authority over the Churches he had founded. He *was* against immorality and idolatry. The Jerusalem Church *did* have needy persons. The Gentile Churches *ought* to learn to share what God had given them. Each element of our suggested agreement is entirely defensible—and yet subject to misinterpretation by persons obligated but not benefited by the arrangement.

ally and limited in their free conduct by a decision to which they were not a party and from which they gained nothing, except the doubtful privilege of remaining under Paul's control. It may well be that, had they been given their choice, they might have chosen Apollos, for example.[1]

TABLE 6B

Paul's Jerusalem Agreement—Corrected

Parties to the agreement	Collection	Decree	Comity
Paul	$(-)$	$(-)$	$+$
Jerusalem Church	$+$	$+$	$-$
Corinthian Church	$-$	$-$	?

We suggest, therefore, that the nature of the agreement which appears to have produced the Previous Letter was such that to have informed the Corinthians about it would only have angered them without serving any useful purpose.

Galatians 2 and the Previous Letter

We have, we believe, shown that there is a certain probability that the Previous Letter implies some sort of antecedent agreement concerning (i) moral and dietary regulations and (ii) the Collection. The fact that such an agreement would have obligated, but not benefited, the Corinthians would explain, we suggested, Paul's silence about the circumstances surrounding the agreement. These suggestions lie some distance from our original starting point, 1 Corinthians, but we believe that the existence of the Decree in Acts provides a measure of confirmation for our attempt to penetrate behind the Previous Letter. Now we reach a second area of confirmation. In his letter to the Galatians Paul wrote as follows:

> After fourteen years I went up again to Jerusalem with Barnabas, taking Titus along with me. I went up by revelation; and I laid before them (but privately before those who were of repute) the gospel which I preach among the Gentiles, lest somehow I should be running or had run in vain. . . . And from those who were reputed to be something (what they were makes no

[1] Cf. the discussion of their query concerning Apollos, pp. 206–7 above.

difference to me; God shows no partiality)—those, I say, who were of repute added nothing to me; but on the contrary, when they saw that I had been entrusted with the gospel to the uncircumcised, just as Peter had been entrusted with the gospel to the circumcised (for he who worked through Peter for the mission to the circumcised worked through me also for the Gentiles), and when they perceived the grace that was given to me, James and Cephas and John, who were reputed to be pillars, gave to me and Barnabas the right hand of fellowship, that we should go to the Gentiles and they to the circumcised; only they would have us remember the poor, which very thing I was eager to do (Gal. 2.1, 2, 6–10).

To quote this passage is to open Pandora's box, for a library could be filled with what has been written concerning this account. To deal with the problems of Galatians in any systematic way would require another book. Yet Paul's account here is so important that we feel bound to sketch briefly the connections between this passage and our hypothesis. There are two obvious points of contact:

(i) Gal. 2.1–10 describes just the sort of agreement of comity which, we suggested, lay behind the Previous Letter. James and Cephas and John are to go to the circumcised; Paul and Barnabas, to the Gentiles.

(ii) In addition, a number of scholars believe that Paul's statement, "only they would have us remember the poor, which very thing I was eager to do" (Gal. 2.10), marks the beginning of the Collection for the poor among the Saints of Jerusalem.[1]

It is significant that these two items are exactly the two aspects of our proposed agreement which, we suggested, were "for publication" as far as Paul was concerned. The remaining item is the Decree. The reasons which were suggested above to explain the absence of any direct reference to the Decree in 1 Corinthians apply even more forcibly to Galatians. We argued in Chapter 1 that the main purpose of Gal. 1.13—2.1 was to deny all but the slightest dependence of Paul on the Jerusalem Church.[2] One could hardly expect Paul to mention in

---

[1] So Holl, *Gesammelte Aufsätze*, II, 58, with references to earlier scholars; Dodd, *Rom.*, pp. 229–30 ("He had made a 'gentlemen's agreement' with Peter, James and John, whereby he was to be free to conduct his mission to the Gentiles without interference from the headquarters of Jewish Christianity. In return, the 'pillars' of the Church stipulated that he should 'remember the poor'—in other words, that he should undertake to raise funds for the support of the impoverished community at Jerusalem"); Franklin, *Kollekte*, pp. 7–16 (in detail); Minear, "Jerusalem Fund," p. 391; Héring, *1 Cor.*, p. 183; J. Knox, *Chapters*, pp. 54–8 (in detail); Buck, "Collection," p. 12; John A. Allan, *The Epistle of Paul the Apostle to the Galatians* ("Torch"; London: SCM Press Ltd, 1951), p. 38 ("The idea seems to have been to provide a pledge of unity."); Grosheide, *1 Cor.*, p. 397; Craig, "1 Cor.," p. 255 (perhaps); and Sanders, "Peter and Paul," pp. 140–1; Crownfield, *Historical Approach*, p. 270; Bornkamm, "Paulus," *RGG*³, V, 171–2; and C. S. C. Williams, "Corr," §842a.

[2] See pp. 20–1 above.

such a polemical context an agreement which would have placed him in such a compromising position. The argument from silence on this point establishes even less probability than on the question whether the western mission might fall between Gal. 1.21–4 and 2.1.[1]

But Paul goes beyond silence. In Gal. 2.6–10 stands his explicit statement: "Those . . . of repute added *nothing* to me . . . *only* they would have us remember the poor." This statement has been designated by many scholars as one of the major obstacles to the identification of Gal. 2.1–10 with Acts 15. Kümmel, for example, considers Gal. 2.6 and the Decree in Acts 15.20, 25 to be the one main point of contradiction between the two narratives. He concludes, "There must therefore be an error here in the account given in Acts; it is probable that the "apostles' decree" was issued at a later time . . . and had nothing to do with the Council at Jerusalem."[2] On the other hand, Munck comments on this sort of argument: "It is by no means certain that the two meetings are identical, but the supposition from which people start here is certainly wrong. The expression "added nothing" has nothing to do with the remaining decisions reached in the negotiations—they could, if they liked, have laid down a whole *corpus juris canonici*—but means that nothing was added of what, in the opponents' opinion, Jerusalem would have been bound to demand."[3] Paul's opponents in Galatia, Munck explains, have claimed that Paul originally preached circumcision and the Law (Gal. 5.11), but then as a man-pleaser (Gal. 1.10) omitted these demands, to make his message easier for the Gentiles. Munck continues, "A meeting face to face between Paul and the leaders in Jerusalem must therefore lead, in the Judaizers' view, to some arrangement by which anything that Paul left out of his preaching was again 'added.' In that sense—but in our context in that sense only—nothing was added."[4] Paul, according to this understanding of the passage, was arguing that he had left no essential element out of the gospel which he preached "among the Gentiles" (Gal. 2.2). Therefore

---

[1] See pp. 19–22 above.

[2] Dibelius-Kümmel, *Paul*, p. 130. Other scholars who consider that Gal. 2.6 excludes the Decree from the meeting described in Gal. 2.1–10 include: Burton, *Gal.*, p. 116; Dibelius, *Studies in Acts*, p. 100, who noted that with the Decree eliminated from the Council, "we no longer need the very strained exegesis of the words in Gal. 2.6—'they have imposed nothing upon me', " the sort of exegesis which makes the hair-splitting distinction that the Decree was not imposed upon Paul but upon his churches (for the sense of this passage refer to the German original); Crownfield, *Historical Approach*, p. 270; and Bornkamm, "Paulus," *RGG*³, V, 172.

The relatively rare verb προσανέθεντο has occasioned considerable scholarly debate. The translation assumed above is that of the RSV and Arndt/Gingrich among many others, and is the sense which appears most difficult to our hypothesis.

[3] *Paul and the Salvation of Mankind*, p. 100.   [4] Ibid.

there was nothing to be "added" to his message by "those who were reputed to be something" (2.6).

Leaving aside the *corpus juris canonici*, we can observe that our analysis of Paul's conversation with the Corinthians on the matters contained in the Decree supports Munck's conclusions. There is no sign in I Corinthians that Paul ever admitted that he had changed his mind at any point or on any principle. It was the Corinthians who had pointed out his inconsistencies to him. Paul in reply protested that they had failed to understand him, failed to mature in the faith, failed to appreciate the dangers of idolatry, and failed to safeguard themselves sufficiently against immorality. Even after presenting the Corinthians with the provisions of the Decree (without indicating their source) he still could claim a higher consistency (I Cor. 9.19–23).[1] How much more, when writing to the Galatians in an attempt to counter the subversions of his Judaizing opponents, would he say, "Those . . . of repute added nothing to me".

Munck's argument coincides at a number of points with, and makes reference to, Olof Linton's analysis of the problem.[2] Linton, however, takes an important step further. In seeking to reconstruct what Paul's opponents in Galatia had been saying about him, Linton uses the device of omitting the emphasized negatives in Gal. 1.11—2.10. The result is a coherent picture which agrees at a number of points with traditions which were later included in Acts. In the statement which presently concerns us stands one such negative. Paul says explicitly that *nothing* was added to his gospel by the Jerusalem apostles. The implication is that Paul's Judaizing opponents had been saying that *something* had been added to his message on that occasion. As Linton puts it, "The Galatian version presumably argued that Paul had acknowledged some quite indispensable conditions."[3] Paul, on the other hand, denied that he had preached circumcision either before or as a result of the Council of Gal. 2.1–10, and, since he could maintain that he had always been opposed to idolatry and immorality, he affirmed that the Jerusalem apostles "added nothing" to his message. Otherwise, Paul might well have said that "those of repute" approved his gospel, or found nothing to condemn, or challenged nothing, or subtracted nothing, or changed nothing. What he did say was that they "added nothing", and this phrase is a hint that some who were unsympathetic to Paul had claimed that at this point in his career something *had* been added.

[1] See above, pp. 127–8.
[2] "The Third Aspect: A Neglected Point of View."   [3] Ibid., p. 90.

Although we cannot discuss further the complicated problems concerning the letter to the Galatians and its relationship to Acts, we may claim that Gal. 2.1–10 affords confirmation of our hypothesis about the origin of the Previous Letter. Conversely, the Previous Letter is evidence, we believe, that agreement on the Decree and the commencement of the Collection occurred simultaneously, a fact which is obviously of great importance in the reconstruction of the course of Paul's ministry. One further problem concerning the Previous Letter remains to be discussed.

The "parties" at Corinth

Paul opened 1 Corinthians with a reference to the divisions within the Corinthian Church (1.12). We argued in Chapter 4 that Paul had the names of three "parties" in mind: "Those of Paul", "those of Apollos", and "those of Cephas"; the so-called Christ party probably did not exist.[1] Further, we noted in Chapter 3 that Paul's reference to divisions in 11.18, in direct connection with his condemnation of the Corinthians' broken table fellowship, appears somewhat unlike his reference to the divisions of 1.12. In 1.12 the parties are named, but the behaviour for which Paul reprimanded them is vague; in 11.18 the conduct disapproved of is specified, but the groups are vague.[2] We concluded that either the rationale behind these divisions was based on a dispute concerning the manner of observance of the Lord's Supper (as Lietzmann believed), or these divisions were not parties, but simply reflected a general Corinthian tendency toward factiousness (as Munck contends). Throughout the course of our discussions of Paul's dialogue with the Corinthians we have emphasized repeatedly that Paul appeared to combat a single, apparently unified point of view, a conclusion which seems to favour Munck's hypothesis. We have not, however, examined Lietzmann's type of suggestion, and, in fact, none of those things on which the Corinthians appear unified directly concerns the observance of the Lord's Supper. Now that we have reconstructed the Previous Letter, and compared it with the Apostolic Decree and with Gal. 2.1–10, we may make the following suggestion. The Previous Letter with its moral and ritualistic restrictions might have been expected to affect the Corinthians' observance of the Lord's Supper and to evoke three types of reaction in this respect. Corinthians might have contended

(i) That the Previous Letter provided a basis for table fellowship within the Church between Jew and Gentile, or

[1] See pp. 102–6 above.　　[2] See pp. 80–2 above.

(ii) That, since the Previous Letter had not required circumcision of the Gentiles, table fellowship was still not possible, or

(iii) That table fellowship ought to be possible without regulations of any kind.

Of these the first, we may presume, was Paul's position when he wrote the Previous Letter. The second may be recognized as the position adopted by Peter, Barnabas, and "the rest of the Jews" at Antioch when Peter withdrew from table fellowship with Gentile Christians, "fearing the circumcision party" (Gal. 2.11–13). The third represents Paul's original position (Stage 1). The implication of Paul's agricultural and architectural metaphors in 1 Cor. 3.5–10 is that Apollos continued in the tradition of teaching begun by Paul. Thus Apollos might naturally have represented the position of freedom. Notice that these three positions do not form the "weak" and the "strong" parties which some scholars believe to have existed at Corinth. Persons from any one of these three groups might believe it to be ridiculous, for example, to require Gentiles suddenly to begin to avoid idol meat at all times, or that they all should somehow cut off contact with unbelievers. Formerly, we may suppose, the Corinthians who were circumcised ate by themselves when they met to celebrate the Lord's Supper, and the uncircumcised ate by themselves. The Previous Letter, we suggest, was intended to bridge this separation, but Paul's commands were not well received, and the separation itself became an issue.

Because of the scantiness of the evidence, and because we have not been able to discuss Gal. 2 and the Apostolic Decree in any detail, the above can only be offered as a tentative suggestion. Next we return to the main stream of the dialogue between Paul and the Corinthians, and attempt to reconstruct those items in Paul's original preaching (Stage 1) which later became points of contention between himself and the Corinthian Church.

PART 4

Conclusions

CHAPTER 8

Paul's First Preaching in Corinth

THE SHAPE OF THE DIALOGUE

From 1 Corinthians we have moved backward in time, stage by stage, through Paul's relationship with the Corinthians until at last we now reach Stage 1, Paul's original visit to Corinth. In our survey of Paul's Corinthian ministry to this point we have discussed the three stages which formed a dialogue between Paul and the Corinthians from the Previous Letter to 1 Corinthians. Reviewing these stages we may notice that if we characterize them solely according to the degree of cautiousness or strenuousness which they express, the series is somewhat symmetrical. The Previous Letter (Stage 2) lay, we suggested, well in the direction of an extreme cautiousness in matters of conduct. The Christian was directed to observe what amounted to taboos concerning his diet and his relationship to the world. The Corinthian Reply (Stage 3), on the other hand, lay a considerable distance toward the extreme of freedom. The Corinthians advocated the higher way, the dangerous, bold course for Christian behaviour. Midway between these two statements stood 1 Corinthians (Stage 4), expressing as it did both freedom and caution. Paul warned the Corinthians of the various dangers involved in the conduct they advocated, but in the end he allowed them to continue very much as they were. These three expressions of Christian morality form, we believe, a natural series: statement, counter-statement, and compromise. Stage 3 is a direct reaction to Stage 2; Stage 4, to Stage 3 (in the light of Stage 2). These stages appear to form a self-contained dialogue; there is no evidence that there were other parties to the discussion whose contributions are missing. When we move behind these three stages, however, the situation changes sharply, for here a third party has to be considered—the Jerusalem Church. No longer can we consider each stage to be a reaction to the preceding stage. Between Stage 1 and Stage 2 occurred the agreement which resulted in the adoption of the Decree by Paul and his decision to undertake the Collection. Previous to this agreement, we may suppose that the views of Paul and the Corinthians concerning Christian behaviour were similar, perhaps slightly in tension. The Decree, however, upset this equilibrium and produced the deflection in Paul's position which resulted in the oscillation we have labelled Stages 2–4. Our problem, therefore, is to try to estimate how far toward the Corinthians' position expressed in their Reply Letter, Paul had stood prior to the Decree.

Much scholarly work has been done on the two passages in 1 Corinthians in which Paul explicitly referred to his earliest preaching at Corinth (1 Cor. 11.23–5 and 15.1–8). Each of these passages is marked by the formula, "I delivered to you . . . what I also received . . ." (15.3), indicating that the content of Paul's teaching on these two points was traditional and pre-Pauline. We are not principally concerned with these passages, however, for they occur only in 1 Corinthians and do not form a part of the argument between Paul and the Corinthians in Stages 2 and 3. The area where our investigation of this dialogue does cast new light concerns primarily the life and manner of worship of the earliest Corinthian Church, together with something of its eschatological beliefs. Only indirectly does this reconstruction increase our knowledge of the content of the Corinthians' faith. For the outline of our investigation, therefore, we return to the familiar series of topics found in the Corinthian Reply and in 1 Corinthians (with the exception, of course, of those concerning the Collection and Apollos). We return to the topics of the Corinthian Reply rather than those of the Previous Letter, because the Reply contains those points about which the Corinthians protested that Paul had been inconsistent with his earlier preaching; the topics of the Previous Letter, on the other hand, were occasioned mainly by Paul's Jerusalem agreement and are less closely related to the topics of Stage 1.

CONCERNING SEXUAL MORALITY

Paul's position

From the discussions of topics relating to sexual morality in Chapters 5 and 6[1] we may reconstruct with fair probability the nature of Paul's earliest teaching on the subject.

[1] See above, pp. 154–82 and pp. 222–5.

In the first place, apparently Paul had said in some connection, "It is best for a man not to touch a woman". It is most improbable that Paul would have refrained from attacking this slogan, which was so important to the Corinthians, if it had been an alien element in the tradition of that Church. In outline his argument in 1 Corinthians was that, in spite of the general truth of this principle, practical considerations made less rigorous conduct advisable. By this line of argument he reaffirmed the caution of the Previous Letter, without abandoning what we must assume to be the principles he had advocated when he founded the Corinthian Church. Moreover, it is not probable that Paul had used this slogan only in some special situation. In 1 Cor. 7.1–7 Paul accepted the Corinthians' use of the principle as an argument against sexual intercourse within marriages. Clearly if it could apply in this situation, then how much more to every other form of sexual relationship. Apparently then Paul had taught that, in general, "it is best for a man not to touch a woman". Paul's own unmarried status confirms this supposition. Jeremias has argued that it would have been unlikely for a Jew of Paul's background and education to have remained unmarried and that, therefore, Paul was a widower.[1] It would be even more unlikely, however, for a man who had been married to hold such an ascetic point of view. Since Jeremias' argument is not actually based on evidence from Paul's letters, it seems preferable to accept the implication of 1 Corinthians that Paul in general would have preferred total sexual abstinence among his converts, if such were feasible. Those Corinthians who were single he advised to remain single (if in Stage 4, how much more so in Stage 1 !). To those who were already married he advocated continence, that they might devote themselves more fully to the things of the Spirit.

Spiritual marriages

Our discussions of "spiritual marriages" leave the strong impression that during Stage 1 Paul was much in favour of this institution. The way in which the Corinthian Reply referred to these relationships indicates that Paul was already well informed about their nature. Probably, therefore, they existed during his first visit to Corinth, unless we are to postulate some otherwise unknown contact between Paul and the Corinthians prior to Stage 2. Further, Paul's attitude in 1 Corinthians

---

[1] "War Paulus Witwer?" *ZNW*, XXV (1926), 310–12; "Nochmals: War Paulus Witwer?" *ZNW*, XXVIII (1929), 321–3. Fascher's counterstatement to which the second of Jeremias' articles was a reply has been cited above, p. 158, n. 2.

toward this institution is significant. Because of the danger of immorality, Paul advised married couples to resume sexual relations. Since the spiritual couples were in special danger of immorality, one might have expected Paul in 1 Corinthians strongly to urge them to marry, but his advice to them was of a different order. They were to preserve their relationship unless extreme temptation forced them to marry (7.36). Those couples who refrained from physical marriage, he believed, did "better" (7.38). Clearly these relationships occupied a special place in Paul's thought. Since he defended the institution in 1 Corinthians, we must assume he was still more in favour of these arrangements during his first visit to Corinth.

Indeed we strongly suspect that Paul was instrumental in inaugurating these relationships. We have argued that the vow undertaken by these couples was a result of their Christian enthusiasm.[1] This peculiar institution, therefore, was created during Paul's original stay in Corinth. It is doubtful whether anything so significant for the life of the congregation could have been inaugurated without his full consent and approval. Moreover, since Paul was at that time the undisputed leader of the Corinthian Church, it is natural to suppose that he himself was responsible for creating this new Christian institution.

Like the angels

The picture which appears from this analysis of the Corinthian sexual mores resembles that described in the following pair of passages from the Synoptic Gospels:

> Jesus said to them, "Is not this why you are wrong, that you know neither the scriptures nor the power of God? For when they rise from the dead, they neither marry nor are given in marriage, but are like angels in heaven" (Mark 12.24, 25).

> [Jesus said,] "As it was in the days of Noah, so will it be in the days of the Son of Man. They ate, they drank, they married, they were given in marriage, until the day when Noah entered the ark, and the flood came and destroyed them all" (Luke 17.26, 27).

Thus there is evidence both in the Markan and in the Q traditions that it was believed that marriage as an institution would cease when the Kingdom came.[2] Since the "spiritual" couples at Corinth were not

---

[1] See above, pp. 179–80.

[2] Cf. also Matt. 19.10–12. For parallels with the Dead Sea sect see Matthew Black, *The Scrolls and Christian Origins: Studies in the Jewish Background of the New Testament* (London: Thomas Nelson and Sons Ltd, 1961), pp. 27–9, 83–8; and Cross, *Library of Qumrân*, pp. 73–4. Cross describes the Qumrân sectarian as follows: "The Essene in his

married as the world understood marriage, they were, therefore, living like angels.[1] It is hard to overestimate the enthusiasm which appears to have existed in this early Christian community. The same enthusiasm we shall see expressed in their manner of worship, their contempt for this Age, and their intense expectation of the speedy return of "the Lord Jesus Christ". The strenuous nature of their sexual asceticism implies that they believed they did not have long to wait. Later, the passage of time and Jewish Christian apprehensions about Gentile Christian sexual morality led Paul to move somewhat reluctantly toward a wiser doctrine of Christian marriage.

This reconstruction of the sexual morality of the community established by Paul contrasts sharply with the scholarly opinions summarized in Chapter 4. In tracing the course of the debate between Paul and the Corinthians we have found no evidence of outside influences at work in Corinth drawing the Corinthians away from Paul, introducing gnostic ideas, and allowing, or even encouraging, gross immorality. Instead we have found an earnest group of pioneers who felt themselves challenged by Paul's first preaching into a strenuous, ascetic form of sexual behaviour. This first reaction to the Christian message they wished to preserve, in spite of the dangers about which Paul was made increasingly aware. The shocking scandals and the libertinism which most commentators believe to have existed in the Corinthian Church are an illusion, in our opinion, created (a) by Paul's remarks in 1 Cor. 6.12–20 about the theoretical and possible consequences of taking the motto, "All things are lawful", as an absolute principle, and (b) by his repeated warnings against immorality. These last, we concluded, were not comments about the Corinthians' conduct, but resulted from the Apostolic Decree, that is, from Jewish Christian fears about the future results of the new morality at Corinth. The only concrete example of sexual immorality that Paul can point to, in spite of having what appear to have been willing informants, is the man described as "having his

daily life . . . girds himself to withstand the final trial, purifies himself to join the holy armies, anticipates the coming conditions in God's inbreaking kingdom. This is the situation which prompts counsels against marriage, at least for some. . . . In this new age the righteous live like the angels without need of procreation." And he comments: "Both in the New Testament and at Qumrân we discover counsels against marriage in *this* decisive moment when *this* world is passing away. In neither community is to be found a theoretical ascetic doctrine of universal validity. Rather we may call Essene (or New Testament) practice an 'apocalyptic' asceticism."

For the gnostic development of this idea see Robert M. Grant with David Noel Freedman, *The Secret Sayings of Jesus According to the Gospel of Thomas* (London: Fontana Books, 1960), pp. 75, 83, 136–7 (Saying No. 23), and 185–6 (Saying No. 112).

[1] Did they also believe that they were already resurrected as Hans von Soden, for example, suggested? See above, p. 198, and below, pp. 284–6.

father's wife" (1 Cor. 5.1). We have it directly from Paul that the Corinthians had not troubled themselves about this problem, whatever the exact situation may have been. It is impossible at this distance to judge whether this relationship was innocent or not. There is a real possibility, however, that the pair—a man and, presumably, his (widowed?) stepmother—were joined in spiritual marriage. Such a relationship could have been considered by the Corinthians as exempt from the usual prohibitions, because the union was not a marriage in the physical sense. At the same time, of course, this arrangement could attract the severest censure from moralists, whether or not the parties remained faithful to their vows. But even granting the most unsympathetic interpretation of this man's conduct, the libertinism of the Corinthian congregation seems to have consisted of but one individual case. Thus, while they might possibly be called naïve, or impractical, or too enthusiastic, they cannot be denounced as licentious.

CONCERNING THE WORLD

As on the preceding topic there is double evidence to support a reconstruction of Paul's original preaching about the relationship of Christians to the world: the slogans of the Corinthian Reply and Paul's own conduct.

Slogans

Of all the slogans listed in Table 5 above, those relating to idol meat (8.1, 4; 10.23) are most widely recognized to be quotations from the Corinthian Reply.[1] Yet the manner in which Paul argued around but not against these principles in 1 Cor. 8.1—11.1 implies that their ultimate source was Paul himself. As a number of scholars have suggested, it is very probable that he had himself told the Corinthians when he founded the Church, "All things are lawful", "We have knowledge", "An idol has no real existence", and "There is no God but one".[2] What more effective argument could the Corinthians use to protest Paul's inconsistency than to quote Paul against himself?[3]

[1] See Table 5, p. 68 above.

[2] So, e.g., for some or all of the above slogans, Lock, "I Cor. 8.1-9," p. 69; Findlay, as quoted above, p. 115; von Dobschütz, *Primitive Church*, pp. 51, 65; Bacon, *Story*, p. 278; J. Weiss, *Primitive Christianity*, p. 327 ("In these statements he hears echoes of his own preaching."); Héring, *1 Cor.*, p. 46; and F. C. Grant, *N. T.*, p. 79.

[3] Simon, *1 Cor.*, p. 33, contributes the following comment without, however, giving the reference: " 'A brilliant inconsistency' is how Wilfred Knox once described I Corinthians, a letter in which the Apostle 'deals with the disorders which have arisen out of a perfectly logical interpretation of his own teaching.' "

The last two slogans quoted above are neither surprising nor peculiarly Pauline; the other two, however, are somewhat unexpected. "All things are lawful" is a slogan which is certainly Pauline in principle, but which appears nowhere in Paul's later letters. We may recognize in this early setting aside of legal restrictions one root of his later doctrine that "a man is not justified by works of the law but through faith in Jesus Christ" (Gal. 2.16). Yet even in Galatians, where he expressed his most negative opinion of the value of the law, he was careful to give his converts long lists of "the works of the flesh" and of "the fruit of the Spirit", so that they would not be without ethical guidance (Gal. 5.19–24). And he concluded, "Bear one another's burdens, and so fulfill the law of Christ" (Gal. 6.2). It appears that Paul learned from experience what his converts could do with the slogan, "All things are lawful". This principle, appearing as it very probably did in Paul's earliest preaching, creates for the modern an impression of enthusiasm and freshness with perhaps a touch of naïveté, the same impression as that afforded by Paul's earliest teachings concerning Christian marriage.

The second slogan, "We all have knowledge", is similar to the first. Concerning earthly customs and scruples the Christian could say, "All things are lawful"; concerning his relationship to the heavenly he could say, "We all have knowledge (γνῶσις)". In this latter slogan we catch again the impression of enthusiasm and overconfidence which appear to have characterized Paul's first preaching in Corinth. What Paul meant by this slogan we can gather from his later writings, just as we can see from Galatians what Paul meant by freedom from the law. Thus, for example, he explained to the Corinthians:

> Among the mature we do impart wisdom, although it is not a wisdom of this age or of the rules of this age who are doomed to pass away. But we impart a secret and hidden wisdom of God which God decreed before the ages for our glorification (1 Cor. 2.6, 7).

His earliest preaching had been bold and challenging. He had declared to the Corinthians that he had saving "knowledge" to share with them. Later, to curb what he took to be overconfidence and boastfulness among the Corinthians, he called this knowledge milk for babies (3.2), the ABC's of the gospel. He maintained that he had a higher "wisdom" to impart to the "mature" (2.6). It is especially important to notice that in this later stage he was careful to specify that this wisdom was the means by which God glorified his saints; it was not grounds for self-glorification (2.7). In the case of both these early slogans, therefore,

Paul appears to have matured, and later found ways of expressing his message which were less open to exploitation and misunderstanding. Thus Paul learned to say concerning his own knowledge,

> Love never ends; as for prophecy, it will pass away; as for tongues, they will cease; as for knowledge, it will pass away. For our knowledge is imperfect and our prophecy is imperfect; but when the perfect comes, the imperfect will pass away. When I was a child, I spoke like a child, I thought like a child, I reasoned like a child; when I became a man, I gave up childish ways. For now we see in a mirror dimly, but then face to face. Now I know in part; then I shall understand fully, even as I have been fully understood (1 Cor. 13.8–12).

It is a long way from the bold slogan, "We all have knowledge", to the humble passage above. In our survey of Paul's Corinthian ministry we have discovered some of the pressures which produced this change.

Paul's conduct

It seems clear from the nature of the Corinthians' objections to the proscription of idol meat in the Previous Letter that Paul had never raised this issue before. On the contrary, it appears that during his first stay in Corinth he was "as one outside the law" (1 Cor. 9.21). He himself ate meat without inquiring as to its history; his Gentile converts naturally did the same. There may have been no particular occasion for him to have attended banquets where idol meat was served, but he does not seem to have forbidden the practice to Church members. Thus his own behaviour seems entirely consistent with his slogans, "An idol is nothing", and "All things are lawful".

Therefore, Paul in his earliest preaching at Corinth appears to have forbidden idolatry but not idol meat, unbelief but not contact with unbelievers, in the same way that he had forbidden immorality, but had allowed, and even encouraged, situations in which temptation toward immorality might easily grow. This failure to provide a second line of defence against sin by which the resolve of new Christians might be protected marks this phase of Paul's preaching as both early and temporary. The confidence and enthusiasm suggest an early date for these teachings; the lack of concern for the years ahead implies perhaps, inexperience but, even more, a conviction that the end of all human institutions lay in the near future.

CONCERNING WORSHIP

Glossolalia

The aspect of the Corinthians' manner of worship which became the major issue between Paul and the Corinthians was their exaggerated emphasis on speaking with tongues. This ability was for them the real mark of the Spirit. In our discussion of 1 Cor. 12—14 we noted that Paul was careful never directly to criticize glossolalia.[1] The clear implication is that here again is a topic on which he did not wish to contradict himself. Paul himself said of his first visit to Corinth, "My speech and my message were not in plausible words of wisdom, but in demonstration of the Spirit and power" (1 Cor. 2.4). The nature of this "demonstration of the Spirit" is indicated by his statement, "I thank God that I speak in tongues more than you all" (1 Cor. 14.18). It appears, therefore, that Paul spoke with tongues, that he considered glossolalia a prime "demonstration of the Spirit", and that he encouraged the Corinthians to follow his example. Very probably, therefore, the Corinthians had grounds for their complaint that prior to the Previous Letter Paul had never criticized the practice of speaking with tongues. Here once again is the enthusiasm which marked Paul's founding visit to Corinth.

Veils

Concerning veils the Corinthians had protested that they had simply been following the traditions given them by Paul in allowing their women to go without veils (1 Cor. 11.2).[2] Clearly Paul had at least allowed the practice when he inaugurated Christian worship at Corinth. The question, however, is whether he merely allowed the practice, or whether he actively advocated it. His later criticism of the custom (1 Cor. 11.3–16) implies that he then considered it indecent and unnatural. Moreover, the vigour of his attack seems to indicate that the practice was not a positive element in his earliest preaching. The fact that he chose in the Previous Letter to forbid this practice, in what appears to be the context of a general warning against idolatry, may indicate that the Corinthians had brought the custom with them from paganism. Paul at the time had seen no more reason to change this practice than to alter the Corinthians' eating habits. The Corinthians, therefore, with some justification interpreted his silence as consent.

[1] See p. 188 above.   [2] See pp. 184–6 above.

It is, of course, possible that the practice of allowing women to go unveiled during worship may have been connected with the belief that in the Kingdom there would be "neither male nor female" (Gal. 3.28). We have seen that Paul in his early preaching seems to have considered marriage no longer necessary or desirable. Moffatt probably goes too far, however, in speaking of a "feminist party" at Corinth.[1] It is probable that the mention of divorce (1 Cor. 7.10–16) did not come from such a group as he suggests, but was involved in the Corinthians' protest against avoiding unbelievers.[2] The other two points at which women figure in 1 Corinthians (the matter of veiling and speaking during worship) do not make a party. These practices may, however, have evolved from a general conviction that sexual differences should be set aside in preparation for the Kingdom soon to come. We can attach only limited significance to this observation, however, for Paul's later criticism implies that these customs had only been tacitly permitted in the first enthusiastic days of the Corinthian Church. Later reflection convinced Paul that they were definitely undesirable.

Thus the manner of the Corinthians' worship was an expression of the same enthusiasm and unconcern for social mores which we saw expressed in the areas of sexual and social ethics. We next discuss the cause of this enthusiasm.

CONCERNING ESCHATOLOGY

Our discussion of the Corinthians' question concerning resurrection has led us to the conclusion that prior to the Previous Letter Paul had never preached to them the resurrection of believers.[3] Their reaction on this subject in the Corinthian Reply indicates both that they had never had the doctrine presented to them before, and that the doctrine as contained in the Previous Letter was expressed in its simplest form. Paul had simply assured them that the dead in Christ would be resurrected as Christ had been resurrected. We suggested that his statement was probably similar to 1 Thess. 4.13-18.[4] The Previous Letter and 1 Thessalonians both appear to have originated from the brief period which lay between the time when the first Christian died, and the point at which the Corinthians challenged (Stage 3) Paul's simple statement (Stage 2) that believers would be resurrected. Now we move behind this period and seek to learn what our analysis implies about Paul's original preaching at Corinth.

[1] *1 Cor.*, pp. 78, 149, and 233.   [2] See p. 224 above.
[3] See pp. 195–200, 229–33 above.   [4] See pp. 231–33 above.

It seems to us clear that just as Paul's dialogue with the Corinthians concerning matters of discipline moved through discrete stages, so too his eschatological instruction to them changed to meet new problems. It is not sufficient to say that Paul happened to deal with one aspect of the problem in one letter and another aspect in another letter, or that different Churches had differing problems. We have now established a sequence of exchanges between Paul and a single Church. This sequence extends back to a very early stage in Paul's ministry, a stage at which he had not yet faced the problem of the future of Christian marriage, for example. We are therefore in a far better position to establish the probability of a development in Paul's eschatological teaching than those scholars who have no chronological sequence of letters other than that afforded by Acts. As we have noted, a number of scholars have held such a theory of development,[1] but their work has always been open to the criticism (which we summarized in Chapter 1) that Paul's extant letters are all from the period of his mature thought.[2] Now on the basis of our reconstructed correspondence between Paul and the Corinthians, we believe that we are justified in extrapolating the evidence of 1 Corinthians back to a very early stage.

We have suggested that Paul's simple statement in the Previous Letter affirming the resurrection of believers was occasioned by the death of the first few Christians (whether at Corinth or elsewhere[3]). What had Paul taught prior to this stage? We listed in Chapter 3 the series of ten questions in 1 Corinthians beginning οὐκ οἴδατε ὅτι. Those which relate to matters of Christian faith presumably referred to instruction which Paul had given the Corinthians at an earlier stage. No less than three of these concern the future:

6.2: Do you not know that the saints will judge the world?

6.3: Do you not know that we are to judge angels?

6.9: Do you not know that the unrighteous will not inherit the kingdom of God?

Clearly we are in the realm of apocalyptic eschatology. Each Christian can look forward to the day when he joins with Christ to pass judgement upon the unrighteous and upon angels.[4] An apocalyptic calendar undoubtedly accompanied this representation of the Last Judgement. In view of this fact, and because of the reference to the "trumpet" in 1 Cor. 15.52, in a manner which indicates that the Corinthians had

---

[1] See p. 8, nn. 2, 3, and pp. 232–3 above.   [2] See pp. 7–12 above.
[3] Cf., however, 1 Cor. 11.30.   [4] On the latter see p. 184, n. 4, above.

already heard of this trumpet and at least some of the events connected with it, we are probably justified in believing that the apocalyptic programme in 1 Thess. 4.13–18 was also part of Paul's preaching to the Corinthians. 1 Thessalonians and the Previous Letter represent, however, a second stage in his apocalyptic teaching, for by this point he had modified what he had taught earlier by adding the doctrine of the resurrection of believers.

What was the earlier stage? Behind 1 Thess. 4.13–18 stands an apocalyptic calendar which Paul was certainly not presenting to the Thessalonians for the first time.

> We believe that Jesus died and rose again . . . [and revealed as] the Lord . . . will descend from heaven with a cry of command, with the archangel's call, and with the sound of the trumpet of God. . . . We . . . shall be caught up . . . in the clouds to meet the Lord in the air; and so we shall always be with the Lord (1 Thess. 4.14, 16, 17).[1]

With this proclamation we find ourselves at a very early point in Christian history. It was assumed that those who were converted to Christ would live to enter the Kingdom when the Lord came. There was no need of a doctrine of the resurrection of believers, just as there was no need for a sexual ethic which envisioned the conception and raising of children in Christian homes. Whether or not Jesus taught an apocalyptic eschatology, it is clear that Paul in his early preaching was enthusiastically apocalyptic. Very probably the Resurrection of Jesus focused the attention of the early Church on the immediate future and heightened their expectation of an imminent Parousia. Certainly the Synoptic Gospels contained a large number of sayings which are apocalyptic in their present wording, whatever may have been their original form. Undoubtedly many of these sayings contained substantially their present meaning at the time of Paul's first stay at Corinth. Thus Paul's earliest eschatological preaching correlates well with apocalyptic traditions in the early Church which later found a place in the Synoptic Gospels.

Earlier we noted Hans von Soden's suggestion that the Corinthians had objected to the doctrine of the future resurrection of Christians because they believed that they all had been resurrected already.[2] J. Héring goes further and attributes this belief to Paul:

---

[1] With this picture may be compared 2 Thess. 1.7–10; 2.1–12. The similarity between these systems favours the theory of the scholars listed above, p. 27, n. 1, that 2 Thessalonians was written before 1 Thessalonians.

[2] See p. 198 above.

We do not err in affirming that Paul himself at an early period had expressly denied the future resurrection and that the anti-resurrectionists at Thessalonica and Corinth were after all only the representatives of the unchanged Pauline belief. It is no less true that their position was strongly placed in line with the fundamental conceptions of the Apostle—a fact which explains both their influence and the difficulty that Paul had to convince them.[1]

Héring's insight into the origin of the Corinthians' belief is, we believe, important, but the suggestion that Paul believed that he and his fellow Christians were already resurrected requires closer examination. Our investigations have brought us to a position which at many points supports this suggestion. Thus, for example, the following characteristics of the Corinthian community may be taken as reflecting a belief that they were living proleptically in the Kingdom: (a) spiritual marriages, (b) women unveiled and speaking in church, (c) speaking in tongues by the power of the Spirit, (d) freedom from law ("All things are lawful"), (e) belief in the immunity of believers from contamination by idolaters and idol meat ("An idol is nothing"), (f) belief in the gospel as saving knowledge, (g) acceptance of the designation "holy" (i.e., "saints') following baptism into Christ, (h) participation in the Lord's Supper as an eschatological sacrament, and (i) conviction that the Church was an island of life in Christ surrounded by a sea of death ruled by Satan (5.5). These items generally favour the positions of von Soden and Héring. The key issue, however, is the Corinthian expectations concerning the future. By tracing back the dialogue between Paul and the Corinthians we reached in the Previous Letter what appeared to be Paul's first statement to them that Christians will be resurrected.[2] As we have frequently argued, it is unlikely that the Corinthians had been greatly influenced by any teachers besides Paul. The question is, therefore: What did Paul teach before he taught the resurrection of believers? It seems simplest to suppose that he had assured the Corinthians of the imminence of the Parousia, but had said nothing of any need for a change of bodies or for resurrection to enter the Kingdom. There was no reason to talk of resurrection, since the time before the end was so short that there was no expectation of death; nor was there any reason to discuss a change of bodies, since this subject (as 1 Thessalonians and 1 Corinthians indicate) was dependent upon Paul's later explanation of the resurrection of those believers who had died. Thus

---

[1] "Saint Paul a-t-il enseigné deux résurrections?" *Revue d'Histoire et de Philosophie Religieuse*, XII (1932), 318 (as translated by W. D. Davies, *Paul and Rabbinic Judaism*, p. 292).
[2] See pp. 229–33 above.

there would have been no reason for him to deny a doctrine the need for which had not yet arisen. The Corinthians' antipathy to the idea of the resurrection of believers was in large measure simply antipathy to a new idea. We, therefore, can now set aside the suggestions of von Soden and Héring to the extent that they attribute to Paul and the Corinthians more than the simple conviction that Christians would live until Christ came.

Héring does, however, make the interesting suggestion that the Corinthians may have had a positive reason for believing that they would survive to the day of Christ's return. In discussing the meaning of Rom. 6.3, 4 he writes, "Baptism . . . was an assurance against death (a φάρμακον ἀθανασίας if one should care to put it so, but certainly not in the Hellenistic sense) that guaranteed the prolongation of the terrestrial life until the moment when the Parousia of our Lord and the transfiguration of the surviving Christians should take place."[1] In the light of our discussions both of baptism for the dead and of the incestuous man,[2] we believe it would be more accurate to say that in the period we are investigating baptism was believed to guarantee salvation whether before or after death. However, 1 Cor. 11.30, to which Héring refers in this connection,[3] suggests a better hypothesis.

> Any one who eats and drinks without discerning the body eats and drinks judgment upon himself. That is why many of you are weak and ill, and some have died (11.29, 30).

Without involving a doctrine of resurrection at all, we may simply suggest that the Corinthians believed that the regular eating and drinking of the Lord's body and blood prevented their death before the Parousia. In this sense the bread and the cup were a φάρμακον ἀθανασίας.[4] Paul, writing 1 Corinthians after some believers had died, suggested that the Eucharist had failed to preserve these persons alive because they had not "discerned the body".[5] That the improper reception of the body and blood should cause death (or allow Christians to die) implies that the proper reception of the sacrament would prevent death. The vigour, crudeness, and naïveté of this belief may be taken as evidence that it belonged to the earlier stage of Paul's preaching.

[1] "Deux résurrections," pp. 316–17 (again as translated by Davies, *Paul and Rabbinic Judaism*, p. 291).

[2] See pp. 136–7 above.   [3] *1 Cor.*, p. 181, n. 64.

[4] See the references above to Allo and to Lietzmann, p. 136, n. 1 and n. 2.

[5] Cf. the incestuous man in 1 Cor. 5.1–5, discussed above, p. 137. Paul apparently believed that when this man was excluded from the Church (i.e., delivered to Satan) he would die (i.e., his flesh would be destroyed).

We conclude, therefore, that when Paul first visited Corinth he preached a fervent apocalypticism and assured his converts that they would live to see Christ's return to earth. Very probably the basis of this assurance was the belief that the power of the Lord's Supper held death in check and guaranteed that all who believed would remain alive to the end.

CONCLUSION

The result of our reconstruction of the above portion of Paul's original preaching at Corinth is that we gain a new understanding of these early Corinthian Christians. Ordinarily it is assumed that the Corinthians were a troublesome, quarrelsome group, immoral and licentious, who plagued Paul with their objections and infidelities. There is some justification for this view as we have seen. Certainly the Corinthians were aggressive and argumentative. They rejected Jewish scruples and favoured a daring, strenuous form of Christian life. On the other hand, it is easy to see that from their point of view Paul appeared vacillating and cautious in the Previous Letter and in 1 Corinthians. Further, we have suggested that much of the "wisdom" and "knowledge" to which they clung had been given them by Paul himself during his first visit to Corinth. We have also suggested that in his understandable desire to strengthen the Gentile mission Paul had entered into an agreement with the Jerusalem Church about which he could not tell the Corinthians. His sudden change in perspective and his demand for observance of a cautious list of prohibitions puzzled and angered them. They desired to preserve their original enthusiasm; they resented any diminution of the importance of the Spirit in the guidance of the Church. We can see with the wisdom of hindsight that the future clearly lay with Paul, but as we look back across the years we cannot help admiring the spirit of those spiritual Corinthian Christians.

Conversely, we have by our reconstruction of Paul's early Corinthian ministry gained an insight into a period of Paul's life about which little has been written. Here we meet a younger, more vigorous Paul, fired with enthusiasm in his new faith, less cautious in his theological statements than he later became, little conscious of the weaknesses of human nature. Boldly speaking with tongues, he demonstrated the power of the risen Christ and preached that his Lord would soon put an end to human history and establish God's Kingdom. It is clear that

in many of the areas we have discussed Paul came to revise his presentation, and even his understanding, of the gospel which he preached.
These revisions were the direct result of the succession of problems
which confronted him in his ministry. He said of himself that he bore
on his body "the marks of Jesus" (Gal. 6.17). It can also be said that his
later thought bore the marks of his past campaigns in the service of
Christ. To understand Paul in this fashion makes the work of presenting
his formal theology immensely more difficult. But the gain outweighs
the loss. We understand and admire Paul more as we see more clearly
how he grew.

Yet however grateful we are to Paul for his mature thought, it is
somehow sad that "the first fine careless rapture of the Christian
Church", as C. S. C. Williams called it,[1] had to change and give way
to theological and institutional readjustment and redefinition. Sad, too,
that Paul and his early converts never saw the Lord descend from
heaven, never heard the trumpet's call in the manner of their first
dreams.

[1] "Corr.," §834e.

CHAPTER 9

Retrospect and Prospect

PAUL'S CORINTHIAN MINISTRY

By the necessities of the argument we have had to work backwards through Paul's relationship with the Corinthian Church. We need to remember, however, that to understand this interaction more accurately we must view it chronologically as it originally developed. Much of the discussion of the preceding chapters has been involved and detailed. In order to point up the pattern which has gradually emerged we present at this point Table 7, which proceeds in vertical columns from Stage I at the left through Stage IV at the right. The items of the dialogue between Paul and the Corinthians which concern a single point are to be found opposite one another horizontally. Thus Paul's original advice to the Corinthians, "It is best for a man not to touch a woman," is modified by his later command (in the light of the Decree forbidding "immorality") that Christians should marry. Opposite this pair of items will be found the Corinthians' objection to Paul's change of attitude, an objection based on his original slogan. Finally in the last column appears a reference to the section of 1 Corinthians which was Paul's answer to the Corinthians' objection. The Table thus speaks for itself, and may serve as a summary and conclusion to our investigation of Paul's early Corinthian ministry.

A few comments, however, may be added. Three results of our survey appear particularly important.

(i) In the first place, we can see more clearly the effect of the Apostolic Decree upon Paul. Our reconstructed sequence covers precisely the period during which the Decree was adopted and presented to the Corinthian Church. The Corinthian response was so negative, however, and their reaction so vigorous that in 1 Corinthians Paul in effect withdrew most of the practical regulations by which he had tried in his Previous Letter to implement the Decree. Thus the ethical effect of

U oc

TABLE 7

Paul's Dialogue with the Corinthian Church

Stage 1 PAUL'S FOUNDING MISSION	Stage 2 THE PREVIOUS LETTER
Sexual Morality Preaching: "It is best for a man not to touch a woman." Encouraged intramarital asceticism. Discouraged marriage for single persons. Founded institution of "spiritual" (i.e., celibate) marriage. Conduct: Remained unmarried on principle.	1. APOSTOLIC DECREE *Avoid Immorality* (πορνεία) Christians should be married because of the danger of immorality.
Concerning the World Preaching: "All things are lawful."	Avoid all association with immoral men, i.e., unbelievers.
Preaching: Christians have "knowledge". "An idol is nothing." "There is no God but one." "All things are lawful." Conduct: Ate meat from the public market.	*Avoid Idolatry* Do not eat idol meat (εἰδωλόθυτα). (Avoid Blood?)

TABLE 7—*Continued*

Stage 3	Stage 4
THE CORINTHIAN REPLY	I CORINTHIANS

Stage 3	Stage 4
Concerning Marriage But it is best for a man *not* to touch a woman.	*1 Cor. 7* 7.1–7. Yes, but because of the danger of immorality, asceticism should not be attempted except perhaps for short periods.
Do you mean that married couples should forego asceticism?	
Do you mean that the unmarried should search for spouses?	7.8, 9. It is best for them to remain single, unless they lack self-control.
Do you mean that our spiritual couples should abandon their vows?	7.25–38. It is well that they remain as they are, although marriage is no sin.
But you yourself are unmarried.	7.7, 8. I wish that all were as I myself am, but each has his gift.
Do you mean that Christians married to unbelievers should obtain divorces?	7.10–16. Christians should not talk of divorce. Only if an unbeliever desires it is a separation permissible.
But it is neither possible nor necessary to avoid all contact with the world.	5.9–13a. I did not mean avoid contact with all immoral men; shun immoral Christians.
But all things are lawful for us.	6.12. Yes, but not all things are helpful.
Concerning Idol Meat But we have knowledge.	*1 Cor. 8.1—11.1* 8.1–13. Yes, but knowledge puffs up.
But an idol is nothing.	Yes, but there are so-called gods.
But there is no God but one.	Yes, but not all have this knowledge.
But all things are lawful.	10.23. Yes, but not all things build up.
But you yourself ate idol meat when you were with us.	9.1–27. "Am I not free? Am I not an apostle?"
Do you mean that we may not even buy meat in the market or eat with our friends?	10.25. Eat whatever is sold in the market, or served at banquets.

TABLE 7—*Continued*

Stage 1 PAUL'S FOUNDING MISSION	Stage 2 THE PREVIOUS LETTER
Concerning Worship Conduct: Allowed women to go unveiled during worship.	Do not let your worship be contaminated by the influence of pagan worship. (*a*) Women should wear veils.
	(*b*) Do not quench the Spirit, but test everything. Do not abandon yourselves to pagan enthusiasm.
Spoke with tongues more than all the others.	
Concerning Eschatology The End is at hand. We shall enter the Kingdom soon. The Body and Blood of the Lord will preserve us until the Day.	2. RESURRECTION OF BELIEVERS Do not mourn for those who have died. At the Parousia they shall be resurrected as Christ was resurrected. We shall enter the Kingdom together.
	3. COLLECTION I am making a collection for the poor of the saints in Jerusalem. Your generosity will be pleasing to God.

TABLE 7—*Continued*

Stage 3	Stage 4
THE CORINTHIAN REPLY	I CORINTHIANS

Concerning Worship But we have been following the traditions you gave us. But our women never have been required to wear veils in the household of the church.	*1 Cor. 11.2–16* 11.2. I am glad you maintain the traditions I gave you, 11.3. but it is unnatural and dangerous for women to be unveiled during worship.
Concerning Spiritual Men But how is it possible to test for the Spirit or to distinguish between spiritual men?	*1 Cor. 12—14* 12.1–3. No one speaking by the Spirit says "Jesus be cursed!" But there are many better gifts of the Spirit than glossolalia. 13. Seek the higher gifts, especially love.
You yourself spoke freely in the Spirit without making such distinctions.	14.18. I am glad that I speak in tongues, but I would rather prophesy.
Concerning Bodily Resurrection We do not believe in bodily, fleshly resurrection. The idea is gross and unspiritual.	*1 Cor. 15* 15.1–28. But you do believe in the Resurrection of Christ. 15.35–57. Resurrection will be in a spiritual, not a fleshly body.
Concerning the Collection We shall be glad to join in your undertaking, although, of course, our resources are limited. Are you to receive this money in person? Perhaps others should share this responsibility.	*1 Cor. 16.1–9* 16.1, 2. Save something every week. 16.3–9. I will send your accredited representatives with it to Jerusalem. I may not go myself.
Concerning Apollos Will it be possible for Apollos to return to us?	*1 Cor. 16.12* I urged Apollos to go, but he did not wish to at this time.

the Decree, although real, was short lived. This observation, together with the reasons discussed in Chapter 7 for Paul's silence as to the nature of his agreement with the Jerusalem Church, go a long way toward explaining the lack of any direct reference to, or even advocacy of, the provisions of the Decree in Paul's extant letters.

(ii) Particularly important are the hints which our study has produced concerning the earliest stage of Paul's Gentile mission. Apparently at the very first Paul ignored the requirements of the Law for his converts, and considered that their salvation depended not on the manner of their living but on their new relationship to God through Christ. He seems to have attached great importance to Baptism and the Lord's Supper as the sacramental guarantees of this relationship. But in the apocalyptic enthusiasm of his first visit he gave the Corinthians little ethical guidance. To this early presentation of Christianity the Decree and the pressure of the Jewish Christian Church in general stood as a counter-statement and a challenge. Clearly his Corinthian congregation did stand in need of ethical direction. The Previous Letter, including, as seems probable, the provisions of the Decree, represented the high-water mark of Paul's attempt to apply Jewish legal answers to his converts' ethical needs. After the Corinthian reaction Paul sought more and more to find independent theological bases for ethical action. The principle of the "weaker brother" was a first attempt in this direction. Other more mature attempts are found in Paul's later letters. In other words, between Stages 1 and 2 occurred perhaps the most radical shift of emphasis in Paul's Christian ministry, and, in a sense, the rest of Paul's career was a return at a far more mature level to the positions he held in his first preaching. Thus Paul's earliest Corinthian mission is important evidence of the type of Christianity Paul presented while still free of the influence of the Jerusalem Church. More and more in his later ministry he attempted to return from Stage 2 and all that it represented to Stage 1. His relations with Jewish Christianity convinced him that he had been right at the very beginning.

(iii) It appears that the *whole* of 1 Corinthians was directly or indirectly the result of Paul's disagreements with the Corinthians. The Corinthian Reply was, of course, the immediate occasion for much of 1 Corinthians as we have seen (and in a summary fashion as Table 7 shows). The remainder of 1 Corinthians resulted from oral information which Paul had received. Now we can see that the news Paul received was not a random group of observations, but that each item about which Paul was informed related directly to the Previous Letter. He had told them to avoid immoral men. 1 Cor. 5.1–8, 13b concerns their behaviour in this area. He had warned them to avoid unbelievers. 1 Cor. 6.1–11 concerns this aspect of their conduct. 1 Cor. 1—4 and 11.17–34 concern the "parties" which we suggested were the result of disagreement over the effect of the Previous Letter on table fellowship between Jewish and Gentile Christians. In addition, 1 Cor. 1—4 rebukes the Corinthians' general stubbornness (or constancy, depending on one's point of view) which Paul characterized as pride and arrogance. Thus it appears that the Previous Letter was responsible for the whole spectrum of the early difficulties between Paul and the Corinthians, and that Paul had perhaps gone out of his way to inform himself of the Corinthians' conduct in just those areas covered by that letter. 1 Corinthians, therefore, is not a miscellaneous group of observations on the Corinthians' manner of life, together with a series of answers to an assorted collection of questions from Corinth; every section of this letter relates to the group of disputes which resulted from Paul's attempt to obtain the Corinthians' conformity to the Apostolic Decree.

OTHER TIMES AND OTHER PLACES

The scope of our investigation has necessarily been limited. We believe, however, that the method which has been applied toward the recovery of Paul's early Corinthian ministry may prove useful in further studies of Paul's life and thought. The most immediate opportunity for the type of analysis which we have used is the reconstruction of Paul's relationship with the Thessalonian Church. A number of scholars have suggested that 1 Thessalonians, like 1 Corinthians, was written in answer to a letter which Paul had received.[1] Moreover, it is the present writer's conviction that 2 Thessalonians stood in somewhat the same relationship to 1 Thessalonians as the Previous Letter did to 1 Corinthians. Thus it may well be that 1 Thessalonians was preceded by stages which may be identified and recovered in the same manner as in our present investigation of 1 Corinthians. We have already noted the similarity between the Previous Letter and 1 Thessalonians with respect to their eschatological statements. These Thessalonian Stages would therefore be of particular importance as providing additional light on the earliest period of Paul's preaching.

At the other end of our series of Stages, 2 Corinthians offers further

[1] See above, p. 64, n. 2.

evidence for the reconstruction of the later stages in Paul's relationship with the Corinthian Church. 2 Cor. 2.3, for example, refers back to an earlier letter in the same manner as does 1 Cor. 5.9. This letter invites reconstruction along the lines of our attempted recovery of the Previous Letter. Thus when 2 Corinthians and the Thessalonian letters are brought into relationship with 1 Corinthians, our sequence of four Stages may be elaborated at the beginning and extended at the end.

Moreover, others of Paul's letters are linked to Paul's Corinthian ministry. Both 1 and 2 Corinthians refer to the Collection which began, we suggested, in Stage 2 of our series. John Knox has shown the type of chronological reconstruction which may be made on the basis of references to the Collection in these letters and in Romans.[1] In addition, the agreement over the Decree which appears to have preceded the Previous Letter leads us directly into the whole problem of the letter to the Galatians and Paul's conflict with Judaizers (a further link with 2 Cor. 10—13). Thus, of Paul's letters only Philippians, Ephesians, Colossians, and Philemon appear to stand outside the web of interconnecting relationships which tie Paul's Corinthian ministry to other areas and other periods of his total Christian ministry. In the opinion of the present writer this lack of connection is in the case of Philippians more apparent than real. We may hope, therefore, that the reconstruction of Paul's early Corinthian ministry we have attempted will one day provide the basis for a more adequate background for the understanding of Paul's life and thought than the usually accepted views of Pauline chronology analysed in Chapter 1.

[1] See especially *Chapters*, pp. 47–88.

Appended
Notes to Chapter 1

Bibliography

Indexes

Appended Notes to Chapter 1

1. (The form of this and the succeeding appended notes is explained in the Preface, p. xi.)
When authorities assign 1 Thessalonians to Corinth, it is clearly on the evidence of Acts, since the letter itself does not mention Corinth and refers to Achaia and Macedonia together (1 Thess. 1.7–8) in a way which, if anything, implies that Paul had left Achaia as he had Macedonia. The following authorities place the writing of 1 Thessalonians in Corinth:

(a) *Authorities before 1900.* The "Euthalian" subscription to the letter as given in the Nestle text (on Euthalius [fl. A.D. 458] see Sir Frederick Kenyon, *Our Bible and the Ancient Manuscripts*, rev. A. W. Adams [London: Eyre and Spottiswoode, 1958], pp. 201, 214); J. D. MICHAELIS, *Intro. N. T.*, IV, 24; W. PALEY, *Horae Paulinae*, Ch. 9, sec. 4; H. BÖTTGER, *Beiträge*, Pt. 3, p. 22; H. EWALD, *Sendschreiben*, p. 33; T. LEWIN, *Fasti Sacri*, pp. 297–8; H. C. G. MOULE, *Rom.* ("Camb."), p. 15; J. R. LUMBY, *Acts* ("Camb."), p. 236; G. LÜNEMANN, *Thess.* ("Meyer"), pp. 8–9; B. WEISS, *Intro. N.T.*, I, 218; W. BORNEMANN, *Thess.* ("Meyer"), pp. 17–18; M. DODS, *Intro. N.T.*, p. 161; P. W. SCHMIEDEL, "Thess.", *HCNT*, II, 1, p. 3; G. G. FINDLAY, *Thess.* ("Camb."), p. 27; J. B. LIGHTFOOT, *Biblical Essays*, p. 222; C. FOUARD, *St. Paul*, p. 169; S. DAVIDSON, *Intro. N.T.*, I, 10; W. J. CONYBEARE and J. S. HOWSON, *St. Paul*, I, 383–409; A. SABATIER, *Paul*, p. 21; W. M. RAMSAY, *St. Paul the Traveller*, p. 260; F. W. FARRAR, *St. Paul*, pp. 325–51; E. A. PLUMPTRE, "Acts," p. xv; L. ABBOTT, *Paul*, p. 83.

(b) *Authorities to 1910.* R. J. KNOWLING, "Acts," *ExposGk*, II, 386; J. V. BARTLET, *Acts* ("Cent."), p. 307; W. F. ADENEY, *Thess.*, ("Cent.") pp. 21–5; E. HATCH, "Paul," *EnBib*, III, 3616; A. C. MCGIFFERT, "Thess.," *EnBib*, IV, 5037; A. JÜLICHER, *Intro. N.T.*, p. 56; B. W. BACON, *Story*, p. 170; HERMANN VON SODEN, *Early Christian Literature*, p. 31; R. B. RACKHAM, *Acts* ("West."), p. 325; G. WOHLENBERG, *Thess.* ("Zahn"), p. 8; L. DUCHESNE, *History*, I, 22; E. VON DOBSCHÜTZ, *Thess.* ("Meyer"), p. 17.

(c) *Authorities to 1920.* J. E. FRAME, *Thess.* ("ICC"), p. 9; A. C. HEADLAM, *St. Paul and Christianity*, p. 3; R. D. SHAW, *Pauline Epistles*, pp. xi, 24–5, 35; K. LAKE, *Earlier Epistles*, pp. 75, 101; J. WEISS, *Primitive Christianity*, pp. 293–4; R. ST. J. PARRY, *1 Cor.* ("Camb."), p. lxxv; W. LUEKEN, "1 Thess.," *Schrift*, II, 5; T. ZAHN, *Intro. N. T.*, I, 215; J. MOFFATT, *Intro. N.T.*, p. 73; B. W. ROBINSON, *Paul*, p. 140; D. PLOOIJ, *Chronologie*, pp. 155–6; D. SMITH, *St. Paul*, pp. 149–88; A. H. MCNEILE, *St. Paul*, pp. 123, 129; H. T. ANDREWS, "Thess.," *Peake's Commentary*, p. 876; C. W. EMMET, "Apostolic Age," *Peake's Commentary*, p. 771.

(d) *Authorities to 1930.* A. S. PEAKE, *Intro. N.T.*, p. 11; F. C. GRANT, *Early Days*, p. 159; A. W. F. BLUNT, *Acts* ("Clar."), p. 219; H. T. FOWLER *Intro. N.T.*, p. 127; M. GOGUEL, *Intro. N.T.*, IV. 1, pp. 308–12; W. L. KNOX, *Jerusalem*, p. in 42; O. HOLTZMANN, *Das N.T.*, p. 1059; E. JACQUIER, *Acts* ("EB"), p. 545; A. DEISSMANN, *Paul*, p. 262, n. 7; M. JONES, "Thess.," *New Commentary*, p. 567; C. C. MCCOWN, "Thess.," *Abingdon Commentary*, p. 1236.

(e) *Authorities to 1940.* C. H. DODD, "Chronology," p. 195; E. J. BICKNELL, *Thess.* ("West."), p. xvi; E. F. SCOTT, *Intro. N.T.*, p. 114; K. LAKE and H. J. CADBURY, "Acts," *BC*, IV, 224; A. STEINMANN, "Thess.," *HSNT*, V, 19; P. BACHMANN, *1 Cor.* ("Zahn"), p. 480; C. A. A. SCOTT, *St. Paul*, p. 44; B. H. STREETER, "Rise of Christianity," *Cambridge Ancient History*, XI, 258; A. LOISY, *Origins*, p. 240; F. J. BADCOCK, *Pauline Epistles*, pp. ix, 44, 52; M. DIBELIUS, *Thess.* ("HNT"), pp. 32–3; M. S. ENSLIN, *Beginnings*, pp. 234, 240.

(f) *Authorities to 1950.* C. T. CRAIG, *Beginning*, p. 236; A. D. NOCK, *St. Paul*, pp. 129, 147; A. E. BARNETT, *The N.T.*, p. 36; E. J. GOODSPEED, *Paul*, pp. 92–9, 222; J. DE ZWAAN, *Intro.*

N.T., II, xi; W. G. ROBINSON, *Intro. N.T.*, p. 107; R. KNOPF, H. LIETZMANN, and H. WEINEL, *Intro. N.T.*, p. 80; P. FEINE and J. BEHM, *Intro. N.T.*, p. 130; R. HEARD, *Intro. N.T.*, pp. 181, 185; H. G. G. HERKLOTS, *Fresh Approach*, p. 106; W. NEIL, *Thess.* ("Moffatt"), p. xiv.

(g) *Authorities to 1963.* W. H. P. HATCH, "Life of Paul," *Interp.*, VII, 196; F. V. FILSON, *Opening the N.T.*, p. 97; T. HENSHAW, *N.T. Literature*, p. 223; W. K. L. CLARKE, *Concise Bible Commentary*, p. 173; A. H. MCNEILE, *Intro. N.T.*, rev. C. S. C. WILLIAMS, pp. 125–8; T. W. MANSON, *Studies*, p. 264; B. ORCHARD, "Thess.," *Catholic Commentary*, p. 1137; H. F. D. SPARKS, *Formation N.T.*, p. 32; A. WIKENHAUSER, *N.T. Intro.*, p. 364; R. A. KNOX, *N.T.*, *Commentary*, II, 295–8; M. C. TENNEY, *The N.T.*, p. 295; J. STIRLING, *Atlas*, p. 15; J. HUBY, "Books of the N.T.," p. 421; J. W. BAILEY, "Thess.," *Interp.*, XI, 248–51; F. F. BRUCE, *Book of Acts*, p. 370, n. 19; K. GRAYSTON, "Thess.," *20th Cent. Commentary*, p. 494; W. HENDRIKSEN, *Thess.*, pp. 15–16; E. W. HIPPISLEY, "Chronological Scheme," rev. G. H. DAVIES and A. RICHARDSON, *20th Cent. Commentary*, p. 538; A. SCHLATTER, *Church in the N.T. Period*, p. 150; A. OEPKE, *Thess.* ("NTD"), p. 446; B. RIGAUX, *Thess.* ("EB"), pp. 29–32; D. T. ROWLINGSON, *Intro. N.T. Study*, p. 223; E. KRAELING, *Atlas*, p. 446; P. CARRINGTON, *Early Christian Church*, I, 122–5; A. M. HUNTER, *Intro. N.T.*, p. 86; R. H. FULLER, *Acts of God*, p. 287; H. C. KEE and F. W. YOUNG, *Understanding N.T.*, pp. 474–5; R. S. KINSEY, *With Paul in Greece*, p. 71; C. MASSON, *Thess.* ("CNT"), p. 6; L. MORRIS, *Thess* ("Tynd."), p. 14; L. D. TWILLEY, *Origin and Transmission N.T.*, p. 14; J. T. HUDSON, *Pauline Epistles*, p. 36; G. RICCIOTTI, *Acts*, p. 281; J. CAMBIER, "S. Paul," p. 383; W. VON LOEWENICH, *Paul*, p. 96; F. R. CROWNFIELD, *Historical Approach*, pp. 264–5; J. L. PRICE, *Interpreting the N.T.*, p. 360; G. BORNKAMM, "Paulus," *RGG³*, V, 166; F. W. BEARE, *St Paul*, pp. 25, 30; D. J. SELBY, *Understanding St. Paul*, p. 250; W. D. DAVIES, "Apostolic Age," *Peake's Commentary²*, §765c; J. KNOX, "1 Thess.," *DB²*, p. 995b; and R. M. GRANT, *Historical Introduction*, p. 172. In defence of the genuineness, integrity, and usual dating on the basis of Acts: W. G. KÜMMEL, "Das Problem des ersten Thessalonicherbriefes," in *Neotestamentica et Patristica*, pp. 213–27, with his usual bibliographic thoroughness.

Many scholars are absent from the above list either because they have not investigated, or because they have not written on, the subject. Opinions contrary to the general consensus are exceedingly rare, namely: WILHELM HADORN, *Die Abfassung der Thessalonicherbriefe in der Zeit der dritten Missionsreise des Paulus* ("Beiträge zur Förderung christlicher Theologie," XXIV, 3/4; Gütersloh: C. Bertelsmann Verlag, 1919); and WILHELM MICHAELIS, *Die Gefangenschaft des Paulus in Ephesus und das Itinerar des Timotheus: Untersuchungen zur Chronologie des Paulus und der Paulusbriefe* ("Neutestamentliche Forschungen," hrsg. von Otto Schmitz, 1. Reihe: Paulusstudien. 3. Hft.; Gütersloh: C. Bertelsmann Verlag, 1925), pp. 27ff, 65ff; BUCK, "Collection," pp. 24–5; H. L. RAMSEY, *Place of Galatians*, pp. 186–9; and WALTER SCHMITHALS, "Zur Abfassung und ältesten Sammlung der paulinischen Hauptbriefe," *ZNW*, LI (1960), 225–36.

2. (a) *Authorities before 1890.* Although the subscription in Koine MSS. assigns the letter to Philippi (apparently on the basis of 1 Cor. 16.5), the uncial P and some minuscules read απο Εψεσου. In 1546 CALVIN decisively turned the tide in favour of a dating based on Acts 19 with his comment on 1 Cor. 16.5: "The generally accepted view is that this letter was sent from Philippi. . . . But to me it seems more likely that the letter was written from Ephesus, for a little afterwards he says that 'he will stay there until Pentecost ' " (*The First Epistle of Paul the Apostle to the Corinthians*, trans J. W. Fraser ["Calvin's Commentaries," ed. D. W. Torrance and T. F. Torrance; Edinburgh: Oliver and Boyd, 1960], p. 351). So also with reliance upon Acts 19: J. D. MICHAELIS, *Intro. N.T.*, IV, 42; W. PALEY, *Horae Paulinae*, Ch. 9, sec. 2; H. EWALD, *Sendschreiben*, p. 101; T. LEWIN, *Fasti Sacri*, p. 298; J. J. LIAS, *1 Cor.* ("Camb."), pp. 15–16; H. C. G. MOULE, *Rom.* ("Camb."), p. 16; C. F. G. HEINRICI *1 Cor.* (1880), pp. 57–69; H. A. W. MEYER, *Corr.* ("Meyer"), I, 8; J. R. LUMBY, *Acts* ("Camb."), pp. 256–7; B. WEISS, *Intro. N.T.*, I, 269, n. 2.

(b) *Authorities to 1900.* M. DODS, *Intro. N.T.*, p. 104; J. B. LIGHTFOOT, *Biblical Essays*, p. 222; F. GODET, *1 Cor.*, I, 11–16; W. J. CONYBEARE and J. S. HOWSON, *St. Paul*, II, 30–68; S. DAVIDSON, *Intro. N.T.*, I, 24; C. FOUARD, *St. Paul*, p. 262; W. M. RAMSAY, *St. Paul the Traveller*, p. 275; A. SABATIER, *Paul*, p. 21; F. W. FARRAR, *St. Paul*, pp. 376–84; T. C. EDWARDS, *1 Cor.*, p. xviii; E. A. PLUMPTRE, "Acts," p. xv; W. SANDAY, "Corr.," *EnBib*, I, 899.

(c) *Authorities to 1910.* R. J. KNOWLING, "Acts," *ExposGk*, II, 403; J. H. KENNEDY, *2 & 3*

Cor., p. 31; J. V. BARTLET, *Acts*, p. 318; E. HATCH, "Paul," *EnBib*, III, 3616; A. JÜLICHER, *Intro. N.T.*, p. 80; B. W. BACON, *Story*, pp. 266–7; HERMANN VON SODEN, *Early Christian Literature*, p. 37; R. B. RACKHAM, *Acts* ("West."), p. 347.

(d) *Authorities to 1920.* H. L. GOUDGE, *1 Cor.* ("West."), p. 168; G. G. FINDLAY, "1 Cor.," *ExposGk*, II, 735; A. MENZIES, *2 Cor.*, p. xi; R. D. SHAW, *Pauline Epistles*, pp. xi, 134, 136; K. LAKE, *Earlier Epistles*, pp. 139–43; A. ROBERTSON and A. PLUMMER, *1 Cor.* ("ICC"), p. xxxi; R. ST. J. PARRY, *1 Cor.* ("Camb."), p. lxxv; T. ZAHN, *Intro. N.T.*, I, 259; J. MOFFATT, *Intro. N.T.*, p. 109; B. W. ROBINSON, *Paul*, p. 159; D. SMITH, *St. Paul*, pp. 234–325; A. H. MCNEILE, *St. Paul*, p. 135; C. W. EMMET, "Apostolic Age," *Peake's Commentary*, p. 771.

(e) *Authorities to 1930.* A. S. PEAKE, *Intro. N.T.*, p. 31; F. C. GRANT, *Early Days*, p. 173; A. W. F. BLUNT, *Acts* ("Clar."), p. 224; H. L. WINDISCH, *2 Cor.* ("Meyer"), p. 28; W. L. KNOX, *Jerusalem*, p. 316; H. T. FOWLER, *Intro. N.T.*, p. 158; E. JACQUIER, *Acts* ("EB"), p. 568; O. HOLTZMANN, *Das N.T.*, p. 1059; E. J. BICKNELL, "Acts," *New Commentary*, p. 367; J. K. MOZLEY, "1 Cor.," *New Commentary*, p. 485; W. F. HOWARD, "Corr.," *Abingdon Commentary*, p. 1169; E. EVANS, *Corr.* ("Clar."), pp. 21, 26.

(f) *Authorities to 1940.* C. H. DODD, "Chronology," p. 195; F. J. FOAKES-JACKSON, *Acts* ("Moffatt"), pp. 181, 185; J. SICKENBERGER, *Corr.* ("HSNT"), pp. 2–4; E. F. SCOTT, *Intro. N.T.*, p. 114; R. H. STRACHAN, *2 Cor.* ("Moffatt"), p. xxxix; E.-B. ALLO, *1 Cor.* ("EB"), p. lxxxvi; B. H. STREETER, "The Rise of Christianity," *Cambridge Ancient History*, XI, 258; C. A. A. SCOTT, *St. Paul*, pp. 47–9; P. BACHMANN, *1 Cor.* ("Zahn"), pp. 479–81; A. LOISY, *Origins*, p. 241; F. J. BADCOCK, *Pauline Epistles*, pp. x, 61; M. S. ENSLIN, *Beginnings*, pp. 247–8; T. W. MANSON, "The N.T.," *Companion*, pp. 102–3.

(g) *Authorities to 1950.* C. T. CRAIG, *Beginning*, p. 236; A. D. NOCK, *St. Paul*, pp. 132–3; A. E. BARNETT, *The N.T.*, p. 50; E. J. GOODSPEED, *Paul*, pp. 115–22; J. DE ZWAAN, *Intro. N.T.*, II, xi; H. LIETZMANN, *Corr.*, rev. W. G. KÜMMEL ("HNT"), p. 89; R. KNOPF, H. LIETZMANN and H. WEINEL, *Intro. N.T.*, p. 83; P. FEINE and J. BEHM, *Intro. N.T.*, p. 155; R. HEARD, *Intro. N.T.*, pp. 181, 189; A. SCHLATTER, *Corr.*, p. 1.

(h) *Authorities to 1963.* W. H. P. HATCH, "Life of Paul," *Interp.*, VII, 197; M. DIBELIUS and W. G. KÜMMEL, *Paul*, p. 81; T. HENSHAW, *N.T. Literature*, p. 234; F. V. FILSON, *Opening the N.T.*, p. 114; A. H. MCNEILE, *Intro. N.T.*, rev. C. S. C. WILLIAMS, pp. 132–3; W. K. L. CLARKE, *Concise Bible Commentary*, p. 174; H. F. D. SPARKS, *Formation N.T.*, p. 36; M. C. TENNEY, *The N.T.*, pp. 305–9; J. STIRLING, *Atlas*, p. 17; F. W. GROSHEIDE, *1 Cor.* ("Internat."), p. 13; H.-D. WENDLAND, *Corr.* ("NTD"), p. 2; R. A. KNOX, *N.T. Commentary*, II, 46; J. HUBY, "Books of the N.T.," p. 427; W. MICHAELIS, *Intro. N.T.*, p. 175; F. F. BRUCE *Books of Acts*, p. 394; K. GRAYSTON, "Corr.," *20th Cent. Commentary*, p. 478; E. W. HIPPISLEY, "Chronological Scheme," rev. G. H. DAVIES and A. RICHARDSON, *20th Cent. Commentary*, p. 538; E. G. KRAELING, *Bible Atlas*, p. 449; D. T. ROWLINGSON, *Intro. N.T. Study*, p. 114; A. M. HUNTER, *Intro. N.T.*, p. 86; R. H. FULLER, *Acts of God*, p. 287; R. S. KINSEY, *With Paul in Greece*, p. 148; L. D. TWILLEY, *Origin and Transmission N.T.*, pp. 16–17; H. C. KEE and F. W. YOUNG, *Understanding N.T.*, pp. 474–5; P. CARRINGTON, *Early Christian Church*, I, 132–9; J. H. ROPES, "Corr.," *Encyclopedia Britannica*, VI, 443; L. MORRIS, *1 Cor.* ("Tynd."), p. 28; A. WIKENHAUSER, *N.T. Intro.*, pp. 389–90; G. RICCIOTTI, *Acts*, p. 297; J. T. HUDSON, *Pauline Epistles*, p. 10; J. CAMBIER, "S. Paul," p. 383; W. VON LOEWENICH, *Paul*, p. 91; J. L. PRICE, *Interpreting the N.T.*, p. 369; G. BORNKAMM, "Paulus," *RGG³*, V, 166, 173; F. W. BEARE, *St Paul*, pp. 66, 84; D. J. SELBY, *Understanding St. Paul*, p. 218; W. D. DAVIES, "Apostolic Age," *Peake's Commentary²*, §766a; G. STÄHLIN, *Acts* ("NTD"), pp. 258–9; R. M. GRANT, *Historical Introduction*, p. 172; and P. FEINE/J. BEHM/W. G. KÜMMEL, *Intro. N.T.*, p. 206.

The following scholars do not regard 1 Corinthians as a single letter. They agree, however, in using Acts 19 to date at least the first part of the Corinthians' correspondence: J. WEISS, *Primitive Christianity*, p. 323; M. GOGUEL, *Intro. N.T.*, IV. 2, pp. 5–9; W. SCHMITHALS, *Gnosis*, pp. 22–34; and E. DINKLER, "Corr.," *RGG³*, IV, 18–19.

H. BÖTTGER, *Beiträge*, pp. 28–31, seems to be the only scholar who has not followed Calvin's lead in assigning 1 Corinthians to Ephesus (or its neighbourhood). He depends on Acts, however, to date the letter from South Achaia (cf. Acts 19.21) between Acts 19.22 and 19.23.

3. (a) *Authorities before 1900.* J. D. MICHAELIS, *Intro. N.T.*, IV, 89; W. PALEY, *Horae Paulinae*, Ch. 2, secs. 1–2; H. EWALD, *Sendschreiben*, p. 314; T. LEWIN, *Fasti Sacri*, p. 313; H. C. G. MOULE, *Rom.* ("Camb."), p. 17; B. WEISS, *Intro. N.T.*, I, 294; M. DODS, *Intro. N.T.*, p. 86; J. B. LIGHTFOOT, *Biblical Essays*, p. 222; S. DAVIDSON, *Intro. N.T.*, I, 117; W. J. CONYBEARE and J. S. HOWSON, *St. Paul*, II, 154–7; C. FOUARD, *St. Paul*, p. 330; W. M. RAMSAY, *St. Paul the Traveller*, p. 288; F. W. FARRAR, *St. Paul*, p. 425; A. SABATIER, *Paul*, pp. 187–8; E. A. PLUMPTRE, "Acts," p. xv; L. ABBOTT, *Paul*, p. 213; C. GORE, *Rom.*, I, 1.

(b) *Authorities to 1910.* J. DENNEY, "Rom.," *ExposGk*, II, 568; A. E. GARVIE, *Rom.* ("Cent."), p. 17; J. V. BARTLET, *Acts* ("Cent."), p. 323; W. SANDAY and A. C. HEADLAM, *Rom.* ("ICC"), pp. xxxvi–xxxvii; E. HATCH, "Paul," *EnBib*, III, 3617; A. JÜLICHER, *Intro. N.T.*, p. 106; B. W. BACON, *Story*, pp. 291–2; HERMANN VON SODEN, *Early Christian Literature*, p. 97; R. B. RACKHAM, *Acts* ("West."), p. 373; L. DUCHESNE, *History*, I, 23.

(c) *Authorities to 1920.* R. D. SHAW, *Pauline Epistles*, pp. xi, 204; K. LAKE, *Earlier Epistles*, p. 369; J. WEISS, *Primitive Christianity*, pp. 357–63; R. ST. J. PARRY, *1 Cor.* ("Camb."), p. lxxv; T. ZAHN, *Intro. N.T.*, I, 434–8; B. W. ROBINSON, *Paul*, pp. 177–8; J. MOFFATT, *Intro. N.T.*, p. 144; D. SMITH, *St. Paul*, pp. 371–3, 656; G. G. FINDLAY, "Rom.," *Peake's Commentary*, p. 817; A. H. MCNEILE, *St. Paul*, pp. 181–9; C. W. EMMET, "Apostolic Age," *Peake's Commentary*, p. 771.

(d) *Authorities to 1930.* A. S. PEAKE, *Intro. N.T.*, p. 39; F. C. GRANT, *Early Days*, p. 183; A. W. F. BLUNT, *Acts* ("Clar."), p. 229; H. T. FOWLER, *Intro. N. T.*, p. 191; M. GOGUEL, *Intro. N.T.*, IV. 2, pp. 202–5; W. L. KNOX, *Jerusalem*, p. 347; E. JACQUIER, *Acts* ("EB"), p. 593; O. HOLTZMANN, *Das N.T.*, p. 1059; E. J. BICKNELL, "Acts," *New Commentary*, p. 368; N. P. WILLIAMS, "Rom.," *New Commentary*, p. 442; C. A. A. SCOTT, "Rom.," *Abingdon Commentary*, p. 1135; M.-J. LAGRANGE, *Rom.* ("EB"), p. xvii.

(e) *Authorities to 1940.* F. J. FOAKES-JACKSON, *Acts* ("Moffatt"), pp. 181, 184; J. SICKEN-BERGER, *Rom.* ("HSNT"), p. 170; E. F. SCOTT, *Intro. N.T.*, p. 114; C. H. DODD, *Rom.* ("Moffatt"), p. xxv; H. LIETZMANN, *Beginnings*, p. 111; P. FEINE and J. BEHM, *Intro. N.T.*, p. 171; B. H. STREETER, "The Rise of Christianity," *Cambridge Ancient History*, XI, 258; A. LOISY, *Origins*, p. 247; F. J. BADCOCK, *Pauline Epistles*, pp. x, 106; K. E. KIRK, *Rom.* ("Clar."), p. 11; M. S. ENSLIN, *Beginnings*, p. 267.

(f) *Authorities to 1950.* C. T. CRAIG, *Beginning*, p. 253; A. D. NOCK, *St. Paul*, p. 207; A. E. BARNETT, *The N.T.*, p. 61; E. J. GOODSPEED, *Paul*, pp. 149–54; T. W. MANSON, *Studies*, p. 226; J. DE ZWAAN, *Intro. N.T.*, II, 10; R. KNOPF, H. LIETZMANN, and H. WEINEL, *Intro. N.T.*, p. 86; G. O. GRIFFITH, *Rom.*, pp. 173–4; W. G. ROBINSON, *Intro. N.T.*, p. 108; R. HEARD, *Intro. N.T.*, pp. 182, 196.

(g) *Authorities to 1963.* W. H. P. HATCH, "Life of Paul," *Interp.*, VII, 197; M. DIBELIUS and W. G. KÜMMEL, *Paul*, p. 82; T. HENSHAW, *N.T. Literature*, p. 259; F. V. FILSON, *Opening the N.T.*, p. 132; W. K. L. CLARKE, *Concise Bible Commentary*, pp. 174, 821; R. T. STAMM, "Gal." *Interp.*, X, 439; A. H. MCNEILE, *Intro. N.T.*, rev. C. S. C. WILLIAMS, p. 154; H. F. D. SPARKS, *Formation N.T.*, pp. 43–4; M. C. TENNEY, *The N.T.*, p. 315; J. STIRLING, *Atlas*, p. 19; P. ALTHAUS, *Rom.* ("NTD"), p. 3; G. H. C. MACGREGOR, "Acts," *Interp.*, IX, 264; R. A. KNOX, *N.T. Commentary*, II, 68; J. HUBY, "Books of the N.T.," pp. 434–5; K. GRAYSTON, "Rom.," *20th Century Commentary*, pp. 475–6; F. F. BRUCE, *Book of Acts*, p. 405; A. SCHLATTER, *Church in N.T. Period*, p. 206; E. W. HIPPISLEY, "Chronological Scheme," rev. G. H. DAVIES and A. RICHARDSON, *20 Cent. Commentary*, p. 538; H. W. BEYER, *Acts* ("NTD"), p. 121; E. G. KRAELING, *Bible Atlas*, p. 449; D. T. ROWLINGSON, *Intro. N.T. Study*, p. 114; R. H. FULLER, *Acts of God*, p. 287; H. C. KEE and H. W. YOUNG, *Understanding N.T.*, pp. 269, 474–5; P. CARRINGTON, *Early Christian Church*, I, 144–5; F. J. LEENHARDT, *Rom.* ("CNT"), p. 9; O. MICHEL, *Rom.* ("Meyer"), p. 1; A. M. HUNTER, *Intro. N.T.*, p. 87; R. S. KINSEY, *With Paul in Greece*, p. 149; L. D. TWILLEY, *Origin and Transmission N.T.*, p. 18; C. K. BARRETT, *Rom.* ("Black"), p. 3; A. WICKENHAUSER, *N. T. Intro.*, p. 405; J. T. HUDSON, *Pauline Epistles*, p. 7; G. RICCIOTTI, *Acts*, p. 312; E. M. BLAIKLOCK, *Acts* ("Tynd."), p. 163; J. CAMBIER, "S. Paul," p. 383; W. VON LOEWENICH, *Paul*, p. 93; J. L. PRICE, *Interpreting the N.T.*, p. 360; G. BORNKAMM, "Paulus," *RGG³*, V, 166, 173; F. W. BEARE, *St Paul*, p. 26; D. J. SELBY, *Understanding St. Paul*, p. 227; W. D. DAVIES, "Apostolic Age," *Peake's Commentary²*, §766b; G. W. H. LAMPE, "Acts," *Peake's Commentary²*, §797d; R. T. STAMM,

"Rom.," *DB²*, p. 859b; G. STÄHLIN, *Acts* ("NTD"), p. 263; O. MICHEL, *Rom.* ("Meyer"), p. 1; R. M. GRANT, *Historical Introduction*, p. 188; and P. FEINE/J. BEHM/W. G. KÜMMEL, *Intro. N.T.*, p. 222.

Counter-opinion is rare: WILHELM MICHAELIS, "Kenchreä (Zur Frage des Abfassungsortes des Rm)," *ZNW*, XXV (1926), 144–54, and his *Intro. N.T.*, p. 165 (in Philippi at Acts 20.6); THEOPHILUS MILLS TAYLOR, "The Place of Origin of Romans," *JBL*, LXVII (1948), 281–95 (same opinion as Michaelis); LINDSEY P. PHERIGO, "Paul and the Corinthian Church," *JBL*, LXVIII (1949), 347 (just before Acts 20.5); BUCK, "Collection," pp. 10, 28 (in Macedonia before completion of the collection); and G. FRIEDRICH, "Rom.," *RGG³*, V, 1138 (same opinion as Michaelis). All but Buck rely on the Acts chronology, however.

4. The theory is not traditional and is now rare. KIRSOPP and SILVA LAKE, *An Introduction to the New Testament* (London: Christophers, 1938), p. 138, however, report that it was once dominant. Scholars before 1900 who held this theory for some or all of these letters include: T. BEZA, H. BÖTTGER, E. HAUPT, A. HAUSRATH, S. HILGENFELD (Plm. only), O. HOLTZMANN, J. MACPHERSON, H. A. W. MEYER, H. C. G. PAULUS (Phil.), O. PFLEIDERER, E. REUSS, A. RILLIET (Phil.), A. SABATIER, D. SCHENKEL, SCHNECKENBURGER, SCHOTT, D. SCHULZ, F. SPITTA, THIERSCH, B. WEISS, J. WIGGERS, ZÖCKLER. More recently the following scholars have adopted this view: P. FEINE and J. BEHM, *Intro. N.T.*, pp. 177–92 (except Phil.); W. L. KNOX, *Jerusalem*, p. 362, n. 17 (for Col. and Plm. if genuine); M. GOGUEL, *Intro. N.T.*, IV. 2, pp. 310, 430; M. DIBELIUS and W. G. KÜMMEL, *Paul*, p. 138 (except Phil.); and E. LOHMEYER, *Phil.* ("Meyer"), p. 3, and *Col. and Plm.* ("Meyer"), p. 14; L. JOHNSON, "The Pauline Letters from Caesarea," *ET*, LXVIII (1956/57), 24–6; and P. FEINE/J. BEHM/W. G. KÜMMEL, *Intro. N.T.*, pp. 239, 250 (Col., Plm., and perhaps Phil.).

5. This is the opinion of tradition as early as the Marcionite prologues (mid-second century) which place Philippians, Philemon, and Ephesians ("Laodicians") at Rome. So also almost all scholars except the few mentioned in the preceding note and a second small group who assign these letters to a hypothetical Ephesian imprisonment. See the following note.

6. The Marcionite prologue to Colossians (only) assigns the letter to Ephesus. The reference attracted no notice, however, so that DEISSMANN can be credited with originating the theory in a lecture at Herborn in 1897. In his *Paul* (p. 17, n. 1) he gave a full bibliography of scholars who had adopted his position through 1925, including among others: M. ALBERTZ (who later reverted to the traditional opinion, however: *Botschaft*, II.2, p. 230), B. W. ROBINSON, K. and S. LAKE, B. W. BACON, M. JONES, P. FEINE (Phil. only), C. R. BOWEN, and T. W. L. DAVIES. To this list can now be added M. GOGUEL, *Intro. N.T.*, IV.1, p. 376, n. 1 (Phil. only); O. HOLTZMANN, *Das N.T.*, p. 736 (Eph.); J. H. MICHAEL, *Phil.* ("Moffatt"), pp. vii, xii–xxi; G. S. DUNCAN, *St. Paul's Ephesian Ministry*, p. 298; "Important Hypotheses Reconsidered: VI. Were Paul's Imprisonment Epistles Written from Ephesus?" *ET*, LXVII (1955/56), 163–6; "Paul's Ministry in Asia—the Last Phase," *NTS*, III (1956/57), 211–8; "Chronological Table to Illustrate Paul's Ministry in Asia," ibid., V (1958/59), 43–5; F. J. BADCOCK, *Pauline Epistles*, pp. 54–71; M. S. ENSLIN, *Beginnings*, pp. 279–80, 283–5; D. W. RIDDLE, *Paul, Man of Conflict*, pp. 113–5; J. HÉRING, *1 Cor.* ("CNT"), p. 181, n. 64 (for Col.); P. BONNARD, *Phil.* ("CNT"), p. 10; A. MASSON, *Col.* ("CNT"), pp. 85–6; D. T. ROWLINGSON, "Paul's Ephesian Imprisonment: An Evaluation of the Evidence," *ATR*, XXXII (1950), 1–7; *Intro. N.T. Study*, p. 115; F. C. SYNGE, *Phil. and Col.* ("Torch"), pp. 14–15 (Phil. only); M. DIBELIUS and W. G. KÜMMEL, *Paul*, p. 81 (Phil. only); F. F. BRUCE, *Acts of the Apostles*, p. 40 (Phil., probably); A. H. MCNEILE, *Intro. N.T.*, rev. C. S. C. WILLIAMS, pp. 180–5 (Phil. only); W. MICHAELIS, *Intro. N.T.*, pp. 199, 204–11, 215–18; P. N. HARRISON, "The Pastoral Epistles and Duncan's Ephesian Theory," *NTS*, II (1955/56), 250; J. T. HUDSON, *Pauline Epistles*, p. 5; P. BENOIT, *Phil., Plm., Col., and Eph.*, pp. 11–13 (Phil. only); A. R. C. LEANEY, *Tim., Tit., and Plm.* ("Torch"), p. 136 (for Col. and Plm.); B. RIGAUX, *Saint Paul et ses Lettres*, p. 148, n. 1 (Phil. only); and D. J. SELBY, *Understanding St. Paul*, pp. 219–21, 283 ("attractive").

7. Holders of the North Galatian hypothesis before 1916 include H. A. W. MEYER, F. SIEFFERT, R. A. LIPSIUS, E. SCHÜRER, A. HILGENFELD, H. J. HOLTZMANN, P. W. SCHMIEDEL (*EnBib*, II, cols. 1596–1618), TH. MOMMSEN, E. VON DOBSCHÜTZ, A. JÜLICHER, H. H. WENDT, and A. LOISY. Of particular importance are the discussions of J. B. LIGHTFOOT, *St. Paul's*

Epistle to the Galatians (9th ed.; London: Macmillan and Co., 1887), pp. 18–56; and *St. Paul's Epistles to the Colossians and to Philemon* (9th ed.; London: Macmillan and Co., 1890), p. 24, n. 2; and of ALPHONS STEINMANN, *Der Leserkreis des Galaterbriefs* ("Neutestamentliche Abhandlungen," bgt. August Bludau, 1. Bd., 3/4. hft.; Münster: Verlag der Aschendorffschen Verlagsbuchhandlung, 1908). Since 1916 the theory has been defended by W. BOUSSET, "Gal.," *Schrift.*, II, 31–2; R. KNOPF, "Acts," *Schrift.*, III, 76; J. MOFFATT, *Intro. N.T.*, p. 102 (reluctantly); M.-J. LAGRANGE, *Gal.* ("EB"), pp. xiii–xxvii; M. GOGUEL, *Intro. N.T.*, IV. 2, pp. 150–66; H. LIETZMANN, *Gal.* ("HNT"), p. 4; K. LAKE, "Paul's Route in Asia Minor," *BC*, V, 234–6 (Earlier he had held the South Galatian hypothesis as noted below.); M. S. ENSLIN, *Beginnings*, p. 226; C. T. CRAIG, *Beginning*, p. 227; A. D. NOCK, *St. Paul*, pp. 115, 119; M. DIBELIUS and W. G. KÜMMEL, *Paul*, p. 75; P. FEINE and J. BEHM, *Intro. N.T.*, p. 143; H. SCHLIER, *Gal.* ("Meyer"), pp. 5–6; P. BONNARD, *Gal.* ("CNT"), pp. 9–12; A. WICKENHAUSER, *Intro. N.T.*, pp. 374–6; G. RICCIOTTI, *Acts*, p. 289; L. CERFAUX, "Gal.," pp. 404–6; G. STÄHLIN, *Acts* ("NTD"), p. 214; F. C. GRANT, *N.T.*, pp. 140–2, (who comments in reversing the position he held in 1922, "It is not improbable that the 'North Galatian' hypothesis will eventually prevail."); R. M. GRANT, *Historical Introduction*, p. 185; and P. FEINE/J. BEHM/W. G. KÜMMEL, *Intro. N.T.*, pp. 191–3.

8. This phrase is important to those who hold the "South Galatian" hypothesis (see below) as well. Scholars who translate as above include J. B. LIGHTFOOT, *Gal.*, pp. 41, 174–5; C. VON WEIZSÄCKER, *Apostolic Age*, I, 252; W. M. RAMSAY, *St. Paul the Traveller*, p. 92; J. MOFFATT, *Intro. N.T.*, p. 84; E. DE W. BURTON, *Gal.* ("ICC"), pp. xiv, 239–41; T. ZAHN, *Gal.* ("Zahn"), p. 216; E. MEYER, *Ursprung*, III, 203; H. LIETZMANN, *Gal.* ("HNT"), p. 28; G. S. DUNCAN, *Gal.* ("Moffatt"), p. xxii; H. SCHLIER, *Gal.* ("Meyer"), p. 148; P. BONNARD, *Gal.* ("CNT"), p. 14; G. RICCIOTTI, *Acts*, p. 289; and STÄHLIN, *Acts* ("NTD"), p. 214.
The necessity of this interpretation in the Hellenistic period, however, is denied by K. LAKE, *Earlier Epistles*, pp. 265–6; MOULTON/MILLIGAN, p. 554; A. H. MCNEILE, *Intro. N.T.*, rev. C. S. C. WILLIAMS, p. 147; HOERBER, "Gal. 2.1–10," p. 488; and R. M. GRANT, *Historical Introduction*, p. 185.

9. In defence of his first statement, *Prolusio de Galatis, ad quos Paulus literas misit*, Schmidt wrote *Prolusionem suam de Galatis—ad objectionibus doctissimorum virorum vindicare conatur* in 1754. The theory was not well received and waited for its second statement until Danois Mynster, *Einleitung in den Brief an die Galater* in his *Kleine Theologische Schriften*, 1825. Then followed Miemeyer, 1827; Paulus, 1827, 1831; Ulrich, 1836; and H. Böttger, 1837. The theory received its most ardent and detailed defence from Sir William Mitchell Ramsay in a vast series of articles and books beginning with "St. Paul's first Journey in Asia Minor," *Expositor*, Ser. 4; VI (1892), 164. By 1920 C. H. Turner could say that the South Galatian hypothesis had "swept the opposing theory from the field" (Inaugural Lecture at Oxford quoted by Duncan, *Gal.*, p. xx). The theory has remained immensely popular, but time has proven Turner's optimism premature. A number of prominent scholars have remained unconvinced (see above on the North Galatian hypothesis). South Galatianists include among others: E. RENAN, *St. Paul*, p. 25; C. CLEMEN, "Die Adressaten des Galaterbriefes," *Zeitschrift für wissenschaftliche Theologie*, XXXVII (1894), 396–423; V. WEBER, *Die Adressaten des Galaterbriefes: Beweis der rein südgalatischen Theorie*; A. C. MCGIFFERT, *Apostolic Age*, pp. 177–82; J. V. BARTLET, *Apostolic Age*, pp. 71, 84–5; C. VON WEIZSÄCKER, *Apostolic Age*, I, 270–5; W. J. WOODHOUSE, "Galatia," *EnBib*, II, 1589–92; F. RENDALL, "Gal.," *ExposGk*, III, 127; HERMANN VON SODEN, *Early Christian Literature*, pp. 58–62; O. HOLTZMANN, "Die Jerusalemreisen des Paulus," *ZNW*, VI (1905), 102–4; B. W. BACON, *Intro. N.T.*, pp. 58–60; R. B. RACKHAM, *Acts* ("West."), pp. 334–6, 360; K. LAKE, *Earlier Epistles*, pp. 254–65, 309–16 ("The balance of evidence in favour of the South Galatian theory seems to be overwhelmingly strong" [p. 265.] He later changed to the North Galatian hypothesis as noted above!); J. WEISS, *Primitive Christianity*, pp. 297–304; E. DE W. BURTON, *Gal.* ("ICC"), pp. xxi–xliv; T. ZAHN, *Gal.* ("Zahn"), pp. 9–22; C. W. EMMET, "Tradition," *BC*, II, 282–6; F. C. GRANT, *Early Days*, pp. 138–9 (later he reversed his position as noted above); E. MEYER, *Ursprung*, III, 197–203; F. C. BURKITT, *Christian Beginnings*, pp. 116–18; A. W. F. BLUNT, *Gal.* ("Clar."), p .21; W. L. KNOX, *Jerusalem*, pp. 236–9; G. S. DUNCAN, *Gal.* ("Moffatt"), pp. xviii–xxi; F. J. BADCOCK, *Pauline Epistles*, p. ix; C. J. CADOUX, "Tentative Synthetic Chronology," p. 184; R. T. STAMM, "Gal.,"

Interp., X, 435–7; G. H. C. MACGREGOR, "Acts," *Interp.*, IX, 150–2; W. MICHAELIS, *Intro. N.T.*, pp. 183–7; R. A. KNOX, *N.T. Commentary*, II, 211; F. F. BRUCE, *Book of Acts* ("Internat."), p. 287, n. 5; C. S. C. WILLIAMS, *Acts* ("Black"), pp. 26–30, 175–6; P. CARRINGTON, *Early Christian Church*, I, 91; H. C. KEE and F. W. YOUNG, *Understanding N.T.*, p. 235; J. T. HUDSON, *Pauline Epistles*, p. 16; E. M. BLAIKLOCK, *Acts* ("Tynd."), p. 122; R. G. HOERBER, "Gal. 2.1–10," pp. 485–8; J. L. PRICE, *Interpreting the N.T.*, p. 391; F. W. BEARE, *St Paul*, p. 52; D. J. SELBY, *Understanding St. Paul*, pp. 192–6; W. D. DAVIES, "Apostolic Age," *Peake's Commentary*[2], §765b; and A. C. PURDY, "Gal.," *DB*[2], p. 312.

Bibliography

A. TEXTS AND TRANSLATIONS

Ägyptische Urkunden aus den Köninglichen Museen zu Berlin: Griechische Urkunden. 7 vols. Berlin: Weidmann, 1895–1926.

Chrysostom, Saint John. *Homilies on the Epistles of Paul to the Corinthians.* Translated by H. K. Cornish, J. Medley, and J. Ashworth. Revised by Talbot W. Chambers. ("A Select Library of the Nicene and Post-Nicene Fathers of the Christian Church," ed. Philip Schaff, 1st Ser., Vol. XII.) New York: The Christian Literature Company, 1889.

Clark, Albert Curtis. *The Acts of the Apostles: A Critical Edition with Introduction and Notes on Selected Passages.* Oxford: The Clarendon Press, 1933.

Goodspeed, Edgar Johnson. *The New Testament: An American Translation.* Chicago: The University of Chicago Press, 1923.

Grenfell, Bernard Pyne, and Hunt, Arthur Surridge (eds.). *The Oxyrhynchus Papyri.* London: Egypt Exploration Fund, 1898——.

Jerome, Saint. *The Principal Works of St. Jerome.* Translated by W. H. Fremantle. ("A Select Library of Nicene and Post-Nicene Fathers of the Christian Church," 2nd Ser., Vol. VI.) New York: The Christian Literature Company, 1893.

Nestle, Erwin, and Aland, Kurt (eds.). *Novum Testamentum Graece.* Edition founded by Eberhard Nestle. 25th ed. Stuttgart: Würtembergische Bibelanstalt, 1963.

Ropes, James Hardy. *The Text of Acts.* Vol. III of *The Beginnings of Christianity.* Edited by F. J. Foakes-Jackson and Kirsopp Lake. London: Macmillan and Co., Limited, 1926.

Soden, Hermann von. *Die Schriften des Neuen Testaments in ihrer ältesten erreichbaren Textgestalt hergestellt auf Grund ihrer Textgeschichte.* 2 Teile in 4 Abteilungen. Göttingen: Vandenhoeck und Ruprecht, 1902–1913.

Souter, Alexander (ed.). *Novum Testamentum Graece: Textui a Retractatoribus Anglis Adhibito Brevem Adnotationem Criticam Subiecit.* 2d ed. Oxford: The Clarendon Press, 1947.

Tertullian. "On Monogamy," translated by S. Thelwall, in *Fathers of the Third Century,* Vol. IV of *The Ante-Nicene Fathers: Translations of the Fathers down to A.D. 325,* edited by A. Roberts and J. Donaldson (American reprint revised by A. C. Coxe; 10 vols.; Buffalo: The Christian Literature Publishing Company, 1885), pp. 59–72.

Tischendorf, Constantine. *Novum Testamen um Graece.* Editio VIII critica maior. 3 vols. in 5 parts. Leipzig: Giesecke & Devrient, 1869–1894.

B. COMMENTARIES

Allan, John A. *The Epistle of Paul the Apostle to the Galatians*. "Torch Bible Commentaries." London: SCM Press Ltd, 1951.

Allo, Ernest-Bernard. *Saint Paul: Première Épître aux Corinthiens*. "Études Bibliques." Paris: J. Gabalda et Cⁱᵉ, Éditeurs, 1935.

—— *Saint Paul: Seconde Épître aux Corinthiens*. "Études Bibliques." Paris: J. Gabalda et Cⁱᵉ, Éditeurs, 1937.

Bachmann, Philipp. *Der erste Brief des Paulus an die Korinther*. ("Kommentar zum Neuen Testament," herausgegeben von Theodor Zahn; VII. Bd.; 3. Aufl.) Leipzig: A. Deichertsche Verlagsbuchhandlung (Dr. Werner Scholl), 1921.

Barclay, William. *The Letters to the Corinthians*. 2d ed. Philadelphia: The Westminster Press, 1956.

Barrett, Charles Kingsley. *A Commentary on the Epistle to the Romans*. "Black's New Testament Commentaries." London: Adam & Charles Black, 1957.

Beyer, Hermann Wolfgang. *Die Apostelgeschichte*. ("Das Neue Testament Deutsch," herausgegeben von Paul Althaus, 5. Abt., 8. Aufl.) Göttingen: Vandenhoeck & Ruprecht, 1958.

Bicknell, Edward John. *The First and Second Epistles to the Thessalonians*. "Westminster Commentaries." London: Methuen & Co. Ltd., 1932.

Billerbeck, Paul. *Die Briefe des Neuen Testaments und die Offenbarung Johannis erläutert aus Talmud und Midrasch*. Vol. III of *Kommentar zum Neuen Testament aus Talmud und Midrasch* by Hermann L. Strack and Paul Billerbeck. München: C. H. Beck'sche Verlagsbuchhandlung, 1926.

Blunt, Alfred Walter Frank. *The Acts of the Apostles in the Revised Version*. "The Clarendon Bible." Oxford: The Clarendon Press, 1923.

Bonnard, Pierre. *L'Épître de Saint Paul aux Galates*. ("Commentaire du Nouveau Testament," Vol. IXa.) Neuchâtel: Delachaux & Niestlé S. A., 1953.

Bousset, Wilhelm. "Der erste Brief an die Korinther," in *Die Schriften des Neuen Testaments neu übersetzt und für die Gegenwart erklärt*, in 3. Aufl. hrsg. von Wilhelm Bousset und Wilhelm Heitmüller (4 Bde.; Göttingen: Vandenhoeck & Ruprecht, 1917–1918), II, 74–167.

Bruce, Frederick Fyvie. *Commentary on The Book of Acts: The English Text with Introduction, Exposition and Notes*. "The New International Commentary on the New Testament." Grand Rapids, Mich.: Wm. B. Eerdmans Publishing Company, 1955.

Burton, Ernest de Witt. *A Critical and Exegetical Commentary on the Epistle to the Galatians*. "The International Critical Commentary." Edinburgh: T. & T. Clark, 1921.

Craig, Clarence Tucker. "The First Epistle to the Corinthians: Introduction and Exegesis," in *The Interpreter's Bible*, edited by George Arthur Buttrick et al. (12 vols.; New York: Abingdon Press, 1951–1957), X, 1–262.

Dodd, Charles Harold. *The Epistle of Paul to the Romans*. "The Moffatt New Testament Commentary." New York: Harper and Brothers Publishers, 1932.

Duncan, George Simpson. *The Epistle of Paul to the Galatians.* "The Moffatt New Testament Commentary." London: Hodder and Stoughton, 1934.

Edwards, Thomas Charles. *A Commentary on the First Epistle to the Corinthians.* 3d ed. London: Hodder and Stoughton, 1897.

Evans, Ernest. *The Epistles of Paul the Apostle to the Corinthians.* "The Clarendon Bible." Oxford: The Clarendon Press, 1930.

Ewald, Georg Heinrich. *Die Sendschreiben des Apostels Paulus übersetzt und erklärt.* Göttingen: Verlag der Dieterichschen Buchhandlung, 1857.

Findlay, George Gillanders. *The Epistles to the Thessalonians with Introduction, Notes and Map.* "The Cambridge Bible for Schools and Colleges." Cambridge: The University Press, 1891.

—— "St. Paul's First Epistle to the Corinthians," in *The Expositor's Greek Testament,* edited by W. Robertson Nicoll (5 vols.; London: Hodder and Stoughton, 1897–1910), II, 727–953.

Foakes-Jackson, Frederick John. *The Acts of the Apostles.* "The Moffatt New Testament Commentary." London: Hodder and Stoughton, Limited, 1931.

—— and Lake, Kirsopp (eds.). *The Beginnings of Christianity: The Acts of the Apostles.* 5 vols. London: Macmillan Co., Limited, 1920–33.

Frame, James Everett. *A Critical and Exegetical Commentary on the Epistles of St. Paul to the Thessalonians.* "The International Critical Commentary." Edinburgh: T. & T. Clark, 1912.

Godet, Frédéric. *Commentary on St. Paul's First Epistle to the Corinthians.* Translated by A. Cusin. 2 vols. ("Clark's Foreign Theological Library," N. S., Vols. XXVII, XXX.) Edinburgh: T. & T. Clark, 1893.

Goudge, Henry Leighton. *The First Epistle to the Corinthians with Introduction and Notes.* 3d ed. revised. "Westminster Commentaries." London: Methuen & Co. Ltd., 1911.

Grant, Frederick Clifton. *The New Testament: The Letters and the Revelation to John* ("Nelson's Bible Commentary," edited by Frederick C. Grant, Vol. VII). New York: Thomas Nelson & Sons, 1962.

Grosheide, Frederik Willem. *Commentary on the First Epistle to the Corinthians.* "The New International Commentary on the New Testament." Grand Rapids, Mich.: Wm. B. Eerdmans Publishing Company, 1953.

Haenchen, Ernst. *Die Apostelgeschichte.* ("Kritisch-exegetischer Kommentar über das Neue Testament," begründet von H. A. W. Meyer, 3. Abt., 13. Aufl.) Göttingen: Vandenhoeck & Ruprecht, 1961.

—— *Idem.* 10. Aufl., 1956.

Hanson, Richard Patrick Crosland. *II Corinthians.* "Torch Bible Commentaries." London: SCM Press Ltd, 1954.

Heinrici, C. F. Georg. *Der erste Korintherbrief.* ("Kritisch-exegetischer Kommentar über das Neue Testament," begründet von H. A. W. Meyer, 5. Abt., 8. Aufl.) Göttingen: Vandenhoeck & Ruprecht, 1896.

—— *Das erste Sendschreiben des Apostel Paulus an die Korinther.* Berlin: Wilhelm Hertz, 1880.

Héring, Jean. *The First Epistle of Saint Paul to the Corinthians.* Translated by A. W. Heathcote and P. J. Allcock. London: Epworth Press, 1962.

—— *La Seconde Épître de Saint Paul aux Corinthiens.* ("Commentaire du Nouveau Testament," VIII.) Neuchâtel: Delachaux & Niestlé S. A., 1958.

Lake, Kirsopp, and Cadbury, Henry Joel. *The Beginnings of Christianity: The Acts of the Apostles*, Vol. IV: *English Translation and Commentary*, edited by F. J. Foakes-Jackson and Kirsopp Lake. London: Macmillan and Co., Limited, 1933.

Lampe, Geoffrey W. H. "Acts," in *Peake's Commentary on the Bible*, edited by Matthew Black and H. H. Rowley (London: Thomas Nelson and Sons Ltd, 1962), §771–803.

Leenhardt, Franz J. *The Epistle to the Romans*. Translated by Harold Knight. London: Lutterworth Press, 1961.

Lietzmann, Hans. *An die Korinther I/II*. Enlarged by Werner Georg Kümmel. ("Handbuch zum Neuen Testament," 9. Bd.; 4. Aufl.) Tübingen: Verlag von J. C. B. Mohr (Paul Siebeck), 1949.

Lightfoot, Joseph Barber. *Notes on the Epistles of St. Paul*. Edited posthumously by J. Rendel Harris. London: Macmillan and Co., 1895.

—— *St. Paul's Epistle to the Galatians*. 9th ed. London: Macmillan and Co., 1887.

MacGregor, George Hogarth Carnaby. "The Acts of the Apostles," in *The Interpreter's Bible*, edited by George Arthur Buttrick *et al.* (12 vols.; New York: Abingdon Press, 1951–1957), IX, 1–352.

Masson, Charles. *Les Deux Épîtres de Saint Paul aux Thessaloniciens*. ("Commentaire du Nouveau Testament," XIa.) Neuchâtel: Delachaux & Niestlé S. A., 1957.

Meyer, Heinrich August Wilhelm. *Critical and Exegetical Handbook to the Epistles to the Corinthians*. Translated by D. D. Bannerman and D. Hunter. Edited by W. P. Dickson. 2 vols. ("Critical and Exegetical Commentary on the New Testament," by H. A. W. Meyer.) Edinburgh: T. & T. Clark, 1881-1883.

Meyer, Werner. *Der erste Korintherbrief*. 2 Bde. "Prophezei: Schweizerisches Bibelwerk für die Gemeinde." Zürich: Zwingli Verlag, 1947, 1945.

Michel, Otto. *Der Brief an die Römer*. ("Kritisch-exegetischer Kommentar über das Neue Testament," begründet von H. A. W. Meyer, 4. Abt., 12. Aufl.) Göttingen: Vandenhoeck & Ruprecht, 1963.

Milligan, George. *St. Paul's Epistles to the Thessalonians*. London: Macmillan and Co., Limited, 1908.

Moffatt, James. *The First Epistle of Paul to the Corinthians*. "The Moffatt New Testament Commentary." London: Hodder and Stoughton Limited, 1938.

Morris, Leon. *The First Epistle of Paul to the Corinthians*. "The Tyndale New Testament Commentaries." London: The Tyndale Press, 1958.

Neil, William. *The Epistle of Paul to the Thessalonians*. "The Moffatt New Testament Commentary." London: Hodder and Stoughton, 1950.

Olshausen, Hermann. *Biblical Commentary on St. Paul's First and Second Epistles to the Corinthians*. Translated by J. E. Cox. ("Clark's Foreign Theological Library," Vol. XX.) Edinburgh: T. & T. Clark, 1885.

Osty, Émile. *Les Épîtres de Saint Paul aux Corinthiens*. 3d ed. revised. "La Sainte Bible traduite en français sous la direction de l'École Biblique de Jérusalem." Paris: Les Éditions du Cerf, 1959.

Parry, Reginald St. John. *The First Epistle of Paul the Apostle to the Corinthians in the Revised Version with Introduction and Notes.* "The Cambridge Bible for Schools and Colleges." Cambridge: The University Press, 1916.

—— *The First Epistle of Paul the Apostle to the Corinthians with Introduction and Notes.* 2d ed. "The Cambridge Greek Testament for Schools and Colleges." Cambridge: The University Press, 1926.

Plummer, Alfred. *A Critical and Exegetical Commentary on the Second Epistle of St. Paul to the Corinthians.* "The International Critical Commentary." Edinburgh: T. & T. Clark, 1915.

Preuschen, Erwin. *Die Apostelgeschichte.* ("Handbuch zum Neuen Testament," Bd. IV.1.) Tübingen: J. C. B. Mohr (Paul Siebeck), 1912,

Rackham, Richard Belward. *The Acts of the Apostles.* 3d ed. "Westminster Commentaries." London: Methuen & Co., 1906.

Ramsay, William Mitchell. "Historical Commentary on the Epistles to the Corinthians," *The Expositor,* Ser. 6; I (1900), 19–31, 91–111, 203–17, 273–89, 380–87; II (1900), 287–302, 368–81, 429–44; III (1901), 93–110, 220–40, 343–60.

Rigaux, Béda. *Saint Paul: Les Épîtres aux Thessaloniciens.* "Études Bibliques." Paris: J. Gabalda et Cⁱᵉ, Éditeurs, 1956.

Robertson, Archibald, and Plummer, Alfred. *A Critical and Exegetical Commentary on the First Epistle of St. Paul to the Corinthians.* 2d ed. "The International Critical Commentary." Edinburgh: T. & T. Clark, 1914.

Sanday, William, and Headlam, Arthur Cayley. *A Critical and Exegetical Commentary on the Epistle to the Romans.* 5th ed. "The International Critical Commentary." Edinburgh: T. & T. Clark, 1902.

Schlatter, Adolf. *Paulus, der Bote Jesu: Eine Deutung seiner Briefe an die Korinther.* Stuttgart: Calwer Vereinsbuchhandlung, 1934.

Schmiedel, Paul Wilhelm. "Die Briefe an die Thessalonicher und an die Korinther," in *Hand-Commentar zum Neuen Testament,* bearbeitet von H. J. Holtzmann et al. (4 Bde.; Freiburg i. B.: J. C. B. Mohr [Paul Siebeck], 1889–1891), II. 1, pp. i–xvi, 1–276.

Selwyn, Edward Gordon. *The First Epistle of Peter: The Greek Text with Introduction, Notes and Essays.* 2d ed. London: Macmillan & Co. Ltd., 1955.

Sickenberger, Joseph. *Die Briefe des heiligen Paulus an die Korinther und Römer.* 4. Aufl. ("Die heilige Schrift des neuen Testamentes," VI. Bd.) Bonn: Peter Hanstein, Verlagsbuchhandlung, 1932.

Simon, William Glyn Hughes. *The First Epistle to the Corinthians.* "Torch Bible Commentaries." London: SCM Press Ltd, 1959.

Stählin, Gustav. *Die Apostelgeschichte.* ("Das Neue Testament Deutsch," herausgegeben von Paul Althaus und Gerhard Friedrich, 5. Abt., 10. Aufl.) Göttingen: Vandenhoeck & Ruprecht, 1962.

Strack, Hermann Leberecht, and Billerbeck, Paul. *Das Evangelium nach Markus, Lukas und Johannes und die Apostelgeschichte erläutert aus Talmud und Midrasch.* Vol. II of *Kommentar zum Neuen Testament aus Talmud und Midrasch* by Hermann L. Strack and Paul Billerbeck. München: C. H. Becksche Verlagsbuchhandlung, 1924.

Weiss, Johannes. *Der erste Korintherbrief.* ("Kritisch-exegetischer Kommentar über das Neue Testament," begründet von H. A. W. Meyer, 5. Abt., 10. Aufl.) Göttingen: Vandenhoeck und Ruprecht, 1925.

Wendland, Heinz-Dietrich. *Die Briefe an die Korinther.* ("Das Neue Testament Deutsch," herausgegeben von Paul Althaus und Gerhard Friedrich, 7. Abt., 8. Aufl.) Göttingen: Vandenhoeck & Ruprecht, 1962.

Wendt, Hans Hinrich. *Die Apostelgeschichte.* ("Kritisch-exegetischer Kommentar über das Neue Testament," begründet von H. A. W. Meyer, 3. Abt., 9. Aufl.) Göttingen: Vandenhoeck & Ruprecht, 1913.

Williams, Charles Stephen Conway. *A Commentary on the Acts of the Apostles.* "Black's New Testament Commentaries." London: Adam & Charles Black, 1957.

—— "I and II Corinthians," in *Peake's Commentary on the Bible,* edited by Matthew Black and H. H. Rowley (London: Thomas Nelson and Sons Ltd, 1962), §§829-49.

Windisch, Hans Ludwig. *Der zweite Korintherbrief.* ("Kritisch-exegetischer Kommentar über das Neue Testament," begründet von H. A. W. Meyer, 6. Abt.; 9. Aufl.) Göttingen: Vandenhoeck & Ruprecht, 1924.

Wohlenberg, Gustav. *Der erste und zweite Thessalonicherbrief.* ("Kommentar zum Neuen Testament," herausgegeben von Theodor Zahn, XII. Bd., 2. Aufl.) Leipzig: A. Deichert'sche Verlagsbuchhandlung Nachf. (George Böhme), 1909.

C. BOOKS AND ARTICLES

Achelis, Hans. *Virgines Subintroductae: ein Beitrag zum VII. Kapitel des I. Korintherbriefs.* Leipzig: J. C. Hinrichs'sche Buchhandlung, 1902.

Albertz, Martin. *Die Botschaft des Neuen Testamentes.* 2 vols. in 4 parts. Zollikon-Zürich: Evangelischer Verlag AG., 1947-1957.

Allmen, Jean Jacques von. *Pauline Teaching on Marriage.* Translated from the French. ("Studies in Christian Faith and Practice," VI.) London: The Faith Press, 1963.

Alzas, E. "L'Apôtre Paul et le Célibat," *Revue de Théologie et de Philosophie,* N. S. XXXVIII (1950), 226-32.

Bacon, Benjamin Wisner. "The Apostolic Decree against Πορνεία," *The Expositor,* Ser. 8; VII (1914), 40-61.

—— "The Christ-Party in Corinth," *The Expositor,* Ser. 8; VIII (1914), 399-415.

—— "The Chronological Scheme of Acts," *The Harvard Theological Review,* XIV (1921), 137-66.

—— *An Introduction to the New Testament.* New York: The Macmillan Company, 1900.

—— *The Story of St. Paul.* Boston: Houghton, Mifflin and Company, 1904.

Badcock, Francis John. *The Pauline Epistles and the Epistle to the Hebrews in Their Historical Setting.* London: S. P. C. K., 1937.

Baljon, Johannes Marius Simon. *De Tekst der Brieven van Paulus aan de Romeinen, de Corinthiërs en de Galatiërs als Voorwerp van de Conjecturaalkritiek Beschouwd.* Utrecht: Kemink & Zoon, 1885.

Barnett, Albert Edward. *The New Testament. Its Making and Meaning.* New York: Abingdon Press, 1946.

Barr, James. *The Semantics of Biblical Language*. London: Oxford University Press, 1961.

Barrett, Charles Kingsley. "New Testament Eschatology," *Scottish Journal of Theology*, VI (1953), 136–55.

—— *The New Testament Background: Selected Documents*. London: S. P. C. K., 1957.

Baur, Ferdinand Christian. *Paul, the Apostle of Jesus Christ: His Life and Work, His Epistles and His Doctrine*. Revised by Eduard Zeller. Translated by A. Menzies. 2 vols.; 2d ed. London: Williams and Norgate, 1875–76.

Beare, Francis Wright. *St Paul and his Letters*. London: Adam & Charles Black, 1962.

Beasley-Murray, George Raymond. *Baptism in the New Testament*. London: Macmillan & Co Ltd, 1962.

Belkin, Samuel. "The Problem of Paul's Background: III, Marrying One's Virgin," *Journal of Biblical Literature*, LIV (1935), 49–52.

Bernard, John Henry. *Studia Sacra*. London: Hodder and Stoughton, 1917.

Black, Matthew. *The Scrolls and Christian Origins: Studies in the Jewish Background of the New Testament*. London: Thomas Nelson and Sons Ltd, 1961.

Bleek, Friedrich. "Erörterungen in Beziehung auf die Briefe Pauli an die Korinther," *Theologische Studien und Kritiken*, III (1830), 614–32.

Bludau, August, "Die Quellenscheidungen in der Apostelgeschichte," *Biblische Zeitschrift*, V (1907), 166–89, 258–81.

Boman, Thorleif. "Hebraic and Greek Thought-Forms in the New Testament," in *Current Issues in New Testament Interpretation: Essays in Honor of Otto A. Piper*, edited by W. Klassen and C. F. Snyder (New York: Harper & Brothers, Publishers, 1962), pp. 1–22.

Bonsirven, Joseph. *Exégèse Rabbinique et Exégèse Paulinienne*. "Bibliothèque de Théologie Historique." Paris: Beauchesne et ses fils, 1939.

Bornkamm, Günther. "Paulus," in *Die Religion in Geschichte und Gegenwart: Handwörterbuch für Theologie und Religionswissenschaft*, 3. Aufl. herausgegeben von H. v. Campenhausen *et al.* (6 Bde.; Tübingen: J. C. B. Mohr [Paul Siebeck], 1957–1962), V, 166–90.

Braun, Herbert. "Zur nachpaulinischen Herkunft des zweiten Thessalonicherbriefs," *Zeitschrift für die neutestamentliche Wissenschaft und die Kunde der älteren Kirche*, XLIV (1952/53), 152–56.

Bristol, Lyle O. "Paul's Thessalonian Correspondence," *The Expository Times*, LV (1944), 223.

Broneer, Oscar. *The South Stoa and its Roman Successors*. Vol. I, Pt. 4 of *Corinth: Results of Excavations Conducted by the American School of Classical Studies at Athens*. Princeton, N. J.: The American School of Classical Studies, 1954.

—— "Studies in the Topography of Corinth at the Time of St. Paul," *ΑΡΧΑΙΟΛΟΓΙΚΗ ΕΦΗΜΕΡΙΣ*, CIV (1937), 125–33.

Bruce, Frederick Fyvie. "The Epistles of Paul," in *Peake's Commentary on the Bible*, edited by Matthew Black and H. H. Rowley (London: Thomas Nelson and Sons Ltd, 1962), §§804–14.

Brun, Lyder. "Apostelkoncil und Aposteldekret," in *Paulus und die Urgemeinde*, "Beiheft I zu Norsk Teologisk Tidsskrift" (Giessen: Alfred Töpelmann Verlag, 1921), pp. 1–52.

Buck, Charles Henry, Jr. "The Collection for the Saints," *Harvard Theological Review*, XLIII (1950), 1–29.

—— "The Date of Galatians," *Journal of Biblical Literature*, LXX (1951), 113–22.

Bultmann, Rudolf. *Exegetische Probleme des zweiten Korintherbriefes.* ("Symbolae Biblicae Upsalienses," 9.) Uppsala: Wretmans Boktryckeri A.-B., 1947.

—— *Offenbarung und Heilsgeschehen: Die Frage der natürlichen Offenbarung: Neues Testament und Mythologie.* ("Beiträge zur Evangelische Theologie," Bd. 7.) München: A. Lempp, 1941.

—— *Der Stil der Paulinischen Predigt und die Kynischstoische Diatribe.* Göttingen: Vandenhoeck und Ruprecht, 1910.

—— *Theology of the New Testament.* Translated by Kendrick Grobel. 2 vols. New York: Charles Scribner's Sons, 1951–1955.

—— "Zur Frage nach den Quellen der Apostelgeschichte," in *New Testament Essays: Studies in Memory of Thomas Walter Manson*, edited by A. J. B. Higgins (Manchester: Manchester University Press, 1959), pp. 68–80.

Burn, J. H. "1 Corinthians xv. 51," *The Expository Times*, XXXVII (1925/26), 236–7.

Burkitt, Francis Crawford. *Christian Beginnings.* London: University of London Press, Ltd., 1924.

Cadbury, Henry Joel. "Acts and Eschatology," in *The Background of the New Testament and Its Eschatology*, edited by W. D. Davies and David Daube (Cambridge: The University Press, 1956), pp. 300–21.

—— "The Macellum of Corinth," *Journal of Biblical Literature*, LIII (1934), 134–41.

—— *The Making of Luke–Acts.* London: Macmillan & Co., Limited, 1927.

—— "Overconversion in Paul's Churches," in *The Joy of Study: Papers on New Testament and Related Subjects Presented to Honor Frederick Clifton Grant*, edited by Sherman E. Johnson (New York: The Macmillan Company, 1951), pp. 43–50.

Cadoux, Cecil John. "The Chronological Divisions of Acts," *Journal of Theological Studies*, XIX (1918), 333–41.

—— "A Tentative Synthetic Chronology of the Apostolic Age," *Journal of Biblical Literature*, LVI (1937), 177–91.

Caird, George Bradford. *The Apostolic Age.* "Studies in Theology." London: Gerald Duckworth & Co. Ltd., 1955.

—— *Principalities and Powers: A Study in Pauline Theology.* Oxford: The Clarendon Press, 1956.

Campenhausen, Hans von. *Die Begründung Kirchlicher Entscheidungen beim Apostel Paulus: zur Grundlegung des Kirchenrechts.* ("Sitzungsberichte der Heidelberger Akademie der Wissenschaften: Philosophisch–historische Klasse," 1957, 2. Abhandlung.) Heidelberg: Carl Winter, Universitäts-verlag, 1957.

Carrington, Philip. *According to Mark: A Running Commentary on the Oldest Gospel.* Cambridge: The University Press, 1960.

—— *The Early Christian Church.* 2 vols. Cambridge: The University Press, 1957.

—— *The Primitive Christian Calendar: A Study in the Making of the Marcan*

Gospel. Vol. I: *Introduction and Text.* Cambridge: The University Press, 1952.

—— *The Primitive Christian Catechism: A Study in the Epistles.* Cambridge: The University Press, 1940.

Cerfaux, Lucien. "Le Chapitre XVe du Livre des Actes à la Lumière de la Littérature Ancienne," in *Recueil Lucien Cerfaux* ("Bibliotheca Ephemeridum Theologicarum Lovaniensum," Vols. VI-VII; Gembloux: Éditions J. Duculot, S. A., 1954), II, 105–24.

Chadwick, Henry. " 'All Things to All Men' (I Cor. ix. 22)," *New Testament Studies,* I (1954/55), 261–75.

Charles, Robert Henry. *A Critical History of the Doctrine of a Future Life in Israel, in Judaism, and in Christianity.* 2d ed. revised. London: Adam and Charles Black, 1913.

Cleary, Patrick. "The Epistles to the Corinthians," *The Catholic Biblical Quarterly,* XII (1950), 10–33.

Clemen, Carl. *Die Einheitlichkeit der paulinischen Briefe.* Göttingen: Vandenhoeck und Ruprecht, 1894.

—— *Paulus: sein Leben und Wirken.* 2 Bde. Giessen: J. Ricker'sche Verlagsbuchhandlung (Alfred Töpelmann), 1904.

Conybeare, William John, and Howson, John Saul. *The Life and Epistles of St. Paul.* 2 vols. in 1. New York: Scribner, Armstrong & Co., 1874.

Couchoud, Paul-Louis. "Reconstitution et Classement des Lettres de Saint Paul," *Revue de l'Histoire des Religions,* LXXXVII (1923), 8–31.

Craig, Clarence Tucker. *The Beginning of Christianity.* New York: Abingdon Press, 1943.

Cross, Frank Moore, Jr. *The Ancient Library of Qumrân and Modern Biblical Studies.* ("The Haskell Lectures," 1956–1957.) Garden City, N. Y.: Doubleday & Company, Inc., 1958.

Crownfield, Frederic R. *A Historical Approach to the New Testament.* New York: Harper & Brothers, Publishers, 1960.

Cullmann, Oscar. *Peter: Disciple—Apostle—Martyr: A Historical and Theological Study.* Translated by Floyd V. Filson. 2d ed. revised. ("The Library of History and Doctrine") London: SCM Press Ltd, 1962.

Davies, Arthur Powell. *The First Christian: A Study of St. Paul and Christian Origins.* New York: Farrar, Straus and Cudahy, 1957.

Davies, William David. *Christian Origins and Judaism.* London: Darton, Longman & Todd, 1962.

—— *Paul and Rabbinic Judaism: Some Rabbinic Elements in Pauline Theology.* 2d ed. with additional notes. London: S. P. C. K., 1955.

Deems, Mervin Monroe. "The Sources of Christian Asceticism," in *Environmental Factors in Christian History,* edited by J. T. McNeill, M. Spinka, and H. R. Willoughby (Chicago: The University of Chicago Press, 1939), pp. 149–66.

Deissmann, Gustaf Adolf. *Bible Studies.* Translated by Alexander Grieve. Edinburgh: T. & T. Clark, 1901.

—— *Light from the Ancient East.* Translated by Lionel R. M. Strachan. 2d ed. revised. New York: George H. Doran Company, 1927.

—— *Paul: A Study in Social and Religious History.* Translated by William E. Wilson. 2d ed. revised. London: Hodder and Stoughton, Ltd., 1926.

Delling, Gerhard. art. παρθένος, in *Theologisches Wörterbuch zum Neuen Testament,* hrsg. Gerhard Kittel (Stuttgart: Verlag von W. Kohlhammer, 1933——), V, 824-35.

—— *Paulus' Stellung zu Frau und Ehe.* ("Beiträge zur Wissenschaft vom Alten und Neuen Testament," 4. Folge, Heft 5.) Stuttgart: W. Kohlhammer Verlag, 1931.

De Zwaan, Johannes. *Inleiding tot het Nieuwe Testament.* 3 vols.; 2d ed. rev. ("Volksuniversiteitsbibliotheek," 2d series, Nos. 15, 16, 17.) Haarlem: De Erven F. Bohn N. V., 1948.

Dibelius, Martin. *A Fresh Approach to the New Testament and Early Christian Literature.* (No translator named.) "The International Library of Christian Knowledge." London: I. Nicholson and Watson, 1936.

—— *Paul.* Edited and completed by Werner Georg Kümmel. Translated by Frank Clarke. London: Longmans, Green and Co., 1953.

—— *Studies in the Acts of the Apostles.* Edited by Heinrich Greeven. Translated by Mary Ling. London: SCM Press Ltd, 1956.

Dinkler, Erich. "First Letter to the Corinthians," in *Dictionary of the Bible,* edited by James Hastings; revised ed., edited by F. C. Grant and H. H. Rowley (New York: Charles Scribner's Sons, 1963), pp. 177-80.

—— "Korintherbriefe," in *Die Religion in Geschichte und Gegenwart: Handwörterbuch für Theologie und Religionswissenschaft,* 3. Aufl. herausgegeben von H. v. Campenhausen et al. (6 Bde.; Tübingen: J. C. B. Mohr [Paul Siebeck], 1957–1962), IV, 17-23.

—— "Zum Problem der Ethik bei Paulus," *Zeitschrift für Theologie und Kirche,* XLIX (1952), 167–200.

Dobschütz, Ernst von. *Christian Life in the Primitive Church.* Translated by G. Bremner. Edited by W. D. Morrison. London: Williams and Norgate, 1904.

—— "Zum Wortschatz und Stil des Römerbriefes," *Zeitschrift für die neutestamentliche Wissenschaft und die Kunde der älteren Kirche,* XXXIII (1934), 51-66.

Dodd, Charles Harold. *The Apostolic Preaching and its Developments.* 2d ed. London: Hodder & Stoughton Limited, 1944.

—— "Chronology of the Acts and Pauline Epistles," in *Helps to the Study of the Bible,* by A. W. F. Blunt et al. (2d ed. rev.; London: Oxford University Press, 1931), pp. 195-7.

—— "The Mind of Paul: II." Chapter v of his *New Testament Studies* (Manchester: Manchester University Press, 1953), pp. 83–128.

Duncan, George Simpson. *St. Paul's Ephesian Ministry.* London: Hodder & Stoughton Limited, 1929.

Dupont, Jacques. *Gnosis: La Connaissance Religieuse dans les Épîtres de Saint Paul.* (2d ed.; "Universitas Catholica Lovaniensis Dissertationes," Ser. 2, Vol. XL.) Louvain: E. Nauwelaerts, 1960.

—— *The Sources of Acts: The Present Position.* Translated by Kathleen Pond. London: Darton, Longman & Todd, 1964.

Easton, Burton Scott. *Early Christianity: The Purpose of Acts and Other Papers.* Edited by Frederick C. Grant. London: S. P. C. K., 1955.

Eckart, Karl-Gottfried. "Der zweite echte Brief des Apostels Paulus an die Thessalonicher," *Zeitschrift für Theologie und Kirche,* LVIII (1961), 30–44.

Ellis, Edward Earle. *Paul's Use of the Old Testament.* Grand Rapids, Mich.: Wm. B. Eerdmans Publishing Company, 1957.

Emmet, Cyril William. "The Case for the Tradition," in *The Beginnings of Christianity,* Vol. II: *Prolegomena, II: Criticism,* edited by F. J. Foakes-Jackson and Kirsopp Lake (London: Macmillan and Co., Limited, 1922), pp. 265–97.

Enslin, Morton Scott. *Christian Beginnings.* New York: Harper & Brothers Publishers, 1938.

—— *The Ethics of Paul.* New York: Harper & Brothers Publishers, 1930.

Erbt, Wilhelm. *Von Jerusalem nach Rom: Untersuchungen zur Geschichte und Geschichtsdarstellung des Urchristentums.* ("Mitteilungen der Vorderasiatischen Gesellschaft [E.V.]," 1912.2, 17. Jahrgang.) Leipzig: J. C. Hinrichs'sche Buchhandlung, 1912.

Fahnenbruch, F. "Zu I. Cor. 7, 36–38," *Biblische Zeitschrift,* XII (1914), 391–401.

Farrar, Frederic William. *The Life and Work of St. Paul.* New York: E. P. Dutton and Company, 1902.

Fascher, Erich. "Zur Witwerschaft des Paulus und der Auslegung von I Cor 7," *Zeitschrift für neutestamentliche Wissenschaft und die Kunde der älteren Kirche,* XXVIII (1929), 62–9.

Faw, Chalmer E. "The Anomaly of Galatians," *Biblical Research,* IV (1960), 25–38.

—— "On the Writing of First Thessalonians," *Journal of Biblical Literature,* LXXI (1952), 217–25.

Findlay, George Gillanders. "The Letter of the Corinthian Church to St. Paul," *The Expositor,* Ser. 6; I (1900), 401–7.

Fitzmyer, Joseph A. "A Feature of Qumrân Angelology and the Angels of I Cor. XI. 10," *New Testament Studies,* IV (1957/58), 48–58.

—— "Qumrân and the Interpolated Paragraph in 2 Cor 6,14–7,1," *The Catholic Biblical Quarterly,* XXIII (1961), 271–80.

Flemington, William Frederick. *The New Testament Doctrine of Baptism.* London: S. P. C. K., 1948.

Foschini, Bernard M. " 'Those who are baptized for the Dead.' 1 Cor. 15:29," *The Catholic Biblical Quarterly,* XII (1950), 260–76, 379–88; XIII (1951), 46–78, 172–98, and 276–83.

Franklin, Wilbur Mitchell. *Die Kollekte des Paulus.* Scottdale, Pa.: Mennonite Publishing House, 1938.

Funk, Robert W. "The Enigma of the Famine Visit," *Journal of Biblical Literature,* LXXV (1956), 130–6.

Geyser, A. S. "Paul, the Apostolic Decree and the Liberals in Corinth," in *Studia Paulina in Honorem Johannis de Zwaan Septuagenarii,* edited by J. N. Sevenster and W. C. van Unnik (Haarlem: De Erven F. Bohn N. V., 1953), pp. 124–38.

Goguel, Maurice. *The Birth of Christianity.* Translated by H. C. Snape. London: George Allen & Unwin Ltd, 1953.

—— *Introduction au Nouveau Testament.* 4 Pts. in 5 Vols. Paris: Ernest Leroux, 1922–1926.

Goodspeed, Edgar Johnson. *Paul.* Philadelphia: John C. Winston Company, 1947.

—— *Problems of New Testament Translation.* Chicago: The University of Chicago Press, 1945.

Grässer, Erich. "Die Apostelgeschichte in der Forschung der Gegenwart," *Theologische Rundschau,* XXVI (1960), 93–167.

Grafe, Eduard. "Geistliche Verlöbnisse bei Paulus," *Theologische Arbeiten aus dem rheinischen wissenschaftlichen Prediger-Verein,* N. F. III (1899) 57–69.

Grant, Robert McQueen. "Hellenistic Elements in I Corinthians," in *Early Christian Origins: Studies in Honor of Harold R. Willoughby,* edited by Allen Wikgren (Chicago: Quadrangle Books, 1961), pp. 60–6.

—— *A Historical Introduction to the New Testament.* New York: Harper & Row, Publishers, 1963.

—— "The Wisdom of the Corinthians," in *The Joy of Study: Papers on New Testament and Related Subjects Presented to Honor Frederick Clifton Grant,* edited by Sherman E. Johnson (New York: The Macmillan Company, 1951), pp. 51–5.

—— and Freedman, David Noel. *The Secret Sayings of Jesus According to the Gospel of Thomas.* London: Fontana Books, 1960.

Grundmann, Walter. art. καλός, in *Theologisches Wörterbuch zum Neuen Testament,* herausgegeben von Gerhard Kittel (Stuttgart: Verlag von W. Kohlhammer, 1933——), III, 539–53.

Gyllenberg, Rafael. "Die einleitenden Grussformeln in den paulinischen Briefen," *Svensk Exegetisk Arsbok,* XVI= 1951 (1952), 21–31.

Hadorn, Wilhelm. *Die Abfassung der Thessalonicherbriefe in der Zeit der dritten Missionsreise des Paulus.* ("Beiträge zur Förderung christlicher Theologie," 24. Bd., 3/4 Hft.) Gütersloh: C. Bertelsmann Verlag, 1919.

Haenchen, Ernst. "Quellenanalyse und Kompositionsanalyse in Act 15," in *Judentum—Urchristentum—Kirche: Festschrift für Joachim Jeremias,* edited by Walther Eltester ("Beihefte zur Zeitschrift für die neutestamentliche Wissenschaft und die Kunde der älteren Kirche," Beiheft XXVI; Berlin: Verlag Alfred Töpelmann, 1960), pp. 153–64.

—— "Das 'Wir' in der Apostelgeschichte und das Itinerar," *Zeitschrift für Theologie und Kirche,* LVIII (1961), 329–66.

Hagge. "Die beiden überlieferten Sendschreiben des Apostels Paulus an die Gemeinde zu Korinth," *Jahrbücher für protestantische Theologie,* II (1876), 481–531.

Hamilton, Neill Quinn. *The Holy Spirit and Eschatology in Paul.* ("Scottish Journal of Theology Occasional Papers," No. 6.) Edinburgh: Oliver and Boyd Ltd., 1957.

Harnack, Adolf von. "Das Aposteldekret (Act. 15,29) und die Blass'sche Hypothese," in his *Studien zur Geschichte des Neuen Testaments und der alten Kirche, I: Zur neutestamentlichen Textkritik* ("Arbeiten zur Kirchengeschichte," Bd. 19, herausgegeben von E. Hirsch und H. Lietzmann; Berlin: Walter de Gruyter & Co., 1931), pp. 1–32.

—— *New Testament Studies, III: The Acts of the Apostles.* Translated by J. R. Wilkinson. ("Crown Theological Library," Vol. XXVII.) London: Williams & Norgate, 1909.

Harris, James Rendel. "A Study in Letter-Writing," *The Expositor,* Ser. 5; VIII (1898), 161–80.

Hart, J. H. A. "Apollos," *Journal of Theological Studies,* VII (1906), 16–28.

Hausrath, Adolf. *Der Vier-Capitelbrief des Paulus an die Korinther.* Heidelberg: Bassermann, 1870.

Headlam, Arthur Cayley. "Acts," in *A Dictionary of the Bible,* edited by James Hastings (5 vols.; Edinburgh: T. & T. Clark, 1898–1904), I, 25–35.

Heard, Richard. *An Introduction to the New Testament.* New York: Harper & Brothers Publishers, 1950.

Heitmüller, Wilhelm. "Die Quellenfrage in der Apostelgeschichte (1886–1898)," *Theologische Rundschau,* II (1899), 47–59, 83–95, 127–140.

Hettlinger, R. F. "2 Corinthians 5.1–10," *Scottish Journal of Theology,* X (1957), 174–94.

Hirsch, Emanuel. "Petrus und Paulus," *Zeitschrift für die neutestamentliche Wissenschaft und die Kunde der älteren Kirche,* XXIX (1930), 63–76.

Hoeber, Robert G. "Galatians 2:1–10 and the Acts of the Apostles," *Concordia Theological Monthly,* XXXI (1960), 482–91.

Holl, Karl. *Gesammelte Aufsätze zur Kirchengeschichte:* Bd. II, *Der Osten.* Tübingen: J. C. B. Mohr (Paul Siebeck), 1928.

Hollmann, Georg. "Die Unechtheit des zweiten Thessalonicherbriefs," *Zeitschrift für die neutestamentliche Wissenschaft und die Kunde des Urchristentums,* V (1904), 28–38.

Holtzmann, Heinrich Julius. "Zum zweiten Thessalonicherbrief," *Zeitschrift für die neutestamentliche Wissenschaft und die Kunde des Urchristentums,* II (1901), 97–108.

Holtzmann, Oskar. *Das Neue Testament nach dem Stuttgarter griechischen Text übersetzt und erklärt.* 2 Bde. Giessen: A. Töpelmann, 1926.

Holzhey, Karl. "Zur Exegese von I Co[r 7,] 36–37," *Theologie und Glaube,* XIX (1927), 307 ff.

Hunter, Archibald Macbride. *Interpreting the New Testament, 1900–1950.* Philadelphia: The Westminster Press, 1951.

—— *Paul and his Predecessors.* Revised edition. London: SCM Press Ltd, 1961.

Jeremias, Joachim. " 'Flesh and Blood Cannot Inherit the Kingdom of God' (I Cor. XV. 50)," *New Testament Studies,* II (1955/56), 151–9.

—— "Nochmals: War Paulus Witwer?" *Zeitschrift für die neutestamentliche Wissenschaft und die Kunde der älteren Kirche,* XXVIII (1929), 321–3.

—— "Untersuchungen zum Quellenproblem der Apostelgeschichte," *Zeitschrift für die neutestamentliche Wissenschaft und die Kunde der älteren Kirche,* XXXVI (1937), 205–21.

—— "War Paulus Witwer?" *Zeitschrift für die neutestamentliche Wissenschaft und die Kunde der älteren Kirche,* XXV (1926), 310–12.

—— "Zur Gedankenführung in den paulinischen Briefen: (3) Die Briefzitate in I. Kor 8, 1–13," in *Studia Paulina in Honorem Johannis de Zwaan Septuagenarii,* edited by J. N. Sevenster and W. C. van Unnik (Haarlem: De Erven F. Bohn N. V., 1953), pp. 151–3.

Jülicher, Adolf. *An Introduction to the New Testament*. Translated by Janet P. Ward. New York: G. P. Putnam's Sons, 1904.

—— "Die Jungfrauen im ersten Korintherbrief," *Protestantische Monatshefte*, XXII (1918), 97–119.

Juncker, Alfred. *Die Ethik des Apostels Paulus*. 2 vols. in 1. Halle a. S.: M. Niemeyer, 1904–1919.

Kähler, Else. *Die Frau in den paulinischen Briefen (unter besonderer Berücksichtigung des Begriffes der Unterordnung)*. Zürich: Gotthelf-Verlag, 1960.

Käsemann, Ernst. "Die Legitimität des Apostels. Eine Untersuchung zu II Kor. 10–13," *Zeitschrift für die neutestamentliche Wissenschaft und die Kunde der älteren Kirche*, XLI (1942), 33–71.

Kee, Howard Clark, and Young, Franklin Woodrow. *Understanding the New Testament*. Englewood Cliffs, N. J.: Prentice-Hall, Inc., 1957.

Ketter, Peter. "Syneisakten in Korinth? Zu I Cor 7, 36–38," *Trierer Theologische Zeitschrift*, LVI (1947), 175–82.

Kilpatrick, George Dunbar. "Galatians 1:18 *ΙΣΤΟΡΗΣΑΙ ΚΗΦΑΝ*," in *New Testament Essays: Studies in Memory of Thomas Walter Manson*, edited by A. J. B. Higgins (Manchester: Manchester University Press, 1959), pp. 144–9.

Klausner, Joseph. *From Jesus to Paul*. Translated by William F. Stinespring. London: George Allen & Unwin, Ltd., 1944.

Knopf, Rudolf; Lietzmann, Hans; and Weinel, Heinrich. *Einführung in das Neue Testament*. ("Sammlung Töpelmann," Bd. 2; 5. Aufl.) Berlin: Alfred Töpelmann Verlag, 1949.

Knox, John. *Chapters in a Life of Paul*. New York: Abingdon-Cokesbury Press, 1950.

—— "'Fourteen Years Later': A Note on the Pauline Chronology," *The Journal of Religion*, XVI (1936), 341–9.

—— "The Pauline Chronology," *Journal of Biblical Literature*, LVIII (1939), 15–29.

—— *Philemon among the Letters of Paul: A New View of Its Place and Importance*. 2d ed. revised. New York: Abingdon Press, 1959.

Knox, Wilfred Lawrence. *The Acts of the Apostles*. Cambridge: The University Press, 1948.

—— *St. Paul and the Church of the Gentiles*. Cambridge: The University Press, 1939.

—— *St. Paul and the Church of Jerusalem*. Cambridge: The University Press, 1925.

Koch, Hugo. "Vater und Tochter im ersten Korintherbrief," *Biblische Zeitschrift*, III (1905), 401–7.

Kümmel, Werner Georg. "Die älteste Form des Aposteldekrets," in *Spiritus et Veritas*, edited by Auseklis (Eutin: Societas Theologorum Universitatis Latviensis [in exile], 1953), pp. 83–98.

—— "Urchristentum," *Theologische Rundschau*, XIV (1942), 167–73.

—— "Verlobung und Heirat bei Paulus (I. Cor 7, 36–38)," in *Neutestamentliche Studien für Rudolf Bultmann* ("Beihefte zur Zeitschrift für die neutestamentliche Wissenschaft und die Kunde der älteren Kirche," Beiheft XXI; Berlin: Alfred Töpelmann, 1954), pp. 275–95.

Kuhn, Karl Georg. "Les Rouleaux de Cuivre de Qumrân," *Revue Biblique*, LXI (1954), 193–205.

Lake, Kirsopp. "The Apostolic Council of Jerusalem." In *Additional Notes to the Commentary*: Vol. V of *The Beginnings of Christianity*, edited by F. J. Foakes-Jackson and Kirsopp Lake (London: Macmillan and Co., Limited, 1933), pp. 195–212.

—— "The Chronology of Acts," in *Additional Notes to the Commentary*: Vol. V of *The Beginnings of Christianity*, edited by F. J. Foakes-Jackson and K. Lake (London: Macmillan and Co., Limited, 1933), pp. 445–74.

—— *The Earlier Epistles of St. Paul: Their Motive and Origin*. 2d ed. London: Rivingtons, 1914.

—— and Lake, Silva. *An Introduction to the New Testament*. London: Christophers, 1938.

Lewin, Thomas. *The Life and Letters of St. Paul*. 2 vols. 5th ed. London: George Bell & Sons, 1890.

Lietzmann, Hans. *The Beginnings of the Christian Church*. Translated by B. L. Woolf. 3d ed. revised. London: Lutterworth Press, 1953.

—— *Mass and Lord's Supper: A Study in the History of the Liturgy*. Translated by D. H. G. Reeve. Leiden: E. J. Brill, 1953– 1955.

—— "Der Sinn des Aposteldekrets und seine Textwandlung," in his *Kleine Schriften, II: Studien zum Neuen Testament*, herausgegeben von Kurt Aland ("Texte und Untersuchungen zur Geschichte der altchristlichen Literatur," LXVIII; Berlin: Akademie Verlag, 1958), pp. 292–8.

Lightfoot, Joseph Barber. "The Chronology of Paul's Life and Epistles," in his *Biblical Essays*, edited posthumously by J. Rendel Harris (London: Macmillan and Co., 1893), pp. 213–33.

—— "The Mission of Titus to the Corinthians," in his *Biblical Essays*, edited posthumously by J. Rendel Harris (London: Macmillan and Co., 1893), pp. 271–84.

Linton, Olof. "The Third Aspect: A Neglected Point of View: A Study in Gal. i–ii and Acts ix and xv," *Studia Theologica*, III (1950), 79–95.

Lock, Walter. "I Cor. 8:1–9. A Suggestion," *The Expositor*, Ser. 5; VI (1897), 65–74.

Loisy, Alfred. *Les Livres du Nouveau Testament*. Paris: Émile Nourry, 1922.

—— *The Origins of the New Testament*. Translated by L. P. Jacks. London: George Allen and Unwin Ltd, 1950.

Lowe, John. "An Examination of Attempts to Detect Development in St. Paul's Theology," *The Journal of Theological Studies*, XLII (1941), 129–42.

Lütgert, Wilhelm. *Freiheitspredigt und Schwarmgeister in Korinth: ein Beitrag zur Charakteristik der Christus Partei*. ("Beiträge zur Förderung christlicher Theologie," XII, 3.) Gütersloh: C. Bertelsmann, 1908.

Lund, Nils Wilhelm. *Chiasmus in the New Testament*. Chapel Hill: The University of North Carolina Press, 1942.

MacGregor, George Hogarth Carnaby. "Principalities and Powers: The Cosmic Background of Paul's Thought," *New Testament Studies*, I (1954/55), 17–28.

McCown, Chester Charlton. "The Current Plight of Biblical Scholarship," *Journal of Biblical Literature*. LXXV (1956), 12–18.

McGiffert, Arthur Cushman. *A History of Christianity in the Apostolic Age.* "International Theological Library." Edinburgh: T. & T. Clark, 1897.

McNeile, Alan Hugh. *An Introduction to the New Testament.* 2d ed. revised by C. S. C. Williams. Oxford: The Clarendon Press, 1953.

Manson, Thomas Walter. "'*IΛΑCΤΗΡΙΟΝ*," *The Journal of Theological Studies,* XLVI (1945), 8–9.

—— *On Paul and John.* ("Studies in Biblical Theology," No. 38.) London: SCM Press Ltd, 1963.

—— *Studies in the Gospels and Epistles.* Edited by Matthew Black. Manchester: Manchester University Press, 1962.

Massie, John. "Did the Corinthian Church Advocate Universal Marriage? A Study in Interpretation," *The Journal of Theological Studies,* II (1901), 527–38.

Matheson, George. *The Spiritual Development of St. Paul.* 4th ed. Edinburgh: W. Blackwood and Sons, 1897.

Menoud, Philippe-Henri. "Le Plan des Actes des Apôtres," *New Testament Studies,* I (1954/55), 44–51.

Meyer, Eduard. *Ursprung und Anfänge des Christentums.* 3 Bde. Stuttgart: J. G. Cotta'sche Buchhandlung Nachfolger, 1921–1923.

Michaelis, John David. *Introduction to the New Testament.* Translated and edited from the 4th German ed. of 1788 by Herbert Marsh. 6 vols. Cambridge: John Burges, Printer to the University, 1801.

Michaelis, Wilhelm. *Einleitung in das Neue Testament.* 2. Aufl. Bern: Berchthold Haller Verlag, 1954.

Minear, Paul Sevier. "The Jerusalem Fund and Pauline Chronology," *Anglican Theological Review,* XXV (1943), 389–96.

Moffatt, James. *An Introduction to the Literature of the New Testament.* 3d ed. revised. "International Theological Library." Edinburgh: T. & T. Clark, 1918.

Morrison, Clinton Dawson. *The Powers That Be.* ("Studies in Biblical Theology," No. 29.) London: SCM Press Ltd, 1960.

Müller, Karl. *Kirchengeschichte.* 1. Bd., 1. Halbbd. 3. Aufl. in Gemeinschaft mit H. von Campenhausen. Tübingen: J. C. B. Mohr (Paul Siebeck), 1941.

Munck, Johannes. *Paul and the Salvation of Mankind.* (Translated by the author.) London: SCM Press Ltd, 1959.

Nestle, Eberhard. *Einführung in das Griechische Neue Testament.* 4. Aufl. völlig umgearbeitet von Ernst von Dobschütz. Göttingen: Vandenhoeck & Ruprecht, 1923.

Nock, Arthur Darby. *St. Paul.* "The Home University Library." London: Oxford University Press, 1946.

Norden, Eduard. *Agnostos Theos: Untersuchungen zur Formengeschichte religiöser Rede.* Stuttgart: B. G. Teubner, 1912.

O'Neill, J. C. *The Theology of Acts in Its Historical Setting.* London: S. P. C. K., 1961.

Paley, William. *Horae Paulinae: or the Truth of the Scripture History of St. Paul, Evinced by a Comparison of the Epistles Which Bear His Name with The Acts of the Apostles, and with One Another.* 8th ed. London: J. Faulder et al., 1812.

Pierce, Claude Anthony. *Conscience in the New Testament.* ("Studies in Biblical Theology," No. 15.) London: SCM Press Ltd, 1955.

Porter, Joshua Roy. "The 'Apostolic Decree' and Paul's Second Visit to Jerusalem," *The Journal of Theological Studies,* XLVII (1946), 169–74.

Preisker, Herbert. *Christentum und Ehe in den ersten drei Jahrhunderten: eine Studie zur Kulturgeschichte der alten Welt.* ("Neue Studien zur Geschichte der Theologie und der Kirche," hrsg. Reinhold Seeberg, 23. Stück.) Berlin: Trowitzsch & Sohn, 1927.

Preuschen, Erwin. " 'Und liesse meinen Leib brennen' I Kor. 13,3," *Zeitschrift für die neutestamentliche Wissenschaft und die Kunde des Urchristentums,* XVI (1915), 127–38.

Ramsay, William Mitchell. *The Letters to the Seven Churches of Asia and Their Place in the Plan of the Apocalypse.* New York: A. C. Armstrong & Son, 1905.

—— *St. Paul the Traveller and the Roman Citizen.* New York: G. P. Putnam's Sons, 1896.

Ramsey, Howard Lyn. *The Place of Galatians in the Career of Paul.* (Ph.D. Thesis, Columbia University, 1960.) Ann Arbor, Mich.: University Microfilms, Inc., 1961.

Reicke, Bo. "Der geschichtliche Hintergrund des Apostelkonzils und der Antioch-Episode, Gal. 2, 1–14," in *Studia Paulina in Honorem Johannis de Zwaan Septuagenarii,* edited by J. N. Sevenster and W. C. van Unnik (Haarlem: De Erven F. Bohn N. V., 1953), pp. 172–87.

Reitzenstein, Richard. *Die hellenistischen Mysterienreligionen nach ihren Grundgedanken und Wirkungen.* 3d ed. of 1927 reprinted photographically. Stuttgart: B. G. Teubner Verlagsgesellschaft, 1956.

Richard, L.-A. "Sur I *Corinthiens* (VII, 36–38). Cas de Conscience d'un Père Chrétien ou 'Mariage Ascétique'? Un Essai d'Interprétation," in *Memorial J. Chaine* ("Bibliothèque de la Faculté Catholique de Théologie de Lyon," Vol. 5; Lyon: Facultés Catholiques, 1950), pp. 309–20.

Richardson, Alan. *An Introduction to the Theology of the New Testament.* New York: Harper & Brothers, Publishers, 1958.

Riddle, Donald Wayne. *Paul: Man of Conflict: A Modern Biographical Sketch.* Nashville: Cokesbury Press, 1940.

Rigaux, Béda. *Saint Paul et ses Lettres: État de la Question.* ("Studia Neotestamentica," Subsidia II.) Paris: Desclée de Brouwer, 1962.

Robinson, H. Wheeler. *The Christian Doctrine of Man.* 3d ed. Edinburgh: T. & T. Clark, 1926.

Robinson, John Arthur Thomas. *The Body: A Study in Pauline Theology.* ("Studies in Biblical Theology," No. 5.) London: SCM Press Ltd, 1952.

—— *Jesus and His Coming: The Emergence of a Doctrine.* London: SCM Press Ltd, 1957.

Roller, Otto. *Das Formular der paulinischen Briefe: Ein Beitrag zur Lehre vom antiken Briefe.* ("Beiträge zur Wissenschaft vom Alten und Neuen Testament," Bd. LVIII.) Stuttgart: W. Kohlhammer Verlag, 1933.

Rouge, J. "La Navigation hivernale sous l'Empire Romain," *Revue des Études Anciennes,* LIV (1952), 316–25.

Rowlingson, Donald T. "The Jerusalem Conference and Jesus' Nazareth Visit," *Journal of Biblical Literature*, LXXI (1952), 69–74.

Rylaarsdam, John Coert. "The Problem of Faith and History in Biblical Interpretation," *Journal of Biblical Literature*, LXXVII (1958), 26–32.

Sabatier, Auguste. *The Apostle Paul: A Sketch of the Development of his Doctrine.* Translated by A. M. Hellier. 3d ed. London: Hodder and Stoughton, 1896.

Sahlin, Harald. *Der Messias und das Gottesvolk: Studien zur protolukanischen Theologie.* ("Acta Seminarii Neotestamentici Upsaliensis," XII.) Uppsala: Almquist & Wiksells Boktryckeri AB, 1945.

Sanday, William. "The Apostolic Decree (Acts XV. 20–29)," in *Theologische Studien Theodor Zahn zum 10. Oktober 1908 dargebracht* (Leipzig: A. Deichert'sche Verlagsbuchhandlung Nachf. [Georg Böhme], 1908), pp. 317–38.

Sanders, Joseph Newbould. "Peter and Paul in the Acts," *New Testament Studies*, II (1955/56), 133–43.

Scharlemann, Martin H. *Qumran and Corinth.* New York: Bookman Associates, 1962.

—— Review of Ulrich Wilkens, *Weisheit und Torheit, Journal of Biblical Literature*, LXXIX (1960), 189–90.

Schlier, Heinrich. "Über das Hauptliegen des I. Korintherbriefs," *Evangelische Theologie*, VIII (1948/49), 462–73.

Schmiedel, Paul Wilhelm. "Acts of the Apostles," in *Encyclopaedia Biblica*, edited by T. K. Cheyne and J. Sutherland Black (4 vols.; New York: The Macmillan Company, 1899–1903), I, 37–57.

Schmithals, Walter. *Die Gnosis in Korinth: Eine Untersuchung zu den Korintherbriefen.* Göttingen: Vandenhoeck & Ruprecht, 1956.

—— "Zur Abfassung und ältesten Sammlung der paulinischen Hauptbriefe," *Zeitschrift für die neutestamentliche Wissenschaft und die Kunde der älteren Kirche*, LI (1960), 225–45.

Schoeps, Hans-Joachim. *Paul: The Theology of the Apostle in the Light of Jewish Religious History.* Translated by Harold Knight. London: Lutterworth Press, 1961.

Schubert, Paul. *The Form and Function of the Pauline Thanksgivings.* ("Beihefte zur Zeitschrift für die neutestamentliche Wissenschaft und die Kunde der älteren Kirche," Beiheft XX.) Berlin: Alfred Töpelmann, 1939.

Schwartz, Eduard. "Zur Chronologie des Paulus," in *Nachrichten von der Königlichen Gesellschaft der Wissenschaft zu Göttingen: Philologisch-historische Klasse* (Berlin: Weidmannsche Buchhandlung, 1907), pp. 269–74.

Schweitzer, Albert. *The Mysticism of Paul the Apostle.* Translated by William Montgomery. New York: Henry Holt and Company, 1931.

—— *Paul and His Interpreters: A Critical History.* Translated by W. Montgomery. London: Adam and Charles Black, 1912.

Scott, Ernest Findlay. *The Literature of the New Testament.* New York: Columbia University Press, 1932.

Scranton, Robert Lorentz. *Monuments in the Lower Agora and North of the Archaic Temple.* Vol. I, Pt. 3 of *Corinth: Results of Excavations Conducted by the*

324   BIBLIOGRAPHY

American School of Classical Studies at Athens. Princeton, N. J.: The American School of Classical Studies, 1951.

Selby, Donald Joseph. *Toward the Understanding of St. Paul*. Englewood Cliffs, N. J.: Prentice-Hall, Inc., 1962.

Shaw, R. D. *The Pauline Epistles*. 4th ed. Edinburgh: T. & T. Clark, 1914.

Shepherd, Massey Hamilton, Jr. "A Venture in the Source Analysis of Acts," in *Munera Studiosa*, edited by Massey Hamilton Shepherd, Jr. and Sherman Elbridge Johnson (Cambridge, Mass.: Published by the Episcopal Theological School, 1946), pp. 91–105.

Sickenberger, Joseph. "Syneisaktentum im ersten Korintherbrief?" *Biblische Zeitschrift*, III (1905), 44–69.

Smith, David. *The Life and Letters of St. Paul*. New York: George H. Doran Company, [1919].

Snape, Henry Currie. "The Composition of the Lukan Writings: A Reassessment," *The Harvard Theological Review*, LIII (1960), 27–46.

Soden, Hans von. "Sakrament und Ethik bei Paulus: Zur Frage der literarischen und theologischen Einheitlichkeit von 1 Kor. 8–10," in *Urchristentum und Geschichte: Gesammelte Aufsätze und Vorträge*, herausgegeben von Hans von Campenhausen (2 Bde.; Tübingen: J. C. B. Mohr [Paul Siebeck], 1951–1956), I, 239–75.

Soden, Hermann von. *The History of Early Christian Literature: The Writings of the New Testament*. Translated by J. R. Wilkinson. Edited by W. D. Morrison. ("Crown Theological Library," Vol. XIII.) London: Williams & Norgate, 1906.

Souter, Alexander. *The Text and Canon of the New Testament*. Revised by C. S. C. Williams. "Studies in Theology." London: Gerald Duckworth & Co. Ltd., 1954.

Stählin, Gustav. art. ἀσθενής, in *Theologisches Wörterbuch zum Neuen Testament*, hrsg. Gerhard Kittel (Stuttgart: Verlag von W. Kohlhammer, 1933———), I, 488–92.

Stauffer, Ethelbert. *New Testament Theology*. Translated by John Marsh. New York: The Macmillan Company, 1956.

Steck, R. "Geistliche Ehen bei Paulus? (I Cor 7:36–38)," *Schweizer Theologische Zeitschrift*, XXXIV (1917), 177–89.

Stendahl, Krister. "Implications of Form-criticism and Tradition-criticism for Biblical Interpretation," *Journal of Biblical Literature*, LXXVII (1958), 33–38.

Streeter, Burnett Hillman. "The Primitive Text of Acts," *Journal of Theological Studies*, XXXIV (1933), 232–41.

Suggs, M. Jack. "Concerning the Date of Paul's Macedonian Ministry," *Novum Testamentum*, IV (1960), 60–8.

Taylor, Vincent. *The Text of the New Testament: A Short Introduction*. London: Macmillan & Co Ltd, 1961.

Thacheray, Henry St. John. *The Relation of St. Paul to Contemporary Jewish Thought*. London: Macmillan and Co., Limited, 1900.

Titus, Eric Lane. *Essentials of New Testament Study*. New York: The Ronald Press Company, 1958.

Trocmé, Étienne. Le "Livre des Actes" et l'Histoire. ("Études d'Histoire et de Philosophie Religieuses Publiées sous les Auspices de la Faculté de Théologie Protestante de l'Université de Strasbourg," No. 45.) Paris: Presses Universitaires de France, 1957.

Turner, Cuthbert Hamilton. "Chronology of the New Testament," in A Dictionary of the Bible, edited by James Hastings (5 vols.; Edinburgh: T. & T. Clark, 1898–1904), I, 403–25.

Van Manen, W. C. "Paul: Later Criticism," in Encyclopaedia Biblica, edited by T. K. Cheyne and J. Sutherland Black (4 vols.; New York: The Macmillan Company, 1899–1903), III, 3620–38.

Vischer, Lukas. Die Auslegungsgeschichte von I. Kor. 6, 1–11: Rechtsverzicht und Schlichtung. ("Beiträge zur Geschichte der neutestamentlichen Exegese," No. 1.) Tübingen: J. C. B. Mohr (Paul Siebeck), 1955.

Weber, Valentin. Die antiochenische Kollekte, die übersehene Hauptorientierung für die Paulusforschung. Würzburg: Buchhandlung Bauch, Echterhaus, 1917.

Weiss, Johannes. The History of Primitive Christianity. Translated and edited by Frederick C. Grant with A. H. Forster, P. S. Kramer, and S. E. Johnson. 2 vols. New York: Wilson-Erickson, 1936.

Weizsäcker, Carl von. The Apostolic Age of the Christian Church. Translated by James Millar. 2 vols. ("Theological Translation Library," Vols. I, V.) London: Williams and Norgate, 1894–1895.

Wellhausen, Julius. "Noten zur Apostelgeschichte," in Nachrichten von der Königlichen Gesellschaft der Wissenschaften zu Göttingen: Philologisch-historische Klasse (Berlin: Weidmannsche Buchhandlung, 1907), pp. 1–21.

West, J. C. "The Order of 1 and 2 Thessalonians," The Journal of Theological Studies, XV (1914), 66–74.

Westcott, Brooke Foss, and Hort, Fenton John Anthony. The New Testament in the Original Greek. Vol. II: Introduction and Appendix. New York: Harper & Bros., 1882.

Wilckens, Ulrich. Weisheit und Torheit: Eine exegetisch-religionsgeschichtliche Untersuchung zu 1. Kor. 1 und 2. ("Beiträge zur historischen Theologie," hrsg. Gerhard Ebeling, 26. Hft.) Tübingen: J. C. B. Mohr (Paul Siebeck), 1959.

Wilder, Amos Niven. "Biblical Hermeneutic and American Scholarship," in Neutestamentliche Studien für Rudolf Bultmann ("Beihefte zur Zeitschrift für die neutestamentliche Wissenschaft und die Kunde der älteren Kirche," Beiheft XXI; Berlin: Alfred Töpelmann, 1954), pp. 24–32.

Williams, Charles Stephen Conway. Alterations to the Text of the Synoptic Gospels and Acts. Oxford: Basil Blackwell, 1951.

Wilson, William E. "The Development of Paul's Doctrine of Dying and Rising again with Christ," The Expository Times, XLII (1930/31), 562–5.

Windisch, Hans Ludwig. "The Case against the Tradition," in Prolegomena II: Criticism. Vol. II of The Beginnings of Christianity, edited by F. J. Foakes-Jackson and Kirsopp Lake (London: Macmillan and Co., Limited, 1922), pp. 298–348.

Wrede, William. Die Echtheit des zweiten Thessalonicherbriefs untersucht. ("Texte und Untersuchungen zur Geschichte der altchristlichen Literatur," N. S., IX. Bd., 2. Hft.) Leipzig: J. C. Hinrichs'sche Buchhandlung, 1903.

Zahn, Theodor. *Introduction to the New Testament.* Translated by J. M. Trout *et al.* Edited by M. W. Jacobus. 3 vols. 2d ed. New York: Charles Scribner's Sons, 1917.

Zuntz, Günther. *The Text of the Epistles: A Disquisition upon the Corpus Paulinum.* ("The Schweich Lectures of the British Academy," 1946.) London: The British Academy, 1953.

D. REFERENCE WORKS

Arndt, William Frederick, and Gingrich, Felix Wilbur. *A Greek-English Lexicon of the New Testament and Other Early Christian Literature.* A translation and adaptation of the fourth revised edition of Walter Bauer's Griechisch-Deutsches Wörterbuch zu den Schriften des Neuen Testaments und der übrigen urchristlichen Literatur. Cambridge: The University Press, 1957.

Blass, Friedrich, and Debrunner, Albert. *A Greek Grammar of the New Testament and Other Early Christian Literature.* Translated and revised by Robert W. Funk. Cambridge: The University Press, 1961.

Kittel, Gerhard, and Friedrich, Gerhard (eds.). *Theologisches Wörterbuch zum Neuen Testament.* Stuttgart: W. Kohlhammer Verlag, 1933————.

Liddell, Henry George, and Scott, Robert. *A Greek-English Lexicon.* A new (9th) edition revised and augmented by Henry Stuart Jones with Roderick McKenzie. 2 vols. Oxford: The Clarendon Press, 1940.

Morgenthaler, Robert. *Statistik des neutestamentlichen Wortschatzes.* Zürich: Gotthelf-Verlag, 1958.

Moule, Charles Francis Digby. *An Idiom Book of New Testament Greek.* 2d ed. Cambridge: The University Press, 1959.

Moulton, James Hope, and Howard, Wilbert Francis. *A Grammar of New Testament Greek:* Vol. II, *Accidence and Word-Formation.* Edinburgh: T. & T. Clark, 1929.

—— and Milligan, George. *The Vocabulary of the Greek Testament Illustrated from the Papyri and Other Non-Literary Sources.* London: Hodder and Stoughton, Limited, 1930.

Moulton, William Fiddian, and Geden, Alfred Sherington. *A Concordance to the Greek Testament according to the Texts of Westcott and Hort, Tischendorf and the English Revisers.* 3d ed. Edinburgh: T. & T. Clark, 1926.

Souter, Alexander. *A Pocket Lexicon to the Greek New Testament.* Oxford: The Clarendon Press, 1917.

E. BIBLIOGRAPHY TO CHAPTER I, APPENDED NOTES

The following works are cited only in that part of Chapter I designated as "The Evidence for the Usual Chronology of Paul's Letters" (i.e., pp. 12–19). They are included to show how widespread is the agreement among scholars on the use of Acts to date Paul's letters.

Abbott, Lyman. *The Life and Letters of Paul the Apostle.* Boston: Houghton, Mifflin and Company, 1898.

Adeney, Walter Frederic. *Thessalonians and Galatians: Introduction, Authorized Version, Revised Version with Notes, Index and Map.* "The Century Bible." Edinburgh: T. C. & E. C. Jack, [1902?].

Althaus, Paul. *Der Brief an die Römer* ("Das Neue Testament Deutsch," herausgegeben von Paul Althaus, 6. Abt., 8. Aufl.) Göttingen: Vandenhoeck & Ruprecht, 1954.

Andrews, Herbert Tom. "I. and II. Thessalonians," in *A Commentary on the Bible*, edited by Arthur S. Peake (London: Thomas Nelson and Sons, Ltd., 1920), pp. 876–80.

Bailey, John William. "The First and Second Epistles to the Thessalonians: Introduction and Exegesis," in *The Interpreter's Bible*, edited by George Arthur Buttrick *et al.* (12 vols.; New York: Abingdon Press, 1951–1957), XI, 243–340.

Bartlet, James Vernon. *The Acts: Introduction, Authorized Version, Revised Version with Notes, Index and Map.* "The Century Bible." Edinburgh: T. C. & E. C. Jack, 1901.

—— *The Apostolic Age: Its Life, Doctrine, Worship and Polity.* "Eras of the Christian Church." Edinburgh: T. & T. Clark, 1902.

Benoît, Pierre (trans.). *Les Épîtres de Saint Paul aux Philippiens, à Philémon, aux Colossiens, aux Éphésiens.* 3d ed. "La Sainte Bible." Paris: Les Éditions du Cerf, 1959.

Bicknell, Edward John. "The Acts of the Apostles," in *A New Commentary on Holy Scripture Including the Apocrypha*, edited by Charles Gore, Henry Leighton Goudge, and Alfred Guillaume (London: S. P. C. K., 1928), pp. 320–78.

Blaiklock, Edward Murgrave. *The Acts of the Apostles.* "The Tyndale New Testament Commentaries." Grand Rapids, Mich.: Wm. B. Eerdmans Publishing Company, 1959.

Blunt, Alfred Walter Frank. *The Epistle of Paul to the Galatians.* "The Clarendon Bible." Oxford: The Clarendon Press, 1925.

Böttger, Heinrich. *Beiträge zur historisch kritischen Einleitung in die Paulinischen Briefe.* 5 Abteilungen und Supplemente. Göttingen: Vandenhoeck und Ruprecht, 1837–1838.

Bonnard, Pierre. *L'Épître de Saint Paul aux Philippiens.* ("Commentaire du Nouveau Testament," Vol. Xa.) Neuchâtel: Delachaux & Niestlé S. A., 1950.

Bornemann, Friedrich Wilhelm Bernard. *Die Thessalonicherbriefe.* ("Kritischexegetischer Kommentar über das Neue Testament," begründet von H. A. W. Meyer, 10. Abt., 5. u 6. Aufl.) Göttingen: Vandenhoeck & Ruprecht, 1894.

Bousset, Wilhelm. "Der Brief an die Galater," in *Die Schriften des Neuen Testaments neu übersetzt und für die Gegenwart erklärt*, in 3. Aufl. hrsg. von Wilhelm Bousset und Wilhelm Heitmüller (4 Bde.; Göttingen: Vandenhoeck & Ruprecht, 1917–1918), II, 31–74.

Bruce, Frederick Fyvie. *The Acts of the Apostles: The Greek Text with Intro duction and Commentary.* 2d ed.; London: The Tyndale Press, 1952.

Calvin, John. *The First Epistle of Paul the Apostle to the Corinthians*. Translated by John W. Fraser. "Calvin's Commentaries," edited by D. W. Torrance and T. F. Torrance. Edinburgh: Oliver and Boyd, 1960.

Cambier, J "La Vie et l'Oeuvre de Saint Paul," in *Introduction à la Bible*, Tome II: *Nouveau Testament*, by C. Bigaré et al. (Tournai, Belgium: Desclée & Cie., Éditeurs, 1959), pp. 377–84.

Cerfaux, Lucien. "L'Épître aux Galates," in *Introduction à la Bible*, Tome II: *Nouveau Testament*, by C. Bigaré et al. (Tournai, Belgium: Desclée & Cie., Éditeurs, 1959), pp. 403–16.

Clarke, William Kemp Lowther. *Concise Bible Commentary*. London: S. P. C. K., 1952.

Clemen, Carl. "Die Adressaten des Galaterbriefs," *Zeitschrift für wissenschaftliche Theologie*, XXXVII (1894), 396–423.

Davidson, Samuel. *An Introduction to the Study of the New Testament: Critical, Exegetical, and Theological*. 2 vols.; 3d ed. rev.; London: Kegan Paul, Trench, Trübner & Co. Ltd., 1894.

Davies, William David. "The Apostolic Age and the Life of Paul," in *Peake's Commentary on the Bible*, edited by Matthew Black and H. H. Rowley (London: Thomas Nelson and Sons Ltd, 1962), pp. 870–81.

Denney, James. "St. Paul's Epistle to the Romans," in *The Expositor's Greek Testament*, edited by W. Robertson Nicoll (5 vols.; London: Hodder and Stoughton, 1897–1910), II, 555–726.

Dibelius, Martin. *An die Thessalonicher I/II. An die Philipper*. ("Handbuch zum Neuen Testament," 11. Bd., 3. Aufl.) Tübingen: J. C. B. Mohr (Paul Siebeck), 1937.

Dobschütz, Ernst von. *Die Thessalonicher-Briefe*. ("Kritisch-exegetischer Kommentar über das Neue Testament," begründet von H. A. W. Meyer, 10. Abt., 7. Aufl.) Göttingen: Vandenhoeck & Ruprecht, 1909.

Dods, Marcus. *Introduction to the New Testament*. ("The Theological Educator," ed. W. Robertson Nicoll.) London: Hodder and Stoughton, 1890.

Duchesne, Louis. *The Early History of the Christian Church from its Foundation to the End of the Fifth Century*. Translated from the 4th French edition. 3 vols.; London: John Murray, 1909–1924.

Duncan, George Simpson. "Chronological Table to Illustrate Paul's Ministry in Asia," *New Testament Studies*, V (1958/59), 43–5.

—— "Important Hypotheses Reconsidered: VI. Were Paul's Imprisonment Epistles Written from Ephesus?" *The Expository Times*, LXVII (1955/56), 163–6.

—— "Paul's Ministry in Asia—the Last Phase," *New Testament Studies*, III (1956/57), 211–18.

Emmet, Cyril William. "The Apostolic Age and the Life of Paul," in *A Commentary on the Bible*, edited by Arthur S. Peake (London: Thomas Nelson and Sons, Ltd., 1920), pp. 766–75.

Feine, Paul. *Einleitung in das Neue Testament*. Revised and edited by Johannes Behm. 9. Aufl. Leipzig: Quelle & Meyer, 1950.

Feine, Paul, and Behm, Johannes. *Einleitung in das Neue Testament*. 12., völlig neu bearbeitete Auflage von Werner Georg Kümmel. Heidelberg: Quelle & Meyer, 1963.

Filson, Floyd Vivian. *Opening the New Testament*. Philadelphia: The Westminster Press, 1952.

Findlay, George Gillanders. "Romans," in *A Commentary on the Bible*, edited by Arthur S. Peake (London: Thomas Nelson and Sons, Ltd., 1920), pp. 817–31.

Fouard, Constant. *Saint Paul and His Missions*. Translated by George F. X. Griffith. New York: Longmans, Green, and Co., 1894.

Fowler, Henry Thatcher. *The History and Literature of the New Testament*. New York: The Macmillan Company, 1925.

Friedrich, Gerhard. "Römerbrief," in *Die Religion in Geschichte und Gegenwart: Handwörterbuch für Theologie und Religionswissenschaft*, 3. Aufl. herausgegeben von H. v. Campenhausen *et al.* (6 Bde. Tübingen: J. C. B. Mohr [Paul Siebeck], 1957–1962), V, 1137–43.

Fuller, Reginald Horace, and Wright, George Ernest. *The Book of the Acts of God: Christian Scholarship Interprets the Bible*. Garden City, N. Y.: Doubleday & Company, Inc., 1957.

Garvie, Alfred Ernest. *Romans: Introduction, Authorized Version, Revised Version with Notes, Index and Map*. "The Century Bible." Edinburgh: T. C. & E. C. Jack, [1901?]

Gore, Charles. *St. Paul's Epistle to the Romans: A Practical Exposition*. 2 vols.; London: John Murray, 1899–1900.

Grant, Frederick Clifton. *The Early Days of Christianity*. "The Abingdon Religious Education Texts." New York: The Abingdon Press, 1922.

Grayston, Kenneth. "The Epistle to the Romans," "The Epistles to the Corinthians," "The Epistles to the Thessalonians," in *The Twentieth Century Bible Commentary*, edited by G. Henton Davies, Alan Richardson, and Charles L. Wallis (rev. ed.; New York: Harper & Brothers, Publishers, 1955), pp. 474–82; 492–6.

Griffith, Gwilym Oswald. *St. Paul's Gospel to the Romans*. Oxford: Basil Blackwell, 1949.

Harrison, Percy Neale. "The Pastoral Epistles and Duncan's Ephesian Theory," *New Testament Studies*, II (1955/56), 250–61.

Hatch, Edwin. "Paul," in *Encyclopaedia Biblica*, edited by T. K. Cheyne and J. Sutherland Black (4 vols.; New York: The Macmillan Company, 1899–1903), III, 3606–20.

Hatch, William Henry Paine. "The Life of Paul," in *The Interpreter's Bible*, edited by George Arthur Buttrick *et al.* (12 vols.; New York: Abingdon Press, 1951–1957), VII, 187–99.

Headlam, Arthur Cayley. *St. Paul and Christianity*. New York: Longmans, Green & Co., 1913.

Hendriksen, William. *New Testament Commentary: Exposition of I and II Thessalonians*. Grand Rapids, Mich.: Baker Book House, 1955.

Henshaw, Thomas. *New Testament Literature in the Light of Modern Scholarship*. London: George Allen and Unwin Ltd, 1952.

Herklots, Hugh Gerard Gibson. *A Fresh Approach to the New Testament*. New York: Abingdon-Cokesbury Press, 1950.

Hippisley, Evelyn Waters. "Chronological Scheme of Dates for Old Testament, Apocrypha (and Apocalyptic) and New Testament," revised and supplemented by G. Henton Davies and Alan Richardson, in *The Twentieth Century Bible Commentary*, revised edition edited by G. Henton Davies, Alan Richardson, and Charles L. Wallis (New York: Harper & Brothers, Publishers, 1955), pp. 519–41.

Holtzmann, Oskar. "Die Jerusalemreisen des Paulus und die Kollekte," *Zeitschrift für die neutestamentliche Wissenschaft und die Kunde des Urchristentums*, VI (1905), 102–4.

Howard, Wilbert Francis. "First and Second Corinthians," in *The Abingdon Bible Commentary*, edited by F. C. Eiselen, E. Lewis, and D. G. Downey (New York: Abingdon–Cokesbury Press, 1929), pp. 1169–1206.

Huby, Joseph. "The Books of the New Testament," in *Guide to the Bible: An Introduction to the Study of Holy Scripture*, edited by A. Robert and A. Tricot, translated by E. P. Arbez and M. R. P. McGuire (2 vols; 2d ed. rev.; Paris: Desclée Company, 1960————), I, 382–474.

Hudson, James T. *The Pauline Epistles, Their Meaning and Message: Introduction, Translation, Marginal Analysis and Paraphrase.* London: James Clarke & Co. Ltd., 1958.

Hunter, Archibald Macbride. *Introducing the New Testament.* 2d ed. rev. London: SCM Press Ltd, 1957.

Jacquier, Eugène. *Les Actes des Apôtres.* "Études Bibliques." Paris: Libraire Victor Lecoffre (J. Gabalda, Éditeur), 1926.

Johnson, Lewis. "The Pauline Letters from Caesarea," *The Expository Times*, LXVIII (1956/57), 24–6.

Jones, Maurice. "I. and II. Thessalonians," in *A New Commentary on Holy Scripture Including the Apocrypha*, edited by Charles Gore, Henry Leighton Goudge, and Alfred Guillaume (London: S. P. C. K., 1928), pp. 566–73.

Kennedy, James Houghton. *The Second and Third Epistles of St. Paul to the Corinthians with Some Proofs of their Independence and Mutual Relation.* London: Methuen & Co., 1900.

Kenyon, Frederick. *Our Bible and the Ancient Manuscripts.* Revised by A. W. Adams. London: Eyre and Spottiswoode, 1958.

Kinsey, Robert S. *With Paul in Greece.* Nashville, Tenn.: The Parthenon Press, 1957.

Kirk, Kenneth Escott. *The Epistle to the Romans.* "The Clarendon Bible." Oxford: The Clarendon Press, 1937.

Knopf, Rudolf. "Die Apostelgeschichte," in *Die Schriften des Neuen Testaments neu übersetzt und für die Gegenwart erklärt*, in 3. Aufl. hrsg. von Wilhelm Bousset und Wilhelm Heitmüller (4 Bde.; Göttingen: Vandenhoeck & Ruprecht, 1917–1918), III, 1–157.

Knowling, Richard John. "The Acts of the Apostles," in *The Expositor's Greek Testament*, edited by W. Robertson Nicoll (5 vols.; London: Hodder and Stoughton, 1897–1910), II, 1–554.

Knox, John. "First Epistle to the Thessalonians," in *Dictionary of the Bible*, edited by James Hastings; revised ed., edited by F. C. Grant and H. H. Rowley (New York: Charles Scribner's Sons, 1963), pp. 995–6.

Knox, Ronald Arbuthnott. *A New Testament Commentary for English Readers.* Vol. II: *The Acts of the Apostles; St. Paul's Letters to the Churches.* New York: Sheed & Ward, 1954.

Kraeling, Emil Gottlieb Heinrich. *Bible Atlas.* Chicago: Rand McNally & Company, 1956.

Kümmel, Werner Georg. "Das literarische und geschichtliche Problem des ersten Thessalonicherbriefes," in *Neotestamentica et Patristica: Eine Freudesgabe, Herrn Professor Dr. Oscar Cullmann zu seinem 60. Geburtstag überreicht.* ("Supplements to Novum Testamentum," Vol. VI; Leiden: E. J. Brill, 1962), pp. 213–27.

Lagrange, Marie–Joseph. *Saint Paul: Épître aux Galates.* 2d ed. "Études Bibliques." Paris: Librairie Lecoffre (J. Gabalda et Cie, Éditeurs), 1925.

—— *Saint Paul: Épître aux Romains.* "Études Bibliques." Paris: Librairie Lecoffre (J. Gabalda et Cie, Éditeurs), 1930.

Lake, Kirsopp. "Paul's Route in Asia Minor," in *The Beginnings of Christianity,* Vol. V: *Additional Notes to the Commentary,* edited by F. J. Foakes-Jackson and Kirsopp Lake (London: Macmillan and Co., Limited, 1933), pp. 224–40.

Leaney, Alfred Robert Clare. *The Epistles to Timothy, Titus and Philemon.* "Torch Bible Commentaries." London: SCM Press Ltd, 1960.

Lewin, Thomas. *Fasti Sacri: A Key to the Chronology of the New Testament.* London: George Bell and Sons, 1865.

Lias, John James. *The First Epistle to the Corinthians with Notes, Map and Introduction.* "The Cambridge Bible for Schools." Cambridge: The University Press, 1879.

Lietzmann, Hans. *An die Galater.* ("Handbuch zum Neuen Testament," 10. Bd.; 3. Aufl.) Tübingen: Verlag von J. C. B. Mohr (Paul Siebeck), 1932.

Lightfoot, Joseph Barber. *St. Paul's Epistles to the Colossians and to Philemon.* 9th ed. London: Macmillan and Co., 1890.

Loewenich, Walther von. *Paul: His Life and Work.* Translated by Gordon E. Harris. Edinburgh: Oliver and Boyd, 1960.

Lohmeyer, Ernst. *Die Briefe an die Philipper, an die Kolosser und an Philemon.* Corrected from the author's notes by Werner Schmauch. ("Kritisch-exegetischer Kommentar über das Neue Testament," begründet von H. A. W. Meyer, 9 Abt., 12. Aufl.) Göttingen: Vandenhoeck & Ruprecht, 1961.

Lueken, Wilhelm. "Der erste Brief an die Thessalonicher," in *Die Schriften des Neuen Testaments neu übersetzt und für die Gegenwart erklärt,* in 3. Aufl. herausgegeben von Wilhelm Bousset und Wilhelm Heitmüller (4 Bde.; Göttingen: Vandenhoeck & Ruprecht, 1917–1918), II, 5–21.

Lünemann, Gottlieb. *Critical and Exegetical Handbook to the Epistles of Paul to the Thessalonians.* ("Critical and Exegetical Commentary on the New Testament," ed. H. A. W. Meyer.) Translated by Paton J. Gloag. Edinburgh: T. & T. Clark, 1884.

Lumby, Joseph Rawson. *The Acts of the Apostles with Maps, Introduction and Notes.* "The Cambridge Bible for Schools." Cambridge: The University Press, 1882.

McCown, Chester Charlton. "First and Second Thessalonians," in *The Abingdon Bible Commentary,* edited by F. C. Eiselen, E. Lewis, and D. G. Downey (New York: Abingdon–Cokesbury Press, 1929), pp. 1263–73.

McGiffert, Arthur Cushman. "Thessalonians (Epistles to)," in *Encyclopaedia Biblica*, edited by T. K. Cheyne and J. Sutherland Black (4 vols.; New York: The Macmillan Company, 1899–1903), IV, 5036–46.

McNeile, Alan Hugh. *St. Paul: His Life, Letters, and Christian Doctrine.* Cambridge: The University Press, 1920.

Manson, Thomas Walter. "The New Testament and Other Christian Writings of the New Testament Period," in *A Companion to the Bible*, edited by T. W. Manson (Edinburgh: T. & T. Clark, 1939), pp. 97–129.

Masson, Charles. *L'Épître de Saint Paul aux Colossiens.* ("Commentaire du Nouveau Testament," Xb.) Neuchâtel: Delachaux & Niestlé S. A., 1950.

Menzies, Allan. *The Second Epistle of the Apostle Paul to the Corinthians.* London: Macmillan and Co., Limited, 1912.

Michael, John Hugh. *The Epistle of Paul to the Philippians.* "The Moffatt New Testament Commentary." London: Hodder and Stoughton Limited, 1928.

Michaelis, Wilhelm. *Die Gefangenschaft des Paulus in Ephesus und das Itinerar des Timotheus: Untersuchungen zur Chronologie des Paulus und der Paulusbriefe.* ("Neutestamentliche Forschungen," herausgegeben von Otto Schmitz I. Reihe: Paulusstudien, 3. Hft.) Gütersloh: C. Bertelsmann Verlag, 1925.

—— "Kenchreä (Zur Frage des Abfassungsortes des Rm)," *Zeitschrift für die neutestamentliche Wissenschaft und die Kunde der älteren Kirche*, XXV (1926), 144–54.

Morris, Leon. *The Epistles of Paul to the Thessalonians: An Introduction and Commentary.* "The Tyndale New Testament Commentaries." Grand Rapids, Mich.: Wm. B. Eerdmans Publishing Company, 1957.

Moule, Handley Carr Glyn. *The Epistle of Paul the Apostle to the Romans with Introduction and Notes.* "The Cambridge Bible for Schools." Cambridge: The University Press, 1879.

Mozley, John Kenneth. "I. Corinthians," in *A New Commentary on Holy Scripture Including the Apocrypha*, edited by Charles Gore, Henry Leighton Goudge, and Alfred Guillaume (London: S. P. C. K., 1928), pp. 484–515.

Mynster, Danois. *Einleitung in den Brief an die Galater.* "Kleine Theologische Schriften." 1825.

Oepke, Albrecht. "Die Briefe an die Thessalonicher," in *Die kleineren Briefe des Apostels Paulus*, von Hermann W. Beyer et al. ("Das Neue Testament Deutsch," herausgegeben von Paul Althaus; 8. Abt.; 7 Aufl.; Göttingen: Vandenhoeck & Ruprecht, 1955), pp. 127–58.

Orchard, Bernard. "1 and 2 Thessalonians," in *A Catholic Commentary on Holy Scripture*, edited by Bernard Orchard et al. (New York: Thomas Nelson & Sons, 1953), pp. 1137–41.

Peake, Arthur Samuel. *A Critical Introduction to the New Testament.* New York: Charles Scribner's Sons, 1922.

Pherigo, Lindsey P. "Paul and the Corinthian Church," *Journal of Biblical Literature*, LXVIII (1949), 341–50.

Plooij, Daniël. *De Chronologie van het Leven van Paulus.* Leiden: E. J. Brill, 1918.

Plumptre, Edward Hayes. "The Acts of the Apostles," in *A New Testament Commentary for English Readers by Various Writers*, edited by Charles John

Ellicott (3 vols.; London: Cassell and Company, Limited, 1897), Vol. II, pp. v–xvi, 1–192.

Price, James L. *Interpreting the New Testament*. New York: Holt, Rinehart and Winston, 1961.

Purdy, Alexander Converse. "Epistle to the Galatians," in *Dictionary of the Bible*, edited by James Hastings; revised ed., edited by F. C. Grant and H. H. Rowley (New York: Charles Scribner's Sons, 1963), pp. 311–13.

Ramsay, William Mitchell. "St. Paul's First Journey in Asia Minor," *The Expositor*, Ser. 4; VI (1892), 161–75.

Renan, Ernest. *The History of the Origins of Christianity*. Book III: *Saint Paul*. Translated from the French. London: Mathieson & Company, n. d.

Rendall, Frederic. "The Epistle to the Galatians," in *The Expositor's Greek Testament*, edited by W. Robertson Nicoll (5 vols.; London: Hodder and Stoughton, 1897–1910), III, 121–200.

Ricciotti, Giuseppi. *The Acts of the Apostles: Text and Commentary*. Translated by Laurence E. Byrne. Milwaukee: Bruce Publishing Company, 1958.

Robinson, Benjamin Willard. *The Life of Paul*. Chicago: The University of Chicago Press, 1918.

Robinson, William Gordon. *An Introduction to the New Testament*. "Merlin Books." London: Edward Arnold & Co., 1949.

Ropes, James Hardy. "Epistles to the Corinthians," in *Encyclopaedia Britannica: A New Survey of Universal Knowledge* (24 vols.; Chicago: Encyclopaedia Britannica, Inc., 1958), VI, 443–4.

Rowlingson, Donald T. *Introduction to New Testament Study*. New York: The Macmillan Company, 1956.

—— "Paul's Ephesian Imprisonment: An Evaluation of the Evidence," *Anglican Theological Review*, XXXII (1950), 1–7.

Sanday, William. "Epistles to the Corinthians," in *Encyclopaedia Biblica*, edited by T. K. Cheyne and J. Sutherland Black (4 vols.; New York: The Macmillan Company, 1899–1903), I, 899–907.

Schlatter, Adolf. *The Church in the New Testament Period*. Translated by Paul P. Levertoff. London: S. P. C. K., 1955.

—— *Die Korintherbriefe ausgelegt für Bibelleser*. ("Schlatters Erläuterungen zum Neuen Testament," 6. Teil.) Stuttgart: Calwer Verlag, 1950.

Schlier, Heinrich. *Der Brief an die Galater*. ("Kritisch-exegetischer Kommentar über das Neue Testament," begründet von H. A. W. Meyer, 7. Abt., 11. Aufl.) Göttingen: Vandenhoeck & Ruprecht, 1951.

Schmidt, John Joachim. *Prolusio de Galatis, ad quos Paulus literas misit*. 1748.

—— *Prolusionem suam de Galatis—ad objectionibus doctissimorum virorum vindicare conatur*. 1754.

Scott, Charles Archibald Anderson. "Romans," in *The Abingdon Bible Commentary*, edited by F. C. Eiselen, E. Lewis, and D. G. Downey (New York: Abingdon-Cokesbury Press, 1929), pp. 1135–68.

—— *Saint Paul: The Man & the Teacher*. Cambridge: The University Press, 1936.

Sparks, Hedley Frederick Davis. *The Formation of the New Testament*. New York: Philosophical Library, 1953.

Stamm, Raymond T. "The Epistle to the Galatians: Introduction and Exegesis," in *The Interpreter's Bible*, edited by George Arthur Buttrick *et al.* (12 vols.; New York: Abingdon Press, 1951–1957), X, 427–593.

—— "Letter to the Romans," in *Dictionary of the Bible*, edited by James Hastings; revised ed., edited by F. C. Grant and H. H. Rowley (New York: Charles Scribner's Sons, 1963), pp. 859–62.

Steinmann, Alphons. *Die Briefe an die Thessalonicher und Galater.* 4. Aufl. ("Die heilige Schrift des neuen Testamentes," V. Bd.) Bonn: Peter Hanstein, Verlagsbuchhandlung, 1935.

—— *Der Leserkreis des Galaterbriefs.* ("Neutestamentliche Abhandlungen," bgt. August Blundau, I. Bd., 3/4. Hft.) Münster: Verlag der Aschendorffschen Verlagsbuchhandlung, 1908.

Stirling, John. *An Atlas Illustrating the Acts of the Apostles and the Epistles.* 2d ed.; London: George Philip and Son Limited, 1954.

Strachan, Robert Harvey. *The Second Epistle of Paul to the Corinthians.* "The Moffatt New Testament Commentary." London: Hodder and Stoughton Limited, 1935.

Streeter, Burnett Hillman. "The Rise of Christianity," in *The Cambridge Ancient History*, Vol. XI: *The Imperial Peace, A. D. 70–192*, edited by S. A. Cook, F. E. Adcock, and M. P. Charlesworth (Cambridge: The University Press, 1936), pp. 253–93.

Synge, Francis Charles. *Philippians and Colossians.* "Torch Bible Commentaries." London: SCM Press Ltd, 1951.

Taylor, Theophilus Mills. "The Place of Origin of Romans," *Journal of Biblical Literature*, LXVII (1948), 281–95.

Tenney, Merrill Chapin. *The New Testament: A Historical and Analytic Survey.* London: The Inter-Varsity Fellowship, 1954.

Twilley, Leslie Douglas. *The Origin and Transmission of the New Testament: A Short Introduction.* Edinburgh: Oliver and Boyd, 1957.

Weber, Valentin. *Die Adressaten des Galaterbriefes: Beweis der rein-südgalatischen Theorie.* Ravensburg: Verlag von Hermann Kitz, 1900.

Weiss, Bernhard. *A Manual of Introduction to the New Testament.* Translated by A. J. K. Davidson. 2 vols. "The Foreign Biblical Library." New York: Funk & Wagnalls, 1889.

Wikenhauser, Alfred. *New Testament Introduction.* Translated by Joseph Cunningham. New York: Herder and Herder, 1958.

Williams, Norman Powell. "The Epistle to the Romans," in *A New Commentary on Holy Scripture Including the Apocrypha*, edited by Charles Gore, Henry Leighton Goudge, and Alfred Guillaume (London: S. P. C. K., 1928), pp. 442–84.

Woodhouse, William John. "Galatia," in *Encyclopaedia Biblica*, edited by T. K. Cheyne and J. Sutherland Black (4 vols.; New York: The Macmillan Company, 1899–1903), II, 1589–96.

Zahn, Theodor. *Der Brief des Paulus an die Galater.* 3. Aufl. durchgesehen von Friedrich Hauck. ("Kommentar zum Neuen Testament," herausgegeben von Theodor Zahn, IX. Bd.) Leipzig: A. Deichertsche Verlagsbuchhandlung (Dr. Werner Scholl), 1922.

Indexes

Bold face page numbers indicate major discussions.
Superior numerals refer to notes.

BIBLICAL REFERENCES

AUTHORS

Woodhouse, W. J., 304[9]
Wrede, W., 27[2]
Wright, G. E., see R. H. Fuller.

Young, F. W., see H. Kee.

Zahn, T.:
Intro. N. T., 50[1], 55[3], 57[1], 64[1], 68, 80[4],
83[1], 90[2], 91[2], 100[6], 102, 102[3], 106, 106[2], 116[4], 139[1, 3], 147[1], 151[1], 155[3], 157[4], 158[2], 159[2], 161, 161[3], 167[1], 187, 187[3], 215[3], 216[4], 299[1(c)], 300[2(d)], 302[3(c)]
Gal., 304[8, 9]
Zeiller, J., 100[5]
Zöckler, O., 303[4]
Zuntz, G., 14[3], 77[4], 123[2], 129[1], 230[1]

SUBJECTS

Achaia, 14, 31, 49
Acts: cities visited by Paul in, 28–31; chronological patterns in, 22; chronological vagueness, 22, 23; and Gal., 15–19, 33–5; itinerary source, 28, 30, 41; literary patterns in, 32, 37–40; omitted information, 23–7; purpose of author, 32, 33; sources, 27, 28; speeches in, 32, 36–41; textual problems, 34, 35, 246–50; theology, 32, 33, 40; and 1 Thess., 13, 14, 25–7; uncertain arrangements of events, 28–31; unrealiability, 22–41; usual basis of Pauline chronology, 12–19, 299–305; "we" source, 12
Affliction in Asia, 24
Alexandria and Apollos, 98
Angels, 184[4]; judgement by Christians, 85, 229, 231, 283
Antioch (Pisidia), 17, 29
Antioch (Syria), 24, 29, 33, 36, 37, 39, 270
Apocalypticism: at Corinth, 277; in Paul's teaching, 283–4, 287, 294
Apollos: at Corinth, 14, 53, 54, 97–9, 213–14, 245; Corinthians' request concerning, 63, 74, 108, **206–7**, 209; Paul's relationship to, 53, 54, 98, 99, **207**, 214; popularity, 206–7, 265
Apollos party, 75, 97–9, 104, 108, 213–14, 269–70
Apostleship, Paul's, 109–11; questioned by Corinthians? 43, 70, 109–11
Apostolic Decree: ethical interpretation, 250–1; intention, 250–3; Levitical interpretation, 252–3; occasion for Previous Letter, 259–62; Paul's abandonment of, 289, 294; Paul's silence concerning, 16, 253–9, **262–7**, 294; separable from Acts 15, 40–1; source of Paul's disagreements with the Corinthians, 289, 294; text, **246–50**
Arabia, Paul's sojourn, 15, 20, 24
Asceticism: at Corinth, 156–7, 164–8, 179–

82; within marriage, 156–69, 181, 275–7, 284; Paul's ideal, 161–3, 181, 274–8
Athens, Paul in, 13, 25, 26
Authority: Paul's, 70, 108–9, 263; Paul's appeals to, 66, 70, 87, 90–1

Baptism: for the dead, 136–7, 286; guarantee of salvation, 137, 286, 294; administered by Paul, 54, 104, 105, 242
Barnabas, 24, 29, 34, 37–41, 266
Belial/Beliar, 236, 236[1]
Blood, clause in Apostolic Decree, 247, 250–1, 259[2], 290
Body, metaphor of unity/diversity, 88, **190–2**

Caesarea, imprisonment letters from, 14, 303[4]
Calendar, Christian, 139–41
Celibate, Corinthians' question concerning: 63, 68, 69, **169–82**; contents, 180–1, 208; nature, 181–2; origin, 217–18, 224–5; previous reconstructions, 169–71
Cephas, 20, 21 (see also Peter)
Cephas party, 75, 81, 97, **99–101**, 104, 118, 155, 213–14, **269–70**
Childishness vs. maturity, **111–13**, 189, 243–4, 279
Chloe's people, 46, 48–50, 52, 72, 75, 77, 81–2
Christ party, 75, **101–6**, 269
Chronology of Acts: accepted, 10–19, 299–305; disputed, 11[1(a)], 19–42
Chronology, Pauline: Gallio inscription, 31; letters as basis, 12[3], 42, 295–6; theological significance, 11, 12; usual assumptions, 12–19
Circumcision: not required of Gentile Christians, 264, 294; party of, 37, 38, 100, 101, 270; Paul accused of preaching, 267–8